Selling Empire

L.A.
CALIFORNIA
AUGUST 2016

(MORTON PRIZE
FOR WMQ
PIECE)

Selling Empire

India in the Making of Britain and America,
1600–1830

JONATHAN EACOTT

Published for the

Omohundro Institute of Early American History and Culture,

Williamsburg, Virginia,

by the University of North Carolina Press, Chapel Hill

*The Omohundro Institute of Early American History and Culture is
sponsored by the College of William and Mary. On November 15, 1996,
the Institute adopted the present name in honor of a bequest from
Malvern H. Omohundro, Jr.*

Jacket illustration: Detail of stamp for United East India Company on back
of *"Tree of Life" Textile Panel,* India, 1740–1760, India chintz, accession
1954-494 (Photo by Jonathan Eacott with the permission of The Colonial
Williamsburg Foundation)

Library of Congress Cataloging-in-Publication Data
Eacott, Jonathan, author.
Selling empire : India in the making of Britain and America, 1600–1830 /
Jonathan Eacott.
pages cm
Includes bibliographical references and index.
ISBN 978-1-4696-2230-9 (cloth : alk. paper) —
ISBN 978-1-4696-2231-6 (ebook)
1. Imperialism—Economic aspects. 2. Great Britain—Colonies—India.
3. Great Britain—Colonies—America. 4. Great Britain—Colonies—History.
I. Omohundro Institute of Early American History & Culture, sponsoring
body. II. Title.
DA16.E23 2016
382'.609540903—dc23
2015035748

cloth   20 19 18 17 16   5 4 3 2 1

Acknowledgments

I am not sure anymore when, exactly, I began thinking about the issues raised and addressed by this book, but I am sure that I am only finishing it thanks to more people than I can name. I would not have been in a position to even imagine writing this book without Brian Lewis at McGill University, and Sandra den Otter, at Queen's University, Kingston, who transformed how I thought about history and encouraged me, with suitable caution, to pursue a Ph.D. This book would not have been possible without David Hancock's interest in my curious proposal to bring India to the study of the Atlantic world, his willingness to work with me for that Ph.D. at the University of Michigan, and his unparalleled advice and guidance many years later. I simply cannot imagine a better dissertation adviser and mentor. The University of Michigan itself, where much of the research and many of the ideas for this book developed, was also a model of academic support. Dena Goodman, Kali Israel, David Porter, as well as Allison Abra, Maya Jasanoff, Jeff Kaja, and Amanda Moniz, provided incisive commentary on much of my early research and writing. I also had the great fortune while a Michigan student to spend a year affiliated with the University of London's Institute for Historical Research. My IHR adviser, dissertation committee member, and indefatigable reader Peter Marshall brought his encyclopedic knowledge and judicious comments to bear on my often inexcusably rough chapters, patiently reading multiple drafts from the dissertation through the manuscript to save me from countless mistakes. With his warm hospitality and irrepressibly good humor, he makes every stay in England brighter. I cannot thank them all enough.

This book took on its present shape through two productive years as a postdoctoral fellow at the Omohundro Institute of Early American History and Culture in Williamsburg, Virginia. For me, as for many others, the Omohundro Institute provided invaluable time, support, and guidance to fundamentally reimagine the possibilities and expansion of my dissertation research. I thank everyone at the Institute, in particular, Ron Hoffman, for his extraordinary generosity and support, and my editors Fredrika Teute, Nadine Zimmerli, and Virginia Chew, who have worked through my inordinate number of changes with saintly patience but, most of all, with great insight—often seeing much more clearly than I did the best path forward. At Colonial Williamsburg, Linda Baumgarten thoughtfully guided me through the fabric collections. I was also lucky that my time in Williamsburg overlapped with Mark Hanna, Dan Livesay, and Molly Warsh and that while there I also got to know Amanda Herbert and Nick Popper, all of whom through conversation, careful reading, shared sources, and warm friendship put their imprints throughout this book.

The long process of researching and writing would have been impossible without funding and intellectual support from a number of institutions on three continents. In America, I am indebted for residential fellowship support from the Program in Early American Economy and Society and the Library Company of Philadelphia; the Winterthur Museum, Delaware; and the Peabody Essex Museum, Salem, Massachusetts. My research in Britain was enabled by a Mellon Humanities Fellowship at the IHR in London, a dissertation fellowship from the North American Conference on British Studies, the Omohundro Institute, and grants from the American Historical Association, the University of Michigan, and the University of California, Riverside. This support allowed me to spend many happy and productive months benefiting from the patient advice of librarians and archivists throughout Britain, including at the British National Archives, British Library, National Library of Scotland, National Archives of Scotland, Glasgow City Archives, Gloucestershire Archives, Bedfordshire and Luton Archives, John Rylands Library, Guildhall Library, Keele University Special Collections, Christie's Auction House Archives, Bodleian Library, and Cambridge University Library. For taking my requests, humoring my ideas, imparting their knowledge, and even inviting me for dinner or drinks, I am grateful to them all. In India, my thanks to the Deputy Director of the State Archives of West Bengal as well as to the staff at the Ahmedabad Calico Museum, Asiatic Society of Kolkata, and National Library for helping me within the tight confines of my schedule and despite the ambiguity of many of my requests. My research in India was facilitated by funding from the History Department at the University of Michigan.

My deep appreciation extends to a great many people who read various versions of this book at various times in various states of incompleteness. The book as a whole benefited immeasurably from the input of James Allegro, Zara Anishanslin, John Brewer, Cary Carson, Alison Games, Paul Mapp, Cathy Matson, Jane Merritt, Tillman Nechtman, David Ormrod, Brett Rushforth, Robert Travers, and Karin Wulf. Audiences and seminar participants at Oxford and Georgetown heard or read versions of Chapter 2, on which they kindly and helpfully commented. An earlier version of

Chapter 2 also benefited immensely from Chris Grasso and Meg Mussel-white at the *William and Mary Quarterly,* where it appeared in October 2012. Chapter 4 benefited from input from John Brooke and the Ohio State University Seminar in Early American History and Culture and from the charitable readings of Rob Parkinson and Alexander Haskell, who helped focus my disparate (and often desperate) thoughts. Chapter 5 was improved in countless ways by Carole Shammas, Peter Mancall, and the USC-EMSI American Origins Seminar at the Huntington Library. An early version of some of the material in Chapter 6 benefited from the guidance of Maxine Berg and the editors of *Quaderni Storici,* in which it appeared in December 2006. Many other parts of the book benefited from audiences and conversations with colleagues at universities and conferences throughout North America and Europe. Several anonymous reviewers generously gave their time and thoughtful comments, without which this book would have been much poorer.

I have been incredibly fortunate, too, to be finishing this book at the University of California, Riverside, among the most welcoming and smart colleagues one could ask for. UCR gave me precious leave as a new hire to accept the Omohundro Institute's fellowship and provided funding to travel to London to complete the book's research. It also provided funding so that Jillian Azevedo, Andrew Frantz, Samuel Fullerton, and Leanna McLaughlin, graduate students from UCR, and Hendrik Isom, from Brown University, could provide vital and much appreciated assistance in tracking down citations, entering data, and digging through archives for me. My thanks also to Rebecca Wrenn, another UCR graduate student, who transformed my graphs for publication. I am honored to have been able to test out and toss around many of the ideas in this book with undergraduate and graduate students at the University of Michigan, the College of William and Mary, and UCR.

For much longer than it has taken to research and write this book, my family has always been there for me, sharing their love, kindness, and support. I cannot possibly thank them appropriately. Most of all, I thank Amy, for inspiring me to always be the best version of myself and for putting up with what has seemed the never-ending process of writing this book. This book is for M and N, who find joy in all books (in many ways) and melt worries with their smiles. Still, I know it could have used more pictures.

Contents

Illustrations

FIGURES

Abbreviations and Short Titles

APS   American Philosophical Society, Philadelphia

BL   British Library, London

CO   Colonial Office, National Archives, Kew

CSPC   Great Britain, Public Record Office, *Calendar of State Papers, Colonial Series*, ed. W. Noel Sainsbury et al. (London, 1860–): *America and West Indies*, I, *1574–1660*, IX, *1675–1676*, XIII, *1689–1692*, XVI, *1697–1698*, XVIII, *1700*, XXXI, *1719–1720*; *East Indies, China, and Japan*, III, *1617–1621*; *East Indies and Persia*, VIII, *1630–1634*

DNB   David Cannadine, gen. ed., *Oxford Dictionary of National Biography*, Online ed. (Oxford, 2004–)

EHR   *Economic History Review*

Fort William–India House Correspondence
    National Archives of India, *Fort William–India House Correspondence and Other Contemporary Papers Relating Thereto*, 21 vols. (Delhi, 1949–1985)

HSP   Historical Society of Pennsylvania, Philadelphia

IOR   India Office Records

JBS   *Journal of British Studies*

NA   National Archives, Kew

NAS   National Archives of Scotland, Edinburgh

NLS   National Library of Scotland, Edinburgh

PCC   *The Papers of the Continental Congress, 1774–1789*, microfilm, M247 (Washington, D.C., 1959)

PEM   Peabody Essex Museum, Salem, Massachusetts

RAC   Royal African Company

SR   sicca rupee

VOC   Vereenigde Oost-Indische Compagnie (Dutch East India Company)

WMQ   *William and Mary Quarterly*

Selling Empire

Introduction

"The discovery of an India" could do more, for better or worse, than anything else for the English people, wrote Captain Edward Wynne to his king, Charles I, in 1623. The world did not have one India, it had many awaiting English discovery. Wynne explained that the "low-Countrymen," meaning the Dutch, "have made the Sea their India; and by that sole waie of Fishing, have raised themselves to such an unweildlie Treasure." The Dutch had found their India near Newfoundland. Wynne was sure that Newfoundland itself would be England's India. It was more southerly than England, and it had, he claimed, mild winters with rare snows. Its potential wealth most made Newfoundland an India. Still, that wealth could be risky. The newfound wealth of the Dutch, he wrote, might lead to "lazyness, the readie waie to povertie." But the benefits were worth such a risk. Wynne explained that, through territory in America, Charles I's harbors would fill with ships and merchants, and "their houses with outlandish Commodities." The king's "Dominions" would gain "infinite wealth," and he would gain great "coffers" of "Treasure." For Wynne and other imperial thinkers and adventurers in Elizabethan and early Stuart England, India was a set of variable and sometimes competing ideas about wealth, trade, wondrous commodities, and potential corruption, more than it was a place. During the seventeenth and eighteenth centuries, however, Britons came to see India much more as the subcontinent of Asia—a place of cultivation, manufacturing, conquest, and potential religious allies and converts—than as a set of transferable ideas. America the India and India the place might have many of the same potential benefits and dangers in common.[1]

1. Edward Wynne, "The British India; or, A Compendious Discourse Tending to Advancement," 1623? Royal MS 17 A LVII, fols. 6, 18, 32–33, BL. Wynne was part of George Calvert's expeditions to Newfoundland. See Peter E. Pope, *Fish into Wine: The Newfoundland Plantation in the Seventeenth Century* (Chapel Hill, N.C., 2004), 2–57. Wynne was not alone in using a very broad definition of India as a source of wealth. Sir John Eliot advised the House of Commons that "the war with Spain is our Indies, that there shall we fetch wealth." See Sir John Eliot, Spring Diary, Mar. 19, 1624, 124–125, Houghton Library, Harvard University,

Scholars have long debated the definition of *empire* and when English and, after the 1707 Act of Union between Scotland and England, British activity in the Indian Ocean might best be considered imperial. They have often concluded that the British empire existed only in the northern half of the Atlantic Ocean until Robert Clive's conquests in India during the Seven Years' War started the so-called second British Tudor empire. Certainly, until the late 1750s, the Governor and Company of Merchants of London, Trading into the East Indies (founded 1600) and its subsequent English and British iterations, better known collectively as the East India Company, had limited strength or influence in India. Mostly the Company had a legal monopoly over English and, later, British, trade with a vast area from the east of the Cape of Good Hope to the Pacific coast of the Americas, a monopoly that was often porous and difficult to enforce. Nevertheless, historians have also shown that many British people, including within the Company, saw conquest and colonization in the Indian Ocean along roughly Atlantic models as appropriate courses of action long before Clive's conquests. The Company behaved in several imperial ways, and certainly some within it, and supporting it, had strongly imperial motives. Historians of the early United States have also begun to show that Britain retained significant political and cultural influence in its former North American colonies, alongside the Atlantic colonies that remained and became British. There was no sharp imperial turn to the east after the American Revolution. These important interventions encourage reconsideration of the when and where of British imperialism.[2]

---

quoted in Thomas Cogswell, *The Blessed Revolution: English Politics and the Coming of War, 1621–1624* (Cambridge, 1989), 204, 287. The influential Samuel Purchas used a broad definition more anchored to land, not wealth, writing, "The name of *India*, is now applyed to all farre-distant Countries, not in the extreme limits of Asia alone; but even to whole America." See Purchas, *Purchas His Pilgrimage; or, Relations of the World and the Religions Observed in Al Ages and Places Discovered, from the Creation unto This Present; in Foure Parts; This First Contayneth a Theologicall and Geographicall Historie of Asia, Africa, and America, with the Ilands Adiacent* (London, 1617), 541. Others also described the Atlantic fishery as the "Myne" for Dutch wealth. See, for example, John Smith, *A Description of New England; or, The Observations, and Discoveries, of Captain John Smith (Admirall of That Country) in the North of America* . . . (London, 1616), 11–12.

2. In his classic statement, Vincent T. Harlow argued that the "process of founding what may be termed for convenience's sake the Second British Empire began some thirty years before the collapse of the First." Harlow also argued that the system of trade with Asia, which he saw as a hallmark of the second empire, revived an "abandoned" Tudor ambition. See Harlow, *The Founding of the Second British Empire, 1763–1793*, 2 vols. (London, 1952), I, 3 (quotation), 11. This book makes a different case that the system certainly did not go away, and what was revived after the American Revolution was the dream of cultivating Asian commodities

This book suggests a new approach to the British empire by pursuing a set of related but also rather different questions about the relationship between the geography of rule and the mainsprings of imperial strength. It explores, in particular, whether and how thinking and actions regarding India fostered, propelled, and supported English and British imperial expansion and power in America. Such an approach considers the importance of parts of the world that the English and British could not readily influence in the rise of British power in addition to tracking the development of the exercise of imperial influence, power, and rule itself. It addresses, not when Britain built a first or second empire, but to what extent activities in one ocean shaped and made possible—or at times perhaps only seemed to make possible to those involved—activities in the other.

India was in many ways essential to the making of the British empire in America, and, to a lesser extent, America the empire in India, even when they were, respectively, not officially parts of the empire. Many merchants and adventurers suspected that America might provide the spigot to tap Asian riches. India's wealth, agricultural products, and manufactured goods inspired many of the goals of English expansion in the Americas in the seventeenth century as well as British industrialization in the eighteenth century. The popularity of Indian goods in the colonies has attracted little attention, but, encouraged by imperial policy, that popularity grew during the seventeenth and eighteenth centuries. India's goods were also vital to the Atlantic slave trade upon which much of the Atlantic's colonial production depended. Many of the enslaved that worked colonial fields around the Atlantic were as tied to the India trade as the Company's servants in Bengal, although their experiences were hardly alike. The Company's trade with India came to be an integral part of a system intended to generate financial strength for the empire and maintain the loy-

---

in America. P. J. Marshall argues for a lengthy transitionary period in the middle of the eighteenth century as opposed to a swing to the east. See Marshall, *The Making and Unmaking of Empires: Britain, India, and America, c. 1750–1783* (Oxford, 2005), 1–9. On Indian Ocean colonization, see Alison Games, *The Web of Empire: English Cosmopolitans in an Age of Expansion, 1560–1660* (New York, 2008), 181–218. On the Company's ambition as a state, see Philip J. Stern, *The Company-State: Corporate Sovereignty and the Early Modern Foundation of the British Empire in India* (New York, 2011), 6–7, 10–14, 23, 42, 58–60, 74–75, 83–214. On continuing British influence in America, see Eliga H. Gould, "Entangled Atlantic Histories: A Response from the Anglo-American Periphery," *American Historical Review*, CXII (2007), 1415–1422; Sam W. Haynes, *Unfinished Revolution: The Early American Republic in a British World* (Charlottesville, Va., 2010); Elisa Tamarkin, *Anglophilia: Deference, Devotion, and Antebellum America* (Chicago, 2008); Kariann Akemi Yokota, *Unbecoming British: How Revolutionary America Became a Postcolonial Nation* (New York, 2011).

alty and identity of the Atlantic colonists as active participants in British power and expansion. And, all the while, concern over the supposedly corrupting influence of India's wealth, goods, and cultures remained, too, a central generative force within Britain and its colonies.[3]

Understanding the development of the British empire in the Atlantic and Indian Oceans requires paying close attention to the shifting connections among what Britons and Americans thought, what they did, and what they bought. India and its goods were at the center of conversations and decisions about the trade, economy, politics, and daily life of the British empire. India was in the grandest policies and close to the skin in the most intimate places. As India influenced the British Atlantic, moreover, the British Atlantic influenced British approaches to India. Nevertheless, a story of ever-increasing interconnections would be as misleading as one of few connections. The nodes, characters, implications, and strengths of connections among goods, thoughts, and policies as well as among India,

3. Maxine Berg began to draw out the connections among global trade, rising consumerism, and the consumption of Asian goods in the rise of British industry; see Berg, "In Pursuit of Luxury: Global History and British Consumer Goods in the Eighteenth Century," *Past and Present*, no. 182 (February 2004), 85–142; see also Berg, *Luxury and Pleasure in Eighteenth-Century Britain* (Oxford, 2005). On India's cotton fabric specifically, see Giorgio Riello, "The Globalization of Cotton Textiles: Indian Cottons, Europe, and the Atlantic World, 1600–1850," in Riello and Prasannan Parthasarathi, eds., *The Spinning World: A Global History of Cotton Textiles, 1200–1850* (Oxford, 2009), 261–287; Beverly Lemire, *Fashion's Favourite: The Cotton Trade and the Consumer in Britain, 1660–1800* (Oxford, 1991); and Lemire, "Fashioning Cottons: Asian Trade, Domestic Industry, and Consumer Demand, 1660–1780," in David Jenkins, ed., *The Cambridge History of Western Textiles*, 2 vols. (Cambridge, 2003), I, 493–512. On consumption rates of India cottons in the colonies, see Robert S. DuPlessis, "Cottons Consumption in the Seventeenth- and Eighteenth-Century North Atlantic," in Riello and Parthasarathi, eds., *Spinning World*, 229–231; Jonathan P. Eacott, "Making an Imperial Compromise: The Calico Acts, the Atlantic Colonies, and the Structure of the British Empire," *WMQ*, 3d Ser., LXIX (2012), 731–762. On calicoes in the Spanish empire, see Marta V. Vicente, *Clothing the Spanish Empire: Families and the Calico Trade in the Early Modern Atlantic World* (New York, 2006). On India cottons in the trade for enslaved Africans, see Marion Johnson, *Anglo-African Trade in the Eighteenth Century: English Statistics on African Trade, 1699–1808*, ed. Thomas Lindblad and Robert Ross, *Intercontinenta*, XV (Leiden, 1990), 29, 54–55, 61, 72–73.

The men working for the East India Company were described as, and described themselves as, servants of the Company. They were not indentured servants; instead, they were more akin to employees. The modern notion of employee did not yet exist. Company servants were often appointed through patronage, did not necessarily see salary as the main perk, and often operated extensive businesses that competed with the Company. On the changing understanding of the term *servant* in America, see Lucy Maynard Salmon, "Domestic Service since the Colonial Period," in Salmon, *History and the Texture of Modern Life: Selected Essays*, ed. Nicholas Adams and Bonnie G. Smith (Philadelphia, 2001), 30–38, esp. 37.

Britain, and America shifted over time. They not only intensified and pro-liferated; they also attenuated, decreased, and realigned. Company servants, adventurers, planters, weavers, armies, navies, pirates, merchants, consumers, inventors, industrialists, missionaries, and governments continually created, short-circuited, and rewired such connections. The independence of the thirteen colonies and the growth and mechanization of British industry, prominent topics for historians of America and Britain that are rarely discussed together or with India, illustrate this point. Studying these places and topics together reveals that, as the American Revolution broke some connections, industrialization created new ones.

My selection of India, as opposed to the Ottoman empire, China, or elsewhere, is driven by India's role as the namesake of the mutable place of wealth in early modern England; the perceived importance of its trade in seventeenth- and eighteenth-century Europe; its importance, particularly via the East India Company, in major political controversies of the period; the significance of its goods in stimulating the development of consumer societies and factory production in Britain and, later, America; and its eventual conquest by Britain. India was consistently, and in many remarkably different ways, important for Britain and America from 1600 to 1830. India, it is true, did not exist in the past with the same borders or meanings as in the early twenty-first century. Nevertheless, India is not an anachronistic term, as it was used by Britons following the ancient Greeks, Romans, and Persians to describe much of modern Pakistan, India, and beyond; the places it denoted could vary widely. Britons increasingly saw India as the subcontinent, more or less following the territory of the former Mughal empire, including present-day Pakistan and Bangladesh, most of the region we would today describe as South Asia. India, in short, is often the term of my sources, and its mutability and increasing narrowness in the English language is part of the story.[4]

4. This is not a comprehensive study of Britain's interactions with the whole globe or even with the whole East Indies, although at times I consider China and Southeast Asia in some detail. The so-called Near East, Middle East, China, and other parts of Asia held prominence for Britons and Americans at different times and in some similar and many different ways from India. I do not intend to suggest that Britons and Americans ignored China. Scholars have carefully explored the importance of China's goods in Britain, Europe, and America. See, in particular, David Porter, *Ideographia: The Chinese Cipher in Early Modern Europe* (Stanford, Calif., 2001); Porter, *The Chinese Taste in Eighteenth-Century England* (New York, 2010). Though China was undoubtedly important, Caroline Frank overstates the case that China was the goal of English adventurers and that "its exported manufactures were the crown jewels of the East Indies trades." For England and Britain, in the early seventeenth century such crown jewels were Indonesian and Indian spices and pepper and then, from

Arguing that India was an important part of English, British, and American thinking and the development of consumer culture and industrialization is not to argue that India was thereby subject to substantial informal or cultural imperialism. Notions of informal and formal empire have tended to lead scholars away from recognizing the importance of parts of the world not subject to forms of British power to the development of British power elsewhere. If there were any empires effectively exerting much informal power in the seventeenth through mid-eighteenth centuries, at least, they were mostly the Mughal empire of India, the Ottoman empire of the Mediterranean, and the Ming and Qing empires of China over parts of Asia, Western Europe, and its colonies. Few English people initially imagined formal or informal colonization of extensive territories on the subcontinent, although they did imagine smaller island colonies in the Indian Ocean. English people were aware of their kingdom's relative weaknesses. Nevertheless, it does not follow that India was unimportant to English thinking about Europe and empire more broadly, somewhat as Spain was vital to English thinking about power and empire, even though the English did not expect to conquer Spain.[5]

Scholars working in the global history paradigm have detailed the many ways in which India's Mughal empire was economically, demo-

---

the middle of the seventeenth until the middle of the eighteenth century, Indian fabrics. See Frank, *Objectifying China, Imagining America: Chinese Commodities in Early America* (Chicago, 2011), 5–6. For thoughts on the connections between American literature and "the East" broadly, see Jim Egan, *Oriental Shadows: The Presence of the East in Early American Literature* (Columbus, Ohio, 2011). Studies of colonial and early American trading connections with the East Indies have often used the term "China Trade," as opposed to "India trade." See, for example, Jonathan Goldstein, *Philadelphia and the China Trade, 1682–1846: Commercial, Cultural, and Attitudinal Effects* (University Park, Pa., 1978); Sydney Greenbie and Marjorie Barstow Greenbie, *Gold of Ophir: The China Trade in the Making of America*, rev. ed. (New York, 1937). Much like India, America for Britons often included the West Indies, and then came to be often only the United States, a pattern this book also follows.

5. A welcome surge of publications has shown that Mediterranean Muslims ventured to England, English people ventured throughout the Mediterranean, Mediterranean Muslim merchants and governments alike worked with their English counterparts, and Mediterranean Muslim seamen both captured and joined in league with English seamen and pirates. English people often depicted Mediterranean Muslims on stage and in literature. This work has not yet been accompanied by a similar surge on English interactions with and thinking about the Mughal empire, ruled by Muslims, though largely peopled by Hindus. For more, as well as criticism of the misleading application of postcolonial theory to pre-eighteenth-century English relations with Muslim powers, see, for example, Nabil Matar, *Turks, Moors, and Englishmen in the Age of Discovery* (New York, 1999), 8–13, 20–82; Linda Colley, *Captives: Britain, Empire, and the World, 1600–1850* (London, 2002), esp. 103–104.

graphically, and militarily more impressive than England or any other power in Europe or the Americas. The Mughal empire's strength rested largely on its impressive production of rice, cloth, and other goods. Its economy at the beginning of the seventeenth century supported a population of more than 100 million people, approximately twenty-five times that of England's 4.1 million people. The Asian Indian population was more numerous and much more resistant to European diseases than the native populations of the Americas. Furthermore, the Mughal and, later, Mysore and Maratha empires proved more resilient against European warfare than the increasingly sparse and disjointed indigenous populations in North America. India's agricultural bounty inspired English hopes of finding such American places populated by less formidable societies to cultivate similar commodities, and India's fashions frequently provided new models and modes in England and Britain as a whole. English adventurers sought to turn India's productive strength to their benefit long before Britain superseded India's production and conquered India.[6]

Global history also suggests the need for new narratives of the history of the British empire, building studies and stories of separate "worlds" of empire into studies and stories of the British empire in the world. Part of the push here has come from the fruitful development of Atlantic world approaches, which have shown the strength, variety, and importance of interconnections and communities across the Atlantic Ocean, particularly within European empires, but, to a lesser extent, also among them. Atlantic approaches, like a more insular American historiography, have, however, tended to position the Indian Ocean as, at most, tangential and have often ignored it altogether. The Indian Ocean, like the Atlantic, has become a burgeoning field of study. And, as in the Atlantic, good and real reasons exist for the study of the Indian Ocean as a semidistinct region.

6. For more on the relative strength of Asian polities in the early modern period, see Andre Gunder Frank, *ReOrient: Global Economy in the Asian Age* (Berkeley, Calif., 1998), esp. 52–130; Gerald MacLean, ed., *Re-Orienting the Renaissance: Cultural Exchanges with the East* (New York, 2005); Victor Lieberman, "Transcending East-West Dichotomies: State and Culture Formation in Six Ostensibly Disparate Areas," in Lieberman, ed., *Beyond Binary Histories: Re-imagining Eurasia to c. 1830* (Ann Arbor, Mich., 1999), 28. On seventeenth- and eighteenth-century India's economic advantages and difficulties, see, in particular, David Washbrook, "India in the Early Modern World Economy: Modes of Production, Reproduction and Exchange," *Journal of Global History*, II (2007), 87–111. For population estimates, see Irfan Habib, "Population," in *The Cambridge Economic History of India, c. 1200–c. 1750*, ed. Tapan Raychaudhuri, Irfan Habib, Dharma Kumar (Cambridge, 1982), I, 165–167; E. A. Wrigley and R. S. Schofield, *The Population History of England, 1541–1871: A Reconstruction*, new ed. (Cambridge, 1989), 210, 569.

Nevertheless, such worlds were not isolated from one another, and the term "world" suggests a bounded system that is often too limiting when applied to a single ocean.[7]

Global comparative and integrative perspectives have been more common in histories of English adventurers in the seventeenth century than the eighteenth, but historians have also begun to open new approaches to such perspectives for the latter century from a variety of directions. P. J. Marshall and Jack Greene, in particular, have explored global perspectives of the empire from London and Britain, and scholars of the United States have increasingly looked at the early Republic's relationship with the Pacific Ocean and Asia, alongside the older and more entrenched Atlantic approaches. Historians have developed the most integrative perspectives of Britain, the Americas, Africa, and Asia by tracking individuals

---

7. The idea of the British empire in the world was proposed by C. A. Bayly in his pathbreaking *Imperial Meridian: The British Empire and the World, 1780–1830* (New York, 1989). Bayly's world was still largely Eurasian, leaving room for considerable new work on relations with the Americas and Africa. Most of the essays in Nicholas Canny, ed., *The Oxford History of the British Empire*, I, *The Origins of Empire: British Overseas Enterprise to the Close of the Seventeenth Century* (Oxford, 1998), and P. J. Marshall, ed., *The Oxford History of the British Empire*, II, *The Eighteenth Century* (Oxford, 1998), except for a few on warfare and Marshall's introduction to the second volume, also had little to say about America and India together, or India before British conquest. The selection of fine essays in Douglas M. Peers and Nandini Gooptu, eds., *India and the British Empire*, the Oxford History of the British Empire—Companion Series (Oxford, 2012), likewise gives the impression that America and Africa have little significance in understanding India's place in the British empire, or that India mattered to the British empire or economy before 1750. For other ideas on how Indian and Atlantic Ocean histories might be integrated, see Peter A. Coclanis, "Atlantic World or Atlantic / World?" *WMQ*, 3d Ser., LXIII (2006), 725–742; H. V. Bowen, "Britain in the Indian Ocean Region and Beyond: Contours, Connections, and the Creation of a Global Maritime Empire," in Bowen, Elizabeth Mancke, and John G. Reid, eds., *Britain's Oceanic Empire: Atlantic and Indian Ocean Worlds, c. 1550–1850* (Cambridge, 2012), 46–47.

The dean of British Atlantic history, George Louis Beer, did not look to India in his *Old Colonial System, 1660–1754* (New York, 1912). Charles M. Andrews considered India but did little with its connections to America; see Andrews, *The Colonial Period of American History* (New Haven, Conn., 1934), 87, 330–332, 342. For a brief overview of British Atlantic historiography, see David Armitage, "Three Concepts of Atlantic History," in Armitage and Michael J. Braddick, eds., *The British Atlantic World, 1500–1800* (New York, 2002), 11–27. A few studies explore the relationship between the early American Republic and India; see, for example, Susan S. Bean, *Yankee India: American Commercial and Cultural Encounters with India in the Age of Sail, 1784–1860* (Salem, Mass., 2001); James R. Fichter, *So Great a Proffit: How the East Indies Trade Transformed Anglo-American Capitalism* (Cambridge, Mass., 2010); Rosemarie Zagarri, "The Significance of the 'Global Turn' for the Early American Republic: Globalization in the Age of Nation-Building," *Journal of the Early Republic*, XXXI (2011), esp. 10–37.

and commodities, particularly cotton, that moved about the British empire, methods used to great success for the eighteenth century by historians such as Linda Colley, Maya Jasanoff, and Sven Beckert. Building on these global approaches, I simultaneously work through the deeply integrated—but generally separated by scholars—histories of ideas, politics, religion, production, trade, fashion, and consumer culture.[8]

The India trade had vital and prominent roles in the development of English and British Atlantic consumer society, which began largely in the seventeenth century with the introduction of more and more globally sourced and standardized goods, including sugar, cottons, and silks. A broadening range of people regularly purchased such goods. Despite this expansion, consumer spending was most substantial among the middling and upper sorts, people with wealth placing them in the top 10 percent and, eventually, 20 percent of the population. The middling sorts established and managed new interactions among the state, merchants, producers, and consumers. Histories of these interactions suggest that de-

8. For the seventeenth century, Charles Wilson, *Profit and Power: A Study of England and the Dutch Wars* (London, 1957), explored both oceans but alternated between them (see 44, 117). Kenneth R. Andrews, whose work *Trade, Plunder, and Settlement: Maritime Enterprise and the Genesis of the British Empire, 1480-1630* (New York, 1984) helped revitalize more global approaches to empire, took a similar regional approach (269-270). A strong model of an integrative approach for the seventeenth century remains: Robert Brenner, *Merchants and Revolution: Commercial Change, Political Conflict, and London's Overseas Traders, 1550-1653* (Princeton, N.J., 1993). For the eighteenth century, P. J. Marshall has produced two integrative narratives largely using the view from London; see Marshall, *Making and Unmaking of Empires;* Marshall, *Remaking the British Atlantic: The United States and the British Empire after American Independence* (New York, 2012). Jack P. Greene explores a set of British intellectual currents critical of British activities in Ireland, India, Africa, and the Americas, with a regional organization; see Greene, *Evaluating Empire and Confronting Colonialism in Eighteenth-Century Britain* (New York, 2013). Linda Colley's work on Elizabeth Marsh shows that some Britons circulated throughout the global empire, and not within inscribed worlds; see Colley, *The Ordeal of Elizabeth Marsh: A Woman in World History* (New York, 2007). Colley's *Captives* also ranges broadly, though it largely moves from one geographic location to another over time. Maya Jasanoff tracks the global British loyalist diaspora from the thirteen colonies instigated by the American Revolution; see Jasanoff, *Liberty's Exiles: American Loyalists in the Revolutionary World* (New York, 2011). Books on single commodities have also successfully illustrated interconnections across space. For excellent commodity studies of cotton, see Giorgio Riello, *Cotton: The Fabric that Made the Modern World* (New York, 2013); and Sven Beckert, *Empire of Cotton: A Global History* (New York, 2014). As studies focused on cotton, neither explores other India goods or British notions of India and its peoples in encouraging and shaping British trade and imperialism. On the importance of approaches to imperial history that include culture, see Kathleen Wilson, ed., *A New Imperial History: Culture, Identity, and Modernity in Britain and the Empire, 1660-1840* (New York, 2004), 10-16.

mand and supply-side theories alike oversimplify the process of growing consumption. In the eighteenth century, such interactions continued to multiply and thicken, and changes in retailing, advertising, and branding followed, all of which can be seen readily through India goods. Industrialization, itself driven by simulating India goods, then transformed production, eventually lowering prices, increasing output, and standardizing products further.[9]

Historians of India and America have separately stressed that Britons and Americans in each place adopted an increasingly British consumer culture and aesthetic. Discussions of this process, called "Anglicization," tend to gloss over more complex and geographically wide-ranging interconnections. Most economic and cultural historians of colonial and early American trade, for instance, use the terms "British" or "European" to describe the imports flooding into America from London, Bristol, and Liverpool in the eighteenth and early nineteenth century. Many of these goods, however, were imported into Britain from elsewhere in the world and then reexported to America. As their global trade and consumption of goods expanded, Britons developed complex imperial and not essentially British consumer aesthetics that combined manufactured goods and

9. Such historians as Joan Thirsk, Chandra Mukerji, Simon Schama, Lorna Weatherill, and Carole Shammas have documented substantial growth in the diversity and quantity of consumer goods in seventeenth-century Europe and America. See Thirsk, *Economic Policy and Projects: The Development of a Consumer Society in Early Modern England* (Oxford, 1978), esp. 106–107; Mukerji, *From Graven Images: Patterns of Modern Materialism* (New York, 1983); Schama, *The Embarrassment of Riches: An Interpretation of Dutch Culture in the Golden Age* (London, 1988), 289–323, 351–371; Weatherill, *Consumer Behaviour and Material Culture in Britain, 1660–1760* (New York, 1988); Shammas, *The Pre-industrial Consumer in England and America* (Oxford, 1990). Peter Earle estimated that only 10 percent of the English population could afford to engage in significant consumer spending in the late seventeenth century; see Earle, *The Making of the English Middle Class: Business, Society, and Family Life in London, 1660–1730* (Berkeley, Calif., 1989), 335. Meanwhile, Neil McKendrick, John Brewer, and J. H. Plumb argued for a mid-eighteenth-century consumer revolution; see McKendrick, Brewer, and Plumb, *The Birth of a Consumer Society: The Commercialization of Eighteenth-Century England* (Bloomington, Ind., 1982). For America, see Richard L. Bushman, *The Refinement of America: Persons, Houses, Cities* (New York, 1992), esp. xii, 70–115; Cary Carson, "The Consumer Revolution in Colonial British America: Why Demand?" in Carson, Ronald Hoffman, and Peter J. Albert, eds., *Of Consuming Interests: The Style of Life in the Eighteenth Century* (Charlottesville, Va., 1994), esp. 486–487. For an example of the interactions among producers, traders, and consumers in developing markets for a pre-industrial good, see David Hancock, "Commerce and Conversation in the Eighteenth-Century Atlantic: The Invention of Madeira Wine," *Journal of Interdisciplinary History*, XXIX (1998), 197; see also Hancock, *Oceans of Wine: Madeira and the Emergence of American Trade and Taste* (London, 2009), 144–171.

styles from Europe, India, and China with Atlantic produce such as tobacco, sugar, and mahogany. Passing goods through London did not make
them British. Anglicization was therefore influenced significantly by what
might be termed "Indianization," and both were subsets of a larger process
of "imperialization"—the development and circulation of Britain's imperi-
ally shaped consumption practices and aesthetics.[10]

The adoption, adaptation, and rejection of different India goods in different places at different times within this imperial consumer culture had
important implications for the ideological and political discourses of empire. Objects and ideas were mutually constitutive. The politics of consumer society connected people and things, ideas and experiences, and
spaces and places. Decisions about buying, owning, using, and rejecting
goods factored into decisions about domestic manufacturing and protec-
tionism, trade policies, and the maintenance of social, racial, and sexual
hierarchies. The acts and ideas associated with consumer goods, moreover, were part of debates over justifications for imperial rule and the conversion of other peoples to Christianity. British and American people did
not simply define themselves against other peoples and cultures. They recognized not only difference but also sameness, and they intentionally and

10. Colin Kidd noted in 1999, "From the Glorious Revolution until 1763 the principal
dynamic of colonial development was Anglicisation"; see Kidd, *British Identities before Na-
tionalism: Ethnicity and Nationhood in the Atlantic World, 1600–1800* (New York, 1999),
263. Timothy Breen, like most scholars of colonial America, consistently describes all of the
various goods imported from Britain as British. See Breen, *The Marketplace of Revolution:
How Consumer Politics Shaped American Independence* (New York, 2004), 34–71. The Anglicization of British communities in India has also been widely accepted. George D. Bearce
saw this Anglicization at an abstract level: a major shift in the social and political values of
Britons who turned against Indian politics, law, and learning. For Suresh Chandra Ghosh
and E. M. Collingham, major changes occurred in how people lived, in what they thought
about Indian goods, and in what they owned, used, and wore in the early nineteenth century. Collingham suggests, with William Dalrymple, a sort of feedback mechanism in which
increased access to European material culture and increasing numbers of European people,
particularly women, reinforced ideological change. See Bearce, *British Attitudes towards
India, 1784–1858* (Oxford, 1961), 65–68, 153–162; Collingham, *Imperial Bodies: The Physical
Experience of the Raj, c. 1800–1947* (Cambridge, 2001), 50–80; Dalrymple, *White Mughals:
Love and Betrayal in Eighteenth-Century India* (New York, 2004), 394–395. My argument
imperializes Cary Carson's point that consumer society emerged in part to standardize "social communications" in a dramatically new world of human mobility; see Carson, "The
Consumer Revolution," in Carson, Hoffman, and Albert, eds., *Of Consuming Interests*, 523,
553–664. The classic study of Britain as an imperial consumer culture remains James Walvin,
Fruits of Empire: Exotic Produce and British Taste, 1660–1800 (New York, 1997). On limited
colonial manufacturing and the myth of colonial self-sufficiency, see Shammas, *The Pre-
industrial Consumer*, 4–8, 52–65.

unintentionally claimed sameness to obscure difference and claimed difference to obscure sameness.[11]

Studying only Indian products popular in Britain and America therefore creates incomplete pictures of producer and consumer decision making as well as of imperial economies and politics. Cottons, shawls, umbrellas, curry, and tea (cultivated in huge plantations by Britons and Indians in India after this period) have come to be considered quintessentially British. They were all adopted from Asia and primarily from India at various times in various ways. Hookah pipes and palanquins, however, were not adopted in Britain or America but were nevertheless embraced by Britons and Americans in India, and frequently used by other Britons and Americans for thinking about India and themselves and for creating ideological space for the acceptance of other India goods. The less commonly studied and less commonly adopted hookah pipes and palanquins are as essential to this book as the more commonly studied cottons and more widely adapted umbrellas and curries.

Britons sought to sell the idea of empire using ideas about India, and they built their empire in large part out of notions of using, and when possible exploiting, lands and peoples for the cultivation and production of Indian commodities to sell to themselves, their colonists, and others. More than that, they transported and sold the manufactured goods of India itself as a means of expanding and integrating British imperial strength and culture. Selling empire metaphorically and materially encouraged fears of imperial corruption and decadence and also provided tools to rebut such fears. The importance of ideas about India and the importance of India's goods and simulations of India's goods alike continued in the United States even after the American Revolution. Britain lost the American Revolutionary War, but, with the aid of old and new relations with India and its goods, it hardly lost America.[12]

11. Barbara Fuchs, *Mimesis and Empire: The New World, Islam, and European Identities* (New York, 2001), 1–4, 164. For more on the move beyond simple binaries of English and others and toward an understanding of early modern English culture and identity formation as a complicated process of rejection, adoption, and adaptation that often followed the experiences of powers in the Mediterranean, see Daniel Vitkus, *Turning Turk: English Theater and the Multicultural Mediterranean, 1570–1630* (New York, 2003), esp. 6–14, 23. As Alison Games explains, cultural adaptation and adoption could also be a strategic move of "dissimulation," not a shift in identity; see Games, *Web of Empire*, esp. 52–79.

12. America's relations with India both support and complicate Eliga H. Gould's claim that, "in important respects, the center of the American Republic was still in Britain and the British Empire." See Gould, "Entangled Atlantic Histories," *AHR*, CXII (2007), 1422. Jonathan Dull has also argued that the thirteen colonies and Britain both won the Revolu-

Those suffering the greatest loss under imperial power were not British colonists or the majority of U.S. citizens; they were enslaved peoples, native Americans, and, increasingly, British subjects in India and Britons working in factories in Britain. Britain's drive to emulate India's wealth and manufactures caused substantial suffering, although cheap cottons, for instance, also improved, in some measure, the lives of the expanding numbers of people who wore them. The imperial dream was a nightmare for many in Britain, in the colonies Britain conquered, and in the territories that became the United States and its empire. Historians have increasingly recovered the incredible and painful stories of some of the sufferers of the British empire and of early industrialization, but most individual stories are irretrievably lost. I do not try to recover them here, but instead I try to reveal the centrality of the British use of India in the making of the imperial schemes, cultures, and systems of which such stories were a fundamental part.[13]

---

tionary War and that France and Holland lost. Dull's focus did not stray far from the Atlantic. See Dull, *A Diplomatic History of the American Revolution* (New Haven, Conn., 1985), 161–162.

13. Some historians of early America have explicitly recognized the duality of British colonists as violent conquerors and as subjects of British rule in the Atlantic. See, for example, William Appleman Williams, *The Tragedy of American Diplomacy* (Cleveland, Ohio, 1959), 19–20; Francis Jennings, *The Creation of America: Through Revolution to Empire* (New York, 2000), 42, 79. On enslavement in the Atlantic, see, for example, Eugene D. Genovese, *Roll, Jordan, Roll: The World the Slaves Made* (New York, 1976); Philip D. Morgan, *Slave Counterpoint: Black Culture in the Eighteenth-Century Chesapeake and Lowcountry* (Chapel Hill, N.C., 1998). The material on the early working classes and eighteenth-century urban poor in Britain is also staggering; see, for example, Anna Clark, *The Struggle for the Breeches: Gender and the Making of the British Working Class* (Berkeley, Calif., 1995); Peter Linebaugh, *The London Hanged: Crime and Civil Society in the Eighteenth Century* (London, 1991). Debendra Bijoy Mitra argued that the Company failed to gain monopolistic control over Indian weavers and that the weavers already struggled financially before the Company. Hameeda Hossain then argued that the Company effectively reduced the weavers' freedoms and incentives to produce cloth. Most recently, Prasannan Parthasarathi has demonstrated that the Company increasingly exploited the weavers. See Mitra, *The Cotton Weavers of Bengal, 1757–1833* (Calcutta, 1978), 5–8, 130–150, 216–217; Hossain, *The Company Weavers of Bengal: The East India Company and the Organization of Textile Production in Bengal, 1750–1813* (Delhi, 1988), xv, 173–178; Parthasarathi, *The Transition to a Colonial Economy: Weavers, Merchants, and Kings in South India, 1720–1800* (New York, 2001).

1 "Those Curious Manufactures That Empire Affords"

India Goods and Early English Expansion

Thomas Abbay's dedication to his 1612 revision of John Smith's *Map of Virginia* asked English people "to consider, to conceave, and apprehend Virginia, which might be, or breed us a second India." Abbay recalled the mistaken doubters of Columbus and warned English people not to similarly doubt the value of Virginia. Smith thought Virginia to be on the same latitude as Rome, Greece, Constantinople, and Asia's currently most wealthy kingdoms—a promising situation to be sure. Virginia would be a godly Protestant India fully under English control, in Edward Wynne's sense as a source of wealth as well as in the Asian commodities that it produced.[1]

In the same work, Smith's companions explained that by labor and trade, instead of "spoile and pillage," Virginia would become as valuable as the West Indies were to Spain. English wealth in Virginia would be created by teaching the local people "to be tractable, civil, and industrious" or by planting colonies of Englishmen to "bring to perfection the commodities of the countrie." Virginia was not stocked with "mines of gold and silver, nor such rare commodities as the Portugals and Spaniards found in the East and West Indies," but this was for the better. Indeed, Edward Waterhouse argued that the Spanish empire's wealth now came, not so much from gold and silver mines, but from transplanting, cultivating (often with enslaved labor), and trading such commodities as sugar,

---

1. Edward Terry, *A Voyage to East-India; Wherein Some Things Are Taken Notice of in Our Passage Thither, but Many More in Our Abode There, within That Rich and Most Spacious Empire of the Great Mogol* . . . (London, 1655), 253; John Smith, *A Map of Virginia; with a Description of the Countrey, the Commodities, People, Government and Religion* . . . *Whereunto Is Annexed the Proceedings of Those Colonies, Since Their First Departure from England, with the Discourses, Orations, and Relations of the Salvages, and the Accidents that Befell Them in All Their Journies and Discoveries* . . . (Oxford, 1612), dedication page by Thomas Abbay. On the authorship, revision, and publication of *Map of Virginia*, see Lyon Gardiner Tyler, ed., *Narratives of Early Virginia, 1606–1625* (New York, 1907), 75. Smith also figured that Virginia was on the same northern latitude as the southern latitude that was home to some of South America's richest gold mines. See Smith, *The Generall Historie of Virginia, New-England, and the Summer Isles* . . . (London, 1624), 210–211.

ginger, indigo, cotton, tobacco, and drugs. A lot of these same commodities, many of them previously obtained from Asia, would be gained instead in Virginia. Smith included Waterhouse's work in his own. In this model, England's Atlantic empire would avoid the dual moral dangers of plundering the Americas and dealing directly with Asia's non-Christian powers.[2]

Smith's desire to colonize America to cultivate commodities needs to be seen alongside his attacks on Ottoman Muslims and Spanish Catholics and his fears of Asian-inspired avarice. Before going on the first ships to Jamestown in 1607, Smith had traveled eastward to join the Austrian forces at war with the Ottoman empire. In his *True Travels, Adventures, and Observations of Captaine John Smith* (1630), which recounted these activities, Smith disdained various non-Protestant cultures and spoke out against the English pirates who joined the enemy "Turks" and "Moores." Envy of Ottoman and Asian commodities and wealth could be a motivating force for adventurers, but so, too, could envy of Spanish success and of the success of other English people. Many English thinkers, however, did not envy what they saw as the implications of Muslim and Catholic forms of wealth and power accumulation. English humanists, in particular, often believed that Asian luxury and tyranny had undone Rome and may now undo England. Even Smith, who agreed with Spanish exploitation of native peoples and countered humanist belief in the need for just possession in the Americas, argued that Rome failed when its people became idle, inexperienced, self-adulating, jealous, politically corrupt, and lewd. He similarly explained the early failures at Jamestown in part by connecting the Indies to such corruption, noting, "For all the *China* wealth, nor *Indies* can / Suffice the minde of an av'ritious man."[3]

2. The section from Smith's companions is attributed in the text to Richard Wiffin, William Phettiplace, and Anas Todkill; see Smith, *Map of Virginia*, 76–77. On trade as the source of Spanish wealth, see Smith, *Generall Historie of Virginia*, 147–149. The material on Spanish trade was reprinted along with considerable other material, though not including the specific material on latitude, from Edward Waterhouse, *A Declaration of the State of the Colony and Affaires in Virginia* (London, 1622), 5, 22–33. Smith and Waterhouse agreed that native American attacks on English settlers justified conquest, displacement, and enslavement following the Spanish example in their colonies. For similar hopes to obtain East Indian pepper, silk, and cotton at Saint Christopher, see Smith, *The True Travels, Adventures, and Observations of Captaine John Smith; in Europe, Asia, Affrica, and America . . .* (London, 1630), 51, 54. Steve Pincus also addresses Smith's understanding of the origin of wealth in labor; see Pincus, "Rethinking Mercantilism: Political Economy, the British Empire, and the Atlantic World in the Seventeenth and Eighteenth Centuries," *WMQ*, 3d Ser., LXIX (2012), 16.

3. Smith, *True Travels*, esp. 30, 39, 58–60; John Smith, *A Description of New England;*

In *True Travels,* Smith also confused the Ottoman and Mughal empires, China, and elsewhere in the East Indies. Smith apparently thought the Mughal emperor and the Great Turk were one and the same. He skipped over describing the Mughal empire itself, then hoped to use the accounts of other authors to tell his readers about "*Cathay* towards the North-east, and *Chyna* towards the South-east, where are many of the most famous Kingdomes in the world; where most arts, plenty, and curiosities are in such abundance, as might seeme incredible." Such confusion helped to encourage the broadness of early English expansion attempts, but it also dissipated as the English came to focus more on the Mughal empire. As Smith alluded to, a small but growing number of English people had direct experiences with the Mughal empire and the Indian Ocean more broadly, experiences that were increasingly reported in print. India itself, as opposed to more general conceptions of the East Indies, would become a vital engine driving English trade, colonization, and fashion. That vitality would be tied tightly to English adventures in Africa and, particularly, the Atlantic colonies, but not necessarily in the ways that many English people, including Smith, had hoped or expected.[4]

Throughout the seventeenth century, as England embedded enclaves in North America and the West Indies, English adventurers, thinkers, and leaders rethought India. No longer was it so much a mutable place of wealth or a place of marvelous commodities to be reproduced in America. Failure to find gold or cultivate Asian commodities in the Atlantic colonies, as well as religious and economic contests with other European powers, helped to stimulate new ideas and new structural systems of empire and trade. English people increasingly tried to use India's manufacturing superiority to their own and England's benefit. At the same time, India became an important part of the solution for wringing more value

---

or, The Observations, and Discoveries, of Captain John Smith (Admirall of That Country) in the North of America . . . (London, 1616), 32, 43–44; Smith, *Generall Historie of Virginia,* 53 ("*China* wealth"). In London, Smith became an important member of Robert Bruce Cotton's learned, powerful, and connected circle that was opposed to Charles I's absolutist and Catholic tendencies. According to David S. Shields, Smith published *True Travels* to entrench support for colonization and naval power and to elevate himself as an "an avatar of primitive virtue" endowed with the heroic heritage of Anglo-Saxon English liberty. See Shields, "The Genius of Ancient Britain," in Peter C. Mancall, ed., *The Atlantic World and Virginia, 1550–1624* (Chapel Hill, N.C., 2007), 494–504. For the definitive biography of Smith, see Philip L. Barbour, *The Three Worlds of Captain John Smith* (Boston, 1964). For more on Smith's critiques of humanism, see Andrew Fitzmaurice, *Humanism and America: An Intellectual History of English Colonisation, 1500–1625* (New York, 2003), 168, 177–186.

4. Smith, *True Travels,* 31, 49.

out of the Atlantic colonies by facilitating the trade in enslaved Africans and more money out of English consumers throughout the Atlantic by popularizing new fashions. Stimulating such consumer demand, however, was not as simple as it often appears. People did not automatically want nor could they necessarily afford India's goods. Demand for new fashions, such as cotton calicoes, needed to be carefully cultivated, much like the growth of commodities needed to be cultivated in new colonies and trade itself needed to be cultivated to open sources of supply and drive down prices. Successfully expanding demand for India's goods, moreover, might exacerbate fears of India's supposedly dangerous luxury corrupting England. Opportunities for profit and material satisfactions, on the one hand, and of potential economic and moral impoverishment from the pursuit of those satisfactions, on the other, together shaped the ways in which English adventurers, merchants, leaders, and consumers thought about and pursued their empire and trade. From the late sixteenth century, English conceptions of Indias, India, and India's products alike were instrumental in this dialectical relationship.[5]

Indias Everywhere

In English thinking and expeditions, the alluring and dangerous wonder of Indias fused Catholic and Muslim, Europe and Asia, past and present, Old World and New. English promoters and adventurers considered religious divisions not only between Protestants and Catholics but also between Protestants and Muslims, and they saw Catholics and Muslims as similar in many ways. The Muslim-ruled Ottoman empire was part of the known ancient Mediterranean classical world and was tied tightly into European trade and politics. As Smith exclaimed, Constantinople was "the most pleasant and plentifull Citie in Europe." The Levant Company, founded in 1581, dramatically enhanced English connections to the Ottoman empire by tapping into large diasporic networks of Jewish, Greek

---

5. On the importance of the marvelous for Europeans as a tool to understand the unfamiliar and to position it as terrible or desirable, see Stephen Greenblatt, *Marvelous Possessions: The Wonder of the New World* (Chicago, 1991), 22. Gerald MacLean has argued for European imperial envy of the Ottomans; the idea also applies to English imperial envy of Spain. See MacLean, *Looking East: English Writing and the Ottoman Empire before 1800* (New York, 2007), 20–23, 44. Many scholars have explored the fear of "turning Turk" or "going native," both on an individual and a national level. See, for example, Daniel Carey, "Questioning Incommensurability in Early Modern Cultural Exchange," *Common Knowledge*, VI (1997), 32–50.

Orthodox, Armenian, and Muslim traders interested in English woolens and, particularly, English bullion. Many of the goods available in the Ottoman empire, however—including spices, pepper, raw silk, and cottons—might be had cheaper and in greater variety in Asia and the Spice Islands, even if the markets for English goods in these more distant polities were also weaker. America, too, might offer similar wealth and commodities; it might replicate or defuse the risks of supposedly Asian dangers of moral and political corruption; or it might not do any such things.[6]

Influential imperial promoter Richard Hakluyt and many English leaders shared understandings of a twin threat presented by Catholic and Muslim tyranny. First published in 1589, Hakluyt's *Principal Navigations* was the most important public document encouraging English imperial expansion and trade around the world. Hakluyt used his lengthy discussion of Asiatic riches and rule in part to reinforce English concerns over Catholicism and Islam. Hakluyt constructed both an accessible geographic space that covered the globe known to Europeans as well as a national English history and future providential global legacy. Spain, with expansionary tendencies in Europe, was an imminent threat. Spain's Catholic Philip II, as Queen Mary's husband, had been England's king. Later, as king of Spain and Portugal, he believed the world was quite literally and rightfully his to rule as God's appointed and absolute earthly overlord. The English needed to contend with principal Catholic enemy

6. Smith often included the "Turke" in lists of European powers, and the Ottoman empire does not appear to be part of his discussions of Spanish and Portuguese exploration in the East and West Indies, Africa, America, and "Terraincognita." See, for example, Smith, *Description of New England*, 43–44. More broadly, Daniel Goffman explains that after the fifteenth century the Ottoman empire was considered European, a designation that changed beginning with the nineteenth-century Orientalists. See Goffman, *The Ottoman Empire and Early Modern Europe* (New York, 2002), esp. 1–20, 169–188 (on trading diasporas in the Ottoman empire). On imports, see Ralph Davis, "English Imports from the Middle East, 1580–1780," in M. A. Cook, ed., *Studies in the Economic History of the Middle East: From the Rise of Islam to the Present Day* (New York, 1970), 193–206. In addition to woolens and tin, historians have debated the scale of English weapon and gunpowder exports to the Ottoman empire. These exports appear to have been significant in particular moments and as models for emulation, but overall they do not seem to have rivaled woolens and tin in value. For an overview of the debate and a careful assessment, see Gábor Agoston, "*Merces Prohibitae*: The Anglo-Ottoman Trade in War Materials and the Dependence Theory," *Oriente Moderno*, n.s., XX (2001), 177–179, 183–192. On bullion exports to the Ottoman empire, see Robert Brenner, *Merchants and Revolution: Commercial Change, Political Conflict, and London's Overseas Traders, 1550–1653* (Princeton, N.J., 1993), 31–32. On the raw silk trade, see Halil İnalcık and Donald Quataert, eds., *An Economic and Social History of the Ottoman Empire*, II (New York, 1994), 502–505.

Spain, but they also had to contend with potential Muslim allies and ene-mies as well. Martin Luther had drawn equivalence between the Spanish and Ottoman empires, and some English and Scottish thinkers steeped in classical literature equated the Ottomans with the barbarians who had overrun Rome. In the mid-1580s, Elizabeth I's secretary of state, Francis Walsingham, and William Harborne sought an English-Ottoman alliance against the Spanish so that these *"limbs of the devil"* might turn against each other to "advantage" Protestant England and the "true Church and doctrine of the gospel may . . . have leisure to grow to such strength as shall be requisite for *suppression of them both.*" Harborne was to impress upon the sultan that the king of Spain now ruled much of Europe and *"the whole Indias* both *east and west* whence he draweth infinite treasures, the sinews of war." Religious conflict among Protestants, Catholics, and Mus-lims was thereby bound up with notions of wealth-producing Indias.[7]

For Hakluyt, trade with Asia and colonization in America would be complementary countervailing Protestant forces to the leading Catholic and Muslim powers. In dedicating *Principal Navigations* to Walsingham, Hakluyt noted that the interest expressed by the rulers and people of the Moluccas, Java, Japan, and the Philippines to interact with England was "a pledge of Gods further favour both unto us and them: to them especially,

---

7. For more on Hakluyt's influence, see David Armitage, *The Ideological Origins of the British Empire* (Cambridge, 2000), 72–80. On Hakluyt's construction of geography, memory, and providential mission, see Mary C. Fuller, *Voyages in Print: English Travel to America, 1576-1624* (Cambridge, 1995), 148–153; Louis B. Wright, *Middle-Class Culture in Elizabe-than England* (Chapel Hill, N.C., 1935), 526–533; David Harris Sacks, "Discourses of West-ern Planting: Richard Hakluyt and the Making of the Atlantic World," in Mancall, ed., *The Atlantic World and Virginia*, 450–451. On Philip II, see Geoffrey Parker, "The Place of Tudor England in the Messianic Vision of Philip II of Spain: The Prothero Lecture," Royal Histori-cal Society, *Transactions*, 6th Ser., XII (2002), 172–221; Marie Tanner, *The Last Descendant of Aeneas: The Hapsburgs and the Mythic Image of the Emperor* (New Haven, Conn., 1993), 131–145. There was significant disagreement in Spain over the monarch's right to rule the world. See Anthony Pagden, *Lords of All the World: Ideologies of Empire in Spain, Britain, and France, c. 1500-c. 1800* (New Haven, Conn., 1995), 43–62. On English alliances with the Ottoman empire, see Conyers Read, *Mr. Secretary Walsingham and the Policy of Queen Elizabeth*, 3 vols. (Cambridge, Mass., 1925), III, 225–230 (quotations from a transcribed let-ter from Walsingham to Harborne, Oct. 8, 1585). For more, see Daniel Vitkus, *Turning Turk: English Theater and the Multicultural Mediterranean, 1570-1630* (New York, 2003), 59–62; Jerry Toner, *Homer's Turk: How Classics Shaped Ideas of the East* (Cambridge, Mass., 2013), 79–92; Nabil Matar, *Islam in Britain, 1558-1685* (New York, 1998), 123–125. Similarly, in 1603 the Moroccan ruler Ahmad al-Mansur suggested to Elizabeth that Morocco and En-gland should join forces to conquer the West Indies from Spain; see Matar, *Turks, Moors, and Englishmen in the Age of Discovery* (New York, 1999), 9.

unto whose doores I doubt not in time shalbe by us caried the incomparable treasure of the trueth of Christianity, and of the Gospell, while we use and exercise common trade with their marchants." England's influence would be godly, but its treasure would be of the earthly kind. Portuguese success in western India throughout the sixteenth century suggested that the English could achieve Hakluyt's promise. In America, meanwhile, excess English labor would cultivate commodities on supposedly excess land. These colonies would make productive the poor (who seemed to Hakluyt to be a drain on the kingdom's treasure), convert American Indians to create more Protestant supporters, purchase English cloth, and generate tremendous wealth for England. In his 1584 "Particuler Discourse concerninge the Greate Necessitie and Manifolde Commodyties That Are Like to Growe to This Realme of Englande by the Westerne Discoveries Lately Attempted," Hakluyt claimed, "I may well and truly conclude with reason and aucthoritie that all the commodities of all our olde decayed and daungerous trades in all Europe, Africa, and Asia" could be obtained in Virginia. Cultivating Asian commodities in Virginia would outflank all of England's broadly Old World rivals. It would be the plan that Smith would later follow, but it was different from other contemporary ideas, such as Sir Walter Ralegh's plan to use colonization in the Atlantic to extract gold directly, as the Spanish had done. Hakluyt and many others also hoped for the discovery of a Northwest Passage through or around North America to gain Asia's goods. A Northwest Passage, however, would only give English merchants a fleeting advantage over other European traders and do nothing to reduce the economic imbalance between England and Asia. Cultivating Asian commodities in America could solve economic problems that a Northwest Passage could not.[8]

8. Richard Hakluyt, *The Principal Navigations Voyages Traffiques and Discoveries of the English Nation* . . . (1589) (Glasgow, 1903), I, xxi; Hakluyt, *A Particuler Discourse concerninge the Greate Necessitie and Manifolde Commodyties That Are Like to Growe to This Realme of Englande by the Westerne Discoveries Lately Attempted, Written in the Yere 1584*, ed. David B. Quinn and Alison M. Quinn (London, 1993), 27. The commonly used title "Discourse of Western Planting" deemphasizes Hakluyt's focus on the variety of commodities. For arguments about trade, see Richard Helgerson, *Forms of Nationhood: The Elizabethan Writing of England* (Chicago, 1992), 181–187; Sacks, "Discourses of Western Planting," in Mancall, ed., *The Atlantic World and Virginia*, 423. For more, see Peter C. Mancall, *Hakluyt's Promise: An Elizabethan's Obsession for an English America* (New Haven, Conn., 2007). On gold extraction, see Pincus, "Rethinking Mercantilism," *WMQ*, 3d Ser., LXIX (2012), 15–16. The positions of theorists on sources of wealth were also not necessarily fixed; see Cathy Matson, "Imperial Political Economy: An Ideological Debate and Shifting Practices," *WMQ*, 3d Ser., LXIX (2012), 36.

Before Asian goods could be cultivated in America, or at least gained from India, the English first had to secure a foothold in each territory, and their initial forays were less than successful. English attempts at colonization in North America at Roanoke in the 1580s had dissolved in the face of efforts back home to thwart the famous invasion plans of the Spanish Armada. In 1590, the first English attempt to emulate the successes of the Portuguese in sailing to India by way of the Cape of Good Hope only reached Madeira. A group of London merchants then dispatched three more ships to attempt the journey. One ship, captained by James Lancaster, made it beyond Mozambique. Lancaster opted for piracy instead of trade, and his crew successfully attacked several local and Portuguese vessels in the Indian Ocean. Nevertheless, they suffered severe hardships, and many died. Another attempt to sail east in 1596 led by Benjamin Wood and financed by Robert Dudley failed completely. The Levant Company and other regulated chartered companies suggested part of the means forward by pursuing expansion at little state cost and limited direct state control while still offering potential state benefits. But failure in America and in the Indian Ocean trade also suggested the need, in these two pursuits alike, for joint-stock companies that pooled capital and spread risks and profits.[9]

The charters for the joint-stock East India Company (1600) and Virginia Company (1606) reflected the geographic, political, religious, and demographic reports from English adventurers, particularly those recounted in *Principal Navigations*. Elizabeth I chartered the East India Company for "the Honour of our Nation, the Wealth of our People, and the Encouragement of them, and others of our loving Subjects in their good Enterprizes, for the Increase of our Navigation, and the Advancement of lawful Traffick, to the Benefit of our Common Wealth." The charter granted the Company the right to purchase and sell goods and territory east of the Cape of Good Hope. James I's Virginia charter for the North American coast, in contrast, empowered colonists to simply seize "all the

9. William Foster, "A Forgotten Voyage of John Davis," *Geographical Journal*, II (1893), 146–149; Clements R. Markham, ed., *The Voyages of Sir James Lancaster, Kt., to the East Indies* . . . (London, 1877), 1–34; J. Horton Ryley, *Ralph Fitch, England's Pioneer to India and Burma: His Companions and Contemporaries, with His Remarkable Narrative Told in His Own Words* (London, 1899), 248; David Beers Quinn, *Set Fair for Roanoke: Voyages and Colonies, 1584–1606* (Chapel Hill, N.C., 1985); David B. Quinn and A. N. Ryan, *England's Sea Empire, 1550–1642* (London, 1983), 80–91, 138–145. For a brief overview of the advantages of joint-stock companies, see Michael J. Braddick, *State Formation in Early Modern England, c. 1550–1700* (New York, 2000), 398–401.

Lands, Woods, Soil, Grounds, Havens, Ports, Rivers, Mines, Minerals, Marshes, Waters, Fishings, Commodities, and Hereditaments" within the charter's bounds. The Virginia charter encouraged colonists to develop agricultural cultivation and extract timber, minerals, and fish to transport to England. Additionally, James I expected the propagation of *"Christian Religion* to such People, as yet live in Darkness and miserable Ignorance of the true Knowledge and Worship of God." The lack of Christianity and of supposedly Christian use of the land helped to justify English claims. Some English people believed in the goal of conversion and peaceful trade, but on the ground in the English colonies violent displacement was a more common form of interaction. Similar religious language did not appear in the East India Company's 1600 charter, nor in James I's 1609 charter to renew the East India Company's rights. Religious cover was less necessary for trading forts and factories that did not depend on seizing large tracts of land from other people. Still, religion helped encourage the trade to Asia, as it did colonization in America, as a means of challenging Catholic and Muslim powers.[10]

Cross investments and leadership roles in the companies similarly suggest the symbiosis of the different economic approaches in the charters,

10. The Virginia Company initially referred to two companies. One company, based in London, focused on present-day Virginia; the other, based in Plymouth, focused on present-day New England, but it quickly went dormant. For more on the English history of using charters, particularly for imperial expansion, see Philip J. Stern, "British Asia and British Atlantic: Comparisons and Connections," *WMQ*, 3d Ser., LXIII (2006), 700–702. On the formation of the East India Company and its charter, see Kenneth R. Andrews, *Trade, Plunder, and Settlement: Maritime Enterprise and the Genesis of the British Empire, 1480–1630* (New York, 1984), 256–264; John Shaw, ed., *Charters Relating to the East India Company from 1600 to 1761*, new ed. (Madras, 1887), 2, 16–31. For the Virginia charter, see Charles W. Eliot, ed., *American Historical Documents, 1000–1904*, XLIII (New York, 1910), 49–53. On early English missionary activity and violence in America, see Francis Jennings, *The Invasion of America: Indians, Colonialism, and the Cant of Conquest* (Chapel Hill, N.C., 1975), esp. 53–54, 228–253; Alden T. Vaughan, "'Expulsion of the Salvages': English Policy and the Virginia Massacre of 1622," *WMQ*, 3d Ser., XXV (1978), 61–84; Martin H. Quitt, "Trade and Acculturation at Jamestown, 1607–1609: The Limits of Understanding," *WMQ*, 3d Ser., LII (1995), 229–231. Andrew Fitzmaurice argues that the Virginia Company "was not an essentially commercial enterprise," though this contention seems to put a little too much weight on public pronouncements from the company's supporters and the number of gentry investors. Such pronouncements were intended in part to steel the investors against their lack of monetary returns and to persuade skeptics that the venture had a higher calling and would not be corrupting. Still, Fitzmaurice is undoubtedly correct that Virginia Company supporters also sought glory, virtue, and the betterment of the common good, and some of them likely cared more for these motives than for financial wealth; all of their pronouncements did not simply paper over a bare profit motive. See Fitzmaurice, *Humanism and America*, 61, 75–78, 187.

hedging against one or another region becoming the dominant profit center for tropical and subtropical goods. A strong cohort of Levant Company members helped launch the East India Company. By 1608, likewise, approximately forty-six of the East India Company's slightly more than two hundred investors also participated in the Virginia Company. The smaller Plymouth Company of 1620 had only a few East India Company investors, though Thomas Roe, former ambassador to the Mughal court, served on the Plymouth Company's council. Thomas Smythe, meanwhile, served as the leader of both the Levant Company and the East India Company, the latter from 1603 until 1621. In 1609, he obtained the Virginia Company's second charter and became its treasurer. Later, in 1615, Smythe also became the leader of the Somers Isles Company to settle Bermuda, putting him in charge of or in a position of significant power over trade to the Ottoman empire, Mughal empire, Virginia, and Bermuda. Smythe also briefly led the Northwest Passage Company seeking to reach Asia through America.[11]

George Chapman, Ben Jonson, and John Marston played upon such English hopes to find and cultivate Asian goods in America and to find a Northwest Passage in their 1605 satirical play *Eastward Ho*. In one scene, a drunken goldsmith's apprentice in London yells out to his master, "Eastward Ho! 'Holla, ye pampered jades of Asia!'" The apprentice referred to the popular belief in England that Asia, with its great wealth, was a place of emasculating luxury. His accusation that the goldsmith was such a "pampered jade," combined with further immodesties, prompted the goldsmith to ask, "Do ye know where you are?" and explain that "'Eastward Ho' will make you go Westward Ho!" The goldsmith simultaneously implied that the apprentice would likely end up in the Tyburn gallows in the west of London for his insolence and that getting India's riches by going west

---

11. On the role of Levant Company members in the launching of the East India Company and on Smythe, see Brenner, *Merchants and Revolution*, 21–22, 98; K. N. Chaudhuri, *The English East India Company: The Study of an Early Joint-Stock Company, 1600–1640* (New York, 1965), 34. The figures on overlapping participation cannot be precise owing to inconsistent spelling and the potential for two men to share the same name. Cross investment in the companies is calculated from Henry Stevens, *The Dawn of British Trade to the East Indies as Recorded in the Court Minutes of the East India Company, 1599–1603 . . .* (London, 1886), 58–60; George Birdwood, ed., *The Register of Letters etc. of the Governour and Company of Merchants of London Trading into the East Indies, 1600–1619* (London, 1893), 275–281; and Samuel M. Bemiss, *The Three Charters of the Virginia Company of London with Seven Related Documents, 1606–1621* (Williamsburg, Va., 1957), 28–42. This list includes investors, planters, and other immigrants. Overlap in the Plymouth Company is calculated from Theodore K. Rabb, *Enterprise and Empire: Merchant and Gentry Investment in the Expansion of England, 1575–1630* (Cambridge, Mass., 1967), 232–410.

was a fool's death. Later the goldsmith mocked both the leader of an expedition to colonize Virginia and its implicit confusion of geography. He wondered to himself, "Do we not know north-north-east, north-east-and-by-east, east-and-by-north, nor plain eastward? Ha! Have we never heard of Virginia? Nor the *Cavallaria?* Nor the *Colonoria?* Can we discover no discoveries?" Similarly, in his 1609 burlesque *Discovery of a New World,* Joseph Hall mocked the Virginia Company's propaganda and described Virginia using the terms that English people commonly applied to Asia. Hall's characters find only "a land of vice and luxury, inhabited by gluttony, lechery and women."[12]

Also in 1609, in his "Entertainment at Britain's Burse," Jonson both celebrated and questioned the as yet largely unfulfilled desires to import, consume, and profit from Asian and American commodities and curiosities. He wrote the "Entertainment" for James I's opening of London's New Exchange, built, in part, to accommodate an expected growing importation of goods. It was a seemingly unlikely moment for any hint of critique, and Jonson's willingness to use a mocking tone in the "Entertainment" suggests the broad ambivalence with which many English people saw their imperial and trading projects. Jonson intended the performance to include a satirical exchange between Asian curiosity sellers, who would then distribute curiosities to the audience. The import of curiosities into London, however, was still more imagined than real. Thomas Wilson, tasked with procuring appropriate curiosities for the performance, wrote, "We have sought out diverse toys whereupon conceits are ministered, yet doth not the town afford such plenty as we expected." The show nevertheless cataloged and made fun of imports from abroad, which included dishes from the Ottoman empire that broke if they detected poison, a mechanical elephant salt shaker, carpets made of parakeet feathers, "umbrellas made of the winge of the Indian Butterfly," and a collection of famous beards. Jonson mocked how the English obtained the Asian goods—notably, not

12. George Chapman, Ben Jonson, and John Marston, *Eastward Ho* (1605), ed. R. W. Van Fossen (Manchester, 2006), 94–95, 163. The slippage in direction in the play's title echoed the title of another popular satire, *Westward Ho.* The apprentice is quoting Christopher Marlow's *Tamburlaine,* IV.iii.I. For brief discussions of *Eastward Ho* and *Discovery of a New World* as critiques of the English desire to plunder in Virginia, see Fitzmaurice, *Humanism and America,* 79–80; Rebecca Ann Bach, *Colonial Transformations: The Cultural Production of the New Atlantic World, 1580–1640* (New York, 2000), 137. On attempts occurring at this time to find a Northwest Passage involving the East India Company and its investors, see Andrews, *Trade, Plunder, and Settlement,* 343–346.

from English traders, but from the capture of a Dutch ship by "Warde the man of warre, for that is nowe the honorable name for a pyrate." Near the end of the performance, one actor explained, "I ame goeing shortlye for Verginnia to discover the Insecta of that countrye, the kind of Flye they have ther, and so over land for China: to compare him for comoditie, and but see wher paradice stood." He jokingly expected that America and Asia were in fact the same continent, perhaps referencing Columbus's mistaken belief that he had found Asia as well as English hopes to cultivate Asian goods in America. He ended by beseeching, "God make me Rich, which is the sellers prayer / ever was and wilbe." Here, Jonson implicitly criticized the merchant for pursuing lucre under the cover of faith, a criticism that many English Protestants shared.[13]

The court poet and playwright Samuel Daniel wrote that the expected windfall from America was a strong argument against colonization; he asked rhetorically whether America "may not unto Christendome / As Fatall be, as Asia was to Rome." Daniel was part of a conversation including the king, playwrights, religious leaders, and imperial adventurers that frequently associated James, England, and Britain with Rome and selected Roman emperors. For many, such as Virginia Company promoter Robert Johnson and preacher William Symonds, James would be heir to Constantine's defense of Christianity or Augustus's supposed benevolence in a unified Britain, Ulster, America, and "places most remote." But, for Daniel, wealth would corrupt England as it did other European powers. Even if America did not offer luxuries similar to Asia, American wealth and the means of obtaining it could cause the debasement of English virtue. Moreover, many English humanists believed that freedom from luxury was one of the many virtuous qualities of American Indians. As Daniel explained, they, too, would be corrupted by a new desire for luxury introduced by the already corrupted English people. At least some Virginia Company promoters, such as William Crashaw, both acknowledged and shared humanist concerns about the threat to English virtue from

13. Thomas Wilson to Robert Cecil, earl of Salisbury, Mar. 31, 1609, Cecil Papers, 195/100, Hatfield House Library and Archives, Hertfordshire, in United Kingdom, Royal Commission on Historical Manuscripts, *Calendar of the Manuscripts of the Most Honourable the Marquess of Salisbury . . . Part XXI (1609–1612)* (London, 1970), 37; Letters and papers published in the Calendar of State Papers Domestic, James I, 1603–1610, SP14/44/62, 144r–147r, NA, printed as Ben Jonson, "The Entertainment at Britain's Burse," in James Knowles, "Jonson's *Entertainment at Britain's Burse,*" in Martin Butler, ed., *Re-Presenting Ben Jonson: Text, History, Performance* (London, 1999), 115–116, 132–140.

conquest. Crashaw argued that the settlers would not steal land or life from the native peoples.[14]

Related, but also notably different, concerns from those expressed over colonization in Virginia appeared in works on India, such as the title page to Thomas Coriat's 1618 *Mr. Thomas Coriat to His Friends in England Sendeth Greeting* (Plate 1). The poem and image on the title page reflected worries that trading with India would possess English people with delusions of glory, give them false understandings of value, feminize their masculinity, and put them unwittingly under the control of India's people. The poem made fun of the comical traveler's report of his journey from Jerusalem to Agra. It posited that no animal, and indeed only the whole earth, could "beare" Coriat's oversized ambition for fame. The poem questioned whether Coriat's fame, his supposed worth, was actually "worthlesse." It also questioned his masculinity by placing him metaphorically upon a "Palfrey," a small horse often for women. The last line of the poem, "Thou rid'st the World, and all the World rides thee," made Coriat simultaneously a rider and a beast of burden. As the steed taking his readers around the world, Coriat gained a sort of power, but the people in foreign lands also had power in directing his knowledge and experiences—and his readers had power in deciding whether to buy his work. The accompanying plate depicts Coriat riding upon a camel, locating him in the foreignness of India and promoting him as a traveler. Coriat is the highest and whitest figure. He is the only one armed, and his prominent sword is impossibly long. But, as in the poem, the plate suggests that Coriat's power may not be what it seems. Although he appears to be astride the camel, Coriat's torso is turned, as if he is riding sidesaddle. The camel, too, appears to be mincing, further effeminizing Coriat and mirroring the use of the word "palfrey" in the poem. A black man has a firm grip on the camel's reigns, leading the beast. By extension, this man controls Coriat and takes on the masculine power in the scene. He also grins, suggesting devious awareness that he is in control.[15]

14. Samuel Daniel, "Epistle: To Prince Henry," in H. R. Woudhuysen, ed., *The Penguin Book of Renaissance Verse* (London, 1992), 433–436; Fitzmaurice, *Humanism and America*, 81–82, 162–166; Karen Ordahl Kupperman, *Indians and English: Facing Off in Early America* (Ithaca, N.Y., 2000), 2, 18–20, 23, 27–31, 109. On positive associations of James, Britain, and Rome, see Tristan Marshall, *Theatre and Empire: Great Britain on the London Stages under James VI and I* (Manchester, 2000), 19, 36–40, 64–68, 116–122, 132, 145.

15. Thomas Coriat, *Mr. Thomas Coriat to His Friends in England Sendeth Greeting: From Agra the Capitall City of the Dominion of the Great Mogoll in the Easterne India, the Last of October, 1616* (London, 1618). For more on Coriat, see Jyotsna G. Singh, *Colonial Narra-*

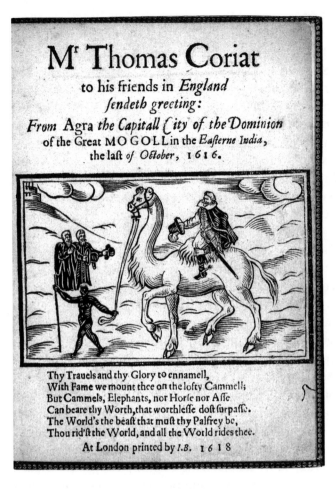

Plate 1.
Title page from
Thomas Coriat,
*Mr. Thomas
Coriat to His
Friends in
England Sendeth
Greeting...*
(London, 1618).
By permission
of the Folger
Shakespeare
Library

Even the Company's and king's ambassador to the Mughal empire, Thomas Roe, doubted the benefits of trading with India. Roe was already experienced in the Americas; he had traveled up the Amazon River in 1610, hoping to find gold for Prince Henry. Suitably impressed, Roe left twenty men to claim the river for England. Roe had also helped draft a constitution for Virginia. In 1615, Roe traveled to Surat to establish strong forts to entrench and defend English access to this impressively productive region and to encourage Indian peoples to purchase English goods. The Portuguese objected, but Roe persuaded the emperor to allow the English to stay and trade. Roe argued that the Company should not follow

---

tives/Cultural Dialogues: 'Discoveries' of India in the Language of Colonialism (London, 1996), 40–47.

the model of the Portuguese and Dutch, who built forts and "seeke Plantation heere by the Sword." Such conquest would ultimately sap money and strength. "Let this be received as a Rule," he enjoined, "that if you will profit, seeke it at Sea, and in quiet trade." Nevertheless, the productive and imitative abilities of the Indian people, and their disdain for most of what England had to trade in return, suggested that the East India Company would be hard-pressed to profit. Roe was clearly taken aback that people with such different beliefs and practices from Europeans could easily emulate Europe's finest products. He wrote that the emperor's painters copied European paintings "beyond all expectation." The emperor's workers also easily copied and improved upon an English coach that Roe had provided. Roe warned the Company's directors in London, "Let not your servants deceive you, [English] Cloth, Lead, Teeth, Quick-silver, are dead Commodities here, and will never drive this Trade." The prospects for using India, similar to the Ottoman empire, as a profitable market for English manufactures in exchange for Asian commodities did not look good.[16]

For its exports from the Indian Ocean, meanwhile, the Company was turning away from its initial efforts in the pepper and spice trades, which the VOC had begun to control, and toward the Mughal empire's fabrics. In 1614, the Company sought to distribute information for selecting "Callicoes and Pintathoes," or painted cloth, which could be "vented into Turkey and sundry other parts." The Company quickly succeeded in many of Surat's trades to ports on the Indian Ocean and Red Sea and gained access to Persia through violence, diplomacy, and trade. In its trade to England, the Company likewise began to seriously pursue a broader range of luxury cotton and silk fabrics, quilts, and hangings. These piece goods included three main types: white muslin, dyed and printed calicoes, and painted chintz. The designs popular in Indian Ocean markets typically emphasized Asian flowers interspersed with small animals on dark backgrounds. Such designs did not appeal strongly to English consumers. In any case, Roe wrote that Parliament rightly valued ten thousand pounds in bullion to be worth more than one hundred thousand pounds in the East India Company's "China dishes, silkes, spices, dyes and trash." These goods

16. Roe crossed paths in India with Coriat—one the comical traveler, the other the royal diplomat. On Roe in the Americas, see Louis B. Wright, "Colonial Developments in the Reign of James I," in Alan G. R. Smith, ed., *The Reign of James VI and I* (London, 1973), 126–127. For Roe in India, see Samuel Purchas, ed., *Hakluytus Posthumus; or, Purchas His Pilgrimes* . . . (1625; rpt. Glasgow, 1905), IV, 344–345, 376, 464–467 ("seeke" and "let"). On the establishment of English trade in Surat and the effectiveness of Roe's diplomacy, see Andrews, *Trade, Plunder, and Settlement*, 271–273.

simply "fuell . . . pride and gluttony . . . none of these will sett out a fleete to sea nor pay an army." For many English thinkers, leaders, and merchant adventurers, whether Indian consumer goods fostered or sapped England's strength was an essential question.[17]

Defending India Trades

Asia and America had substantial political and economic differences, but the extent of their ecological differences and moral implications remained debatable. In Asia, the English had to reckon with the many advantages of Asian powers, particularly the Mughal empire, as well as the increasing trade of the Dutch. In America, they had to find or grow valuable commodities and deal with native peoples already on the land. Humanist fears of corruption and notions of colonies as places of communal good might have delayed profit demands, but those demands still existed. Promoters, including London's heavily invested mayors and the East India Company's directors, pushed hard to show that colonization and long-distance trade would generate wealth and knowledge, bring desirable and salutary new products, build on England's heroic past, and provide a benevolent check to Catholic and Muslim powers. England could have its spices and eat them too. Within this process, competition was inherent, not simply between England and Catholic and Muslim powers, but between England and the Protestant Dutch as well as among England's own adventures to India and America.

These tensions are apparent in the work of Samuel Purchas, Hakluyt's heir as England's leading imperial promoter. In his third edition of *Pyrchas His Pilgrimage* (1617), which described all of the regions, people, and religions known to Europeans, Purchas explained that English trade with the world was both the will of God and Elizabeth I. James I apparently treasured the book and read it several times. Purchas asked, "Is it not a profit to our Nation, to vent Clothes, Iron, Lead, and other Commodities? To set on worke so many of all Trades and Professions? To employ

17. Court Minute Book III, Jan. 19, 1614, IOR/B/5, 13, BL; Chaudhuri, *English East India Company*, 140–190, 199–203; Thomas Roe to Surat, Aug. 20, 1616, Additional Manuscripts 6115, fol. 114, BL, quoted in William Foster, ed., *The Embassy of Thomas Roe to the Court of the Great Mogul, 1615–1619 as Narrated in His Journal and Correspondence* (London, 1899), I, 167n; Samuel R. Gardiner, *History of England from the Accession of James I to the Outbreak of the Civil War, 1603–1642* (London, 1907), III, 162–168. On competition with the Dutch, Dutch success, and English control over local trading routes from Surat, see Andrews, *Trade, Plunder, and Settlement*, 265–268, 273–276.

so many Mariners? To build so many, so able, so capable Ships? To enrich the King's Coffers and publike Treasurie, in Customes, Imposts, and other Duties?" Purchas's rhetorical line of questioning continued beyond economic benefits for England. He wondered, "Is it not for the Honor of our Nation, that the English Name hath pierced the remotest Countries, and filled the Indians with admiration of the English?" He saw "the Sea becomming an Amphitheatre; where the Easterne World might be Spectators of the Westerne Worth." Purchas also turned to Asia's goods as specifically beneficial to England, explaining that "Asia clothes us with her Silkes, feedes us with her Spices, cures us with her Drugges, adornes us with her Jewels." In exchange for importing Asian goods, English people enjoyed more economic prosperity, better lives, better reputations, and more honor—a good bargain by any measure.[18]

The lord mayors of London, and particularly those from the Grocers' livery company, increasingly encouraged the broader public to embrace this vision of England's benefiting from commerce with Asia to become the world's most benevolent power, a vision in which they had personal interests. Back in 1605, Anthony Munday's *Triumphes of Re-United Britania*, performed to introduce Lord Mayor Leonard Holliday, a Merchant Taylor and an East India Company founder and director, already included a scene titled "The Shippe Called the *Royall Exchange.*" A large model ship "Laden with *Spices, Silkes,* and *Indico,*" supposedly returned from the East Indies, was crewed by children and led a procession so large that it required the removal of parts of buildings along the route. Pepper, cloves, and mace might have been distributed to the crowd. Famous playwright Thomas Middleton expanded on such presentations in his introductory public entertainments for three mayors from the Grocers' company, Thomas Myddleton in 1613, George Bowles (or Bolls) in 1617, and Peter Broby in 1622. *The Triumphs of Truth* to introduce Myddleton, an investor in the East India Company, included a river scene of "five Islands art-fully garnished with all manner of Indian Fruite-Trees, Drugges, Spiceries, and the like." In another scene, a fictional king and queen of the Moors converted to Protestant Christianity because of the good effects of English trade.[19]

18. Samuel Purchas, *Pyrchas His Pilgrimage; or, Relations of the World and the Religions Observed in Al Ages and Places Discovered, from the Creation unto This Present; in Foyre Parts; This First Contayneth a Theologicall and Geographicall Historie of Asia, Africa, and America, with the Ilands Adiacent* (London, 1617), 550. On James I's reading the book, see Samuel Purchas, *Purchas His Pilgrimage . . .* (London, 1626), n.p.

19. On the popularity, pageantry, and format of the shows and on the difficulty of gauging audience understanding of the meanings, see Tracey Hill, *Pageantry and Power: A Cul-*

In *The Tryumphs of Honor and Industry* to introduce Bowles, Middleton stressed that India's advantages in cultivation were the key to London's global wealth and Christian community. Bowles had interests in the East India Company, as well as the Virginia, Irish, Russia, and Northwest Passage companies. The performance began with a pageant of scantily dressed people who were supposed to be Asian Indians growing spices, collecting fruits, and packing pepper. The Indians danced "to give content to themselves and the spectators." Next entered "a rich personage presenting *India*, (the Seate of Merchandise)." India carried gold, while her associate, "Trafficke," brought a globe, and "Industry" brought love. Next, representatives from France and Spain, England's Catholic opponents, gave brief speeches celebrating London's achievements because they simply could not be "content with a silent joy." Love had clearly overcome them.[20]

Middleton's *Triumphs of Honor and Vertue* for Peter Broby celebrated merchants who traded not only in spices but also in knowledge and in the creation of a greater, inclusive, Protestant community in India and America alike. The Grocers internally titled the performance "The East Indian Paradise," but perhaps simply for consistency the published title followed the pattern of Middleton's other mayoral pageants. In any case, the subject and claims were unmistakable: the first part portrayed India, and the second honor and virtue. It began, "A blacke Personage representing *India*, call'd for her odours and riches, the Queene of Merchandize,"

---

tural History of the Early Modern Lord Mayor's Show, 1585–1639 (Manchester, 2010), 1–26, 129–130, 174–193. The primary focus of *Triumphes of Re-United Britania* was, as the title suggests, the supposed reunion of Britain brought about by James; see A[nthony] Munday, *The Triumphes of Re-United Britania* (London, 1605), n.p. On the model ship (which likely appeared in several mayoral pageants, the texts for which do not survive) and its crew, see R. T. D. Sayle, *Lord Mayors' Pageants of the Merchant Taylors' Company in the 15th, 16th, and 17th Centuries* (London, 1931), 74, 78–80, 83, 89. Thomas Myddleton and Thomas Middleton were different people; see Thomas Middleton, *The Triumphs of Truth: A Solemnity Unparaleld for Cost, Art, and Magnificence, at the Confirmation and Establishment of That Worthy and True Nobly-Minded Gentleman, Sir Thomas Middleton . . .* (London, 1613), n.p.

20. [Thomas Middleton], *The Tryumphs of Honor and Industry . . .* (London, 1617), n.p. Barbour suggests that the dancing and love represent the powerful eroticism of the East; see Richmond Barbour, *Before Orientalism: London's Theatre of the East, 1576–1626* (Cambridge, 2003), 95–98. The dancing might have suggested erotic savagery, but the rest of the performance celebrates India as a wealthy commercial power that in many ways would make an ideal trading partner, not a place of inferior peoples awaiting colonization. For more on how literary scholars have debated the colonial resonances of such performances, see Hill, *Pageantry and Power*, 292–294. For Bowles's memberships, see Rabb, *Enterprise and Empire*, 249.

who "advanceth . . . upon a bed of Spices, attended by *Indians* in Antique habits: *Commerce, Adventure* and *Traffique*." Three merchants then brought forward "a bright Figure, bearing the inscription of *Knowledge*." The "Queene" explained, "As Wise men shoote their beames forth, you'le then find / A change in the complexion of the mind; / I'me beauteous in my blacknesse." And, through trade with "English Merchants," she had been led to the knowledge of all wealth, "Christian holynesse." By trading with India, England would gain merchandise, wealth, understanding, loving Christian fellows, and, indeed, the world. This was both an acknowledgment of India's advantages and a vision of the means to Protestant England's rise to global preeminence. At the pageant's finale, the "Cardinall" virtues of wisdom, justice, fortitude, and temperance were attached to four banners displaying the arms of London, the lord mayor, the Grocers, and the "Noble" East India Company. This display accompanied a large globe "shewing the Worlds Type," English ships, and "that prosperous Plantation in the Colonie of *Virginia*, and the *Bermudaes* . . . those Christianly Reformed Islands," suggesting that Indian trade and American colonization were complementary in bringing virtue, honor, commerce, and global Protestant expansion.[21]

Similarly, John Webster's mayoral sea show, *Monuments of Honor*, for Mayor John Gore in 1624 encouraged the notion that an integrated network of adventurers and companies brought wealth and glory, raising London up as the virtuous leader of the world against Spain. Gore was a Merchant Taylor invested in the East India, Virginia, Barbary, and Spanish Companies, among others. The show opened with two spectacles. One celebrated the mayor's local power. The second spectacle, a globe "Circled about" by the famous Elizabethan seamen Francis Drake, John Hawkins, Martin Frobisher, Humphrey Gilbert, Thomas Cavendish, Christopher Carleill, and John Davis, connected that local importance to global expansion. The goal was to "wed our *Empire* with a Ring of Gold." With their daring sea fights and "Rich Lading," England's adventurers brought the whole world to London from every "Navigable Sea." Webster was pointedly tapping into and furthering a triumphalist public mythology of Elizabethan expansion, war, and piracy against Catholic Spain to support a new war on the world's oceans—despite James I's apparent unwillingness. Webster suggested that the world was not angered by English pirates;

21. Grocers' Company, Charges of Triumphs 1613–1614, MS 11, 590, fol. 21, Guildhall Library, London, quoted in Hill, *Pageantry and Power*, 217; Tho[mas] Middleton, *The Triumphs of Honor and Vertue* . . . (London, 1622), n.p.

it was in happy awe of English navigation and mercantile successes. In Saint Paul's churchyard, Webster built a temple with a figure representing London at its apex. Beneath London, individuals representing all the great cities of Europe, including Constantinople, looked up to admire her, similar to the speeches from the Frenchman and Spaniard in Middleton's show for Bowles. The globe, poems, and temple explained that, through its virtuous overseas exploits, London had overtaken the greatest ports in Europe and poked fun at England's rivals. It was a generous view of England. It was also more in keeping with ideas of accumulating wealth through gold and treasure rather than through labor and trade.[22]

In 1621, Thomas Mun, an East India Company director, provided a sophisticated intellectual accompaniment to such public performances. Mun sought to mollify those in the English public and in positions of power, such as Roe, concerned with the Company's export of bullion to pay for imported luxuries. By trading directly to the source, Mun explained, the Company avoided paying higher prices to the Dutch or Muslim Ottoman traders, "the common enemie of *Christendome*." This trade, he believed, saved England nearly £75,000 per year. Mun emphasized, moreover, that the East India trade "is a meanes to bring more treasure into this Realme then al the other trades of this kingdome (as they are now mannaged) being put together." In exchange for £100,000, the East India Company imported every year India goods worth £500,000. Merchants then annually reexported India goods worth £380,000 from London, thereby sending away much of the luxury and netting great wealth

22. James denounced piracy. Many English pirates worked together with the Barbary corsairs with little regard for English law or imperialism, but the mythology longed for Elizabethan exploits over Spain in the world's oceans more than adventures in Europe. The pageant also celebrated the defense of Christendom against Muslims as well as riches, dead heroes, liberality, navigation, unanimity, industry, chastity, justice, peace, fortitude, loyalty, and obedience, represented notably by an elephant, "the strongest Beast, but most observant to man." See John Webster, *Monuments of Honor* . . . (London, 1624), n.p. On James I's dislike of all piracy, see David Delison Hebb, *Piracy and the English Government, 1616–1642* (Aldershot, U.K., 1994), 8–11, 16–20. On the memory of Elizabethan triumphs in the Atlantic against Spain, see Thomas Cogswell, *The Blessed Revolution: English Politics and the Coming of War, 1621–1624* (New York, 1989), 14, 181–182, 287; Cogswell, "The Path to Elizium 'Lately Discovered': Drayton and the Early Stuart Court," *Huntington Library Quarterly*, LIV (1991), 220–221. For more on popular English portrayals of pirates during James's reign, including ambivalence over the English-Barbary pirates, see Barbara Fuchs, *Mimesis and Empire: The New World, Islam, and European Identities* (New York, 2001), 2, 118–137. For more on poking fun at France and Spain to delight the assembled crowds, see Hill, *Pageantry and Power*, 301–302.

back to England. Instead of accounting by single countries, the balance of trade needed to be accounted among all countries at once. Additionally, Mun explained, "Money is the prize of wares, and wares are the proper use of money; so that their Coherence is unseparable." Despite being the manufacture of "Infidells," India's calicoes simply had too much value to shun. They drove down the price of linens and were exported to foreign places. Mun also argued that India goods helped to solidify the nation's defense by requiring great warlike ships and by training seamen. Giving up the trade would mean giving up all of these advantages to the Dutch, England's biggest competitors in the Indian Ocean.[23]

As defenses of the trade ramped up in England, the Company further sharpened its focus on the Mughal empire's calicoes. The Company had sold several thousand pieces of calicoes in London in 1613. By 1621, it had increased exports to London dramatically to 123,000 pieces. In 1622, the directors asked how "to advance the vent of them." One director suggested that the Company sell them cheaply to English drapers, "who might be thereby encouraged to take off good quantities and would disperse them throughout the lande." The pressure to use India as a base and its calicoes as a staple increased further when, in 1623, the Dutch arrested, tortured, and killed ten English traders and ten accused Japanese and Portuguese collaborators at Amboyna in the Spice Islands. Protestant English expansionists, including Purchas, blamed misguided and Spanish-supporting Dutch individuals for the affair and advocated against Catholic and Muslim powers in Eurasia, not Protestant ones. Some continued to hope that the English and Dutch would develop shared trading companies. Instead, by 1625 Company calico exports to London reached 221,500 pieces. The directors pushed to open new domestic and foreign markets where calico "use is not generally known."[24]

23. Mun was a Company director and he wrote his economic tracts to defend his own and the Company's interests. Joan Thirsk suggested that Mun and other political economists followed, and did not drive, economic change. See Thirsk, *Economic Policy and Projects: The Development of a Consumer Society in Early Modern England* (Oxford, 1978), 133–136. In working from his position of interest, however, Mun sought to and did influence English economic policy. See T[homas] M[un], *A Discourse of Trade, from England unto the East-Indies: Answering to Diverse Obiections Which Are Usually Made against the Same* (London, 1621), 8, 25–26, 30, 34–35, 40, 43, 48. See also E[dward] M[isselden], *The Circle of Commerce; or, The Ballance of Trade, in Defence of Free Trade: Opposed to Malynes Little Fish and His Great Whale, and Poized against Them in the Scale* ... (London, 1623); P. J. Thomas, *Mercantilism and the East India Trade* (1923; rpt. London, 1963), 10–11.

24. On selling more calicoes, see Court Minute Book, Mar. 18, 1622, IOR/B/7, 375, BL;

Difficulties in the spice trade and increased cotton imports also encouraged further interest in America's ability to replace India. Purchas, a strong India trade supporter, was also bullish on America and surmised that North America and Asia might be physically connected in the parts that Europeans had not yet explored. He relayed that Smith "holds Virginia by the natural endowments, the fittest place for an earthly Paradise." Virginia would offer access to the "South Sea" and plentiful silk grass, silkworms, and a long list of other commodities. Though the Virginia colony had struggled, Purchas portrayed solid improvement, particularly in the colonial government. He related from Thomas Dale that early settlement in Virginia was like the "peepe and creepe" of Rome to its eventual "height of Majesty" and could also be compared to the growth of Spanish power in America. The dangers of "Aristocratical Government" in Virginia had contributed to its early difficulties, but by 1617 the colony was "correspondent to their [English] constitutions" not only physically but also politically. Virginia was now settled by the "milde Law of Nature not that violent Law of Armes." In Purchas's words, Virginia's supposedly "Virgin soile not yet polluted with Spaniards lust" had been in danger of pollution from misguided English leadership. Yet English people in Virginia had now begun to prevent the emerging empire from slipping toward Catholic, or supposedly similar Muslim or Asiatic, tyranny. With proper support, unpolluted Virginia, the transmogrification of Elizabeth herself, Purchas explained, would be a fertile success.[25]

Patrick Copland argued in a sermon in 1622 that Virginia promised to supply the goods of India without the complications of dealing with

---

Chaudhuri, *English East India Company*, 193–195, 201. Calico was initially used in England for decor, expanded by an interest in floral designs; see Beverly Lemire, "Domesticating the Exotic: Floral Culture and the East India Calico Trade with England, c. 1600–1800," *Textile: The Journal of Cloth and Culture*, I (2003), 67–71; Giorgio Riello, "The Globalization of Cotton Textiles: Indian Cottons, Europe, and the Atlantic World, 1600–1850," in Riello and Prasannan Parthasarathi, eds., *The Spinning World: A Global History of Cotton Textiles, 1200–1850* (Oxford, 2009), 267. On Amboyna and reactions to it, see Cogswell, *Blessed Revolution*, 182–183, 275; Armitage, *Ideological Origins*, 87; Christopher Grayson, "James I and the Religious Crisis in the United Provinces, 1613–1619," in Derek Baker, ed., *Reform and Reformation: England and the Continent c. 1500–c. 1750* (Oxford, 1979), 205; Steve Pincus, "From Holy Cause to Economic Interest: The Study of Population and the Invention of the State," in Alan Houston and Pincus, eds., *A Nation Transformed: England after the Restoration* (Cambridge, 2001), 280–283. On the success of the Dutch against the English in the Spice Islands, see Charles Wilson, *Profit and Power: A Study of England and the Dutch Wars* (London, 1957), 43–44; Andrews, *Trade, Plunder, and Settlement*, 269–270.

25. Purchas, *Purchas His Pilgrimage*, 912, 937, 942, 945–946, 948.

dangerous Muslims and Catholics. Copland had been to India, where he was impressed by the Mughal emperor's wealth and cruelty as well as by the many good qualities of the Indian peoples and their clothing. Based on his own assessments, Copland, even more strongly than Roe, doubted that extensive trade to or attempted settlement in India would be in the best interests of England. Copland asked: Does not Virginia promise "great hopes of abundance of Corne, Wine, Oyle, Lemons, Oranges, Pome-granats, and all maner of fruites pleasant to the eye, and wholesome for the belly? And of plentie of Silke, Silke Grasse, Cotton-wooll, Flax, Hempe etc. for the backe?" He explained that Virginia could provide nearly every-thing "which I have heard and seene abroad in my travailing to *India* and *Japan*," goods of more value than those of Europe itself. Copland argued that Virginia would not only provide employment for English people; it would provide goods more securely than Asia could. Copland did not put as much weight on the threat of luxury or other European powers in the Atlantic as on the safety from "Turkes" and "Pyrates" that Virginia would provide. The success of "poysoning" Jesuit Catholics in Asia, he further ex-plained, was additional incentive for the careful "planting" of the gospel in an English Virginia.[26]

Efforts to cultivate Protestantism and, notably, as the East India Com-pany looked to fabric for its own trade, silk and cotton in the supposed safety of Virginia were already afoot. In 1610, the Council of Virginia in-structed the Jamestown settlers to pursue silk grass. Of earlier samples sent back and woven into cloth in England, some "who have lived in the *East Indies* affirme, that they make all their *Cambaya* Stuffes of this, and Cotton-wooll." Mayor Bowles had then subsidized and overseen the trans-portation of "over one hundred persons" of London's "over-flowing multi-tude to Virginia" as laborers. The leadership of the Berkeley Hundred plantation sent cotton seeds from London to Virginia. A report from the Berkeley plantation in 1622 outlined that settlers successfully planted cot-ton "trees" from the West Indies as well as the "Cotton-wooll-seeds from the *Mogols* Countrey," most likely those sent via London. They hoped to quickly bring the cotton to "a good perfection and quantity." Additionally, a "*China* box" at a native American king's house, which supposedly came

26. Patrick Copland, *Virginia's God Be Thanked; or, A Sermon of Thanksgiving for the Happie Successe of the Affayres in Virginia This Last Yeare; Preached by Patrick Copland at Bow-Church in Cheapside, before the Honorable Virginia Company, on Thursday, the 18. of Aprill 1622; and Now Published by the Commandement of the Said Honorable Company* (London, 1622), 12–30 (quotations on 12–13).

from the west over both sea and land, fueled expectations of the discovery of the "*South Sea*, so long talked of."[27]

Purchas, in his 1625 *Hakluytus Posthumus; or, Purchas His Pilgrimes*, modified and expanded his support of England's global exploration, trade, and colonization, and he also recognized that at least some English people were thereby in "danger to travell from God and themselves." *Hakluytus Posthumus* had "a World for the subject, and a World of Witnesses for the Evidence." By exhaustively documenting the global exploits of English adventurers, Purchas tightened the connection between global commerce, Protestantism, and national wealth and glory. In his dedication to Prince Charles, Purchas refrained from Hakluyt's attacks on the Spanish. The dedication, like the collection itself, suggested that England should try to refocus outside Western Europe. These non–Western European interests reflected those of other Englishmen, such as Francis Bacon, who believed that the energies directed against fear of Catholic influence might better be directed against the Muslim Ottomans, enemies to all Christianity. As part of this extra-European focus, Purchas included and apparently agreed with Mun's defense of England's trade with the East Indies. It certainly fit Purchas's earlier strong statements of support. But Purchas was also careful to note that he did not celebrate those useless travelers for whom travel was "an excellent Ornament." These people "bring home a few smattering termes, flattering garbes, Apish crings, foppish fancies, foolish guises and disguises, the vanities of Neighbour Nations . . . without furthering of their knowledge of God, the World, or themselves." Global adventures without a godly, positive, and ordered purpose could fall to useless and dangerous temptations.[28]

---

27. "Instructions Given By Way of Advice . . . for the Intended Voyage to Virginia" and "Instructions for Such Things as Are to Be Sent from Virginia, 1610," CO 1/1, fol. 86a, NA, in Edward Wright Haile, ed., *Jamestown Narratives: Eyewitness Accounts of the Virginia Colony: The First Decade, 1607–1617* (Champlain, Va., 1988), 23–26; Ralph Hamor, *A True Discourse of the Present Estate of Virginia . . .* (London, 1615), reprinted ibid., 828–829; Richard Berkeley and John Smyth, "A Commission to George Thorpe for the Government of the Plantation," Sept. 10, 1620, and Virginia Company, "A Note of the Shipping, Men, and Provisions Sent and Provided for Virginia," May 1622, in Susan Myra Kingsbury, ed., *The Records of the Virginia Company of London* (Washington, D.C., 1906–1935), III, 400, 641–642; Copland, *Virginia's God Be Thanked*, 31. The East India Company also sought to use Virginia to support its India trade at least as early as 1619. The Court of Directors had heard that maize was "much commended for an excellent strong meat, and hearty for men at sea, and more wholesome than beef." They asked the Virginia Company to obtain some for trial. See Court Minute Book, Mar. 5, 1618, IV, 306, *CSPC*, IX, no. 103, 57–58.

28. Purchas, ed., *Hakluytus Posthumus*, I, xliv ("bring" and "danger"), x1iii ("World"),

Indeed, many of Purchas's "pilgrimes" suggested that the Mughal emperor's impressive and alien consumption practices showed him to be corrupted and emasculated by just such temptations and luxury. These were not exactly endorsements of trading in India goods or adopting aspects of its material culture. Elephants, for instance, appeared regularly in the adventurers' accounts as markers of both India's fantastic wealth and power and of the concentration of this wealth and power in the hands of the despotic and cruel emperor. William Hawkins claimed that the emperor owned twelve thousand elephants and that he spent a staggering fifty thousand rupees per day to dress his few personal elephants in gold and velvet and feed them butter, grain, and sugarcane. Many authors reported that the emperor took great joy in daily watching his elephants fight one another and tear unarmed men into pieces. Hawkins also described the emperor's "infinite numbers of Dromedaries" as well as his oxen, dogs, lions, and birds as further evidence of the emperor's wealth, power, and excess. Copland, who supported Virginia over the East Indies trade, reported a luxurious feast of four hundred different dishes served in copper and gold. Roe, on record against much of the trade with the Mughal empire, explained that the rulers traveled with fantastic tent cities that covered spaces greater than London and accommodated two hundred thousand people. These tent cities suggested great wealth, excessive luxury, self-indulgence, and a lack of permanence and solidity. "This is all their pride," wrote Roe. Roe snuck a peek into the emperor's private area, writing, "The beauty thereof, which I confesse was rich, but of so divers pieces, and so unsutable, that it was rather patched then glorious, as if it seemed to strive to shewe all, like a Lady that with her Plate, set on a Cupboord her imbroydered Slippers." The emperor's wealth betrayed a lack of sophistication and taste, while associating him with an English woman undermined his masculinity. Several authors marveled that on his birth-

---

V, 262–303. Purchas published *Hakluytus Posthumus* at a high point of English anti-Catholicism spurred by the planned marriage of Prince Charles and the Spanish infanta and by Charles's actual marriage to the French Catholic Henrietta Maria. Many in England already feared Charles I's Catholic and absolutist ambitions, which would eventually lead to the English Civil War. See Thomas Cogswell, "England and the Spanish Match," in Richard Cust and Ann Hughes, eds., *Conflict in Early Stuart England: Studies in Religion and Politics, 1603-1642* (London, 1989), 109–130. On the differences between Hakluyt's and Purchas's conceptions of monarchy, historiography, religion, and time, and on anti-Catholicism, see Armitage, *Ideological Origins*, 81–92. As the title suggests, Purchas owed a significant debt to Hakluyt for collecting, preserving, and handing over many of the accounts of English adventurers that Purchas published. For more on calls for an all-Christian union against the Turks, including Bacon's thinking, see Cogswell, *Blessed Revolution*, 38–39.

day the emperor weighed himself against a range of jewels and commodities, directly relating his person to the value of India's luxury goods. These and similar accounts positioned India's goods as marks of tyranny, corruption, and effeminacy, creating a sort of vicious cycle where the supposed behavior of Indian rulers was manifested in their consumption habits, and the same consumption habits further corrupted the rulers.[29]

Despite the efforts of Purchas, London's mayors, Mun, the East India Company, and Virginia's supporters, it still remained unclear whether India was worth trading with, or whether America would, or should, be a new India. William Camden, Elizabeth I's chronicler, wrote that the East India trade had "for the honour of the *English* Nation . . . placed Empories in *Lurat [Surat]*, in the Empire of the great *Mogoll*, in *Mossolupatan, Bantan, Patane, Siam, Sagad, Mecassar*, and also in *Japan;* and have with happy victories repressed the insolency of the enemy, and *Turkish* treachery." But, he went on, "whether to the good of the Common wealth, so great a masse of silver being exported out of *England*, and such a multitude of Saylers consumed every yeere, let the wise speake and posterity see."[30]

Civil War, Imperial Structure, and India Goods

Posterity soon saw a series of dramatic upheavals in England from 1629 through the early 1660s that stimulated further connections and competition among English adventures in the Indian and Atlantic Oceans, new ways of thinking about India's goods, and new systems of trade. Many Protestant leaders saw the margins of the empire in the Atlantic as a space of relative freedom and godly potential. Atlantic colonies might still cultivate India's goods, particularly its silks and cottons, but, if English Protestants were to consume these goods, the goods themselves needed to be defensible as uncorrupting. Attempts to solve the problems of reproducing India in America and of defending India's goods, however, might also clear a path for an expanded trade to the subcontinent. By the 1660s, England would be transformed, and a mixture of old ideas and new systems would increase prospects for a global English imperial and trading system with

29. Purchas, ed., *Hakluytus Posthumus*, III, 30–49 ("infinite" on 36), IV, 149–151, 322–328 ("beauty" on 332–333), 440 ("pride"), 561.

30. William Camden, *Annals; or, The Historie of the Most Renowned and Victorious Princesse Elizabeth, Late Queen of England . . .* (1625), 3d ed., trans. R. N. Ghent (London, 1635), 528.

fundamentally different products coming to England from the Atlantic and Indian Oceans.

In 1629, Protestant adventurers, disgusted with Charles I's turn toward absolutist rule and concerned about a popish plot, began planning a new godly colony where the faithful could prosper, harry the Spanish, and cultivate spices and cotton otherwise bought from the problematic peoples of the Indian Ocean. They selected Providence Island off the coast of what is now Nicaragua. They thought carefully about approaching the East India Company for assistance in bringing a variety of plants from the Indian Ocean "for the enriching of the island." There was reason to hope for assistance: several shareholders invested in both of the companies, and John Dike, a Providence Island Company director, was a member of the East India Company as well as the Levant and Virginia Companies. The Providence Island Company was likely cognizant, however, that the East India Company might view the former as a potential competitor in Indian Ocean goods. The Providence Island adventurers intended such competition, much like settlers in Virginia and Barbados. These settlers were already optimistically pursuing their own nascent cotton trades with English and, later, Dutch merchants. The leaders of Providence Island instructed their colonists to try to make use of local cotton and to bring in different cotton seeds as experiments instead of relying on tobacco. They sent machines to aid in the processing of cotton as well as two weavers and a spinner to teach colonists to work the cotton. Even as reports detailed struggle and failure, some in England continued to hope that cotton would be the island's profitable staple. Other Protestant reformers in England, however, identified cotton closely with supposed Indian and, also, English debasement.[31]

The former East India Company preacher Henry Lord, for instance, associated the religions and material culture of India with Catholicism,

---

31. The Providence Island adventurers hoped to cultivate a huge range of commodities, including oilseeds, madder, and silkgrass; see Karen Ordahl Kupperman, *Providence Island, 1630–1641: The Other Puritan Colony* (New York, 1993), 1–12, 33, 38–39, 83–93, 105–112, 198–201, 296–297, 310–311, 357–360; Kupperman, "Errand to the Indies: Puritan Colonization from Providence Island through the Western Design," *WMQ*, 3d Ser., XLV (1988), 70–85. On trading cotton to the Dutch, see Christian J. Koot, *Empire at the Periphery: British Colonists, Anglo-Dutch Trade, and the Development of the British Atlantic, 1621–1713* (New York, 2011), 53–54. On Providence Island and the East India Company, see Minutes of a Court for Providence Island, Nov. 21, 1631, Colonial Entry Book, II, 38–39, *CSPS*, I (1574–1660), no. 29, 135–136 (quotation). On John Dike, see Rabb, *Enterprise and Empire*, 280. The Spanish conquered the colony in 1641.

tyranny, and downfall to craft a thinly veiled argument against Charles I. Lord's descriptions in *A Display of Two Forraigne Sects in the East-Indies* complemented the earlier negative descriptions of India's peoples and rulers in Purchas's accounts. The work's frontispiece was divided in two with Surat's "Banians" on one side and Persia's "Persees" on the other. The Banians, described in the text as "effeminate," were naked except for turbans on their heads. Three male figures representing *"Bremaw, Uystney, and Ruddery,"* the Banians' creator, guardian, and destroyer of the creatures, had their hands positioned near one another's genitalia in suggestive motions. A picture of the devil was nailed to the wall behind a *"Bramane"* figure pointing to a cow. The Parsee figures were depicted clothed, but again wearing turbans, with a *"Daroo"* apparently acting as *"Zertoost"* holding "the heavenly fire." Lord concluded that many Catholic rites were shared by these two Satanic "Sects." The English must not be like the "Gnats" who were drawn to such fires and to their own destruction. Instead, the English must follow their own light of God, which was brighter than all other stars. In case there was any doubt of the point in the English political context, the title page included Isaiah 9:16, "The Leaders of this people cause them to erre: and they that are led of them are destroyed." Lord's association of Charles I with India's peoples, fashions, and ways of life and all of them with Satan extended the English twinning of Catholicism and Islam to other Asian faiths, and it militated against trade with India. Such associations had particular salience given Charles I's actions.[32]

The king's suspension of Parliament between 1629 and 1640, the Eleven Years' Tyranny, encouraged him to identify the India trade as a possible means to support his government without parliamentary revenue. The first attempt to dramatically expand calico imports in the early 1620s had been short-lived. Weakness against the Dutch, plague in London, famine in India, and bad investments combined to drive down the Company's trade and profits substantially through the late 1630s. Stung by the lack of royal help against the VOC, the Company had also rebuffed Charles I's desire to become a member in 1628 and his request for a loan of ten thousand pounds. Against this background, the king chartered a new venture in 1637, Courteen's Association, headed by Endymion Porter, a royal favorite, and William Courteen, a merchant instrumental in initial English

---

32. Henry Lord, *A Display of Two Forraigne Sects in the East-Indies viz: The Sect of the Banians the Ancient Natives of India and the Sect of the Persees the Ancient Inhabitants of Persia Together with the Religion and Maners of Each Sect* (London, 1630), I, n.p., 34–39, II, 19, 52–53. There is no indication that the Company supported the publication.

settlements in Barbados in the 1620s. The Association was granted the right to operate in areas previously part of the Company's charter but that the Company was not using. The Association and other planners believed that the Indian Ocean trade could best be developed with a combination of trading factories and plantation colonies modeled on those of the Dutch at Batavia or the English in the Atlantic.[33]

The East India Company, meanwhile, continued to focus primarily on trading factories and cottons instead of plantations, as the soon-to-be director Lewes Roberts reflected in his 1638 commercial guide book. For Roberts, any potential moral shortcomings of India's people had no bearing on whether their goods should be purchased and traded. Roberts expounded upon the bounty of India, commenting frequently on its cottons. In Khambhat ("Cambia"), one would find a "great quantitie" of cotton cloth, "which we terme *callicoes*," from the coarsest to the finest quality, and in Bengal, "*cloth of cotton* of infinite sorts, made here in great quantitie." He complimented the "industriousness" of the people of Machilipatnam ("Masulipatam") and their "excellent *fine cotton linen*, made here in great aboundance, and of all colours, and interwoven with divers sorts of loome workes and flowers, very fine and cunningly wrought . . . better esteemed there then *silke*." At the same moment as Roberts's work, however, more Protestant English attacks on India and its material culture were steadily appearing.[34]

William Bruton, for example, who had established a Company trading factory in Bengal, directly associated what he saw as the horrific tyranny and immorality of India with Indian goods. The title of his work promised revelations on *Their Detestable Religion, Mad and Foppish Rites, and Ceremonies, and Wicked Sacrifices and Impious Customes*. Notably, Bruton did not see Indians as lacking industry or wealth. A depiction of the "great City of Jaggarnat" showed an impressive city with large and ornate buildings, domed rooftops, stone walls, and seven large bridges with multiple arches. He described well-paved streets, great feasts, and well-stocked markets. Nevertheless, he saw Muslims and Hindus as untrustworthy, "foolish," uncultured, and wicked. The frontispiece to his book

33. William Foster, "The East India Company, 1600–1740," in H. H. Dodwell, ed., *The Cambridge History of the British Empire*, V, *British India, 1497–1858* (Cambridge, 1929), 90; Chaudhuri, *English East India Company*, 66–73, 193; Robert Ashton, *The City and the Court, 1603–1643* (Cambridge 1979), 128; Alison Games, *The Web of Empire: English Cosmopolitans in an Age of Expansion, 1560–1660* (New York, 2008), 191.

34. Lewes Roberts, *The Merchants Mappe of Commerce: Wherein the Universal Manner and Matter of Trade Is Compendiously Handled* (London, 1638), 179, 191, 193.

The Grand Idoll Iagernat.

Plate 2. "The Grand Idoll Iagernat." Frontispiece of William Bruton, *Newes from the East-Indies; or, A Voyage to Bengalla, One of the Greatest Kingdomes under the High and Mighty Prince Pedesha Shassallem, Usually Called the Great Mogull ...* (London, 1638). By permission of the Folger Shakespeare Library

depicted several people in turbans pulling the car of Juggernaut over sacrificial victims (Plate 2). Upon the car a frightening idol sat sheltered by a large umbrella carried by a man. In the text, Bruton described Juggernaut as "the Mirrour of all wickednesse and Idoltary" and as the "house of Sathan." Some worshippers, he explained, dragged the cart over crowds of other worshippers, crushing them to death. Through association with the horrible and pagan practice, the umbrella and turbans in the frontispiece became fearful and disgusting emblems, much like the ones employed in Lord's frontispiece.[35]

35. William Bruton, *Newes from the East-Indies; or, A Voyage to Bengalla, One of the Greatest Kingdomes under the High and Mighty Prince Pedesha Shassallem, Usually Called the Great Mogull, with the State and Magnificence of the Court of Malcandy, Kept by the Nabob Viceroy, or Vice-King under the Aforesayd Monarch: Also Their Detestable Religion,*

Thomas Herbert similarly represented the supposed debasement of Asian peoples by pointing to their easy and luxurious ways of life, surroundings, and commodities. Goa, he wrote, had much wealth but "narrow and nasty" neighborhoods. The countryside around the city had "grasse, corne, groves, cattell, fruits, and such sence ravishing delights a reasonable man can require." For Herbert, the bounty of India was "ravishing" and dangerous, like the temptations in the Garden of Eden. In Surat, "the crafty *Bannyan*" sold an incredible selection of calicoes, porcelain, fine inlaid wooden furniture, mother of pearl, ivory, rice, sugar, plantains, and arrack (a sweet liquor). The merchants, "above measure superstitious," wore long hair and white turbans; the women wore alluring veils and jewelry in their ears and noses and on their arms and legs, and they were "silently modest, but full gorg'd with libidinous fantasies and distempers." The alien dress of the people, for Herbert, physically manifested their inner baseness. He mocked the men for praying that their wives "may prove as gentle and fruitfull as a Cow." He marveled that Bengal was "most famous, rich, and populous . . . spacious, noble, and fruitfull" but that its people were "addict to Mars and Merchandize." They were "well cloathed, extremely lustfull; jealous, crafty, and suspicious," driving home his linkage between the outwardly excellent cloth and fashion of India and the low morals of Indian people. In the face of such criticisms of India and its goods, as England became increasingly unstable, and as war wracked reexport markets in Europe, the East India Company found itself debating how to manage the "sale of the calicoes, now a dead commodity."[36]

In 1641, the directors exclaimed in a petition to Parliament, "Disasters

---

Mad and Foppish Rites, and Ceremonies, and Wicked Sacrifices and Impious Customes Used in Those Parts (London, 1638), 3–34. English writers working from many different sides in England's Civil War also associated their enemies with the supposed negative qualities of Ottoman Muslims; see Matar, *Islam in Britain*, 103–107.

36. Tho[mas] Herbert, *Some Yeares Travels into Divers Parts of Asia and Afrique, Describing Especially the Two Famous Empires, the Persian, and the Great Mogull: Weaved with the History of These Later Times as Also, Many Rich and Spatious Kingdomes in the Orientall India, and Other Parts of Asia; Together with the Adjacent Iles. Severally Relating the Religion, Language, Qualities, Customes, Habit, Descent, Fashions, and Other Observations Touching Them; with a Revivall of the First Discoverer of America* (London, 1638), 33–46, 55, 94; Ethel B. Sainsbury, ed., *A Calendar of the Court Minutes etc. of the East India Company, 1640–1643* (Oxford, 1909), vi–xlii, A Court of Committees, June 3, 1640, 45. Herbert might also have meant *ravishing* in the more positive sense of transporting, but his comments on licentiousness suggest that he likely had the more common meaning at least partly in mind.

at Sea, Encounters of Enemies, the undue Proceedings and Actions of our professed Friends and Allies, with other Interruptions, have infinitely damnified the said Traffique." These supposed friends included the Dutch, but the directors particularly disliked the "causeless Complaints in the mouths of many of His Majesties subjects of all degrees and in all Places of the Realm" against the Company and its export of coin for India goods. The directors felt thereby "much discouraged to Trade any longer under the evil Censure of the multitude." They wanted the government to either end the India trade or support the Company. They instructed Thomas Mun, who had crafted their earlier defenses, to succinctly state the Company's importance to the country. Mun added a series of new justifications to his arguments about the balance of trade, the strengthening of the national defense, and competition with the Dutch. He explained that India goods generated considerable customs revenue, raised the value of the gentry's land, and generated wealth for shippers, insurers, and others involved in the trade. He claimed that India provided a market for English lead "and other things," though he struggled to specify those "things." The Company also "spread His Majesties Fame into *Persia, Japan, China*, the Dominions of the Great *Mogul*, and many other remote Nations of the Eastern world." Also in 1641, Roberts dedicated to Parliament his *Treasure of Traffike*, in which he argued in favor of trade, home manufactures, and reexports, and explained that the "want of due and timely protection, and incouragement from the Estate, hath reduced them [the East India Company] to that bad point, and low passe, wherein we now observe them to bee." The Company hoped desperately for further state support.[37]

Within months, however, the outbreak of the English Civil War and broader economic malaise further limited the Company's prospects. England in the 1640s endured several poor harvests, high food prices, and economic depression. In 1643, hoping to increase demand, the directors requested that Indian producers replace "sad red" backgrounds with bright white ones. The change had little immediate effect. Hopes for new,

---

37. *The Petition and Remonstrance of the Governour and Company of Merchants of London Trading to the East-Indies, Exhibited to the Right Honourable the Lords and Commons in the High Court of Parliament Assembled* (London, 1641), 2–25 (quotations on n.p., 23–25). On the petition in Parliament, see *Journals of the House of Commons*, Aug. 24, 1641, II, *1640–1643* (London, 1802), 270. See also Henry Robinson, *Englands Safety, in Trades Encrease; Most Humbly Presented to the High Court of Parliament* (London, 1641), 20–24, 49–50; Lewes Roberts, *The Treasure of Traffike; or, A Discourse of Forraigne Trade* (London, 1641), 88.

more open or plantation-based models of the India trade, instead, continued to develop.[38]

Maurice Thompson, a confidant of Oliver Cromwell, the victor of the Civil War, took up a leadership role in the East India Company in 1649 intending to replicate English Atlantic colonies in the Indian Ocean, not Indian cultivation in Virginia. Thompson had been to Virginia, was extensively involved in trade and colonization in both the Atlantic and Indian Oceans, and had taken over Courteen's Association. In 1644, the association had attempted to imitate the settlement of Atlantic colonies in Madagascar, but patterns of disease, starvation, conflict with local peoples, and death were also replicated from the early Atlantic colonies. Only 40 percent of the colonists survived to be evacuated from Madagascar after fourteen months. Thompson was not deterred. In 1649, he helped launch an East India Company adventure to set up an Atlantic-style sugar colony, using enslaved African labor, and an entrepôt for trade between the Atlantic and Indian Oceans at Assada, near Madagascar. He further planned to use enslaved Africans to operate spice plantations in Pulo Run—which the VOC had seized from the English three decades earlier—and, later, in India itself. He also worked to use English positions in West Africa to secure gold and ivory to trade in the Indian Ocean. The colonization plans, in particular, would fail rapidly, but the Guinea trade and its gold held more promise. The Guinea Company agreed to buy two thousand or more pieces of Indian longcloth on hand in London "for an experiment" to western Africa.[39]

Despite his friend Thompson's plans, Cromwell paid more attention to the multiplying English adventures in the Atlantic over those in the Indian Ocean. The first English Navigation Act, passed by Cromwell's Rump Parliament (composed of only those members that opposed a settlement with Charles I) encoded a new system of global regulation that particularly affected English trade in the Atlantic. The Navigation Act manifested the Rump Parliament's disgust for the Dutch Orangists (who supported the

38. John Irwin, "Origins of the 'Oriental Style' in English Decorative Art," *Burlington Magazine*, XCVII (1955), 110–111. For more on England's economic difficulties, see J. P. Cooper, "Social and Economic Policies Under the Commonwealth," in G. E. Aylmer, ed., *The Interregnum: The Quest for Settlement, 1646–1660* (London, 1972), 123.

39. On Thompson in Virginia, see Lyon Gardiner Tyler, ed., *Encyclopedia of Virginia Biography* (New York, 1915), I, 339–340. On Thompson's plans for the East India Company, see Ethel B. Sainsbury, ed., *A Calendar of the Court Minutes, etc., of the East India Company, 1650–1654* (Oxford, 1913), iii, 9–12, 52, 57, 62–63, 66, 73, 93, 143. On Madagascar and Assada, see Games, *Web of Empire*, 191–217.

Prince of Orange and were seen as sinful monarchists) and distrust of the Dutch pursuit of global economic power. The act was politically motivated, though it nevertheless had many economic implications. The act required goods from "Asia, Africa or America" to be brought to England only on English vessels. The disintegration of many of the Atlantic colonial monopoly companies soon after they were formed, while the colonies themselves often survived, had stimulated competitive private trade in the English Atlantic. Tobacco flowed from Virginia and sugar from Barbados, followed by Antigua and Montserrat. More colonies were successfully settled in Connecticut and Rhode Island, providing mostly fish and wood. The act was targeted to ensure that England, and not other European powers, benefited from these colonial trades. Goods on English vessels from Asia, meanwhile, were exempted from a clause requiring that goods brought from foreign places to England had to arrive directly from their country of origin. English vessels needed the freedom to bring goods from throughout the Indian and Pacific Oceans via the English factories in India. Nevertheless, the Company's monopoly rights were in limbo. After the act's passage, negotiations over various types of alliances with the Dutch broke down, leading to the First Anglo-Dutch War. Many traders, particularly the East India Company without protection from London, suffered severely at the hands of the Dutch.[40]

Through the mid-1650s, Cromwell continued to focus on the Atlantic in

40. Goods from the Spanish and Portuguese colonies were also allowed to come from Iberia, underscoring that the Dutch were the primary targets of the act. Continuing attempts at alliance with the Dutch further strengthen the case that, even if some English merchants and shipowners might have hoped to benefit from the act economically, it was intended to gain political leverage for a reformed Protestant Anglo-Dutch union. On the political motivations for the act, the outbreak of the First Anglo-Dutch War, merchant suffering, and negotiations with the Dutch, see Steven C. A. Pincus, *Protestantism and Patriotism: Ideologies and the Making of English Foreign Policy, 1650-1668* (New York, 1996), 24–79, 172–186; Menna Prestwich, "Diplomacy and Trade in the Protectorate," *Journal of Modern History*, XXII (1950), 104–106, 120–121; Cooper, "Social and Economic Policies," in Aylmer, ed., *Interregnum*, 133–135. Ralph Davis saw the act as the fulfillment of long-standing demands by shipowners; see Davis, *The Rise of the English Shipping Industry in the Seventeenth and Eighteenth Centuries* (New York, 1962), 304–306. For the largely circumstantial argument that interloping English merchants crafted the Navigation Acts, and particularly Maurice Thompson, see J. E. Farnell, "Navigation Act of 1651, the First Dutch War, and the London Merchant Community," *EHR*, n.s., XVI (1963–1964), 440–454. For the text of the Navigation Act, see Henry Scobell, *A Collection of Acts and Ordinances of General Use, Made in the Parliament Begun and Held at Westminster the Third Day of November, Anno 1640 and Since, unto the Adjournment of the Parliament Begun and Holden the 17th of September, Anno 1656 . . .* (London, 1658), 176–177.

both his negotiations with the Dutch and in his military pursuits outside Europe. In trying for peace with the Dutch in 1653, Cromwell offered to form a union against Spain and Portugal in which the Dutch would gain exclusive rights to Asia and Brazil and the English would gain exclusive rights to the rest of the Americas. The Dutch rebuffed Cromwell's offer to divide the world, but when peace came the Navigation Act largely fell out of use. In 1654 and 1655, Cromwell turned to increasing England's presence in the Atlantic through force without the Dutch, launching the expedition known as the Western Design, which targeted the Spanish West Indies. The expedition suffered defeat in Hispaniola, shifted more trade with the Spanish empire from the English to the Dutch, and led to a lengthy war with Spain, netting Jamaica for England. Jamaica would become a useful hub to move European and Indian goods into the Spanish colonies, trades for which the English increasingly gained concessions. During this same period, Cromwell effectively allowed an open India trade. He might have hoped that this decision would increase trade for some of his close supporters, but the lack of a powerful state-chartered company also lessened the state's involvement in the trade.[41]

Hopes were again rising to domesticate in the Atlantic colonies the supply of India goods from Muslim and other Asian powers. Efforts to grow indigo in Barbados and the West Indies had begun to provide a little Atlantic competition to the Indian Ocean trade. Trials were afoot in Jamaica to cultivate cloves and nutmegs brought from the Spice Islands. Additionally, influential English Protestant writer Samuel Hartlib and Virginia Company investor John Ferrar and his daughter Virginia reinvigorated plans to produce silk in Virginia. In their aptly titled *The Reformed Virginian Silk-Worm* (1655), Hartlib and the Ferrars explained that silk cultivation and the production of other Asian goods in Virginia would "contract all the riches of the South-sea, the *Molocos, Philipines, China, etc.*" The Virginia colony would also supply the commodities currently im-

---

41. Cornelius Vermuyden, a Dutch immigrant, authored the proposal on which the offer to the Dutch to divide the world was based; see Samuel Rawson Gardiner, *History of the Commonwealth and Protectorate, 1649–1660* (London, 1901), III, 349–354; for the text, see "A Paper Delivered by Sir Cornelius Vermuyden, Relating to a Treaty between England and the States General," in Thomas Birch, ed., *A Collection of the State Papers of John Thurloe . . .* (London, 1742), II, 125–126. For more on war with Spain, see Prestwich, "Diplomacy and Trade," *Journal of Modern History*, XXII (1950), 107–112, 117. On the Western Design, see Kupperman, "Errand to the Indies," *WMQ*, 3d Ser., XLV (1988), 88–99. See also Stanley J. Stein and Barbara H. Stein, *Silver, Trade, and War: Spain and America in the Making of Early Modern Europe* (Baltimore, 2000), 60–67.

ported from powers in southern Europe and from the Ottoman empire. As the title suggests, the reform of the silkworm in Virginia would be an integral part of England's broader reformation, and the authors hoped that it would employ the poor and convert native Americans to Christianity. The Virginia colony reinstated an old Virginia Company law requiring the planting of mulberry trees and promising bounties for silk and other commodities. Still, dreams of significant silk production in America remained elusive for centuries.[42]

For Edward Terry, not silk in Virginia, but trade with India would best serve as a moral guide and prophylaxis against corruption in an age of "Reformation." In 1655, the same year as *The Reformed Virginian Silk-Worm*, Terry published *A Voyage to East-India*, in which he carefully refined the contradictory English views of India's peoples, simultaneously wealthy and poor, enviable and pitiable, admirable and disgusting, harmless and frightening, and in a most godly place but misguided in their religions. Terry found the Muslim rulers corrupted, though Muslim Indians still had many moral habits. More strikingly, Hindus were in many ways closer to godliness than Muslims and many Christians. The pitiable and poor Hindus, he explained multiple times, grew the food and made the "curious Manufactures" upon which the Mughal empire depended, and which the empire afforded to its rulers and traders. This celebration of Hindu labor reflected English Protestant hopes of a positive labor-based empire in America cultivating silk, cotton, and spices, but Terry's description of the corruptions of India's Muslim rulers also fit with humanist warnings of the declension that an English empire in America might bring to its English rulers. In this view, an independent noncolonized India with

42. William Foster, *The English Factories in India, 1655–1660* (Oxford, 1921), 322; Foster, *The English Factories in India, 1661–1664* (Oxford, 1923), 224n; [Samuel Hartlib], *The Reformed Virginian Silk-Worm; or, A Rare and New Discovery of a Speedy Way, and Easie Means, Found Out by a Young Lady in England, She Having Made Full Proof Thereof in May, Anno 1652. for the Feeding of Silk-Worms in the Woods, on the Mulberry-Tree-Leaves in Virginia . . .* (London, 1655), 8–12, 14 (quotation); Linda Levy Peck, *Consuming Splendor: Society and Culture in Seventeenth-Century England* (Cambridge, 2005), 103–107. David R. Ransome suggests that John Ferrar, not Virginia, was the author of the works on silk in Virginia's name, which were attributed to Virginia by John Ferrar and Samuel Hartlib; see Ransome, "Ferrar, John (c.1588–1657)," *DNB*. For a brief survey of ongoing attempts to develop silk production in North America, see Kathleen A. Staples and Madelyn C. Shaw, *Clothing through American History: The British Colonial Era* (Santa Barbara, Calif., 2013), 160–166. On later attempts, see James Etheridge Callaway, *The Early Settlement of Georgia* (Athens, Ga., 1948), 30; Joyce E. Chaplin, *An Anxious Pursuit: Agricultural Innovation and Modernity in the Lower South, 1730–1815* (Chapel Hill, N.C., 1993), 160–167.

its godly laborers and corrupted rulers was a safer trading partner than a colonized English Virginia.[43]

Terry positioned India's often Hindu-produced export commodities, such as cottons, spices, and furniture as well as its dress, as godly and beneficial and its nonexport Muslim cultural traits and some of its religious practices as marks of corruption and degrading luxury. Terry agreed with earlier authors that the Indians were "the best Apes for imitation in the world," but he also stressed that they "shew very much ingenuity" in their furniture, fabrics, carpets, and other manufactures. He celebrated the cloth and, particularly, Muslim clothing not only for its beauty and quality but also because it was less prideful, wanton, and deforming than English fashions, and was therefore closer to godliness. He appreciated the Indians' "curious" and "excellent" furniture. And he admired their curry cooking, writing, "They stew all their flesh . . . cut into sippets, or slices, or little parts, to which they put Onions and Herbs and Roots, and Ginger . . . and other Spices, with some Butter, which ingredients when as they are well proportioned, make a food that is exceedingly pleasing to all Palates." Further positioning the food positively to his Protestant readers, he averred that curry was "happily" the food that Jacob made for his father in Genesis 27. Coffee and betel, too, offered many healthful benefits. In contrast, he exclaimed of Indian palanquins in which local Muslim elites reclined while carried by human bearers: "They make the shoulders and joints of those that feel their heavy weight, to bow and buckle under their burdens. This as it should seem was an ancient, but a base effeminacy sometimes used in *Rome*." He criticized English people in India for adopting palanquins and in England for vanity in dress, which were both evidence of a Roman-style decline through corrupt luxury. India and England alike were the source of such corruption, but India also offered many godly products and styles from which the English could benefit.[44]

43. Terry, *Voyage to East-India*, n.p. [iv, vi–vii, x–xii], 252–253, 319. Terry seems to have been somewhat uncomfortable with the Protectorate and celebrated the restoration of Charles II. For more on Terry, see William Foster, ed., *Early Travels in India, 1583–1619* (London, 1921), 288–290.

44. Terry, *Voyage to East-India*, 106–107, 134–136, 155, 206–207, 214–231. Terry had given a relation of his experiences as Thomas Roe's chaplain privately to the Prince of Wales, the future Charles I. It became the basis for another version published in Purchas, ed., *Haklwytus Posthumus*, IX, 1–54. This earlier version did not commend Indian clothing, nor Indians for their ingenuity as producers, focusing instead only on their abilities as imitators. It also included a much more muted description of curry, though the connection to Jacob appeared. With the meal, Jacob tricks his father Isaac into blessing him instead of his brother. The food could thus have been associated with sin, but the choice of the term "happily" and the

Curiosity collections also encouraged a blurry split between commodities from India suitable for consumption and assimilation in Protestant England, on the one hand, and natural specimens and specific manufactures that supposedly represented important human and ecological differences to be studied to further universal knowledge, on the other. Collections of curiosities rose in importance dramatically after the English Civil War, particularly among men on the make. Collectors drew on an understanding of a biblical human empire over all nature, and their collections increasingly manifested an interest in England's imperial pursuits. By 1656, John Tradescant, Jr., owned England's largest museum, and one of the largest museums in Europe. Tradescant depended on English exploits in the Americas and East and West Indies to stock his shelves. In the 1650s, the museum's Indian items included an umbrella, hookahs, birds, musical instruments, statues, shoes, vests, a range of gurgolets (water bottles with long spouts), stones, a tiger's head, an elephant's head, a flying squirrel, and various plants. Notably, these collected items did not tend to include pepper and calicoes, common East India Company trade goods. Instead, collectors accumulated arts and crafts that they associated with heathenness and immorality and specimens that brought them closer to a universal understanding of the natural world. Tradescant's museum became connected to England's institutions of empire when it landed, after several decades, at Oxford University as the Ashmolean Museum.[45]

The Company soon answered another of the strongest criticisms against it by exporting precious metals to India directly from western

---

overall context show that Terry meant to use Genesis 27 to support curry. The earlier version also contained a simpler palanquin description, referencing Rome but without the "bow and buckle" phrase. In sum, the earlier version was less favorable to India's peoples and their products. See Purchas, ed., *Hakluytus Posthumus*, IX, 30–33, 45–46. Many English people resisted general moral reformation under the Protectorate; see Derek Hirst, "The Failure of Godly Rule in the English Republic," *Past and Present*, no. 132 (August 1991), 33–66. Terry's framing, however, made Indian luxury moral in an attempt to appeal to both those embracing and resisting moral reformation. For more on luxury consumption during the Protectorate, see Linda Levy Peck, "Luxury and War: Reconsidering Luxury Consumption in Seventeenth-Century England," *Albion*, XXXIV (2002), 1–23.

45. John Tradescant, *Musaeum Tradescantianum; or, A Collection of Rarities, Preserved at South-Lambeth Neer London* (London, 1656), 4–8, 42–54; Arthur MacGregor, "The Cabinet of Curiosities in Seventeenth-Century Britain," in Oliver Impey and Arthur MacGregor, eds., *The Origins of Museums: The Cabinet of Curiosities in Sixteenth- and Seventeenth-Century Europe* (Oxford, 1985), 147–152. On godly universal knowledge, see *Gesta Grayorum; or, The History of the High and Mighty Prince, Henry Prince of Purpoole . . .* (London, 1688), 35; Marjorie Swann, *Curiosities and Texts: The Culture of Collecting in Early Modern England* (Philadelphia, 2001), 194–200.

Africa, a change enabled by newfound support from Cromwell. Cromwell rechartered the Company monopoly in 1657 to strengthen England's position in the Indian Ocean, particularly against the Dutch, with his old friend Thompson in charge. Cromwell thus turned to actively embrace ideas of Protestant English action in the Indian Ocean espoused by Hakluyt, Purchas, Thompson, and the East India Company. The Company had continued to struggle through most of the 1650s, and Thompson's ambitious plans had largely failed. With its new charter and a new stock issue, the Company now quickly facilitated Thompson's plans to join the Atlantic and Indian Ocean trades by purchasing the Guinea Company. The East India Company then reexported significant quantities and values of Indian goods from London to the western coast of Africa. Indian fabrics, particularly longcloth, typically accounted for between one-fifth and one-half of the value of all goods shipped, with the proportion generally increasing. The Company sold the fabric in Africa primarily for gold and ivory to take directly to India to purchase more India goods for European and Atlantic markets. It was a promising new model.[46]

After the Restoration, however, Charles II wanted western Africa's gold for England, and he understood that the Company was little interested in developing the English Atlantic trading and enslaved labor plantation system. In 1660, the king chartered the RAC under the leadership of the duke of York. The charter granted the RAC the rights to western Africa and was focused on the development of gold mines, the shipment of gold to England instead of India, and the general expansion of trade between Africa and England. All of that might further the cause against the Dutch, but it also threatened to usurp the East India Company's already patented operations in Africa. The East India Company directors fruit-

46. William Foster, "Introduction," in Ethel Bruce Sainsbury, ed., *A Calendar of the Court Minutes etc. of the East India Company, 1644–1649* (Oxford, 1912), xi. For the purchase of the Guinea Company, see Foster, *English Factories in India, 1655–1660*, 141. For examples of Company exports to Africa in which Indian cottons accounted for approximately one-fifth of the total value, see Directors to Fort Cormantine, July 16, 1658, IOR/E/3/85, fol. 67r, BL; approximately one-third, Directors to Fort Cormantine, Sept. 13, 1658, IOR/E/3/85, fol. 76r, BL, Dec. 27, 1658, IOR/E/3/85, fol. 84v, June 23, 1659, IOR/E/3/85, 225–228/fols. 113v–114v (both page and folio numbers are provided, as here, when available), Nov. 8, 1659, IOR/E/3/85, 256/fol. 128v, Sept. 12, 1660, IOR/E/3/85, fol. 163; approximately half the value, Directors to Fort Cormantine, Nov. 10, 1661, IOR/E/3/86, fol. 31r, BL. Considerable work remains to be done on the Company and its servants' involvement in the trade in enslaved people from western Africa. On the Company's trade in Indian Ocean enslaved people, see Richard B. Allen, "Satisfying the 'Want for Labouring People': European Slave Trading in the Indian Ocean, 1500–1850," *Journal of World History*, XXI (2010), 55.

lessly petitioned the duke to buy up and resell to them all of the RAC's shares, noting western Africa's important role in supplying gold for the India trade, claiming that the Gold Coast was worthless without India, and not mentioning human trafficking. Indeed, in September 1660, the Company directors forbade their factors and all English people in Ghana from "the buying and selling of any Negroes, as hath byn formerly practized, by some of our factors (in private) to our great prejudice"—hardly a policy designed to maximize the trade in enslaved people. The RAC charter itself, likewise, did not mention trafficking in enslaved people, though it mentioned other commodities. In 1663, however, Charles II rechartered the RAC with a clearly specified monopoly to stimulate the demand for and supply of enslaved people to the Atlantic colonies. Charles II was not the first English ruler to support an expanded English trade in enslaved Africans, but his backing would help make an expanded trade a reality. When the East India Company's preexisting access to western Africa expired in 1664, it was cut out of the trade and cut off from its western African gold.[47]

India goods were not as central to the RAC's trade as they had been to the Company's trade in Africa, but enslaved African labor in European Atlantic colonies had other importance in the India trade. The RAC's exports to Africa varied considerably based on local African market demands. At this time, only on the so-called Slave Coast did the RAC purchase Africans primarily with cottons and cowrie shells from India via London. In other points in western Africa, India goods made up a much smaller portion of the RAC's exports, though they could still be high in value. Many of the enslaved people were taken to the English and Spanish Atlantic colonies to produce sugar and tobacco, and some to mine silver and gold. Products of a brutal labor regime, and also less ideal from the

47. Directors to Roger Chappell, Sept. 14, 1660, IOR/E/3/85, 330/fol. 165v, BL. The Company did export small numbers of people from Africa to India; see, for example, Directors to Fort Cormantine, Sept. 12, 1660, IOR/E/3/85, 239/fol. 165r, BL. On the development of the RAC, see P. E. H. Hair and Robin Law, "The English in Western Africa to 1700," in Nicholas Canny, ed., *The Oxford History of the British Empire*, I, *The Origins of Empire: British Overseas Enterprise to the Close of the Seventeenth Century* (Oxford, 1998), 255–257; Joseph E. Inikori, *Africans and the Industrial Revolution: A Study in International Economic Development* (New York, 2002), 219–224. On the royalist directorship of the RAC, see Wilson, *Profit and Power*, 113–114; Pincus, *Protestantism and Patriotism*, 248–249. For the terms of the first two RAC charters, see Cecil T. Carr, *Select Charters of Trading Companies, A.D. 1530–1707* (London, 1913), 172–181. For the directors' petitions, see Ethel B. Sainsbury, ed., *A Calendar of the Court Minutes, etc., of the East India Company, 1660–1663* (Oxford, 1922), 202–203.

Company's perspective than direct access to African gold, these precious metals from the Americas helped enable the Company's trade with the monetized Indian and Chinese economies.[48]

Meanwhile, Charles II also passed a new Navigation Act in 1660 to revive and enhance Cromwell's system regulating the trade of English, American, Asian, and African commodities, but it was a system with a small hole as far as India goods and the English colonies were concerned. Though rarely studied together by historians, the East India Company monopoly and the Navigation Acts worked together. For bilateral trades without major settlement colonies, like that to the Indian Ocean, company monopolies offered the state simplified policing and revenue opportunities. The Navigation Acts, in contrast, did not grant a monopoly to a single company. They did, however, intend to advance a national monopoly over the empire's imports and exports. The 1660 act mandated that "no Goods or Commodities whatsoever, of the Growth, Production or Manufacture of *Africa, Asia* or *America* . . . be imported into *England*" unless on English vessels with crews that were three-quarters English. These goods must come into England directly from their country of production, although the East India Company was again allowed to bring goods produced anywhere east of the Cape of Good Hope from any port east of the Cape of Good Hope. Any goods from anywhere must also be imported and exported from English colonies on English vessels with three-quarters English crews. The act enumerated several products, including tobacco, indigo, cotton, and sugar, that could be legally shipped only among English colonies and to England. Nevertheless, merchants could still legally reexport Asian goods from continental Europe to the English colonies and to English bases in Africa as long as those goods went on English vessels. In 1660, the English trade in enslaved Africans and the demand for India goods among English people throughout the Atlantic was much smaller than it would become. This regulatory hole, therefore, does not seem to have alarmed the Company, although it would become increasingly important.[49]

---

48. Chaudhuri suggests that calicoes already dominated the RAC trade in the seventeenth century, but David Eltis has shown that was not yet the case, except on the Slave Coast. The vital importance of Indian fabric in the trade of enslaved Africans would be more an eighteenth-century development. See Chaudhuri, *English East India Company*, 9, 201; Eltis, *The Rise of African Slavery in the Americas* (Cambridge, 2000), 168–169, 176, 184, 224.

49. Another act in 1663 required that goods produced in Europe destined for English ports in America, Asia, or Africa be landed in England and shipped on English vessels with

In the meantime, Charles II still intended to use the East India Company in the Indian Ocean to his benefit, and he significantly enhanced the Company's authority to collect new territories. Plans were proposed to limit the Company's export of bullion by imitating the Dutch, who used military power to create colonies and force people in the East Indies to buy the "Manufactures of Christendom, the Dutch being in the East-Indies as Potent, and numerous as they are in Christendom." Charles II gave the Company a new charter in 1661 that included the express right of the Company to expand its power by starting wars and making peace with non-Christian peoples and, following the attempts of Thompson and others, to create "Colonies or Plantations." This right, like the trading right, extended only eastward from the Cape of Good Hope to the Straights of Magellan. Eastern Africa was inside the Company's own charter territory, and western Africa was outside it. The Company's position in India was further strengthened by the king's marriage to Catherine of Braganza, the daughter of John IV of Portugal, which gained for the Company the major Portuguese factory and settlement of Bombay. Significantly, the charter also noted that the king could terminate it with three years' notice if the Company failed to be "profitable to the realm."[50]

The realm's profit demands, though potentially damaging to the Company's trade, ensured the Company's continuing importance to the state. Parliament increased duties on all linens, including calico. The king borrowed £10,000 from the Company at a rate of 6 percent. The Company loaned a further £120,000 to be paid using customs receipts on the Company's trade during the Second Anglo-Dutch War. In the decade from 1669, the state borrowed more than £290,000 of saltpeter and money. These loans confessed Charles II's grace in allowing the charter monopoly; they also made the Company and its trade essential to the state. Private

---

crews that were three-quarters English, but this rule did not apply to Asian-made goods. See [Owen Ruffhead, ed.], *The Statutes at Large . . .* , 14 vols. (London, 1786–1800), III, 166–169, 246–249.

50. K. N. Chaudhuri, *The Trading World of Asia and the English East India Company, 1660–1760* (Cambridge, 1978), 508; Tho[mas] Violet, *A Petition against the Jewes, Presented to the Kings Majestie and the Parliament; Together with Several Reasons, Proving the East-India Trade, the Turkey Trade, the East-Country Trade, May All Be Driven without Transporting Gold or Silver out of England; and Also Some Abuses in the Managing Those Trades Set Down . . .* (London, 1661), 9–10 ("Manufactures"); Shaw, ed., *Charters Relating to the East India Company*, 45–46. For more on Bombay as a colony, see Philip J. Stern, *The Company-State: Corporate Sovereignty and the Early Modern Foundation of the British Empire in India* (New York, 2011), 23–40.

merchants trading to Asia could not provide similar loans, particularly in times of war.[51]

Cromwell had begun, and Charles II more fully executed, a plan to codify a global English empire of colonization, enslaved labor plantations, and national monopoly trades operating in the interests of the state. The opportunities for this global empire and its integration seemed nearly boundless to some. In 1671, for example, William Petty proposed "a Grand House of Peers," including Scots, Irish, and "10 or more out of the rest of His Ma'tys Dominions in Asia, Affrica and America, all Men of the best Estates within the respective Provinces." In reality, English dominions were confined primarily to Britain and small territories around the northern half of the Atlantic Ocean. But, through trade, these places could be profitably tied to the even smaller English claims in India, and the India trade did not necessarily require much, if any, dominion in India. India's value to England depended on considerable consumer demand for its goods in the English Atlantic, including England, its colonies, and its trading forts in Africa as well as in Europe. The replacement of hopes of using the Atlantic colonies to cultivate Asian goods with real productivity in tobacco and sugar, meanwhile, meant that India goods had little competition, though the East India Company certainly had competition in the India trade. European demand for pepper and spices was already largely filled by the VOC, but India offered many more products. The new distinction between manufactured goods from India to be consumed and assimilated, such as silks, cottons, and furniture, and India's supposed luxury and corruption, a distinction developed by supporters of Atlantic colonial silk and of the India trade alike, took on substantial new significance. Here, at the intersection of the India trade, English regulation, and the potential of popularizing more India goods in the Atlantic, was an opportunity.[52]

51. On duties, see Thomas, *Mercantilism and the East India Trade*, 66. Glenn O. Nichols argued that the loans were proof of the Company's dependence on the state for its charter, but the state was also dependent on the charter for the cash to pursue its aims. Leaning on the Company for state borrowing was part of a larger pattern, including the Corporation of London and goldsmith bankers. See Nichols, "English Government Borrowing, 1660–1688," *JBS*, X, no. 2 (May 1971), 85–88. The war was fought over royalist English fears of Dutch radical nonconformist republicanism and pretensions to a sort of neopapist universal Dutch dominion based on economic power in the East and West Indies. See Pincus, *Protestantism and Patriotism*, 260–267, 291–293, 299–317, 443.

52. Wealthy representatives, William Petty figured, would be unmovable by corruption and bribery, and the peers would "superintend" the assemblies of England and its colonies alike. See Petty, "Of a Grand House of Peers," 1671, Add. MS 72866, fols. 8–10v, BL. For

"A Most Useful and Necessary Commodity": The Calico Conquest

The English and other challengers, John Evelyn wrote in 1674, "have driven the Trade of the *East-Indies*, with his [Spanish] Treasure of the *West*, and uniting, as it were, Extreams, made the *Poles* to kiss." In the two decades after the mid-1660s, the East India Company's trade to England exploded in size. This was not a foregone conclusion. Historians have examined the price and material benefits of calico as well as England's position at the vanguard of the calico fashion in Europe, but the timing of the shift toward calico and the rise of the Company's trade needs further explanation. Much as English colonial promoters persuaded people to adventure to the Atlantic colonies, the East India Company also needed to persuade the English public to buy Mughal India's goods. The groundwork for popularizing calicoes in England had already been laid by Edward Terry and others. Still, the Company needed to further adapt these goods to consumer tastes and sell consumers on the goods' benefits. Asian-Indian consumers, for their part, were simply not going to buy English woolens or substantial quantities of any other English goods. The Company, therefore, also needed to convince English consumers and leaders throughout the Atlantic that India's goods were worth buying with bullion, especially without the Company's direct access to African gold, and that they were not corrupting.[53]

---

more comments on the plan, see Armitage, *Ideological Origins*, 152–153. For more on the Dutch domination of the spice trade, see Chaudhuri and Israel, "English and Dutch East India Companies," in Israel, ed., *Anglo-Dutch Moment*, 410. On merchant reactions to these changes, see Pincus, "From Holy Cause to Economic Interest," in Houston and Pincus, eds., *Nation Transformed*, 295–296; Bernard Bailyn, *The New England Merchants in the Seventeenth Century* (Cambridge, Mass., 1955), 112–113, 126–142; David Harris Sacks, *The Widening Gate: Bristol and the Atlantic Economy, 1450–1700* (Berkeley, Calif., 1991), 251, 259–270.

53. [Thomas Papillon], *The East-India-Trade a Most Profitable Trade to the Kingdom; and Best Secured and Improved in a Company, and a Joint-Stock* . . . (London, 1677), 10; J[ohn] Evelyn, *Navigation and Commerce, Their Original and Progress: Containing a Succinct Account of Traffick in General; Its Benefits and Improvements: Of Discoveries, Wars and Conflicts at Sea, from the Original of Navigation to This Day; with Special Regard to the English Nation; Their Several Voyages and Expeditions, to the Beginning of Our Late Differences with Holland; in Which His Majesties Title to the Dominion of the Sea Is Asserted, against the Novel, and Later Pretenders* (London, 1674), 15. Pincus suggests that the English understanding that economic gains through trade to the East and West Indies created the basis and strength of universal monarchy was new in the 1650s, but some Englishmen had been theorizing Spain's success and England's future rise to global power on a similar premise since the turn to the seventeenth century. As discussed above, John Smith and Edward Waterhouse, for example, had earlier argued that Spain's wealth and power came from trade

The directors did not rely on price or physical fabric advantages to stimulate greater English demand for calico. When the East India Company began trading with India in the early 1600s, prices of calicoes in England fell by more than half. Calicoes enjoyed a long period of price advantage over both woolen and linen, but English demand fluctuated and rose to only relatively modest peaks. Between 1665 and 1688, when calico popularity in England spiked, the average sale prices of Indian textiles in London generally fluctuated between twelve and sixteen shillings per piece with no clear downward trend. Many woolens and fustians, in contrast, fell in price sharply. From a price perspective, calico had become, if anything, less competitive. Similarly, calico had more or less the same advantages of color fastness, easy washing, limited shrinkage, cool wearing, and potential to imitate silk in 1603 as it did in 1683. Rather than relying on these long-term advantages, the East India Company repositioned calico in the English marketplace by refining colors and patterns, taking advantage of market opportunities, and both stimulating and capitalizing on an increasingly positive sense of both Indian style and the importance of the India trade on English terms.[54]

In 1662, the directors built upon their earlier strategy of requesting light-colored fabrics by shipping patterns, drawn up in London, to be copied by Indian weavers. These "muster patterns," or "musters," translated Indian production and design into a vernacular more readily understood and appreciated among English people and other Europeans. The Company might have obtained the idea from foreign Persian and Arabic merchants who already operated a large calico trade in the Indian Ocean. In recounting his 1638–1643 journey to India, Jean-Baptiste Tavernier noted that local workers printed cottons "according to the Patterns which the Forreign Merchants give them." Under the muster system, the Company doubled fabric imports from India between the early 1660s and the early 1670s. Much of the focus was on well-priced calicoes and chintzes,

---

in both Indies (Smith, *Generall Historie of Virginia*, 147–149; Waterhouse, *Declaration of the State of the Colony and Affaires in Virginia*, 32–33). See Pincus, *Protestantism and Patriotism*, 256–259, 448–449. For an excellent overview of calico's benefits, see Beverley Lemire, "Fashioning Cottons: Asian Trade, Domestic Industry, and Consumer Demand, 1660–1780," in David Jenkins, ed., *The Cambridge History of Western Textiles* (Cambridge, 2003), I, 496–500.

54. Carole Shammas, *The Pre-industrial Consumer in England and America* (Oxford, 1990), 97; Shammas, "The Decline of Textile Prices in England and British America Prior to Industrialization," *EHR*, 2d Ser., XLVII (1994), 484, 492; Chaudhuri, *English East India Company*, 201; Chaudhuri, *Trading World of Asia*, 547.

such as that shown in Plate 3, made in particular in the eastern and western parts of the subcontinent (now Bangladesh and the Indian states of West Bengal and Gujarat) where the Company had more strength than the VOC. The importance of the Company's fabric trade in these regions was further elevated as the Dutch Company militantly reengrossed the pepper trade in Bantam, Sumatra, and the Malabar Coast. Additionally, the current heavily pleated dress fashions from France required light fabrics. Silks and calicoes readily fit the need. The Company increased imports again after new legal restrictions hit French silks in the English market in 1678.[55]

To defend the Company's growing imports of consumer goods, Thomas Papillon and Josiah Child wrote detailed tracts amplifying and expanding on Thomas Mun's earlier arguments. Papillon and Child were Whigs, longtime members of the Company, and business partners vying to be elected respectively as the Company's deputy-governor and governor. In 1677, Papillon wrote that the East India trade "renders us Rich, Honourable and Great . . . makes us Masters of the Treasures of other Countries, and begets and maintains our Ships and Seamen, the Walls and Bulwarks of our Country." India provided saltpeter essential for gunpowder, and the

55. Raymond Head, "Indian Crafts and Western Design from the Seventeenth Century to the Present," *RSA Journal*, CXXXVI (1988), 118. Company servants from India had previously sent musters as samples to London for approval. See, for example, Fras. Fetiplace and Robert Hughes to the East India Company, Dec. 20, 1617, *CSPC*, III, no. 220, 87–89; John Norris, Raphe Cartwright, and Thomas Clarke to Thomas Colley, Feb. 5, 1633, *CSPC*, VIII, no. 397, 363. Unfortunately, since he published the work in the mid-1670s it is unclear whether Tavernier actually witnessed the printing of the cottons based on foreign patterns in the 1630s or 1640s. The nationalities of the foreign merchants in question are also unclear. See Jean-Baptiste Tavernier, *The Six Voyages of John Baptista Tavernier, Baron of Aubonne; through Turky, into Persia and the East-Indies, for the Space of Forty Years; Giving an Account of the Present State of Those Countries . . . to Which Is Added, a New Description of the Seraglio*, trans. J. P. (London, 1677), part 2, 33. On the Dutch, see Chaudhuri and Israel, "English and Dutch East India Companies," in Israel, ed., *Anglo-Dutch Moment*, 413–418. The directors also sent artisans to India to train Indians to produce for European markets. The extent of their influence in India remains unclear, but it was likely minimal. Indians had much better dying technologies and were already skilled in reproducing requested designs. The directors quickly recalled the artisans, suggesting they were of little use. See Thomas, *Mercantilism and the East India Trade*, 39; John Irwin and Margaret Hall, *Indian Painted and Printed Fabrics* (Ahmedabad, 1971), 24–42. Chandra Mukerji put a lot of weight on a "vacuum" created in the market by the restrictions on French silks needed to make French-style dresses. The restrictions likely did increase demand for calicoes and silks from India, but the surge had begun much earlier, and the peak of imports did not come until the mid-1680s. See Mukerji, *From Graven Images: Patterns of Modern Materialism* (New York, 1983), 189–190. Data is from Chaudhuri, *Trading World of Asia*, 286–287.

Plate 3. Palampore Textile Fragment, India. Circa 1690–1710. Cotton. Accession no. 1930-685. The Colonial Williamsburg Foundation. Museum Purchase

trade in fashionable goods supported the English military and state interests as well. Calico generated customs revenue and displaced nationally damaging French, Dutch, and Flemish linen from the English market. Papillon claimed that reexports of India goods from London to "France, Holland, Spain, Italy, Turky, etc." brought back more value in goods and money than the Company sent to India to purchase them. These transactions, moreover, needed warehousing, lighters, carts, porters, and a whole range of facilities and workers, all of which generated economic activity that added to the wealth of the nation. Furthermore, he explained that merchandise and money were equally part of the national "Stock and Riches." A man with ten thousand pounds in land and property might have only one hundred pounds of money, but everyone would agree he was worth ten thousand pounds. Gold and silver, he explained, had value primarily as "Merchandise, to be traded with." Papillon and Child were elected in 1680. Papillon remained a Whig critic of the Stuarts, whereas in 1681 Child turned to support the now dominant Tories and the Stuart regime to solidify his leadership over the Company. Child repeated Papillon's arguments in defense of the East India Company and claimed that, since the Dutch, French, Danes, Portuguese, and Swedes all wanted to be major India traders, the trade must have considerable national value.[56]

56. [Papillon], *East-India-Trade*, 2–12; [Josiah Child], *A Treatise Wherein Is Demonstrated I. That the East-India Trade Is the Most National of All Foreign Trades. II. That the Clamors, Aspersions, and Objections Made against the Present East-India Company, Are Sinister, Selfish, or Ground-less. III. That . . . the Dominion of the Sea Depends Much upon the Wane or Increase of That Trade . . . IV. That the Trade of the East-Indies Cannot Be Carried on . . . in Any Other Way Than by a General Joynt-Stock. V. That the East-India Trade Is More Profitable and Necessary to the Kingdom of England, Than to Any Other Kingdom or Nation in Europe* (London, 1681), 2–38. John Houghton similarly explained the value of money in terms he expected the average Englishman to understand: people pay butchers with money because the meat is more useful than the money, and more money will be obtained from other places. See "A Real and Hearty Lover of His King and Countrey" [John Houghton], *England's Great Happiness; or, A Dialogue between Content and Complaint . . .* (London, 1677), 6–7. On the value of reexports, see also Roger Coke, *England's Improvements; in Two Parts; in the Former Is Discoursed, How the Kingdom of England May Be Improved, in Strength, Employment, Wealth, Trade . . . in the Latter Is Discoursed, How the Navigation of England May Be Increased, and the Soveraignty of the British Seas More Secured to the Crown of England* (London, 1675), 58. On Papillon and Child, see A. F. W. Papillon, ed., *Memoirs of Thomas Papillon, of London, Merchant (1623–1702)* (Reading, 1887), 78–84; David Ormrod, "Puritanism and Patriarchy: The Career and Spiritual Writings of Thomas Papillon, 1623–1702," in Alec Detsicas and Nigel Yates, eds., *Studies in Modern Kentish History* (Maidstone, U.K., 1983), 123–137; Irene Scouloudi, "Thomas Papillon, Merchant and Whig, 1623–1702," Huguenot Society of London, *Proceedings*, XVIII (1947–1952), 49–72; Richard Grassby, "Child, Sir Josiah, first baronet (bap. 1631, d. 1699)," *DNB*.

Under Child's leadership, the directors expanded the muster system with increasingly large and diversified textile orders, including a range of ready-made fabric goods. In 1682, they ordered a stunning 2.8 million pieces of Indian textiles. These cottons and silks poured into London through the middle of the 1680s. The directors also ordered one hundred fashionable ready-made coordinated room sets—each including matching curtains, counterpanes, two carpets, and twelve cushions—needing only the wooden furnishings to complete them. Additionally, Child requested 200,000 ready-made shifts of various qualities and values suitable for everyone from seamen and laborers to the gentry. The shifts did not sell well in England. The directors complained that the shifts were 40 percent too expensive and "basely made up by the Taylers" as if they wanted to "discourage the Company in trading in that Commodity." Even if the ready-made shifts proved unprofitable, the directors observed "that their cheapness have introduced the wearing of Callico in shifts" among the poor. The distribution of these Indian fabrics in England radiated outward from London and then other major urban centers. By the 1670s and 1680s, shopkeepers and chapmen as remote as Penrith, Cumberland, sold Bengals, calico, and muslin from India alongside domestic and European fabrics as well as Scottish linens as a popular, cheaper alternative to calicoes. People at a range of income levels used calicoes for curtains, furniture, shirts, and gowns, and they used muslin for handkerchiefs, neckclothes, aprons, and decorative embroideries.[57]

A rash of works written in, or at this time translated into, English made the case that India's superior value and quality fabrics, foods, and furniture should not be rejected, despite the supposed shortcomings of Muslims and Hindus. These arguments were typically less generous than Terry's earlier argument that Indian producers were models of morality, but they were not necessarily less supportive of Indian products. In 1665,

57. Geo. P. Baker, *Calico Painting and Printing in the East Indies in the XVIIth and XVIIIth Centuries* (London, 1927), I, 33; Chaudhuri, *Trading World of Asia*, 286–287. A second attempt at selling ready-made shifts a few years later also failed. See John Styles, "Production Innovation in Early Modern London," *Past and Present*, no. 168 (August 2000), 136–140; Thomas, *Mercantilism and the East India Trade*, 41; "List of Coast Goods to Be Provided for the Year 1690," IOR/E/3/91, 570/fol. 284v, BL (quotation). On distribution, see Margaret Spufford, *The Great Reclothing of Rural England: Petty Chapmen and Their Wares in the Seventeenth Century* (London, 1984), 21, 90, 92, 108–109, 121–122; Audrey W. Douglas, "Cotton Textiles in England: The East India Company's Attempt to Exploit Developments in Fashion, 1660–1721," *JBS*, VIII, no. 2 (May 1969), 29–35, 41–43. Douglas saw well-placed gifts, variety, and quality as the primary means through which the company popularized cottons.

for instance, George Havers translated Pietro Della Valle's experiences in India, notably ignoring the first two parts of Della Valle's work that were on Egypt and Syria. Della Valle wrote that India's white cottons were as they had been since ancient times, "for the most part very fine in comparison of those of our Countries." As for the style of garments, he was "so taken with this India dress, in regard of its cleanness and easiness, and for the goodly shew me-thought it had on hors-back" that he had an outfit made for himself to show in Italy. Like Terry, he praised Indian curries as exceedingly healthy and better than European food. Nevertheless, Della Valle criticized the "foolish devotions" of India's peoples. Similarly, in 1670 Richard Blome wrote that Indian peoples were under the hold of Satan and "averse to *Law,* and *Morality*," but, unlike Della Valle, he thought the men of India and Persia dressed like women. Still, Blome explained that Gujarat and Bengal were extraordinarily rich with fine and valuable crops, industrious people, and excellent cotton cloth.[58]

In 1676, John Speed wrote that people came from all over the world to buy India's "Silks, and other curious Stuffs, and rich Commodities." India's people also grew to incredibly old ages, "notwithstanding their addiction, above all other people in the World, to luxury and venereal exercises." This was not necessarily a defense of luxury, perhaps, but certainly a sign of doubt that Mughal luxury itself was debilitating. Tavernier explained that, unlike other fabrics, "the more you wash them, the fairer the colours shew," giving those from "Seronge," in particular, unique "beauty and liveliness." Some such fabric could become corrupting when it was made so thin that the wearer appears "as if he were naked," as the local rulers supposedly dressed their many wives to dance. However, the emperor, Tavernier explained, forbade merchants to export this immoral and sketchy material. The English translation of Jean de Thévenot's work on India from the 1660s appeared in 1687 and noted that India's cottons washed well, keeping them neat, as in ancient India. Still, the fruitful climate and soil of Bengal made its people lazy, and Islam corrupted them. John Ovington averred in 1696, "In some things the Artists of *India* outdo all the Ingenuity of *Europe, viz.* in the painting of Chites or Callicoes,

---

58. Pietro Della Valle, *The Travels of Sig. Pietro Della Valle, a Noble Roman, into East-India and Arabia Deserta; in Which, the Several Countries . . . Are Faithfully Described: In Familiar Letters to His Friend Signior Mario Schipano; Whereunto Is Added a Relation of Sir Thomas Roe's Voyage into the East-Indies* (London, 1665), 20 ("foolish"), 23 ("very fine" and "taken"), 48–49, 146, 164–165; Richard Blome, *A Geographical Description of the Four Parts of the World Taken from the Notes and Workes of the Famous Monsieur Sanson, Geographer to the French King . . .* (London, 1670), 2, 45, 49, 51, 55, 60, 66 ("averse").

which in *Europe* cannot be parallell'd." He also remarked on Indian abilities to imitate almost any European manufacture, including ships built with superior wood. Indians built good enough furniture, although it was not shellacked as well as that from Japan. Ovington, like Terry, criticized palanquins as pompous, but he noted that they were also more comfortable and regal, and they were quicker than London's sedan chairs. Such detailed textual descriptions considerably increased the level of information, if not its accuracy, about Indian cultures, ways of life, and commodities. More than that, they contributed to a sense of a growing ability to access India's goods on English terms without running great risks of corruption, which apparently came from India's religions or climate and soil, not from its fine export manufactures.[59]

The importance of a positive sense of India goods on English terms can be seen in the English elite's adoption of Indian-style banyans and banyan gowns as well as furniture that they took to be Indian-style. Samuel Pepys, for instance, rented a banyan for his 1666 portrait. Banyans could be long loose robes, such as that worn by Pepys, or more tailored knee-length buttoned shirts. English people imported banyans ready-made from India or had them made in England from imported or domestic fabrics. The king and queen, for instance, hired Robert Croft and Mary Mandove as their personal "Indian Gown" makers. The East India Company also imported growing quantities of cane, worked by an emerging group of craftsmen skilled in producing cane chairs with elegant spiral-turned wooden frames. Furniture makers often painted the wooden frames black to simulate Asian ebony, or "Japanned" them with lacquer and paint. Ebony and lacquered chests, tables, and desks, though often made in Japan and elsewhere in Asia, were generally imported from India and imitated in Europe to supply a growing fashion among the middling and upper sorts after the 1650s.[60]

59. John Speed, *An Epitome of Mr. John Speed's Theatre of the Empire of Great Britain; and of His Prospect of the Most Famous Parts of the World* (London, 1676), 257; Tavernier, *Six Voyages*, part 2, 31–33 (quotations), 36, 90, 126–128; [Jean de Thévenot], *The Travels of Monsieur de Thevenot into the Levant; in Three Parts; viz. into I. Turkey. II. Persia. III. The East-Indies* (London, 1687), part 3, 36, 68; J[ohn] Ovington, *A Voyage to Suratt, in the Year, 1689; Giving a Large Account of That City, and Its Inhabitants, and of the English Factory There, Likewise a Description of Madeira, St. Jago, Annobon, Cabenda and Malemba* (London, 1696), 255–256, 280–282 (quotation).

60. Samuel Pepys, *Diary of Samuel Pepys . . .* , Mar. 30, 1666 (London, 1906), II, 24; Aileen Ribeiro, *Dress in Eighteenth-Century Europe, 1715–1789* (New Haven, Conn., 2002), 26–27; Beverly Lemire, *Dress, Culture, and Commerce: The English Clothing Trade before the*

The importation and display of India's live animals in England, particularly its elephants, further enlivened English terms for understanding India and its material culture. In 1683, Randolph Taylor circulated a broadside of a "Strange and Wonderful SHE-ELEPHANT, Sent from the INDIES." The headline and text connected the elephant's arrival to English access to India and noted that this was only the second elephant ever in England. The text noted that the elephant "exceedeth all other beasts in the World" and described the elephant's strength, sagacity, habits, and diet. Unlike earlier accounts of elephants as the tools of cruel Indian despots, this elephant was not associated with tyranny. Around the same time, another East India Company ship brought London's first rhinoceros. No known elephants or rhinoceroses came to the Atlantic colonies, but colonial writers did discuss such beasts, suggesting a transatlantic interest. One 1650 collection recounted the story of Alexander's war elephants in verse, and Increase Mather intimated that horses "abominate" camels, and "mighty" elephants were terrified of mice.[61]

The Atlantic colonies were hardly disconnected from English engagement with India's commodities and fashions. Merchants reexported considerable quantities of spices, pepper, muslin, calico, cane, and lacquered furniture from London to the colonies. Probate inventories, lists of goods owned at a person's death, provide ample evidence of the consumption of India goods in colonial America in the 1670s and 1680s. Spices, like many other groceries, rarely appeared in probate inventories, but more durable consumer goods can be more readily tracked. In Plymouth Colony, New England, Captain Thomas Willett owned calico "pillowbeares," a calico coverlet, three "boxes of Indian Glasse Jewells," and several Turkey-work chairs made from snippets of fabric. Willett also consumed India through

---

Factory, 1660–1800 (New York, 1997), 63; Edw[ard] Chamberlayne, Angliae Notitia; or, The Present State of England . . . , 15th ed. (London, 1684), 179, 226.

61. A True and Perfect Description of the Strange and Wonderful She-Elephant, Sent from the Indies, Which Arrived at London, August 1, 1683, with the True Portraicture of That Wonder in Nature (London, 1683); Anthony Farrington, Trading Places: The East India Company and Asia, 1600–1834 (London, 2002), 119–120 (for the rhinoceros); [Anne Bradstreet], The Tenth Muse Lately Sprung Up in America; or, Severall Poems, Compiled with Great Variety of Wit and Learning . . . (London, 1650), 27, 140; Increase Mather, An Essay for the Recording of Illustrious Providences: Wherein an Account Is Given of Many Remarkable and Very Memorable Events, Which Have Hapned in This Last Age; Especially in New-England (Boston, 1684), 100. English kings and queens had intermittently kept a menagerie in the Tower of London since 1235. In 1255, the Tower housed its first elephant. See The Tower Menagerie: Comprising the Natural History of the Animals Contained in That Establishment; with Anecdotes of Their Character and History (London, 1829), xiv.

print as he perused his copies of *Purchas His Pilgrimes* and "Smithe's *eastindia Voyages.*" Upper-sort men and women in New England, as they did throughout the English Atlantic, also owned India muslin neckwear and aprons. Even people with few possessions might own calico, such as James Ford of Ispwich, whose 1677 inventory included a small collection of clothing, a chest, a few weapons, and several yards of serge, calico, and silk. The Hudson's Bay Company purchased hundreds of calico shirts for its trading stations in the north. New England colonists also turned their hands toward making their own cotton fabric, continuing the hopes of using America to produce India's commodities. Samuell Fuller of Plymouth, for example, owned six pounds of cotton wool, a pair of cotton cards to clean and align the fibers, and six and a half skeins of cotton thread. Joseph Coleman owned cotton and sheep's wool as well as cotton and linen yarn. Homespun cotton, however, had a different place in the market from cotton imported from India. It was neither as fine as India muslin, nor dyed, printed, and painted like India calico and chintz.[62]

Mid-1680s probate inventories for New York and the southern colonies list Indian silk and cotton gowns, gloves, stockings, and hangings as well as lacquered furniture and India pictures. In 1685, Mrs. De Lange owned "three flowered calico samare" gowns, "three calico nightgowns—two flowered and one red"—as well as silk and calico waistcoats, cotton stockings, six calico aprons, and "five small East India boxes." With her husband, Jacob, she also owned silk and calico curtains, calico bed hangings,

62. Willett's library also contained works on the Ottoman empire, Rome, and London. Unfortunately, most inventories did not specifically detail the fabric that clothing was made from or the covering or style of furniture, which makes a statistical analysis of rates of India goods ownership impossible. For examples of personal probate inventories containing calicoes and other India goods, see Inventory of Thomas Willett, Aug. 25, 1674, Plymouth Colony Records, Wills, Inventories, and Estates, 1633–1686, III, 117–128, Plimoth Plantation, Plymouth, Mass., Inventory of Samuell Fuller, Aug. 29, 1676, III, part 2, 47, Inventory of Joseph Coleman, Nov. 9, 1674, III, 141–142; *The Probate Records of Essex County Massachusetts* (Salem, Mass., 1920), III, 121, 154, 156, 178, 206, 208, 364, 412, 424; Patricia Trautman, "Dress in Seventeenth-Century Cambridge, Massachusetts: An Inventory-Based Reconstruction," *Early American Probate Inventories,* Dublin Seminar for New England Folklife, *Annual Proceedings,* XII (1987), 55–57, 61; Abbott Lowell Cummings, ed., *Rural Household Inventories: Establishing the Names, Uses, and Furnishings of Rooms in the Colonial New England Home, 1675–1775* (Boston, 1964), 56, 59 (see also 10–11, 28, 33, 52). On the Hudson's Bay Company purchases, see Lemire, "Fashioning Cottons," in Jenkins, ed., *Cambridge History of Western Textiles,* I, 497–498. Good reexport data for the period remains elusive; see Nuala Zahedieh, "London and the Colonial Consumer in the Late Seventeenth Century," *EHR,* 2d Ser., XLVII (1994), 248.

a variety of calico spreads and counterpanes, a lacquered East India trunk, an "East India Cupboard," five framed East India pictures, and "thirteen East India prints past upon paper." In 1688, Ann Watkins owned three "calico heads," or headcloths, and an "alamode" silk hood. In addition to these goods imported from India or made after Asian styles, many inventories also contained chinaware imported from Canton via Europe. Further south, Sarah Willoughby of lower Norfolk County, Virginia, owned five petticoats, one of which was made partly from India silk and another partly from India calico. Colonists in Virginia also owned India-caned and Turkey-work chairs and many diamonds, emeralds, and pearls that might have come from India. Inventories for Charleston, South Carolina, in the 1680s contain numerous references to calico window curtains, the most common curtain material. The inventories also listed calico and muslin clothing.[63]

The Company was, however, becoming too successful in popularizing such goods for its own good. Impassioning the poles' "kiss" revived discomforts with India's seductive luxuries and its appetite for bullion. The economic writer Carew Reynell explained in 1674, "Finding us fantastical and voluptuous, they tempt us with all sorts of *French* Toyes, *Indy* and *Japan* trifles, stain'd Callicoes, Silks and such pleasant things, and fetch away our Money and solid wealth." Reynell not only attacked the spending of bullion on useless luxury but also aligned the East India Company's stimulation of demand for India goods with the frivolous fashions of Catholic France, a historic enemy of Protestant England. England would be "undone" by consuming India goods. Andrew Yarranton wrote that England sent "vast quantities of our great Monies and Gold, to keep the Heathens poor at Work" instead of England's poor.[64]

63. Esther Singleton, *Dutch New York* (1909; rpt. New York, 1968), 60–64, 90–93, 105–106; Annie Lash Jester, *Domestic Life in Virginia in the Seventeenth Century* (Williamsburg, Va., 1957), 54, 64, 66–67; Teresa C. Farris, *From England to Barbados, to Carolina, 1670–1700: Recovering the Material Culture of First Generation Carolinians* (Gadsden, Ala., 2000), 84, 96.

64. Carew Reynell, *The True English Interest; or, An Account of the Chief National Improvements; in Some Political Observations, Demonstrating an Infallible Advance of This Nation to Infinite Wealth and Greatness, Trade and Populacy, with Imployment, and Preferment for All Persons* (London, 1674), 12; Andrew Yarranton, *England's Improvement by Sea and Land; the Second Part . . .* (London, 1681), 187–189. See also *The Allegations of the Turky Company and Others against the East-India-Company, Relating to the Management of That Trade: Presented to the Right Honourable the Lords of His Majesties Most Honourable Privy Council, the 17th of August, 1681; Together with the Answer of the Said East-India-Company*

In his 1680 *Britannia Languens,* William Petyt echoed old fears about the similar dangers that Asia and America presented to England, though colonists saw America as fundamentally different. Petyt attacked colonization in America for weakening English manufacturers and state power through emigration. Likewise, he attacked the East India Company for creating competition for domestic manufacturers, importing goods in exchange for bullion, and impoverishing the nation. For Petyt, the empire's supposed benefits in America and India were a mirage. Not surprisingly, the few colonists in America who intervened in these debates tended to point the finger only outside America. Cotton Mather referred to the influx of East and West Indian goods and wealth as distracting from God's promise to save people at *"All the Ends of the Earth,"* which was worth more than *"the Riches of both the India's."* His position reflected longstanding strands of Protestant thought alarmed by the potential corrupting wealth of Indias and encouraged by America as outside this corrupting potential.[65]

Nevertheless, to the benefit of the Company and the state, consumers on both sides of the Atlantic showed little fear of and much pleasure in the Company's growing flow of calicoes, Asian-style furniture, and other commodities from the Indian Ocean. The Company had increased its importance to the Atlantic trade primarily by aggressively cultivating English Atlantic demand for the Mughal empire's cottons. Through its muster system, bulk purchases, and experimental orders, the Company used Mughal India's strength to its advantage, outdistancing the Dutch spice and pepper trades in importance. Writers enhanced the English Atlantic public's sense of participation in an ever more successful and impressive empire of trade and colonization, on English terms. To some extent, at least, the Company's defenders had also proven more right than its de-

---

Thereunto, Delivered in Writing the 22th. Instant according to Their Lordships Order, upon Which a Hearing Was Had before Their Lordships the 24. of the Said Month (n.p., [1681]), 1–2.

65. [William Petyt], *Britannia Languens; or, A Discourse of Trade: Shewing the Grounds and Reasons of the Increase and Decay of Land-Rents, National Wealth and Strength; with Application to the Late and Present State and Condition of England, France, and the United Provinces* (London, 1680), 333–344, 350, 414; Cotton Mather, *Call of the Gospel Applyed unto All Men in General, and unto a Condemned Malefactor in Particular . . .* (Boston, 1686), 1. See also Samuel Lee, *Chara Tes Pisteos The Joy of Faith; or, A Treatise Opening the True Nature of Faith, Its Lowest Stature and Distinction from Assurance, with a Scripture Method to Obtain Both; by the Influence and Aid of Divine Grace: With a Preliminary Tract Evidencing the Being and Actings of Faith, the Deity of Christ, and the Divinity of the Sacred Scriptures* (Boston, 1687), 98.

tractors. India's goods were helping to support the state's army and navy in Europe and beyond. In 1685, Parliament levied an additional 10 percent duty on Indian fabrics, which was doubled in 1690 for the "Defence of your Realms, the perfect reducing of *Ireland*, and the effectual Prosecution of War against *France*." England's Atlantic colonies, meanwhile, expected at the beginning of the century to compete with India as fabulous new sources of Asian raw materials, had, by the end of the century, transitioned to cultivating other commodities and consuming India's goods in the mold of England.[66]

IN 1695, THE EAST INDIA COMPANY faced the possibility of competition from a new and global company, the Darien Company, chartered by the Scottish Parliament. This new company, like English efforts before it, was targeted in part at universal Spanish dominion. It also represented both the extent to which England's own imperial adventures had failed to reproduce Asia's commodities in the Atlantic colonies and its success in using North America instead to reproduce markets for India's goods. It was this latter model that the Darien Company would pursue with a colony on the Isthmus of Panama. The colony would export bullion from Central America to Asia to exchange for "spices and goods" to take back to the Americas without passing through Europe, as the English did. The Darien Company's motto sounded similar to Coriat's from nearly a century before, "To unfold Scotland and its company's strength over the world." The company would also allow Britons to avoid English trading restrictions and duties. The House of Lords thus sought regulations to ban Englishmen from participating in the Darien Company in any capacity. Without access to English capital, the company's settlement expedition ended in disaster. Not surprisingly, the company received no assistance when it called on the English East India Company for help. From being the weedy upstart challenging Spain, England had become one of many global powers provoking its own flailing challenger by attempting to use Asia and the Americas together.[67]

66. [Ruffhead, ed.], *Statutes at Large,* III, 426.

67. Stern, "British Asia and British Atlantic," *WMQ,* 3d Ser., LXIII (2006), 705–707 (the motto was translated by Stern); Reynell, *True English Interest,* 13; *Journals of the House of Lords,* Dec. 20, 1695, XV (1691–1696) (London, 1771), 618–619. See also David Armitage, "The Scottish Vision of Empire: Intellectual Origins of the Darien Venture," in John Roberston, ed., *A Union for Empire: Political Thought and the British Union of 1707* (Cambridge, 1995), 97–113, 117. On the influence of English colonization, the growth of the Dutch and English empires, and the Navigation Acts as motivation and justification for Scottish imperial

English ambivalence over empire and, particularly, over the India trade had not gone away. Many people in England feared that global fantasies and desires would possess English people with delusions of glory, give them false understandings of value, feminize their masculinity, and put them unwittingly under the control of both other people and seductive luxuries. English leaders spun their discomfort of trading with Asia and colonization in America alike in part from their understanding of the central role expansion to Asia played in Rome's collapse and in their understandings of both Catholic and Muslim luxury and tyranny. Like the positive fantasies of expansion, trade, and consumption, the negative fantasies of economic and moral impoverishment had real, tangible elements. Political crisis in England in the middle of the seventeenth century led to the codification of an empire of national commercial monopolies in the Atlantic and Indian Oceans. These monopolies were worthless without high levels of demand for staples from each region of trade, and an increasingly clear separation between positive and negative India goods created the possibility for new Indian staples. The East India Company's popularization of calicoes and other India goods in the English Atlantic as well as its supply of calicoes for the trade in enslaved Africans did much more than other failed English attempts at linking the Americas and Asia. It created an imperial fashion and helped to create an empire.

English subjects not only brought Europe to America; they brought India to America as well. They brought India in their economic schemes to cultivate cottons, silks, and spices, and as consumers they brought Indian goods into their homes. The English also brought America to India. They brought gold and silver from Spanish America, and, more than that, in the middle of the seventeenth century they attempted to bring models of colonization that they had used in Virginia, New England, and the West Indies to Madagascar and Assada in the Indian Ocean and to some extent to Bombay on the subcontinent. They also brought India to Africa so that they could send Africans to America and the West Indies to, among many other activities, cultivate sugar and tobacco and mine precious metals, under horrific conditions. Despite the takeover of Bombay, changes in the Company charter, and the ideas of some in the Company, India was not in any immediate danger of being conquered by the much smaller and weaker England. India's strength was, nevertheless, essential to the conceptualization and, after the 1660s, the operation and defense of the

pursuits, see David Armitage, "Making the Empire British: Scotland in the Atlantic World, 1542–1707," *Past and Present*, no. 155 (May 1997), 50–51, 56–58.

　　　India Goods and Early English Expansion

English empire. The Company's popularization of India goods, especially cotton cloth, generated increasing customs revenue and backed substantial loans to the state, particularly for wars with European powers. The popularization of calicoes and other India goods between the 1660s and the 1690s altered the Company, English fashion, ideas about India, and the management, trading, and revenue structures of the English empire itself. India cottons, silks, furniture, and curiosities supported and shaped a broadly imperial fashion and consumption system. From the mid-1660s, competition in this system had increasingly emerged—ominously for many—not between India and the Atlantic colonies, but between Indian and English textile manufacturers.[68]

68. Some still believed, as did John Ovington, that with proper encouragements and the protection of infants, Bombay "might in time be peopled with the *Europeans* transmitted thither, as the Western Islands are, which belong to the Crown of *England*"; see Ovington, *Voyage to Suratt,* 142–147.

2 An Imperial Compromise
The Calico Acts, the Company, and the Atlantic Colonies

"The Company had not made a Dividend for some years, but they would make one now," shouted a "rabble" storming the East India Company's office in London in January 1697. The attackers intended to "rifle the Treasury," and a small group managed to break open the Company's gate and get into the courtyard. The Company, despite its stunning rise in the previous three decades, had not, in fact, paid dividends to its shareholders for six years. These attackers, however, did not own shares; instead, they represented London's woolen and silk producers. Their goal was to force their own special dividend from the Company. They believed that the Company had taken treasure from England and that its calico had taken away the demand for English-made fabrics, throwing England's spinners and weavers into poverty. By pointing out the Company's failure to pay its regular dividends, the rabble also reflected on the Company's own struggles. The Company and English weavers both had suffered as larger economic forces and the Nine Years' War against France (1688–1697) temporarily contracted the markets for all fabrics. The Glorious Revolution, moreover, displaced James II, the Company's most powerful champion, and stimulated intense legal, political, and economic reactions against monopoly companies, including the RAC and the East India Company. At the turn to the eighteenth century, the East India Company faced a range of English adversaries, from the weavers, to interlopers and rival traders, to pirates operating in the Indian Ocean and Red Sea.[1]

1. Trial of William Norman, Feb. 24, 1697 (t16970224–34), *Old Bailey Proceedings Online,* www.oldbaileyonline.org; *Post Boy* (London), Jan. 21–23, Mar. 20–23, 1697; [Owen Ruffhead, ed.], *The Statutes at Large . . .* , 14 vols. (London, 1786–1800), IV, 44. Those attacking the Company had apparently come after raising "tumults" in Parliament. The participants were described as a "rabble" by several master weavers who claimed "their Dislike and Abhorrence" of the violent actions; see *Journals of the House of Commons . . .* , Jan. 29, 1696/7, XI (1693–1697) (London, 1802), 681–684. For more on the RAC and the political and ideological shifts of the Glorious Revolution, see William A. Pettigrew, *Freedom's Debt: The Royal African Company and the Politics of the Atlantic Slave Trade, 1672–1752* (Chapel Hill, N.C., 2013), 5, 12–22, 64, 89–99. This chapter is adapted from my previously published

The pirates, hailing from ports throughout the English Atlantic, had stimulated another "rabble" and a "great noise" against the Company in Surat, and stories about them arrived in Company offices as English weavers intensified their protests. In 1695, the infamous English pirate commander John Avery and the crew of the *Fancy*, with another pirate vessel from Rhode Island, pillaged two Mughal treasure ships returning from Mecca on the annual Hajj pilgrimage. On one ship owned by the Mughal emperor Aurangzeb, the *Ganj-i-Sawai*, the pirates raped several women and took from £155,000 to £180,000 of plunder. The Company's men explained that the pirates "barbarously used" those aboard. They then reported that the Surat rabble "barbarously used" a group of Company merchants and Englishmen, fatally wounding one. Aurangzeb's representative imprisoned the English factors for most of a year. It made some sense to use similar language to describe the actions of English weavers, English Atlantic pirates, and Surat protesters who acted violently against the Company's interests—even if indirectly, in the pirates' case. Together, such stories of fashions, rabbles, and pirates suggest that the allure of India's wealth and its fabulous goods stirred popular violence from America to India among a startling range of people. These distant people, both as participants and as subjects of discussion, further encouraged long, broad, and heated debates centered in London over the Company and, in particular, its Indian calico. Concerns that calicoes weakened Protestant England's manufacturers and that pirates weakened England's already weak position in India would ultimately redefine and realign the relationships among England, its Atlantic colonies, and its India trade.[2]

The strong and intensifying demand for inimitable calicoes that the East India Company had stimulated posed a set of problems outside the terms of the Navigation Acts and the Company's charter. These English regulations forbade independent English merchants from trading to the

article, "Making an Imperial Compromise: The Calico Acts, the Atlantic Colonies, and the Structure of the British Empire," *WMQ*, 3d Ser., LXIX (2012), 731–762.

2. John Avery was also known as Henry Every. On the actions of Avery and his men, see Khafi Khan, "Capture of a Royal Ship: The English at Bombay," in J. N. Das Gupta, *India in the Seventeenth Century: As Depicted by European Travellers* (Calcutta, 1916), 233–238; Robert C. Ritchie, *Captain Kidd and the War against the Pirates* (Cambridge, Mass., 1986), 87–88, 131; Joel H. Baer, "'Captain John Avery' and the Anatomy of a Mutiny," *Eighteenth-Century Life*, n.s., XVIII, no. 1 (February 1994), 1–3; Baer, ed., *British Piracy in the Golden Age: History and Interpretation, 1660–1730* (London, 2007), II, 109–110. For the responses of the Company servants and the "rabble," see "Abstract, E. I. Co. Letters from Bombay, October 12, 1695," Privy Council, Unbound Papers, I, 46, in John Franklin Jameson, ed., *Privateering and Piracy in the Colonial Period: Illustrative Documents* (New York, 1923), 157–158.

Indian Ocean and required Asian goods consumed in England to come from the Company directly from any port east of the Cape of Good Hope. Colonists and those trading to Africa, however, could legally import such goods from continental Europe on English ships with crews that were three-fourths English, and, increasingly, they could illegally import goods from pirates operating out of colonial ports. The Navigation Acts had codified the assumption that the Atlantic colonies were most valuable as supporters of English shipping, suppliers of raw materials, and consumers of English manufactures. They created forms of imperial monopoly, but they did not specifically or directly regulate consumption.

In the first decades of the eighteenth century, Parliament would pass two Calico Acts that would, alongside other new trading regulations, codify new functions and positions for colonists as distinct consumers of India goods within the empire's economic system. By compromising to protect both English manufacturers and the Company's trade to Asia, the acts would further shift the political, legal, and economic emphasis away from using the colonies to cultivate Asian raw materials for English manufacturing and toward using them as reexport markets for Asian manufactured goods imported to London by the East India Company. English writers asserted similar producing and consuming differences between the English and Scots, but the 1707 Act of Union positioned Scots under the umbrella of the British metropole. On the one hand, the Calico Acts gave colonists more consumer freedom than their counterparts in Britain. On the other, that freedom depended on an increasingly entrenched belief that colonists were not equal to English or, after 1707, British people as either producers or consumers. They were, instead, different types of subjects to be used to support not only English or British shippers and manufacturers but also the East India Company through the consumption of goods increasingly considered by many leaders economically, morally, and politically unacceptable in England and, later, Britain itself.[3]

3. Historians have explored how the calico debates reflected the remarkable rise of the calico fashion, followed general patterns of late-seventeenth- and eighteenth-century political protest, focused concerns about women's consumption, and might have contributed to the development of factory production, but they have not considered the important Atlantic implications of the Calico Acts. For a classic account of the weavers' struggle, see P. J. Thomas, *Mercantilism and the East India Trade* (1926; rpt. London, 1963). For a more recent and brief overview, see Tim Keirn, "Parliament, Legislation, and the Regulation of English Textile Industries, 1689–1714," in Lee Davison et al., eds., *Stilling the Grumbling Hive: The Response to Social and Economic Problems in England, 1689–1750* (New York, 1992), 1–24. On riots in English political culture, see Robert B. Shoemaker, *The London Mob: Vio-*

The Colonies and the First Calico Act

After the Glorious Revolution, Parliament needed to navigate a course among the competing interests of domestic weavers seeking protected markets, the Company and English-Atlantic traders seeking access to the Indian Ocean, and consumers seeking India fashion—all of whom might generate revenue for the state. The Company was not waiting. In 1688, the directors commissioned Colonel Thomas Dungan in New York to operate "against all Interlopers that have been, or shall be found trading within the limits of the Company's Charter, and particularly at Madagascar." They empowered him to seize ships and cargoes and arrest men that departed for or arrived from the Indian Ocean in "New York, Pennsylvania, New Jersey, or any of the adjacent Provinces." They told their servants in Bengal that "Interloping not only ruins Trade but never fails to turn into Piracy at last." Some of these English people in India were traders, others were pirates, and still others were both. The interlopers, in particular, hoped that the post-Revolution Parliament would end the Company's monopoly. They argued that monopoly companies were wasteful, that Magna Carta had made the seas a free space for all English traders, and that competition (even if regulated) resulted in the biggest economic benefits. The erstwhile Whig director Thomas Papillon supported the interlopers, but he hoped that interloping might lead Parliament to establish a new, more inclusive India company. The Company, for its part, hoped that the growing number of pirates "will prove a good effect of an ill cause" by pushing Parliament to act in its favor. Indeed, the activities of English pirates often

---

lence and Disorder in Eighteenth-Century England (London, 2007), 114–115, 242. On the calico fashion in England, see Beverly Lemire, *Fashion's Favourite: The Cotton Trade and the Consumer in Britain, 1660–1800* (Oxford, 1991), 3–42; and, for Britain and America, see Phyllis Whitman Hunter, *Purchasing Identity in the Atlantic World: Massachusetts Merchants, 1670–1780* (Ithaca, N.Y., 2001), 96–101. For the classic account of the linkages among the calico debates, fashion, and the rise of materialism as well as a brief survey of the debates over the importance of cotton cloth production in Britain, see Chandra Mukerji, *From Graven Images: Patterns of Modern Materialism* (New York, 1983), 166–250. On the Calico Acts and women, see, in particular, Chloe Wigston Smith, "'Callico Madams': Servants, Consumption, and the Calico Crisis," *Eighteenth-Century Life*, XXXI, no. 2 (Spring 2007), 29–55. On the Calico Acts and economic change, see Patrick O'Brien, Trevor Griffiths, and Philip Hunt, "Political Components of the Industrial Revolution: Parliament and the English Cotton Textile Industry, 1660–1774," *EHR*, 2d Ser., XLIV (1991), 395–423. Among imperial historians, neither George Louis Beer nor his many followers noted the connections between the Calico Acts and the Atlantic colonies; see Beer, *The Old Colonial System, 1660–1754* (New York, 1912).

based out of colonial ports, problems for both the Company and England's weavers alike, would unwittingly and eventually help point toward a compromise among the empire's competing interests.[4]

Ironically, the Company's own war against the Mughal empire in the late 1680s suggested the wealth of opportunities for seizing booty from Mughal shipping. The war also helped to establish the Muslim empire as an enemy in the minds of many in England and America, even after the end of the war. The directors themselves continued to argue that their monopoly was necessary to help protect England from Asian *"Infidels,* that by the Laws of the Land are accounted *perpetual Enemies."* In a typical pirate voyage in 1691, the vessel *Bachelor's Delight* departed from either Jamaica or South Carolina for the Red Sea. It attacked a "Moors" ship and netted each crew member a prize rumored between eleven hundred and two thousand pounds, approximately one hundred times more than an average seaman made in a year. The *Bachelor's Delight* returned to South Carolina, and from there the crew dispersed along the Atlantic seaboard.

---

4. Commission to Colonel Thomas Dungan, New York, Mar. 23, 1687/8, IOR/E/3/91, 283–284/fol. 141, BL; Directors to Fort St. George, Oct. 3, 1690, IOR/E/3/92, 116/fol. 58v, BL. For more on interlopers, see Philip J. Stern, *The Company-State: Corporate Sovereignty and the Early Modern Foundations of the British Empire in India* (New York, 2011), 44–60, 144–145. On Papillon, see A. F. W. Papillon, [ed.], *Memoirs of Thomas Papillon, of London, Merchant (1623–1702)* (Reading, 1887), 81–90. Child and the Tory faction of the Company had evicted Papillon from the Board of Directors. For the effects of the Glorious Revolution on the Company, see K. N. Chaudhuri and Jonathan I. Israel, "The English and Dutch East India Companies and the Glorious Revolution of 1688–9," in Israel, ed., *The Anglo-Dutch Moment: Essays on the Glorious Revolution and Its World Impact* (Cambridge, 1991), 433–437; Steve Pincus, *1688: The First Modern Revolution* (New Haven, Conn., 2009), 385–398. For examples of attacks on the Company monopoly, see *A Regulated Company More National Than a Joint-Stock in the East-India-Trade* ([London], [circa 1690]); *Companies in Joynt-Stock Unnecessary and Inconvenient: Free Trade to India in a Regulated Company, the Interest of England; Discours'd in a Letter to a Friend* ([n.p.], [1691]); "To the Queens Most Excellent Majesty: The Humble Petition of Several Merchants, in Behalf of Themselves and Others," "To the Queens Most Excellent Majesty: The Humble Reply of Several Merchants and Others (Who Petitioned Your Majesty in Council on the 17 and 31 of August Last) to the Answer of Certain Persons Stiling Themselves the Governour and Company of Merchants of London Trading into the East-Indies," and more are included in *A Journal of Several Remarkable Passages, before the Honourable House of Commons, and the Right Honourable the Lords of Their Majesties Most Honourable Privy Council: Relating to the East-India Trade* ([n.p.], [1693]), 22–39, 51; *Reasons Humbly Offered against Establishing, by Act of Parliament, the East-India-Trade, in a Company, with a Joint-Stock, Exclusive of Others, the Subjects of England* ([n.p.], [1693]); R[oger] C[oke], *A Treatise concerning the Regulation of the Coyn of England; and How the East-India Trade May Be Preserved and Encreased* (London, 1696), 36–43.

More vessels left the colonies for the Indian Ocean in 1692 and 1694. The directors' hopes that Parliament would see such activity as necessitating a powerful monopoly company, however, were soon dashed. The post-Revolution Parliament looked askance at the Company, which was seen as a Tory establishment. In 1694, Parliament ended the Company's monopoly. Private trading was now permitted, but piracy remained illegal. The fight was certainly not over.[5]

The Company's leader, Josiah Child, defended calicoes and the monopoly alike as vital parts of a trading system encompassing India and the Atlantic colonies. Child, like many Company leaders before him, undertook schemes to trade with North America and produce sugar in Jamaica, and he was a founding investor of the RAC. Child claimed, "The *Dutch* with good reason esteem the trade of the *East-Indies* more profitable to them than are the Mines of Gold and Silver in *America* to the *King of Spain*." Since trading and not hoarding bullion brought in more wealth and ultimately more bullion, Child argued, banning the calico trade would reduce the wealth of England and enrich the Dutch, who would become the sole carriers of India goods. For Child, the North American colonies were primarily valuable as markets. Of all the trades with the Atlantic colonies and India, Child saw New England's manufacturing and illicit trade as the main competitive threat to English producers and merchants. He claimed that Indian calicoes did not create significant competition for English woolens or silks because they were so different in quality and price. Child blamed the general recession for the weavers' difficulties, and

5. "The Humble Answer of the Governour and Company of Merchants of London, Trading into the East-Indies; to the Several Petitions Delivered until Your Majesty in Council, the 17th and 31st of August Last," Sept. 7, 1693, in *Journal of Several Remarkable Passages*, 17; "Deposition of Adam Baldridge, May 5, 1699," in Jameson, ed., *Privateering and Piracy*, 180–187; Lieutenant-Governor Francis Nicholson to the Lords of Trade and Plantations, July 16, 1692, *CSPC*, XIII, no. 2344, 674–675, esp. 674. According to an East India Company officer, the piracy problem began in earnest around 1690 or 1691; see "Officer of an East-India Ship," *Piracy Destroy'd; or, A Short Discourse Shewing the Rise, Growth, and Causes of Piracy of Late; with a Sure Method How to Put a Speedy Stop to That Growing Evil* (London, 1701), 2. On sailors' wages, see George F. Steckley, "Litigious Mariners: Wage Cases in the Seventeenth-Century Admiralty Court," *Historical Journal*, XLII (1999), 315–345, esp. 319. For more on pirates in this period, see Ritchie, *Captain Kidd*, 83, 112–120. Historians agree that the Commons disliked the East India Company in the 1690s, but they do not agree on whether Whigs or Tories disliked the Company more. For the case that Whigs and Tories acted out of self-interest with regard to the Company and not according to party lines, see Thomas, *Mercantilism and the East India Trade*, 94–97. For Whig hatred, see Pincus, *1688*, 386, 398. On the opening of the trade, see *Journals of the House of Commons . . .* , Jan. 19, 1693 [1694], XI (1693–1697) (London, 1802), 64–65.

he feared that the India trade would collapse without a strong monopoly company to deal with India's powerful rulers.[6]

The weavers, meanwhile, focused less on questions of global trading systems and much more on the threat that they saw calicoes posing to woolen production, the fount of English wealth. The weavers argued that the woolen industry employed perhaps as many as a quarter of a million English people. Some wealthy individuals, such as India goods dealer William Arnold, who held calico worth ten thousand pounds sterling, might lose their fortunes or livelihoods under a calico prohibition. But, if the Company and its allies wanted to argue over the number of people employed domestically, the woolen interest claimed the advantage. Additionally, high demand for sheep meant high demand for land, which meant high rents for landowners. This latter point no doubt attracted the attention of the members of Parliament (MPs), many of whom were substantial landowners. The weavers agreed with Child that New England's manufactures posed a threat and persuaded Parliament to curtail the trade in woolens manufactured in the colonies and Ireland. But, unlike Child, they saw imported colonial woolens and Indian calicoes as similarly destructive to England—both put England's woolen producers out of work, which would eventually impoverish the kingdom.[7]

6. Josiah Child, *A New Discourse of Trade, Wherein Is Recommended Several Weighty Points Relating to Companies of Merchants . . .* (London, 1693), 81, 143–153 (quotation on 143–144), 165–208; C[hild], *The Great Honour and Advantage of the East-India Trade to the Kingdom, Asserted* (London, 1697), 21–33. *A New Discourse of Trade* appeared in multiple editions throughout the 1690s. Most of Child's arguments can be traced back through the work of Company supporters throughout the seventeenth century. Beer discussed the treatises of Josiah Child and Charles Davenant at length, without analyzing the purpose of these works to defend the East India trade; see Beer, *The Old Colonial System,* I, 13–17, 34–35, 48–58, 106–107. On bribery, see Henry Horwitz, *Parliament, Policy, and Politics in the Reign of William III* (Manchester, 1977), 149–151. For more on Child's life, see Richard Grassby, "Child, Sir Josiah, first baronet (bap. 1631, d. 1699)," *DNB.*

7. *The Interest of England Considered: In an Essay upon Wooll, Our Woollen-manufactures, and the Improvement of Trade; with Some Remarks upon the Conceptions of Sir Josiah Child* (London, 1694), 1–6; John Cary, *An Essay on the State of England, in Relation to Its Trade, Its Poor, and Its Taxes, for Carrying on the Present War against France* (Bristol, 1695), 52–56; *Journals of the House of Commons,* Mar. 7, 1695 [1696], XI, 495–498. For later examples, see [John Pollexfen], *England and East-India Inconsistent in Their Manufactures; Being an Answer to a Treatise, Intituled, "An Essay on the East-India Trade"* (London, 1697), 4, 20; T[homas] S[mith], *Reasons Humbly Offered for the Pasing a Bill for the Hindering the Home Consumption of East-India Silks, Bengals etc. . . .* (London, 1697), 3; "Answer of the Commissioners of Trade and Plantations," Mar. 22, 1699/1700, CO 389/17, fol. 13v, NA. On landholding and Parliament, see Eveline Cruickshanks, Stuart Handley, and D. W. Hayton, *The House of Commons, 1690–1715,* 5 vols. (Cambridge, 2002), I, 288–289. On

The Bristol merchant and influential trade writer John Cary argued, following a century of similar claims, that the Atlantic colonies should instead provide raw cotton to support English manufacturers, reducing the need to import India's calicoes. Cary explained that, overall, no trade was as "profitable to to [sic] us as that we manage to *Africa* and our own Plantations in *America*" for raw materials, "and none so detrimental as that to the *East-Indies*" for manufactures. He explained in more detail, "I take *England* and all its Plantations to be one great Body, those being so many Limbs or Counties belonging to it, therefore when we consume their Growth we do as it were spend the Fruits of our own Land." "No doubt we might in time," he argued, "make Calicoes equal in their sorts with those Imported from *India,* and afford them as cheap as that Company now sells them, enough not only for our home Expence, but also for Exportation."[8]

Indeed, colonists in North America and the West Indies had finally enjoyed some success in cultivating cotton. In 1690, for instance, agricultural innovator John Stewart reported from South Carolina, "There is not on[e] planter in this province South of Wina river to the Yamasies bot hes Les or more of Cotton planted," enough, he hoped, to "load 2 ships by this year's produce." Stewart expected to make Carolina a "2nd Persia" with "India's Rice Italy and Asia's silk America and Cyprus and Smyrna's cotton Lahore Indigo," and the wine, oranges, currants, and capers of Europe and China. From his experiments on cotton, he claimed to have found "a certain Rule" of distances between plants to maximize the yield per acre. He claimed, too, "a Rationall and cheapr way for distilling Rice than is in India." The governor asked the lords proprietor of the colony to grant Stewart five hundred acres for his overall efforts.[9]

The West Indies, however, became England's leading supplier of cotton wool, providing 849,598 pounds of it in 1697–1698 alone. Thomas Tryon, merchant and influential health-book author, laid out a detailed plan to further transfer cotton growth, spinning, and weaving from the East Indies to the West. He proposed the construction of schools "for the

colonial and Irish woolen restrictions, see "Answer of the Commissioners of Trade and Plantations on Order of the Honorable the House of Commons," Mar. 22, 1699/1700, CO 389/17, fol. 13v, NA; H. F. Kearney, "The Political Background to English Mercantilism, 1695–1700," *EHR,* 2d Ser., XI, no. 3 (1958–1959), 494.

8. Cary, *Essay on the State of England,* 6, 15, 25, 47, 59–70, esp. 59, 60, 66–67.

9. "Letters from John Stewart to William Dunlop," *South Carolina Historical and Genealogical Magazine,* XXXII (1931), 1, 6–7, 16–17, 82, 99, 110. For more on Stewart, see S. Max Edelson, *Plantation Enterprise in Colonial South Carolina* (Cambridge, Mass., 2006), 39–40, 46, 53–83.

Dressing, Spinning and Weaving of Cotton, one for the Children of the *English,* the other for the Children of the Slaves, Black Servants." Diverted from the brutality of the sugarcane fields, the enslaved people of the West Indies, particularly the women, would enjoy an "easy and soft Employment" and produce more valuable children. Their fabrics would rival the *"Blacks* in the *East Indies,"* who, Tryon thought, "do as it were wonders." But Tryon's plan to locate manufacturing in the colonies would do little for weavers in England. It was not at all clear, moreover, that Cary's plan for raw cotton imports would help England's weavers either. England had few cotton-cloth producers, and they produced literally and figuratively pale imitations of India's goods. The lack of experienced cotton manufacturers in England, Cary's qualification "in time," and the simple fact that cotton would still be competing with English woolens and silks were serious problems.[10]

Some weavers pointed to the other old hope of colonial cultivation of silk, not cotton, as the answer. England's cotton industry might have been decidedly weak, but its silk industry was not. Supporters agreed that the use of colonial raw silk instead of foreign raw silk would help the industry to expand and make it a much more clear and valuable benefit to the kingdom. Stewart, for example, expected planters in South Carolina to embrace silk "universally" after he presented his demonstrations on its production. Yet, colonial silk cultivation consistently failed to deliver, leaving London's silk weavers to import raw silk from outside the empire. Additionally, London's silk production involved large numbers of politically difficult French Protestant immigrants. Far more communities in England participated in woolen production, and wool itself was a largely domestic raw material. Silk weavers were a major force in the London Weavers' Company and a growing force in Canterbury, but in the political debate woolens had the advantage of being unimpeachably English. Not surprisingly, then, England's woolen producers had the loudest public voices.[11]

10. Alfred P. Wadsworth and Julia de Lacy Mann, *The Cotton Trade and Industrial Lancashire, 1600–1780* (Manchester, 1931), 520; Tho[mas] Tryon, *Tryon's Letters, Domestick and Foreign, to Several Persons of Quality: Occasionally Distributed in Subjects, Viz. Philosophical, Theological, and Moral* (London, 1700), 183–186.

11. "Letters from John Stewart to William Dunlop," *South Carolina Historical and Genealogical Magazine,* XXXII (1931), 6. The woolen weavers of East Anglia joined the silk interests of London and Canterbury to target the East India Company, whereas woolen weavers from the southwest of England primarily targeted competition from Irish woolen producers; see Linda Levy Peck, *Consuming Splendor: Society and Culture in Seventeenth-Century England* (Cambridge, 2005), 103–107; Natalie Rothstein, "The Calico Campaign of 1719–1721,"

The weaving interest focused blame on the East India Company not only for the collapse of the English economy but also for the moral corruption of Englishwomen seduced by non-Christian Indians, a powerful charge among English Protestants on both sides of the Atlantic. They did not see the Company as protection against infidels but as enablers of infidel corruption. In 1692, for instance, Massachusetts Puritan minister Cotton Mather argued against debilitating foreign luxuries such as silks and calicoes. English production did not necessarily domesticate such goods. He dreamed of a time when "the *Vertuous woman*" would spin wool and flax to occupy her hands and her soul. Influential clothier John Blanch explained that the rakish Company corrupted Englishwomen by teaching low-paid Indian weavers to produce cotton cloth that was "impossible to be withstood by a Feminine Power." Blanch imagined a sort of reverse colonialism, writing that Englishmen must "redeem our Female-Sex from the Government of the *Indians*." Action needed to be taken "against the *Syrenian* Charms of these bewitching Commodities." A few years later, another author wrote that the East India Company had been "forced to ransack all *Christendom* for Silver" to pay for India "Muzlins." Another dubbed the Company's directors "Enemies to the Nation" for employing people in the *"Indies"* to make cloth to English patterns, thereby putting English people out of work. Such notions resonated with long-standing fears of Muslim and Asian threats against Europe.[12]

As English people attacked the Company in print for aligning with Indians, English Atlantic pirates further expanded their operations against Mughal shipping in the Indian Ocean and Red Sea. Avery pursued

---

East London Papers, VII, no. 1 (July 1964), 3–21, esp. 13–19; Alfred Plummer, *The London Weavers' Company, 1600–1970* (London, 1972), 9–10, 16, 144–158; Kearney, "Political Background to English Mercantilism," *EHR*, 2d Ser., XI (1958–1959), 486. The silk weavers did send many petitions to Parliament. See *Journals of the House of Commons*, Mar. 7, 1695 [1696], XI, 495–498.

12. Cotton Mather, *Ornaments for the Daughters of Zion; or, The Character and Happiness of a Vertuous Woman* . . . (Cambridge, Mass., 1692), 9; [John Blanch], *An Abstract of the Grievances of Trade Which Oppress Our Poor; Humbly Offered to the Parliament* (London, 1694), 10–11, 13 ("impossible" and "redeem"); [John Blanch], *The Naked Truth, in an Essay upon Trade: With Some Proposals for Bringing the Ballance on Our Side, Humbly Offered to the Parliament* (London, 1696), 5 ("against"); *Britania Expirans; or, A Brief Memorial of Commerce Humbly Offer'd to the Parliament* (London, 1699), 19 ("forced" and "Muzlins"); *A Reply to a Paper, Intituled, Reasons against the Prohibiting the Wearing East-India and Persian Wrought Silks, etc. Humbly Offer'd to the Honourable House of Commons* ([London], [1700?]), 4 ("Enemies"). Blanch was an MP from 1710 to 1713. On Blanch, see Cruickshanks, Handley, and Hayton, *House of Commons*, III, 230.

a version of holy war against the Mughal's Muslim subjects. He issued a declaration that he would not attack English or Dutch ships and instructed English captains to run up the ensign to signal that he should not attack. Nevertheless, he signed the declaration ominously, "As yet an Englishmans Friend." Presumably, Englishmen seeming to be in league with his enemies might become targets, and the Company's ships circulated Avery's declaration. Additionally, more English Atlantic pirates headed east, driven by the sensational story of the *Ganj-i-Sawai*, increased penalties for nonpiratical illicit trade, and a sharp reduction in legal privateering opportunities against the French with the end of the Nine Years' War. There was clearly wealth to be gained from India, but the relationship between English Atlantic pirates and the solution to the weavers' complaints against calico was not yet clear.[13]

Throughout 1696, Parliament attempted to negotiate a middle course between the weavers and the Company, and it used the colonies as a bargaining chip. In March, Henry Hobart, MP for Norfolk, reviewed petitions from the woolen and English silk interests and proposed a bill to restrain "the Wearing of all Wrought Silks, Bengals, and dyed, painted, or stained Callicoes, imported into this Kingdom of *England,* and the Plantations belonging thereunto, of the Product and Manufacture of *Persia,* and the *East Indies.*" Charles Davenant, economic writer and friend of the Company, responded that the Company deserved access to the domestic market. He also specifically elaborated on the value of the colonial markets. Davenant explained that gold and silver from South America paid for goods in India, which were then exported to Europe and the Americas for profit. "Callicoes," Davenant explained, "are a useful wear at Home, and in our own Plantations, and for the *Spaniards* in *America.*" Indeed, under the 1648 Treaty of Münster the Spanish were not allowed to trade to India by way of the shorter Cape of Good Hope route but only by the longer Pacific route, opening opportunities for other Europeans to act as middlemen in the India trade. The House of Commons amended Hobart's bill to strip the language involving the colonies, but it ultimately failed in the House of Lords.[14]

13. Several of Avery's men were eventually captured, and others escaped to the colonies. See Declaration of Henry Every, Feb. 28, 1694, copied in "Petition of the East India Company, July 1696," Privy Council, Unbound Papers, I, 46, in Jameson, ed., *Privateering and Piracy,* 154; Ritchie, *Captain Kidd,* 88–89; Baer, "'Captain John Avery,'" *Eighteenth-Century Life,* n.s., XVIII, no. 1 (February 1994), 17–18; Baer, ed., *British Piracy in the Golden Age,* II, 110.

14. *Journals of the House of Commons,* Mar. 7, 11, 24, 25, 1695/6, XI, 497, 502, 529–531; [Charles Davenant], *An Essay on the East-India-Trade* (London, 1696), 12–15 (quotation on

In December, Hobart, now a leader of the Rose Club that orchestrated the Whig ministry, presented another bipartisan calico bill, assisted by the Tory MP for Norwich, Thomas Blofield. The new bill also exempted the colonies from the ban. The Company convinced the House of Lords to add amendments forbidding all imported cottons and silks, not just those from India, and to levy a penalty of fifty pounds against wearers. The latter amendment impinged on the House of Commons' prerogative over fiscal policy, and the amended bill failed primarily on this constitutional issue. The Company had won its point on the Atlantic colonies and defeated both bills, but it faced an increasingly agitated weavers' interest that had by then stormed Parliament and attacked the Company's offices.[15]

The Company also faced a growing piracy problem. In 1697, tensions escalated to a new high in the Red Sea and Indian Ocean. Six ships hailing from Boston, Philadelphia, Rhode Island, and New York again attacked the Hajj pilgrimage fleet. The Company servants in Bombay wrote of a "Nest of Rogues Settled on the Island St Mary's . . . from New York, New England, and the West Indies." But they anticipated that a naval fleet could regain control, as "we believe their strength is not very great." The pirates' outright robbery and abuse, however, stimulated well-placed and well-founded fears among the Company directors that Aurangzeb might banish all English traders from his dominions. The directors encouraged their servants to stress to Indian leaders "the great care cost and charge the Company have been at to bring those Pyraticall Villains to Justice." Then, in 1698, the notorious pirate Captain William Kidd took the *Quedah Merchant* off the coast of Malabar. The ship was carrying 160 bales of calico, which Kidd sold off for markets throughout the Atlantic world. With English piracy escalating, protestors rioting over the India trade in England, and a need for revenue at home, Parliament had to act. Yet Parliament did not pass another of Hobart's attempts to restrain the importation and use of India cottons and silks.[16]

---

14), 51–55; Cruickshanks, Handley, and Hayton, *House of Commons*, IV, 369–370. For Davenant's connection with the Company, see David Waddell, "Charles Davenant and the East India Company," *Economica*, n.s., XXIII (1956), 261–264.

15. *Journals of the House of Commons*, Dec. 4, 1696, Feb. 22, 1696/7, Mar. 25, 1697, XI, 612, 716, 755–756; *Journals of the House of Lords* . . . , Mar. 12, 19, 23, 1696/7, XVI (1696–1701) (London, 1767–1830), 121, 129, 132–133; Horwitz, *Parliament, Policy, and Politics*, 190–191; Cruickshanks, Handley, and Hayton, *House of Commons*, I, 756, III, 247. The Rose Club was named for the Rose Tavern, where large numbers of Whig MPs often met.

16. Bombay Castle to the Directors, Dec. 18, 1697, IOR/E/3/53, fol. 219 ("Nest"), BL; "General Letter to Fort St. George," Apr. 16, 1697, *Despatches from England*, Records of Fort

Instead, Parliament legally closed the India trade to private English merchants and opened bidding for the monopoly rights. This decision was not what either the weavers or the Company had in mind. The Company continued to see its monopoly charter as a royal, not a parliamentary, prerogative, the latter established by Chief Justice John Holt in 1689. Nevertheless, the Company offered Parliament seven hundred thousand pounds at 4 percent interest. A group of Whig merchants, in league with Papillon, then offered two million pounds at 8 percent. Parliament took the richer deal, and most of the private merchants soon incorporated themselves into a new East India Company, competing with the old.[17]

The old Company now pursued a multipronged strategy to reclaim its monopoly: increase the volume and quality of its purchases, campaign to sway Indian leaders, and take a major financial stake in the new Company. The directors told their factors in Surat, Madras, and Calcutta to buy all the available gruff goods and silk, creating a shortage to drive up the prices faced by the new Company. They directed care and attention to quality and standardization, writing, for example, "Send us all you can but let them be as fine as these and full nine yards long and yd. wide which makes them a fitt pattern for a gown and Petticoat." They chastised their servants in Bencoolen for sending benjamin resin that was "the Refuse of the Place a great part of it be[ing] adulterated and mixed with Dammer [another resin]." The directors also had their servants impress upon Indian leaders that the Company's forts and warehouses backed its credit, in contrast to the new Company, which had no history and no significant assets in India. The new Company, for its part, claimed that the king had dissolved the old Company as punishment for its violence against the Mughal empire and for being "thieves and Confederates with the pyrates." Nicholas Waite, dis-

St. George, XI (Madras, India, 1929), 13 ("great"), "General Letter to Fort St. George," Jan. 26, 1698, XI, 38–39. On Kidd's cloth, see "Examination of Edward Buckmaster, June 6, 1699," Rawlinson Manuscripts A 272, fol. 48, Bodleian Library, Oxford, in Jameson, ed., *Privateering and Piracy*, 198; "Information of Henry Bolton, February 4, 1701," Duke of Portland, Welbeck Abbey Collection, ibid., 246–247; Ritchie, *Captain Kidd*, 167.

17. For more on the politics of the two companies in London, see Bruce G. Carruthers, *City of Capital: Politics and Markets in the English Financial Revolution* (Princeton, N.J., 1996), 150; Philip Lawson, *The East India Company: A History* (London, 1993), 55–56. For the Company's belief in its monopoly rights, see "General Letter to Fort St. George," Apr. 16, 1697, *Despatches from England*, XI, 5–18, esp. 13, "General Letter to Fort St. George," Jan. 26, 1698, XI, 36–42, esp. 39, "General Letter to Bombay," July 19, 1698, XI, 21–24, esp. 22. On the conflicted legal footing of the Company's monopoly, see William Wilson Hunter, *A History of British India*, II, *To the Union of the Old and New Companies under the Earl of Godolphin's Award* (London, 1900), 313–315; Pincus, *1688*, 385–386.

missed by the old Company and now working for the new, boasted that he was chosen to be the "Chiefe Captain of all the English Nation at Suratt." Back in London, however, the old Company bought more than £300,000 of the new Company's stock. The old Company's directors assured their servants "that we don't intend to cross the Cudgells to the New Gamesters." This multipronged strategy might defeat the new Company, but it also increased the ire of English weavers against calico, as Indian cloth imports soared in quantity and in value from £74,667 in 1697 to £273,071 in 1699.[18]

Print attacks claiming calico as effeminizing, Indianizing, and impoverishing escalated. "The Effeminate Trade of the *East Indies* and *Levant"* had destroyed other "Noble" trades, one author explained. He went on, "The Money of the Rich is laid out to feed *Indians* abroad, and enrich men of unbounded desires at home." As a result, "they have debauch'd the Nation with Cobwebs and Cockle-shells, in return for their Gold and Silver; in which, tho' the Luxurious and Effeminate are made *Indians."* A century's worth of nightmares about the India trade turning English people into Indians was apparently coming to life. The author agreed with Davenant that the reexport of India goods was valuable, but that was not enough. Quite simply, he did not agree "That whoever hath the Trade of the *East-Indies,* will command the Trade of the whole World." Like many before him, he also doubted the worth of the Atlantic colonies; only the extractive process in the fisheries of Newfoundland surely enriched England. "A Weaver of London" explained that the India trade used to be in spices,

18. "General Letter to Bombay," July 19, 1698, *Despatches from England,* XI, 22, "General Letter to Bombay," Aug. 26, 1698, XI, 43, "General Letter to Fort St. George," Oct. 28, 1698, XI, 60–65, "General Letter to Fort St. George," Dec. 15, 1698, XI, 73, Addendum, Jan. 6, 1698/9, to "General Letter to Fort St. George," Dec. 15, 1698, XI, 75 ("Send"), "General Letter to Bengal," Aug. 26, 1698, XI, 80–81 ("intend"), "General Letter to Bencoolen," Oct. 28, 1698, XI, 66 ("Refuse"); J. Hiller to Thomas Bowrey, Feb. 26, 1700, fol. 345, Thomas Bowrey Papers, MSS Eur D1076, BL. The factors responded that the weavers would not alter their looms to make the widths that European consumers demanded; see Bombay General Letter to the Directors, Aug. 21, 1699, IOR/E/3/55, fol. 195v, BL. For the Companies' competing spin campaigns, see President and Councill of Fort William at Calcutta, Jan. 5, 1699/1700, IOR/E/3/93, 272–273/fols. 136v–137r, BL; Benjamin Mews and Charles Brooke, Surat, to the New Company, Dec. 12, 1699, IOR/E/3/55, fol. 363, BL; Nicholas Waite to Emperor Aurganzeb, May 14, 1700, and a copy of a second letter from Waite to Emperor Aurganzeb, n.d., IOR/E/3/57, #7057–8 ("thieves"), BL. On redoubled agitation from the weavers, see Thomas, *Mercantilism and the East India Trade,* 112–113. For the data on the Company's increased purchasing of goods, see K. N. Chaudhuri, *The Trading World of Asia and the English East India Company, 1660–1760* (Cambridge, 1978), 286.

pepper, drugs, and raw silk; only for the last thirty years had the Company succeeded in bringing in calicoes. Substituting such foreign manufactures for domestic manufactures "is like drawing out the pure and spirituous Blood of a Man's Veins, and filling them with Hydropick Humours." Domestic manufactures were pleasing to God and best for England's poor and the nation.[19]

Critics of Indian calicoes also continued to argue that consumers in the colonies and England were economically the same and wanted the same fashions; they therefore needed to be under the same new prohibition. Thomas Smith, who identified himself as a weaver, wrote that India goods "have Spoiled our Foreign Trade for Fine Stuffs made in *Norwich* and *London* . . . And for our *American* Plantations, all Persons dealing there, know they will imitate the Gentry of *England*." He clearly recognized the Atlantic imperial aesthetic for India goods, writing, "If our Nobility and Gentry wear *India* Manufactures, our *West India* Plantations will wear the same." Similarly, another author responded to Davenant, "As to our *Plantations* and *Ireland*, to which we send great quantities of our Manufactures, if the *East India Silks, etc.* are the Mode here, they will be so there, the orders that are sent from thence, being to send over such Manufactures, as are most Fashionable in *England*." The India fashion was, the author claimed, displacing English woolens throughout the empire. Another advocate for the weavers argued that "a great part of the *India* Manufactured Goods were spent in *England*, and our Plantations, in the room of our own Manufactures." A prohibition must, therefore, include the colonies.[20]

In reality, the 412,000 people in the colonies could not consume as many calicoes as the 132 million people of Europe, though how much less the colonists consumed remains unclear. Customs records for 1700 show that approximately £17,000 in India calicoes were reexported from England to England's Atlantic colonies each year, compared to approximately £284,000 in calicoes reexported to Europe. There are many rea-

19. *An Answer to a Late Tract, Entituled, [An Essay on the East-India Trade]* (London, 1697), 4–5, 8, 19–20; N. C., a Weaver of London, *The Great Necessity and Advantage of Preserving Our Own Manufacturies; Being an Answer to a Pamphlet, Intitul'd the Honour and Advantage of the East-India Trade, etc.* (London, 1697), 6–8, 30.

20. S[mith], *Reasons Humbly Offered for the Pasing a Bill*, 6–7; *An Answer to the Most Material Objections against the Bill for Restraining the East-India Wrought Silk; etc. Humbly Offered to the Consideration of the Lords* ([London?], [1699?]), 2–3; *Reasons Humbly Offered for Restraining the Wearing of Wrought Silks, Bengals, and Dyed, Printed, and Stained Callicoes, of the Product and Manufacture of Persia and the East-Indies, in England and Our Planta[t]ions* (n.p., [1699]), 1.

sons to expect these statistics to be inaccurate. Fraud was frequent, merchants had little reason to accurately report goods upon which they paid few or no export duties or received negligible drawbacks (refunds of duties to merchants when goods were reexported from England), and customs had no record of goods that came to the colonies from pirates, smugglers, or traders in Europe. Regardless, the broad outlines in the data are clear enough: Europe imported many more calicoes from England, but the colonies imported several times more per person. Furthermore, with imports from Europe, interlopers, and pirates added, colonial consumption was even higher than it appeared. English merchants also reexported calicoes from London through Barbados and Jamaica into the Spanish colonies, the trade that Davenant had expounded upon as Parliament debated whether the colonies should be under a calico prohibition.[21]

Stories that sensationalized the pirates' activities and the colonists' demand for India goods circulated throughout the government, despite the comparatively low total quantity of consumption. Robert Quary, admiralty judge in Pennsylvania, claimed that at multiple points along the Atlantic seaboard vessels loaded with India goods sat at anchor offshore, awaiting smaller coastal boats that eagerly took on and disbursed the cargo. He wrote that an "abundance of East India goods" had been landed in small New Jersey ports such as Cape May, Cohanzy, and Salem. The India goods were packed "so as that they may pass for other goods" and brought to Philadelphia "without the least no(tice) taken of't." Quary reported that not a single cask or bale had been searched in Philadelphia for two years and that twenty thousand pounds' worth of India goods were smuggled through Cape May in one summer alone. Richard Coote, the earl of Bello-

---

21. Customs data aggregated from Ledgers of Imports and Exports, CUST 3/1–4, NA. The disparity between the value of calicoes reexported to the Atlantic colonies and the value of those reexported to Europe was typical for surrounding years as well. The data is useful only in suggesting the broad outlines of English calico reexports per capita. Population data from Jean-Pierre Bardet and Jaques Dupâquier, eds., *Histoire des populations de l'Europe*, II, *La révolution démographique, 1750–1914* (Paris, 1998), 196; John J. McCusker and Russell R. Menard, *The Economy of British America, 1607–1789* (Chapel Hill, N.C., 1985), 54. For more on the importance of reexports of goods through Jamaica before the 1692 Port Royal earthquake, see Nuala Zahedieh, "The Merchants of Port Royal, Jamaica, and the Spanish Contraband Trade, 1655–1692," *WMQ*, 3d Ser., XLIII (1986), 570–593, esp. 576–583. Certainly many of the India goods from the pirates also flowed into Europe. Of ninety-two bales of calicoes brought back by one pirate ship in 1698, only "some" remained in America, with the majority going to Hamburg. See "Abstract of Several Depositions, Taken before Sir Charles Hedges, as to the Ship Frederick, Belonging to Frederick Phillips [Flypse] of New York," Sept. 6, 1698, *CSPC*, XVI, no. 794, 413–414.

mont and governor of New York, accused colonial officials and other colonial governors of sheltering pirates bringing booty from the east and colluding with "plain breaches of the Acts of Trade and Navigation." He also wrote that "great quantities of East India goods" came into New York from Madagascar. Indeed, Captain Kidd arrived in New York with dozens of bales of India fabrics as well as gold and silver. Kidd claimed one of the bales to be worth two thousand pounds. He promised to bring in more such goods from "a great Ship near the Coast of Hispaniola" if Bellomont pardoned him. New York merchants denied that their colony protected pirates and argued that their India goods had been purchased legally in Madagascar. A rabble confined customs officials attempting to seize the illicit India goods of merchant Ouzel van Sweeten. Bellomont described the piracy problem as being too large for him to handle without a few men-of-war, a new judge, and an attorney general. Similarly, in September 1699, "the East India Company came down in a full body . . . to the Lords Justices" to demand redress from Kidd, and the Company intended "to make all the bustle about it they can." Such bustle was not lost on Parliament, but it had heard the weavers' bustle too.[22]

The colonies, as both a location to help solve the Companies' pirate problem and as a valuable market to bolster the calico trade, offered the means of compromise between the East India Companies and the weavers. English Atlantic pirates and private traders had reinforced the notion that Asia was a source of fantastic treasure, illustrated the risks of allowing an open India trade, and sensationalized the size and importance of colo-

22. Robert Quary to the Commissioners of Customs, Mar. 6, 1700, *CSPC*, XVIII, no. 190, 106–109 (quotations on 108). The Board of Trade also received from Quary letters and depositions on India goods coming into America. See, for example, Quary to the Board of Trade, Aug. 25, 1698, CO 5/1267, fols. 132r–133v, NA. For Bellomont on piracy, see "Report of the Earl of Bellomont, on the Irregularities of Rhode Island," Nov. 27, 1699, in John Russell Bartlett, ed., *Records of the Colony of Rhode Island, and Providence Plantations, in New England* (Providence, R.I., 1858), III, 385–388 (quotation on 387); Earl of Bellomont to the Board of Trade, May 18, 1698, *CSPC*, XVI, no. 472, 221–224 (quotation on 222); Lord Bellomont to the Board of Trade, July 26, 1699, CO 5/860, no. 64, NA, in Jameson, ed., *Privateering and Piracy*, 225, 228–229. Quary, Bellomont, and others might have trumped up the prevalence and atrocities of pirates and gubernatorial and colonial corruption in the hope of personal political gains in London. Bellomont himself had previously supported Captain William Kidd, but he changed his mind when Kidd returned to New York. For more, see Patrick Pringle, *Jolly Roger: The Story of the Great Age of Piracy* (New York, 1953), 132–134, 167; Ritchie, *Captain Kidd*, 168–175; James Vernon to the Duke of Shrewsbury, Oct. 7, 1697, Sept. 21, Dec. 2, 1699, in G. P. R. James, ed., *Letters Illustrative of the Reign of William III . . .*, 3 vols. (London, 1841), I, 423, II, 353–354, 372–374.

nial markets that might offset those lost to the East India Companies by a potential calico prohibition in England. Between 1695 and 1700, the government appointed governors to enforce laws prohibiting pirates from returning to the Atlantic colonies, routed the Madagascar pirate settlement, and established special courts and commissions of oyer and terminer in the Atlantic colonies and Company factories in India.[23]

With so much done to project and protect the rule of English law and the Companies' trades, in 1700 the calico measure came back to the floor of the Commons, where the MPs "calmly debated . . . without shewing any great regard to either company." The Lords this time added no amendments. The preamble to the resulting first Calico Act affirmed the weavers' arguments that the calico trade weakened the nation by draining bullion and pushing domestic manufacturers out of employment. Parliament included new language exempting white Indian fabric printed in England to protect England's nascent calico-printing industry. The act thus prohibited the retail of Asia's dyed, stained, and printed cottons and silks in England, although it did not penalize their wear. The Board of Trade, established by William III in 1696 to advise the government on colonization and trade and to provide administrative services, firmly supported the weavers against Indian competition and objected that omitting the colonists from the prohibition would be a mistake. The colonists were, after all, English, and they might resupply England as they had done already. But Parliament need not, and did not on this point, follow the Board's advice. Parliament exempted the Atlantic colonies from the prohibition. Parliament's compromise reaffirmed the importance of domestic English producers, whether woolen makers or calico printers, while creating a new precedent for Atlantic colonists to distinctly support the trade of the two East India Companies.[24]

23. The show trials of a few of John Avery's men and of Captain Kidd might have reduced piracy somewhat, but shows of maritime force likely mattered more. In 1699, a royal fleet under Commodore Thomas Warren arrived off Madagascar to destroy the pirates' primary supply base at Saint Mary's "and seiz on all such Pyraticall Villains as they can meet with" in the region ("General Letter to Fort St. George," Jan. 26, 1697/98, *Despatches from England*, XI, 39). A sort of show battle also occurred in June 1700, when Virginia's governor Francis Nicholson, on HMS *Shoreham*, defeated a powerful pirate vessel off the Virginia coast; for more on these attacks on pirates, see Pringle, *Jolly Roger*, 166–174.

24. Thomas, *Mercantilism and the East India Trade*, 113–116; Vernon to the Duke of Shrewsbury, Jan. 23, Feb. 16, 1700, in James, *Letters*, II, 417–418 ("calmly"), 434. Hobart had been killed in a duel in 1698; the winning bill was prepared by Blofield. See Cruickshanks, Handley, and Hayton, *House of Commons*, III, 247, IV, 371. For the text of the act, see [Ruffhead, ed.], *Statutes at Large*, IV, 44. For the Board's opinion, see "Answer of the Commis-

The Breakdown of the First Calico Act

After the Calico Act passed, the new Company canceled all of its Bengal chintz orders. The leaders in London complained to their servants that they expected to incur devastating losses on the great quantities of chintz that had been sent despite their warnings that such goods would be prohibited under the new law. The old Company was much less concerned. Indeed, within two years the Board of Trade had received petitions complaining that the Calico Act "hath not had the good Effect which was expected thereby." Since the act did not prohibit calicoes and chintz in the colonies, "great Quantities" were being shipped to the English West Indies. The consumption of calicoes in the colonies "greatly obstructed" the sale of woolens and undermined the protection of English woolen and silk producers. In England, meanwhile, the rapid growth of interloping traders, smugglers, and English calico printers served by the old Company would make the act increasingly ineffectual. The old Company's success would also drive the new Company toward a merger with important implications for the Indian Ocean and Atlantic calico trades alike. For the Companies, only the smuggling of non-Company goods posed a problem; smugglers reimporting and passing off Company goods as English prints helped to further undermine the prohibition. For the weaving interests, in contrast, smuggling suggested the need for a more complete prohibition. Calicoes were unacceptable regardless of how they came into England, where they were printed, or where they were manufactured. Ultimately, this pressure against domestic calico printers and manufacturers would operate against hopes for colonial cotton cultivation.[25]

The directors of the old Company had confidence in the porousness of the prohibition. They wondered, for example, if the prohibition language effectively banned fabrics woven of previously dyed thread or only fabrics dyed or printed after weaving. In any case, cottons or silks that could not be sold domestically could be reexported. They planned to hold prohibited goods in the London warehouses and release them into the market when

---

sioners of Trade and Plantations," Mar. 1699/1700, CO 389/17, fol. 14, NA. The Board was more directly involved in administrative services for the Atlantic colonies since the old East India Company, in particular, had its own administrative apparatus.

25. New Company Directors to Edward Littleton President and the rest of the Councill at Hugley in the Bay of Bengal, Aug. 2, 1701, IOR/E/3/94, 315/fol. 163, BL; "The Humble Memorial of George Morley," Oct. 23, 1702, CO 389/17, fol. 220, NA; Board of Trade, "Representation Relating to the Woollen Manufactory," Oct. 28, 1702, CO 389/17, fol. 232, NA.

An Imperial Compromise

reexport demand was high. Although a new duty of 15 percent was applied to white muslin, they explained that it did not apply to reexports. When they did cut orders on Madras merchandise they claimed that the prices at Madras were simply too expensive relative to similar piece goods from the other settlements. Indeed, they expected that prices in India would fall and that the factors could then "pick and cull" the fabrics. They did not see any need for a reduction in the number of the Company's trading factories. In case the Calico Act was repealed, as they hoped it would be, the local skills in manufacturing needed to be maintained, even if the Company lost some money in the short term.[26]

The old Company also continued to try to reduce its politically difficult reliance on bullion by better adapting its exports, such as English glassware, to Indian markets. "It will look more popular," they explained, "to be sending out Goods than Money." In 1696, the servants in Bombay had sent the directors an "Earthen Huble Buble," or hookah pipe, that a local "Umbran" wanted reproduced in London "of this bigness and fashion made of flint glass." A few decades earlier, George Ravenscroft had perfected flint glass, or lead crystal. Glass cutters soon arrived in London from Germany and settled along fashionable streets, helping England to become an important producer of luxury glassware. The Bombay servants therefore expected that they had hit upon a lucrative idea and noted that an additional two chests of hookahs would sell easily for high profits. They also sent a chime bowl and "Earthen Cusar" to be copied in flint glass and requested twelve of each as an experiment. The servants also requested flint glass for the emperor of Persia and explained that he was desperate to enjoy it. The Company servants in Surat warned the directors that the local Mughal officials seized one of the glass shipments and sold it themselves for large profits. This information, however, would have arrived too late for the shipment the directors sent in early 1698, which included crystal hookah pipes and a full collection of crystal glassware for the emperor. The directors, meanwhile, futilely encouraged their servants to "Endeavour the Consumption of Woollen Goods by Selling at low rates if you can Hereby advance their Wear." Instead, the Surat servants requested more glass

26. "List of Coast Goods to Be Provided for the Year 1702," *Despatches from England,* XII/XIII, 19–20, "Despatch from the Company to Fort St: George," Mar. 6, 1702, XII/XIII, 23–24 ("pick and cull"), "Despatch from the Company to Fort St. George," Jan. 12, 1705, XII/XIII, 67; "Directions for Providing a List of Surratt Goods Proper for Europe," Aug. 21, 1700, IOR/E/3/93, 346–347/fols. 173v–174r, BL; Directors to Our President and Council of Fort William, Mar. 5, 1701/2, IOR/E/3/93, 536–538/fols. 268v–270, BL.

hookahs, rose bottles, candlesticks, bowls, basins, pawn boxes, lanterns, mirrors, and gurgolets as well as clockwork and muskets, with woolens at the end of the list.[27]

The new Company was behind the curve and chastised its servants in Bengal for not mentioning, in particular, the "extraordinary demand for flint glass." Their returning ship captains claimed to have earned profits of 700 percent on their personal exports of English glass. Such trade on the personal accounts of the ship's officers, the so-called privilege trade, was allowed by both Companies in set but often exceeded limits. Like the old Company directors, the new Company directors hoped that larger Company exports of glass might reduce the need to export silver, "whereas we Shall advance the Nations interest as well as our own." They sent a trial shipment, but when their servants sent a specific order back, the directors had considerable difficulty filling it since many of the items were too big or otherwise unsuited for glass construction. Overall, the old Company responded more effectively than the new Company to the Calico Act and, though with modest success, to the pressure to find new markets in India for English goods.[28]

By 1701, the Companies had begun cooperating to improve their political and economic positions in both England and India. As the cost of the War of the Spanish Succession (1701–1714) mounted and Indian imports resurged, Parliament increased duties on white cottons in 1701, 1704, and 1708. In 1708, Parliament also authorized the merger of the Companies in exchange for a further £1,200,000 added to the £2,000,000 from 1698, but with a new lower interest rate of 5 percent on the total. The Company (formally known as the United Company of Merchants of England Trading to the East Indies) now enjoyed the support of Tories as well as

27. Directors to Agent and Councill in Bengall, Dec. 20, 1699, IOR/E/3/93, 251–252/ fol. 126, BL; Bombay Castle to Directors, June 17, 1696, IOR/E/3/52, fol. 79, BL; Francis Buckley, *A History of Old English Glass* (London, 1925), 23–45; Directors to Chief and Councill at Ispahan [Persia], Sept. 1, 1697, IOR/E/3/92, 609/fol. 305, BL; Bombay Castle to Directors, Dec. 18, 1697, IOR/E/3/53, fol. 228, BL; Suratt Council to the Company, Jan. 12, 1697/8, IOR/E/3/53, fol. 281, BL; Directors to Generall and Council of India, Bombay, Mar. 10, 1697/8, IOR/E/3/93, 48/fol. 24v, BL; "Extract of the Suratt Committee of Buying," circa July 1700, #7107, IOR/E/3/57, BL. The directors also sent glassware to their other factories; see, for example, Directors to Agent and Councill in Bengall, Jan. 26, 1697/8, IOR/E/3/93, 27/fol. 14r, BL.

28. New Company Directors to Edward Littleton President and the Rest of the Council at Hugley in the Bay of Bengal, Sept. 7, 1700, IOR/E/3/94, 219/fol. 115, BL; New Company Directors to Nicholas Waite President and the Rest of the Councill at Suratt, Mar. 24, 1700/1, IOR/E/3/94, 287/fol. 149, BL.

An Imperial Compromise

of those Whigs whose rival new Company had become part of the unified Company. By the late 1710s, several new members of the Board of Trade also looked more kindly on the Company's trade than had their predecessors, reflecting the Company's broadening political support. To further entrench their political position, the unified Company continued its troubled efforts to export glassware, hookahs, and woolens to India. The directors sent, for example, four large and complicated woolen tents and portable banqueting houses based on reports of elite Indian tent complexes. Despite efforts to modify the designs based on Indian feedback, the woolen tents were a failure. Indians still had little interest in English woolens, while English people continued to strongly desire Indian calicoes. Indeed, smugglers importing prohibited calicoes and heavily dutied white goods became a growing issue.[29]

During the 1710s, the directors investigated and sought to impede a "new sort of Interlops," Britons evading the Company monopoly and the prohibition by trading through Ostend and using the flag of the Austrian Netherlands as cover. Some worked with or were Jacobites, and therefore were doubly enemies. The ships, recognizable as Indiamen by their style of construction and sheathing, had British names, officers, and crews, and many even fitted out in the Thames. These traders often worked with the Company's own servants in India. According to the Company's foreign buyers, the cargo of the interloper *Heathcote*, for example, contained the same types and qualities of piece goods in the same packaging as the Company itself shipped from India. If, as had been claimed, the goods came from French settlements in India, they would have been sorted for the

29. On duties passed, see O'Brien, Griffiths, and Hunt, "Political Components of the Industrial Revolution," *EHR*, 2d Ser., XLIV (1991), 406. On the cost of union, see *Charters Relating to the East India Company from 1600 to 1761* (Madras, 1887), xv. On the Company's new political breadth, see Carruthers, *City of Capital*, 150–151. For more on the makeup of the Board, see I. K. Steele, *Politics of Colonial Policy: The Board of Trade in Colonial Administration, 1696–1720* (Oxford, 1968), 150–152. On the tents, see Directors to President and Council of Ft. St George, Jan. 8, 1718, IOR/E/3/99, 332/fol. 166v, BL; Directors to President and Council of Bengal, Apr. 26, 1721, IOR/E/3/100, 583–584/fols. 293–293v, BL. In 1717, the servants in Madras related that "they have lately seen Hubblebubbles rightly made according to the Moors Pattern," which earned a great profit, but that there were still problems with the glass sorts sent out. See Directors to President and Council of Bengal, Jan. 18, 1717, IOR/E/3/99, 76/fol. 38v, BL; Directors to President and Council of Bengal, Feb. 16, 1722, IOR/E/3/101, 154/fol. 77v, BL. For the greater strength of the unified Company in India, see "Despatch from the Company to Fort St. George," Mar. 6, 1702, *Despatches from England*, XII/XIII, 23, "Instructions from the Company to Fort St. George," Mar. 9, 1703, XII/XIII, 45.

French market, not the English. The directors told their servants to "do what ever lyes in your power to disappoint" the Ostend traders' "expectations of Trade." The directors explained that Britons' trading from Europe to India threatened the nation's seafaring strength, reduced the state's revenue, and imperiled the Company. Anyone caught participating in this "flagrant Peice of Perfidiousness" should be deported immediately. But the directors apparently had little sense of the identities of the participants. They wrote to their servants praising, for instance, private merchant and active interloper John Scattergood, junior, and his partner for their good behavior.[30]

The directors gave Scattergood permission to live and trade around the Indian Ocean, but they specifically forbade him from trading to Madagascar, Africa, the Comoro Islands, Europe, and the Americas. Nevertheless, he shipped goods to Ostend, directing the revenue to be remitted to his agents in England. He used a broad range of smuggling methods to move India goods into Britain from the Netherlands as well as directly from India on Company ships. In 1712, he sent a bundle containing twenty-five pieces of high-quality chintz for making bedding, gowns, and petticoats as well as two pieces of gold-striped dimity, which he intended for his mother and wife. He instructed the ship's captain to either deliver the goods in Amsterdam to his associates to be run into England from there or to hide them in packages of other goods that could then be purchased. Scattergood soiled muslin to make it appear old and had silk made into a nightgown "the easier to gett it ashoare." He developed a relationship with Captain Charles Kesar, "an excellent man for running things ashoare." Kesar promised to smuggle into Britain more prohibited "fine chintz" and tea without duty. Scattergood also worked with Governor Isaac Pike at Saint Helena. Pike agreed to hold onto a bale of fabric and two bundles of shirts

---

30. "General Letter to Fort Marlborough," Mar. 14, 1717, *Despatches from England,* XXII/ XXIII, 33 ("new"), "General Letter to Fort St. George," Oct. 17, 1718, XXII/XXIII, 54, "Account of Ships Which the East India Company Have Very Great Reason to Believe Are Designd for the East Indies as Well from Private Informations to Be Depended on as Because They Are Full Sheathed and Filled with Nails Which Are Never Done Except for East India Voyages," XXII/XXIII, 67, "General Letter to Fort Marlborough," Mar. 14, 1717, XXII/ XXIII, 33 ("do" and "expectations"), "General Letter to Fort St. George," Feb. 16, 1721, XXII/ XXIII, 108–109 ("flagrant"); Directors to the Council at Fort St. George, Jan. 8, 1718, in Richard Carnac Temple, Lavinia Mary Anstey, and Bernard P. Scattergood, eds., *The Scattergoods and the East India Company: Being a Selection from the Private Letters and Business Correspondence of John Scattergood, East India Merchant, 1681–1723* (Bombay, 1935), 172. On the Jacobite connection, see Paul Monod, "Dangerous Merchandise: Smuggling, Jacobitism, and Commercial Culture in Southeast England, 1690–1760," *JBS,* XXX (1991), 172–173.

and shifts for one of Scattergood's friends until a way might be contrived to get them into England without paying the duty. The governor's collusion suggests the extent of the difficulty that the East India Company, Parliament, and the weaving interest faced in controlling trade and suppressing the demand for smuggled goods.[31]

Indeed, woolen and English silk supporters regularly described and bemoaned calico smugglers. One author reported, for instance, that an English vessel pretended to be Dutch (perhaps part of the Ostend trade), to sell six thousand pounds' worth of "Callicoes, silks and spices" in a few days on the English coast. The "ship was like a faire, all ready mony," and the captain intended to return in six weeks with more fabrics. Several London mercers reported to the Board of Trade, "The Running of the Said Prohibited Goods is Increased to that Degree that Wee have Dayly great Quantities of Patterns brought to our Shopps to Match for Lining . . . and used in Furniture." They had piles of English silks on hand that were simply too expensive to compete with the smuggled goods. Most damningly, they recounted receiving "Great Quantities of English Manufactured Silks Dayly Offered us at a lower Price then they can Possibly be made at." In other words, the goods were either run from India as English or, if really English, their makers would soon be run out of business.[32]

31. *The Scattergoods and the East India Company*, 167, 183, 226, 232, 242, John Scattergood to James Wendey and Osmond Beavoir, Oct. 8, 1712, 84, to his mother, 1714, 143 ("excellent" and "fine"), to Edward Arlond, January 1716, 153, to Mrs. Farmerie, November 1718, 182 ("easier"), to Dr. Manston, Nov. 2, 1721, 242. Scattergood was born in India and raised in England.

32. "Copy of a Letter from Dorchester to a Mercer in London," Apr. 28, 1720, CO 388/21, fol. 179, NA; A Lover of the Manufacture, *Reasons Humbly Proposed to the Honourable House of Commons, for Laying a Duty upon East-India Silks, etc. Exported into Her Majesty's Dominions; and That No Drawback Be Allow'd upon Callicoes, Muslins, etc. When Exported to America and Ireland* ([n.p.], [1714]); David Clayton, *A Short System of Trade; or, An Account of What in Trade Must Necessarily Be Advantageous to the Nation, and What Must of Consequence Be Detrimental* (London, 1719), 12; A Citizen [Henry Elking], *The Interest of England Consider'd, with Respect to Its Manufactures and East-India Callicoes Imported, Printed, Painted, Stained, and Consumed Therein; or, An Essay Shewing from Whence the Decay of Trade, the Melting of Coin, the Scarcity of Silver, the Increase of Poor Do Proceed* (London, 1720), 29; Memorial from Mr Badcock, Mr Feary, and Other Mercers of London, received Oct. 14, 1719, CO 388/21, fol. 143, NA. The Company also complained; see [Charles Davenant], *New Dialogues upon the Present Posture of Affairs, the Species of Mony, National Debts, Publick Revenues, Bank and East-India Company, and the Trade Now Carried on between France and Holland* (London, 1710), 195–196; R. S——le, *An Essay upon Trade, and Publick Credit; Shewing the Advantages of the East-India Prohibition, Bankrupts Affidavits, etc.* . . . (London, 1714), 9–10.

Such smuggling also operated via the Atlantic colonies, Ireland, and the straits. Cary explained that smugglers reimported East India Company goods illegally into Britain from open markets in "*Ireland,* our Plantations, and other Places to which they are sent." Another author pointed to ships passing between the "*Straits, etc.*" and the colonies, claiming that "notwithstanding the Laws against taking in any of the Manufactures or Merchandize of those [foreign] Countries, Sailors and Super-Cargoes will break thro them; . . . and they never want Opportunities of buying *Italian* Silks, *French* Silks, Stuffs and Druggets, *Indian* Silks and Callicoes, *French, Dutch,* and *Hamburgh* Linens." Smugglers thus bought India and other goods outside Britain, "by which means the Money that should be brought to us, is laid out in foreign Countries." Additionally, "this irregular Navigation" encouraged sailors to settle in the colonies, where they would avoid serving in the Royal Navy, weakening the national defense.[33]

Smuggling and interloping generated enough concern to stimulate a range of responses by the government and Company. From 1714, Parliament required customs officers to strip off the customs marks on goods to be reexported to deter their being relanded in England. George I issued a proclamation in 1718, "Recalling and Prohibiting" British sailors from working under foreign flags, whether in navies or private merchant vessels. The interlopers even stimulated cooperation between the English and Dutch East India Companies, which in all other matters were generally bitter rivals. The two companies exchanged names of reputed interloping vessels and captains and sent this information to their servants in India. Those in the Ostend trade quickly realized, however, that such words and plans lacked any effective means of enforcement. One of Scattergood's associates wrote, for instance, that a recent law against the Ostend trade "you will find to be of little purpose," and many India traders continued "from thence."[34]

The Company itself does not appear to have engaged in smuggling to avoid the prohibition, and it did not need to since the directors saw in the Calico Act the potential to sell vastly more white cottons in England to serve the expanding and improving domestic printers. They wrote to their

33. John Cary, *An Essay towards Regulating the Trade, and Employing the Poor of This Kingdom* (London, 1717), 43–44; *A Letter to a Member of Parliament, concerning The Naval Store-Bill, Brought in Last Session* . . . (London, 1720), 37, 38.

34. *London Gazette,* July 27–31, 1714; King George I, "A Proclamation, for Recalling and Prohibiting Seamen from Serving Foreign Princes and States," in *Despatches from England,* XXII/XXIII, 68, "General Letter to Fort St. George," Oct. 17, 1718, XXII/XXIII, 54; William Phipps to Scattergood, Jan. 14, 1720, *The Scattergoods and the East India Company,* 213.

An Imperial Compromise

servants in Surat: "The Prohibition on Chints or painted or printed Callicoes is only on those manufactured beyound the Seas; because We have a great many persons here do the same work almost as good as India, so that you will do well to send us the more white Callicoes and fewer Chints if readily procurable." French printers escaping a complete and vigorously enforced French calico ban that had begun in 1686 to protect French woolen, linen, and silk producers further bolstered the London industry. With great demand now for white cottons, from 1704 to 1720 the Company's imports of Indian fabrics trended upward at levels similar to those during the surge from 1660 to 1680, reaching more than 700,000 pieces per year in both periods. The sharp peak of more than 1.7 million in 1684 would not, however, be matched. English printed calicoes went to *"Africa, and other hot Countries"* and were used in England for "Childrens Frocks, Handkerchiefs and Aprons." English prints were inferior imitations, but they were acceptable for some purposes.[35]

The Company's importation of white cottons served England's burgeoning printers, but the weaving interest made clear that it served smugglers as well. As Daniel Defoe, eloquent new defender of the domestic weavers explained, private merchants claimed for export at the customhouse white calicoes purchased at the East India Company's sales. They took the export drawback on the duties before shipping the goods out and running them back ashore. Once back in England, they had the calicoes printed and again entered at the customhouse for export. The merchants then ran the fabric back ashore one last time, pocketing the export drawbacks to the detriment of the nation's treasury and weavers alike. Defoe claimed that a single merchant house gained ten thousand pounds in drawbacks between June 1717 and June 1718 for goods to Holland and Hamburg that had never made it beyond the coast of England. He reported that smug-

35. Directors to the President and Council at Surat, Aug. 21, 1700, IOR/E/3/93, 338/fol. 169v, BL ("Prohibition"); Directors to the President and Council of Bengal, Aug. 21, 1700, IOR/E/3/93, 345/fol. 173, BL; *The Stuff Weaver's Case against Printing Callicoes Examined* ([London?], [1704]), *("Africa")*. See also "Humble Memorial of George Morley," Oct. 23, 1702, CO 389/17, fol. 220, NA; Thomas, *Mercantilism and the East India Trade*, 126. On French printers, see Wadsworth and Mann, *Cotton Trade and Industrial Lancashire*, 122–123. The import trends are derived from data charted in Chaudhuri, *Trading World of Asia*, 286. Printers copied and adapted the Indian practices of using a mordant on the fabric to make dyes permanent and resists to repel dyes from areas for which they were not intended, knowledge that came via Armenian printers; see Giorgio Riello, "Asian Knowledge and the Development of Calico Printing in Europe in the Seventeenth and Eighteenth Centuries," *Journal of Global History*, V (2010), esp. 6–23. The most famous description of the French ban is Eli F. Heckscher, *Mercantilism* (1935; rpt. New York, 1994), I, 172–175.

gling "is now become such a *customary Stealing*, that many, who in other Things, call themselves honest Men, make no Conscience of this Kind of Robbery." Economic writer Simon Clement, who attacked the calico trade for creating a "Famine of Silver," similarly claimed that "some are grown so dextrous in this Business, as that they will undertake to ship off any Man's Goods, recover the Debenture, reland them, and deliver them at his own House, for a very moderate *Premio*."[36]

The success of England's calico printers also revitalized hopes for the development of an English cotton spinning and weaving industry, using Indian and, particularly, Atlantic colonial cotton. The directors encouraged their servants to send back from India as much raw silk and cotton yarn as they could, explaining that such goods had "a Popular reputation, because they may be further Manufactured here." One proposal to Queen Anne explained that if British producers had enough raw cotton they could spin and weave it to make "as good Muslane [muslin], as any the Indys afford; and some of our weavers have actually done it." The calico printers' supporters claimed that not only did the printers increasingly print linens; they also printed on cotton cloth made from colonial cotton. The former member of Parliament John Asgill explained in 1719 that the nascent cotton and fustian spinning and weaving industries in England used raw cotton imported from "our Plantations in *America*." Additionally, he claimed, printing white cottons from India generated almost as much wealth for the nation. English cotton weavers and printers, therefore, both deserved protection more than English silk weavers who used foreign spun silk. Prohibitions on wearing calicoes, he argued, severely stunted the domestic cotton industry's growth.[37]

36. [Daniel Defoe], *The Just Complaint of the Poor Weavers Truly Represented, with as Much Answer as It Deserves, to a Pamphlet Lately Written against Them Entitled "The Weavers Pretences Examined, etc."* (London, 1719), 34; [Defoe], *A Brief State of the Question between the Printed and Painted Callicoes, and the Woollen and Silk Manufacture, as Far as It Relates to the Wearing and Using of Printed and Painted Callicoes in Great-Britain* (London, 1719), 7; Defoe, *The Case of the Fair Traders, Humbly Represented to the Honourable the House of Commons: Being a Clear View and State of Clandestine Trade, as Now Carry'd on in Great Britain* (n.p., [1720]), n.p. (quotation); [Simon Clement], *Remarks upon a Late Ingenious Pamphlet, Entituled, "A Short but Thorough Search into What May Be the Real Cause of the Present Scarcity of Our Silver Coin, etc."* . . . (London, 1718), 19–24 (quotations on 20–21). See also *The Case of the Printers of Callicoes and Linens* ([n.p.], [1720?]). For more on Defoe and the London weavers, see Plummer, *London Weavers' Company*, 298–301.

37. Directors to Our President and Councill of Bengall, Aug. 21, 1700, IOR/E/3/93, 345/ fol. 173 ("Popular"), BL; *Case of the Printers of Callicoes and Linens*; "The Means of a Most Ample Encrease of the Wealth and Strength of England, in a Few Years," 1706, MS84, fol.

Some proponents expected that the supply of colonial cotton could be dramatically increased through the use of joint-stock companies to cultivate cotton plantations and train cotton spinners and weavers, much as the East India Company used a joint-stock to overcome the challenges of trading to the Indian and Pacific Oceans. Several men requested a charter in 1720 to start a calico manufacturing company in Britain protected by a complete ban on calico imports. They claimed that this manufacturing company would employ 38,160 people in Britain as spinners and weavers as well as a vast number of enslaved people in the West Indies to grow cotton. Additionally, it would require more ships and sailors, produce £125,000 for the treasury, "greatly Diminish the number of Poor," and ultimately "*Transplant* a very considerable Branch of the Treasures of the *Indies* into *Great Britain.*" The woolen and silk interests published a notice in London's newspapers to "utterly disown and reject any such Proposal." They did not need to worry. The government did not grant the charter and remained unconvinced that such schemes could work. It was not alone in such doubts.[38]

Writers increasingly saw the colonies more in the terms set by the first Calico Act, as either positive or problematic markets for calicoes, not as cultivators of raw cotton for Britain. In his 1710 work promoting colonization in South Carolina, Thomas Nairne did not mention cotton cultivation, although he discussed efforts at rice and silk cultivation and suggested that coffee, tea, and drugs from Asia would all be suitable staples for the colony. He reported that twenty-two ships a year arrived in South Carolina from Britain laden with woolens, linen, calico, and muslin, among many other goods. This focus on the colonies as consumers of finished cotton rather than providers of the raw material for its production was frequently repeated. "A Lover of the Manufacture" claimed in 1714 that domestic silk weavers suffered from "very great Quantities of *East-India* Silks, and Silks

---

50 ("good"), Special Collections, Senate House Library, University of London; [John] Asgill, *A Brief Answer to a Brief State of the Question between the Printed and Painted Callicoes, and the Woollen and Silk Manufactures: As Far as It Relates to the Wearing and Using Printed and Painted Callicoes in Great Britain* (London, 1719), 7–9, 14–15, 20.

38. *Daily Post* (London), May 26, 31, June 1 ("utterly"), 6, 8, 1720; *Daily Courant* (London), June 6, 1720; "The Memorial of Jonathan Wrightson, Richard Score, Thomas Ollive, James Warren, Abraham Vanmildert, Richard Coxeter, Oliver Hurst and Joseph Stephenson, on Behalf of Themselves, Many Eminent Merchants, Linnen Drapers and Other Considerable Traders and Manufacturers of This Kingdom," CO 388/23, fols. 134–135, NA. See also Wrightson and Hurst, "A Short State of the Advantages Which Will Arise by Manufacturing Callicoes in Great Brittain," Nov. 23, 1720, CO 388/22, fol. 307, NA.

mixt with Cotten, etc. . . . bought cheap at the *East-India-House*" and "Exported into all Her Majesty's Dominions." He went on, "There are great Quantities of Callicoes, Muslins, etc. Exported into *America* and *Ireland.*" Another wrote that the Dutch took to Spain and America "a World of fine and coarse Callico, stain'd in *Holland* with all Sorts of Colours." Similarly, a supporter of England's printers claimed that "great Quantities" of silk handkerchiefs made in England and India and printed in England "daily are exported to Her Majesty's Dominions Abroad" and consumed at home to the benefit of the poor printers. In this reading of the situation, consumers on both sides of the Atlantic were thought to fulfill the same economic role as purchasers of English manufactured goods, although there was clear disagreement over whether English printed goods counted as manufactured.[39]

Parliament had sought a balance between competing interests, but it had underestimated the potential weight of smugglers and calico printers in upsetting the entire mechanism. By the late 1710s, the Company and the woolen and English silk interests alike were pushing in earnest for the balance to be reset. The continuing popularity of cotton calicoes and the strengthening position of the now united Company in the state through its lending power and bipartisan politics suggested that garnering support for enhanced restrictions on cottons would not be easy. Indeed, while smuggling was undoubtedly widespread, the state still collected nearly £1.5 million in duties on white India cottons from the end of 1708 to the end of 1718. From this amount, the government netted more than £0.5 million in the ten-year period, or £51,081 per year, after drawbacks on reexports. These figures suggest that the legal trade was both sizable and

39. [Thomas Nairne], *A Letter from South Carolina; Giving an Account of the Soil, Air, Product, Trade, Government, Laws, Religion, People, Military Strength, etc. of That Province; Together with the Manner and Necessary Charges of Settling a Plantation There, and the Annual Profit It Will Produce; Written by a Swiss Gentleman, to His Friend at Bern* (London, 1710), 11, 15, 58; A Lover of the Manufacture, *Reasons Humbly Proposed;* Francis Cawood, *An Essay; or, Scheme: Towards Establishing and Improving the Fishery and Other Manufactures of Great-Britain; Humbly Offered and Dedicated to the North-Sea Company; and All True Lovers of Their Country, Nature, and Art; What Goods and Merchandize Are Proper for Maritime Traffick . . . the Which Will Produce a Far Greater Treasure to the Crown . . .* (London, 1713), 106 ("a World"); *Reasons Humbly Offer'd . . . to the Honourable House of Commons, against a Duty Intended to Be Laid . . . upon Silks, Manufactured, Printed, or Stained, as far as It Concerns Handkerchiefs* (n.p., [1712]), broadside ("great"). See also John Haynes, *Great Britain's Glory; or, An Account of the Great Numbers of Poor Employ'd in the Woollen and Silk Manufacturies, to the Increase of Trade, the Enlargement of the Revenues of the Crown, and Augmenting Our Navigation . . .* (London, 1715), 82–86.

an important revenue stream for the state, accounting for approximately 3 percent of all net customs revenue. Additionally, the government netted approximately a further £24,470 per year, or 1.5 percent of all duty revenue, from printed calicoes reexported. In contrast to the strength of the Company's trade and its importance to state revenue, hopes to use the Atlantic colonies to provide raw cotton to be spun and woven in Britain remained unfulfilled—and, indeed, were now ignored by most imperial thinkers and leaders. Still, the Atlantic colonies might offer the means to refine the compromise between the weavers and the Company, if not as favored cultivators, then as even more distinct, protected consumers.[40]

An Empire of Difference: The Second Calico Act

In mid-1719, the Board of Trade embarked on a serious reevaluation of the India trade for Britain and its empire, including India's relationship to the Atlantic colonies. It invited David Martin, a leading mercer from Ludgate Hill, to speak with its members directly. Martin's presentation outlined the weaving interests' new approach to the calico question, alongside older arguments about the weavers' poverty and economic value to the kingdom. Martin did not blame the powerful East India Company for the resurgence of calicoes; instead, he targeted those with little political capital in the metropole. Martin and the weaving interests more broadly elevated their own self-fashioned identities as the nation's defenders against fashionable women, supposedly Catholic Scots, false manufacturers, and insufficiently regulated Atlantic colonists. He told the Board to cast their "eyes" upon "the Ladies and all their Sex in general dressed in these Calicoes and Linnens." Women wearing these goods, he explained, encouraged smuggling and reduced the demand for domestic silks and woolens in proportion. They needed to be controlled by the government. Martin also derided the calico printers' claims that they employed the poor to manufacture goods, exclaiming, "These Men know not what belongs to

40. The net revenue data does not compare exactly analogous periods owing to differences in the data reported. Annual averages are calculated for white cottons for the period December 1708–1718 and for net customs revenue during 1713–1719. The annual averages for printed calicoes are from June 1714 to June 1719. Year-to-year data did vary, but the averages smooth out much of the variance. The figures of 3 and 1.5 percent are nevertheless an estimate. The average combined net calico duty revenue was within a few tenths of a percent of the tea duty revenue. The Company's goods overall from 1716 to 1720 accounted for more than 13 percent of the state's gross duty revenue. Data is from *Journals of the House of Commons*, XIX (1718–1721) (London, 1803), 188, 202, 218, 480.

a Manufacture." He argued, moreover, that a strict prohibition needed to be enforced in "Our Plantations" so that "they are made subservient to the main Interest of the Kingdom." That the colonists should be subservient (in Martin's argument, similar to women) was not really in question, but the means through which colonists would best serve the kingdom remained unclear. Indeed, such arguments might help to secure a more stringent calico prohibition over newly unified Scotland and England, but they might also help to further solidify the position of colonists as unlike both British producers and British consumers at home. Martin's case to the Board and its development among the weaving interests in the debate over the second Calico Act contributed to shifting understandings of the empire, its power structures, and its peoples from India to America.[41]

Events in the press and the streets paralleled Martin's statements. John Blanch, an old hand from the 1690s debate, switched in 1718 from blaming Indians for seducing British women to indicting British women from "the City" for determining "Fashions in the Consumption of *India* Silks and Calicoes." The London Weavers' Company also targeted British women, offering cash rewards to people reporting Indian calico furniture and women in calico dresses to Henry Soames, a ribbon weaver. Given such instructions, it is not surprising that more and more people soon began seizing goods and assaulting fashionable women. In June 1719, the weavers doused women's calico gowns with aqua fortis, tore their clothing asunder, and threatened to pull down a house in which several victims had taken cover. The weavers also marched on the increasingly successful calico printing workshops in Lewisham. Witnesses saw Thomas Hardy "with a Piece of Callicoe in his Hand flourishing it over his Head, crying, *down with the Callicoes.*" Witnesses also saw John Humphreys, an avowed Jacobite, distributing money and alcohol to the rioters, stirring fears in the city that the weavers had joined a popish plot. Some of the rioters did not have the weavers' best interests at heart. The weaving interest was, nevertheless, disingenuous when it attempted to distance itself from the attacks on women. Claudius Rey, a leading weaver, claimed that "these petit Disturbances are properly *among* the *Women themselves;* which *proceeds* from the *foolish Fancy* of some, and the *Madness and Rage* of others." Rey

41. Martin to the Board of Trade, Oct. 30, 1719, CO 389/27, 250–268, 279–280, NA; "The Humble Petition of the Bailiffs, Wardens, Assistants, and Comonalty of the Trade, Art, and Mistery of Weavers, London," to the Board of Trade via the Lord Justices, Oct. 17, 1719, CO 389/27, 229–231, NA.

falsely blamed women on both sides of the debate to diffuse criticisms of the weavers' violence. He further sought to reduce the complexity of the problem to a women's tiff, thereby making a total prohibition seem an easy solution for men to enact.[42]

Affordable and stylish Indian calicoes also seemed to critics to dangerously cloak the social differences among Britain's women like few goods had before. The notion that fabrics reflected the quality of the person wearing them had existed across Asia and Europe and had underwritten sumptuary laws for centuries. Weaver supporter Henry Elking fretted, "Do we not daily observe Persons of Quality and Distinction, and all intermediate Ranks and Degrees, to the meanest Servant Maid, clad in what is painted, stained or printed?" He further explained, in response to arguments that the cheapness of Indian cotton benefited the nation, that expensive silk offered a more important social and political advantage by more clearly marking status. These attacks amplified general charges of the dire effects of rising and broadening consumer spending patterns. In particular, Richard Steele's popular and widely distributed *Tatler* and *Spectator* vigorously pushed the case for restrained fashion, especially for women. Published verses in defense of woolens associated women who wore calico with promiscuity and prostitution, cheating the king, and confusing the social order.[43]

42. [John Blanch], *A Dialogue between Sir Arthur Cleaveland and Sir Gilbert Proteus, at Garraways* (n.p., [1718?]), [1]; [Clement], *Remarks upon a Late Ingenious Pamphlet*, 20; *Weekly-Journal; or, Saturday's-Post* (London), Mar. 29, 1718, 405; A Weaver [Claudius Rey], *The Weavers True Case; or, The Wearing of Printed Callicoes and Linnen Destructive to the Woollen and Silk Manufactures . . .* (London, 1719), 30–41 (quotation on 41). On the riots in June 1719, see Trial of John Humphreys, Sam Bains, George Picket, Tho. Hardy, Charles Child, July 8, 1719 (t17190708–56), *Old Bailey Proceedings Online*, www.oldbaileyonline.org; *Post Boy* (London), June 11–13, 1719. An author defending the calico trade shot back that the real victims were the calico-wearing women and children thrown "into Fitts, insomuch that some of them, as I'm informed, died soon after." See A Merchant, *The Weavers Pretences Examin'd; Being a Full and Impartial Enquiry into the Complaints of Their Wanting Work, and the True Causes Assign'd . . .* (London, 1719), 16.

43. [Elking], *Interest of England Consider'd*, 26, 32–33; "The Weaver's Complaint against the Calico Madams," *Weekly Journal, Or, British Gazetteer* (London), Nov. 7, 1719, 1444. As the anthropologist Grant McCracken explains, "Clothing forms a 'system of material difference' that corresponds to and so communicates a 'system of conceptual difference'"; see McCracken, *Culture and Consumption: New Approaches to the Symbolic Character of Consumer Goods and Activities* (Bloomington, Ind., 1988), 98. In India, cottons had symbolized status and were often thought to have transformative powers over their wearers. Tight and smooth silks and cottons were seen to offer greater protection from caste pollution than loose

Nevertheless, the Glorious Revolution had encouraged a shift from a premodern, pan-Eurasian emphasis on social inequalities and sumptuary restrictions to a fundamental humanist faith in individual market freedoms (though not necessarily free trade) as central to Englishness. As an author writing under the pseudonym "A Merchant" explained, "What signifies all our Riches, and that Liberty and Property that we so justly boast of, except we have the liberty of eating and drinking, or wearing what we please, and thinking or believing what we please?" The Scottish linen makers similarly asked why free Britons would champion despotic Catholic French models of prohibition.⁴⁴

Pointing to the primary importance of men in overseeing and ordering society helped the weaving interest overcome the problem that prohibitions and arguments against fashion seemed to be at odds with notions of English and British liberty. The Glorious Revolution had also empowered some women politically, and here the weaving interest saw its opportu-

---

and coarse ones, for example. See C. A. Bayly, "The Origins of Swadeshi (Home Industry): Cloth and Indian Society, 1700–1930," in Arjun Appadurai, ed., *The Social Life of Things: Commodities in Cultural Perspective* (New York, 1986), 286–293.

According to Daniel Kuchta, in the decades following the Glorious Revolution, sartorial simplicity became a marker of English masculinity, and critics directed less concern at women's fashionable consumption; see Kuchta, "The Making of the Self-Made Man: Class, Clothing, and English Masculinity, 1688–1832," in Victoria de Grazia with Ellen Furlough, ed., *The Sex of Things: Gender and Consumption in Historical Perspective* (Berkeley, Calif., 1996), 54–78, esp. 56–62. Women's dress, however, was a significant political issue. Not only did critics use it as evidence of women's supposed foolishness; they also argued that women should be directed to dress in simple fashions made from English fabrics, which were less conspicuous and vibrant than Indian ones. See Erin Mackie, *Market à la Mode: Fashion, Commodity, and Gender in "The Tatler" and "The Spectator"* (Baltimore, 1997), esp. 7, 121–202. Steele started the *Spectator* with Joseph Addison. For more on Steele, see Cruickshanks, Handley, and Hayton, *House of Commons*, V, 559–564. For more on calicos and the social order, see Smith, "'Callico Madams,'" *Eighteenth-Century Life*, XXI, no. 2 (Spring 2007), 33, 39–47.

44. A Merchant, *Weavers Pretences Examin'd*, 6; and for a similar statement in a letter to the press, see *Weekly Journal; or, British Gazetteer*, June 27, 1719, 1389. For the critique of the prohibitions as French, see *The Answer of the Scots Linnen Manufacturers to the Report of the Lords Commissioners of Trade and Plantations; and to a Paper Falsly Call'd, "The Case of the Printing of Linnen in Great-Britain, etc. . . ."* ([London], [1720?]), [1], which follows similar statements such as [Davenant], *Essay on the East-India-Trade*, 26. On English conceptions of individuals and the market, see Craig Muldrew, *The Economy of Obligation: The Culture of Credit and Social Relations in Early Modern England* (New York, 1998), 134–147, 319–320. For a brief review on fashion and market freedom, see Beverly Lemire, "Second-Hand Beaux and 'Red-Armed Belles': Conflict and the Creation of Fashions in England, c. 1660–1800," *Continuity and Change*, XV (2000), 391–417, esp. 400–403. On the Glorious Revolution, see Hannah Smith, "Politics, Patriotism, and Gender: The Standing Army Debate on the English Stage, circa 1689–1720," *JBS*, L (2011), 48–75, esp. 66.

An Imperial Compromise

nity. It responded to arguments that sartorial freedom was part of British liberty by claiming that, in giving such liberty to women, men had lost their own freedom. Steele, speaking in the character of a boy from India, wrote, "I cannot see . . . in what the People of this Country excell those of ours, except it be that they are govern'd by their Wives; they go to our Country to bring home to their Women fine Dresses from Head to Foot." By not controlling their wives' desires for foreign luxuries, Englishmen had relinquished their masculinity, even more than supposedly effeminate Indian men. Defoe argued that "A Merchant" made a "Demand of exorbitant Liberty" that enabled the "folly of our Women" in consuming calicoes. This line of argument received an unexpected boost when a purchasing frenzy over the shares of the South Sea Company in 1720 created a stock bubble. The South Sea Company had been set up to improve the finances of the state in part through the promise of a monopoly trade with South America. With the promise unfulfilled, the resulting South Sea Bubble soon burst, costing countless fortunes in Britain. Critics blamed women and effeminate men for causing the bubble through emotional instead of rational purchasing behavior. In the context of the South Sea Bubble, Defoe furthered his case that fathers, husbands, and the government needed to work together to constrain women's consumer freedom and "FORCE" them to wear woolens for the good of the kingdom.[45]

Similarly, the woolen and English silk interests argued that Protestant Englishmen needed to exert their control over Catholic French printers and Scottish linen makers. Rey, for one, described most calico printers in London as *"French Roman Catholicks,* who were forced to fly from their Country," not because of religious persecution like the beneficial French Protestant weavers, but because of the sensible French ban on calico consumption. He advised Parliament against protecting these few Catholic people at the expense of the poor Protestant English and Huguenot French weavers. Supporters of the ban also focused on the Scots, often aligned with the bugbears of Catholicism and Jacobinism for producing linens that looked like Indian calicoes. They argued that English manu-

---

45. [Richard Steele], *The Spinster: In Defence of the Woollen Manufactures; to Be Continued Occasionally,* no. 1 (London, 1719), 16; Defoe, *Just Complaint of the Poor Weavers,* 6 ("folly"), 9 ("Demand"); Monsieur de Brocade of Paris [Daniel Defoe], *The Female Manufacturers Complaint: Being the Humble Petition of Dorothy Distaff, Abigail Spinning-Wheel, Eleanor Reel, etc. Spinsters, to the Lady Rebecca Woollpack* . . . (London, 1720), 11 ("FORCE"). See also [Rey], *Weavers True Case,* 30–31, 34, 48. On the South Sea Bubble, see Catherine Ingrassia, "The Pleasure of Business and the Business of Pleasure: Gender, Credit, and the South Sea Bubble," *Studies in Eighteenth-Century Culture,* XXIV (1995), 191–210.

facturers should not be subordinated to the Scots, who had only recently been brought within a unified Britain. Besides, the weaving interest claimed, 90 percent of the linen consumed in England came from Europe, not Scotland, making Scottish linen simply a screen for foreign goods. The Scots pointed out the inconsistency of the attacks against them, writing of the woolen and English silk interests, "Sometimes they tell us, That *Scots* Printed Linnen is become a general Wear . . . in *England*," but, when they wanted the Scots to voluntarily give up the trade, they called it a "Trifle."[46]

As the Scots were to be subjected to the interests of England's weavers, David Clayton, Henry Elking, and Ephraim Parker argued that the colonists needed to be as well. This vigorous burst of arguments built on the sense of the colonists as great consumers of India goods that had begun in the 1690s and continued to develop through the late 1710s. "The supplying our Collonies, Plantations, or Settlements, in *America*, with foreign Manufactures, doth tend to the Detriment, and in time will, if not prevented, to the Ruin of the Nation," Clayton exclaimed. Of all the calicoes exported to Europe, "not one tenth Part of those Goods are consum'd in the whole *United Provinces*, with their Appendixes on the whole *German* Empire; but 'tis *Great-Britain, Ireland*, and our Islands and Collonies in *America*, take, as I may say, the whole." Clayton made clear that the colonies should have the same economic role in consuming English manufactures as England, since they were "part of our selves." Besides, American merchants could easily substitute English "Silks, Crapes, Stuffs, etc." for Indian fabric without any loss of business. Elking wrote that England had "many advantagious Colonies in *America*, which would (if due Care were taken to prevent the sending thither printed Callicoes) take from us far greater Quantities of our Woollen and Silk Manufactures than at present they do." Parker argued that the greatest barrier to the success of England's

46. [Rey], *Weavers True Case*, 23, 38; *An Essay on Trade, Wherein the Present Dispute about Callicoes, etc. Is Consider'd* (n.p., [1719?]), 8; *The Weavers Reply to the Linen-Drapers, and Other Dealers in Printed Callicoes and Linens; Wherein Their Case Is Considered, and Answered Paragraph by Paragraph* . . . (London, 1720), 12; *The Case of the Printing of Linnen in Great Britain, as It partic[u]larly Relates to the Printing of Linnens Made in Scotland and in Ireland* ([n.p.], [1720?]); *The Farther Case of the Woollen and Silk Manufacturers* ([London], [1720?]); *Answer of the Scots Linnen Manufacturers*, [1], [2]. Before the Act of Union, one critic of the calico prohibition argued that it would cause the Scots, not the French, to take control of the India trade and overrun England with their supposedly Catholic religion; see *A Speech without Doors, Which Would Be Spoken within Doors, if the Author Had the Honour to Be a Member of This House of Commons, and Therein to Offer His Sense of the Bill for the More Effectual Encouragement of the Manufactures of England, and Setting the Poor at Work* (n.p., [1704]), 3.

weaving industry "is, by allowing all sorts of foreign wrought Goods . . . to be sent to our own Plantations, . . . in Effect we have almost lost the Supplying our Fellow-Subjects in those Parts, with our own Goods." English woolens, not Indian calicoes, were England's equivalent to the gold and silver mines of the Spanish empire.[47]

Meanwhile, the Board of Trade solicited accounts of the tax revenue provided by calicoes and silks printed in England, the reexport of the East India Company's goods in general, and the reexport of India goods specifically to America. The Board learned that from June 1717 to June 1719 cottons and silks dyed, stained, and printed in England netted nearly forty thousand pounds per year to the state. The accounts showed as yet comparatively modest markets for India calicoes shipped legally from Britain to the colonies. The customs office could not measure the extent of the trade to the colonies from Europe and from interlopers returning from India. The Board asked the East India Company directors for their input. The directors appeared exasperated with the weavers' demand for further relief from Indian competition. They produced a one-page statement explaining that they had "purchased" the right to trade to India from Parliament at considerable expense and for the benefit of the "Nation." They expected to unfairly lose a "very great Branch" of their trade if the government further restricted calico consumption.[48]

Still, the directors and other Company supporters hoped that the Atlantic markets were bigger than they had previously thought. In the early 1700s, the Company had brought to London few calicoes suitable for the African and West Indian markets, and many British merchants looked to reexports from Holland instead. By the late 1710s, however, the Company

47. Clayton, *Short System of Trade*, 16, 19, 20, 23; [Elking], *Interest of England Consider'd*, 37, 44; Ephraim Parker, *Proposals for Increasing the Trade of the Silk, Woollen, and Cotten Manufactories of This Nation, Both at Home and Abroad, and Consequently the Whole Trade of the Kingdom; Humbly Presented to the Consideration of the Honourable House of Commons* (n.p., [1720]), [1]. See also *A Brief State of the East India Trade, as It Relates to Other Branches of the British Commerce* . . . ([London], [1710/1715]).

48. For the Board's account of duty revenue, see "Duties on Silks, Silk-Handkerchiefs, Calicoes, Linnens, and Stuffs, Printed, Painted, Stain'd, or Dyed," July 10, 1719, CO 388/21, fol. 110, NA. For the Board's knowledge of exports to the Atlantic colonies, see "An Accompt Shewing the Species and Quanties of Prohibited East India Goods Re-Exported from England to Ireland, the Isles of Guernsey, Jersey, and His Majesties Plantations in America, Since the Peace of Utrecht to Christ, 1716," CO 390/8, fols. 237r–248v, NA. For the directors' statement, see Court of Directors to the Board of Trade, Nov. 20, 1719, CO 388/21, fol. 278, NA. The Board's thirst for information followed its new overall approach in the later 1710s. See Steele, *Politics of Colonial Policy*, 153.

had begun to pay more attention to the suitably colored and patterned calicoes and polished cowrie shells that had high demand in several West African markets. In 1720, an author writing as "A Merchant" amplified Charles Davenant's arguments from the 1690s that the Company added to the nation's prosperity by bringing calicoes to London to be reexported throughout the Atlantic. The author explained that the reexport of calicoes was generally beneficial and that "there are some Trades especially, which cannot be carried on with any Success without them; as the *Guinea, West India* and *South-Sea;* which Trades every one must allow, to be highly beneficial to the whole Nation." These "highly beneficial" trades involved the reexport of calicoes to Africa to purchase enslaved people necessary to the valuable West Indian plantations and to the Spanish Atlantic colonies. The author expected that a prohibition on calicoes in the colonies would destroy these important trades. Additionally, the colonists would simply purchase India fabrics illegally from the French, Dutch, and Germans. The empire would lose substantial revenue and the East India Company's financial backing, and many people in London would lose their livelihoods. "There's hardly any one Trade in *London* that does not receive some Benefit by the fitting out of an *East India* Ship," A Merchant explained.[49]

Indeed, some continued to debate whether the India trade might be more successful and beneficial to Britain without the prohibition and the Company monopoly alike. Whig economic writer Henry Martin's 1701 discourse supporting an end to the calico prohibition and the beginning of an open India trade, more like that in the Atlantic, reappeared in 1720. Martin argued that consuming and trading India's calicoes drove down prices, stimulated innovation, and bolstered the kingdom's wealth. Real profit came from "trading to the *Plantations,* to the *Straights,* to *Africa,* to the *East-Indies*" as much as possible. "Bullion," Martin explained, echoing the East India Company's defenders, "is only secondary and dependant, Cloaths and Manufactures are real and principal Riches." The monopoly, he argued, separating here from the Company's defenders, artificially constrained the India trade. If an open trade succeeded in expanding the calico trade, as Martin hoped, and as other Whigs supporting the weavers feared, it would make the weavers' plight worse. The East India Company's monopoly gave it a greater ability to control the India trade whether or not

49. Richard Harris to Mr. Popple, Sept. 21, 1719, *CSPC,* XXXI, no. 388, 223–224, esp. 223. On cowries, see, for example, Directors to President and Council at Bombay, Nov. 4, 1719, IOR/E/3/100, 25/fol. 13, BL; A Merchant, *Weavers Pretences Examin'd,* 13–14; see also *Letter to a Member of Parliament, concerning the Naval Store-Bill,* 37–38.

it was better at expanding it, and, besides, it had developed real financial value as a state lender. An open India trade was now politically unlikely.[50]

Whatever the organization of the India trade, Defoe, in particular, understood that if Britons continued to desire Indian calicoes they would continue to try to evade the prohibition, and so he sought to embarrass Britons for not wanting domestic woolens. He described Indians as stupid but still capable of understanding the economic benefits of consuming their own manufactures. He explained that *"Indians*, who, as uncapable as they may be to judge of their National Interests, are yet wiser in this part, by the Strength of meer Nature, than we are." Indians refused to wear woolens, despite Defoe's unlikely claims that fine woolens were "much Cooler, and much more suited to the Heat of the warmest Climate, than the uncouth Passions, great Sleeves and pleated Gowns of the *Indians*." He sought to overturn Indian manufacturing superiority by imagining that Indians defended their interests only by "meer Nature" and that, despite living in cool Britain, he knew better than Indians the proper clothing for the tropics. Defoe described calico as "a tawdery, Pie-spotted, flabby, ragged, low-priz'd Thing . . . a Foreigner by Birth; made the L[or]d knows where, by a Parcel of *Heathens* and *Pagans*, that worship the Devil, and work for a Half-penny a Day." He personified calico as ugly, lowly, and un-English, while dehumanizing Indians as a "parcel," like fabric, and as groveling devil worshippers.[51]

50. [Henry Martin], *Considerations upon the East-India Trade* (London, 1701), 12–21, esp. 17 ("only"), 34–40, 67, 102 ("trading"). Martin's text was reprinted in 1720 as *The Advantages of the East-India Trade to England, Consider'd* . . . (London, 1720). Calls for an open trade to Africa, it turned out, resonated more easily with the public and Parliament. Unlike the India trade, the Africa trade provided significant outlets for English goods, labor for English plantations, and no competition to English manufactures. How best to expand the trade to Africa was not caught up much in the question of whether to expand the trade. Defoe, for instance, supported the RAC's monopoly at least in part for the same reason that he attacked the East India Company. Both companies furthered trade, but the former furthered a positive trade, wheareas the latter, a negative one. For more on the Africa trade and Defoe and Davenant's support for the RAC, see Pettigrew, *Freedom's Debt*, esp. 102–118. See also [Davenant], *New Dialogues*, 194–197; Davenant, *A Report to the Honourable the Commissioners for Putting in Execution the Act, Intitled, "An Act, for the Taking, Examining, and Stating the Publick Accounts of the Kingdom,"* part I (London, 1712), 36–41. Thomas overstated the case that there was agreement in opposition to open-trade principles in England; some clearly supported such principles publicly. See Thomas, *Mercantilism and the East India Trade*, 173. At this time, the Commons defeated a proposed amendment to eventually open the India trade; see *Journals of the House of Commons*, Jan. 28, 1718/19, XIX, 79.

51. [Defoe], *A Brief State of the Question*, 27–28; [Defoe], *Female Manufacturers Complaint*, 10.

Defoe's understanding of Indians and their fabric as being fundamentally un-English or un-British was paralleled by his understanding of colonists as not fully British. In general, the woolen and English silk weavers' focus on identifying their own interests with that of Englishmen within Britain itself, as well as their opposition to plans for the cultivation of colonial cotton, contradicted their insistence that colonists were equal Britons when it came to consumption. Defoe, in contrast, reversed the argument. He claimed that, as producers, colonists were not to be treated differently from people in Britain. Whether calicoes were made in the British Atlantic colonies or, importantly, in Britain itself with colonial cotton, they should still be prohibited in Britain for competing with ancient British woolens that employed more people. He similarly argued against printed linen, which was made in Scotland. The weaker industries, whether in Britain or America, were to be subordinated to the stronger. On consumption, however, colonists were not British. Aligning with the Company instead of the general weaving lobby, Defoe wrote, "Not only great Quantities [of calicoes] should be exported, but all of them; for let us but be deliver'd from the Use of them here, we care not whether they send them, whether to *Africa, America, Germany,* or any where." For Defoe, colonists in America were no more equivalent to domestic consumers than Indians, Africans, and Germans. Subordinating the interests of colonial cultivators and cotton manufacturers throughout Britain and its colonies to British woolen producers might seem to limit the value of the Atlantic colonies to Britain, but positioning colonists as non-British consumers made them valuable in other ways to the Company and the government.[52]

In the Atlantic colonies themselves, meanwhile, newspapers carried stories about the calico debates, and religious leaders attacked consumer spending. Reverend Thomas Paine, for instance, identified the *"extravagant consumption of imported Commodities"* as the main cause of New England's economic "difficulties." Explaining that the colonists had erred when they blamed paper money for economic decline, he argued instead that merchants had ruined the people by encouraging the consumption of ever "greater Quantities of European, and East and West-India Goods." Much like woolen supporters in England, he wrote, "Thus often are the most distant Indies searched with the greatest cost and peril, for the finest

---

52. As part of this argument, Defoe called claims that the calicoes were made in British colonies in India a "wretched Piece of Trade-Nonsense," since the Company only had factories and not colonies; see [Defoe], *Just Complaint of the Poor Weavers,* 17–19, 24, 35 ("Not"). On linen, see also [Defoe], *Female Manufacturers Complaint,* 17.

Sattins, Silks or at least Chences [Chintzes] and Callicoes to fit up thousands of Women, who really are not worthy to be advanced one Ace above the Dunghill." And yet, without a major woolen or silk interest threatened by these imports, colonial consumption of Indian fabrics continually increased both in real terms and as a relative share of all fabrics. Although many colonists knew something of the English calico debates and the more general charges against luxury from the press and the pulpit, most simply did not demand that they be included in the prohibition, and it is difficult to imagine why they would have.[53]

In mid-1720, the House of Lords requested that the Board of Trade follow up on its investigations and "prepare a Scheme" to prevent "the Wearing and Using of Callicoes" while "better enabling" the East India Company to "carry on a Trade so beneficial to the Kingdom." This scheme would become the basis for substantial regulatory reforms involving both the India trade and the Atlantic colonies. The directors proposed to the Board a suite of benefits to strengthen the regulation and enforcement of the Company's monopoly as well as London's position as the hub for private merchants to reexport the Company's goods. The directors asked for a small extension of the monopoly to the west of the Cape of Good Hope so that colonial and other ships could not pick up India goods from the Dutch settlements in southern Africa and for a disallowance on India goods going to America without passing through the Company's London sales. They also requested improvements in the rate and payment periods of duties, new laws against interlopers, and the right to "bear up" against the Dutch at Bantam. In a face-to-face meeting, the Board affirmed most of the ideas presented by the directors, except for the ending of the calico prohibition. The meeting also produced other potential concessions, such as the prompt payment of back interest owed to the Company by the gov-

53. Philopatria [Thomas Paine], *A Discourse, Shewing, That the Real First Cause of the Straits and Difficulties of This Province of the Massachusetts Bay, Is It's Extravagancy, and Not Paper Money* . . . (Boston, 1721), 4–6. See also *Boston Gazette,* May 2–9, 1720. Perry Miller has described more general concerns about materialism and economic growth in New England; see Miller, "Declension in a Bible Commonwealth," in Miller, *Nature's Nation* (Cambridge, Mass., 1967), 14–49, esp. 27, 29–49. For more on fabric consumption in the colonies, see Robert S. DuPlessis, "Cottons Consumption in the Seventeenth- and Eighteenth-Century North Atlantic," in Giorgio Riello and Prasannan Parthasarathi, eds., *The Spinning World: A Global History of Cotton Textiles, 1200–1850* (Oxford, 2009), 227–246, esp. 229–231; Susan Prendergast Schoelwer, "Form, Function, and Meaning in the Use of Fabric Furnishings: A Philadelphia Case Study, 1700–1775," *Winterthur Portfolio,* XIV (1979), 25–40; Adrienne D. Hood, *The Weaver's Craft: Cloth, Commerce, and Industry in Early Pennsylvania* (Philadelphia, 2003).

ernment. The Board tendered the ideas to the commissioners of customs for further comment and obtained agreement from the secretary to the Treasury. In late January 1721, the Board and the directors settled on fifteen points. Nearly half of the points were specifically intended to defend the Company against interlopers and smugglers and to otherwise enhance its monopoly, through London, in supplying the merchants who shipped to colonial markets around the Atlantic.[54]

On January 24, the House of Commons reviewed a slew of petitions from the weaving interests complaining about calicoes and formed a committee to introduce a bill for the weavers' relief. The Commons already had in hand a report from the Board on the need to improve the prohibition to aid the weavers. The Commons also requested that the Board present the "Scheme" that it had prepared, referring to the plan prepared in response to the request to the Board from the Lords. A few days later, the Norwich Whig Waller Bacon presented the bill that would become the second Calico Act. The directors responded to the Commons with their standard complaint that the Company would be "greatly damaged" by the enhanced prohibition, without gain to the woolen interests.[55]

At this point, hopes for colonial cotton manufactured in Britain were not dead, and a petition arrived from Weymouth, Dorset, representing the "Merchants, Masters of Ships, Master Workmen, Weavers and Spinners of Cotton Wool imported from the *British* Plantations." The petitioners explained that hundreds of people worked raw cotton from the colonies into fabric, "which have been usually printed, or dyed blue." They urged the Commons to encourage this production, not discourage it. In response, Parliament exempted blue calicoes from the bill. London's merchants trading to the colonies further asked Parliament whether "a Clause, or Clauses, may be added to the said Bill, that all Cloth and Stuffs mixed with or made of Cotton Wool, imported from the *British* Plantations in

---

54. *Weekly Journal, Or, Saturday's-Post* (London), May 7, 1720, 448 ("prepare"); *Journals of the House of Commons*, Mar. 4, 1720/1, XIX, 465; Directors to the Board of Trade, Sept. 15, 1720, CO 388/22, fols. 137–140, NA; "Account of Ships (according to the Advices Which the East India Company Have Rec'd) Sent out to the East Indies under Foreign Commissions—with English and Irish Officers, Supra Cargo's, and Mariners," Nov. 15, 1720, CO 388/22, fol. 285, NA; "Copy of a Report of the Commissioners of Customs," Jan. 20, 1720/1, CO 388/23, fols. 29r–32v, NA; Great Britain, Board of Trade, *Journal of the Commissioners for Trade and Plantations, from November 1718 to December 1722, Preserved in the Public Record Office* (London, 1925), Sept. 20, Oct. 13, Nov 16, 17, 1720, Jan. 6–10, 26, 30, 31, 1720/1, 212, 216, 230–231, 240–241, 245–247.

55. *Journals of the House of Commons*, Jan. 24, 31, Feb. 1, 3, 1720/1, XIX, 408, 414–416.

America, and manufactured in *Great Britain, may be printed, painted, stained, dyed, and wore, as usual."* The Manchester cotton manufacturers and dealers in cotton wool made the same request, noting that "it will effectually answer the Intent of the Bill, by employing great Numbers of His Majesty's Subjects; will greatly increase His Majesty's Revenue, be a very great Improvement to the said Plantations, and an Advancement to Trade and Navigation in general." Parliament refused these requests to dramatically broaden the exemption for all fabrics made from colonial cotton, though it continued to allow much less desirable fustians manufactured in Britain that were only partly cotton. The bill banned both Indian and British-made or printed calicoes in Britain and also included clear penalties for wearers. It also continued to exempt consumption in the American colonies, now with the Board's blessing.[56]

While the Lords considered the calico bill, the Commons heard from the Board's scheme, in its possession since February 1: "As the Prohibition . . . will be a great Restraint upon the *East India* Trade, it might be reasonable, that some Advantages should be allowed to the *East India* Company." These new "Privileges" would require companion legislation to the calico bill. The Commons did not accede to everything in the scheme, such as the plan to shift the charter line to the west and permission for the Company to trade in slaves from Madagascar to the Atlantic plantations. Nevertheless, the Commons largely used the Board's recommendations to prepare An Act for the Further Preventing His Majesty's Subjects from Trading to the *East-Indies* under Foreign Commissions; and for Encouraging and Further Securing the Lawful Trade Thereto. This legislation would extend and equalize the time for drawbacks to three years, reinforce the illegality of transshipping (delivering to ports outside England goods taken at sea from "homeward bound" India ships), and end the issuance of certificates allowing tea to be imported from Ostend. These were modest adjustments and attempts to correct past mistakes. More striking, the Commons agreed to "prohibit the Importation of all *East India* Goods into any of the *British* Colonies in *America,* except such as shall be carried thither directly from *Great Britain.*" Stiff penalties and laws of forfeiture would be applied, with "proper Encouragement" for catching cheaters. The second Calico Act and the act to secure the Company's trade both soon passed.[57]

56. Ibid., Feb. 8, 17, 1720/1, XIX, 418 ("Merchants"), 423; *Journals of the House of Lords,* Feb. 25, 27, Mar. 8, 1720/1, June 16, 1721, XXI, 448, 450, 463, 544.

57. *Journals of the House of Commons,* Mar. 4, 1720/1, XIX, 465–466, 492; Board of Trade to the Earl of Stanhope, Feb. 1, 1720/1, CO 389/28, 17–22, NA. The Commons also con-

The old loophole allowing the colonists to import India goods from Europe, which had survived for decades, was now closed. The directors feared that the expanded prohibition would not be offset by this full and more rigorously protected monopoly over the supply of India goods. The Board of Trade was more sanguine. It noted that its two-pronged plan of prohibition in Britain and enhancements to the Company's monopoly over the supply to the Atlantic colonies would stop the "Evil" caused to domestic weavers while "securing to the said Company their carrying on successfully a Trade so beneficial to this Kingdom." The Company's ships soon seized the British merchant vessel *Postillion,* returned to the Atlantic laden with enslaved people and goods from Madagascar. A Royal Navy vessel in Virginia seized the *Eugene,* also returning from Madagascar, having sold goods to pirates and brought back a similar cargo. The *American Weekly Mercury* reported that the captain was taken to England and tried, "not for any Dealings with the Pyrates, but for having on Board East India Goods." This shift in charge reflected the government's new-found interest in backing the Company's monopoly over the British Atlantic supply of India goods. The warning to future interlopers was clear.[58]

In the preamble to the second Calico Act, Parliament followed the lead of the woolen and English silk interests and no longer focused on the East India trade or a debilitating drain of bullion. Instead, Parliament attacked consumers for "wearing and using . . . Callicoes in Apparel, Houshold

----

sidered the report from the Commissioners of Customs, which had little to say on the points targeted at the trade to the Atlantic colonies; see ibid., Mar. 10, 1720/1, XIX, 473–475. For the texts of the acts, see [Ruffhead, ed.], *Statutes at Large,* V, 229–231, 238–239. Virginia Bever Platt discussed the Company's (Board supported) desire to trade in enslaved people from Madagascar at length. It was, nevertheless, a minor issue in the negotiations compared to goods from Asia. Parliament did not act in a momentary pique against the Company, as Platt claimed. Parliament was in fact reinforcing the Company monopoly at many points. Her supposition that a future Parliament might have allowed trade in calicoes to the colonies, if a trade to the Atlantic in enslaved Madagascar people had been permitted at this juncture, also runs up against the reality that Parliament routed the India trade through the monopoly and London to better restrict, regulate, duty, and profit from it. See Platt, "The East India Company and the Madagascar Slave Trade," *WMQ,* 3d Ser., XXVI (1969), 548–577.

58. Board of Trade to the Earl of Stanhope, Feb. 1, 1720/1, CO 389/28, 17, NA; "Philadelphia, August 3," *American Weekly Mercury* (Philadelphia), July 27–Aug. 3, 1721 ("not"). For more on the *Postillion* and *Eugene,* see Platt, "East India Company and the Madagascar Slave Trade," *WMQ,* 3d Ser., XXVI (1969), 566–575. It should be noted that the *Eugene* was breaking multiple statutes, including the Company's monopoly rights. For the Company's efforts against Ostenders in India and China at this time, see Directors to President and Council of Fort St. George, Feb. 24, 1721, IOR/E/3/100, 503–507/fols. 253–255, BL.

Stuff, [and] Furniture" and for putting weavers out of work. By framing women's freedom of consumer choice in opposition to both men's freedom to rule and the country's social and economic well-being, the defenders of the woolen and English silk industries suggested that a stronger domestic prohibition was in the interests of all British, especially English, men. Such arguments for exercising authority dovetailed neatly with metropolitan concerns over controlling Atlantic colonial trade, cultivation, and consumption. The Scots, now part of a united Britain, would be subjected to the prohibitions of the second Calico Act and Company monopoly and would remain free to produce and sell their linens. The colonists, now more clearly different, would not be subject to the second Calico Act and would remain unable to broadly export their manufactured woolens. The Board and Parliament alike had privileged the woolen and English silk interests over those of colonial producers and the East India Company. In elevating the political and moral stakes of consumption and trying to widen the many divisions among the different peoples within and outside the empire, the woolen and English silk interests played into the notion that cultivators, producers, and consumers in the Atlantic colonies differed in valuable ways from those in Britain. Colonists were to consume Indian cottons, but only in very circumscribed limits were they to be encouraged to supply the production of very specific imitations in Britain.[59]

THE POPULARIZATION OF THE NOTION that the Atlantic colonists should and did consume large quantities of India goods reexported from London was an important part of an imperial compromise involving the Atlantic colonists, Indian producers, the East India Company, and British spinners, weavers, landowners, and consumers. That compromise, moreover, built new legal structures and reinforced old ones that together changed the colonists' place in the empire. More than fifty years before the famous Tea Act, Parliament had decided that American consumers would support the East India Company in the interests of the metropole. The government, Company, and others in the public hoped that a monopolization of the supply of East India goods imported into America and the West Indies would create wealth in London. The Company supplied white and printed cottons, domestic printers employed the poor, and the Atlantic colonies provided markets. By funneling everything through London, the state could harness, control, and benefit from the complex calico trade.

59. [Ruffhead, ed.], *Statutes at Large*, IV, 44, V, 229 (quotation).

Newspapers celebrated the increase of reexports even before the second Calico Act officially took effect, but confusion remained over which markets would most support the East India Company. *Applebee's Original Weekly Journal* printed statistics showing that 207,035 pieces of calico had been exported to foreign places, excluding the colonies, during just four days in April 1721. The report noted that "the Account might otherwise seem incredible," but the customs data proved the "good Effect of the late Callico Act." A few months later, the *Weekly Journal: or, British Gazetteer* reported considerable exports of calicoes "for the West-Indies, Germany, Holland, New-England, New-York, Jamaica, and other Countries." Not only did the West Indies come first in the list, four of the six listed markets were colonial, giving readers the impression that the colonies absorbed large quantities of calicoes. In reality, the American and West Indian markets consumed at high rates per capita, but they were still smaller than Europe, and too small to offset the domestic British market that the Company and the calico printers lost to prohibition. Yet the potential of a monopoly over growing colonial markets seemed to brighten the prospects of the East India Company and the calico printers. This complex trading structure made the distant and threatening calico producers in India a benefit to the state, while giving colonial consumers the very fashions that Londoners had taught them to desire but that Londoners could no longer legally own.[60]

The acts, regulations, and enforcement efforts surrounding calico increasingly differentiated and structured people in Britain, India, and the Atlantic colonies as producers and consumers and as different types of producers and consumers subject to different moral and economic arguments. The Calico Acts and the regulatory and enforcement efforts against pirates and interlopers also increasingly subjected British and smaller numbers of non-British people to British laws in the Atlantic and Indian Oceans alike. The government's approach to the calico problem initially might have been inspired by the ideals expressed in the Navigation Acts, but positioning Atlantic colonists more as consumers of goods manufactured in India and banned in Britain than as cultivators of India's raw cotton for British production suggested something rather different. Unlike people in Britain, Atlantic colonists were to enjoy supposedly dangerous Indian luxuries without trading to India, without gaining the labor value

60. *Applebee's Original Weekly Journal* (London), May 6, 1721, 2050 (a Tory paper) (see also Mar. 11, 1721, 2003); *Weekly Journal: or, British Gazetteer*, Sept. 16, 1721, 2031 (a Whig paper).

An Imperial Compromise

added through manufacturing, and without cultivating Indian cotton for Britain. Atlantic colonists were to be the ultimate imperial consumers.[61]

In accepting the Calico Acts and the East India Company monopoly in the early eighteenth century, colonists accepted the making of an imperial compromise that rendered them outlets for goods seen as immoral by many in Britain and that structurally subordinated their economic interests as cultivators, producers, and merchants to the interests of the Company and its Indian producers. On the surface, the compromise gave every contingent something of what they wanted—including the colonists, who kept the right to buy Indian calicoes, though only because of the Company. During the next several decades, however, trade and conflict with the colonies would both nest in this arrangement that tied together differing conceptions of the morality of consumer choice, the apparent colonial right to consumer freedom, and the legal structures that limited the benefits of colonial cotton cultivation while requiring Asian goods to come via Britain and to support a powerful British company.

61. The argument here for the development of regulations in response to pressure from English interest groups and colonial behavior adds to Alison Gilbert Olson's contention that the imperial government at this time became more "more responsive" and "more assertive"; see Olson, *Making the Empire Work: London and American Interest Groups, 1690–1790* (Cambridge, Mass., 1992), 61.

3 Enforcement, Aesthetics, and Revenue

Barbados's new governor, Henry Worsley, arrived shortly after the British government issued a lengthy set of instructions to all colonial governors on the regulation of the India trade in the Atlantic Ocean. The Order in Council for these instructions, published in 1721, noted specifically that a ship from Ostend brought from the East Indies to Barbados a full cargo of India goods. Several ships from Britain and the British Atlantic colonies, it explained, had also pretended to sail to Guinea to purchase enslaved people, but instead they went to Madagascar to trade weapons and supplies to pirates in exchange for cheap India goods. They then sold the goods "at good Prices" in the British West Indies. All of these actions, the order explained, were illegal. The lengthy and detailed instructions that followed in 1722 emphasized that the enforcement of the East India Company's monopoly of the Atlantic colonies, through London, contributed to the well-being of the empire. Similar instructions had not been given after the first Calico Act. Now the government was united in supporting the colonial consumption of the East India Company's goods. The instructions commanded the governors to arrest the captains and crews of ships trading from Madagascar or elsewhere beyond the Cape of Good Hope "directly to Our Plantations in America, to the great Detriment of these Realms, and in Breach of the Several Laws in Force." The cargo, crew, and documents of every ship with India goods on board were to be examined to verify that the goods came only via Britain. Ships carrying India goods that had not passed through Britain as required by law must be turned away without breaking bulk, even if they appeared to "be in distress, Want, Disability, Danger of Sinking or for upon any other Reasons or Pretence whatsoever." Governors and officers found negligent in "an affair of so great Importance to Our Service and the Welfare of Our Subjects" would be removed from office, penalized, and required to forfeit their bond.[1]

1. Order in Council, Oct. 2, 1721, CO 5/1266, fols. 233–234, NA; "Draft of H.M. Additional Instructions to Governors of Plantations, Directing the Strict Observance of the Acts of Trade and Navigation, Particularly in Relation to the East Indian Trade," May 1, 1722, CO

Worsley had surely seen these instructions, and he quickly wrote to the Board of Trade claiming to have seized more smuggling vessels than had been taken in several years. He explained that he enlisted a sloop to hunt smugglers through the night in secluded creeks and bays. He requested another "sloop of ten, or twelve guns with twenty men allowed of, and to be solely under this Government's orders, to visit all ships or vessels that come upon this coast." The French, he wrote, used just such a vessel at Martinique. In particular, Worsley related to the Board "one of the unlawful branches of the trade" wherein British ships loaded "Indian commoditys, and forbidden European goods" in Holland and Ostend before clearing out from English ports and arriving in Barbados. Worsley explained, "'Tis very difficult to learn the truth from people whose interest it is to conceal it"—a problem faced by eighteenth-century officials and present-day historians alike. Certainly many smugglers successfully evaded British regulations from India to America and at countless points in between. Smugglers rarely left good records of their successes, and we know mostly about their failures. Nevertheless, arguing from silences is not necessary to determine whether smugglers were the main source of India goods and whether those goods came directly from the Indian Ocean. The records of colonial courts and particularly of private merchants in Britain and the Atlantic colonies reveal the establishment and continuance of a dominant legal trade.[2]

324/10, 443–453, NA (quotations on 444, 447, 449); "H.M. Additional Instruction to Governors of the Plantations," June 1, 1722, CO 324/34, 136–144, NA. The Order in Council followed a petition from the Company asking the king to "prevent the mischief that threatens the Generall Trade of this Kingdom by the Ostenders visiting the British Ports in America, And clandestinely running in Goods to England"; see Court of Directors, Minutes, June 7, 21, Oct. 6, 1721, IOR/B/56, 379 (quotation), 389, 479, BL.

2. Worsley was also deeply concerned about a smuggling trade between the "Northern" English colonies and Martinique. See Henry Worsley to the Council of Trade and Plantations, Mar. 26, 1723, CO 28/17, fols. 297–298, NA. Historians have long debated the extent of smuggling and its economic importance in the British Atlantic. As Christian J. Koot explains, the weight of evidence suggests that the smuggling of sugars and enslaved people was not particularly common. The extent of smuggling in other goods is much less clear. Koot argues it was significant, with various peaks, but that generally it was in decline in the seventeenth through early eighteenth century. See Koot, *Empire at the Periphery: British Colonists, Anglo-Dutch Trade, and the Development of the British Atlantic, 1621–1713* (New York, 2011), esp. 3–7, 13, 120, 185, 225. Throughout this debate, little consideration has been paid to the question of India goods in America, although Chinese tea has garnered some attention in light of the tea crisis preceding the American Revolution. Lawrence A. Harper warned about the dangers of using sensational stories of smuggling as a measuring stick; see Harper, *The English Navigation Laws: A Seventeenth-Century Experiment in Social Engineering* (New

The problems of controlling trade, production, and consumption were broadly imperial problems stemming from the desire to maximize economic growth and revenue through the relationship between the Indian and Atlantic Oceans. When it came to Atlantic colonists' trading with Asia, the British government did not practice salutary neglect. The government actively regulated, enforced, and to some extent encouraged colonial consumption of India goods. Parliament intended the Company monopoly, the Navigation Acts, the Calico Acts, and the Act for the Further Preventing His Majesty's Subjects from Trading to the East-Indies to direct the India trade. The Company in London was to act as the coachman, yoking together across two oceans individual producers, merchants, consumers, and investors to pull forward the interests of the British state. The calico compromise thereby exacerbated the need for active enforcement and increased the importance of protecting the East India Company's monopoly on reexports to markets in Europe and throughout the Atlantic world. Imperial leaders needed to enforce British laws over Britons and, indeed, other people not only within Britain but outside it as well—whether in America, Africa, or India. Such enforcement was difficult.[3]

The best way to outdo smugglers was to instead outtrade them by obtaining better goods at better prices. This strategy, however, required the Company to tightly control its supply and its Indian producers. Success in controlling supply, prices, quality, and styles also created the potential to further bind the Atlantic colonies to Britain. Done effectively, colonists would gain unequaled access to a broadly imperial consumer aesthetic that made a range of beautiful goods, from japanned furniture, to spices, to printed calico, quickly recognizable as Indian and as provided by London at the center of the India trade. Yet, even if the problems of smuggling, production, supply, and fashion could be solved, questions remained over

---

York, 1939), 263–271. More recently, Thomas M. Truxes has argued that smuggling exploded during the Seven Years' War; see Truxes, *Defying Empire: Trading with the Enemy in Colonial New York* (New Haven, Conn., 2008). From the 1720s through the 1750s, smuggling was not the primary means through which colonists obtained India goods, although tea smuggling increased substantially in the decade or two before the American Revolution.

3. Salutary neglect may better describe other aspects of British government in the Atlantic colonies. The classic statement of salutary neglect remains James A. Henretta, *"Salutary Neglect": Colonial Administration under the Duke of Newcastle* (Princeton, N.J., 1972). For invocations of salutary neglect in a volume dealing with a broader imperial frame, see Stephen J. Hornsby, "Geographies of the British Atlantic World," 38, and Ken MacMillan, "Imperial Constitutions: Sovereignty and Law in the British Atlantic," 84, both in H. V. Bowen, Elizabeth Mancke, and John G. Reid, eds., *Britain's Oceanic Empire: Atlantic and Indian Ocean Worlds, c. 1550–1850* (Cambridge, 2012).

Enforcement, Aesthetics, and Revenue

how to turn successful regulation of the India trade, a recognizable imperial aesthetic, and colonial consumption of imperial goods into revenue for the state.

Enforcing the India Trade in the Atlantic Colonies

Smuggling to avoid the East India Company's monopoly, Navigation Acts, and general customs charges was nothing new, but the Calico Acts and the Company's more complete British Atlantic monopoly changed the stakes. Many imperial officials believed, at least implicitly, in the importance of the East India Company's monopoly to generate profits, economic activity, and state revenue. The effectiveness of the Company's monopoly over the British Atlantic, however, required solutions to the challenges of regulatory enforcement. These challenges included sneaky merchants, complicated and misunderstood laws, duplicitous customs officials, foreign competitors, and eager consumers. After the instructions were sent out to the governors in 1722, policing the regulations became not only more important but also in many ways more contested. A series of court cases throughout the Atlantic colonies from the mid-1720s through the 1730s indicate the importance that a wide variety of people placed on contesting the regulations and many imperial officials placed on enforcing them.

The 1724 case of the ship *Fame,* charged with smuggling Indian and European goods in Philadelphia, stimulated a struggle that continued back and forth across the Atlantic for years over where the case should be tried, how the trials might be fair, who had ultimate authority, and who should get the spoils. The *Fame* departed Holland for Philadelphia ostensibly carrying Palatine families who wanted to settle in Pennsylvania. The ship carried "divers quantitys of East India Goods," including one thousand gallons of arrack and two hundredweight (224 lbs.) of tea as well as some European liquor and cheeses. When the *Fame* arrived in Philadelphia in late October, John Moore, the local customs collector, claimed to have seized it "in obedience to His Majesties Royal Instructions, 1st June, 1722." After Moore seized the vessel, however, "60 or 70 persons in disguise forcibly entered on board the ship cut her away from the wharf and towed her about five miles below the town, where they immediately landed the greater part of the prohibited goods." Moore wrote to Governor William Keith requesting his assistance. At sunrise, Keith rode his horse thirty miles; he then "procured a boat, and came up the River in quest of the Ship Fame." Finally, he boarded the ship at nine o'clock that evening. Keith recounted that Moore told him it was unsafe to seize the *Fame* until a man-of-war could come down from New York. Keith disagreed with Moore, but, like Moore, he referred to the government's 1722 instructions to back up his seizure of the vessel and its subsequent condemnation in the Court of Common Pleas.[4]

The stage was set for a contest over jurisdiction initially involving Keith, Moore, and the Pennsylvania General Assembly. Moore believed that Keith was protecting the smugglers and that the Court of Common Pleas would not offer a suitable venue for a case brought in the name of the king. With the backing of the crown's lawyers, Moore took the case of the *Fame* to the Supreme Court, which also condemned the vessel. Additionally, Moore charged several people with running the goods ashore in the night. The accused smugglers then petitioned the Pennsylvania General Assembly, arguing that the Supreme Court did not have jurisdiction. The assemblymen agreed and passed a new law barring the Supreme Court from being the first court for civil cases, including cases brought by His Majesty's Customs. They also took all Exchequer cases from the Supreme Court's jurisdiction, moving them to the lower courts. Moore pressed for an exemption for customs cases, an exemption that the new governor, Patrick Gordon, who had replaced Keith in 1726, presented to the assembly. Gordon explained, however, that he agreed with the assembly's original bill, especially given "the great uneasiness" the affair had caused in the colony. He signed the bill into law, and the principal smuggler escaped the charges.[5]

4. John Moore to William Keith, Oct. 31, 1724, CO 5/1266, fol. 169, NA; Richard Fitzwilliam to the Board of Trade, Dec. 26, 1727, CO 5/1267, fol. 3, NA; "The Memorial of John Moore Esq. Collector of His Majestie's *[sic]* Customs for the Port of Philadelphia in Answer to the Petition of John Cathcart and William Lea Lately Presented to the Honble Sir William Keith Bart Govr of Pensilvania," n.d., CO 5/1266, fol. 170r, NA. Keith did not mention the letter from Moore requesting assistance. See William Keith to the Board of Trade, Nov. 25, 1724, CO 5/1266, fol. 162r, NA; Keith's account to the Pennsylvania Council, Nov. 12, 1724, signed Patrick Brand, CO 5/1266, fols. 166–168, NA; Court of Common Pleas, Philadelphia, Nov. 19, 1724, CO 5/1266, fol. 163v, NA. For Keith's reference to the instructions from 1722, see Keith to Moore, 1724, CO 5/1266, fol. 171, NA.

5. For Moore's refusal to try in the Court of Common Pleas, see "The Answer of John Moore Esq. Collector of His Majesties Customs for the Port of Philadelphia to a Certain Instrument or [?] Directed to Him by Sir William Keith Baronet Governor of Pensilvania etc.," Nov. 17, 1724, CO 5/1266, fol. 172, NA. On the assembly's new law, see Winfred Trexler Root, *The Relations of Pennsylvania with the British Government, 1696–1765* (New York, 1912), 169–170. Moore and Fitzwilliam believed the law to be specifically "ex post facto" and that it cost the case against the main smuggler, "one Lawrence"; see Fitzwilliam to the Board of Trade, Dec. 26, 1727, CO 5/1267, fols. 3v–4r, NA. For a copy of the act as passed, see CO 5/1267, fols. 6v–14v, NA. On Moore's desire for an exemption and the responses, see "A Clause

Gordon, nevertheless, soon became involved with Moore in disputes with the Vice Admiralty Court over more such smuggling cases. In January 1727, Moore used Pennsylvania's Vice Admiralty Court to condemn one hundred India "Cherry Derries" (fabric made from a combination of cotton and silk in Bengal), forty pieces of calico, two pieces of muslin, ten casks of pepper, and a variety of European goods. Judge Joseph Brown awarded Moore, Governor Gordon, and the king each one-third of the spoils after the judge took his share. But Gordon and Brown disagreed sharply over Brown's proper share, and Gordon ordered the execution of the decision to be stopped. Soon, Moore, who in the *Fame* case had wanted to use the higher courts, charged that Brown was incompetent. In July, the power struggle escalated over the case of the schooner *Sarah*, with Moore and Gordon again aligned against Brown. The *Sarah* case landed in front of the Court of Common Pleas, the same court Moore had earlier disparaged in the *Fame* case. The accused smugglers were acquitted. These jurisdictional, judgment, and personal disputes were enabling smugglers.[6]

Moore and Richard Fitzwilliam, the surveyor of customs, especially needed clear jurisdictional rules to successfully perform their duties, and they decided to pursue the matter of the *Fame* with the Board of Trade in London. Keith had already defended his actions to the Board, claiming, "It would seem as if he [Moore] intended the Fame should have escaped a legal condemnation in order to cast the blame upon me and maliciously to asperse my character." Keith attacked Moore's "notorious Neglect and Connivance in the Affair" and his "indecent behaviour." Fitzwilliam coun-

---

Proposed to be Inserted in the Bill of Courts, Delivered to the Gov. Of Pensilvania by the Collector of Philadelphia," CO 5/1267, fol. 16, NA; Fitzwilliam to Patrick Gordon, Aug. 25, 1727, CO 5/1267, fol. 17, NA; Robert Charles, Extract of Minutes at the Pennsylvania Council, Aug. 18, 1727, CO 5/1267, fol. 132, NA; Gordon to Fitzwilliam, Aug. 25, 1727, CO 5/1267, fols. 17v–18, NA. Imperial officials had found since the seventeenth century that colonists could not be relied upon for support in smuggling cases, and, indeed, colonists often impeded the arrest and conviction of smugglers. The debate over the appropriate courts for smuggling trials had gone on for decades, with particular tension between London and the Pennsylvania General Assembly. For more, see Matthew P. Harrington, "The Legacy of the Colonial Vice-Admiralty Courts (Part I)," *Journal of Maritime Law and Commerce*, XXVI (1995), 589–600. Moore was also following precedent. In 1685, the governor of Saint Christopher, Sir Nathaniel Johnson, gained conviction of one group of smugglers by moving the case from a civil court to an Admiralty court. See Koot, *Empire at the Periphery*, 124–125.

6. John Moore's exhibit to the Philadelphia Court of Vice Admiralty, Feb. 2, 1726/7, CO 5/1267, fols. 146–148, NA; Gordon to ?, July 7, 1727, CO 5/1267, fol. 153v, NA; H. Penrice to the Lords Commissioners of the Admiralty, June 10, 1730, CO 5/1267, fols. 138r–140r, NA. For the definition of "Cherry Derries," see K. N. Chaudhuri, *The Trading World of Asia and the English East India Company, 1660–1760* (Cambridge, 1978), 503.

tered that the lower courts could not be trusted to bring convictions against evaders of the trading regulations, so Moore had correctly placed the trials in the Supreme Court. He reasoned that, "as the judges of those Courts [the lower courts] are men but of mean circumstances, and of as mean capacities, so are the jurys more apt to be biassed in favour of those who transgress the Law." "The common people," Fitzwilliam claimed, believed that "those who bring goods from forreign parts can afford them better pennyworths than others who import the like commodities from Great Britain where the dutys and customs are high." Moore and Fitzwilliam believed that Governor Keith was in cahoots with the colonists and had "pretended" to seize the vessel, which he sold off for only six hundred pounds. Colonial proprietor Springett Penn, through his agent, explained to the Board in detail that the colonists had the right to pass laws to establish local courts as they saw fit and that Gordon, the king's own chosen representative, had signed the act putting smuggling cases in the Court of Common Pleas.[7]

Fitzwilliam, with the support of the Board's legal adviser in London, nevertheless succeeded in persuading the Board and the Privy Council to repeal the Pennsylvania law. It had taken six years. The message was finally clear: local juries could not be trusted to act against their own self-interest in supporting smugglers who brought highly desirable goods, particularly those from Asia, for low prices. The range of people involved— from local customs officials, to smugglers, assemblymen, governors, the Board of Trade, the Board's legal adviser, and the Penn family—shows that undermining the regulations, or controlling the trade by enforcing the regulations, seemed vital to the interests of individuals and the state alike.[8]

In Jamaica, meanwhile, Governor Henry Bentinck (the duke of Portland) and the customs officials responded to the British government's 1722 instructions by seizing the ship *Chandos*, a case that raised questions

7. Fitzwilliam to the Board of Trade, Dec. 26, 1727, CO 5/1267, fol. 4, NA. Keith was a popular governor among Pennsylvanians, indicated in part by his election to the colonial assembly after he was replaced as governor in 1726. This popularity and the low value of the condemnation together suggest that he might have been colluding with the smugglers, but it is difficult to know. For Keith's censure of Moore, see Keith to Moore, Nov. 18, 1724, CO 5/1266, fol. 172v, NA. Penn's agent, Ferdinand John Paris, claimed that the law was not retroactive, but that, in any case, the Supreme Court never had a right to try Moore's cases; see Ferdinand John Paris to the Board of Trade, May 12, 1730, CO 5/1267, fols. 123–130v, NA; Francis Fane to the Board of Trade, Nov. 3, 1730, CO 5/1268, fols. 8–11v, NA.

8. For more on the decision to veto the law in London, see Root, *Relations*, 171–173.

about who in the empire knew about which laws. The *Chandos*'s master, John Kerfoot, had purchased four hundred gallons of arrack and two pieces of silk in Barbados from a Royal Navy fourth-rate ship of the line, the *Salisbury*. The *Salisbury* had just returned from the Indian Ocean, and by bringing India goods back to the Atlantic it illegally broke the East India Company's monopoly. It should have been arresting smugglers, not participating in smuggling. The openness of Kerfoot's dealings in Jamaica certainly suggests that he little feared the customs officials. Kerfoot apparently paid a duty of one hundred pounds and entered the arrack in the customs books. He also offered tastings of his arrack to interested merchants on the ship and in the town. Kerfoot's actions could have been based on the officials' previous failure to enforce the laws or on a reasonable belief that, since he purchased the goods from a Royal Navy vessel, the deal was either legal or legal enough to cause no problem in Jamaica. Either way, there was considerable uncertainty not only among merchants but within the Royal Navy about which trades were now legal or accepted.[9]

As in Pennsylvania, the case also raised questions over which courts had the proper jurisdiction over which laws, questions that underscored the differences among the older Navigation Acts and the more recent laws demanding colonial conformity to the East India Company's monopoly. A separate but simultaneous trial for breaking the Navigation Acts created "so much Noise, Clamour and even threats" from the local people that the regular operation of the Vice Admiralty Court proved difficult and unsafe. The governor decided to move both trials to Saint Jago Dela Vega so that they could be near him and his authority. The prosecution brought motion against Kerfoot on the basis of three primary acts. The first two acts were older Navigation Acts from the seventeenth century. The third act was the Act for the Further Preventing His Majesty's Subjects from Trading to the East-Indies passed in 1721, shortly after the Calico Act, to enhance the Company's monopoly over the Atlantic colonies via London. The prosecutor explained, "By virtue of severall Acts of Parliament

9. The *Chandos* was a sizable four-hundred-ton vessel partly owned by the duke of Chandos. It primarily brought enslaved people from Africa and participated in the intercolonial slave trade. Motion against the Ship *Chandos*, Vice Admiralty Court, Saint Jago Dela Vega, Jamaica, Mar. 26, 1724, CO 137/15, fol. 96, NA. On the ownership of the *Chandos* and its size, see Richard Lockwood to John Stewart and Jonathan Perrie, June 25, 1725, CO 137/15, fols. 150r, NA. For the *Salisbury* and tastings, see Deposition of Second Mate George Stewart, May 2, 1724, CO 137/15, fols. 166r–169r(a), NA. For the duty paid, see Deposition of William Strother, May 2, 1724, CO 137/15, fols. 171r–174r. For the tastings, see the Deposition of William Townsend, May 2, 1724, CO 137/15, fol. 180, NA.

and Ltres Pattents the whole trade to and from the East Indies and other places beyond the Cape of Good Hope . . . is now solely vested in the united Company of Merchants of England trading to the East Indies." The defense countered that the Admiralty Court had no jurisdiction over the 1721 act. The judge seemed to concur: "He was in some doubt whether the Court of Admiralty was within the words and meaning of that Statute. The words seeming to Common Law Terms therefore in his judgement the Prosecutions against the Ship Chandos on that Statute had been more Regularly brought in a Court of Common Law." But he ruled that, since he had clear jurisdiction over the other two acts, he could readily rule on all three. Indeed, such a judgment was important for a conviction, since the vessel was more clearly in contravention of the latter than the former acts. It also almost certainly reflected the government's intent to protect the East India Company's monopoly, even if it needed to be protected from Britain's own navy.[10]

In the preceding cases, smuggled goods passed through Europe or from one ship to another in the Atlantic Ocean, but the Board of Trade and Parliament had also been concerned with goods coming directly to the Atlantic colonies on Company vessels from the Indian Ocean, as in the test case of the *Princess Amelia* in Barbados in 1727. The *Princess Amelia* had come from the ports of Mocha (in Yemen), Bombay, and Tellicherry. After a routine stop in Saint Helena, a leak was discovered in the hold. In their depositions, the three ship's mates, the boatswain, and the carpenter claimed that, though "the said leak then was Six or Seven foot under water it was easy to perceive the day light through it and it was not safe . . . to proceed directly for England." The ship's officers claimed that enough cargo must be unloaded temporarily in Barbados to raise the leak above the waterline and effect the repair. The attorney general in Barbados, Jonathan Blenman, advised the collector of customs, Henry Lascelles, that the law clearly forbade the ship from stopping or unloading anything. Nevertheless, Blenman concluded that the spirit of the law surely did not intend a huge and valuable East India Company ship and cargo to sink for want of an easy repair. In arguing that the law did not apply in this case, Blenman was either unaware that Company ships contained so-called privilege goods traded on the officers' accounts that the officers had vested

10. Henry Bentinck, Duke of Portland, to the Council of Trade and Plantations, July 13, 1724, CO 137/15, fols. 1–3v, NA; Motion against the Ship *Chandos*, Mar. 26, 1724, CO 137/15, fol. 105, NA; Minutes, Vice Admiralty Court, Saint Jago Dela Vega, Jamaica, Apr. 28, 1724, CO 137/15, fols. 156–157, NA.

Enforcement, Aesthetics, and Revenue

interests in smuggling or he was involved in the affair himself. He recommended that the goods be unloaded in a secure environment for the repair to take place.[11]

Governor Worsley, however, had grounds to suspect that the *Princess Amelia's* officers sought to evade the empire's regulations on purpose, using the leaky-ship trick that the government's 1722 instructions had specifically warned against. Worsley feared that the officers of the *Princess Amelia* had exaggerated the danger of the leak in the hope of selling their privilege cargo without passing it through the customs officers and Company sales in London. Indeed, many of the ship's crew claimed the ship to be safe. Robert Jones said in his deposition "that he would with all his heart venture to England" in the ship without repair. Additionally, Worsley related that the captain claimed a cargo of "2,228 bales of coffee and 6 casks of aloes, tho' I am very well informed that there is a very considerable cargo besides." It appears that the captain did not reveal the contents of the large privilege trade on board, the same goods of which the attorney general seemed to be ignorant. Worsley conceded to the repair, but he tended to believe the reports that the leak did not pose a major risk to the ship. To protect against smuggling, he ordered customs officials to guard the cargo and offered a substantial reward of two hundred pounds for any information leading to the seizure of illicit goods. After the repair had been completed, Worsley reported with a noticeable lack of confidence, "If they came here to dispose of their Separate Cargo, I hope I have taken Effectual care to prevent them." Worsley should have sided with his own doubts. The Board of Trade censured him for allowing a ship from the East Indies to stop in the harbor and receive aid. The censure of Worsley illustrates that the government saw its regulations as rigid and necessary defenses against abuses in a trading system stretching from India to America with London as the pivot.[12]

11. Depositions of Phineas Frognall, Charles Windebank, Robert Thompson, John Lee, and William Potter, Apr. 8, 1727, CO 28/44, fols. 386v–387, NA; J[onathan] Blenman to Henry Lascelles, Apr. 15, 1727, CO 28/44, fols. 397–398, NA. On the ship's ports of call, see Anthony Farrington, *Catalogue of East India Company Ships' Journals and Logs, 1600–1834* (London, 1999), 527–528.

12. Deposition of Robert Jones, Apr. 13, 1727, CO 28/44, fol. 393, NA. A further thirteen sailors signed a letter to the governor attesting to the safety of the ship (n.d., fol. 403, NA). See also Worsley to the Board of Trade, Apr. 18, 1727, CO 28/18, fols. 356v, 357v, 359, NA; Worsley to the Duke of Newcastle, May 6, 1727, CO 28/44, fol. 404 ("If they came"), NA; Governor Lord Howe to the Council of Trade and Plantations, May 31, 1733, CO 28/23, fol. 102v, NA.

The government had made its point, though it might not have been exactly what the East India Company had in mind. The directors thanked Lascelles for pushing to allow the *Princess Amelia* to be repaired despite the governor's doubts. They sided firmly with their own supercargo from which they had received information that the ship would sink. The Company simply wanted its cargoes and profits protected. If a ship was sinking, the directors wanted the flexibility to save it. If the danger was being faked, however, they wanted the full force of the law to guard the Company from smugglers and foreign competitors alike. Nevertheless, when Worsley's successor, Emanuel Howe, second Viscount Howe, faced a similar decision in 1733, he cited the censure of Worsley as his reason for turning away "two large East-India Ships in the Greatest distress." One ship with a cargo valued by its captain at three hundred thousand pounds was supposedly "in danger of sinking even in the Bay." The ships would not follow Howe's orders until the fort fired "Several Shot at them." Howe had been told to "duly and strictly observe" similar instructions to those granted to Worsley, and he wrote back to his superiors, "Cou'd that Instruction be alter'd it woud not only be of service to the East India Company but even to the Nation in General for if these Ships do not get into some of the Islands to refitt it will be Impossible for 'em by all Accounts to reach England." The ships went a short distance to Pigeon Island, immediately off the coast of Saint Lucia, where substantial repairs to a serious leak were undertaken under the protection of HMS *Fox*. Some illegal trading might have taken place with the French at Saint Lucia, and, judging from the case of the *Chandos*, the *Fox* would not necessarily have intervened.[13]

In any case, goods being smuggled off of British East Indiamen in the British Atlantic colonies appears to have been rare, but the political importance of claims of other Europeans smuggling India goods into the British colonies continued into the 1730s. In 1731, for example, Jeremiah Dunbar, deputy surveyor of the woods in America, explained to the Board of Trade that there were more than one hundred Frenchmen at Boston importing rum, molasses, French silks, and East India goods in exchange for vessels built in New England. He noted that "the chief ware . . . among

13. Company Minutes, Directors, June 7, 1727, IOR/B/59, 269, BL, Oct. 25, 1727, IOR/B/59, 349; Governor Lord Howe to the Council of Trade and Plantations, May 31, 1733, CO 28/23, fols. 101v–102v (quotations), NA. For the instructions, see Instructions to Lord Howe from the Board of Trade, Nov. 29, 1732, CO 29/15, 403–409, NA. The two ships were the *Aislabie* and the *Francis;* see Journal of the *Aislabie*, May 13–June 12, 1733, IOR/L/MAR/B/683B, BL.

the lower sort, [was] East India calicoes." As the Board of Trade had anticipated, the French merchants "always pretend some misfortune at sea" to get their illegal goods ashore, and "it is connived at by the Government." The extent of smuggling and local government complicity cannot be judged by such testimonies alone, however. Dunbar's brother, David Dunbar, was surveyor general of the woods in America, and the Dunbars had a continuing feud with Massachusetts governor Jonathan Belcher and several other men in New England over new settlements and land claims between New England and Nova Scotia. The Dunbars thus might have been exaggerating the extent of the smuggling problem to gain favor in London for their position. Nevertheless, that they expected such charges to be particularly effective against their enemies' characters suggests the importance that they believed the Board put on proper enforcement of the trading regulations, including those on India goods. Indeed, the office of surveyor of the woods made them particularly well placed to understand the Board's concerns: their main task was to identify and defend pines in America suitable to be masts for the Royal Navy, which was supposed to protect and police Britain's global trade.[14]

Governors Keith in Pennsylvania, Bentinck in Jamaica, and Worsley in Barbados vigorously claimed that they cracked down on illicit trade in India goods, and, whether they acted duplicitously, they believed that such claims raised their favor in London. The cases of the *Fame, Chandos,* and *Princess Amelia* all reflected the importance of the laws regulating the Atlantic trade in India goods and the manifold difficulties and confusions in enforcing those laws. Many of the difficulties appear to have been, or to have become, connected to personal conflicts over shares of the spoils and other interpersonal issues. Moore and Keith, for instance, seem to have had a serious falling out, as did Moore, Gordon, and Brown. Indeed, these

14. The ships built in New England sold in exchange for the goods would register and clear out for a British port before being turned over to the new French owners. David Dunbar was later appointed by the East India Company to be governor of Saint Helena. See Great Britain, Board of Trade, *Journal of the Commissioners for Trade and Plantations* . . . (London, 1920–1938), Jan. 5, 1730/1, 172. On the Dunbars' feud with Belcher and several New Englanders, see Governor Belcher to the Board of Trade, Jan. 13, 1730, and Westmoreland and Others [P. Doeminique, M. Bladen, E. Ashe, and O. Bridgeman] to the Duke of Newcastle, Mar. 5, 1730/1, in *Documentary History of the State of Maine,* XI, *Containing the Baxter Manuscripts,* ed. James Phinney Baxter (Portland, Maine, 1908), 6–9, 17–18; Great Britain, Board of Trade, *Journal,* 1728–1734, Oct. 13–26, Nov. 4, 1731, 237–242, Mar. 16, 1731/2, 285–286. See also Joseph J. Malone, *Pine Trees and Politics: The Naval Store and Forest Policy in Colonial New England, 1691–1775* (Seattle, 1964), 91–128.

difficulties might have been even more important than confusion over the jurisdiction of different courts, a confusion mentioned but overcome with relative ease in Jamaica. But these were not just any personal conflicts; they ultimately made their way to the top of the British government, involving, for instance, the Penn family and the Privy Council. The intensity and longevity of the conflicts over the jurisdiction and enforcement of the laws surrounding India goods in Pennsylvania, the resistance of the colonists in Jamaica to regulation and the governor's efforts to thwart them, the Board of Trade's unyielding response to Worsley, and the attempts made by the Dunbars to drag down their enemies by pointing to collusion in the smuggling of India goods—all provide considerable evidence that the regulation of the India trade in the Atlantic was considered serious business to colonists and the state.

Enforcing the India Trade in Britain and Beyond

The compromise over the Calico Acts not only required increasingly effective enforcement of the East India Company's monopoly over the Atlantic colonies; it also created a new incentive to smuggle East India goods into Europe and Britain, goods that might make their way back and forth to the colonies. In Britain itself the problem was twofold: merchants were locked out of the legal trade to India by the monopoly, and consumers were locked out of the legal consumption of the Company's calicoes. The latter created an additional incentive for merchants to find means around the former. Whereas the incentive to smuggle India goods in the colonies was based on price, in Britain the incentive to smuggle calicos was based on fulfilling an undying but illegal consumer demand as well as on much greater merchant interest in trading with India directly. The smuggling of India goods around the Company through Ostend, in particular, became institutionalized through a new rival company. Strong incentives to smuggle created a fully global problem for the British government, a problem that encouraged significant extension of British law to non-British subjects and non-British territories.[15]

15. Historians have paid much more attention to tea smuggling in Britain, which was done for reasons of monopoly and price, not prohibition. See the classic exchange between W. A. Cole and Hoh-Cheung Mui and Lorna H. Mui: W. A. Cole, "Trends in Eighteenth-Century Smuggling," *EHR*, 2d Ser., X (1957–1958), 396–407; Hoh-cheung Mui and Lorna H. Mui, "Smuggling and the British Tea Trade before 1784," *American Historical Review*, LXXIV (1968–1969), 44–73; Hoh-Cheung Mui and Lorna H. Mui, "'Trends in Eighteenth-Century

Customs agents could not easily control British demand for banned Indian calicoes, nor for other Indian Ocean goods smuggled around the duties. Throughout the middle of the eighteenth century, a wide range of individuals, from common sailors to wealthy women, participated in countless episodes of smuggling from the East India Company's own ships. Soon after the second Calico Act went into effect, for example, customs and Company officers in the Downs seized smuggled handkerchiefs and cotton fabric that had been thrown off the ship *Swallowfield* into a small boat as well as similar goods hidden in chests among the seamen's hammocks. Similarly, in the 1730s "a large Parcel of rich India Goods" were discovered "artfully conceal'd on board the Bedford." In Barking, customs officers seized "A vast Quantity of Tea and India Goods" from the yard of a "Fisherman's House." The fisherman claimed he did not know about the goods and offered as proof that someone had previously stashed brandy and lace in the same place. He drank the brandy and showed the customs officials "one of his Wife's Pinners with the same Lace." Middling- and upper-sort women also went to the East India Company docks in Deptford, rode out to the great ships with watermen, and purchased textiles directly from the ships' officers and crew. These women clearly knew that their activities were illegal. Their willingness to go to such lengths provides strong evidence of the intensity of their desire for calico.[16]

Government officials participated in smuggling as well, and men on both sides put their lives at risk for India goods. A customs officer nabbed a justice of the peace, for instance, smuggling India goods worth three hundred pounds. Customs officers, too, could be bought off and also smuggled. The customs collector at Kirkonbright in Scotland was caught running "Pearl Shells, Tea, etc." from Ostend in June 1723. Several men

---

Smuggling' Reconsidered," *EHR*, 2d Ser., XXVIII (1975), 28–43; W. A. Cole, "Rejoinder: The Arithmetic of Eighteenth-Century Smuggling," *EHR*, 2d Ser., XXVIII (1975), 44–49. See also Chapter 4, below. On the scale of smuggling of East India goods on Company ships and attempts at control during a later period, see H. V. Bowen, "'So Alarming an Evil': Smuggling, Pilfering, and the English East India Company, 1750–1810," *International Journal of Maritime History*, XIV (2002), 1–31.

16. For the *Swallowfield*, see Company Minutes, Directors, June 19, 1723, IOR/B/57, 350, BL. Crewmen also reported the presumably disliked Captain Mabbot for illegally breaking bulk at sea to smuggle India goods; see Company Minutes, Directors, July 3, 1723, IOR/B/57, 368, BL. For the *Bedford*, see *Daily Post* (London), May 31, 1738, [1]. For the fisherman in Barking, see *Read's Weekly Journal, or, British-Gazetteer* (London), Sept. 6, 1735, [4]. For an example of several women being caught hiding calico under their seats on a waterman's boat, see *Daily Post*, Sept. 3, 1736, [1].

were convicted for smuggling "great Quantities of East-India Goods out of several East-India Ships, with the Assistance of some Officers of the Customs, Excise, and the East-India Company, whom they had corrupted," echoing continuing fears that Asia would corrupt England. In Dublin in 1727, the commissioners of the customs offered a reward of fifty pounds for the conviction of people using "false Stamps to stamp and seal Callicoes, Hollands, etc. to the great Prejudice of the Revenues, and the fair Trader." In 1734, Mr. Bird, "a noted Smuggler," tried to defend six bales of India fabric, four casks of tea, and a considerable quantity of brandy that he was smuggling from the Isle of Man. Bird engaged in a firefight with officials in which he was killed by a swivel gunshot "under the Left Breast." His men escaped.[17]

Newspapers printed stories for political effect to suggest that India goods caused irrational frenzy and needed to be further banned or taxed. In 1729, an anonymous author wrote to London's *Daily Journal* that, "in open Defiance of Law, East-India Silks and Callicoes may be daily seen on the Backs not only of some Ladies of the first Rank, but Multitudes of other Persons in all Parts of this Kingdom." Recalling the earlier calico debates, the author explained that the use of such goods encouraged thieves and took jobs from the poor. He put much of the blame on the hawkers going door to door to peddle smuggled goods as well as on the wealthy who agreed to buy them. One story in the *Universal Spectator and Weekly Journal,* founded by Daniel Defoe and his son-in-law Henry Baker, implausibly claimed that peasants in Cornwall stripped a marooned Dutch ship of its cargo of calicoes and fruit as well as its rigging and timber in fifteen minutes. Weavers, and probably others looking for cover to attack the wealthy, continued to assault supposedly calico-clad women in the streets for decades.[18]

---

17. For the justice of the peace, see *London Journal*, Aug. 3, 1723, 3. For Kirkonbright, see Company Minutes, Directors, June 19, 1723, IOR/B/57, 349, BL. For several India ships, see *Evening Post* (London), Feb. 21–23, 1723, [1]. For an especially charming, albeit later, attack on the customs officials, see Eliza Hamilton, *Translation of the Letters of a Hindoo Rajah; Written Previous to, and during the Period of His Residence in England; to Which Is Prefixed a Preliminary Dissertation on the History, Religion, and Manners, of the Hindoos* (London, 1796), 47–49. For Dublin, see *Daily Journal* (London), Nov. 3, 1727, [1]. For Mr. Bird, see, *Read's Weekly Journal, or, British-Gazetteer,* Aug. 24, 1734, [2].

18. *Daily Journal*, May 7, 1729, [1]; *Fog's Weekly Journal* (London), Oct. 18, 1729, [1]. Defoe had passed away, but the *Universal Spectator* continued under Baker; see *Universal Spectator and Weekly Journal* (London), Feb. 26, 1737, [2]. Officials did find India goods aboard Dutch ships intended to be run, as had been done for decades; see *Read's Weekly*

Such stories and assaults were not, however, necessarily signs that legal enforcement was totally ineffective, since they had political purposes to support British weavers, and in some of the instances of attack the women turned out not to be wearing calico at all. The Calico Acts had stimulated increasingly successful linen and fustian imitations. Mixing cotton thread with linen thread created fustian, a fabric that looked and felt like an inferior imitation of cotton but with linen's more difficult care and washing. Nevertheless, linen and fustian producers likely benefited more from the Calico Acts than did woolen producers. The laws were clearly constraining supply and encouraging not only smuggling schemes but also domestic production innovations to meet demand.[19]

Fustian was not illegal, and small-scale smuggling was one thing; the Ostend trade and other large-scale interloping was quite another. After the passage of the act strengthening the Company's monopoly in 1721, Ostend traders initially feared smuggling goods into England. Elihu Trenchfield, for example, found himself overseeing a range of goods intended for several people, including the junior John Scattergood. Trenchfield explained that "at present its dangerous to run 'em over from Ostend." He also informed Scattergood that some people were "obliged" to send their goods to the East India Company warehouse. Some of Scattergood's merchandise, too, had to be turned over to the Company. One of his associates, who had managed to smuggle Scattergood's "white and red taffatys" ashore, dared not expose them for sale, thinking "it not safe as yet to remove 'em." Indeed, the barons of the Exchequer convicted the owners of the ship *Coker* for interloping and ordered them to pay £3,900 in fines plus double damages. The directors were especially pleased. It was, they claimed, the first significant conviction, and they expected the heavy penalties to set a precedent to "deter all others from future attempting the like unlawfull Trade." They hoped that a reward of 300 guineas to the individual providing the damning evidence would encourage him and others to come forward more often.[20]

Journal, or, British-Gazetteer, Jan. 13, 1739, [3]. For an example of assault, see *Common Sense; or, The Englishman's Journal* (London), Feb. 26, 1737, [3].

19. Those assaulting women who were not wearing calico were eventually required to reimburse them for triple the costs of the damages; see *Daily Advertiser* (London), July 18, 1745, [1], Aug. 26, 1745, [2]. On the Calico Acts benefiting fustian and linen makers, see Patrick O'Brien, Trevor Griffiths, and Philip Hunt, "Political Components of the Industrial Revolution: Parliament and the English Cotton Textile Industry, 1660–1774," *EHR*, 2d Ser., XLIV (1991), 410, 414–415.

20. Elihu Trenchfield to John Scattergood, Dec. 11, 1721, in Richard Carnac Temple,

The directors had reason for concern; they had caught wind of a London subscription for the Ostend Company to bolster the trade from Ostend to Asia with Austro-Dutch charters. Those Britons involved in the new company evaded the East India Company's monopoly and the duties and other charges that the Company faced passing its goods through London. They also ran their goods into Britain illegally, underselling the Company in its home market and evading the calico prohibition. That these activities had become common was hardly a secret, and London newspapers reported on the broad outline of the merchants' plans. Parliament noted that the interlopers preferred "their own Lucre to the Good of their Native Country" and passed an act to prevent British subjects from participating in the Ostend Company. Those caught would have to pay triple their investment: one-third to the Treasury and two-thirds to the Company (or one-third to the Company and one-third as a reward if the case depended on the intelligence of an informer). Anyone caught going to, or in, the East Indies without permission would be charged with a misdemeanor, punishable by death, prison, or fine. These were significant punishments for engaging in trade between India and Europe, two places not formally, at least, under British sovereignty.[21]

Exercising power over British and non-British subjects in other sovereign jurisdictions was a particularly imperial prerogative that in this case also depended on negotiated support from other powers. In the preliminary articles of peace to avoid war over the Ostend Company and Gibraltar in 1727, for instance, British negotiators pressed Charles VI, Holy Roman emperor, to agree to suspend the East India trade from Ostend. The East India Company then petitioned the king for the "proper Powers and Authoritys to take and Seize and in case of Resistance to destroy all such Ships trading from the Austrian Netherlands to the East Indies or any place within the Limits of the Companys Charter." The Company would thereby

Lavinia Mary Anstey, and Bernard P. Scattergood, eds., *The Scattergoods and the East India Company: Being a Selection from the Private Letters and Business Correspondence of J. Scattergood, East India Merchant, 1681–1723* (Bombay, 1935), 247–248; Company Minutes, Directors, Mar. 9, 1722/3, IOR/B/57, 275–276, BL.

21. Company Minutes, Directors, Mar. 27, 1723, IOR/B/57, 291, BL; "An Act to Prevent His Majesty's Subjects from Subscribing, or Being Concerned in Encouraging or Promoting Any Subscription for an *East-India* Company in the *Austrian Netherlands;* and for the Better Securing the Lawful Trade of His Majesty's Subjects to and from the *East-Indies,*" *Despatches from England* . . . , Records of Fort St. George (Madras, 1911–), XXIV–XXVI, 157–161. For an example of a newspaper notice, see *Daily Journal,* Aug. 19, 1726, [1]. For more on the Ostend Company, the potential for war, and the peace negotiation, see Gerald B. Hertz, "England and the Ostend Company," *English Historical Review,* XXII (1907), 255–279.

police both British and non-British subjects trading between Europe and India and incur the costs and benefits of the policy. They also pledged to work together with the VOC, which had already gained such powers. In 1730, the East India Company's directors complained to George II that the trade via Ostend continued, and they petitioned the king once more. Under continued pressure from both the British and Dutch, Charles VI dissolved the Ostend Company in the Treaty of Vienna in 1731. The East India Company had successfully pressured the British government to persuade a European ruler to allow the Company to control the trade not just between Britain and India but also between Ostend and India.[22]

Still, a range of illicit trades in India goods persisted in Europe, Britain, and the colonies. New ventures to India popped up under Swedish, Polish, and Prussian flags, often with considerable English involvement. Additionally, in 1745, the Commons heard that "the Officers in the *East-India* Ships carry out what Money they can raise, and buy Goods in the *Indies,* and run almost all the Goods they bring into this Kingdom." East India Company captains set up moonlit transfers of cargoes along the coast. And, as they had in the Atlantic colonies, they arranged to stop for lengthy and unnecessary repairs in British outports to allow time for their ships to be illegally unloaded. Law-abiding merchants and governors in the colonies also continued to complain about competition from smugglers. Philadelphia merchant Samuel Powel, for instance, explained to an associate in London that he could not sell chinaware reexported from London in the face of "Large Parcels being brought directly from Holland." In 1742, Sir Thomas Robinson, the governor of Barbados, wrote to the Board of Trade that nothing "seems to claim my Circumspection here, or your Lordships' Attention at home more than a certain Branch of Trade, that is carried on by the French, from their Settlements with Barbados." The French came for enslaved Africans and paid for them with Spanish "Pistereens" and goods manufactured in both France and India, including silks, laces, and calicos that competed directly with the same items from Britain. Although Robinson focused on the damage to British manufacturers, the problem extended to the East India Company, whose own goods were being displaced from colonial markets. A few months later, William Shirley, the governor of Massachusetts, reported similar, if even more extensive, illicit trade, fearing that Britain would lose the total supply of its colonies.[23]

22. Company Minutes, Directors, Oct. 29, 1728, IOR/B/60, 125, BL; Company Minutes, Directors, Sept. 4, 1730, IOR/B/61, 106, BL.
23. *Journals of the House of Commons . . .* , XXV (1745–1750) (London, 1803), Mar. 24,

In 1750, John Sharpe, agent for the Island of Nevis, described to the Board of Trade considerable illegal trade among the Dutch, French, and English in the West Indian and North American colonies, particularly Rhode Island. "By means of flags of truce in time of war and of false clearances in times of peace . . . [they] supplied all North America with the manufactures of Europe and the East Indies, bought of the French or Dutch," he explained. Such transactions, according to Sharpe, mainly benefited the French. Therefore, nothing short of a total ban on trade between the northern colonies and foreign nations would ensure that the Atlantic colonies' benefits accrued to Britain. Agents for North Carolina, Massachusetts, and New York disagreed and suggested that people like Sharpe simply did not know what they were talking about. The current laws could perhaps be enforced better, but an outright ban would devastate North America's trade. The Board of Trade agreed, and instead of passing many new restrictions it continued to issue instructions to colonial governors on "all the Acts relating to Trade and Navigation," specifically including "That they endeavour to prevent clandestine Trade to the *East Indies, Madagascar,* etc. and to prevent the unlawful Importation of *East India* Goods."[24]

This was the crux of the problem—how to control trade without stifling economic growth or pushing consumers to seek illicit goods. Consumers throughout the Atlantic pursued their desires in coordination with merchants, sailors, and corrupted officials by any means that seemed to promise success. On the one hand, consumption of India goods could fuel expanding trade networks. On the other hand, if not effectively managed such consumption could undermine legal control and potentially

---

1745, 102–106 (quotation on 106); "Remarks on the Private Trade of the Sea Officers in the Service of the East India Company," MSS Eur D624, II, fols. 311–313, BL; James H. Thomas, *The East India Company and the Provinces in the Eighteenth Century*, I, *Portsmouth and the East India Company, 1700–1815* (Lewiston, N.Y., 1999), 284–287; Samuel Powel to Benjamin Bell, Sept. 6, 1733, Series 1a, Powel Family Papers, Correspondence 1729–1749, I, 277, Collection 1582, HSP; Extract of a Letter from Sir Thomas Robinson to the Board of Trade, Nov. 27, 1742, CO 5/5, fols. 199v–203 (quotation on 199), NA; William Shirley to the Board of Trade [Copy], Feb. 26, 1742/3, CO 5/5, fols. 210–211, NA. On using other flags and the creation of companies for cover, see Holden Furber, *Rival Empires of Trade in the Orient, 1600–1800* (Minneapolis, Minn., 1976), 220–224; Great Britain, Board of Trade, *Journal of the Commissioners for Trade and Plantations*, Nov. 18, 1731, 246–247.

24. Great Britain, Board of Trade, *Journal of the Commissioners for Trade and Plantations*, Dec. 10, 1750, 137–139; "Copy of a Representation of the Board of Trade to the House of Lords," London, 1749, 23, CO 5/5, fol. 43r, NA.

economic strength. Parliament and the crown thus applied British laws to both British and non-British subjects, regardless of where they lived. Some Ostend traders, for example, were certainly British, but they were not in Britain, and others were neither British nor in the British empire. Arms of the law capable of reaching across oceans and into foreign sovereign territory were a hallmark of the development of imperial rule, a development driven in part by the exigencies of the India trade. Indeed, regulating trade and applying law on a global scale needed to happen together. If the government could not exercise some measure of control over trade essentially anywhere in the world, it could not readily enforce trade regulations designed to draw wealth into the metropole and project strength outward. Nevertheless, the best defense against interlopers, smugglers, and foreign rivals, in nonprohibited goods at least, was to beat them competitively as merchants.

The Imperial Supply Chain and the Imperial Aesthetic

Carefully matching colonial demand with Indian supply was central to the global articulation of British imperial power. For such goods as spices and white cottons, the Company retained its British markets. For calicoes and colored silks, however, the end markets were hundreds of miles away in Europe or thousands of miles away in western Africa, the Americas, and the West Indies. Matching supply with British market demands was often difficult enough, matching it with reexport market demands was even more difficult. The long distance that India goods traveled, the legal barriers keeping colonists from trading to India themselves, and the exceptional qualities of India's cottons and silks made these goods, in particular, potentially important economic and aesthetic imperial ties. Colonists negotiated their own specific understandings of the beauty and tastefulness of India goods within the larger British imperial framework, and they demanded goods that met their varied and shifting ideals. Private merchants throughout the Atlantic colonies needed to work through private merchants in London to gain access to the East India Company's goods, and the Company needed to persuade Indians to provide the goods that such distant consumers wanted, and at competitive prices. The legal reexport of India goods from London into America involved four continents, hundreds of ships, hundreds of thousands of people, millions of pounds sterling, and a broad range of goods from arrack to spices, cottons to silks. The Philadelphia merchant Samuel Powel's experiences selling a broad range of India goods, documented in a large archival collection spanning several decades, provides an ideal means to explore the operation of this trade.[25]

In 1733, Powel reported to Benjamin Bell in London that "Arrack for sometime past hath been much in Repute but our Gentry have found it so very expensive that they are returned to Good old Rum and Brandy punch." Arrack was a commonly smuggled and consumed product in the Atlantic, central, for example, in the story of the smuggling ship *Fame*. Arrack's journey began when it was distilled in India from the toddy juice produced by coconut trees and in Batavia from sugarcane. Customs records show that the East India Company brought thousands of gallons of arrack into London from India each year. It poured out from London to the colonies, with quantities increasing substantially between 1720 and 1730, as Powel reported. Arrack could be consumed straight, but most of it was used for producing punches. Both the word "punch" and the process of mixing alcohol with sugar and fruits accompanied arrack from India. Punch recipes typically included arrack, water or wine, lemon or lime juice, sugar, and nutmeg. British Atlantic punch imitated popular Indian recipes, using Indian and local ingredients, and punch drinking became a fashionable, pleasing, and intoxicating staple of genteel gatherings. Demand for arrack for punch rose so high that in the 1730s Company ship captains stowed it dangerously between decks in lieu of additional sails and water casks and sleeping space for the crew. To protect the safety of its cargos, the Company restricted the quantity of arrack allowed on its ships. If an excess amount was discovered, the owners were fined, with the proceeds fittingly supporting the "POPLAR-*Hospital*." Substantial quantities of arrack on board also tempted the crews, and the directors exclaimed that they would *"deeply Resent and Punish"* the opening of any casks below the upper deck.[26]

25. For the claim that consumers did not care or think about the origins of their Asian goods, see Trevor Burnard, "Placing British Settlement in the Americas in Comparative Perspective," in Bowen, Mancke, and Reid, eds., *Britain's Oceanic Empire*, 409–410. It is true that most colonists did not know much about India or the people who produced the cotton fabric they desired; nevertheless, they did care that the fabric came from India, and the fabric was a real, known, and valued connection to India.

26. Powel to Bell, Sept. 6, 1733, Oct. 4, 1733, Series 1a, Powel Family Papers, I, 277 (quotation), 279; "Orders and Instructions Given by the Court of Directors of the United Company of Merchants of England, Trading to the East-Indies; to Captain William Crompton Commander of the Ship *Duke of Lorrain* and the Commander for the Time Being," Oct. 25, 1738, *Despatches from England*, XLII–XLIV, 77–78. Newspaper advertisements for arrack

But, as the fashion for arrack-based punch was reaching its height, colonists began shifting to "Good old Rum and Brandy" to bolster their punches instead, a shift that served to localize a larger imperial fashion. Rum and brandy were local and cheap, a point Powel made to Bell after sitting on his unsalable arrack a while longer. Rum, produced in Britain, the West Indies, and New England and continually circulating around the Atlantic in massive quantities, was simply more readily available than arrack. Such disparities in cost and supply would not have mattered nearly so much, however, if colonists had not determined that arrack and rum were interchangeable sweet alcohols suited to punch recipes. By using rum, colonists adapted not just an East Indian drink but also a broadly British imperial one to their local circumstances. This adaptation continued with the addition of ice, peculiar to American punches. Arrack was an effective short-term economic and fashionable tie, but not an effective long-term tie connecting the Atlantic colonies with India through Britain.[27]

Other goods, such as spices and saltpeter, were even more limited as economic and fashionable ties to empire than arrack. Unlike arrack, they were not particularly fashionable goods, nor were they easy to substitute, although unscrupulous dealers certainly did adulterate them. Powel ordered cloves, nutmegs, cinnamon, and mace, but he did not complain about them. Company officials seem to have typically detected many problems, such as tons of "foul and rotten" turmeric, before the goods traveled further. As for saltpeter, Powel explained that in a crisis America had everything it needed except for this one valuable ingredient for gunpowder. India had significant saltpeter resources, but it was not seen as an Indian good as such, and it had little fashionable or aesthetic value.[28]

---

continued to appear. See, for instance, *American Weekly Mercury* (Philadelphia), May 5–12, 1737, 3. Arrack data aggregated from Ledgers of Imports and Exports, CUST 3/22–55, NA.

27. Powel to Bell, Oct. 4, 1733, Series 1a, Powel Family Papers, I, 279. On rum and the colonies, see John J. McCusker, "The Rum Trade and the Balance of Payments of the Thirteen Continental Colonies, 1650–1775," *Journal of Economic History*, XXX (1970), 244–247. On rum production in Britain, see T. C. Smout, "The Early Scottish Sugar Houses, 1660–1720," *EHR*, n.s., XIV (1961–1962), 240–253. On punch innovations, see Peter B. Brown and Marla H. Schwartz, *Come Drink the Bowl Dry: Alcoholic Liquors and Their Place in 18th Century Society* (York, 1996), 52–55.

28. Powel to David Barclay and Son, July 1, 1739, Series 1a, Powel Family Papers, II, 2–3, to Barclay, July 20, 1746, III, 7; "List of Goods to Be Provided in Bengal for Ships Going Out in the Season 1716," IOR/E/3/99, 5–11/fols. 3–6, BL; "List of Goods to Be Provided at Bombay for the Ships Going Out in the Year 1720," IOR/E/3/100, 369–371/fols. 186–187, BL. On saltpeter, see Powel to Thomas Hyam and Son, May 31, 1747, Series 1a, Powel Family Papers,

Indian calicoes and silks stood out as the most effective long-term mediums to develop an imperial aesthetic of India goods since, unlike arrack, they resisted easy substitution, and, unlike spices, they were specific markers of fashion with difficult problems of quality control. Colonial calico consumers reached into India through local merchants and the East India Company to order goods of particular styles, colors, and designs. In another sense, India, through these styles (albeit modified to colonial tastes), reached into America. True, European and British linens, fustians, and silks were potential substitutes for India cottons and silks, like rum for arrack, and Powel did order a variety of European fabrics. When it came to his silks and cottons, however, he consistently specified that they were to come from the East India Company's sales. Colonial shoppers, particularly women, wanted specifically India calico, muslin, and silks.[29]

Powel's experiments with British silk show the responsiveness of colonial demand to the superior qualities and prices of Indian fabrics. In the 1730s, Powel placed his first order with William Sheldon and Company for English silks. The silks arrived in good condition. Nevertheless, Sheldon and Company had chosen the patterns poorly for Philadelphia, and the prices were uncompetitive. Powel explained that "our people wear Indian Silks vastly cheaper than you can afford any made in England." Powel tried another order the next year. Again, he was disappointed in the selection. Powel enjoyed much better success in meeting colonial demand by ordering Indian fabrics from the Company sales, despite the extended supply chain. His customers also clearly preferred India goods to other potential substitutes. As Powel explained, "The great importation of Indian Silks Lessen the Ware of all English Manufactures fit for Summer." Powel requested a nice silver watch from Sheldon and Company as compensation for the losses that he suffered and recommended that they might trade to the West Indies instead.[30]

By the 1730s, colonial merchants such as Powel consistently obtained

---

III, 77; Directors to President and Council in Bengal, Feb. 14, 1723, IOR/E/3/101, 465/fol. 231v, BL.

29. Forty-seven percent of women shopping at James Bonsall's store between 1722 and 1729, for example, purchased India goods, compared to 17 percent of men, who generally purchased more utilitarian fabric and hardware. See James Bonsall Account Book, 1722–1729, Collection 108, Am.909, HSP.

30. Powel to William Sheldon and Co., Apr. 12, 1736, Series 1a, Powel Family Papers, I, 362, to Sheldon and Co., June 1, 1737, I, 433, to Sheldon and Co., Feb. 2, 1739, I, 498. For a later example, see Gough and Caramault to William Neate, Aug. 8, 1759, Gough and Caramault Letter Book, Am.9181, HSP.

the India goods that their customers desired from buyers at the Company's London sales, just as the Board of Trade and Parliament had intended. Powel placed specific orders for goods through David Barclay, and he allowed Barclay to add goods to the order based on Barclay's assessments of the market and future trends. Sales in Philadelphia generally went well, but occasionally bad goods led to consumer dissatisfaction. In 1728, one shipment caused major problems. Powel wrote to Barclay, "There is not one thing among the India Goods Saleable but the blue Callicos and perhaps . . . many sorts that will never sell." A year later, Powel still could not sell the goods even at 50 percent of their cost. Customers also came back to complain about the goods. Still, this was a rare difficulty, and Barclay sent acceptable goods for about a decade, until again in late 1739 Powel reported, "The Callicoes you sent me were the worst at the Price I have ever had." Such breakdowns in the trading system show the risks and difficulties involved, but their rarity also shows that the system was successful. Bad buying decisions were not necessarily Barclay's fault. Indeed, Barclay and other London buyers relayed concerns over fashion, quality, and size back to the Company, which then relayed them back to India.[31]

As the directors reported to their servants in Bengal, complaints came from "foreign Buyers that their Correspondents abroad are uneasy" about fabric pieces being inferior to the samples at the London sales. Generally, the Company and the merchants it supplied paid for bales assuming they contained fabrics of the same quality and of different patterns, not different qualities of the same patterns. Bales of fabric might appear fine at the sale, but they could contain poorly woven, damaged, or undersized pieces of fabric hidden within. Such uneven bales were often not discovered until the goods had been reexported and unpacked thousands of miles away. Atlantic consumers also wanted specific widths and lengths of fabric. Pieces that did not divide evenly into the dimensions necessary for standard clothing patterns sold much more poorly because large sections of the piece would become waste. Emerties (a mid-tier white cotton cloth), for example, needed to be fourteen yards long to provide the correct amount of fabric for two garments. Additionally, the government adjusted duty rates based on fixed widths. Customs house officials pulled only a few pieces from each bale to ascertain the proper duty. If all the goods in the

31. Powel to Barclay, Mar. 6, 1727, Series 1a, Powel Family Papers, I, 14, to Thomas Caney, Apr. 5, 1728, I, 21, to John Simpson, June 4, 1728, I, 37, to Barclay, Nov. 9, 1728, I, 61, to Barclay, Mar. 30, 1730, I, 148, to Thomas Foster, Apr. 24, 1730, I, 154, to Barclay and Son, May 26, 1739, I, 515.

bale did not conform to the same length and width, the Company could overpay or underpay the duty, which could lead to losses and fines after the sale of the goods. For years, the directors and their servants struggled to impress the importance of standard qualities, lengths, and widths on their weavers and fabric sorters.[32]

In 1723, for example, the directors sharply chastised the sorters in Madras. Sorters had to insert their names into the bales they sorted and packed along with a description of the goods and the prices charged to the Company. The directors could thus easily know which sorters underperformed. In their letters back to India, the directors were disappointed that the most experienced sorter buried rotten fabrics in his bales, and inexperienced sorters judged the finest clothes that required the "greatest skill and nicety." They also noted that the highest-rated goods in the bales were poorer than the lower-rated goods the previous year and that some fabric rated highly had "thick Gouty threads." By charging the Company more for the goods than they should be worth, the sorters and others involved pocketed the difference. The directors returned two sample bales and demanded that all the goods be re-rated and the Company reimbursed. They also dismissed one of the senior sorters who packed the worst bales, citing it as a cautionary example. A few months later, however, they wrote again, distressed that little had been done to address their concerns.[33]

The directors reported that the goods sent from Madras "are, so grievously complained of, that we are afraid they will bring the sortment into a total disuse abroad which will be an irretrievable damage." The Company had already lost more than twenty-four thousand pounds from the sale of Madras cloth. It had on hand in London hundreds of bales of unsalable cotton longcloth. That such terrible cloth was consistently imported from Madras, they concluded, must be due to widespread "bribery, Corruption or piscashes, and want of pains, skill or care." This was a problem of quality control that extended from the weavers, through the factors, and up to the sorters, but the directors placed the blame squarely on the

32. Directors to President and Council in Bengal, Oct. 30, 1717, IOR/E/3/99, 288/fol. 144v, BL; Directors to President and Council in Bengal, Feb. 3, 1719/20, IOR/E/3/100, 225/fol. 113r, BL. For the length of emerties, see "List of Goods to Be Provided in the Bay of Bengal for the Ships Going Out in the Year 1751," Jan. 8, 1752, IOR/E/3/111, 324/fol. 162v, BL. For a general example of the continued problem of widths, see Directors to President and Council of Bengal, Feb. 16, 1721/2, IOR/E/3/101, 164/fol. 82r, BL. For a list of cloth types and characteristics, see Chaudhuri, *Trading World of Asia*, 500–505.

33. "General Letter to Fort St. George," Nov. 29, 1723, *Despatches from England*, XXIV–XXVI, 106–108.

Enforcement, Aesthetics, and Revenue

sorters, the Madras Warehouse keeper, and the president and Council who ultimately oversaw the rating and packing of cloth. In the immediate term, the directors called for an inquiry into who did what and for the punishment of those involved. In the longer term, they laid down a collection of new rules for the sorting process, including stricter supervision, marking unacceptable cloth to prevent resubmission, and stamping the initials of each sorter onto every single piece processed. Still, the problem of bad fabric in good bales occurred across India and continued for decades as reports trickled back from distant merchants to London and from there to India, where the directors struggled to exercise their will.[34]

Indeed, Indian weavers in this period had local strengths. Neither the Company nor local merchants supplying fabrics at this time could easily exploit weavers, who enjoyed high demand for their products, had a long-standing sense of solidarity, were mobile and skilled in tricking merchants, and able to sell to a variety of potential buyers. To get around these advantages, the directors sent musters of goods from Surat to their servants in Bengal to see if the goods could be made cheaper in the east of India than in the west. The results were promising, and Bengal increasingly displaced Surat in what had been Surat goods. In addition, throughout the middle of the eighteenth century the directors ordered their servants in Bengal to supply "fine Jugdea Baftaes" (white cotton cloth) to Madras. The directors told their Madras servants to have the cloth "Printed with variety of Beautifull Patterns [sic], but not in the expensive manner of the Madrass Chints." Thus, the directors made use of the comparative advantages of

34. General Letter to Fort St. George, Feb. 2, 1724, *Despatches from England*, XXIV–XXVI, 122–126. A *piscash*, or *peshkash*, was a gift to a person in authority. For examples of continued problems, see "List of Investment to Be Provided on the Coast of Choromandel for the Ships Going Out in the Year 1747," July 24, 1747, ibid., LI, 21, "List of Goods to Be Provided on the Coast of Choromandel for the Ships Taken Up into the Company's Service in the Year 1756," ibid., LX, 79, 81. For another large case, this time in Bengal, see Directors to President and Council in Bengal, Jan. 23, 1751, IOR/E/3/111, 76–77/fols. 38v–39r, BL. The directors explained that the terrible goods bought at high prices and in inadequate quantities had nearly ruined the Company's vital Bengal trade, leaving the French and Dutch to increasingly control it and reap its profits. See Directors to President and Council in Bengal, Jan. 8, 16, 1752, IOR/E/3/111, 300–302, 309–310/fols. 150v–151, 155, BL; "List of Goods to Be Provided in the Bay of Bengal for the Ships Going Out in the Year 1752," Dec. 15, 1752, IOR/E/3/111, 468–469/fols. 234v–235r, BL. In China, Company supercargoes took a leading role in assessing silks available, and Chinese printers also worked to produce patterns popular in the Atlantic to satisfy the supercargoes' orders. The Chinese weavers already produced highly standardized widths, but lengths and mismatched colors could still be problems. See Leanna Lee-Whitman, "The Silk Trade: Chinese Silks and the British East India Company," *Winterthur Portfolio*, XVII (1982), 22–27.

their different factories, shipping cloth woven in Jugdea (near Dacca) a thousand miles away to be finished by the more highly skilled and perhaps more affordable printers in Madras.[35]

The letters from the directors to the factories also overflowed with criticisms of colors and patterns as well as detailed instructions on fashion trends so that buyers such as Barclay would be able to satisfy their re-export customers. In their annual order to Bengal in 1723, for instance, the directors criticized the Patna chintz with "flowers mostly of Single red or Single peach blossom Colour which are little valued in Europe." The flowers needed to be attached to green sprigs and placed on a white or yellow background with black drawing to make them salable (see Plate 4 for a similar pattern). The Company's fortunes depended upon such aesthetic details. The directors also noted that the designs must run the length of each piece of fabric, instead of being printed from each end and meeting as opposites in the middle of the piece. In 1732, they wrote, "We expect to find the nasty dead Colours of all prohibited Goods amended, the value of those Commoditys depending as much upon the Stripes and Colours as the Frabrick." In 1747, they explained that the baftas must continue to be printed on "White Grounds" with lively colors and with "as much variety as you can." Similarly, they wanted their chintz to be of "as many different and new Patterns as possible." Yet the directors not only chastised their servants in India; they also lauded good decisions and products. Of a "Bale of Chints No. 1 from Vizagapatam," for example, they encouraged similar purchases, explaining, "The patterns were good and a great variety, which is of great advantage in the Sale."[36]

A wide variety of prints helped insulate the Company from fashion

35. Prasannan Parthasarathi, *The Transition to a Colonial Economy: Weavers, Merchants, and Kings in South India, 1720–1800* (New York, 2001), 22–39. On musters from Surat to Bengal, see Directors to President and Council in Bengal, Feb. 14, 1723, IOR/E/3/101, fols. 229–239, BL. On Jugdea baftas, see "List of Goods to Be Provided on the Coast of Choromandell for the Ships Going Out in the Year 1737," Oct. 5, 1737, *Despatches from England,* XLII–XLIV, 26; "List of Investment to Be Provided on the Coast of Choromandel for the Ships Going Out in the Year 1747," July 24, 1747, ibid., LI, 22; "List of Goods to be Provided on the Coast of Choromandel for the Ships going Out in the Year 1750," Nov. 28, 1750, IOR/E/3/111, 12/fol. 6v, BL.

36. "List of Goods to be Provided in the Bay of Bengal for the Ships Going Out in the Year 1723," IOR/E/3/102, 82/fol. 42r, BL; Directors to the President and Council of Bengall, Feb. 11, 1731/2, IOR/E/3/105, 439/fol. 220r, BL; "List of Investment to Be Provided on the Coast of Choromandel for the Ships Going Out in the Year 1747," July 24, 1747, *Despatches from England,* LI, 21–22; "List of Goods to Be Provided on the Coast of Choromandel for the Ships Taken Up into the Company's Service in the Year 1756," ibid., LX, 79.

Plate 4. Textile Fabric, India. Circa 1700–1725. Mordant painted and dyed.
Accession no. 1978-195. The Colonial Williamsburg Foundation.
Gift of F. Schumacher and Company

trends that could change more quickly than fabric could be ordered and received from India and also gave the Company opportunities to stimulate new fashions. In this sense, the Company often ordered goods in India much like Powel ordered goods from Barclay, with a combination of specific requests and a general variety that gave buyers the freedom to pursue purchases of opportunity. Particularly with chintz for the reexport markets, the directors encouraged their servants to "let the Indians Work their own Fancys, which is always preferable before any Patterns We can send you from Europe." Chintzes "must be of the India Taste, and of the newest Patterns." The situation had changed since the 1670s. Indian printers now had a stronger understanding of what consumers in Europe, Africa, and the Americas might like. Additionally, the evidence from Powel suggests that colonial consumers had also become so accustomed to the patterns designed in Britain that more novel patterns invented in India could create new fashions. It was easier for the Company with its significant capital than for merchants such as Powel to hold fabrics aside for later sale and to take risks on new fashions. To stay on top of fashion developments, the directors frequently requested that their servants procure and send home a bale of every sort of fabric sent home on the other European ships.[37]

The demand for different patterns and colors of India goods also varied by place, even reaching well beyond the major colonial ports and into the rural hinterland. Michael Hillegas, for instance, functioned as both a local retailer and a wholesale merchant supplying backcountry Pennsylvania storekeepers with imported goods. Hillegas sold India goods to visiting retailers and used the stagecoach network to send merchandise to the countryside. The coaches' limited cargo abilities economically and easily supplied the quantity of fabric required in backcountry communities and also shifted small amounts of goods among major urban centers. Although they consumed less Indian cloth than their urban counterparts,

37. "List of Goods to Be Provided at Bombay for the Ships Going Out in the Year 1750," IOR/E/3/111, 118/fol. 59v, BL; President and Council of Bombay from the Directors, Mar. 3, 1731/2, IOR/E/3/105, 482/fol. 241v, BL. For more examples, see "Observations upon the Goods Sent by the Ships Cardonnel, Arabella, King George and Dartmouth Arriv'd in the Year 1717," IOR/E/3/99, 279/fol. 140, BL; "List of Goods to Be Provided at Bombay for the Ships Going Out in the Year 1720," IOR/E/3/100, 369–371/fols. 186–187, BL; "List of Goods to Be Provided in the Bay of Bengall for the Ships Going Out in the Year 1732," Nov. 10, 1732, IOR/E/3/105, 585/fol. 293r, BL. For examples of requests for one of every sort, see "List of Goods to Be Provided in the Bay of Bengall for the Ships Going Out in the Year 1732[/3]," Feb. 6, 1732/3, IOR/E/3/105, 591/fol. 296r, BL; "List of Investment to Be Provided on the Coast of Choromandel for the Ships Going Out in the Year 1747," July 24, 1747, *Despatches from England*, LI, 21, 23.

Enforcement, Aesthetics, and Revenue

rural colonial consumers had their own tastes for particular colors and styles of fabric, much like consumers in London and Philadelphia. Hillegas complained that his London suppliers had sent a poor selection of calicoes. His calicoes sported a blue background, whereas rural consumers currently preferred a green background. Additionally, in times of peace, native Americans offered markets for India cottons with their own specific price points and styles.[38]

Back in London, Barclay described the difficulties he faced in meeting the demands of colonial customers for particular fabric fashions—a challenge that extended from America through him and the East India Company to India. In one instance, Powel blamed Barclay for not supplying everything in his orders, causing "Disappointment to many of my Constant Customers who waited long and at last were obliged to be supplyed otherwise." Barclay explained that he had to wait until the Company's next semiannual sale before he could attempt to fulfill Powel's requests, and then the auction did not include everything that Powel's customers in Pennsylvania wanted. Additionally, although the Company did have cossaes (fine white cotton muslin) for sale, which Barclay had on his shopping list from Powel, they sold for too much to leave a profit. Barclay substituted humhums (a finer white muslin) and calicoes, which he thought were good values. The bordered bandanas that Powel had requested, meanwhile, were of very poor quality, so Barclay substituted a different style of bandana that sold cheaply. The goods would arrive later than Powel expected, and they would not match the goods he requested. Both difficulties were a result of the long supply chain linking colonial consumers back to India's producers. The Company's directors had either failed to gauge upcoming demand or, as commonly happened, their ser-

38. Michael Hillegas to Peter Clopp, July 16 and ?, 1757, Hillegas Letter Book, I, Collection 287, HSP; see also Francis Jerdone, Wastebook, Feb. 16, 1749, MS1929.6.2, 40, John D. Rockefeller Jr. Library, Colonial Williamsburg Foundation, Williamsburg, Va. Philip Wilson, for example, advertised an assortment of European and East India goods "extream [sic] cheap . . . for the Indian trade"; see Pennsylvania Gazette (Philadelphia), May 16, 1771, 1. For an excellent analysis of the ownership of imported goods in the backcountry, see Paul G. E. Clemens, "The Consumer Culture of the Middle Atlantic, 1760–1820," WMQ, 3d Ser., LXII (2005), 577–624. Unfortunately, Clemens's probate inventory sources did not frequently itemize cloth items. Considerable work remains to be done on native American consumption of India goods, particularly in the southern colonies. Robert S. DuPlessis has found increasing, but limited, consumption of cottons among native peoples in eastern North America; see DuPlessis, "Cottons Consumption in the Seventeenth- and Eighteenth-Century North Atlantic," in Giorgio Riello and Prasannan Parthasarathi, eds., The Spinning World: A Global History of Cotton Textiles, 1200–1850 (Oxford, 2009), 233–240.

vants in India failed to bother with the details of the directors' orders, or to persuade Indians to produce the goods, or to produce them at moderate prices. In 1752, the directors wrote to their servants in Bengal, "You have looked upon the Lists of Investments sent You from time to time as meer matters of Form, and have regarded them accordingly." But, the directors went on, they are "the most Interesting and Material part."[39]

The directors were acutely aware that the Company's success depended on supplying European and broader Atlantic markets with better products than those of its competitors, who were attracted by the prevalent understanding in Europe that the India trade was vital to developing power globally. The directors feared, in particular, the "furious" expansion of the French East India Company, which, they wrote, threatened to "deprive us of the flower of Our Trade, or to run away with the applause of the World." The directors' plan was to both copy and outspend them. "A Friend" who promised to make large purchases sent the directors "full and rich" patterns of flowered muslins imported by the French, accompanied by the French names. The directors then requested that such goods be purchased at appropriate prices and put in appropriate bales so "that thereby the French and other Nations may be frustrated of having those Goods." This strategy not only undermined competition; it also served to protect the role of the British Company as the provider of India fabric to much of the Atlantic. In effect, it helped keep the colonies harnessed to India through Britain and promoted a sense that colonists in the British empire enjoyed better access than the colonists in other European empires to India goods.[40]

Colonial newspaper advertisements frequently celebrated this success of the British supply chain in providing all manner and quality of India goods—indeed, more variety than was legal in Britain itself. Advertisers regularly displayed that variety on the page through lengthy, detailed lists of available items. These lists often included the place of manufacture of

39. Powel to Barclay and Son, June 3, 1741, Series 1a, Powel Family Papers, II, 89–90; Barclay to Powel, Aug. 18, 1747, ibid., box 1, folder 11, HSP; Directors to President and Council in Bengal, Jan. 8, 16, 1752, IOR/E/3/111, 301/fol. 151r, BL.

40. Directors to President and Council of Fort St. George, Feb. 11, 1731/2, IOR/E/3/105, 404/fol. 202v, BL; Directors to President and Council of Bengall, Feb. 6, 1732/3, IOR/E/3/105, 660/fol. 330v ("furious" and "deprive"), BL; Bosquet and Clerembault to the Directors, circa 1733, IOR/E/3/105, 594/fol. 297v, BL; "List of Goods to Be Provided on the Coast of Choromandell for the Ships Going Out in the Year 1738," Feb. 14, 1738, *Despatches from England*, XLII–XLIV, 39 ("that"). On increasing purchases, see also Directors to the President and Council of Bombay, Nov. 10, 1732, IOR/E/3/105, 552–553/fols. 276v–277r, BL.

the goods. Between 1740 and 1745, for instance, 42 percent of advertisements for cotton cloth in the *Pennsylvania Gazette* and *American Weekly Mercury* mentioned India or some place within India as the location of production. If India did not matter to consumers, advertisers would not have mentioned and often stressed it. Even when an Indian source was not mentioned, it was implied since colonists would have known which types of fabrics came from India by reading other advertisements and through fashionable conversation. Additionally, between 1740 and 1745, and 1768 and 1773, 55 and 56 percent respectively of Philadelphia advertisements for Indian fabric mentioned that it had been imported via London. London provided cache—it was, alternately with Paris, the heart of eighteenth-century Atlantic fashion. It was, moreover, the well-known distribution point for most fashionable Asian and other goods to the colonies, connecting the global origins of the goods with their local availability. These goods were not acclaimed as British, as historians have assumed; they were products of British connections with India and of a much broader, more complicated, and locally adaptable imperial aesthetic. In one typical advertisement from the *Pennsylvania Gazette* (Plate 5), Samuel Neave noted that his goods originated in Europe and India and had arrived recently from "London." He specifically noted the "Great variety" and represented that variety visually through a list. Neave and other advertisers did not specifically reference the empire, but they did not need to; the empire's global trade was everywhere in their advertisements, providing both the variety of goods as well as the access route for them.[41]

Yet the empire did not provide just any goods; it offered particularly fashionable and high-quality goods at prices below other suppliers. Although no good statistical data exists for smuggling, little evidence suggests that a greater quantity of fashionable India goods arrived in British Atlantic colonies from points outside Britain. By the period 1740–1745, the British Company annually exported from Bengal goods worth an average of SR 3,842,856, compared to SR 2,317,180 by the Dutch, their main competitor. Additionally, the British had substantial exports from Madras and Bombay. Other empires simply could not provide as easily, cheaply, or diversely as the British. Indeed, the prices in America on many goods were

---

41. *Pennsylvania Gazette*, 1740–1745; *American Weekly Mercury*, 1740–1745; *Pennsylvania Chronicle, and Universal Advertiser* (Philadelphia), 1768–1773. For Philadelphia examples, see *American Weekly Mercury*, Nov. 26, 1741, [4]. For Boston, see *Boston News-Letter*, Apr. 27–May 4, 1719, [4]. For historians' seeing India goods as British, see note 10 in the Introduction, above.

other goods, not mentioned here.

Philadelphia, October 1. 1747.

Juſt imported from London, in the ſhip Lydia, William Tſſin Commander, and to be ſold by Edward Dowers, at his ſtore, next to Meſſieurs Benjamin and Samuel Shoemakers ſtore, in Water-ſtreet, above Arch-ſtreet, for ready money ;

SUperfine and middling broadcloths, in patterns and pieces, halfthicks, ſhalloons, camblets, callimancoes, cambricks, buckrams, ready made waiſt-coats for ſailors or ſervants ; with a variety of other goods, ſuitable for the ſeaſon. ⊕

Juſt imported in the ſhip Lydia, from London, and to be ſold by

SAMUEL NEAVE,

At the houſe from which Mr. Charles Willing lately remov'd, in Front-ſtreet,

A Great variety of European and Eaſt-India goods, very cheap for ready money, or ſhort credit, viz. Broadcloths, forreſt cloths, 3-4 and 6-4 knap duſſels, ſtrouds, half-thicks, druggets, ſhalloons, flannel, bearſkins, ſilk and worſted camblets, camblettees, florettas, callimancoes, flower'd damaſks, crapes, allopeens, Perſians, black mantua and alamode, oznabrigs, garlix, ſhirting Holland, cambricks, callicoes, cotton and linnen checks, table linnen and clouting diaper, buckrams, buttons and mohair, ſewing ſilk, white tabby and ſtay-trimmings, ſilk, cotton, and linnen handkerchiefs, ſilk ferret, cotton and thread laces, ribbons and ferrets, gartering, thread, bobbins and tapes, needles and pins, mens and womens thread, cotton and worſted hoſe, ſilk, cotton and worſted caps, mens and womens gloves, mens and womens horſewhips, looking glaſſes, gun-powder, lead and ſhot, frying-pans, and London ſteel ; variety of cutlary, ironmongery and haberdaſhery ware, and ſundry other goods, too tedious to mention here.

N. B. Said Neave gives three ſhilings and ſixpence per buſhel for good clean wheat, and ſells Liſbon ſalt at four ſhillings and twopence per buſhel.

Philadelphia, October 1. 1747.

RUn away, on Monday night laſt, from Joſeph Burr, of Burlington county, an Iriſh ſervant man, named John Canada, a well-ſet, likely fellow, about 23 years of age, and has ſhort brown hair : Had on when he went away, a caſtor hat, and white cap, a browniſh coat, with ſlaſh ſleeves, and wrought braſs buttons, a cloth coloured half worn kerſey jacket, a fine ſhirt, and an oznebrigs ditto, good leather breeches, and check trowſers, peak-toed ſingle ſoled ſhoes, and new braſs buckles. Whoever takes up ſaid ſervant, and ſecures him, ſo that his maſter may have him again, ſhall have *Three Pounds* reward, and reaſonable charges, paid by JOSEPH BURR.

N. B. Maſters of veſſels and others, are warned not to carry him off, or harbour him.

Philadelphia, October 1. 1747.

RUn away, on the 20th of September laſt, from Cohanſie Bridge, a very big Negroe man, named Sampſon, about 50 years of age, has ſome Indian blood in him, is hip-ſhot, and goes very lame ; he has taken his ſon with him, a boy about 12 or 14

similar to, even lower than, those in Britain. The government repaid much of the customs duties to merchants when they reexported many types of goods to the colonies. These customs drawbacks lowered effective duty rates and thereby reduced the temptation to smuggle and trade to India illicitly. The drawbacks, especially combined with the lack of a calico prohibition in the colonies, provide substantial evidence of the government's desire to ensure that colonists bought Indian fabrics, and bought them legally from British merchants supplied by the East India Company's sales in London. The condensing power of the empire to provide in America the variety of the world through London fueled an important imperial aesthetic.[42]

It might be argued that the Company's offices on Leadenhall Street attempted to centralize decision making. Frequently, however, the Company's offices served much more as an information clearinghouse, centralizing communications for decisions and demands made by its decentralized customer base, whether in Europe, Africa, or the Americas. The purchase of poor-quality or overpriced fabrics and other goods by the Company in India could throw the whole system into disarray. Bad goods resulted in significant difficulties for reexport merchants in London, and particularly for merchants such as Powel and their consumers in the Atlantic colonies. The end customers, thousands of miles away from India, ultimately applied pressure to India through a range of intermediaries. The goods flowed out from India, the pressure flowed back from consumers, and the cycle repeated. The problems of matching size, style, color, and quality to colonial demands and of stimulating new demands changed little. Despite the inherent difficulties and the occasionally frustrating mismatches, merchants throughout the Atlantic world ordered a wide diversity of fabrics and other India goods from London. Indeed, consumers preferred such goods over English imitations. Consumers had power to sway trends and demand good quality and low prices, but merchants and the Company also worked to exercise control over them— encouraging them to buy more and to embrace new patterns and colors.

The excitement surrounding an unexpected quantity of India goods

42. Data compiled by Indrajit Ray, *Bengal Industries and the British Industrial Revolution (1757–1857)* (New York, 2011), 176. The Dutch exports from Bengal in the previous few decades appear to have been higher than the British, but the Dutch were exporting a much lower proportion of fabrics, making the consumer fabric exports much closer in value; see Om Prakash, *Bullion for Goods: European and Indian Merchants in the Indian Ocean Trade, 1500–1800* (New Delhi, 2004), 288–289.

that arrived directly into North America in 1745 further attests to the general success of the British imperial regulatory system and the stimulation of demand for India goods in America. That year, a force of New England militiamen and British navy vessels seized the French colony of Cape Breton off the coast of Newfoundland. The War of the Austrian Succession, of which the victory was a part, took place among the major European powers in Europe, America, and India—but events on Cape Breton brought all three theaters together. Two French East Indiamen arrived in the port after its capture, apparently unaware that it was now British. Powel reported to Barclay in London, "One if not both the Indiamen are from Bengall and her Cargo Consists of Muslins, Cottons . . . pepper etc." Some local merchants believed that more French Indiamen would arrive and unsuspectingly fall into British hands. Powel explained to another correspondent that "a great many of our People are setting out for the Place expecting to buy great Bargains." The ships were worth getting excited about. They offered goods the Company had helped to make highly desirable at prices typically impossible in the imperial system of trade since neither the prime cost nor the costs of shipping through London had to be accounted for. The French, whose goods had been seized, as well as many British merchants and the British East India Company, whose regular trade had been in this case legally circumvented, would lose from the sale of the French cargos in Cape Breton. Their loss would be the consumers' gain. Powel warned Barclay that from the two French ships "enough of those [India] Commodities will be bought to stock North America for some years." In his excitement and worry, Powel underestimated colonial demand, though undoubtedly colonial markets remained smaller than those in Europe and Africa. Still, colonial markets might offer other benefits.[43]

Conquest, Economic Growth, and Revenue

The extent to which the British state benefited from both the successful enforcement of its regulations and the Company's and merchants' successes in stimulating and supplying colonial markets remained both debatable and important. In the Indian Ocean, the Company's desire for control over

43. Powel to Thomas Hothersall, Aug. 24, 1745, Series 1a, Powel Family Papers, I, 421, to David Barclay, [Aug?] 3, 1745, I, 422–423. Transmission costs through London included duties, wharfage, and the profits of both the East India Company and the private merchants, such as Barclay, who shipped the goods to America.

production, and its ultimate concern for revenue, rejuvenated notions of conquest and colonization. The directors had long before explained the importance of local Indian revenue to support "any English Dominion in India" necessary to allow the Company to do more than "peddle in trade." Only with revenue and dominion could the Company "support a uniform nationall powerfull politicall interest in India" to make "great profit" like the Dutch. Such ideas were not necessarily different from those connecting trade, conquest, and revenue in the Atlantic. Hopes for colonial silk and expanded cotton cultivation, moreover, still reemerged from time to time. British fustian manufacturers, for instance, pointed to the colonial source of their cotton wool in the 1730s to push back against claims by English woolen producers that fustians should be domestically prohibited. They emphasized that the colonial cotton plantations supposedly employed far more "White People" than the sugar plantations. Nevertheless, few were overly concerned anymore with ideas of cotton cultivation for Britain in the Atlantic colonies. The bigger concerns now revolved around benefiting from the colonial consumption of India's goods, particularly calicoes. Those concerns included old questions about whether colonial consumption was equivalent to consumption in Britain itself and newer questions about the proper purposes and rates of revenue generation.[44]

In a 1722 letter to their servants in Bengal, the directors outlined the two main strategies for maximizing revenue in India, strategies that were similar to those used in America: encourage Indians to purchase English goods and, failing that, use force as needed to regulate trade, control producers, create markets, and gain territory to benefit the Company. Selling British manufactures in India had been dreamed of since the beginning of English contact with India, much as the English sold their manufactures to colonists and native peoples in America. Preceding and during the debates over the Calico Acts, pressure had been intense for the Company to export English woolens and other goods, but Indians generally showed little interest in such products. As the directors explained in their letter, products that promised success, such as glassware, quickly saturated the small elite markets and were often "not of right sizes or fashionable." With modest success in exporting goods to India, the directors encouraged instead impressive shows of military force to obtain trading concessions. They expected the resulting trade to repay the military costs. As for con-

44. Directors to President and Council of Ft. St. George, May 30, 1690, IOR/E/3/92, 103/fol. 52r, BL; *The Case of the Importers of Cotton Wool, and the Manufacturers Thereof into Fustian, and of the Traders in That Manufacture* (n.p., [1736]), 1–2.

trolling land, they explained, "We are not fond of much Territory, especially as it lies at a distance from you or is not pretty near the Water side . . . unless you have a moral assurance that it will contribute directly or in consequence to our real benefit." This latter clause allowed considerable discretion to the Company's servants. They could try to purchase, fight for, or take as prize or gift virtually any territory as long as they could offer a justification of benefit to the directors. Indeed, the Company increasingly accepted the use of force and the takeover of territory, following European patterns in the Atlantic. Though territorial acquisitions might have been relatively small as yet, the imposition of force by one people over another was and is imperial and, in India, it had spun out of the desire to obtain India's commodities and Asia's wealth. The directors wanted revenue and profits, and conquest was another tool to achieve those ends.[45]

Written descriptions helped establish India in British minds as a wild space in need of the Company's improvement. If conquest could be defended as increasing revenue and providing benefits to the local people, as Richard Hakluyt had argued more than a century prior, conquest was acceptable. An anonymous author in the second decade of the eighteenth century, for instance, echoed these sentiments, encouraging the conquest of Diviseema, the delta of the Krishna River, where "the tyger, that ravenous animal, and others of the savage host, range without controulment, kil mankind without distinction." The deer, antelope, and rabbits of Diviseema, the author went on, did not even know to fear a person's approach since so few people ventured among them to hunt. The number of people was small, suffering under the purportedly tyrannical rule of the "Moors" and "Rajowe." Diviseema was a place waiting for European development and control, and, with its small and supposedly amenable population, conquest there was possible. Best of all, the annual revenue would increase rapidly "after the English have it for some years in their possession, especially when the whole Island is inhabited with merchants." Perhaps the same anonymous author also described Junkceylon, today Thai Phuket, as being tyrannically governed by the king of Siam. Junkceylon, the author wrote, "is at present such a scene of missery and want, it needs nothing but a good Government to make it a very happy place and the inhabitants very rich." The people "would be glad to joyn or come under any forrainers for

45. Directors to President and Council in Bengal, Feb. 16, 1722, IOR/E/3/101, 154, 163–164/fols. 77v, 81v–82, BL. The instruction to use shows of military force was frequently repeated; see, for another example, Directors to President and Council in Bengal, Feb. 14, 1723, IOR/E/3/101, 466/fol. 232r, BL.

Enforcement, Aesthetics, and Revenue

their protection." Under good British government, the island would become a major exporter of tin, sugar, rice, coconuts, "arackee nutts," pepper, and elephants. Of the elephants, the author estimated that "a great profitt may be made yearly by transporting them to Madrass." Finally, shipbuilding could be started using the island's timber. According to these visions, people would immigrate from Britain, India, and China; much of the produce would be exported, and the property would be taxed. Several hundred miners, planters, and soldiers from Britain could easily begin the whole process of vastly increasing the Company's revenue through conquest.[46]

Revenue, rule, and also religion were intertwined in the directors' thinking. In 1721, the directors wrote to their servants in Fort Saint George explaining that all the "old experienced Indian inhabitants" agree that Indians would pay double the duties to be under the Company's government instead of that of local rulers. Strikingly, the goodness of English government could be measured directly by the willingness of the people to pay for it. The directors went on, however, that Company officials had to act as Christians to inspire the native people to respect and follow them. The directors had already supported several conversion projects and recently allowed the Society for Promoting Christian Knowledge to send silver and books to India to help "propagate the Christian Religion" among the Indians through charity and teaching.[47]

Support for active proselytizing did not remain steady, but the directors continually reminded their servants through the middle of the eighteenth century to present a thrifty Protestant example to the native populations. In 1751, they wrote that the factory at Bengal had become infamously licentious. The Company employees must return to "sound Religion and Morality" and reduce their frivolous expenditures to set an example of virtue and decency for both lower Englishmen and Indians to respect and follow. The directors wanted control of both their own employees and the Indians that produced the goods for export. Only through control did they

46. "A Description of Dewy (Taken Partly from the Natives) of Metchlepatan and the Moors Government with Some Observations in the Medical Art," in *Scattergoods and the East India Company*, 93, "A Description of the Island of Junkzelone and What Vast Profit the Honble. Company May Make by Settling That Place," 103, 104–105.

47. Directors to President and Council of Ft. St. George, Apr. 26, 1721, IOR/E/3/100, fol. 282, BL; Directors to President and Council of Fort St. George, Jan. 25, 1716/7, IOR/E/3/99, 124/fol. 63v, BL. For more on the directors' earlier interest in conversion work, see Philip J. Stern, *The Company-State: Corporate Sovereignty and the Early Modern Foundations of the British Empire in India* (New York, 2011), 100–118.

hope to guarantee the quality of their products and the survival of their business.[48]

In America, meanwhile, the trade in India goods promised opportunities for additional revenue and control as well. Archibald Cumings, a naval officer stationed in Boston, wrote to the Board of Trade in 1722 offering a scheme whereby duties on calicoes and other goods in the colonies would maintain six thousand regular troops for colonial defense, help increase hemp production, and raise "a fund for the better support of Governours and Officers, of the Crown, in the Plantations." Currently, he explained, most of the duties paid on calicoes were drawn back by the merchants when they reexported the goods. Cumings claimed that two hundred thousand yards, or ten thousand pieces of calico and muslin, came into Massachusetts annually, the "drawbacks of which, will amount to a considerable Sume, with the Excise duty, for stamping the same." By removing the drawbacks on duties allowed to foreign linen, calico, muslin, tea, coffee, pepper, paper, and fruit, he expected the British government to raise forty to fifty thousand pounds. The East India goods would bring the most revenue. Echoing the weavers' arguments from the calico debates, he wrote in his cover letter, "The wearing of Callicoes here hurts the Sale of the Brittish manufactorys, so if they will wear them, its no great damage if they pay dearer for them." Cumings concluded that increasing the duties would make little difference to the level of consumption since the colonists "incline much to that Sort of apparel." Cumings also proposed to raise perhaps thirty thousand pounds further through a range of new duties on goods such as rum, foreign sugar, and wine and by extending the stamp duties to the colonies. Cumings hoped to be rewarded for his plan with either a position overseeing the revenue or the title of commissioner of the stamp duties, or both. Cumings took to its logical extension the clause in the Calico Acts allowing goods banned from Britain to be sold

48. Directors to President and Council in Bengal, Jan. 8, 16, 1752, IOR/E/3/111, 309/fol. 155r, BL; Directors to Fort St. David, Jan. 23, 1750/1, IOR/E/3/111, fol. 29v, BL; Directors to President and Council of Bengall, Dec. 3, 1731, IOR/E/3/105, 337/fol. 169, BL; Directors to President and Council of Bengall, Feb. 11, 1731/2, IOR/E/3/105, 454–455/fols. 227v–278r, BL. The Levant Company sent similar instructions to be moral and devout to its men in the Ottoman empire in the mid-seventeenth century. Daniel Goffman argues that such instructions were "hedges" against the influence of foreign cultures on men far from England. In India in the eighteenth century, the directors were similarly concerned about the influence of India's foreign cultures on their servants, but they were also interested in converting and controlling locals by setting Christian examples. See Goffman, *Britons in the Ottoman Empire, 1642–1660* (Seattle, 1998), 99, 108–109, 204.

and consumed in the colonies. His plan foreshadowed many of the revenue ideas that would exacerbate conflict between the British government and its colonists in America in the late 1760s and early 1770s.[49]

Cumings was not alone. In 1728, former Pennsylvania governor William Keith explained in a detailed report that the growing consumption of British and India goods in the colonies benefited Britain by increasing legal trading activity. Charles Townshend, secretary of state for the Northern Department, aided Keith in circulating the report that went before the king and the Board of Trade. Keith explained that the Atlantic colonies had value not only as providers of raw materials but also as valuable markets. These colonies, he wrote, "take off and consume" linen and calicoes exported from Britain, "either the Product of *Britain* and *Ireland,* or partly the profitable Returns made for that Product carried to foreign Countries." He claimed that these exports, a portion of which were India goods, generated more than double the revenue of woolen goods exported. He specifically explained that the colonies took a great variety and "daily" increasing quantities of English silks, haberdashery, and furniture and "also a very considerable Value in *East-India* Goods" reexported from London. The Atlantic colonies, by this reckoning, were major and beneficial consumers of British, European, and India goods in service to British interests. Keith expected that revenue might be raised from this trade to pay for small establishments of regular troops.[50]

Whereas Keith was in agreement with the part of Cumings's plan to pay for troops in the colonies, others saw problems with generating revenue for such ends and were instead in agreement with Cumings's plan to use heavier duties to help pay for the imperial administration. An anonymous person close to the government, for instance, admitted considerable discomfort with plans for replacing the militia in the colonies with a

49. Archibald Cumings to [Richard Plumer?] and "Scheme for Maintaining 5 or 6,000 Regular Troops upon the Continent of America for the Better Defense of the Same," Nov. 3, 1722, CO 323/8, fols. 139–140v, NA; Archibald Cumings to [Richard Plumer?], Nov. 17, 1722, CO 323/8, fol. 143v, NA.

50. William Keith to the king, 1728, CO 5/4, fols. 168, 174–175, NA; William Keith, "A Short Discourse on the Present State of the Colonies in America with Respect to the Interest of Great Britain," 1728, CO 323/8, fols. 302r–307v, NA; published as William Keith, "Discourse on the Present State of the Colonies in America, with Respect to the Interest of Great Britain," in Keith, *A Collection of Papers and Other Tracts, Written Occasionally on Various Subjects* . . . (London, 1740), [168]–184. Townshend's influence was on the decline, however. See Linda Frey and Marsha Frey, "Townshend, Charles, second Viscount Townshend (1674–1738)," *DNB*.

standing army. However, the author argued, "If a fund could be rais'd for payment of Governours, and Judges, so as to make them independent of the people it would be a very great work done." Importantly, he explained, "it has been thought a considerable summe might be raised for those purposes by a duty upon East India goods vended in the Colonys." "I have seen some calculations upon this subject." The use of revenue in this plan would help solve the problem of smuggling, and the plan reemerged before the American Revolution with important consequences.[51]

In 1730, David Dunbar, whose brother claimed that the colonists were in cahoots with the French to import India goods, lobbied for the removal of the drawbacks on the duties on India goods reexported to the Atlantic colonies. Dunbar explained, "All the plantations have one advantage of the people in England, which is that there is a drawback allowed for all India or other goods exported, which pay a duty in England and no duty is payd upon importing them in the plantations." Since people in England had to pay the duty on unprohibited goods, he concluded, "it does not seem unreasonable that either there should be no drawback, or pay Kings duty else where." Thomas Coram, who had lived several years as a shipbuilder in Boston and had also sought to develop a settlement in Maine, similarly wrote to the Board recommending "that the drawbacks on East India goods and foreign goods re-exported to the Plantations, which make goods come cheaper there than in Great Britain be no longer allowed." He explained that an "Allowance might be made in the case of Jamaica" to protect that island's reexport trade with the Spanish colonies. Coram was highly respected on colonial affairs, but his recommendation did not sway the Board of Trade to get rid of the drawbacks.[52]

There were several problems with removing the drawbacks or intro-

51. Response to Sir Wm. Keith's Memorial, Sept. 27, 1729, CO 5/4, fols. 160v–162v, NA. In the 1750s, Charles Townshend (not to be confused with the second Viscount Townshend, above) was thinking about this policy. In 1767, it would become central to the controversial act that bears his name. See Lewis Namier and John Brooke, *Charles Townshend* (London, 1964), 38–40, 173–179.

52. Colonel Dunbar to Mr. Secretary Popple, Sept. 15, 1730, in *Documentary History of the State of Maine*, XI, *Containing the Baxter Manuscripts*, ed. Baxter, 51; Capt. Coram to the Board of Trade, CO 323/9, fols. 89r–92v, NA; James Stephen Taylor, "Coram, Thomas (c.1668–1751)," *DNB*. Published works also made this point, often together with concerns about New Englanders' making their own versions of English goods; India goods and domestic colonial goods posed the same problem to British manufacturers. See, for example, Gentleman of Barbadoes, *The British Empire in America, Consider'd; in a Second Letter, from a Gentleman of Barbadoes, to His Friend in London* (London, 1732), 13–14.

Enforcement, Aesthetics, and Revenue

ducing new duties on India goods in the colonies. Much of the drawback savings were offset by the costs of shipping India goods across the Atlantic, including freight, insurance, interest, commissions, and profits to merchants. The drawbacks might have cost the state in the short term, but, as Keith and others pointed out, and as explored above, the drawbacks encouraged the development of consumer societies in the colonies that both gained from and depended on their economic relationship with Britain. Eliminating the drawbacks on the duties would potentially raise the prices of legal goods compared to smuggled goods from the Dutch or French, and thus the drawbacks helped to keep India goods moving to the colonies largely from the British East India Company through London. As a matter of defensible policy, English colonists had not only the legal right to purchase a wider variety of India goods than people in Britain, including the most fashionable and inimitable dyed, painted, and printed calicoes and silks, but colonists also escaped most of the duties on goods legal in both places.

The economic activity generated by the India trade became a primary justification used by the East India Company's supporters in conjoined debates over the renewal of the Company's charter and continuance of the calico prohibition in the late 1720s and early 1730s. One anonymous author explained that the Company's monopoly was necessary to meet the India trade's capital, settlement, and local negotiating demands, including the need to exercise concerted force. Both domestic consumption and an even more valuable reexport trade, he argued, increased Britain's wealth through the "Chain, and Dependence of one Branch of Commerce upon another." The Company's forty impressive ships employed countless people building, rigging, and fitting them out and five thousand sailors to man them. Each ship, he wrote, cost ten thousand pounds to build, all of which was money that went into the London economy. Similarly, the Company's shipowners had nine ships refitted annually for twenty-six hundred pounds. The trade required the export of stores to India, and Britons often returned home from India to invest the riches that they had gained. The Calico Acts, he claimed, had actually helped European linen producers, not English woolen producers. Chinaware, japanned furniture, arrack, muslin, tea, and coffee were only luxuries in the sense that people could survive without them, but such goods were not corrupting luxuries. Britons would pay triple for such goods if they had to rely on the India trade of other countries. Additionally, the trade netted three hundred thousand pounds per year to the state in customs and excise revenue.

The great improvement of Britain since "Queen *Elizabeth's* Time" was the author's ultimate evidence that the system worked.[53]

Similarly, "A Briton Born" wrote to London's *Daily Journal* defending the East India Company's monopoly as "essentially necessary to the better carrying on our Trade to Africa and America, as well as to our furnishing most Parts of Europe with great Quantities of East India Goods, besides the Abundance which are consumed at home." The author positioned Africa and America first in his list, and, although he indicated that "great Quantities" of India goods went from London to Europe and were consumed in Britain, he argued that India goods were "essentially necessary" to the Atlantic trades. He was certainly correct on the point of Africa. In 1713, the British had gained the *Asiento* for the Spanish trade in enslaved Africans. To fulfill both Spanish and British demand for this enslaved labor, traders needed considerable quantities of India cottons. Immediately after the passage of the first Calico Act, reexports of India piece goods to Africa surged before falling steadily. After the second Calico Act, reexports rose even more impressively. During the 1720s, India piece goods worth £493,580 were reexported to Africa, rising to £775,805 during the 1730s. Exports of calicoes to Africa, however, did not stimulate much concern. These calicoes were not being consumed by British people, and they were necessary for the operation of the trade in enslaved Africans upon which Atlantic colonial production of sugar and tobacco depended.[54]

Two days later, the *Journal* published a response to "A Briton Born" by "Anglicanus" in favor, not of reducing the consumption of India goods, but of eliminating the monopoly Company to increase consumption. The Company, Anglicanus wrote, paid the British government both a lump sum of £200,000 and allowed interest abatements worth another £192,000 over six years for the right to have the monopoly. For some, these payments could be construed as a great service to the nation, but for Anglicanus they were simply another onerous form of taxation since the costs were passed on to consumers. India goods, he claimed, were indeed real luxuries, and,

53. *Some Considerations on the Nature and Importance of the East-India Trade* (London, 1728), 7–9, 17 ("Chain"), 45–55 ("Queen" on 51), 65–78.

54. A Briton Born, "To All My Fellow-Subjects . . . More Especially Those Who Are Proprietors in the Stock of the United Company of Merchants Trading to the East-Indies . . . ," *Daily Journal*, Apr. 9, 1730, [1]; Marion Johnson, *Anglo-African Trade in the Eighteenth Century: English Statistics on African Trade, 1699–1808*, ed. Thomas Lindblad and Robert Ross, *Intercontinenta*, XV (Leiden, 1990), 29, 54–55, 61, 72–73. For a detailed list of India cloth in demand in Africa, see Stanley B. Alpern, "What Africans Got for Their Slaves: A Master List of European Trade Goods," *History in Africa*, XXII (1995), 6–8.

if a monopoly Company was really required to trade to India, it was far better to open the trade and let it decline. He explained, "We could keep our Silver at Home, which we now squander in mere Luxury, and instead of India Goods cloath all Europe and our Dominions in America with our Woollen and Silk Manufactures." But Anglicanus did not want to ban India goods; nor did he expect a decline in their consumption. He argued that it had become abundantly clear that neither in Europe nor in America were consumers willing to give up India goods—demand would always find a way to create supply. Without a monopoly, Britain would take even more control of this supply because other European countries would be fettered to their own inefficient and expensive monopolies. British freedom meant in part the freedom to trade to all places. Through this open trade, Britons would discover new sources of gold and new markets for British goods, the number of British ships and seamen employed would increase, productive investments would be made in trade instead of stock-jobbing, and consumption would steadily rise. The national wealth would thus increase, and the state would generate more revenue without higher taxes.[55]

Fayrer Hall, in his *Importance of the British Plantations in America to This Kingdom* (1731), likewise argued that the export of British and re-export of India manufactured goods benefited the colonists and Britain. Hall was not simply a political writer; he was a well-connected member of the imperial administration. As the commander of a sloop out of South Carolina, Hall had caught several pirates in 1718, and he was soon to be appointed secretary to the governor of Barbados. Hall did not focus on the Company's monopoly but rather meditated on the effectiveness of the Calico Acts, pointing out that every "Man of Sense and Observation" believed that banning calicoes in England did nothing to increase the consumption of woolens either in England or anywhere else. In England, he explained, women either bought illegal calicoes or legally imported linens so that they could look fashionable and, importantly, clean. Turning back to America, he noted, "It is notorious that our own Plantations have not taken, in any degree of Comparison, so much of our Woollen Manufacture as they did before our prohibiting the Wear of printed Callicoes, and other *India* Goods." He went on that the colonists "would be weak not to do as they do, since it is their Interest" to buy the more fashionable, easier to

55. Anglicanus, "Some Observations on the Present Circumstances of Our East-India Trade," *Daily Journal*, Apr. 11, 1730, [1].

clean, and inexpensive calicoes instead of English woolens. In exchange, the plantations provided necessary raw materials.[56]

Other writers, however, saw the ban on calicoes in Britain as a positive model to be followed in the colonies to encourage manufacturing and to avoid the dangerous importation of Indian luxury. Defoe now changed his earlier argument that calicoes needed to be banned only in Britain itself, exhorting that "all the Nations of *Christendom*" needed to band together to prohibit India's cottons and silks. He wrote in 1729 that Indians "have a natural Genius to Industry and Application" and that the "People of *India* and *China* are able to clothe the whole World with their Manufactures." But the only ones enriched by this production was the *"Mogul"* and the *"Grand Tartar."* That same year, a contributor to the *Maryland Gazette* declared the "Wisdom and Policy of our Mother Country, in prohibiting the Wear of Callicoes, to encourage Industry at home, and employ the indigent and necessitous Part of the Nation, A President worthy of our Imitation." The author encouraged the colonies in America to adopt Calico Acts of their own, not to stimulate local consumption of English goods, but to increase local consumption of locally produced goods. Other colonial writers denounced local consumption of calicoes and other India goods for bringing Asiatic luxury and exporting bullion. Such Asiatic luxury was the "Bane of Liberty" and the ruin of the Romans, echoing fears of Asia voiced in seventeenth-century England. Now the Calico Acts had simply displaced the bane to America.[57]

Those on both sides of the calico question in Britain continued to invoke colonial consumption in their arguments through the 1730s and 1740s. As woolen supporter John Munn explained in 1739, "No sooner were Calicoes out of use in *England,* but they were imediately sent to our Foreign Plantations, and many other Places where our Woollen Goods had been formerly wore, so that we sent Calicoes instead of Woollen Goods Abroad." The Calico Acts thus did little to help the woolen industry. East

56. F[ayrer Hall], *The Importance of the British Plantations in America to This Kingdom; with the State of Their Trade, and Methods for Improving It; as Also a Description of the Several Colonies There* (London, 1731), 11, 14, 108. On Hall's service, see *London Evening-Post,* Jan. 11–13, 1732, [1].

57. [Daniel Defoe], *The Advantages of Peace and Commerce; with Some Remarks on the East-India Trade* (London, 1729), 14–17, 37; D. E. to Mr. Parks, July 19, 1729, *Maryland Gazette* (Annapolis), July 15–22, 1729, [5]. On the need to produce linen and wool in the colonies and the difficulties of paying colonists to do the work, see [John Colman], *The Distressed State of the Town of Boston, etc. Considered; in a Letter from a Gentleman in the Town, to His Friend in the Countrey* (Boston, 1720), 4–5, 8.

India Company director Matthew Decker used the same point in 1743 to support the repeal of the Calico Acts. He agreed that the prohibition had caused people outside England to replace woolens with calicoes and had thus "done a World of Harm to some of the Manufactures of *England,* and particularly to the City of *Norwich,* for whose Benefit it was chiefly intended." The state's revenue had also suffered sharply on the loss of potential duties. One of the main proponents, according to Decker, "confessed before he died" that it was a terrible bill, "one of the worst that ever passed." Decker also wanted the repeal of all import and excise duties to be replaced by a single tax on homeowners. The end of prohibitions and duties, he argued, would relieve the poor, increase trade and employment, simplify revenue collection, and end smuggling. The Calico Acts would not, however, be repealed for decades.[58]

Meanwhile, the political economist and future supporter of American independence Josiah Tucker blamed the Company's protection of its monopoly and aggressive military attitude for failing to make India a consumer of British goods and instead for making Britain a consumer of India goods. Climate, he explained, could not be the problem. English people made silks, painted linens, and cottons. It was true, he admitted, that in England goods were not currently made "according to the *Indian* Taste and Fashion, yet this Difficulty might soon be got over." The main problem was that the English goods simply cost too much because of the Company. The solution, therefore, was to open up the trade to all private merchants to increase competition and drive down prices. Trade, he argued like many critics before him, had no need of forts or military displays such as the Company effected. Trade and conquest, he concluded, were incompatible.[59]

---

58. A Manufacturer of Northamptonshire [John Munn], *Observations on British Wool, and the Manufacturing of It in This Kingdom* . . . (London, 1739), 57; A Well-Wisher to the Good People of Great-Britain [Matthew Decker], *Serious Considerations on the Several High Duties Which the Nation in General, (as Well as It's Trade in Particular) Labours under: With a Proposal for Preventing the Running of Goods, Discharging the Trader from Any Search, and Raising All the Publick Supplies by One Single Tax* (London, 1743), 8–24, esp. 22–24. Other critics continued to attack the Company's export of bullion for India goods consumed in Britain and the colonies; see Merchant of London, *Some Thoughts on the Present State of Our Trade to India* (London, 1754), 6–7. William Keith's positive assessments of colonial consumption also continued to reappear in new editions; see William Keath [Keith], *A Collection of Papers and Other Tracts* . . . , 2d ed. (London, 1749), 171–172.

59. Josiah Tucker, *The Elements of Commerce, and Theory of Taxes* ([Bristol?], [1755]), 97–110 (quotation on 101); Rory T. Cornish, "Tucker, Josiah (1713–1799)," *DNB.*

Notions of imperial control and conquest were not, in reality, as diametrically opposed to antimonopoly positions as it might have appeared. Indeed, Tucker himself defended trading regulations, duties, and bounties intended to steer commerce, generate economic growth, and support state revenue. He disdained smugglers and encouraged strict actions against them. Private merchants, moreover, wanted control over product pricing and quality in the interests of maximizing revenue and profits as much as the East India Company did. The Company and private merchants alike supported a strong navy to defend them and, if needed, an army as well, both of which required revenue for the state. Like the Company, private merchants also wanted to expand markets in India for English goods as well as markets for Indian goods in Britain, Europe, Africa, and the Atlantic colonies—the latter, in particular, products of conquest themselves.

In the decades after the passage of the second Calico Act, India was, at times, something akin to the Atlantic colonies. It was not a twin, certainly, but a sibling, a space where British strength, both commercial and military, was to be exercised to gain markets, producers, and revenues, all of which could be under the power of foreign rulers or, some increasingly believed, under the power of the East India Company. At other times, however, India seemed to be a distinct other, more foreign than foreign Europe. Commentators often mentioned India goods and other foreign goods together, but they mentioned both. If they saw India goods as the same as other foreign goods, they would have seen no need to mention India goods specifically. Many of the issues that would later become central to the tea crisis of 1773 were already circulating from the 1720s. Administrators and writers considered the economic and political implications of the Company's military and monopoly tendencies, of increasing defense and control in the Atlantic colonies, of taxing India goods to pay for that defense and control, and of the economic and moral value of those goods. It is tempting to draw a direct line from these discussions to the American Revolution, but before the late 1760s people in Britain and the imperial administration, more than colonists, debated these questions and fretted about their implications. For most colonists with money to spend, the empire was bringing from India exactly the goods that they wanted at prices and duty rates that they accepted.

THE EAST INDIA COMPANY, along with private merchants, shipowners, mariners, and shopkeepers, created a complex supply chain that made India goods mutually profitable within the legal structure created and enforced by the British state. Many people, ranging from government and Company officials to producers, merchants, dockers, customs agents, wholesalers, and retailers, had a vested interest in catering to and stimulating consumer demand for Indian products. For these people, the India trade was clearly worth the trouble. The Company also paid an annual 6 to 8 percent dividend to its stockholders. And, perhaps most significantly, by the War of the Austrian Succession the East India Company's loans to the British government amounted to £4.2 million, largely backed by the value of the trade in piece goods. The Company did not directly rule many cloth producers, who retained significant advantages in negotiating quality and rates, but it did seek to control producers and the size, quality, and prices of fabric to expand the value of its trade. The Company, colonial merchants, and their London suppliers connected customer demand in Europe, the Atlantic colonies, and Africa to artisans producing cloth in India. That this trade operated primarily through London and not, say, Amsterdam, Bristol, or Barbados shows that the carefully regulated trading and consumption system developed in the seventeenth and early eighteenth century had become a more or less effective reality. The British trade with its colonies and Africa appears as triangular only if we ignore the vital Indian components. From the mid-seventeenth century, London had increasingly made itself the knot of a sort of trading bow tie—the so-called triangle in the Atlantic would have unraveled without the other side of the bow tie in India. But, if London was the knot, regulated India goods, especially calico, muslin, and silk were the fabric of the bow joining India and the Atlantic colonies together.[60]

According to a "Poetical Essay" printed in 1744 in the *American Magazine and Historical Chronicle,* India still had "dazzling" wealth and "vast ... strength," and it was known as a place where "elephants obey the curbing reins!" Its manufactures, too, encouraged a "gaudy pride." With so much wealth, power, luxury, and temptation, India was also in need of Protestant Britain's redeeming touch. The poem's couplet, "Ye Christians, as their plenteous wealth you share, / With your blest faith enrich

60. "Dividends on Stock from 1708 (the Union) to 1780," L/AG/18/2/1, 3, BL; "Particulars of the Debt Owing from Government, also the Amount of Annuities and in What Manner the Same Originated," IOR/L/AG/18/2/1, 1, BL. It is an overwhelming, if not impossible, task to disaggregate and quantify the profits generated for retailers through India goods. See Hohcheung and Lorna H. Mui, *Shops and Shopkeeping in Eighteenth-Century England* (Montreal, 1989), 106–121, 135–147.

the natives there," sounded almost like a versed version of Richard Hakluyt. In some ways, the British imagination of America and India had remained relatively static. In other ways, however, a great deal had changed. The East India Company had become a powerful global force. India and America had become more closely connected through London by the empire's regulations. A growing system of enslaved labor plantations using African peoples often purchased with Indian cloth had transformed British labor practices and consumption habits and enhanced the value of many colonies. British colonial populations in America were finally becoming more lucrative markets. Britain itself was becoming capable of using laws, economic practices, fashion, and military force to control more and more people at greater and greater distances away, especially in ports on the Atlantic and Indian Oceans. The colonists' relationship to India, mediated by their empire's laws and traders, was decidedly imperial both economically and aesthetically, regardless of the relationships between the East India Company and its Indian suppliers.[61]

The Treaty of Aix-la-Chapelle that ended the War of the Austrian Succession in 1748 suggested again that the British government saw the East India Company as central to the strength of its empire. British negotiators traded back to the French Cape Breton, which had been captured in large part through colonial exploits and was the sight of the frenzy over the French Indiamen. For the East India Company, however, the negotiators got back from the French the growing entrepôt of Madras. It was not a quid pro quo. Instead, as colonial writer Nathaniel Ames explained, Massachusetts, which had won the Cape, "may be said to give Peace to Europe; since for *Cape-Breton* the *French* yielded all their Conquests in *Flanders*." The return of Cape Breton was intended to focus conflict in Europe instead of in the Atlantic colonies. Colonists remained mostly sanguine about giving up Cape Breton while the Company got back Madras, much as they had seen few dangerous implications in the Calico Acts when the government had positioned the American colonists as markets to prop up the Company. Still, Cape Breton, not Madras, was traded for Flanders. The British government got for the Company territory it had lost in India and gave away territory the colonists had won in America. The next big imperial war, the Seven Years' War, would finally bring to a head four long-standing questions connecting India and America: what positions the East India Company and the Atlantic colonies occupied in the British constitution, whether the India trade or American colonization was more

61. *American Magazine and Historical Chronicle* (Boston), I (August 1744), 522–523.

Enforcement, Aesthetics, and Revenue

valuable to Britain, how to control the East India trade in England and America to profit the state and nation, and what the role of military force should be in exercising that control. Conquest in India would make the East India Company and its revenue take on revolutionary importance in America.[62]

62. Jack M. Sosin, "Louisburg and the Peace of Aix-la-Chapelle, 1748," *WMQ*, 3d Ser., XIV (1957), 516–521, 534–535; Nathaniel Ames, *An Astronomical Diary; or, An Almanack for the Year of Our Lord Christ, 1756* . . . ([Boston], [1755]). Some reports suggested that it was a trade of Madras for Cape Breton; see, for example, *New-York Weekly Journal*, Jan. 25, 1747, [2].

4   A Company to Fear
India and the American Revolution

Neither Siraj-ud-daula, the nawab of Bengal, nor British major-general Robert Clive intended to remake the British empire around the world. After the official beginning of the Seven Years' War in 1756, the new nawab seized the leading East India Company port, Calcutta. The Company was the most successful of the European companies in India, and he wanted to curtail its trading privileges. Upon hearing the news of Calcutta's capture, Clive sailed from Madras with a fleet and army and retook the city. Over the following months, Clive struck a deal with the wealthy banking house of Jagat Seth. Clive sought to secure the East India Company from the dual threats of Siraj-ud-daula and the French, who wanted to displace the British as the primary European power in the region. The house of Jagat Seth was nominally allied to the nawab, though it was unhappy with the nawab's plans to limit British trade. The house and Mir Jafar, the nawab's army paymaster, promised Clive that a large contingent of the nawab's troops, which outnumbered the British forces, would stand down in an upcoming British attack. In return, Mir Jafar would become the new nawab. Clive thereby enjoyed an easy victory at the Battle of Plassey in 1757. The Company consolidated its regional power through the grant of the *diwani,* the proficient revenue administration of Bengal, which it took through victory at the Battle of Buxar. The diwani was believed to be worth approximately £1.7 million annually, equivalent in some years to more than 10 percent of the British government's national budget. Placing parts of India under more effective Company influence, if not outright control, followed a line of British thinking and attempted actions that extended back to the seventeenth century. Nevertheless, this was an unprecedented increase in British power on the subcontinent.[1]

---

1. P. J. Marshall, *Bengal — The British Bridgehead: Eastern India, 1740–1828* (Cambridge, 1987), 76–93. Rice cultivation was the main basis for the revenue; see Rajat Datta, *Society, Economy, and the Market: Commercialization in Rural Bengal, c. 1760–1800* (New Delhi, 2000), 333–338. For the view from a Briton in India close to Clive, see Gerard Gustavus Du-

Historians of early America have long called the conflict of which the conquest of Bengal was a part the "French and Indian War," a title used particularly in popular histories and textbooks. The name French and Indian War, instead of "Seven Years' War," not only reflects American preconceptions that the British conquest of New France was the most important event of the war; it also entrenches a faulty and limiting notion of a British empire with two distinct halves, one in the Americas and West Indies and another in India and Africa. It obscures the global genealogy of the conflict and its legacy. Although a growing number of historians of early America have embraced the title Seven Years' War, the significance of the Indian theater for America remains largely unstudied. Ironically, the older title French and Indian War might be applied fruitfully to the conflict in Asia as well if one thinks not only of American Indians but also of Asian Indians. Between 1756 and 1763, Britain's gains in India added far more people and revenue than its gains in America. India was finally becoming for Britain a directly exploitable mine of wealth—an India following Edward Wynne's definition—with revenue that no British imperial pursuit, perhaps since Elizabeth's pirates, had produced.

The conquest of Bengal and its fallout intensified long-standing debates over the British empire in India, the dangers of Indian corruption, and the best means to enhance the already partly integrated fashion, trade, taxation, and constitutional structures connecting India to America, Africa, and Europe through London. In America, the conquest of Bengal encouraged contradictory impulses for imperial belonging and revolution. The conquest increased access to and encouraged interest in a wide variety of Asian goods. It reinvigorated old plans to generate revenue in America from the colonial consumption of these goods to pay for local imperial administrators. It encouraged conceptions of India as a place of colonies and tax revenue in addition to trading factories. It reduced the political isolation of colonists from India and the Company. These developments would take on dramatic new importance after a catastrophic famine in Company-managed Bengal that would result in heated rhetoric in Britain and America as Parliament increased oversight of the Company, passed the Tea Act (1773), and sought to shore up its oversight in the colonies. The popular tea outcry in America would share many features with the calico outcry in Britain seventy years earlier—both vilified the East India Com-

carel to his mother, Apr. 12, 1767, D2091/F11, Ducarel Family Papers, Gloucestershire Archives, United Kingdom.

pany, invoked exploitation, and sought to alter the balance in the imperial articulations among India, Britain, and the Atlantic colonies. Legislation over India and the India trade would ultimately magnify the different constitutional understandings of the empire in the colonies and in the British government. The East India Company became a company to fear both as an actual example of an unrepresentative and exploitative form of rule within the British empire and as an accompaniment to other colonial fears of Catholicism, native Americans, and slavery.[2]

An Intensifying Imperial Aesthetic

Following the Battle of Plassey, Britons throughout the empire built on symbolic associations and aesthetic elements from as far back as the early seventeenth century to incorporate India itself, as opposed to the India

2. At the beginning of the twentieth century, Arthur Meier Schlesinger argued that the patriots played up the dangers of the East India Company as a monopoly organization after its conquest of Bengal and that this accounted for the sudden opposition to duties on tea in 1773; see Schlesinger, "The Uprising against the East India Company," *Political Science Quarterly*, XXII (1917), 60–79; Schlesinger, *The Colonial Merchants and the American Revolution, 1763–1776* (New York, 1918), 265–278. Eighty-five years later, H. V. Bowen revived Schlesinger's argument; see Bowen, "Perceptions from the Periphery: Colonial American Views of Britain's Asiatic Empire, 1756–1783," in Christine Daniels and Michael V. Kennedy, eds., *Negotiated Empires: Centers and Peripheries in the Americas, 1500–1820* (New York, 2002), 284–295. In 2010, Benjamin L. Carp and James R. Fichter briefly discussed the role of the East India Company in the American Revolution, again focusing in particular on fears of it as a monopoly corporation, not as a model of constitutional changes; see Carp, *Defiance of the Patriots: The Boston Tea Party and the Making of America* (New Haven, Conn., 2010), esp. 3, 10–15, 18–24; Fichter, *So Great a Proffit: How the East Indies Trade Transformed Anglo-American Capitalism* (Cambridge, Mass., 2010), 18–27. For a concise overview of the standing constitutional interpretation of the Revolution, see Jack P. Greene, *The Constitutional Origins of the American Revolution* (New York, 2011), which largely distills Greene, *Peripheries and Center: Constitutional Development in the Extended Polities of the British Empire and the United States, 1607–1788* (Athens, Ga., 1986); see also John Phillip Reid's many works, which are summarized in Reid, *Constitutional History of the American Revolution: Abridged Edition* (Madison, Wis., 1995).

On the rhetoric of slavery, and fear of Catholics and native Americans, see, for example, Christopher Leslie Brown, *Moral Capital: Foundations of British Abolitionism* (Chapel Hill, N.C., 2006), 117–153, 212–226, 240–258; Brendan McConville, *The King's Three Faces: The Rise and Fall of Royal America, 1688–1776* (Chapel Hill, N.C., 2006), 112–119, 261–266; Peter Silver, *Our Savage Neighbors: How Indian War Transformed Early America* (New York, 2008); Vernon P. Creviston, "'No King Unless It Be a Constitutional King': Rethinking the Place of the Quebec Act in the Coming of the American Revolution," *Historian*, LXXIII (2011), 463–479; Owen Stanwood, *The Empire Reformed: English America in the Age of the Glorious Revolution* (Philadelphia, 2011).

India and the American Revolution

trade, more firmly into perceptions of their empire. A celebratory medal produced by the Society of Arts, for instance, employed many of the same symbols used by London's mayoral pageants more than one hundred years earlier. One side of the medal depicts a cornucopia of riches, a rudder that symbolized increased shipping, a globe that represented the new territorial expanse of the empire, and Robert Clive wielding a Union Jack. The opposite side of the medal depicts "a victory seated on an elephant." The medal was a commemorative collectible, but many other objects intended originally for different uses served a similar purpose. The British Museum, founded in 1753 "for the Honor and advantage of this country," displayed a growing collection of Indian artifacts alongside similar specimens from imperial holdings in America and the West Indies and from connections with Africa and the Far East. In 1760, the museum displayed several samples of worked East Indian agates, jewels, chowries (fly whisks), musical instruments, and a palanquin. The museum also accumulated many natural specimens from the East Indies, including birds, shells, pepper, spices, and insects.[3]

Similarly, for-profit museums and displays offered members of the genteel public who lacked the means to own a large collection the opportunity to claim a sense of participation in the empire and its colonies in America and India. Proprietors fused entertainment, education, status, and national pride. In London, one coffeehouse, for example, held natural and manufactured artifacts from America alongside Asian-Indian hookah pipes, "Letters in the Malabar language," an elephant ear, and rupees

3. Description of the medal by its designer, James "Athenian" Stuart, quoted in John Malcolm, *The Life of Robert, Lord Clive: Collected from the Family Papers Communicated by the Earl of Powis*, 3 vols. (London, 1836), II, 247–248. For the British Museum, see parliamentary proceedings accompanying the will of Hans Sloane, C.61.b.13, British Museum, quoted in Edward Miller, *That Noble Cabinet: A History of the British Museum* (London, 1973), 44; *Gentleman's Magazine, and Historical Chronicle*, XVIII (July 1748), 302; [Robert Dodsley], *The General Contents of the British Museum: With Remarks; Serving as a Directory in Viewing That Noble Cabinet*, 2d ed. (London, 1762), 23, 57, 84–96, 132–141, 151, 163, 171, 178; *A Companion to Every Place of Curiosity and Entertainment in and about London and Westminster . . .*, 3d ed. (London, 1772), 104. Many Britons in India, and Clive in particular, accumulated collections of Indian objects as booty, but also to document and celebrate conquests. For much more on the relationship between collections, the possession of empire in India, and personal invention, see Maya Jasanoff, *Edge of Empire: Conquest and Collecting in the East, 1750–1850* (London, 2005), esp. 6–13, 32–43, 74–76, 182–185. On collectors in India, see Michael Edwardes, *The Nabobs at Home* (London, 1991), 39–40. For a catalog of Clive's collection, see Mildred Archer, Christopher Rowell, and Robert Skelton, *Treasures from India: The Clive Collection at Powis Castle* (London, 1987).

seized by Clive. Increasing numbers and species of live animals were also imported from America and India for profitable displays and as gifts for the royal family. For a "few pence," for instance, Londoners could see an elephant on display at the royal stables in Chelsea in the 1760s. Captain Sampson returned from Bengal with an elephant for the king and published an excursive narrative about it that was reprinted as far away as North Carolina. At Portsmouth in 1762, two tigers and a cow were landed for the duke of Cumberland; in 1769, a pair of Indian deer arrived for George III; and, during the 1770s, the king received two elephants, while the Prince of Wales received an Indian cow and calf. Although large live animals from India were not imported into the colonies in North America, one enterprising tavern owner in Philadelphia charged a shilling to see such animals tastefully represented in "A Very fine and elaborate Piece of SUGAR WORK, or DESERT." This impressive dessert represented "the four Quarters of the Globe, who make their Appearance in triumphal Cars, drawn by Lions, Elephants, Camels and Horses." In America, such "triumphal" displays celebrated membership in Britain's increasingly powerful global empire.[4]

A broad cross section of people throughout the British empire also increasingly used a stunning variety of India goods. Indeed, India goods— and progressively more goods from China as well—had an especially prominent place in a broader expansion of consumer spending, particularly in the colonies. Colonial consumers imported ever-growing quantities of Indian cottons and silks (many of which were banned in Britain) to fashionably dress themselves, their furniture, and their homes. Despite the indirect nature of the trade through London, every major port city in North America as well as smaller ports such as York River and Pensacola, cleared a wide variety of India goods. Wealthy families purchased fine calico, muslin, and silk for themselves and inexpensive coarse cotton fab-

4. *A Catalogue of the Rarities to Be Seen at Adams's, at the Royal Swan, in Kingsland Road, Leading from Shoreditch Church*, 3d ed. ([London], 1756), 12; *A Catalogue of the Rarities, to Be Seen at Don Saltero's Coffee-House in Chelsea; to Which Is Added, a Complete List of the Donors Thereof*, 36th ed. ([London, 1785?]), 4, 7, 9, 11; *A Companion to Every Place of Curiosity and Entertainment in and about London and Westminster . . .* (London, 1767), 174; [Captain Sampson], "A Description of the Young Elephant, Lately Presented to His Majesty, by Capt. Sampson, from Bengal," *North-Carolina Magazine; or, Universal Intelligencer* (Newbern), I, no. 14 (Aug. 31–Sept. 7, 1764), 105. On animal gifts, see James H. Thomas, *The East India Company and the Provinces in the Eighteenth Century*, I, *Portsmouth and the East India Company, 1700–1815* (Lewiston, N.Y., 1999), 268. John William Millers, confectioner, crafted the sugar display; see *Pennsylvania Gazette* (Philadelphia), June 20, 1765, [1].

ric for their servants and enslaved laborers. Some enslaved people had the desire and found the opportunity to obtain their own fashionable clothing made from India fabrics, and some used such clothing to pass as free. Lower-sort free families also tailored moderately expensive India fabrics into Sunday clothing or special table linen. For the home, the Philadelphia upholsterer John Webster advertised his skills in covering "Sophias, couches, canopies and canopy-beds, French elbows, stools, [and] chairs" with a range of European and Asian fabrics, and he offered to hang India "chintz, damask, or tapestry" on walls. Colonists also owned palampore bedspreads stitched in India portraying trees of life surrounded by elephants and tigers.[5]

Not just fabrics but fashions from India, too, increased in popularity. Gentlemen from Calcutta, to London, to Philadelphia wore calico or damask banyans in the East Indian style, loose and form fitting "at all times of the day and abroad in the streets" (see Plate 6). This fashion had resurged dramatically since the middle of the seventeenth century. Captain Robert Robinson of the *Oliver*, for example, fell overboard while wearing his "Scotch Plad Banyan" and was eaten by sharks. A servant ran away from Reginold Orton in Yorktown, Virginia, stealing Orton's "gray Cloth Banyan lined with Calimanco of two different Colours." Neal McMullen was described as "sometimes" wearing "a banyan and ruffles" after he stole a horse in New Hampshire. Banyans became so popular as outerwear among students that in 1755 Harvard forbade their use during commencement ceremonies. Prominent men, such as the Boylston brothers in Plates 7 and 8, posed for portraits wearing banyans and accompanying turban caps. Additionally, Atlantic colonists had begun using Indian bandannas as handkerchiefs, neckerchiefs, and headwraps as well as for making bundles. Bandannas were prohibited in Britain.[6]

5. On the general growth of colonial population and prosperity, see John J. McCusker and Russel R. Menard, *The Economy of British America, 1607–1789* (Chapel Hill, N.C., 1985), 11, 267–269, 278–294; R. C. Nash, "Domestic Material Culture and Consumer Demand in the British Atlantic World: Colonial South Carolina, 1670–1770," in David S. Shields, ed., *Material Culture in Anglo-America: Regional Identity and Urbanity in the Tidewater, Lowcountry, and Carribean* (Columbia, S.C., 2009), 250–256. For enslaved peoples, see Anne Adams, who escaped wearing "a dark flowered calico short gown." Notably, Adams was described as wearing, not taking or stealing, these items; see *Pennsylvania Gazette*, June 6, 1771, [4]; Kate Haulman, *The Politics of Fashion in Eighteenth-Century America* (Chapel Hill, N.C., 2011), 25–28. For John Webster's advertisement, see *Pennsylvania Chronicle, and Universal Advertiser* (Philadelphia), Dec. 3, 1767. For examples of palampores, see Acc. nos. 60.784, 60.786, and 60.798, Winterthur Museum and Library, Delaware.

6. "Apparel," extracted from John Fanning Watson's *Annals of Philadelphia* . . . (Phila-

Plate 6. Banyan, circa 1760. Silk and cotton linen lining. Accession no. 2008.75.
Metropolitan Museum of Art, New York, Alfred Z. Solomon–Janet A. Sloane
Endowment Fund and Isabel Shults Fund, 2008.

Several matching blue silk banyans survive, suggesting that this item was
standardized. The silk is Chinese, but the lining and cut suggest that they might
have been produced in India, and certainly many such banyans were made on the
subcontinent and in Britain of local and imported materials. One of these blue
banyans is reputed to have been worn by East India ship Captain William Fernell
(Accession no. C002338.1, Brighton Museum, U.K.).

Plate 7. John Singleton Copley, *Nicholas Boylston.* 1767. Oil on canvas, 127.3 × 101.1 cm. Harvard Art Museums / Fogg Museum, Harvard University Portrait Collection, Bequest of Ward Nicholas Boylston to Harvard College, 1828, H90. Photo: Imaging Department © President and Fellows of Harvard College

Plate 8. John Singleton Copley, *Thomas Boylston II.* Circa 1767–1769. Oil on canvas, 126.9 × 102 cm. Harvard Art Museums / Fogg Museum, Harvard University Portrait Collection, Bequest of Ward Nicholas Boylston to Harvard College, 1828, H29. Photo: Imaging Department © President and Fellows of Harvard College

Britons on both sides of the Atlantic could, however, adopt umbrellas, which had spread from Asia throughout Britain's southernmost colonies. Like the Portuguese before them, Britons in India took the right of using sun umbrellas, a local mark of power and protection from the hot sun, as their own. British people in the eighteenth-century Atlantic learned about the connection between umbrellas and status most prominently through depictions, such as the popular engravings of the Indian King and the Indian Queen. These engravings typically included a dark-skinned person under the shade of an umbrella held aloft by black boys. Palm trees frequently helped to set the tropical environment. Furthermore, the use of European dress, such as in Plate 9, made the user of the umbrella appear genteel and understandable to British audiences. Umbrellas were advertised frequently in the *Charleston Gazette* in the 1730s, but not in the *Philadelphia Gazette*. Reflecting this difference in consumption between the southern and northern colonies, women in 1740s Connecticut reportedly carried sieves on broomsticks to mock a few people who briefly adopted the fashion. Between 1751 and 1765, however, umbrellas suddenly appeared in dozens of advertisements in Philadelphia. Umbrellas were also being made in the colonies, again moving from the south to the north. In Charleston, advertisements for umbrella makers appeared in the 1730s, and in Boston in 1761 an artisan offered "UMBRILLOS of all Sorts made and Sold," targeting local women who could bring in their own silk to be "made up." A 1766 advertisement by hatter Samuel Lund in London for "a person that understands making umbrello's" suggests that finding such

---

delphia, 1830), in Samuel Hazard, ed., *Register of Pennsylvania*, VI (1833), 89 ("all times"); *American Weekly Mercury* (Philadelphia), Aug. 21–28, 1735, [2] ("Scotch"), May 5–12, 1737, [3] ("gray"); *Pennsylvania Gazette*, May 30, 1751, [6] ("sometimes"). On Harvard banyans, see Gertrude Z. Thomas, *Richer Than Spices: How a Royal Bride's Dowry Introduced Cane, Lacquer, Cottons, Tea, and Porcelain to England, and So Revolutionized Taste, Manners, Craftsmanship, and History in Both England and America* (New York, 1965), 56. On bandannas, see *American Weekly Mercury*, Sept. 26 to Oct. 3, 1734, [4]; *Pennsylvania Gazette*, May 8, 1755, [3]; *Pennsylvania Ledger; or The Philadelphia Market-Day Advertiser*, Dec. 24, 1777, [3]; Susan S. Bean, "Bandana: On the Origins of an All American Textile," in Peter Benes, ed., *Textiles in Early New England: Design, Production, and Consumption* (Boston, 1999), 170–172; Florence M. Montgomery, *Textiles in America, 1650-1870: A Dictionary Based on Original Documents, Prints and Paintings, Commercial Records, American Merchants' Papers, Shopkeepers' Advertisements, and Pattern Books with Original Swatches of Cloth* (New York, 1984), 154. For a sense of quantities of bandannas exported to the colonies compared to Europe, where quantities were smaller, see, for example, "London: Exportations of Foreign Goods and Merchandize by Certificate (Out of Time) from Christmas 1756 to Christmas 1757, with an Estimate of the Value in England," Ledgers of Imports and Exports, CUST 3/57, fols. 106r–118r, NA.

Plate 9. "John Cotterell China-Man and Glass-Seller." 1751. John Johnson Collection: Trade Cards 6(18). The Bodleian Libraries, The University of Oxford

people was still not easy, but by the 1760s they were in demand throughout the British Atlantic.[7]

7. On the Portuguese and umbrellas, see T. S. Crawford, *A History of the Umbrella* (Newton Abbot, U.K., 1970), 42–47. On the mockers, see Crawford, *History of the Umbrella*, 119. For umbrella advertisements, see, for example, *South-Carolina Gazette* (Charleston), Oct. 14, 1732, [4], Apr. 19, 1735, [3], June 7, 1735, [4], May 18, 1738, [3]; *Pennsylvania Gazette*, Sept. 4, 1760, [3]; *Boston-Gazette, and Country Journal*, June 8, 1761, [4]; *Gazetteer and New Daily Advertiser* (London), June 7, 1766. The "Indian Queen" engravings appear to be modeled after an engraving of Anne Bracegirdle performing the title character of Robert Howard and John Dryden's 1664 play by the same name. The play took place in Spanish America, not India. Retailers of East India goods adopted the icon in the eighteenth century. See William Vincent, *The Indian Queen* (London, 1683–1729?), mezzotint, NPG D19498, National Portrait Gallery, London. For an example of an Indian King image, see Charles Vere, London, January 1760, Acc. no. 60x008.4, Collection 71, Joseph Downs Collection of Manuscripts and Printed Ephemera, Winterthur Museum and Library (hereafter cited as Downs Collection, Winterthur). For the Indian Queen, see also Lope and Corrall bill to Gordon Esq., London, July 11, 1763, Acc. no. 65x068.2, Downs Collection, Winterthur; Lambden and Woods bill

Criticisms of these goods as frivolous, draining, and immoral foreign luxuries continued, as they had for more than a century, but in America with distinct racial additions. In 1762, Ann Cooper Whitall, a Quaker and future Revolutionary heroine, invoked a leitmotif of un-Christianness, foreignness, and women's fashion, which had been threaded with calico in various strands of British discourse since the seventeenth century. Whitall ranked calico as a drug, writing, "So much excess of tobacco; and tea . . . and there is the calico. Oh, the calico!" Her excitement over calico reflected its prominent place in all aspects of colonial society. She explained of Quakers, "We pretend to go in a plain dress and plain speech; but where is our plainness?" As in Britain earlier, such arguments reflected the popularity of India goods more than they represented a powerful stream of resistance. And Whitall's fulmination shows that fashions for calico and tea had spread even among the Quakers, who advocated against conspicuous consumption. Strikingly she went on to conflate tobacco, tea, and calico "with the negroes, one as bad as the other." Whitall's thinking was a product of the American context, where enslaved Africans were far more numerous than in Britain, and of her Quakerism. Whitehall, like most Quakers, believed that owning people was a sin. Her argument went beyond notions of so-called enslavement to fashion by suggesting that owning tobacco, tea, or calico was as bad as owning people—all were similar marks of ungodliness.[8]

Historians of colonial America have paid much more attention to tea

for Miss Gordon, London, July 13, 1769, Acc. no. 65x068.5, Downs Collection, Winterthur; Thomas and Daniel Blackford receipt for Charles Chisholme, London, 1777, MS 5462, NLS.

Joseph Roach argues that the parasol was a metonym marking non-Europeans as different and hyperindulgent; see Roach, "The Global Parasol: Accessorizing the Four Corners of the World," in Felicity A. Nussbaum, ed., *The Global Eighteenth Century* (Baltimore, 2003), 98–105. The Indian Queen engravings, however, aligned the element of Asian fashion with clearly European dress so that difference was effectively associated as sameness. In the middle of the eighteenth century, skin color did not necessarily mark the Indian Queen as inferior. See Roxann Wheeler, "Colonial Exchanges: Visualizing Racial Ideology and Labour in Britain and the West Indies," in Geoff Quilley and Kay Dian Kriz, eds., *An Economy of Colour: Visual Culture and the Atlantic World, 1660–1830* (Manchester, 2003), 46–48; Wheeler, *The Complexion of Race: Categories of Difference in Eighteenth-Century British Culture* (Philadelphia, 2000), 7–9.

8. Ann Cooper Whitall, "Diary of Ann Cooper Whitall, March, 1762," in H[annah] W[hitall] S[mith], ed., *John M. Whitall: The Story of His Life* (Philadelphia, 1879), 7, 19. On Quaker views of enslavement, see Brown, *Moral Capital*, 87–91. On criticisms of India fabric from Benjamin Franklin, in particular, see Haulman, *Politics of Fashion*, 93. Whitall's criticism of tea also follows earlier models; see Caroline Frank, *Objectifying China, Imagining America: Chinese Commodities in Early America* (Chicago, 2011), 190–191.

consumption than calico, largely because tea was to take on such a prominent role in 1773. Tea consumption had taken off in the colonies somewhat
later than calicoes, but by the 1750s and 1760s it was widely consumed by
men and women at a range of wealth levels. It also brought with it growing
demand for chinaware tea equipage. Colonists did not necessarily recognize that tea came from China, a completely different place in Asia than
Company Bengal, although some certainly did. In any case, as the population and prosperity of the Atlantic colonies increased rapidly in the middle
of the eighteenth century, their value as markets for Asian goods—from
calicoes, to tea, to pepper and spices—increased substantially as well. As
one anonymous author observed in 1763, the Atlantic colonies contributed
to the wealth of Britain through the consumption of *"British* manufactures, *East India* goods, provisions as well as *linens* from *Ireland,"* all paid
for with specie and raw materials.⁹

   In Britain, too, unprohibited muslin, domestic fustian meant to imitate
calico, and a range of Asian drugs, foods, teas, spices, curiosities, and home
furnishings increased in popularity. Drapers and muslin sellers offered a
variety of legal and illegal Indian fabric to the middling and upper sorts.
Meanwhile, street hawkers offered the lower ranks inexpensive white
cottons imported specifically for the bottom of the market. Through the
thriving secondhand clothing trade, the lower sorts also had access to previously enjoyed and affordable India fabrics. Large oilmen, such as Philips
and Atkinson, advertised a tremendous variety of noncloth goods, including "India pepper-pods; capsicums; India mangoes" as well as "ginger
(whole and ground); mace; cinnamon; cloves; nutmegs; sago; rice . . .
[and] petre salt," among other products from Spain, France, the Italian
Peninsula, and Russia. "Chinamen," who were not Chinese and were often
women, sold a selection of goods imported privately and by the Company
from all over Asia. Typical items included tea, chinaware, "chocolate,

---

9. [John Roberts], *Considerations on the Present Peace, as Far as It Is Relative to the Colonies, and the African Trade* (London, 1763), 7 *("British")*. On relative tea values, see K. N.
Chaudhuri, *The Trading World of Asia and the English East India Company, 1660–1760*
(Cambridge, 1978), 538–539, 540–548. For more on the rise of tea and chinaware in the colo-
nies after the 1730s, see Jane T. Merritt, "Tea Trade, Consumption, and the Republican Paradox in Prerevolutionary Philadelphia," *Pennsylvania Magazine of History and Biography*,
CXXVIII (2004), 126–130; Rodris Roth, "Tea-Drinking in Eighteenth-Century America: Its
Etiquette and Equipage," in Robert Blair St. George, ed., *Material Life in America, 1600–1800*
(Boston, 1988), 439–462; T. H. Breen, *The Marketplace of Revolution: How Consumer Politics Shaped American Independence* (New York, 2004), 177–179; Frank, *Objectifying China*,
97, 113–126, 138, 162–173.

snuff, arrack, fans, lacquered cabinets, tea tables, Indian curiosities, and lace." Between 1753 and 1774, the number of such dealers in London directories increased from eighteen to fifty-two. Additionally, shoppers looking for Asian birds and animals could buy directly from importers at the India docks or from men such as James Murdoch, "Dealer in Birds and Beasts." Household furniture auction catalogs listed Indian screens, cabinets, pictures, mats, and umbrellas. Consumption of India goods was certainly not new in the middle of the eighteenth century, but it was continuing to expand in America and Britain as consumers enjoyed a growing quantity and variety of goods and beasts to be used and exhibited.[10]

"The Proper Union of All Their Parts": India Goods and Imperial Revenues

As demand for a growing variety of India and China goods increased, Company servant John Henry Grose hoped that, "under the sanction of proper regulations, the West Indies, and our American colonies, might receive a greater benefit than they do from the East India trade, still preserving to England its right and advantage of being the centrical point of union of both." For Grose, those regulations included low duties on India goods that would encourage colonists to enjoy their own "greater benefit" but that would also expand trade and increase the number of seamen for imperial defense. Such issues were on the minds of many authors and political leaders. The situation was pressing. By 1763, the British debt

10. Hoh-cheung Mui and Lorna H. Mui, *Shops and Shopkeeping in Eighteenth-Century England* (Montreal, 1989), 19, 21–22, 56–79; Parakunnel J. Thomas, "The Beginnings of Calico-Printing in England," *English Historical Review*, XXXIX (1924), 209, 213–216; S. D. Chapman and S. Chassagne, *European Textile Printers in the Eighteenth Century: A Study of Peel and Oberkampf* (London, 1981), 79; Philips and Atkinson, oilmen, Trade Card, London, 1776, item 81 in "A Nation of Shopkeepers" Exhibition, 2001, John Johnson Collection, Bodleian Library, Oxford; Aubrey J. Toppin, "The China Trade and Some London Chinamen," *Transactions of the English Ceramic Circle*, III (1935), 45–53. Although Beverly Lemire's evidence is for an earlier period, the Company continued to import a range of qualities of cotton cloth; see Lemire, *Fashion's Favourite: The Cotton Trade and the Consumer in Britain, 1660–1800* (Oxford, 1991), 17–20, 61–76; Lemire, *The Business of Everyday Life: Gender, Practice, and Social Politics in England, c. 1600–1900* (New York, 2005), 82–140. For Murdoch, see *Indexes of the Fire Insurance Policies of the Sun Fire Office and the Royal Exchange Assurance, 1775–1787* (London, 1986), microform. For examples of auctions, see *A Catalogue of the Genteel Household Furniture . . . of a Gentleman*, Apr. 1, 1773, Christie's Auction House, London; *A Catalogue of all the Neat and Genuine Household Furniture, Plate, Pictures, Prints, Some Linen, China, etc. of Mr Swainton, Gone Abroad at His House, on the West Side of Queen's Square, Bloomsbury*, Apr. 30, 1772, Christie's Auction House, London.

amounted to more than £133 million. Parliament needed to decide how to use its expanding empire to help pay for the costs of its expansion. The goal, however, was not necessarily to use reforms in America to pay down the debt directly. The current system already generated state revenue simultaneously from India's production and from the consumption of India goods at home, in the Atlantic colonies, and elsewhere abroad. The conquest of Bengal now promised far more revenue than America. That conquest, combined with the popularity of India goods, the existing India trade regulations, and long-standing designs to capitalize on that trade would drive a constitutional struggle over colonial legislation and revenue in the decade following the Seven Years' War.[11]

The customs revenue generated by the East India Company's trade bolstered the British Treasury in times of war and peace. According to the Company's records, from 1750–1751 to 1780–1781 the Company's goods generated approximately £36,000,000 in customs and excise revenue for the state. Total government income from all sources during this thirty-year period was £311,317,805. The Company's imports thus generated more than 11 percent of British government income, all with approximately 2 percent of British ship tonnage. But these long-term figures also hide significant growth in customs revenue from Company goods in the 1760s. Customs revenue on goods imported from Asia more than doubled, from £430,123 in 1763–1764 to £886,922 in 1769–1770. In the latter fiscal year, the British exchequer brought in a total of £2,739,257 of customs revenue. The Company thus accounted for about one-third of Britain's customs income in 1769–1770. Part of the answer to the increase can be found in the growing demand for a broad range of Asian goods throughout the Atlantic. But part of the answer also lies in changes to the duties themselves.[12]

11. Malachy Postlethwayt, *Britain's Commercial Interest Explained and Improved; In a Series of Dissertations on Several Important Branches of Her Trade and Police . . .* , 2 vols. (London, 1757), I, 401. John Henry Grose's work appeared in several editions into the 1770s, and the sentence remained. It was also translated into French. See Grose, *A Voyage to the East-Indies, with Observations on Various Parts There* (London, 1757), 402. The debt figure is from John Brewer, *The Sinews of Power: War, Money, and the English State, 1688-1783* (London, 1988), 114–116. For more on the issue of legislative supremacy, see Greene, *Constitutional Origins*, 67–103.

12. "Amount of the Customs and Duties, Also an Estimate as Nearly as May Be, of the Excise Received by Government on Account of the Company's Trade for 16 Years Preceding 1766, and for Years Following That Period," IOR/L/AG/18/2/1, BL. Government income was calculated using "Accounts of Net Public Income and Expenditure of Great Britain and Ireland, 1688–1800; Receipts and Issues from Exchequer; Accounts of Gross Public Income and Expenditure, 1801-69," in Great Britain, House of Commons, *Parliamentary Papers*,

In the early 1760s, the government explored the possibility of reducing drawbacks to increase its net revenue. Colonists were already paying sizable duties on significant imports of calicoes, amounting in 1763 to nearly £27,000 net on 81,140 pieces. Most of the net duty, however, came from dyed, printed, or stained calicoes that did not have big drawbacks. The government asked John Tomkyns, the assistant inspector general of the customs, to work up a series of reports detailing the cost to the Treasury of the drawbacks on foreign goods. For 1761, Tomkyns found that drawbacks on white calicoes were worth more than on all other foreign fabrics reexported to the colonies combined. The white calico drawbacks totaled £39,511.0.7 as well as several hundred more pounds in other India fabrics rated at value—all revenue lost to the state. The drawbacks on spices, in contrast, totaled only several hundred pounds. Altogether, drawbacks on India goods, almost all on white India fabrics, accounted for nearly half the value of total drawbacks on foreign goods reexported to the colonies. Tomkyns also provided reports specifically on calicoes and linens for the years 1761–1763. During these years, the colonies took between 57,588 and 69,310 pieces of "white callicoes." These goods paid nearly £83,000 in duties, but the state only netted approximately £1,300 after drawbacks. An anonymous commentator on the report noted that if a proposal to reduce the drawback by a third was implemented the state would keep approximately £8,667.15.3 more per year from the colonial consumption of India's white calicoes. The government was paying attention to the reports.[13]

XXXV, no. 1 (London, 1869), paper 366, 164, 430–433. Ship tonnage is from Ralph Davis, *The Rise of the English Shipping Industry in the Seventeenth and Eighteenth Centuries* (New York, 1962), 26–27, 266. The Company report did not clearly specify whether the indicated customs revenue paid to the state was gross or net of drawbacks. As H. V. Bowen points out, incoming goods purchased with reexported Company goods paid import duties as well, offsetting much of the revenue lost to drawbacks if indeed the data represented gross revenue. Annual customs revenue data for 1763–1764 and 1769–1770 on India goods is from IOR/L/AG/1/1, XX–XXXI, BL, compiled by H. V. Bowen, *The Business of Empire: The East India Company and Imperial Britain, 1756–1833* (Cambridge, 2006), 39.

13. "An Account of All Foreign Good Exported to the British Colonies in America, Particularly Wines and Callicoes Whether under Certificate or Otherwise from Xmas 1763 to Xmas 1764 with the Amount of the Duties and Drawbacks Paid on the Same," Liverpool Papers, CXCVIII, Add. MS 38387, fols. 61r–63r, BL; John Tomkyns, "An Account of the Amount of the Drawbacks upon Each Article of Foreign Goods Re-exported by Certificate from England to the American Colonies between the 1st of January 1761 and the 1st of January 1762," Apr. 15, 1763, Liverpool Papers, CXLVI, Add. MS 38335, fols. 87r–89r, BL; Tomkyns, "An Account of the Quantity of White Callicoes and Foreign Linen Exported from England to the British Colonies and Plantations in America v of the Duties and Drawbacks Paid

In the often misunderstood 1764 Sugar Act, Parliament duly enacted the proposal to reduce the drawbacks on white calico and muslin reexported to the colonies by a third. Additionally, the act levied duties of 2s on every pound of India wrought silk, and 2s 6d on every piece of colored India calico reexported to the colonies. Historians have paid little attention to the already substantial revenue generated on colored India cloth and the additional new revenue in the Sugar Act from all India cloth. A focus on sugar (the act lowered the duty on all molasses to discourage smuggling and increased the duties on foreign sugar to support colonial planters) elides the duties on calico and many other goods adjusted by the act. The calico revenue and its successful long-term collection helps to explain the two primary reactions to the Sugar Act. Many Britons on both sides of the Atlantic saw the Sugar Act as economically disadvantageous for many colonists but in keeping with a long-standing system. The support of the Sugar Act for the jurisdiction of Admiralty courts over all customs cases, for instance, seemed radical to some, but Admiralty courts had heard smuggling cases before—indeed, sometimes in the face of colonial protests. The precedents established around goods such as calico and arrack in the first three decades of the eighteenth century were for many colonists not part of recent memory, and for those well versed in regulatory and jurisdictional history they were unwelcome. For some people in Britain and America, the Sugar Act's language and focus on many types of revenue and new enforcement efforts suggested a significant constitutional shift toward Parliament's taxing the colonies.[14]

Thomas Pownall proposed much more radical changes to the system

---

Thereon for the Last Three Years Viz from Xmas 1760 to Xmas 1763 Distinguishing Each Year," Mar. 19, 1764, Liverpool Papers, CXLVIII, Add. MS 38337, fols. 221v–222r, BL. The commentator also noted that reducing the drawback on reexports of white calicoes to Europe by a third would keep £51,234.15.7 in revenue for the state; see "Observations on Duties on Callicoes as Stated by Mr. John Tomkyns Assist. Insp. Gen.," Liverpool Papers, CXLIX, Add. MS 38338, fols. 191r–192r, BL.

14. "Clause Relating to the Drawback on Muslin and White Callicoes," Liverpool Papers, CXLVIII, Add. MS 38337, fol. 291r, BL; P. D. G. Thomas, *British Politics and the Stamp Act Crisis: The First Phase of the American Revolution, 1763–1767* (Oxford, 1975), 270–271. For an outstanding overview of colonial responses to the act and how those responses changed over time, see John Phillip Reid, *Constitutional History of the American Revolution: The Authority to Tax* (Madison, Wis., 1987), 2, 194–207. The historian Oliver M. Dickerson argued, following the line of some colonists, that the Sugar Act was "a constitutional revolution" intended to change from "the old system to the new system"; see Dickerson, *The Navigation Acts and the American Revolution* (Philadelphia, 1951), 179–184. On the use of Admiralty courts for smuggling cases, see Chapter 3.

than anything in the Sugar Act. Pownall had been governor of Massachusetts from 1757 to 1759 and was well connected with the Board of Trade. He was one of the colonists' best champions in London, although his later plan for a unified imperial Parliament gained him scorn from several patriots. In his frequently republished and widely read *Administration of the Colonies,* Pownall agreed with the principle that America should be made into "one of the greatest marts in the world, with every attendant advantage to the British general commerce, and the special interest of the East India trade." Pownall argued that strictly enforcing the current laws governing the import of foreign Europe and India goods into the colonies might "bring on the necessity of these Americans manufacturing for themselves." Such an undesirable outcome would drive down the demand for both British and Indian manufactures. Instead, the East India Company should be given a land grant in a new West India conquest, such as Grenada. The Company could send an annual ship from Asia to the island, which would give colonists a direct access point to India goods and the Company direct access to Spanish silver. It would "open a better channel of trade between the East and West-Indies, which our company must command." Prices would be lower, smuggling reduced, and duties readily collected. Grenada, then, would come to better fulfill the role currently filled by London in the India trade.[15]

Thomas Whately, one of the architects of the Sugar Act, rebutted such calls for restructuring the current system and outlined the many ways in which the act followed long-standing pan-imperial policies and practices. That a man with as yet no experience on the Board of Trade so fully understood the global integration of the empire and trading system that Parliament and the Board had devised before he had even been born reflected the extent to which this integration had become entrenched. Whately explained that the "aristocratical Opulence" of West Indian planters "enables them to demand the Products of the *East Indies,* and other Countries, more similar in Climate, in Taste, and in Manners, to their own,"

15. [Thomas Pownall], *The Administration of the Colonies* (London, 1764), 121–129; Pownall, *The Administration of the Colonies,* 2d ed. (London, 1765), 191–199; Pownall, *The Administration of the Colonies . . . ,* 4th ed. (London, 1768), 306–316. Similarly, Thomas Forrest recommended the creation of a new "Circumnavigating East-India Company" to be based in Australia for access to Peru, essentially mirroring Pownall's plan for Grenada. Forrest explained that Peru's inhabitants are "very rich" and would buy all the cottons that they could get. See [Forrest], *Reflections on the Present State of the East-India Trade; and Proposals to Render It of More General Benefit to the British Nation, without Changing the Present System* ([n.p.], [1769]), 3–13.

but he noted that colonists throughout America also enjoyed foreign and, particularly, India goods. Indeed, "the Indulgence . . . of wearing them is not taken away from the Colonies," and the new higher duties were still much lower than those that consumers in England had paid before Parliament had banned colored calicoes domestically. Whately also considered the effect of the duty in potentially ceding to the Dutch the lucrative trade in calicoes with the Spanish colonies, echoing one of the main concerns voiced by opponents to the Calico Acts. He noted that the British East India Company had long since overtaken the abilities of the Dutch and that the British Company alone could provide the calicoes adapted to South America and the West Indies. The Dutch, he pointed out (and as backed up by the customs records), purchased much of their supply at the Company's London sales and would thus be subject to British duties. The duties would also not damage the domestic calico printers because a substantial, though more limited, drawback would continue for them. On the issue of constitutionality, he noted that the colonists had long ago accepted Parliament's duties and trading regulations.[16]

Tomkyns's reports also suggested the benefits of keeping the current system. He explained that the British colonists still did not buy nearly as many calicoes reexported from Britain as continental Europeans did but that their importance had grown since the Calico Acts, particularly indirectly if one included the enslaved people purchased for the colonies with calicoes in Africa. New York, New England, and Pennsylvania had markedly increased consumption. The ex-French colony of Quebec had steadily taken more dyed, printed, or stained calicoes every year after becoming part of the British empire; in 1764 it took 1,907 pieces. Altogether from 1761 to 1763, the British colonies imported 41,349 pieces of calicoes prohibited in Britain, whereas Europe and Africa took 389,920 pieces. Holland was the primary destination, but Africa followed close behind. As the East India Company directors wrote to their servants, "We are desirous of contributing as far as lays in our Power to the Encouragement of a Trade on which the well being of the British Plantations in the West Indies so much depends, and considering the same therefore in a National View." Even older arguments resurfaced in 1765, too. According to these views, Parliament needed to be sure to jealously guard the Indian

16. [Thomas Whately], *The Regulations Lately Made concerning the Colonies, and the Taxes Imposed upon Them, Considered* (London, 1765), 6, 59, 70–73, 104–105. Whately, a rising star in Parliament, became secretary to the treasury and responsible for guiding colonial policy in late 1763; see Rory T. Cornish, "Whately, Thomas (1726–1772)," *DNB*.

reexport trade, which enabled Britain to "exert a naval power in all parts of the world; under the influence of which, by extending our commerce to the more distant territories, we gain such a superiority in the competition with other rivals, as greatly to enlage *[sic]* even our European Trade." Britain benefited from Atlantic consumption of India goods passed through London.[17]

Some colonists celebrated their continued role in supporting the India trade for the empire. Francis Hopkinson, a customs collector and eventual patriot, published *Four Dissertations, on the Reciprocal Advantages of a Perpetual Union between Great-Britain and Her American Colonies* in both Philadelphia and London. Hopkinson asserted that, since the American colonies supplied the bullion to send to Asia and then participated in "the vast consumption of *India* goods, the flourishing condition of that valuable branch of commerce, may, in no small degree, very justly be attributed to the *American* Colonies." Colonists, he claimed, purchased British and British-Indian goods worth two million pounds more per year than the value of the goods they exported back. Colonists thus needed to export two million pounds of bullion to Britain to balance their accounts, bullion that was sent to purchase yet more goods in Asia. Far from resenting this expenditure, Hopkinson trumpeted it as evidence of the highly beneficial integration of India and America in the British imperial system.[18]

Still, other Britons argued that Parliament had gone too far with the duties on India goods consumed in the Atlantic colonies. "A Merchant of

17. Tomkyns noted that, since there were no drawbacks on colored calicoes and silks, merchants did not bother to report their reexports carefully. Still, any underreporting would not likely change the order of the leading destinations. See John Tomkyns, "An Account of All Callicoes Printed, Painted, Stained, or Dyed in the East Indies, Which Have Been Exported from Christmas 1760 to Christmas 1763 Distinguishing Those That Have Been Exported to the British Colonies and the Plantations in America from Those That Have Been Exported to Other Places," Jan. 15, 1765, Liverpool Papers, CL, Add. MS 38339, fol. 17r, BL; Tomkyns, "An Account of Callicoes Painted, Printed, Stained, or Dyed in Persia, China, or East India Exported from Xmas 1760 to Xmas 1764 Distinguishing to What Countries," Mar. 12, 1765, Liverpool Papers, CL, Add. MS 38339, fol. 89, BL; Directors to Ft. St. George, Feb. 15, 1765, IOR E/4/863, 79, BL; Directors to Ft. William, Feb. 15, 1765, *Fort William–India House Correspondence*, IV, 92; [William Mildmay], *The Laws and Policy of England, Relating to Trade, Examined by the Maxims and Principles of Trade in General; and by the Laws and Policy of Other Trading Nations* (London, 1765), 72–83.

18. [Francis Hopkinson], *Four Dissertations, on the Reciprocal Advantages of a Perpetual Union between Great-Britain and Her American Colonies* (Philadelphia, 1766), 57–60; P. M. Zall, "Hopkinson, Francis (1737–1791)," *DNB*.

Plate 10. *The Great Financier; or, British Oeconomy for the Years 1763, 1764, 1765*. [London, 1765]. Library of Congress, Prints and Photographs Division, LC-USZ62-45399

London" argued that higher duty rates would reduce consumption, which would decrease revenue. He also expected that British merchants would be compelled to quit the whole Africa trade owing to a new requirement to cancel their bonds on India goods reexported for Africa within eighteen months to reduce the risk of smuggling. Colonists would suffer doubly as enslaved people would become more expensive (there was no mention of the suffering of those enslaved). Similarly, in the satirical print *The Great Financier; or, British Oeconomy for the Years 1763, 1764, 1765* (Plate 10), Britannia slumps with her head in her hand, disgusted, as Prime Minister George Grenville weighs the national debt against the revenue that he could extract from the Atlantic fisheries, the Atlantic colonies, and India. The Atlantic colonies, represented as a native American woman, and India, personified by Robert Clive wearing a banyan and turban, are both reduced to their knees. The native American protests that with better policies "Commerce will outweigh" the revenue intended to be extracted by heavy taxation. The text explains that Grenville "discharges our Debts by destroying our Trade." The colonists protested in vain, because "for Conquests, or Commerce he [Grenville] cares not a Straw." Parliament's new policies would destroy both the Atlantic and Indian Ocean trades and, thereby, the value of Britain's colonies.[19]

The most effective noises opposing the Stamp Act, which was levied on paper products in 1765, likewise came from trumped-up concerns of economic devastation caused by the tax and colonial nonimportation movement, but for colonists constitutional issues became prominent. Merchants and manufacturers in Britain as well as merchants and mobs in America lobbied much harder for Parliament to rescind the Stamp Act than the Sugar Act. Many colonists, with the support of William Pitt in Parliament, claimed that the new taxes were unconstitutional. Benjamin Franklin, in particular, stressed to Parliament an awkward difference between legal external taxes or duties to regulate trade and illegal internal taxes. The influential writer Richard Bland made the same point and also explained the danger of Parliament's controlling colonial officials. Parliament scrapped the Stamp Act, but it quickly passed the Declaratory Act, which proclaimed Parliament's authority to tax the colonies. The notions of internal and external taxation developed over the Stamp Act would shape future acts dealing with India goods.[20]

Some Britons, meanwhile, returned to calls for more radical revisions of the trade linking India and America. The "Untainted Englishman," for instance, rehashed long-standing arguments that an open trade allowing any Britons anywhere to trade with India would drive down prices through competition and generate more revenue for the state. Additional revenue might also come from a public subscription in celebration of the end of all monopolies, the taxation of true luxuries such as servants and

19. A Merchant of London, *The True Interest of Great Britain, with respect to Her American Colonies, Stated and Impartially Considered* (London, 1766), 8–10.

20. Richard Bland, *An Inquiry into the Rights of the British Colonies . . .* (Williamsburg, Va., 1766), 24–25, 29–30. Edmund S. Morgan and Helen M. Morgan argued that the colonists saw no difference between internal and external taxation, and certainly many, including John Dickinson, disavowed the distinction. See Morgan and Morgan, *The Stamp Act Crisis: Prologue to Revolution* (Chapel Hill, N.C., 1953), 35–40; Robert Middlekauff, *The Glorious Cause: The American Revolution, 1763-1789* (New York, 1982), 69; [Dickinson], *Letters from a Farmer in Pennsylvania, to the Inhabitants of the British Colonies* (Philadelphia, 1768), 18–22. On the importance of trade arguments, the playing down of constitutional arguments in Britain, and Franklin, see Thomas, *British Politics and the Stamp Act Crisis*, 84–100, 214–216, 224.

horses, and the growth in exports from Britain to India. By disbanding the Company, moreover, the British state could take direct control of the Company's Indian conquests and land tax revenue, imaginatively estimated at four million pounds. He admitted that opening the trade would overthrow the imperial system, which had been in place since the Calico Acts. Colonists would "reap very considerable Advantages from the East India Trade; greatly to the Prejudice of Great Britain." These advantages would lead ultimately to "the *Independence* of the Americans," but the Untainted Englishman figured that the Americans wanted to become independent anyway. Besides, this loss would be offset by the projected gains from the Indian conquests. In the short term, this plan might have prevented India goods from becoming a touchstone issue for the larger constitutional debate over legislative power.[21]

Instead of such dramatic reforms, in the late 1760s the government passed several interlocking acts, known collectively as the Townshend Acts (after Charles Townshend, chancellor of the exchequer). These acts were designed to draw more revenue from the Company and to enhance the central government's position in the colonies to better enforce imperial trading regulations. Under the Indemnity Act (1767), Parliament lowered duties on tea sent to the colonies to discourage smuggling and aid the Company's sales. The Company was required to compensate the government for lost revenue, which totaled £299,200 between 1768 and early 1772. Parliament also negotiated a tribute of £400,000 per year from the Company, satisfying the Company's desire to maintain its control over the diwani and its conquests as well as the government's desire for part of the revenue. India was paying out.[22]

---

21. [Untainted Englishman], *The Absolute Necessity of Laying Open the Trade to the East-Indies* . . . (London, 1767), 14–36, 52–55, 60; [Untainted Englishman], *An Attempt to Pay Off the National Debt, by Abolishing the East-India Company of Merchants; and All Other Monopolies; with Other Interesting Measures* (London, 1767), 12–35; *An Infallible Remedy for the High Prices of Provisions; Together with a Scheme for Laying Open the Trade to the East-Indies* . . . (London, 1768), 19–28; [Untainted Englishman], *The Nature of a Quarantine, as It Is Performed in Italy; to Guard against That Very Alarming and Dreadful Contagious Distemper, Commonly Called, the Plague; with Important Remarks on the Necessity of Laying Open the Trade to the East Indies; to Enable the Government (by an Increase of Revenue Arising from an Extension of Commerce) to Take Off the Taxes Which Burthen the Nation, the Only True Means of Providing a Relief for the General Distress* (London, 1767), xiv–xvi.

22. H. V. Bowen, *Revenue and Reform: The Indian Problem in British Politics, 1757–1773* (Cambridge, 1991), 59–65, 109, 122–123; P. J. Marshall, *The Making and Unmaking of Empires: Britain, India, and America, c.1750–1783* (Oxford, 2005), 308.

As for America, in contrast, Townshend did not intend to drain signifi-cant wealth directly out of the colonies. The Revenue Act (1767) increased the duties on a variety of British and East India Company goods, with the total gains expected to be only forty thousand pounds per year. The duties on tea were increased above the Indemnity Act rates, but the total effec-tive duty rate would still be lower than before. Townshend estimated that the duty on tea would generate twenty thousand pounds, less than that generated by the duties already on calicoes sent to the colonies. The gov-ernment expected little complaint since the new taxes were in the pattern of external taxation. He intended to use the modest new revenue to shift the routing of payments to colonial governors, judges, and other officials through Parliament instead of through colonial assemblies, hoping that men paid by Parliament would be less amenable to colonial smuggling and corruption.[23]

Future patriot leader John Dickinson claimed this "NEW SYSTEM OF REVENUE" violated the old system of trade. Instead of focusing on a split between internal and external taxation, he explained that the duties failed the test of regulating commerce for the good of the empire and were there-fore illegal. Many of the duties were on necessaries from Britain, and they did not encourage the consumption of British goods over colonial or other European manufactures. The Sugar Act duties, in contrast, were not ille-gal taxes; they were duties on foreign goods, which were not necessities, and despite generating revenue they were also designed to regulate trade to benefit the empire as a whole. Duties on calicoes and teas, as foreign luxuries, were therefore not necessarily a problem. The use of the Towns-hend revenue to pay colonial officials, however, was a serious usurpation of colonial constitutional rights. What looked like a modest extension of an existing system and an implementation of old ideas in London appeared remarkably different to Dickinson. But these were not the only arguments relating to India goods.[24]

A New York author calling himself a "Linen Draper" argued against the importation of any *"Asiatick Goods"* by applying to America many

23. Peter D. G. Thomas explains that, even had the Townshend duties been put into full operation, they likely would not have significantly increased Parliament's position in the colonies because the affected offices were too small and many colonies would still have chosen which officials would be appointed; see Thomas, *British Politics and the Stamp Act Crisis*, 348–362. For details on the negotiations in London, see Thomas, *The Townshend Duties Crisis: The Second Phase of the American Revolution, 1767–1773* (Oxford, 1987), 9, 26–35.

24. [Dickinson], *Letters*, 7–13, 18–22, 43–48, 64n ("NEW").

arguments used earlier in Britain. The author argued that trade riches came from the biggest imbalance possible between exports and imports — therefore, Britain kept America poor by siphoning off its wealth in exchange for British and Indian manufactures. Echoing those in Britain who had argued in favor of banning calicoes at the beginning of the century, he posited that foreign trade might make sense as a path to wealth for the Dutch, who had little and poor land, but it did not make sense for people in America. A colonist could only achieve the "Deliverance and Salvation of his Country" by manufacturing goods, especially fabrics. Encouraging homespun fabric, he wrote that, instead of "Domestic Trade, which would be attended with Peace, Plenty, Happiness, and Independance on other Countries . . . we chuse to ransack almost half the Globe, and often contrary to the Laws, in pursuit of such Things as we might produce in our own Country." Public spinning meetings bringing together several women to produce thread and cloth to political effect surged in New England. Some colonists fused concerns that had circulated for decades on both sides of the Atlantic about the moral risks of affordable yet luxurious fabric and the belief in the godliness of domestic production with newer colonial worries over imperial control and corruption. This collection of concerns and ideals supported a pan-colonial movement to boycott goods from Britain as a means of applying pressure for the repeal of Townshend's Revenue Act.[25]

Many patriot and loyalist merchants and consumers, however, continued to support the pan-imperial system and did not see India goods as conduits for corruption or dangerous constitutional changes. The Virginia boycotts of 1769, for instance, specifically exempted a range of goods that included inexpensive linen and woolen cloth as well as spices from India. Additionally, the boycotts only applied to "Callico or Cotton Stuffs of more than Two Shillings per Yard," even more generously reset in 1770 at three shillings. In Philadelphia, consumption of Indian cotton cloth continued at a significant rate. Customs records for 1769 show 11,082 pieces and 146 ells of unrated Indian piece goods as well as 4,136 pieces of "calico and muslin variety" and 92 ready-made shirts (probably banyan-style). These various pieces amounted to about 225,000 yards of cotton cloth. Philadel-

25. [Linen Draper], *The Commercial Conduct of the Province of New-York Considered . . .* (New York, 1767), 6–20. On the boycott, spinning meetings, moral risks, and the virtue of domestic production, see Breen, *Marketplace*, 156–166, 198–200, 211–213, 231–268, 282; Laurel Thatcher Ulrich, *The Age of Homespun: Objects and Stories in the Creation of an American Myth* (New York, 2001), 176–184.

phia merchants cleared an additional 92,458 yards of printed and plain calicoes not itemized by piece. Between 1767 and 1772, on either side of the boycott and during it, the *Pennsylvania Chronicle* ran more than one hundred advertisements that denoted specifically Indian fabric, further illustrating its continued popularity. Additionally, advertisers throughout the colonies continued to highlight, with clear block letters, London's importance in supplying India goods. In the early 1770s, after the boycott faded out with the repeal of the Townshend duties, except on tea, Philadelphia advertisers headlined "English and East India Goods." Such advertisements boasted about the ability of the empire to bring to America the most diverse and finest fabrics. In Boston, Gilbert Deblois offered the "Cream of Goods" from London at his "Cheap Shop," including "English, Scots, Irish, Dutch and India Goods."[26]

During and after the boycott, colonists and merchants continued to request specifically India goods, styles, and qualities from powerful London associates to satisfy local consumers. Throughout 1769 and after, the

26. "Virginia Nonimportation Resolutions, 1769, Williamsburg, Wednesday, the 17th May, 1769," and "Virginia Nonimportation Resolutions [22 June 1770]," in Barbara B. Oberg and J. Jefferson Looney, eds., *The Papers of Thomas Jefferson Digital Edition* (Charlottesville, Va., 2008); "Account of all Foreign Goods and Produce Imported into the Several Ports of North America from Great Britain and Ireland, from the 5th of January 1769 to the 5th of Jan. 1770," Ledgers of Imports and Exports, America, 1768–1773, CUST 16/1, 95, NA. For advertisements during the boycott period, see *Pennsylvania Chronicle, and Universal Advertiser*, July 17–24, 1769, 217, Apr. 22–29, 1771, 56; *Nova Scotia Chronicle and Weekly Advertiser* (Halifax), Aug. 7–24, 1770, 264 (Nova Scotia, like several other colonies, did not participate in the boycott). For advertisements after the boycott period, see *Massachusetts Gazette, and the Boston Post-Boy and Advertiser*, Apr. 13, 1772, [3] and *Censor* (Boston), Apr. 25, 1772, [1] ("Cream"); *Nova Scotia Gazette and Weekly Chronicle* (Halifax), Apr. 20, 1773, 2; *Imported in the Last Ships from London, by John Appleton* ([Salem], 1773), American Antiquarian Society, Worcester, Mass. On measurements of cloth, see James and Drinker to Pigou and Booth, Mar. 26, 1774, and June 29, 1774, Drinker Family Papers, Collection 176, HSP; "Invoice of Two Bales and Six Trunks of Merchandise as Shipped by Sargent Chambers and Co. on the Elizabeth, Alex Christie Master, by Order and on Account of Wm Philip Francis at Philadelphia, London, 15 January 1771," (Phi) Amb 3400, Collection 2001, HSP. Pieces typically measured one yard wide and fifteen to twenty-four yards long. Ells measured forty-five inches wide and fifteen to eighteen yards long. In the early 1770s, Philadelphia enjoyed what the historian Kate Haulman calls "a period of conspicuous consumption" marked by "an influx of inexpensive imported goods and the adoption of extravagant, eye-catching styles for men and women"; see Haulman, "Fashion and the Culture Wars of Revolutionary Philadelphia," *WMQ*, 3d Ser., LXII (2005), 625–645; Haulman, *Politics of Fashion*, 127–130. On merchant economic and political acrobatics in supporting and undermining the boycotts, see Merritt, "Tea Trade, Consumption, and the Republican Paradox," *PMHB*, CXXVIII (2004), 134–137.

India and the American Revolution

merchant Samuel Nightingale in Rhode Island ordered spices, bandan-nas, Bengals, romals, and calicoes from the firm of Hayley and Hopkins in London. George Hayley was one of London's wealthiest merchants; he was the brother-in-law of John Wilkes and would soon become a member of Parliament and leader in the movement to avoid war with the Ameri-can colonies. In 1771, Thomas Jefferson ordered specifically Indian cotton stockings, silk stockings, and a "neatly finished" umbrella from Thomas Adams in London. As tensions increased again, the Philadelphia Quaker firm of Abel James and Henry Drinker ordered its India cloth from the powerful London partnership of East India Company directors Frederick Pigou and Benjamin Booth. James and Drinker ordered such India fab-rics as humhums, cossaes, and Patna chintz. They sent patterns, dimen-sions, and prices of locally fashionable fabrics to Pigou and Booth, much as colonial merchants had done for decades. "We have sent the colours to shew what we mean when we say Doves, Leads, Browns, Blues, etc," they explained. James and Drinker asked Pigou and Booth for new India products to introduce to the colonies, including "any neat patterns 12, 16, or 18 yds shipp'd here and to New York (for womens wear or Furniture) which are not high priced and you think are clever and bargains." Through such experiments, James and Drinker continued to introduce new styles from India into colonial fashion. And, as they had also done for decades, the Company directors still demanded from India "improvements in some parts and alterations in others as may in future render our investment more applicable to the European, American, and African markets."[27]

27. For orders, see Mar. 6, Nov. 2, 1769, Aug. 24, 1771, Feb. 20, 1772, Nightingale-Jenckes Papers, MSS 588, box 4, oversized vol. VII, Invoice Book, 1769–1773, Rhode Island Histori-cal Society, Providence. For another example of a Rhode Island merchant's importing India cloth from London, but in this case also struggling to pay for it, see Hayes and Polock to Har-ford and Powell, May 12 and 17, 1769, Henry Marchant Papers, MSS 552, box 2, Rhode Island Historical Society. On Hayley, see Lewis Namier and John Brooke, *The House of Commons, 1754–1790*, 3 vols. (London, 1964), II, 602–603. For Jefferson's order, see Thomas Jefferson to Thomas Adams, June 1, 1771, in Oberg and Looney, eds., *Papers of Jefferson Digital Edi-tion*. See James and Drinker to Pigou and Booth, Oct. 30, 1773, James and Drinker Foreign Letter Book, 1772–1785, Drinker Family Papers, Collection 176, HSP, Mar. 26, June 29, 1774. James and Drinker wound up on the wrong side of the tea crisis, as they won contracts to im-port the Company's tea. On Booth, see Holden Furber, "The United Company of Merchants of England Trading to the East Indies, 1783–96," *EHR*, X (1940), 145; C. H. and D. Philips, "Alphabetical List of Directors of the East India Company from 1758 to 1858," *Journal of the Royal Asiatic Society of Great Britain and Ireland* (1941), 325–336. For the directors' de-mand, see "Extract of General Letter from Court of Directors Dated 7th April 1773," General Letters from the Court of Directors Commercial Department, Dec. 18, 1765–Sept. 15, 1785, State Archives of West Bengal, Kolkata, India.

In the 1760s, the British government had sought to improve its regulation and revenue regime to better control the long-standing reexport trade in India goods to the Atlantic colonies. Substantial colonial resistance did not occur until the Stamp Act brought the paper tax to America and Townshend later increased duties on a large basket of goods to pay colonial officials. Other than the Stamp Act, most of the changes had decreased drawbacks, increased rates, strengthened enforcement, or encouraged the purchase of legal instead of smuggled goods following attempts and debates since the early eighteenth century. From the perspective of most in the imperial government, these changes were modest compared to suggestions for ending the Company monopoly or creating new Atlantic entrepôts for India goods. Certainly the changes intended for America were modest compared to those intended to draw unprecedented wealth from India for Company shareholders and the British government alike. Colonial resistance was, nevertheless, effective in gaining repeal on most of the new Atlantic laws except the tea duty. For the vast majority of colonists, the remaining tea duty, even to pay colonial officials, was worth neither war nor continuing nonimportation. Between 1770 and 1773, colonists paid duties on 787,000 pounds of Company tea. Given the long-standing system of duties on Asian goods funneled through London and the limited effect of the pay change, the colonial response was not surprising. Leaders of the colonial resistance such as Dickinson and Bland had voiced little about the danger of the Company or its regime in India, and concerns about Asian luxury did not sway many.[28]

28. Thomas is likely correct that Dickinson's point about British manufactures was not significant enough in the government's reasoning to rescind most of the Townshend duties; nevertheless, the government's circular letter (which was harsher than intended) to the colonies indicated that the non-tea duties would be removed because they were "'contrary to the true principles of commerce'"; see Thomas, *Townshend Duties*, 92–93, 137–141 (quotation on 139), 173. Dickinson's point, even if it was not the reason for the repeal of the other duties, was valuable because colonists had many different views on the limits of Parliament's duty and tax powers. Only the most extreme denied the right of duties to direct trade. On non-importation falling apart, see Thomas, *Townshend Duties*, 199–206, 210–212. On tea as corrupting and continued consumption, see Merritt, "Tea Trade, Consumption, and the Republican Paradox," *PMHB*, CXXVIII (2004), 126–130, 138–140. On continued consumption, see Schlesinger, "Uprising against the East India Company," *Political Science Quarterly*, XXII (1917), 60–62, 65–66; Benjamin Labaree, *The Boston Tea Party* (New York, 1964), 50–53, 104–106; Thomas, *Townshend Duties*, 246–249, 256.

Debates over taxation and its constitutionality connected India and America, but they were only one part of a more wide-ranging discussion about the similarities and differences in the constitutional positions of British subjects in the Atlantic and Indian Oceans. The question of virtual representation, for instance, was not confined to the Atlantic. In 1765, Thomas Whately drew a parallel between the East India Company, which acted as the colonial government of India, and the American colonies, as virtually represented in Parliament. Daniel Dulany responded that many members of the East India Company lived in Britain and could be, and were, elected to Parliament. Colonists living in America, however, had no such opportunities to be represented. Dulany omitted to mention that the people of India could not vote or be elected to Parliament either. A year later, Josiah Tucker saw no problem in using the East India Company's ability to "dispose of the Fate of Kings and Kingdoms abroad" without direct representation in Parliament to encourage support among American colonists for the beauty of virtual representation. But, again, opponents pointed out that several Company stockholders had been elected as members of Parliament, and therefore the Company enjoyed actual representation, as Americans should, too. The radical Stephen Sayre explained, "Englishmen, and their descendants, wherever they go, and wherever they plant themselves, are Englishmen, with all their rights, privileges, and freedom." Sayre emphasized that he really meant "wherever," writing, "Nor is he less an Englishmen who lives in India, Africa, or America, than he who daily basks in the immediate sunshine of royal presence." This was a broad vision of a shared constitution among English people all over the globe.[29]

---

29. [Richard Clarke], *The Nabob; or, Asiatic Plunderers: A Satyrical Poem, in a Dialogue between a Friend and the Author* (London, 1773), iii; [Whately], *Regulations Lately Made,* 108–109; [Daniel Dulany], *Considerations on the Propriety of Imposing Taxes in the British Colonies* . . . (New York, 1765), 6–7; [Josiah Tucker], *A Letter from a Merchant in London to His Nephew in North America, Relative to the Present Posture of Affairs in the Colonies; in Which the Supposed Violation of Charters, and the Several Grievances Complained of, Are Particularly Discussed, and the Consequences of an Attempt towards Independency Set in a True Light* . . . (London, 1766), 16; [Stephen Sayre], *The Englishman Deceived; a Political Piece: Wherein Some Very Important Secrets of State Are Briefly Recited, and Offered to the Consideration of the Public* (London, 1768), 14–15. See also Maurice Moore, *The Justice and Policy of Taxing the American Colonies, in Great-Britain, Considered: Wherein Is Shewed, That the Colonists Are Not a Conquered People:—That They Are Constitutionally Intituled to Be Taxed Only by Their Own Consent:—and That the Imposing a Stamp-Duty on the Colo-*

William Knox detailed an even broader vision for the empire in which all the people that Britain ruled, not just those with English heritage, were British subjects with similar constitutional positions and responsibilities. Knox was born in Britain, became a colonial official and successful rice planter in Georgia, and served as Georgia's colonial agent in London until he was dismissed for his support of the Stamp Act. In his view, Bengal, Bihar, and Orissa "are British colonies, and the inhabitants are British subjects." He went on: "There is no material difference between the grant of the crown to the proprietor of Maryland, and the grant to the [East India Company] proprietors of the countries to the east of the cape of Good Hope, save in the article of trade. The inhabitants, therefore, of the East India company's possessions, are equally bound with the people of Maryland to contribute to the burdens of the state." Britain, being "the sovereign power over the whole empire," had the right, even the duty, to impose or reduce taxes in both places. He calculated that the Atlantic colonies should contribute £200,000, Ireland £100,000, and India £400,000 to help pay down the national debt, with people in Britain paying a majority share. And so the constitutional question came back to the revenue question.[30]

In *The Importance of the British Dominion in India, Compared with That in America,* an anonymous author argued that the new conquests in India were model colonies compared to those in North America. The author figured that the diwani was worth £1.3 million annually. Additionally, he claimed that Britons in Bengal sent back more than £700,000 in private fortunes, and a net positive balance of trade with Bengal generated a further £300,000. Such high rates of withdrawal from Bengal's economy could not be sustained, he explained, but a total of £1.3 million per year would not impoverish the region. Moreover, the people of Bengal were

nists Is as Impolitic as It is Inconsistant with Their Rights (Wilmington, N.C., 1765), 8–9. Parliament found negotiating with the East India Company, a charter corporation, similar to negotiating with the American colonies, though the Company had more direct representation. See Marshall, *Making and Unmaking of Empires,* 209. According to John Brewer, all the main political groups in Britain, except the radicals who were demanding an expanded franchise, believed in virtual representation; see Brewer, *Party Ideology and Popular Politics at the Accession of George III* (New York, 1976), 17.

30. [William Knox], *The Present State of the Nation: Particularly with respect to Its Trade, Finances, etc. etc. Addressed to the King and Both Houses of Parliament* (London, 1769), 91–93; Leland J. Bellot, "Knox, William (1732–1810)," *DNB.* For a response to Knox's argument, see, for example, [Hercules Langrishe], *Considerations on the Dependencies of Great Britain; with Observations on a Pamphlet, Intitled, "The Present State of the Nation"* (London, 1769), 70–73.

"exceeding mild, pliant, and submissive" as well as "ingenious industrious and frugal . . . possessing the knowlege of arts and manufactures." From America, in contrast, he imagined that Britain netted only £600,000 in national wealth. And "Americans are . . . haughty and insolent, impatient of rule, disdaining subjection, and by all means affecting independance." "America hangs like a wasting disease on the strength of Britain," while Bengal generated great and stable wealth.[31]

This public and private revenue from India was not generated through gentle means, and between 1769 and 1770 the activities of Company servants exacerbated a devastating famine in Bengal. Conquest had largely freed the Company's servants in India from the nawab's customary regulations that previously limited opportunities for corruption and exploitative trade. Britons in India monopolized food supplies to drive up prices, and they strong-armed Indian producers to drive down costs. Those at the top built the largest private fortunes. Harry Verelst and Henry Vansittart, for example, ignored the customary restrictions on the vital local trades in salt and rice while also participating in private cloth exports. In the late 1760s, the Court of Directors and the Company government in Bengal, now including Verelst and Vansittart, attempted to find common ground to limit the private and corporate abuse of the Company's new power. The servants in Bengal agreed to hire only Indian agents in the countryside, and the Court of Directors demanded a ban on European participation in several inland trades. Nevertheless, when drought struck in the late 1760s, the Company "violently" tried to maintain its diwani revenue. Estimates for the death toll in Bengal ran up to ten million, and many witnesses at the time agreed that up to 50 percent of the populations of several districts died of starvation. The Company and its servants had contributed to turning a natural hazard into a human disaster. In the British Atlantic, the famine was important and staggering news.[32]

31. *The Importance of the British Dominion in India, Compared with That in America* (London, 1770), 7–59. For a more balanced assessment, see Arthur Young, *Political Essays concerning the Present State of the British Empire; Particularly respecting I. Natural Advantages and Disadvantages; II. Constitution; III. Agriculture; IV. Manufactures; V. the Colonies and VI. Commerce* (London, 1772), 5–40, 332–338.

32. P. J. Marshall, *East Indian Fortunes: The British in Bengal in the Eighteenth Century* (Oxford, 1976), 112–121, 129–150. On Harry Verelst, see the following from MSS Eur. F218/79, BL: on his trade in salt, Verelst to Robert Huet, Feb. 21, 1761, fols. 6v–7; on rice, Verelst to Morse and Holland, Feb. 26, 1761, fols. 7–8; on the export trade, Verelst to Henry Vansittart, Mar. 17, 1761, fols. 9–11, and to Samuel Middleton, June 19, 1761, fol. 36v. See also "General Opinion of the Board, Consultations Relating to Gomastahs," Fort William, May 3, 1764, MSS Eur. F218/10, fols. 1–4v, BL; "Extract of General Letter to Bengal," Nov.

In a letter of "genuine intelligence" published on both sides of the Atlantic in 1772, an "Asiatic merchant" warned that Bengal had been ruined and millions killed by "extraordinary duties" on food and manufactures levied by Company servants who "oppressed, and plundered without mercy." A Protestant missionary in India noted, "Sins of unrighteousness are universal, and to the wealthy among the Europeans are an alluring contagion. . . . Very few are to be found who have not acquired their wealth unjustly." As the political economist and critic of the Company Henry Pattullo put it: "The most austere American-master treats his slaves with humanity, for his own interest. But the inhuman masters of the unfortunate Asiatics have unhappily hitherto found their avarice more immediately gratified, by sacrificing not only them, but even their country." American chattel enslavement, then, was preferable to the enslavement that the East India Company inflicted. In a sensational exchange in 1772, Parliament questioned Clive for his role in the aggressive activities of the Company's servants. William Pitt the Elder, whose own fortune had been created in large part through his grandfather Thomas Pitt's exploits in India, exclaimed, "The riches of Asia have been poured in upon us, and have brought with them not only Asiatic luxury, but, I fear, Asiatic principles of government."[33]

20, 1767, MSS Eur. F218/7, fol. 23, BL; *Reports from Committees of the House of Commons,* IV, *East Indies—1772, 1773* (London, 1804), 60–61, 98–101, 360. Rajat Datta posits that the Company's tax collection was likely not so severely enforced, though this is more a question of degree. He explains that the Company failed to provide famine relief despite available resources. Datta also concludes that the figure of ten million dead is unrealistic, though certain districts suffered severely. See Datta, *Society, Economy, and the Market,* 256–268. For more on the loss of life and the case that the tax enforcement was more severe, see S. Bhattacharya and B. Chaudhuri, "Eastern India," in Dharma Kumar and Meghnad Desai, eds., *The Cambridge Economic History of India,* II (Cambridge, 1983), 299–300. British rulers acted at least as badly as Bengal's previous rulers, who had subjected the region to what Marshall has called "fiscal terrorism"; see Marshall, *Bengal,* 72. For more on the ways in which people create the preconditions for disasters, see Piers Blaikie et al., eds., *At Risk: Natural Hazards, People's Vulnerability, and Disasters* (London, 1994), 21–45, 113–145.

33. "Honestus" provided the letter of "genuine intelligence" for publication to the *London Evening-Post,* but this name was dropped from reprints in America; see "Postscript," *London Evening-Post,* July 21–23, 1773, [4], published as "Extract of a Real Letter, Lately Received from an Asiatic Merchant, in Bengal, by Another of the Same Country, Now Resident in London," *Pennsylvania Chronicle, and Universal Advertiser,* Oct. 24–31, 1772, VI, no. 41, 166; *Nova Scotia Gazette,* Dec. 1, 1772, [2]. See also *Remains of the Rev. C. F. Schwartz, Missionary in India, Consisting of His Letters and Journals; with a Sketch of His Life,* 2d ed. (London, 1826), 76–77 ("Sins"); Henry Pattullo, *An Essay upon the Cultivation of the Lands, and Improvements of the Revenues, of Bengal* (London, 1772), 27–28. For more on Pattullo, see Ranajit Guha, *A Rule of Property for Bengal: An Essay on the Idea of Permanent Settlement* (New Delhi, 1982), 42–49. Thomas Pitt bought the rotten borough seat of Old Sarum

Indeed, most Company servants thought that their power depended in part on behaving and appearing in a manner similar to their conception of the behavior and appearance of local rulers. After obtaining the diwani in 1765, for instance, Clive held three days of celebrations to help project the Company's right to rule Bengal. Following Indian practice, the days included animal fights and fireworks. Being able to waste elephants in staged combat was possibly the greatest show of wealth and power among Indian princes, and Clive did not intend to disappoint, preparing an elephant battle of his own. Company servants also traveled in palanquins accompanied by extensive retinues, as did local Indian rulers. Clive had attempted to restrict palanquin and umbrella rights to elite Britons in India, in keeping with local customs and to help control Company costs, but he failed, as did all such later attempts. Britons were not willing to give up such symbols of power and protections from the climate. After describing the "Pomp and Magnificence" of elites in India, British army paymaster Gerard Gustavus Ducarel explained in 1768 that it may "not be desirable to fall into it in all Respects yet must be equally improper and disgusting to the Inhabitants [for us] to deviate entirely."[34]

The Company's servants also adopted from local rulers elaborate hookahs and their associated paraphernalia as symbols of wealth, virility, and wisdom. Depictions of Indian rulers at rest or conducting state business often included prominent hookahs, such as in Plate 11. Such a pleasurable mark of distinction attracted Britons eager to establish themselves in

---

to gain a place in the House of Commons. See William Pitt to the House of Lords, Jan. 22, 1770, in William Stanhope Taylor and John Henry Pringle, eds., *Correspondence of William Pitt, the Earl of Chatham* (London, 1839), III, 405. For more on popular attitudes to the Company's conquests and Clive, see Jeremy Richard Osborne, "India, Parliament, and the Press under George III: A Study of English Attitudes towards the East India Company and Empire in the Late Eighteenth and Early Nineteenth Centuries" (Ph.D. diss., University of Oxford, 1999), 91–205.

34. For accounts of the celebration, see Ducarel to his mother, Oct. 6, 1765, Apr. 29, 1768, D2091/F11, Ducarel Family Papers, Gloucestershire Archives; John Grose to Nash [brother], Jan. 31, 1766, MSS Eur. E284, BL. On the use of waste to prove wealth, see Thorstein Veblen, *The Theory of the Leisure Class* (1899; rpt. Boston, 1973), 53, 96–99. On palanquins, see Petition to Lord Clive and his Reply, Governor and Council, Fort William, Nov. 27, 1758, IOR/H/805/25, 855–856, BL; Edward Ives, *A Voyage from England to India, in the Year MDCCLIV; and an Historical Narrative of the Operations of the Squadron and Army in India* . . . (London, 1773), 21–22; Charles Caraccioli, *The Life of Robert Lord Clive, Baron Plassey* . . . , 4 vols. (London, [1775–1777]), I, 283. French officials similarly believed in the need to conform "to the pomp of the Orientals" and traveled in palanquins with extensive retinues, see [M. l'Abbé Guyon (Claude-Marie)], *A New History of the East-Indies, Ancient and Modern* . . . , 2 vols. (London, 1757), II, 97.

Plate 11. Muhammad Reza Hindi, *Nawab Smoking a Hookah.* 1764.
Gouache. 20.7 cm. x 26.1 cm. Add.Or.2410. © The British Library Board

the eyes of Indians as appropriate and respectable rulers of India. David
Anderson sent a hookah home to his brother in Scotland explaining:
"Being obliged from the nature of my occupation to be much in the company of the Indians, I was not long in supplying myself with so material
an instrument. An instrument . . . which is in fact one of the most material
ensigns of there *[sic]* state and grandeur." Using a hookah also required
the assistance of a servant to keep it fueled and smoking while the master
attended to business. Being able to afford a servant to look after one's pipe
further projected wealth, status, and the ability to control other people. In
addition to displaying wealth and control, the hookah "is a machine . . . so
infinitely preferable to our vulgar pipe. . . . It adds so much to the natural
dignity of man by giving his countenance an air of sagacity and wisdom."[35]

35. David Anderson to Fraser Anderson, Feb. 2, 1771, Anderson Papers, Add. MS 45438,
BL. For another similar image, see *A Prince Smoking, Attended by Ladies, 1760–1770,* J.66,
9, India Office Prints and Drawings, BL.

India and the American Revolution

Many Britons feared that what they saw as India's political, economic, and material influence would spread across the empire, particularly with Company servants returning home. The public stereotyped returned Britons as corrupting "nabobs," itself a corruption of the word *nawab*. These men supposedly mimicked Indian despots using fortunes created without virtue through imperial exploitation. This corruption was evidenced by their shocking taste for elephant displays, hookahs, and Indian curries. Mrs. Kindersley, for example, published an account highly critical of 1760s British life in India. Her husband was a Company servant who would later publish translations of "Hindoo Literature." She portrayed Shuja-ud-daula, the wazir of Awadh—who was allied by Clive to the British after the East India Company's victory at the 1764 Battle of Buxar—as a frivolous, lazy, oversexed, and extravagant despot, no proper ally nor model for Britons in India. She wrote, "His chief amusement is in smoking his *hooker*, bathing according to the Mahomedan custom, and his *harram*, in which he passeth the greatest part of his time: when he goes out, which is but seldom, it is with his whole court, himself generally upon an elephant." Although most Company servants who managed to return to Britain blended easily back into society, some men certainly did bring some Indian tastes back with them. The Norris Coffee House began selling prepared curry to a circle of returned migrants in 1773. That same year, Richard Clarke published the poem that established his contemporary fame, *The Nabob*. Clarke wrote:

> Our Liberty, our Lives, our Children sold:
> In *Asia*'s realms let slavery be bound,
> Let not her foot defile this sacred ground,
> Where Freedom, Science, Valour fix'd their seat,
> And taught all Nations how they should be great;
> Now sunk in Vice, indignant thought I own!
> An hireling group in this great realm is grown
> High Lords o'er millions, whose worn hands supply
> Their pride, their pomp, and feast of luxury.

Nabobs represented new and often illicit wealth that threatened to bring slavery and to overturn the social, scientific, and political order in Britain with their pride, profligacy, and purchase of parliamentary seats.[36]

36. Mrs. Kindersley, *Letters from the Island of Teneriffe, Brazil, the Cape of Good Hope, and the East Indies* (London, 1777), 72, 124–125, 155–156, 177, 224, 239; N. E. Kindersley,

Actor, playwright, and theater manager Samuel Foote publicly mocked the British empire in India and chastised those who governed it for giving in to their own corrupt nature. His play, *The Nabob,* first performed in 1772, depicted nabobs as men who saw diamonds as mere trifles and sought seraglios of enslaved Indian women in England. Echoing a century of criticism, the character Lady Oldham feared, "With the wealth of the East, we have too imported the worst of its vices." Foote's criticism, however, also went back to early-seventeenth-century English discomfort that wealth from trade and expansion would draw out negative characteristics already within the English. As a character in the play, aptly named the Mayor of Bribe'em, explained, the Indians "have caught the Tartars in us." The danger, then, was not Asian tyranny and luxury; it was mammon itself.[37]

As in the early seventeenth century, some authors suggested that the solution to the crisis in Bengal and Britain might be found in America—India's government should be patterned from the Atlantic colonies, advancing the notion that colonial Bengal and colonial America were constitutionally similar. Alexander Dow, for example, strongly criticized Clive and the Company for siphoning wealth from Bengal and monopolizing the necessaries of life. He lobbied for the end of monopolies, the introduction of paper money, and the implementation of some British forms of justice. He also advocated the re-parceling of Bengal from nonpermanent grants at pleasure under the Mughal system into private plots of freehold tenure, following the pattern of re-parceling the land of native Americans for colonial settlers. In the Bengali case, however, Indians, not British settlers, would be given ownership over the new plots. Henry Pattullo followed up his attack on the Company by encouraging adoption of Dow's plan. John Henry Grose added a new argument to his *Voyage to the East-Indies,* proposing that each Indian colony should be reformed in the model of American colonies with councils and assemblies chosen

---

Specimens of Hindoo Literature: Consisting of Translations, from the Tamoul Language . . . (London, 1794); Clarke, *The Nabob,* 38; Tillman Nechtman, *Nabobs: Empire and Identity in Eighteenth-Century Britain* (Cambridge, 2010); James Raven, *Judging New Wealth: Popular Publishing and Responses to Commerce in England, 1750–1800* (Oxford, 1992), 147–148, 160–167, 219–247; Percival Spear, *The Nabobs: A Study of the Social Life of the English in Eighteenth Century India* (London, 1932); James M. Holzman, *The Nabobs in England: A Study of the Returned Anglo-Indians, 1760–1785* (New York, 1926), 90.

37. Samuel Foote, *The Nabob; a Comedy, in Three Acts . . .* (London, 1778), 13 ("With"), 33, 37, 40 ("caught"). Notably, the play was published for the first time in 1778, as the American Revolutionary War turned increasingly sour for Britain.

India and the American Revolution

by the people. So governed, "these colonies would soon grow up to such a height as can hardly be conceived."[38]

For retired East India captain and soon-to-be Company director Nathaniel Smith, in contrast, neither the Company's extortion nor the plan to remake India partially in the model of the Atlantic colonies made sense. The natives of India would "enjoy the entire benefit and protection of our laws, or become the mere slaves of the Company, either of which extremes would have a dangerous tendency." Being unused to the freedoms and responsibilities of English laws and living in a hot climate, Indians would "encrease both their licentiousness and their indolence" unless a careful balance could be struck. Alexander Dalrymple claimed that the Company must not govern Indians with English laws and notions of English freedom, for the Indians had developed customs and laws over centuries that suited them. If Indians were to learn English freedom, they would demand independence. They must be enslaved as conquered people, even if lightly governed. Although not necessarily so willing to call the Indians enslaved to Britain in a positive sense, most Britons in power adopted some form of the view that elected assemblies of Indians were completely unsuitable to peoples who supposedly only knew how to live under despotism.[39]

38. Alexander Dow, *The History of Hindostan, from the Death of Akbar, to the Complete Settlement of the Empire under Aurungzebe; to Which Are Prefixed, I. A Dissertation on the Origin and Nature of Despotism in Hindostan; II. An Enquiry into the State of Bengal; with a Plan for Restoring That Kingdom to Its Former Prosperity and Splendor* (London, 1772), xlix, lxxv–lxxvii, cxvii–cl; Pattullo, *Essay upon the Cultivation of the Lands*, 2–21. John Henry Grose's use of "people" is unclear, but he appears to include Indians as he explains that British merchants should be "incorporated with the black merchants, who are excessive rich, and with the Indian artizans, who are sober and industrious"; see Grose, *A Voyage to the East-Indies; Began in 1750; with Observations Continued till 1764 . . .* , 2 vols. (London, 1766), II, 266–267. In early 1773, land speculators also began applying to America the Yorke-Camden legal opinion, which explained the Company's rights to Indian land. The edited version of the opinion in America, however, made the opinion appear to have been about America, not India. The potentially significant constitutional connection that otherwise would have been implied between India and America was thus not part of the debate in America. See Jack M. Sosin, *Whitehall and the Wilderness: The Middle West in British Colonial Policy, 1760–1775* (Lincoln, Nebr., 1961), 229–234.

39. Nathaniel Smith, *General Remarks on the System of Government in India; with Farther Considerations on the Present State of the Company at Home and Abroad . . .* (London, 1773), 64–65; Alexander Dalrymple, *Considerations on a Pamphlet Entitled "Thoughts on Our Acquisitions in the East-Indies, Particularly Respecting Bengal"* (London, 1772), 20–21. For more arguments against elected assemblies for Indians, see Marshall, *Making and Unmaking of Empires*, 201–203.

Instead of reforming Bengal as a new America, in 1773 the British government passed the Regulating Act to reform the terms of the Company's charter and increase Parliament's role in the management of the Indian colonies. The Regulating Act forbade the governors, councillors, and revenue collectors in Bengal, Bihar, and Orissa from participating in any private trade or accepting gifts; it also prohibited all Britons from participating in the inland domestic trade in salt, betel, tobacco, opium, and rice. The act established the primacy of the government in Calcutta over the Company's other India presidencies, with Warren Hastings as governor general and four councillors to guide him. This new executive and a revamped judiciary for India was, at least in a sense, under Parliament and the crown's influence, similar to Townshend's hopes for America.[40]

The Company, meanwhile, needed to be rescued financially because of its own mismanagement and dividend rates, its annual payments to Parliament, and the Townshend boycotts. An increase of 10 percent in the tea duty for the American colonies in 1772 had also further discouraged tea consumption and encouraged smuggling. Credit in London, moreover, had become scarce. The Company's defenders channeled their seventeenth-century forbearers, exclaiming that the Company must be saved to maintain its revenue stream to the British government, preserve the national credit, defeat European rivals, and expand trade, navigation, and naval power. In 1773, Parliament granted the Company a loan of £1.4 million, but the Company still needed answers to its revenue problems.[41]

The directors, for their part, re-imagined India cottons as a means to carry diwani "tribute" from Bengal to the metropole. The directors explained to their servants in Calcutta that the more Indian fabric they had available to sell in London the more money they could draw out of India. This was no longer a normal business concern since Indian tax revenue, levied on Indian people, paid for the fabric. When they sold the cloth in London, the proceeds were thus essentially the proceeds of the Indian tax revenue. More than ever, the "enrichment" of Britain through Bengal required as many people as possible in the Atlantic colonies, Europe, and Africa to own Bengal goods funneled through London. The Atlantic

40. Bowen, *Revenue and Reform*, 189. As Thomas points out, the Regulating Act was a sign of Parliament's willingness to intervene in charter privileges, although Parliament had long interfered in various ways with the Company's business; see Peter D. G. Thomas, *Tea Party to Independence: The Third Phase of the American Revolution, 1773–1776* (Oxford, 1991), 9.

41. Bowen, *Revenue and Reform*, 118–132, 159–168; Thomas, *Townshend Duties*, 248–253.

India and the American Revolution

colonial markets protected in the compromise over the Calico Acts had thus become still more valuable for transferring India's tribute, and it was thought that the colonies might similarly help solve the outstanding problem of excess tea from China.[42]

The Company had faced a large excess of tea before, in the 1730s, and, although America was now a much better potential outlet, Company tea had to compete with large quantities of smuggled tea. Unlike calicoes, which came primarily from British ports in India, the Company did not have any control over the European supply of tea from Canton. Smugglers from other European powers, particularly the Dutch, could thus more easily compete with the Company on tea than on cottons. This smuggling was not a secret. Newspapers throughout the British Atlantic circulated a report by Benjamin Franklin about the growth of tea and other Asian goods smuggled from "the Dutch, Danes and French" into the colonies in the early 1770s. Franklin blamed the British government's duty policy for encouraging the smuggling and thereby injuring the Company, stockholders, the Treasury, and British manufacturers. Smuggling was a sign to many such as Franklin, as it had been for more than a century, of over-aggressive duty rates.[43]

The Tea Act of 1773 followed this understanding, effectively lowering the duty on Company tea and giving the Company the ability to ship tea to America on its own account to reduce smuggling into the Atlantic colonies. The Townshend duty remained, but the Company received its requested removal of the 10 percent duty on tea that had only just been levied in 1772. The Company could apply for licenses to send tea to America without exposing it for sale in public auctions, but the licenses would only be granted when the market for tea in Britain was already glutted. Private merchants thus retained the right to ship tea purchased at the Company

42. "Extract of Consultation Dated 12th April 1773," General Letters from the Court of Directors Commercial Department, Dec. 18, 1765–Sept. 15, 1785, State Archives of West Bengal, Kolkata, India.

43. The Company had sent the earlier two- or three-year supply of excess tea on "round about voyages" in the Indian Ocean; see Directors to President and Council of Fort St George, Dec. 3, 1731, IOR/E/3/105, 325/fol. 163r, BL; "Instructions to Captain Charles Rigby, Commander of the Normanton," Dec. 13, 1732/3, IOR/E/3/105, 638/fol. 319v, BL. On smuggling, see Labaree, Boston Tea Party, 58–67; "Franklin's Preface to the English Edition of the Report of the Committee of Correspondence, Published by Him Immediately after He Received It in London," in Samuel Adams, The Rights of the Colonists, Old South Leaflets no. 173 (Boston, [1906]), VII, 422–424. This preface was reported in many colonial newspapers as "The British Editors Preface"; see Boston Evening-Post, May 3, 1773, [2]; Pennsylvania Packet, and the General Advertiser, May 17, 1773, [1]; Nova Scotia Gazette, June 1, 1773, [2].

sales to America; now, however, they had to compete with the Company on reexports when prices were already low. The price of tea after the Tea Act would be much lower. As a memorandum to the government pointed out, "The Americans will be in some sort compelled to import Tea from us, and consequently pay the 3 % Duty; for so great a difference as there will be in the price, will enable them to import our Tea paying that Duty cheaper than they can buy Dutch Tea." Also, "As far as the Surplus Stock sold so low does actually increase the Consumption in Ireland and America, the Company may expect hereafter to reap a benefit therefrom when the Sales are again made as formerly." The goal in sight for British prime minister Lord North was to make more efficient and entrenched the long-standing system that used the Atlantic colonies as a market for Asian goods to support the Company and generate revenue for the state and, now, also for colonial officials.[44]

The Townshend Acts, the Regulating Act, and the Tea Act all stemmed from a belief that, regardless of their location and charter types, British colonies were constitutionally subservient to Parliament. The government designed these coordinating acts to increase oversight and control over the corrupted Company and wayward Atlantic colonists intent on smuggling and enacting their own constitutional theories. By building on the earlier calico compromise and the old India trading system connecting the colonies to India through London, the colonial consumption of India goods might also further support the state. Indeed, the calico fashion would support the state more strongly than ever through the Company's new plan to use calicoes as tribute. And, much like the colonies had become a market for the Company's calicoes prohibited in Britain, they were now expected to absorb the Company's excess tea. Britain had also used the Calico Acts to help avoid the economic and moral ruin feared to come from the India

44. Owen Ruffhead, *The Statutes at Large, from Magna Charta, to the Twenty-fifth Year of the Reign of King George the Third, Inclusive* . . . , new ed., 10 vols. (London, 1786), VIII, 228–230; "Plan for Enabling the East India Company to Raise Nine Hundred Thousand Pounds by Their Surplus Stock of Teas in the Course of the Present Year, without Reducing the Amount of Their March and September Sales of That Article . . . Wither of a Free Exportation to Foreign States on the Part of the Company, or by Taking off the 3prct Duty in America," Jan. 18, 1773, Liverpool Papers, CCIX, Add. MS 38398, fols. 4r, 5r ("Surplus"), 5v ("Americans"), BL. The authorship of the plan is unknown, but it follows the plan discussed by the Company directors earlier that month. Thomas does not appear to have found this document, but for the directors' discussions of it, the impossibility of using Europe instead of America as the primary outlet, and North's dedication to a revenue to pay colonial officials, see Thomas, *Townshend Duties*, 250–255. For defenses of the Company's importance to the state in 1772 and 1773, see Marshall, *Making and Unmaking of Empires*, 200–201.

trade, but Britain and America now faced new threats posed by the direct influence of Indian wealth, corruption, and tyranny. John Dickinson had already exclaimed that *"the conquered provinces of* Canada *and* Florida, *and the* British *garrisons of* Nova-Scotia . . . do not deserve the name of *colonies."* With its Muslim and Hindu populations and Company rule, Bengal was an even greater departure. In this context, supporters of revolution in America would co-opt the tactic of emphasizing constitutional similarities among the different parts of the empire, especially Bengal and the thirteen colonies, to drive support for their own cause.[45]

The India Trade and the "Bull-Work" of the Empire

In America, most consumers still did not want protection from calicoes or tea, but they did want protection from what they saw as Parliament's constitutional overreach, made particularly alarming by Parliament's involvement with the East India Company. Concerns about luxury consumption, while voiced, took a backseat to concerns about the Company with its monopolies, exploitative practices, and lack of representative assemblies. At precisely the moment that the government passed the Tea Act, American newspapers were filled with stories about the disastrous Company administration of Bengal. Since the East India Company could treat India so poorly, and since imperial policy seemed to both underscore the value of India over America and suggest that America and India might share an increasingly similar place in the imperial constitution, many colonists became concerned about their own future in a universal, exploitative, unrepresentative, and corrupt imperial trading system and constitution. Fear of the Company was ideological, but it was also materially manifested in the Company's behavior in India and its monopoly over the India goods that Atlantic colonists often consumed at per capita rates higher than in Britain or Europe as a whole.[46]

45. [Dickinson], *Letters*, 40–41.

46. A Tradesman, *To the Free-Holders and Free-Men, of the City, and Province of New York* (New York, 1773) ("Bull-Work"); Bernard Bailyn, *Ideological Origins of the American Revolution* (London, 1967), 25, 86, 95–112; for Bailyn's few comments on the Company, see 129–135. On continued consumption after the Tea Party and the ongoing weakness of moral concerns, see Merritt, "Tea Trade, Consumption, and the Republican Paradox," *PMHB*, CXXVIII (2004), 143–147. Few people in America had any direct experience in India, and vice versa, and consumer goods and news stories were the main conduits of knowledge and contact. See Bowen, "Perceptions from the Periphery," in Daniels and Kennedy, eds., *Negotiated Empires*, 287–291.

Pennsylvania and New York merchants, in particular, publicly sought protection from the East India Company's new powers to sell to America (much as woolen and silk producers in England in the 1690s had fought for protection from the Company's calicoes). This shift driven by the Tea Act aligned them more fully with radicals in Boston. Some patriots cheered that the smugglers had "done [a] most important service to their country." One writer explained that North American merchants and colonists alike would be "sacrificed" through the commercial exploitation of the Tea Act, much as Britain had pursued the trade in enslaved Africans, oppression in Ireland, "the cruel despotism exercised over the East-Indians, and the late expedition to St. Vincent." The author only briefly mentioned revenue. The great threat was that the East India Company was the vanguard of a policy to send "Government Factors" to ruin colonial "private traders" and manufacturers. According to "A Mechanic," if the Company was allowed to bring in its tea using its own agents, it would soon "send their own Factors and Creatures, [to] establish Houses amongst US." The Company would sate people's appetites with low prices and drive all the private and illicit merchants out of business. Then the Company would raise prices to unbearable levels. The New York Committee of Correspondence wrote to their counterparts in Boston that lower prices on teas would lead to an effective monopoly that would soon spread to spices and fabrics. The author of the serial the *Alarm* explained that, if the tea came in on the Company's account, colonists would face "an India Warehouse here: and the Trade of all the Commodities of that Country, will be lost to your Merchants, and carried on by the Company; which will be an immense Loss to the Colony." The London papers, the author noted, had already described a radical new East India Company plan to bring India manufactures directly to America from India every year. Such proposals had been circulating long before their emergence in patriot discourse in 1773. Timing made all the difference.[47]

47. A Citizen, "New York, October 28, 1773," *New-York Journal; or, the General Advertiser*, Nov. 4, 1773, [3] (on smugglers as positive); "From the Pennsylvania Packet, of Oct. 27," *Boston-Gazette, and Country Journal*, Nov. 22, 1773, [1]; A Mechanic, *To the Tradesmen, Mechanics, etc. of the Province of Pennsylvania* (Philadelphia, 1773), n.p.; "Letter to Boston Committee of Correspondence, 28 February 1773," Boston Committee of Correspondence MSS, IX, 742–746, cited in Schlesinger, "Uprising against the East India Company," *Political Science Quarterly*, XXII (1917), 75; Hampden, *The Alarm, Number I* (New York, 1773), n.p.; Hampden, *The Alarm, Number III* (New York, 1773), n.p. The idea that the Company would soon raise prices to exploit colonists was widespread. See also Reclusus, *Boston Evening-Post*, Oct. 18, 1773; Scaevola, *To the Commissioners Appointed by the East-India*

"A Student of Law" explained that the East India Company "connived at, if not abetted the starving of thousands of the *Asiatics*, by their servants' monopolizing the absolute necessaries of life." The author made the logical connection for readers that the Company "will have but little compassion on you, if you should be in their power." "They will think every penny they extort from you, as well got as from that miserable and helpless people, whose blood the company's avaricious servants have spilt, with more than savage cruelty," the author declared. John Dickinson likewise argued that the East India Company "has given ample Proof, how little they regard the Laws of Nations, the Rights, Liberties, or Lives of Men. . . . They have, by the most unparalleled Barbarities, Extortions, and Monopolies, stripped the miserable Inhabitants of their Property, and reduced whole Provinces to Indigence and Ruin." The Company had killed one and a half million people in a single year, he claimed, and "they now, it seems, cast their Eyes on *America,* as a new Theatre, whereon to exercise their Talents of Rapine, Oppression and Cruelty." This rhetoric referencing the Company's government of Bengal and the famine was in line with allegations circulating throughout the empire.[48]

Britons on both sides of the Atlantic also frequently associated the East India Company with enslavement. In London, "Rationalis" tied the Company's long-standing export of silver from Britain and its new "rapine and plunder" to plans to "inslave" Britons using Parliament. The Company would ruin Manchester's nascent industrial cotton industry as well as cloth producers in Scotland and Ireland. The trade to "China . . . be both useless and pernicious to this kingdom," but that to India was "more destructive and detestable" and "the mode of carrying it on a reproach not only to a Christian state, but also to human nature." In America, "A Mechanic" explained that the Company needed to be stopped now, for, "once

---

Company, for the Sale of Tea, in America (Philadelphia, 1773). For more on Saint Vincent, see Marshall, *Making and Unmaking of Empires,* 194–196. Ironically, supporters believed that proposals to bring India goods directly to the Atlantic colonies would keep colonists loyal by scrapping regulations, reducing prices, limiting duties, increasing supply, and removing the inclination for local manufacturing; see Pownall, *Administration of the Colonies,* 2d ed., 191–199.

48. A Student of Law, *Fellow Citizens, Friends to Liberty and Equal Commerce* (New York, 1773), 2–4; A Friend to Britain, "To the Printers: May Liberty and Truth Forever Reign!" *Boston Evening-Post,* Feb. 7, 1774, [2]; Rusticus [John Dickinson], *A Letter from the Country, to a Gentleman in Philadelphia* ([Philadelphia?], 1773). For a similar example, see A Citizen, "New York, October 28, 1773," *New-York Journal; or, the General Advertiser,* Nov. 4, 1773, [3].

they get Footing in this (ONCE) happy Country, [they] will leave no Stone unturned to become your Masters." Colonists similarly made racialized claims about tea, which adapted the earlier religious claims about calico in Britain. Some patriots likely combined these threats in their minds with scenes of colonial enslavement of Africans with which they were more immediately familiar—the Company would turn colonists into the people that colonists enslaved.[49]

The loyalist John Vardill responded as "Poplicola," arguing that the colonists had misplaced their anger over the Tea Act and the Company. He noted that it was "too ridiculous" to argue that the Tea Act was a new tax or that it would steal money from American colonists, who, after all, would not be forced to buy the tea. Therefore, following Dickinson's own logic from the 1760s, it was not an illegal tax but a regulatory duty. Besides, they still willingly paid duties on other goods and to other nations that sold them tea. The East India Company was also a most valuable support for the empire, and the colonists needed to sustain it. Many responded to Poplicola. Of course, duties on goods shipped to America were not new, admitted the author of the *Alarm*. The tea duty, however, became a bad tax since it was combined with the goals of raising revenue and monopolizing all tea imports. A New York "Tradesmen" wondered why, if the East India trade was as valuable as Poplicola claimed, it needed special advantages to sell its tea to America. The Company, he suggested, was the *"Bull-Work,"* not the bulwark, of the nation. The loyalist John Randolph, hoping for compromise, explained that the tea coming directly from the East India Company was the real issue. The old, higher duty levied on Company tea bought and shipped by private merchants from London had never been considered a matter worthy of revolution.[50]

49. Rationalis also claimed that the duties on India cottons impoverished consumers and that the drawbacks on reexports negated their revenue potential for the state. See Rationalis, "To the Printer: Letter II," *London Chronicle*, Oct. 12–14, 1773, 364; A Mechanic, *To the Tradesmen, Mechanics, etc.*, 187–194; "New-York, Nov. 5, 1773: To the Friends of Liberty and Commerce" (reprint of handbill), *Rivington's New-York Gazetteer; or the Connecticut, New-Jersey, Hudson's-River, and Quebec Weekly Advertiser*, Nov. 11, 1773, [3]; A Citizen, "New-York, October 28, 1773," *New-York Journal; or, the General Advertiser*, Nov. 4, 1773, [3]. On racialized claims about tea, see Franks, *Objectifying China*, 187–194.

50. Poplicola [John Vardill], *To the Worthy Inhabitants of the City of New-York* [New York, 1773], 1–2; Hampden, *The Alarm, Number V* (New York, 1773), n.p.; Mucius, *To the Freemen of America* [Philadelphia, 1773], n.p.; A Tradesman, *To the Free-Holders and Free-Men, of the City, and Province of New York*, n.p.; [John Randolph], *Considerations on the Present State of Virginia* ([Williamsburg, Va.], 1774), 14.

Another author argued, in contrast, that the Company and colonists should be working together against Parliament. The author rebutted claims that the Company would send factors to the colonies to drive up prices and impoverish the people. Colonial merchants would be able to buy tea at the Company's auctions, and the prices must be low for the Company to gain the intended benefit of underselling foreign competition. Colonists had also paid a range of duties on a variety of goods that generated revenue. The colonists should not be vilifying the Company, the author explained, since it and the colonists shared an interest in getting all tea duties removed.[51]

The author and others further explained that the Company and colonists were engaged in a shared struggle to protect their rights. In pushing back against the Regulating Act, the directors had "exerted themselves in favor of Charter Priviledges." With their wealth and power, "their Influence may be of great use to us in our present Controversy with Great Britain with respect to our Charter Rights." The Boston Committee of Correspondence pointed out that the administration was "desirous of silencing every Opposition to their Measures" in America, particularly in light of how much "that rich and powerful Body the East-India Company resent the Act that was passed in the last Session of Parliament, by which their sacred Charter Rights were arbitrarily taken from them." For these colonists, the Regulating Act was part of the same parliamentary overreach as the Townshend Acts and Tea Act. Notably, comments in support of working with the Company tended to come from Boston, not New York or Philadelphia, where smugglers were more important.[52]

Arguments pointing out parallels regarding charter rights and defending the Company against the Regulating Act were less prominent than arguments that the act failed to substantially reform the Company or punish its wrongdoers. "A Mechanic" explained it would be almost impossible to push the Company out of the colonies for the same reasons that other colonists had encouraged teaming up with the Company: "They are an oppulent Body, and Money or Credit is not wanting amongst them." But, he explained, "They have a designing, depraved, and despotic Ministry to assist and support them. They themselves are well versed in TYRANNY, PLUNDER, OPPRESSION, and BLOODSHED." Furthermore, the leaders

51. Z, "Messrs, Fleets," *Boston Evening-Post*, Oct. 25, 1773, [2].

52. Ibid; Boston Committee of Correspondence for the Town of Boston, *Boston, September 21, 1773* [Boston, 1773].

of the Company failed to defend themselves in Parliament and passed the blame onto their servants in India. Those servants never answered the charges, and the Company continued to employ them. A republished open letter from "Atticus" to Lord North, originally from London's *Public Advertiser,* argued that North was worse even than Clive. Clive had at least gained his wealth by gaining India and "tenfold Advantages" to Britain. The Regulating Act "neither punishes nor restrains a Delinquent; it neither corrects the Influence of Corruption at home, or the Opportunity of Plunder abroad; it only renders that Company . . . *the most dangerous Engine of Oppression that ever a Tyrant ventured to assume."* North had "commenced an East India Merchant" and "connected the Ideas of Profit and Corruption together" to ship tea to America and corrupt the colonists. Atticus also blamed North for turning down the "voluntary Offer" for reconciliation from the colonists in 1769. Instead, North "formed a System . . . to ruin the Company," which now necessitated the Tea Act. If North only had taken the duty off of tea as the colonists had requested, the colonists would have purchased the Company's tea voluntarily, and it would not need rescuing. America must now submit to the new system—or fight for independence.[53]

Indeed, a correspondent supposedly from London claimed to "have told several of the Company that the Tea and Ships will be all burnt" and "strongly disuaded" the Company from proceeding. If the Company persisted, he hoped the "Yorkers will stand their Ground." They did. Those in Boston most famously threw the tea overboard into the harbor. The influential patriot James Warren wrote, in words that make abundantly clear the importance of the Company to the conversation in the colonies at the beginning of 1774: "The Ministry have one way at least to avoid the necessity of Advancing or retreating at this time and that is by laying the

53. A Mechanic, *To the Tradesmen, Mechanics, etc.;* Reclusus, "Messi'rs Fleets," *Boston Evening-Post,* Oct. 18, 1773; Mechanic, *To the Worthy Inhabitants of New-York* ([New York], [1773]), 1; Atticus, "To Lord North," *Public Advertiser* (London), Oct. 14, 1773, [1], reprinted, for example, in *Massachusetts Spy Or, Thomas's Boston Journal,* Jan. 20, 1774, [2]; *Providence Gazette; And Country Journal* (R.I.), Jan. 29, 1774, [1]; *Nova Scotia Gazette,* Apr. 16, 1774, [4]. See also Hampden, *The Alarm, Number I,* n.p.; Hampden, *The Alarm, Number III,* n.p.; Hampden, *The Alarm, Number IV* (New York, 1773), n.p.; and, slightly later, Citizen of New-York, *A Serious Address to the Inhabitants of the Colony of New-York, Containing a Full and Minute Survey of the Boston-Port Act, Calculated to Excite Our Inhabitants to Conspire, with the Other Colonies on This Continent, in Extricating That Unhappy Town from Its Unparalleled Distresses, and for the Actual Redemption and Security of Our General Rights and Liberties* (New York, 1774), 3–7.

Blame of the whole on their own and East India Compy. officers who have drove the People to this desperate step. And this, Justice and Truth . . . will Countenance them in."[54]

In response to the Boston Tea Party, instead of turning against the Company, Parliament passed the so-called Intolerable Acts. These acts closed Boston's port and unilaterally changed the Massachusetts charter to reduce the colony's representative features. Parliament had suspended New York's assembly in 1767, and, although John Dickinson and others raised the alarm, this action had not garnered a scale of reaction similar to the suspensions and changes to the Massachusetts government in 1774. The Intolerable Acts effectively united a large number of colonists in defense of British liberty like nothing else before.[55]

The Intolerable Acts not only illustrated Parliament's belief in its constitutional supremacy, but, importantly, they also seemed to, and in some ways did, parallel the Company's unrepresentative and exploitive government in India, which patriots and others in Britain had been invoking frequently in the previous few months. Speaking to Parliament in 1774, Edmund Burke succinctly expressed that elected assemblies were essential to British liberty and that "popular government, cannot be enforced by an army." "To join together the restraints of an universal internal and external monopoly, with an universal internal and external taxation," he later explained, "is an unnatural union; perfect uncompensated slavery." Monopolies and taxation were the powers exercised by the East India

54. "Extract of a Letter from London," *New-York Journal; or, the General Advertiser,* Oct. 7, 1773, [3]; *Nova Scotia Gazette,* Nov. 2, 1773, [3] (another item from Boston in the *Nova Scotia Gazette* suggested that North would simply be forced to repeal the Tea Act; see "Boston, Oct. 18"); James Warren to John Adams, Jan. 3, 1774, in C. James Taylor, ed., *The Adams Papers Digital Edition* (Charlottesville, Va., 2008).

55. [Dickinson], *Letters,* 4–6; Thomas, *Tea Party,* 62–87, 159, 171 (for an overview of the changes to the Massachusetts charter); David Ammerman, *In the Common Cause: American Response to the Coercive Acts of 1774* (Charlottesville, Va., 1974), 5–22, 67–69, 145–149. Jerrilyn Green Marston's study of 108 sets of colonial resolutions in the summer of 1774 found that 92 percent "specifically condemned" the Boston Port Act or the Intolerable Acts, compared with 64 percent that condemned the preceding revenue acts. See Marston, *King and Congress: The Transfer of Political Legitimacy, 1774-1776* (Princeton, N.J., 1987), 70–75, 88–91, 95, 317; Jack N. Rakove, *The Beginnings of National Politics: An Interpretive History of the Continental Congress* (New York, 1979), 42–62, 80–89. North believed that Parliament had the authority to amend colonial charters at its pleasure, a position not in keeping with that held by many colonists. Colonists largely believed that their own representative assemblies were essential to their liberties as Britons; see Marshall, *The Making and Unmaking of Empires,* 172–174.

Company over Bengal in the preceding decade, and Parliament now intended to exercise them over America. Jonathan Shipley, the bishop of Saint Asaph and a friend of Benjamin Franklin, warned in a piece published in multiple venues: "What misery this right of taxation is capable of producing in a provincial government. We need only recollect that our countrymen in India, have in the space of five or six years, in virtue of this right, destroyed, starved and driven away more inhabitants from Bengal, than are to be found at present in all our American Colonies." The American colonies supposedly had similarly gone from being "instruments of commerce" to "objects of government." Shipley directly connected the Company's tyrannical approach to government in India with Parliament's change toward tax revenue and authority in the Atlantic colonies.[56]

In the same vein, Plate 12, published in London in 1774 and titled *Liberty Triumphant; or, The Downfall of Oppression,* depicts Lord North, the East India Company's directors, and the king in collusion with the devil and some willing colonists to oppress the rest of the colonists. On the British side of the Atlantic Ocean, a "PLAN for an India Warehouse in America" is unfurled prominently in the center of the foreground. One of the Company directors says, "I wish we may be able to establish our Monopoly in America." Poplicola also appears, having "prostituted my reason and my Conscience." On the American side, several colonists intending to import the Company tea discuss their disappointed "hopes of sharing in the Plunder of their Country." The remainder of the colonists, shown as noble native Americans to separate them from the British and loyal colonists, prepare to fight to keep America from being "Fetter'd" by North's chains, clearly invoking fears that the colonists will become enslaved like those that they themselves enslaved and those under Company rule. The print also portrays the patriots as the true guardians of specifically English

56. Edmund Burke, *Speech of Edmund Burke, Esq. on American Taxation, April 19, 1774,* 3d ed. (New York, 1775), 28; Bishop of St. Asaph [Jonathan Shipley], "A Speech, etc.," *Royal American Magazine, or Universal Repository of Instruction and Amusement,* I, no. 13 (August 1774), 289–294; [Shipley], *A Speech Intended to Have Been Spoken on the Bill for Altering the Charters of the Colony of Massachusett's Bay,* 4th ed. (London, 1774), 3–8, 12. Samuel Seabury sharply disagreed with the actions of the Tea Party participants in Boston but still echoed Burke in America; see A. W. Farmer [Samuel Seabury], *The Congress Canvassed; or, An Examination into the Conduct of the Delegates, at Their Grand Convention, Held in Philadelphia, Sept. 1, 1774* (London, 1775), 11. Earlier English arguments that monopolies were taxes do not seem to have been a major part of the debate. John Cary, for example, had explained, "I take that Monopoly to be a Tax." See Cary, *An Essay on the State of England, in Relation to Its Trade, Its Poor, and Its Taxes, for Carrying on the Present War against France* (Bristol, U.K., 1695), 64.

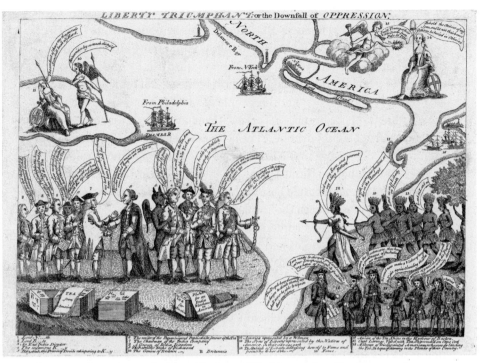

Plate 12. *Liberty Triumphant; or, The Downfall of Oppression.* [London, 1774].
Black-and-white line engraving. Accession no. 1960-44. The Colonial
Williamsburg Foundation. Museum Purchase

liberty. Britannia, represented alongside a Union Jack, turns away from
the scene, ashamed at her "degenerate sons" in Britain, while the patriots
fight for the "Goddess of Liberty," who holds a liberty cap and is flanked by
Saint George's cross. As the seat of the newly massive British empire, the
English had lost touch with themselves.

The Intolerable Acts also dovetailed with the 1774 Quebec Act, and
together these acts confirmed to many patriots the immoral and tyrannical influence of twinned Catholic and Mughal, or, more broadly, Muslim,
ideals in government, an influence long feared by many Britons on both
sides of the Atlantic. The Quebec Act condoned Catholicism and maintained the French code of law instead of installing British common law,
and it did not grant Quebec an elected assembly. From one perspective,
the Quebec Act might suggest an empire of toleration and flexibility. But,
from the perspective of many patriots, the acceptance of Catholicism and
nonrepresentative government in Quebec on the borders of the English-
speaking British colonies in America combined with the luxurious ways

of life of despotic Britons in India amid exploitation and tragedy demonstrated dangerous changes that might soon be applied to the thirteen colonies. These changes appeared to follow supposed Catholic and Muslim ideals of passionate tyranny, not supposed British Protestant ideals of thoughtful regulation and balanced government. Caractacus explained, as a result of the Quebec Act the people of Quebec were "as much *slaves* as the inhabitants of France or Turkey." "We have every thing to fear from living in such a neighbourhood." The act was intended "to prepare the way for universal despotism in the British empire." Patriot language calling the Quebec Act "impolitic, unjust, and cruel" was extraordinarily similar to patriot language about the Company in Bengal. Simultaneously in Quebec, Bengal, and now with the Intolerable Acts within one of the thirteen colonies, the British government was apparently incorporating Catholic and Asiatic Muslim peoples and forms of government.[57]

Some writers and political leaders, meanwhile, sought reconciliation with the patriots by sharpening the differences instead of the similarities between the colonies in the Atlantic and Indian Oceans. Economic writer Thomas Mortimer specifically rebutted *The Importance of British Dominion in India, Compared with That in America.* Mortimer claimed that the East India Company only "pretended dominion" at the pleasure of the Mughal emperor. In the Atlantic, in contrast, "COLONIES are to be considered as large provinces or districts of an extensive empire; they are members of the same body; they are dependencies on one supreme government; and they ought to have but one joint interst in common with the great political head from which they derive their existence." Atlantic colonists purchased far more from the metropole than Indians and "are the primary source of the maritime strength, riches, and prosperity of Great Britain." Even the revenue generated by the diwani did not overtake the value of the Atlantic colonies. Thus, they deserved a much higher position than India in the empire, not a lower one. Edmund Burke agreed that India and the Atlantic colonies were fundamentally different, but he saw neither as useful in generating state revenue. In his lengthy speech on "conciliation with the colonies," Burke explained that America could not

57. Caractacus, "Observations on the Quebec Bill, and on Standing Armies in America," and "Extracts From the Votes and Proceedings of the American Congress . . . ," *Dunlap's Pennsylvania Packet or, the General Advertiser*, Oct. 31, 1774, [1–2]. For a brief overview of the Quebec Act, see Marshall, *The Making and Unmaking of Empires*, 189, 333–334; Thomas, *Tea Party*, 88–117; Ruth H. Bloch, *Visionary Republic: Millennial Themes in American Thought, 1765–1800* (New York, 1988), 57–59. Historians have not noticed its resonance with the long-standing fears of Mughal India.

be expected to produce a great revenue when Bengal had failed to do the same. He wrote: "If ever there was a country qualified to produce wealth, it is India; or an institution fit for transmission, it is the East-India Company. America has none of these aptitudes." The colonies offered value instead, Mortimer and Burke detailed, particularly through the enlargement of trade.[58]

Colonists seeking support for independence in the public and in the First Continental Congress, in which representatives from the colonies met to determine a collective political strategy, continued to publicize the threat of the Company's tyranny, corruption, and monopoly. In 1775, in an exposé on Clive in the *Pennsylvania Magazine*, Thomas Paine proclaimed that "Fear and terror march like pioneers before his camp, murder and rapine accompany it, famine and wretchedness follow in the rear." John Hancock concluded his speech to the people of Boston with a withering attack on the Company and its designs for America. If the colonists had suffered the Company to have its way with tea, "we soon should have found our trade in the hands of foreigners, and taxes imposed on every thing which we consumed; nor would it have been strange, if in a few years a company in London should have purchased an exclusive right of trading to America." In acting against the Company quickly, the patriots had saved America from the Company's "plot" of tyranny. Further pointing to the allegations of rapacious Company employees in India, he exclaimed, "Surely you never will tamely suffer this country to be a den of thieves." The Massachusetts Bay representatives to the Congress later that year urged colonists to "abstain from the consumption of British merchandize and manufactures, and especially of East-India teas and piece goods." The Committee for the City and Liberties of Philadelphia sternly warned residents against purchasing calicoes from the Dutch in early 1775, since the Dutch had reportedly bought them at the British East India Company sales and printed them. This attention paid to the Company's calicoes in Boston and Philadelphia alike reinforces the point that the East India Company and its activities in general, not simply its tea, were at the core of patriot concern.[59]

58. Thomas Mortimer, *The Elements of Commerce, Politics, and Finances, in Three Treatises on Those Important Subjects* (London, 1774), 150–170, 184. The specific paragraph this Burke quotation came from, as well as half of the following paragraph of Burke's speech, was reprinted in Britain and America; see, for example, "London, August 4," *Providence Gazette; and Country Journal*, Nov. 11, 1775, [1].

59. [Thomas Paine], "For the Pennsylvania Magazine: Reflections on the Life and Death of Lord Clive," *Pennsylvania Magazine: or, American Monthly Museum* (Philadel-

The response of the Second Continental Congress to the North ministry's offer for conciliation after armed conflict had broken out at Lexington and Concord in April 1775 stressed not simply the lack of Parliament's right to tax the colonies "but what is of more importance . . . they claim a right to alter our Charters and establish laws, and leave us without any security for our lives or liberties." After opening with taxes, Congress listed the use of military force, Parliamentary revenue streams to pay colonial officials, and the Intolerable Acts and the Quebec Act, and it also explained, as had Burke, the compounded dangers of taxation involving trading monopolies. Congress argued that Parliament had deliberately tried to frame the conflict as being about only one "mode of levying taxes" to distract the colonists and "the world" from these more serious divisions. Certainly colonists themselves had often made much of the issues surrounding duties and taxes, but often historians and others have also fallen for Parliament's emphasis on taxation as the only serious issue, thereby overlooking the root question of the constitution. Consensus jelled around a large basket of concerns, and these concerns had clear linkages with the Company's own behavior in India and Parliament's adjustments of the Company charter, which seemed to reflect Parliament's belief in its supremacy over all charters as well as its general support for the Company's model of exploitative rule.[60]

Throughout 1775 and beyond the signing of the Declaration of Inde-

---

phia) (March 1775), 108; John Hancock, "An Oration; Delivered March 5th, 1774, at the Request of the Inhabitants of the Town of Boston; to Commemorate the Bloody Tragedy of the Fifth of March, 1770," *Royal American Magazine; or, Universal Repository of Instruction and Amusement*, I, no. 5 (March 1774), 86–87; *Journal of the Proceedings of the Congress, Held at Philadelphia, September 5th, 1774 . . .* (London, 1775), 30. For reports of the Dutch "design," see "Philadelphia, March 13: Extract of a Letter from London, dated January 4," *Dunlap's Pennsylvania Packet or, the General Advertiser*, Mar. 13, 1775, supplement, [2]. John Dickinson, one of the strongest American voices against the Company, was a member of the Philadelphia committee; for the committee's warning, see "Committee Chamber, April 3, 1775," *Pennsylvania Evening Post* (Philadelphia), Apr. 4, 1775, I, no. 31, 123. On Congress's generally following popular opinion and the importance of cultivating support for independence, see Rakove, *Beginnings of National Politics*, 108–109.

60. Thomas, for instance, focuses on taxation, and not what the Congress itself claimed to be "of more importance." That this view comes from his approach, looking outward from London, seems to bolster the colonists' claim that Parliament more than the colonies focused on the issue of taxation; see Thomas, *Tea Party*, 252–253. For the text of Congress's statement, see "Answer of the Congress to the Resolutions of the House of Commons of the 20th February Last," in Peter Force, ed., *American Archives: Consisting of a Collection of Authentick Records, State Papers, Debates, and Letters and Other Notices of Publick Affairs . . .*, 4th Ser., II (Washington, D.C., 1839), columns 1900–1902.

pendence, the message circulated on both sides of the Atlantic that the East India Company's violence and despotism, learned from India's previous rulers, had become the new model of imperial government in London. Richard Price, in his highly influential work supporting American independence, *Observations on the Nature of Civil Liberty*, requested of readers:

> Turn your eyes to *India:* There more has been done than is now attempted in *America.* There ENGLISHMEN, actuated by the love of plunder and the spirit of conquest, have depopulated whole kingdoms, and ruined millions of innocent people by the most infamous oppression and rapacity—The justice of the nation has slept over these enormities. Will the justice of Heaven sleep?—Are we not now execrated on both sides of the globe?

One of the anonymous authors in Robert Bell's *Additions to Common Sense* claimed that a list of crimes by history's empires, including "the dreadful famine brought by the East India company upon the poor East Indians, must all be brought into one scale, to serve as any sort of balance to the system of desolation, that you and your brother ministers are meditating and daily practising against the unhappy people of North America." The author of the serial publication *The Crisis*, moreover, provided a lengthy quotation in which George III called the American colonists his hated slaves. The author obliquely admitted to the falsity of the quotation but not its meaning, for "we have fairly cloathed an eastern spirit, in an eastern garb. . . we have not . . . meanly suffered the sentiments of an insolent mogul to be cramped by the poverty of princely diction." To drive home this point, Plate 13, a widely republished print that was produced with at least three different titles, depicted George III as an Asian despot wearing a turban, jeweled crescent and aigrette, and banyan.[61]

---

61. Richard Price, *Observations on the Nature of Civil Liberty, the Principles of Government, and the Justice and Policy of the War with America* (London, 1776), 103; [Robert Bell, ed.], *Additions to Common Sense; Addressed to the Inhabitants of America* (Philadelphia, 1776), 23; *The Crisis, Number XIX* ([New York], [1775]), 159. Price's work was reprinted on both sides of the Atlantic many times. All of section 5 was reprinted in *Continental Journal and Weekly Advertiser* (Boston), July 25, 1776, [4]. On the publication of *Additions to Common Sense*, see Edward Larkin, *Thomas Paine and the Literature of Revolution* (New York, 2005), 54. See also [Hugh Henry Brackenridge], *The Death of General Montgomery, in Storming the City of Quebec* . . . (Philadelphia, 1777), 52. For another example of George III as worse than a "Satrap of an Eastern Despot," see Charles Lee, *General Lee's Letter to General Burgoyne, upon His Arrival in Boston* (New York, 1775), 7–8. For other versions of the

Plate 13.
Ecce Homo. 1779.
Courtesy of The Lewis Walpole Library, Yale University.

Similar images of the king were printed as *The Patriot* and *Behold the Man. Ecce Homo* translates as "Behold the Man," referencing the words of Pontius Pilot at the crucifixion of Jesus. All of the titles were ironic.

Many in London and America thought such fears ludicrous. The Tory writer John Shebbeare, for instance, asked incredulously how patriots failed to see that the example of the East India Company's tyrannical behavior in India proved that the British government had in fact treated its American colonies much more civilly and mildly than any other colonies in the world. In 1776, Joseph Cawthorne attempted to revive the argument for virtual representation by explaining that the Company would soon turn its lands in India over to the crown, and only then would both Americans and Indians be virtually represented. "If it should be said there is a vast difference between the *new* and the *old* acquisitions of a country," Cawthorne mused, "I should be glad to know in what it consists?" From

George III print, see *Behold the Man,* 1779, mezzotint, 1851,0901.14 and *Ecce Homo,* 1779, mezzotint, 1868,0808.4597, Prints and Drawings, British Museum, London.

the patriots' perspective, it must have seemed a strange question to still be asking. Cawthorne's implied answer that there was no difference between colonies augured, for patriots, the exact opposite of his intentions.[62]

The colonists' sense of difference and superiority over nonwhite peoples in the empire made the threat of such despotism over America especially odious, and some clearly hoped that attacks on the Company would continue to buoy support for the burgeoning Revolutionary War. At least one author wondered that patriots on both sides of the Atlantic, who "condemn the universal supremacy asserted by Parliament over the Americans, should feel no compassion whatever for millions of their fellow-subjects who are universally controllable by the same authority in other parts of the British dominions." But patriots believed, as did many in Britain, that such people, including the people of India, had never known freedom and good government. Their political histories were also seen to be products of their race, setting them off as different from white Atlantic colonists. As Dickinson wrote, "Thank GOD, we are not Sea Poys, nor Marattas, but *British Subjects,* who are born to Liberty, who know its Worth, and who prize it high." Reports circulated in the press that the "British goverment had been barbarous enough to offer the prisoners taken at Long-Island, to the East-India company, to be transported to their settlements." The subtext was that Americans were to be enslaved by the Company as the Company had enslaved Indians. George Washington related that a story of deserters purchased by the East India Company and sent to India "has a happy effect," and he encouraged Major General John Sullivan to circulate it.[63]

62. J[ohn] Shebbeare, *An Essay on the Origin, Progress, and Establishment of National Society; in Which the Principles of Government, the Definitions of Physical, Moral, Civil, and Religious Liberty, Contained in Dr. Price's Observations, etc. Are Fairly Examined and Fully Refuted: Together with a Justification of the Legislature, in Reducing America to Obedience by Force* . . . (London, 1776), 191; [Joseph Cawthorne], *Thoughts on America: Together with an Idea of Conciliation, Adapted to the Natural and Legislative Rights of the Colonies, and to the Supremacy of Great-Britain* (London, 1776), 47.

63. *The Plain Question upon the Present Dispute with Our American Colonies,* 2d ed. (London, 1776), 23–24 ("condemn"); Rusticus [Dickinson], *Letter from the Country;* [William Barron], *History of the Colonization of the Free States of Antiquity, Applied to the Present Contest between Great Britain and Her American Colonies* . . . (London, 1777), 149; "Boston, May 5," *Boston-Gazette, and Country Journal,* May 5, 1777, [3]; "Extract of a Letter from Capt. John Fisk," *Boston-Gazette, and Country Journal,* Jan. 27, 1777, [2]; George Washington to John Sullivan, June 7, 1777, in Theodore J. Crackel, ed., *The Papers of George Washington Digital Edition* (Charlottesville, Va., 2008). The directors did hope to reinforce their armies in India by "prevailing on American prisoners to enter as volunteers in our service" and sent several ships to Gibraltar to take up to "one hundred recruits" each. See Direc-

Thomas Paine's publications throughout 1777 and 1778, a collection of essays and letters entitled "The American Crisis," continued to associate the tyrannical East India Company with British designs in America. Paine restated the arguments current in 1773 that the British "had ravaged one part of the globe, till it could glut them no longer; their prodigality required new plunder, and through the East-India article TEA they hoped to transfer their rapine from that quarter of the world to this." In a widely republished public letter to the commander in chief of British forces in America, William Howe, Paine argued that expanding dominion had ruined Britain. He went on that the "late reduction of India under Clive and his successors, was not so properly a conquest as an extermination of mankind. . . . Yet Clive received the approbation of the Last Parliament." Britain, in league with supposedly massacring native Americans, had now turned its "tyranny" and "murders" fully on America's "infancy and innocence," which owed, not Britain, but only God for its claim to the continent's "wilderness." Paine quoted from a "meeting of a reputable number of the inhabitants of the city of Philadelphia." They expressed "astonishment" that tories "should be so fond of living under, and supporting a government and at the same time calling it 'happy,' which is never better pleased than when at war—that hath filled India with carnage and famine,—Africa with slavery—and tampered with Indians and Negroes to cut the throats of the freemen of America." Here, those exploited by white Americans had become the dupes and enablers of British tyranny, which itself exploited everyone.[64]

In his draft address for Congress calling on the support of all the people of the United States in the spring of 1777, North Carolina delegate Thomas Burke similarly warned against Britons and loyalists, who were "unfeeling and mean spirited enough to prefer their present ease and oppulence to the Happiness of Milions now living and of Myriads yet unborn." And, Burke went on, the British government and its supporters "wish you to Submit to the absolute Will of a People whose rapine as appears by their Treatment of Ireland and the East Indies can never be Satisfied, as long as the most Cruel Violence can Extort any thing from you." Burke had

tors to Fort William, Oct. 25, 1776, *Fort William–India House Correspondence*, VII, 157. On the need to buoy popular support, see Rakove, *Beginnings of National Politics*, 114, 123–127.

64. [Thomas Paine], "The American Crisis. (No. V)," *Boston-Gazette, and Country Journal*, June 29, 1778, [1], [2]; [Paine], *The American Crisis*, Number III (Philadelphia, [1777]), 47–49. See also Paine's statement that "the blood of India is not yet repaid, nor the wretchedness of Africa yet requitted," in [Paine], *The American Crisis*, Number II (Philadelphia, [1777]), 18. The letters began again in 1780, but the themes had shifted.

been born to a Protestant family ruined by confiscations in Ireland, where Catholics and Protestants alike saw the British government as corrupt. He had personal reasons to believe that the corruption and despotism of the empire would ruin America.[65]

There was ample evidence to encourage many other British people on both sides of the American Revolutionary conflict to agree with Burke on British behavior in India, at least. After the end of the British occupation of Philadelphia in 1778, the *Pennsylvania Packet* reprinted six- and seven-year-old reports from British magazines on the tragedy in Bengal that placed the blame squarely on the dishonorable, greedy, and tyrannical British. A few months earlier, New York's loyalist *Royal Gazette* had described the Company's men in India in a list *"Of those who have* NOT *made* great Figures *in some particular Action or Circumstance of their Lives."* For loyalists and many in Britain, the actions of the Company and its servants were those of corrupted and rogue Britons and should have had little to do with perceptions of British government in America. Yet, patriots had transformed the arguments of the 1760s over the extent of similarities and differences between the colonies in the Atlantic and Indian Oceans to support revolution. The arguments of Knox, Cawthorne, and the British administration that the British government had similar, if not the same, constitutional powers over America and India backfired terribly once reports about the trauma caused by the East India Company in Bengal began to circulate.[66]

IF COLONISTS HAD BEEN FREE to trade beyond the Cape of Good Hope, if they did not deeply desire India's cottons and silks and China's tea, if Bengal had not been conquered and if it had not suffered a terrible famine

65. Burke's address did not make it out of the committee tasked with its creation; instead, the committee sent James Wilson's address to Congress, which chose not to ratify it. See "Thomas Burke's Draft Address to the Inhabitants of the United States," in Paul H. Smith et al., eds., *Letters of Delegates to Congress, 1774–1789,* 26 vols. (Washington, D.C., 1976–2000), VII, 149–153; Kerby A. Miller et al., eds., *Irish Immigrants in the Land of Canaan: Letters and Memoirs from Colonial and Revolutionary America, 1675–1815* (New York, 2003), 499–501.

66. "From the Gentleman's Magazine, for February 1772 . . . Cruelties Practised by the English in Bengal," *Pennsylvania Packet, Or the General Advertiser,* Oct. 22, 1778, [3]; "From the *Annual Register,* for the Year 1771," ibid., Nov. 7, 1778, [1–2]; "Of Those Who Have Not Made Great Figures in Some Particular Action or Circumstance of Their Lives," *Royal Gazette* (New York), July 1, 1778, [2]. For a patriot comparison of patriot mercy and British violence that invoked the East and West Indies alongside America, see "Fish-Kill, July 29," *Norwich Packet; and the Weekly Advertiser,* Aug. 3, 1779, [3].

under Company rule, the timing and arguments of the American Revolution would have looked significantly different. The early-eighteenth-century decisions regulating the India trade and using colonists as consumers for the Company's India goods had a substantial, even revolutionary, knock-on effect. Since the calico compromise, the desires of colonists in America had been second in London to the perceived need for the colonists to be markets, not only for British manufactures but also for goods from India as well. Parliament dissuaded Americans from making products while encouraging Asian Indians to make them for Americans, supporting the Company in trading for these products and using imperial officials to impose duties on them. The decision to pass the Tea Act was completely in keeping with this system of trade, revenue, and control. For many colonists, the root problem with the Tea Act in America was not so much taxation; rather, the act made more direct the economic and political linkages between America and the monopolistic and sensationally despotic East India Company at precisely the moment that Bengal and America appeared to inhabit similar positions within the imperial constitution.

In America, patriots saw the dangerous old tandem of Mughal and Catholic tyranny spreading through the imperial government, a tyranny that would be further enforced, according to Paine and others, by native Americans and formerly enslaved Africans fighting on the British side. Patriots feared that they would be an equally exploited part of an empire containing native Americans, Africans, French Catholics, and Asian Indians. They also might be victims of a parliamentary-supported monopoly company—a company demonstrably rapacious in Bengal, that had long brought to the colonists the goods of empire that were most in demand, including those illegal in Britain, and that would no longer have to fear the competition of smugglers.

After declaring independence, the patriots and their growing number of European allies hoped to use the American Revolutionary War to destabilize British power in both the Atlantic and Indian Oceans. At least in theory, if not in practice, it made sense to target British India. Disgust over the Company's corruption, concern over its influence in London, and fear of its potential power had fueled Revolutionary sentiment. Near the beginning of the war, Congress had provided instructions to privateers in the Atlantic to "particularly" target British East India Company ships in Atlantic waters. In 1777, Thomas Conway suggested an American assault on British India. When the United States officially allied with France in

1778, the directors warned their servants and allies of potential French attacks in India and advised them to work on defensive plans with Indian rulers. In 1780, the Spanish proposed that Americans should build and man four frigates to be placed under Spanish command for a journey to capture British East Indiamen as partial payment for Spain's assistance to the Revolution. Some patriots hoped for a revolution in Bengal and the collapse of the East India Company, but Congress took few practical steps to that end. It also quashed Conway's proposal. And John Jay, appointed America's first minister to Spain in 1779, explained to the Spanish that too few American sailors possessed enough knowledge of the India trade to track the East India Company's ships. In any case, the patriots needed to focus their already stretched military efforts nearer to home.[67]

At the height of the American Revolutionary War, an author calling himself "Americanus" facetiously celebrated Lord North's success in saving both America and Britain from the corrupting influence of Asian luxury. Americanus explained that Lord North had pushed the Americans to lay "aside, with tea, every other article of needless elegance and refinement." The Americans had become like the ancient Spartans, as proven by their new martial abilities and success in holding off the British armies. Americanus argued that in Britain, meanwhile, the costs of fighting the United States and its European allies had transformed the barest necessities into expensive luxuries. Americans and Britons alike, he scoffed, had thereby been freed from Asiatic corruption and oppression. In contrast, the earl of Sheffield explained that within a few years Britain, with its advantages in prices, production, and patterns, would continue to dominate the great Atlantic markets for Asia's pepper, tea, and calicoes. Yet neither

---

67. The Company assisted the effort to retain the thirteen colonies by offering bounties to seamen and paying for the construction of three men-of-war; see "Account of Sums Paid by the Company to the Government," IOR/H/338, 165, BL. On targeting Company ships, see Marine Committee to Thomas Thompson, Apr. 1777, in Smith et al., eds., *Letters of Delegates to Congress*, VI, 686; W. Robinson to Stephens and Pownall, East India Company, and Lord ? Admiralty, Dec. 28, 1775 (copy), T1/518/11, NA. On Conway's proposal, see Henry Laurens to the Marquis de Lafayette, Dec. 6, 1777, in Smith et al., eds., *Letters of Delegates to Congress*, VIII, 383; Stanley J. Idzerda, ed., *Lafayette in the Age of the American Revolution: Selected Letters and Papers, 1776-1790* (Ithaca, N.Y., 1977), I, 185. On defensive plans in India, see Directors to Fort St. George, Mar. 19, 1778, IOR/E/4/868, 91–92, BL; Directors to Nabob of Arcot, Apr. 13, 1778, IOR/E/4/868, 126–128, BL; Directors to Rajah of Tanjore, Apr. 13, 1778, IOR/E/4/868, 135–136, BL. On the proposal from the Spanish, see Count de Florida Blanca to John Jay, June 7, 1780, *PCC, Transcript of the Letters from John Jay, 1779-1784*, I, 208, Jay to Count de Florida Blanca, June 9, 1780, I, 216–217.

claims that Americans would stay away from India goods nor predictions of resurging British dominance took seriously the interests of the American Republic's European allies. The French and Dutch would not give up easily on seizing the presumed benefits of the India trade to America.[68]

68. Americanus, "On the Progress Made by the Present Administration towards a General Reformation of the Manners of the People, by Compelling Them to Deny Themselves Some Gratifications; To Lord North," *Whig Magazine, or, Patriot Miscellany* (London, 1779), 24–27; [John Holroyd], *Observations on the Commerce of the American States* . . . (London, 1783), 19–21.

5   Empires, Interlopers, Corruption, and America's Early India Trade

"What Profits might be made by the [Dutch] East India Company by carrying their Effects directly to the American Market," asked John Adams rhetorically in his 1781 memorial to the Dutch States General. The memorial was widely published in America and Europe in Dutch, French, and English. Adams knew his European target audiences. Europeans commonly expected that the United States would continue to obtain its India goods from Europe. This expectation reflected the normative entrenchment of the system that had connected India and America through Britain. British colonists had been content with importing India goods from Britain instead of directly from India for decades. Even with the independence of the thirteen colonies, the substantial political and practical difficulties of the Asian trade worked in combination to suggest that Americans would remain within the orbits of European imperial powers.[1]

Importing India goods through Holland or France instead of Britain would reward America's allies and insulate America from India's dangers. The Dutch had provided significant financial backing for the patriots and had a long and strong interest in supplying the North American market for Asian goods. They had been the major supplier of smuggled tea to the colonies before 1773, and during the war their India trade to America, by some accounts, grew larger than before the war. The Fourth Anglo-Dutch War (1780–1784) that resulted from the American Revolution was a final chapter in the long contest between the Dutch and British over global trade. As for the French, they had provided financial backing for the patriot cause as well as decisive military support in North America. But it was also a global war for the French. They hoped to use the American Revolutionary War not only to separate the thirteen colonies from Britain but also to replace British power with French power in India and the India

---

1. John Adams, "Memorial to the States General," Apr. 19, 1781, in C. James Taylor, ed., *The Adams Papers Digital Edition* (Charlottesville, Va., 2008). Adams was a strong proponent of a U.S. India trade after 1783; he might have been making the case in 1781 primarily to keep the Dutch and French happy.

trade. An expanded reexport trade in Asian goods to America formed an important part of the expected payoff from French victory in both theaters. British engagement with India, meanwhile, was still tainted by exploitation, despotism, and scandal. Working through the Dutch or French might further distance Americans from such corruption, which had been so prominently part of Revolutionary politics. British and American merchants wanting to trade with India outside a monopoly company, however, might also gain from an independent America.[2]

During the early years of American independence, then, the public, political leaders, and merchants in Holland, France, Britain, and the United States debated and shaped the extent to which the American Revolutionary War had taken America from Britain and gained India for France, Britain, or America. India remained vitally important, not only in questions of trade but also in questions of personal, local, and global politics. The East India Company monopoly and accusations of the scandalous behavior of its men in India, particularly British India's first governor-general Warren Hastings, continued to shape British and American economic and political development as well as America's constitutional development. The connections among India, Britain, and America continued—both like ever and never before.[3]

War, Corruption, Monopoly

France employed a three-pronged strategy against Britain in the late 1770s and early 1780s: sever the United States from Britain, push the British out

2. The small but growing literature on U.S. engagement with India has often followed a somewhat triumphalist narrative that takes for granted that the United States would want to enter into the India trade as an independent power. Such works typically credit American exceptionalism in free trade and ingenuity. They extend a line that began in the 1780s with works such as J. P. Brissot DeWarville, *New Travels in the United States of America* (Bowling Green, Ohio, 1919), 278–279. See, in chronological order, Winthrop L. Marvin, *The American Merchant Marine: Its History and Romance from 1620 to 1902* (New York, 1902), 33–35; Sydney Greenbie and Marjorie Barstow Greenbie, *Gold of Ophir: The China Trade in the Making of America* (New York, 1937); Daniel Henderson, *Yankee Ships in China Seas: Adventures of Pioneer Americans in the Troubled Far East* (New York, 1946); G. Bhagat, *Americans in India, 1784–1860* (New York, 1970). A few more recent works acknowledge, but downplay, the British participation in the U.S. trade to India. See James R. Fichter, *So Great a Proffit: How the East Indies Trade Transformed Anglo-American Capitalism* (Cambridge, Mass., 2010), 26–27, 39.

3. On the East India Company's behavior as scandal, see Nicholas B. Dirks, *The Scandal of Empire: India and the Creation of Imperial Britain* (Cambridge, Mass., 2006).

of India, and educate Americans on the benefits of buying India goods from France. After victory at Yorktown seemed to complete the first part of the strategy in 1781, the French focused more on the other two parts. They disrupted British trade with India by creating upheaval in India itself, particularly in the Second Anglo-Mysore War (1780–1784), and they actively publicized their plan to funnel the supply of India goods to America through Brittany. This plan would attempt to co-opt both the British and Dutch India trades with America. A letter that ran in several American newspapers late in 1781 reported that Lorient had become a sort of free bazaar for both Dutch and American merchants "in Consequence of the great Obstructions and almost Impossibility of navigating to Holland" against British power. Five Dutch East Indiamen would be arriving in Lorient instead of Holland, making the French port the cheapest and easiest place for Americans to obtain "every Kind of East-India Goods." A similar letter from Nantes ran in newspapers up and down the Atlantic seaboard in 1783 exhorting Americans to buy India goods from France and not to fall into their old prewar lines of trade with Britain. "You may depend," the letter informed readers, "that no part of Europe will be able to furnish America more conveniently or cheaper than France, in the course of a few months after the war."[4]

Trumped-up reports of French victories in India further suggested that France, not Britain, would be the dominant European power in India and in the India trade. Such reports circulated widely in the press and Congress. Congressman Samuel Johnstone proclaimed, "The British have suffered very considerably in the East Indies from an Army of the Asiaticks under the command of a very enterprizing prince, whose Name I do not recollect, in the French Interest." The details might have been hazy, but the "Ruin" of British power in India to the benefit of the French seemed clear. John Adams's brother-in-law wrote, "'Tis remarkable to observe how far the Destruction of the *Indian Weed* at Boston a few Years ago, has operated towards the loss of the very Country itself from whence the Pride of Britain has been so fed and fostered." Rumors circulated that America would help the French finish the job. Citing a source close to the U.S. Congress, an anonymous British author cautioned the East India Company to be alert for congressionally backed American vessels stimulating revolution among the Hindus in India. He warned that Americans

---

4. *Providence Gazette; and Country Journal* (R.I.), Dec. 15, 1781, 3; "From the Freeman's Journal of April 30," *New-Jersey Gazette* (Trenton), May 14, 1783, [1]. On French disruptions, see Robert Robertson to his cousin, Mar. 27, 1777, GD133/168, NAS.

in India would be like "the Devil sowing the Tares amongst the Wheat." Which power would dominate the India trade to America very well could have depended on the outcome of battles in India between the British and French and their allies, though not the Americans.[5]

America's prospects for gaining such goods directly from India instead of Europe, a letter from Paris claimed, likewise depended on French forces successfully ejecting the British from the subcontinent. French victory would supposedly spread the ideals of the American Revolution to India and lead to a free and open trade. Another letter from Paris printed in the *Continental Journal* noted that the American "noble spirit of freedom" had inspired the French to support the Indian nawabs in their struggles for "independence, and a free navigation." The letter went on to explain that "America, as well as other nations, must reap great commercial advantages from it." If they had won in India, however, the French would not likely have empowered local rulers and thrown open the India trade to all comers. The most obvious problem was that, if the French gave Indian rulers full independence, these rulers and not the French would create the laws regulating external trade.[6]

Indeed, before the Treaty of Paris formally recognized U.S. independence, American newspaper reports followed Adams's memorial by suggesting that France or Holland would be given the American India trade in exchange for loans, cash, or other trading privileges. A letter from Paris reported that the people "generally believed" an account "that the French East India Company, which is soon to be established, will, according to Treaty, have the exclusive privilege, of supplying the States of America with oriental commodities." Such was the supposed value of the American markets that the French would forgive all the American debt from the war. Claims also circulated that the Dutch had nearly displaced the British in the reexport of India goods to America. The *Pennsylvania Packet* reported that the Dutch would give another major loan to the cash-strapped American Republic in exchange for "the privilege of sending a greater number of

5. Samuel Johnston to Thomas Burke, June 23, 1781, and Rhode Island Delegates to William Greene, Aug. 28, 1781, in Paul H. Smith et al., eds., *Letters of Delegates to Congress, 1774–1789*, 26 vols. (Washington, D.C., 1976–2000), XVII, 346, 568; John Adams to Abigail Adams, May 22, 1781, in Taylor, ed., *Adams Papers Digital Edition*, Richard Cranch to John Adams, June 22, 1781, and Jean de Neufville and Son to Abigail Adams, July 25, 1781. For the British report, see A Well Wisher to the Company to Directors' Secret Committee, Feb. 4, 1782, IOR/H/157/13, 329–330, BL.

6. *Continental Journal, and Weekly Advertiser* (Boston), Mar. 27, 1783, [3]; see also *Freeman's Journal: or, the North-American Intelligencer* (Philadelphia), May 7, 1783, [3].

East-India ships to America than any other power." The reported Dutch loan was not as generous as the supposed offer of French loan forgiveness, but then the French were said to be expecting a complete monopoly, not just a preeminent position in the trade.[7]

Concerns nevertheless remained that America would continue to be beholden to the British in the India trade. In 1783, "Brutus" wrote to the *Boston Evening-Post*, "In a few years our trade may become so monopolized by British merchants, factors, etc. that the American merchant, though not a hewer of wood, or drawer of water, may become a mere hireling in a compting room." His fears of monopoly and the reduction of American merchants clearly echoed the heated rhetoric of the patriots against the East India Company during the tea crisis a decade earlier. He explained, "We have, through this war, found the British policy has had recourse to mercantile projects; merchants have been used to bring about their measures, as in the case of the East-India Company's tea." There were growing indications in 1783 that as the patriots had correctly expected, Parliament's efforts had failed to reform the Company. Americans were, so far at least, only temporarily freed from the Company monopoly—the Company's scandals remained relevant from Bengal to the United States.[8]

During the 1770s and early 1780s, the Company's governor-general, Warren Hastings, had built on Robert Clive's conquests by reorganizing, consolidating, and expanding British power on the subcontinent. And, like Clive, Hastings was not without powerful critics. In 1774, Lord North appointed one such critic, Philip Francis, to join the council in Calcutta governing Bengal. Francis was the likely author of the Junius letters, which were widely available in America before the Revolution and warned of governmental infringement on British rights and liberties. He also had considered emigrating to New England in 1773 after the circulation of the scandalous stories of East India Company corruption and mismanagement in Bengal. Francis, then, had helped shape and shared patriot impressions of tyranny, constitutional failure, and corruption in the British government, and he took such views with him to India. Francis intended to turn out of power the corrupted Hastings, who he thought showed

7. "Naples, March 10," *Boston Evening-Post: and the General Advertiser*, June 14, 1783, [1] ("generally"); "London, Sept. 14," ibid., Jan. 25, 1783, [2]; "Extract of a Letter from Amsterdam," *Pennsylvania Packet, and General Advertiser* (Philadelphia), Dec. 9, 1783, [2] ("privilege").

8. Brutus, "For the Boston Evening-Post," *Boston Evening-Post, and the General Advertiser*, May 10, 1783, [3].

much less respect for India's local leaders and constitution than had Clive. Once in Calcutta, however, onlookers caught the married Francis hauling himself over the compound wall of Catherine Grand, the wife of another local British official. This scandal concerning Francis's personal life gave Hastings an opportunity to sideline Francis in Calcutta. Back in Britain, however, Francis and his friends did not give up.[9]

One of Francis's friends, William Mackintosh, in *Travels in Europe, Asia, and Africa,* drove a broad attack on Hastings and his Company servants for substantially weakening the British position in India through their adoption of elite Indian attitudes and traits and acceptance of Indian luxury. The Indian people themselves were not to blame for tyrannical government; their rulers were at fault. In an oft-quoted passage, Mackintosh built on the trope of the nabob by claiming that the typical Briton in India under Hastings became so lazy and obsessed with luxury that he employed Indians to do every task for him. A Briton in India dressed "without any greater exertion on his own part, than if he was a statue," and he lazed about smoking a hookah, riding in a palanquin, and sleeping with women. Mackintosh saw corruption and weakness in the elite East Indian way of life embraced by ruling Britons.[10]

In defense of Hastings and elite Indian culture, the India merchant Joseph Price pointed instead to the West Indies and France as the source of corruption in the British empire. Price identified Mackintosh as a "mouth piece of party, and vile scandalizer of private character." Price agreed with Mackintosh that Indians were docile and excellent people and that they must be allowed to retain their customs, but he argued that there was nothing dangerous in India's luxuries. He defended the hookah against Mackintosh's attacks, writing, "The mixture of sweet scented Persian tobacco, sweet herbs, coarse sugar, spice, etc. the smoak of which . . . is so very pleasant, that many ladies take the tube and draw a little of the smoak into their mouths; and almost all ladies like the smell of it, as it goes off directly, and never remains in their cloaths, or the furniture of the rooms." Hookah smoke was pleasant; it did not corrupt. Price saw corruption

9. Sophia Weitzman, *Warren Hastings and Philip Francis* (Manchester, 1929); Robert Travers, *Ideology and Empire in Eighteenth-Century India: The British in Bengal* (Cambridge, 2007), 142–143, 145–149, 179, 208, 210; John Cannon, ed., *The Letters of Junius* (Oxford, 1978); Linda Colley, "Gendering the Globe: The Political and Imperial Thought of Philip Francis," *Past and Present,* no. 209 (November 2010), 117–120.

10. [William Mackintosh], *Travels in Europe, Asia, and Africa; Describing Characters, Customs, Manners, Laws, and Productions of Nature and Art . . . ,* 2 vols. (London, 1782), I, ix, 71–72, II, 214–219.

and intellectual weakness coming particularly from black Africans and French West Indians. He wrote that Mackintosh, the son of a Scots West Indian planter and a French creole, and John Whitehill, the past governor of Madras who defended him, were both "half black" and supported each other on a racial basis. Price positioned the threat to Britain, not in India's luxury, but in the French and the racial mixing of the West Indies, writing that "Mr. Mackintosh himself has never yet been taken for an Englishman before he spoke, and then the puff and gasconade which flow out of his mouth, oblige you to conclude that he is a French renegado." These were the men, Price suggested, that the disgraced—and, after March 1782, former—prime minister, Lord North, consorted with against Hastings.[11]

In 1783, however, the odd pair of Lord North, architect of the failed war with America, and Charles James Fox, patriot supporter and aggressive critic of George III, formed a new coalition government. As they formalized the loss of America through the Treaty of Paris, they proposed an ambitious reform of the East India Company in "A Bill for Vesting the Affairs of the East India Company in the Hands of Certain Commissioners, for the Benefit of the Proprietors and the Public" (Fox's India bill) as well as a companion "Bill for the Better Government of the Territorial Possessions and Dependencies in India." Fox argued that placing the Company more closely under parliamentary control and oversight would reduce corruption in India, better insulate Britain from that corruption, and protect the trade's value to the state.[12]

Price and many others marveled that anyone could think that North, after his policy for America, should be entrusted with more power over India. Members of Parliament raised the same concern on the floor of the House of Commons. In public, too, criticism followed a similar line. *Lord North's Supplication to Mr. Fox* (Plate 14), for example, depicts Fox in

11. [Joseph Price], *Some Observations and Remarks on a Late Publication, intitled, Travels in Europe, Asia, and Africa* . . . (London, 1782), 13, 36, 100. Mackintosh also denounced mixed Anglo-Indians with creole Portuguese parentage as the worst people in India and "impossible to reform"; see Mackintosh, *Travels in Europe, Asia, and Africa*, I, 407. Racial mixing occurred in India as well, but Price appeared to imagine Indians much more positively than Africans. Price also might have been authoring a subtext to position Mackintosh's creole mother as enslaved or as only one generation removed from slavery. Philip Francis became a public supporter of abolition, and he might have been forming and voicing his abolitionist ideals in the 1770s, long before he published them; see T. H. Bowyer, "An Enigmatic Abolitionist: Philip Francis and the British Slave Trade," *Parliamentary History*, XXV (2006), 324–326.

12. For more on Fox's India bill, see Susan Staves, "The Construction of the Public Interest in the Debates over Fox's India Bills," *Prose Studies*, XVIII (1995), 175–198.

Plate 14. *Lord North's Supplication to Mr. Fox.* 1783. Courtesy of The Lewis Walpole Library, Yale University

Asian-style dress, wearing a turban, crescent and aigrette, cummerbund, and long robe. His face is darkened and stubbly, and his hair is unruly. In contrast, North kneels in supplication, wears standard European masculine dress, has a pure white complexion, and sports tidy Georgian hair. From such appearances, Fox seems to represent the corrupting influence of India. North, however, is doing the devil's bidding, wears a sack labeled "Nation's Plunder," begs Fox for his assistance, and promises fealty, exclaiming, "They are going to prosecute me for the American War." Both Fox and North are corrupt and have contributed to the ruin of Britain's economy and power, one in America and the other in India.[13]

Fox's bill had been largely written by Edmund Burke, outspoken critic

13. [Joseph Price], *The Saddle Put on the Right Horse; or, An Enquiry into the Reason Why Certain Persons Have Been Denominated Nabobs* ... (London, 1783), 67–68. For a report on the Commons concern in America, see *Connecticut Journal* (New Haven), Feb. 4, 1784, 2.

America's Early India Trade

of the Company's corruption and tyranny as well as the government's treatment of the thirteen colonies, but the bill seemed to some to be a product of India's corruption, and they associated it with India's supposedly corrupting luxury and way of life. James Sayers, for example, depicted a portly and swarthy Fox as "Carlo Khan," wearing a turban and riding upon an Indian elephant with the face of Lord North (Plate 15). Sayers criticized the unlikely alliance of Fox and North and their India bill, which he believed was intended to transfer wealth from the nabobs to Fox and other members of Parliament. North literally became an Indian beast of burden for Fox, who was his tyrannical Asian rider. Newspapers in Britain and America noted, "The loss of America so much decreased the necessary Influence of the Crown in the Senate, that it became a matter of necessity to seize upon India as an equivalent, whose riches will enable Justice to bribe Truth to her duty." Fox's bill, the papers explained, was not intended to stop corruption so much as to enable the ministry to profit from further patronage in India. Particularly when coupled with the widespread belief in the role of parliamentary corruption in the outbreak of the American Revolution, Fox's India bill made "a Parliamentary reform more requisite than ever." Although the bill passed the Commons, George III successfully encouraged the Lords to block it.[14]

Reports of Fox's India bill in America suggested that Britain would finally be humbled by India. Thomas Jefferson enthusiastically circulated news of the bill's role in bringing down the Fox-North government and the likely benefit to America. Likewise, Congressman William Ellery explained to Rhode Island's governor that some in the British government still wanted to put India more firmly under parliamentary control, whereas others "demand aid in cash and troops to the company." He exclaimed that the situation over India made "certain . . . the bankruptcy of this country [Britain]." John Church (alias John Carter), provisioner to the French and American armies during the Revolution and soon-to-be member of Parliament, wrote to Alexander Hamilton that, as a result of the mess over the India bill, "I think Britain is in a fair way of loosing shortly her Possessions in that Part of the World."[15]

14. Thomas Wright, *England under the House of Hanover* . . . , 2 vols. (London, 1848), II, 82–84. For another example, see *The Fall of Carlo Khan* (London, 1783), in Nicholas K. Robinson, *Edmund Burke: A Life in Caricature* (New Haven, Conn., 1996), 55. For the reprinted newspaper report from London papers, see, for instance, "Boston, January 15," *Massachusetts Spy: Or, Worcester Gazette*, Jan. 22, 1784, [2]. On Burke's authorship, see P. J. Marshall, *The Impeachment of Warren Hastings* (Oxford, 1965), 20.

15. Thomas Jefferson to Benjamin Harrison, Mar. 3, 1784, in Smith et al., eds., *Letters*

CARLO KHAN'S
Triumphal Entry into Leadenhall Street.

Plate 15. [James Sayers], *Carlo Khan's Triumphal Entry into Leadenhall Street.*
[England, 1783?]. Courtesy of The Lewis Walpole Library, Yale University.

    The existence of this less famous mirrored and slightly altered version of the
engraving suggests the extent of the market for the image and the popularity of its
politics.

The Scottish tobacco trader John Woddrop similarly wrote to George Washington that weavers in Britain attacked the Company, inspired by America's success in freeing itself from the Company's devastation. Woddrop claimed to have had many conversations with those involved in the production of linen, fustian, and silk in Britain. They were, he wrote, "reprobating the East India Compy whom they are naming the blood Suckers of the Poor in all parts of this country." He went on that they blamed the Company specifically for the American Revolution: "There Cursed tea, they say, shed the blood of our American friends etc." After devastating both India and America, "they want to Compleat their Murders by a Starvation of many thousand of English and Scotch Weavers etc." This language against the Company sounded like both the calico outcry in the early decades of the century and the patriot outcry before and during the American Revolution. Now, though, Woddrop expected that the Company would finally be destroyed; if not, the weavers would move to America, bringing their industry with them to further impoverish Britain. Woddrop explained, "Theory is, in General, Anihilate that most abominable East India Company. Or Else let them be conveyed over to their brave friends and Country Men in America."[16]

Americans also learned that others in Britain hoped that the two countries might become allies in the India trade. One anonymous writer, for example, wrote that, given the outcome of the American Revolution, "A new system of commerce must take place all over the world." The author predicted that "America will be a medium of trade to all Europe if not in some measure to Asia." America should not look to France to make the most of its new position. Instead, "if Great-Britain, Ireland and the United States of America, form an union of amity, the wealth of the world must circulate under their directions." Certainly there were merchants in Britain and America who would have supported such a plan, but several difficulties needed to be overcome.[17]

As another London writer, republished in America, asked, "How is it possible to frame a code of commercial laws, that shall at once be satisfactory to the Americans, to the people of England, and their friends

of Delegates to Congress, XXI, 405, William Ellery to William Greene, Feb. 1, 1784, XXI, 313; John B. Church to Alexander Hamilton, May 2, 1784, in Harold C. Syrett, ed., *The Papers of Alexander Hamilton Digital Edition* (Charlottesville, Va., 2011).

16. John Woddrop to George Washington, Sept. 16, 1784, in Theodore J. Crackel, ed., *The Papers of George Washington Digital Edition* (Charlottesville, Va., 2008).

17. "London, March 27," *New-Jersey Gazette*, June 18, 1783, [1].

and allies?" This author expected that within a few years "the pride and the enterprize of the Americans" would establish them in the India trade. Britain must be wary of responding with "tameness" to such an event. The Americans would have advantages over the British in not having to work through the East India Company, and so the Americans must either be stopped or the British merchants must be given the same opportunities. This might seem a good idea, but it would ruin the East India Company, and "as our East-India trade is the grand fund that enables us to pay the interest of the national debt, a national bankruptcy would soon follow." Joseph Price likewise noted that those who advocated for a free trade for Britons and Americans alike to India had not thought through the "pernicious and destructive" consequences. Only a continued monopoly and colonies in India, Price argued, would give expanding British industry cheaper prices for Indian raw cotton and silk, and thereby give Britain a competitive advantage over Europe and America. Additionally, Price repeated the old argument that the monopoly fostered the construction of great East Indiamen vital in the defense of Britain and its trades. He also expected that Britain could regain the supply of the American tea market by removing duties and exporting the produce of Company Bengal to China to purchase tea, providing a large advantage over other Europeans forced to use cash.[18]

The French, meanwhile, still claimed that they would be the solution to keep corrupted Britain from resuming its old and tyrannical place as the linchpin between India and America. Stories continued to circulate throughout the United States that France and its allies had greatly reduced British power and trading access in India. An item circulated from Boston in January 1784 claimed: "The accounts from the East Indies appear to be important indeed. . . . The arms of France and their allies, were perhaps never so victorious in the East, both by sea and land, as they have been during the late war." In reality, French military success in India had become largely rhetorical. The British East India Company had gained even more strength on the subcontinent than before. Nevertheless, these reports encouraged the sense that France, not Britain, could provide better access to India goods. "Independent" admitted that Britain had

18. "From the English Review, for 1783," *South-Carolina Weekly Gazette* (Charleston), Sept. 27, 1783, [3]; [Joseph Price], *A Vindication of Gen. Richard Smith, Chairman of the Select Committee of the House of Commons, as to His Competency to Preside over and Direct, an Investigation into the Best Mode of Providing the Investment for the East India Company's Homeward-Bound Bengal Ships* . . . (London, 1783), 81–84, 93, 97–107, 127.

been a beneficial trading partner for the colonies before the Revolution. Now Americans could get goods more cheaply and make greater profits by trading with Holland and France. Leyden offered a good market for India goods for American merchants. But Lorient, he wrote, "is the great East India market and furnishes teas and several kinds of East India goods, cheaper than we can get them from England."[19]

Merchants based in Holland and France trading in India goods and in local reproductions also wrote directly to American merchants to pull business away from the British. On his own account, Jan Van der Werf sent Rhode Island merchant Samuel Nightingale, junior, an unsolicited and unsuccessful shipment of cottons and silks apparently made in Haarlem to imitate India and French fabrics. Nantes merchant Alexander Keith wrote to New York merchant James Beekman in October 1784 to solicit his business. Keith boasted that he could offer excellent prices on "all sorts of teas and other East-India goods." He also claimed a "Considerable Concern . . . in one of the principal Calico and chintz Manufactures in this City," similar to Van der Werf's connections to Haarlem producers. Keith sent Beekman an unsuccessful trial at his own risk of two bales of calico and other sundries through Lorient to try to prove the quality and salability of his merchandise and to encourage further orders. The general failure of many such transactions was due to British success in India against the French, British products of superior value, and the strength of connections that continued between British and American merchants despite the Revolution.[20]

Indeed, the extent to which the fashionable trade in India goods with Britain had collapsed during the war years can easily be overstated. In Philadelphia, for instance, the British occupation gave the city a direct line to new British styles and London's India goods. In the late 1770s, merchants in New York, Philadelphia, and Hartford, Connecticut, had

19. "Boston, January 15," *Massachusetts Spy: Or, Worcester Gazette*, Jan. 22, 1784, [2]; Independent, "To the Citizens of the United States," *Pennsylvania Packet and General Advertiser* (Philadelphia), Mar. 16, 1784, [2]; "To the Citizens of the United States," *South Carolina Gazette, and General Advertiser* (Charleston), Apr. 6–8, 1784, [4].

20. Earlier shipments from Van der Werf during the war when British trade was more restricted had found profitable markets in Philadelphia and Boston. See Jan Van der Werf to Samuel Nightingale, Jr., Oct. 14, 1782, Oct. 4, 1783, Samuel Nightingale, Jr., to Jan Van der Werf, May 15, 1783, Nightingale-Jenckes Papers, MSS 588, subgroup 2, box 2, folder 6, Rhode Island Historical Society, Providence; Alexander Keith to James Beekman, Oct. 15, 1784, in Philip L. White, ed., *The Beekman Mercantile Papers, 1746-1799*, 3 vols. (New York, 1956), III, 1051–1052; on the sale of the goods, see Beekman to Keith, Feb. 16, 1785, III, 1055.

boasted of their "fresh" supplies of India calicoes, chintz, muslin, and shawls specifically imported from London. Smugglers brought "English and India Goods" from British-occupied ports into U.S.-held ports. Certainly, the British trade could have been jeopardized after the war as imperial leaders in London debated their U.S. mercantile policy. Pressure from merchants in Britain, however, quickly helped regain drawbacks on reexports to America common in the colonial period. As "A Merchant" in the *Morning Chronicle* explained, exports to America should be on at least an equal footing with exports to Europe. Otherwise, the goods would simply flow to Europe before they went to America, and Britain would lose the opportunity to carry the goods across the Atlantic. The remaining colonies in British North America, too, needed to enjoy the same drawbacks to remove the temptation of smuggling India goods across the border from the United States.[21]

Within months of the peace, American merchants stocked and advertised India goods from London. In New York, Beekman had already placed orders for Persian taffeties, cossae muslins, cambricks, calicoes, and India chintz from Thomas Pomeroy in London before hearing from Keith in Nantes. In Philadelphia, Thomas Armat ordered Indian and British cottons from British suppliers. A memorandum in his letter book extensively detailed the goods to be ordered from several British ports in contrast to only a few entries for France and Holland. Even in South Carolina, where the war had most recently been most violent, James Gregorie celebrated "European and India GOODS, imported from London" for his Charleston customers.[22]

21. A Merchant, "From the Morning Chronicle, April 23; America Trade," *Royal Gazette* (New York), June 11, 1783, [2]. These goods were advertised alongside other British goods, and sometimes Dutch and French goods as well. See, for examples, *Connecticut Courant, and the Weekly Intelligencer* (Hartford), Nov. 10, 1778, [4]; *New-York Gazette: And the Weekly Mercury*, July 28, 1777, [4], Sept. 13, 1779, [4]; *Royal Gazette* (New York), May 30, 1778, [2], Oct. 31, 1781, [4]; *Pennsylvania Ledger: or The Philadelphia Market-Day Advertiser*, Jan. 28, 1778, [4]; *Royal Pennsylvania Gazette* (Philadelphia), Apr. 17, 1778, [2]. On seized goods from "Long Island, or some other island or place in the possession or under controul of the enemies of this State," see "State of Connecticut; County of Hartford, May 25, 1780," *Connecticut Courant, and the Weekly Intelligencer*, June 27, 1780, [1]. On the formation of British trade policy for the United States, which became bogged down later over the question of the West Indian trade, see Vincent T. Harlow, *The Founding of the Second British Empire, 1763–1793*, 2 vols. (London, 1952), I, 448–470.

22. James Beekman to Thomas Pomeroy, Oct. 5, 1784, in White, ed., *Beekman Mercantile Papers*, III, 1185–1186; Thomas Armat to Champion and Dickason, Aug. 31, 1784, memorandum, n.d., and "Scheme of Sundry Goods to Be Ship'd by Messrs Russels and Smith, Bir-

An American author calling himself "Candidus" argued that both the United States and Britain would benefit from such a renewed mutual friendship, particularly in the India trade. He explained that the United States should not forget its Revolutionary War allies but "should take care not to load ourselves with too partial a connection with any power, for it will be a continued tax upon us." Candidus turned the language of taxation that patriots had used to target Britain before the American Revolution against the notion of a special trading relationship with France. He noted that Britain was vulnerable after losing the thirteen colonies and that British leaders must be aware that "it may be any time in our power more than others, to sow the seeds of dissention amongst them and support a revolution; she will court our favour." He predicted that, in exchange for American friendship and commercial amity, Britain and its matchless navy would "secure our East-India trade, which all the mercantile powers must look upon in a short time with jealousy." Though individual Britons might, the British navy and government would not, as it turned out, nurture and support America's nascent India trade, and "a short time" would prove overly optimistic given the political and economic difficulties of establishing a flourishing trade to Asia. Despite its military setbacks in India, however, the French government had not given up on using America and India together to help weaken the British.[23]

French Connections

In 1784, George Chalmers, prolific author, loyalist returned to Britain, and soon-to-be Board of Trade clerk, argued that, by engaging in the East India trade, the United States would solidify its independence, weaken British trade, and turn the British West Indies against Britain. To support his position, he quoted extensively from Charles Davenant's 1690s claims that colonial pirates and interlopers in the Indian Ocean and Red Sea would have turned the colonies in America into "independent commonwealths" if their activities were left unchecked. The English and later

---

mingham to Philadelphia," Letter Book 1781–1794, (Phi)1971, HSP; "James Gregorie," *South Carolina Gazette, and General Advertiser* (Charleston), Jan. 29–31, 1784, [3]. For more on Armat's business and his use of British suppliers and credit, see Thomas M. Doerflinger, *A Vigorous Spirit of Enterprise: Merchants and Economic Development in Revolutionary Philadelphia* (Chapel Hill, N.C., 1986), 54.

23. "Candidus's Address to the Citizens of New-Jersey," *Political Intelligencer, and New-Jersey Advertiser* (New Brunswick), Apr. 20, 1784, [2].

British government had successfully suppressed colonial participation in British Atlantic piracy and interloping in the Indian Ocean. Now, however, independent Americans might develop their own trade beyond the Cape of Good Hope against British interests. The French government intended to help. The French had failed to overthrow the British in India and were disappointed by American merchants quickly resuming their trade with Britain, but they might yet draw the United States into their imperial orbit in the Indian Ocean. Given the myriad difficulties of the India trade, American merchants and sea captains, for their part, needed experienced associates and capital support as much as the French needed allies and markets.[24]

On February 11, 1784, "a very brilliant and respectable company" celebrated George Washington's birthday on the deck of the *Empress of China* as it prepared to be the first vessel to sail from the United States to Asia. "Hilarity and manly decorum" were punctuated by a thirteen-cannon salute, suggesting the significance of the impending voyage. Nevertheless, the *Empress of China* was not, and could not easily have been, a wholly American venture. The backers had quickly faced the early Republic's significant shortage of capital. Boston merchants, who were expected to provide a third of the investment, could not secure their share. Robert Morris, one of the wealthiest and most influential men in the country, increased his own share to total half of the capital. Still, Morris needed to draw twenty-three thousand dollars in bills on London associates to complete his enlarged investment. The other half of the capital came from the American firm Daniel Parker and Company, of which one of the three partners, John Holker, born in Britain, was a well-connected expatriate French merchant. Holker had arrived in America in 1778 and served as the purchaser for the Royal French Marine during the American Revolution. French support would extend far beyond Holker.[25]

24. George Chalmers, *Opinions on Interesting Subjects of Public Law and Commercial Policy; Arising from American Independence* . . . (London, 1784), 140–141, 193–194. Based primarily on Samuel Shaw's account, Kariann Akemi Yokota suggests that "Americans preferred French to British assistance." This preference was certainly true of some patriots but not of American adventurers to Asia in general, nor even Congress. See Yokota, *Unbecoming British: How Revolutionary America Became a Postcolonial Nation* (New York, 2011), 133–134.

25. "New York, February 14," *Vermont Gazette or Freemans Depository* (Bennington), Mar. 6, 1784, [2]. The calendar under which Washington was born gave the date as February 11, whereas under the new-style calendar it is February 22. The ship sailed on Washington's birthday under the new calendar. See Clarence L. Ver Steeg, "Financing and Outfitting the

The voyage's supercargo, Samuel Shaw, reported that, at the Straights of Sunda, "it was no small Addition to our Happiness . . . to meet there two Ships belonging to our good Allies the French." Several of the French naval officers had experience in the South China Sea. The French captain of the *Triton* had been to Canton eleven times. He "welcomed us in the most affectionate manner" and offered to escort the American vessel on its journey—an offer the Americans, who had limited defensive capabilities and little knowledge of the route, warmly accepted. Shaw reported that at Macao a small party of Frenchmen, including the French consul, congratulated the newcomers and introduced them to the Portuguese governor. The French also provided "Men, Boats and Anchors" to shuttle to the shore, and they invited the Americans to live in their homes at Canton. Additionally, the French vouched for the independence of the Americans to the Chinese government. The easy confusion between American and British citizenship might be productive in some instances, but not in Canton, where it offered no advantages and risked creating local political problems with the Chinese. Overall, the French offered "the most flattering and substantial Proofs of their Friendship."[26]

These proofs of friendship were a considerable aid to the American venture. Sailing east as an independent nation might not have absolutely required such support, but the support made it considerably easier and less risky. The value of the experienced French assistance was underscored on the voyage home. Shaw recounted that they joined a Dutch captain "with the view of availing ourselves of his experience. . . . [But] it was no small mortification to us . . . to find that he was equally a stranger in those seas with ourselves." The mistake cost the Americans time and an anchor. Such was the value of French help that John Jay recommended that Jefferson ask the French minister "to assure his most Christian Majesty that the

First United States Ship to China," *Pacific Historical Review*, XXII (1953), 4, 8; Philip Chadwick Foster Smith, *The Empress of China* (Philadelphia, 1984), 20–23. Similar to the East India Company's crews, the captain and officers were allotted the privilege to trade on their own accounts. See Daniel Parker and others to John Green, Jan. 25, 1784, in Mary A. Giunta, ed., *Documents of the Emerging Nation: U.S. Foreign Relations, 1775–1789* (Wilmington, Del., 1998), 239.

26. *The Journals of Major Samuel Shaw, the First American Consul at Canton; with a Life of the Author, by Josiah Quincy* (Boston, 1847), 152–156, 162–167, 192–195. Before meeting the French, for directions the captain was to rely on the Briton Samuel Dunn's *New Directory for the East Indies*, which had been published in multiple editions. For mention of Dunn, see Daniel Parker and others to John Green, Jan. 25, 1784, in Giunta, ed., *Documents of the Emerging Nation*, 238.

People of the United States will on their part be happy in Opportunities of acknowledging these pleasing Acts of Kindness, and of cultivating and continuing the same spirit of Friendship, which has hitherto so happily subsisted between the two Nations." The French hope that their assistance would draw the Americans away from the British and into the French orbit seemed to be coming true.[27]

The meandering and near catastrophic voyage of the *United States*, which was initially intended to beat the *Empress of China* as the first American ship to China, further demonstrates the importance of French assistance. The successful Philadelphia merchant Philip Moore fitted out the *United States* in March 1784. Two-fifths of the return cargo was financed by European capital, but Moore would have done well to pursue European experience as well. Advice in Madeira redirected the voyage from China to India, which in itself was not a problem. The ship's captain, however, was an American, Thomas Bell, without experience in the India trade. Bell managed to get lost in the Indian Ocean, substantially increasing the length of the outbound voyage beyond that of the *Empress of China* with its French guidance. Compounding problems, on the way home, Bell refused to replenish at the Cape of Good Hope, as most India traders did, and his crew was devastated by scurvy. He was forced to stop in British Barbados for assistance. The governor initially refused, telling Bell he should have gone to America's French allies for help. Eventually, the governor relented, giving Bell forty-eight hours to find a new crew. Inexperience in trading and sailing to India had dramatically lengthened the voyage to nineteenth months and contributed to the ruin of the Moore family's merchant house back in Philadelphia.[28]

In mid-1785, American adventurers and investors developed schemes to spread the raising of capital and the sizable risk of such long voyages and to gain more support from their own states. A group of New York-

27. *Journals of Major Samuel Shaw*, 201; Worthington Chauncey Ford et al., eds., *Journals of the Continental Congress, 1774-1789*, 34 vols. (Washington, D.C., 1904-1937), Sept. 1, 1785, XXIX, 673-674. The interests of the French in providing the Americans with naval protection as well as material and political assistance to keep the Americans from working with the British in China was not lost on the British in Canton, who offered their own assistance; see *Journals of Major Samuel Shaw*, 166-167, 181-182.

28. William Bell Clark, "Postscripts to the Voyage of the Merchant Ship United States," *Pennsylvania Magazine of History and Biography*, LXXVI (1952), 294-310; Lord Macartney to Court of Directors Secret Committee, Jan. 30, 1785, IOR/H/247/23, 373-386, BL; Holden Furber, "The Beginnings of American Trade with India, 1784-1812," *New England Quarterly*, XI (1938), 235-237; *New-Jersey Gazette*, Mar. 16, 1784, [2].

ers got several newspapers to report their proposal for "building and fitting out a ship for the India trade." They met on Wednesday nights and invited anyone interested to bring "only" three hundred dollars for the purchase of a share. In the south, Congressman William Grayson asked James Madison, rhetorically, "Don't you think an exemption from duty on all goods imported immediately from India in Virga. bottoms to our State might have a good effect?" He explained that "most of the mercantile people here" believe the trade to Asia could be done more competitively from America than Europe. He "heartily wish[ed] to see" Virginia merchants successfully smuggling their India goods onward to the West Indies. The plan would require local state support as well as some level of European support in the Indian Ocean for supply bases and protection, and in the West Indies it would depend on European colonial markets. Thomas Jefferson posited that such support was not suitable in the southern states. Merchants in Boston might join those from New York and Philadelphia that had tried the India trade, but "the states south of the Delaware" lacked the ships and sailors to launch an India trade of their own, nor would they purchase India goods from the northern states, which would demand cash as payment. Southern ports would continue to obtain India goods from Europe, Portugal in particular, Jefferson thought, in exchange for agricultural commodities. Although Jefferson was wrong on the point of Portugal, he was correct that the northern states would be more inclined to pursue the India trade.[29]

A widely reprinted piece in the *New-York Gazetteer* opined that more voyages from the United States to Asia would be vital for the country's future. The author exclaimed, "Thank God, the intrigues of a Christian court do not influence the wise decrees of the eastern world." European powers blocking U.S. ships from their colonies in the West Indies made the East India trade especially valuable. He was confident that European powers would not be able to stop the success of American merchants in this "most profitable trade" because they were too committed to protecting their monopoly companies. Such companies, he claimed, could never compete successfully with private traders, and Americans would be the best private traders. U.S. merchants only needed great ships to prosecute

29. The notice also appeared outside New York. See, for example, *Pennsylvania Packet, and Daily Advertiser,* June 15, 1785, [3]; William Grayson to James Madison, May 28, 1785, in Smith et al., eds., *Letters of Delegates to Congress,* XXII, 406–407; Thomas Jefferson to John Adams, Nov. 27, 1785, in Barbara B. Oberg and J. Jefferson Looney, eds., *Papers of Thomas Jefferson Digital Edition* (Charlottesville, Va., 2008).

the trade. Capital and experience were in reality bigger problems, but they were also much more difficult problems to solve. In trying to generate support for an India trade, the author smartly avoided them. He concluded: "Patriotism and private interest here unite, and I wish every citizen could become interested in so great an object; — for instead of importing India goods through Europe, we may, with a moral certainty, supply many parts of it, from this country. We now support their navigation, in proportion as we consume those articles. In the other case, they must in some degree, support ours." The author saw the India trade in the same terms as its supporters had for centuries in Britain, Holland, and France, as a vital means to national strength.[30]

The French government was an increasingly keen partner and stepped up efforts to draw American traders away from buying India goods in Britain or elsewhere in Europe by offering certain incentives to Americans in the Indian Ocean. Louis XVI granted American vessels the freedom to make use of all French islands and ports east of the Cape of Good Hope. According to the congressman Samuel Hardy, the king had opened the ports upon "hearing that Amerrican Vessels on their passage to the East Indies were subject to considerable inconveniences from the want of ports into which they might enter to refresh." Charles Thomson, congressional secretary, noted that the opening of French ports in the Indian Ocean "is the more important to us as we have no factories or ports in those seas to which our vessels in case of any disaster could repair and be sure of meeting with a friendly reception." Newspapers throughout the United States carried notices of the decision and encouraged American merchants to take advantage of the French offer. The standard notice concluded that "this liberal arrangement will be very beneficial to the American India trade, and to the [French] islands." As part of a public relations blitz, newspapers also ran reports celebrating the prospects of Madagascar and the Isle de France (present-day Mauritius). Thomson thought that the opening of French Indian Ocean ports "appears to be a disinterested mark of bounty" from Louis XVI, but the French had significant interests in drawing American vessels away from British ports in Asia and throughout the Indian Ocean. The Isle de France needed all the trade it could get in the midst of "a great Bankruptcy." The Bengal government predicted the French government would need to pay dearly to liquidate the debt and

30. Mercator, "From the New-York Gazetteer: Reflections on a Trade to India," *Freeman's Journal: or, The North-American Intelligencer,* June 22, 1785, [2]; *Independent Chronicle: and the Universal Advertiser* (Boston), June 23, 1785 [3].

avoid the "irretrievable Ruin of a Colony which in its Establishment and protection has cost them many Millions." The French offer, though in part self-serving, was definitely in earnest.[31]

The experience of Salem, Massachusetts, merchant Elias Hasket Derby demonstrates the nevertheless limited effectiveness of French assistance for most private traders as well as the difficulties that American merchants faced in trading to the Indian Ocean without well-capitalized and experienced European associates. Derby had become one of the leading merchants in America during the Revolutionary War. Like many other American merchants, in the months immediately following the peace he lacked support from his creditors in London as well as a ready supply of goods to export, making it difficult to launch any major adventures. By 1785, he had accumulated enough to outfit and load two ships for experimental voyages to the Cape of Good Hope and two to Russia. Money was still "exceedingly scarce," constraining his plans and forcing him to write to several of his associates demanding immediate payment to allow him to move forward. In March, his son, Elias Hasket Derby, junior, arrived on the Cape. He wrote back to his father, confused and disappointed. He found a bustling port "Calculated only to Supply Ships bound too and from India and not purchases of Cargoes." The Derbys had mistakenly expected the Cape to be a rich market at which to buy India goods.[32]

In February 1786, Derby pushed farther into the Indian Ocean by dispatching the large *Grand Turk* for the promised bounty of the Isle de France. Derby had no doubt heard of the French decision to open their ports in the Indian Ocean to American traders, and he might also have seen some of the propaganda for the French islands. He warned his creditors and insurers in London, Lane, Son, and Fraser, "This Voyage is new to us in this part of the world, therefore it is possible my Captain may some

<hr>

31. Samuel Hardy to Benjamin Harrison, July 25, 1784, in Smith et al., eds., *Letters of Delegates to Congress*, XXI, 743, Charles Thomson to Samuel Hardy, July 16, 1784, XXI, 725; "Philadelphia, Nov. 25," *Pennsylvania Packet, and Daily Advertiser*, Nov. 25, 1784, [2]; "Travels of a Philosopher: Containing Observations on the Manners and Arts of Various Nations in Africa and Asia," *Pennsylvania Mercury, and Universal Advertiser* (Philadelphia), Dec. 10, 1784, [1]. On the difficulties in Isle de France, see Fort William to the Court of Directors, Mar. 25, 1785, *Fort William–India House Correspondence*, XV, 405.

32. Elias Hasket Derby, Junior, to Elias Hasket Derby, Apr. 8, 1785, Letter Book, 1783–1788, Derby Family Papers, MSS 37, Series III, box 25, folder 5, XII, 70, PEM; *Journals of Major Samuel Shaw*, 204. On lack of credit and goods, see Derby to Champion and Dickerson, Apr. 15, 1784, Letter Book, 1783–1788, Derby Family Papers, MSS 37, Series III, box 25, folder 5, XII, 22, PEM. On the demand for payment, see Derby to Capt. West, Mar. 20, 1785, ibid., 57, to Nathaniel Lovejoy, Jan. 20, 1785, 67.

way or other deviate from his Intended Voyage." After the ship had been dispatched, however, Derby received a discouraging response from Lane, Son, and Fraser. They explained that their underwriters had knowledge of the Indian Ocean trade and believed that Derby would not find a cargo at the Isle de France. Indeed, upon arrival, Derby's men quickly realized that the Isle de France was, like the Cape, a waypoint more than an export port. They could not find suitable goods to purchase and decided to lease out the ship's cargo space to two Frenchmen, Randall Ouery and Sebier de la Chataignerais. The Frenchmen planned a voyage to Canton and a return voyage back to the United States. This long-distance adventure was "quite unexpected" to Derby, and, as it turned out, somewhat unwelcome. The Frenchmen evidently attempted to take advantage of the Americans and lacked sufficient capital to charter the ship. The parties became embroiled in a complicated dispute at Canton over the payment of fees.[33]

Over the next few years, the Derbys struggled to understand the India trade, using the Isle de France as their Indian Ocean base, much like English sailors and pirates from both sides of the Atlantic had used Madagascar in the 1690s. By encouraging the Derbys to operate out of the Isle de France, the French decision to open their ports in the Indian Ocean had at least part of its desired effect. Derby hoped some of the Frenchmen on the island would offer helpful instructions and advice, but, after the earlier difficulties with the *Grand Turk,* he did not intend to engage them to charter cargo space. The *Grand Turk*'s supercargo, William Vans, still reported accumulating only "some little Information respecting Trade to India." Even this little information needed to be jealously guarded from other Americans. Vans wrote, "This Information I consider you have the first right to, and I have made no communication (agreeable to your Order) to any Person except Captain Nichols in your Ship which I suppous'd wou'd be for your Interest." In 1788, Derby thought perhaps his son might find a good cargo on the Coromandel Coast, though he cautioned, "This I know but little about." There was still much to learn.[34]

33. Derby to Lane, Son, and Fraser, February 1786, Letter Book, 1783–1788, Derby Family Papers, MSS 37, Series III, box 25, folder 5, XII, 106, PEM, to Meir and Co, April 1786, 112, Edward Payne and Son to Derby, Feb. 26, 1787, 149, Derby to Ludlow and Goold, Mar. 8, 1787, 151, to Thomas Randale, Sept. 20, 1787, 174–178; Lane, Son and Fraser to Derby, May 4, 1786, Derby Family Papers, MSS 37, Series I, box 12, folder 1, PEM; Vans and West to Derby, Apr. 27, 1786, Derby Family Papers, MSS 37, Series I, box 3, folder 3, PEM.

34. Derby to Mr. Fleurey, Dec. 6, 1787, and Derby to Monneron and Co., Dec. 6, 1787, Letter Book, 1783–1788, Derby Family Papers, MSS 37, Series III, box 25, folder 5, XII, 192,

Derby was, overall, a highly successful merchant, and his struggles in the India trade were not caused by ineptitude. His ignorance of the trade reflected the long isolation of American merchants from the Indian Ocean and the amount of knowledge and experience required to understand the complicated trades of Asian, Eastern African, and Spice Island ports. Additionally, Americans in the early Republic generally still needed access to British or other European capital to facilitate expensive long-distance trade, as Derby used Lane, Son, and Fraser in London. The problematic assistance of the French, meanwhile, underscored the limits of their own capabilities in these Indian Ocean trades.

An Interloping Empire

Britons in India had conducted business illicitly using other European merchants and companies since the earliest days of the East India Company. After nearly two centuries of trying to check such trade, the directors were still writing, "There is too much reason to suspect that our commercial servants have at times assisted the Investment of foreign European Nations . . . and we do require you to make example of whoever of our Servants shall be discovered to embark in any Transactions of this kind in future." They noted that the Danish ships that arrived in Europe in 1783 brought "those very goods" that the Company ordered but did not receive. In the mid-1780s, Britons and Americans developed networks and activities building on these other interloping trades, and in some ways similar to the late-seventeenth-century English Atlantic traders and pirates in the Indian Ocean that Chalmers referenced. Some writers even expected that piracy was "the only motive that could induce them to think of commencing an intercourse with India." U.S. merchants offered private British merchants a means to operate outside the Company monopoly and more readily participate in their own country's empire in India. In turn, British merchants, many of whom had worked in India for the East India Company, brought unparalleled capital and experience. French capital connections with American merchants were weak. French merchant experience in the Indian Ocean, though greater than American, was also limited, and French ports in the Indian Ocean were inferior to British ports.[35]

PEM, Derby to his son, Jan. 3, 1788, 200; William Vans to Derby, May 19, 1787, Derby Family Papers, MSS 37, Series I, box 3, folder 4, PEM.

35. Directors to Council, Mar. 16, 1784, in Council Meeting, Apr. 21, 1785, IOR/P/3/11,

Britons such as Joshua Williams had already refined several strate-gies to evade the Company monopoly with the help of European associ-ates, including the French, who, like the Americans, could benefit from British strengths and desires. Williams, based in India, used the name of a French friend, Jean Baptiste Esteve, whose proceeds went to Wil-liams's London agent. In a more complicated affair, Williams wrote to Joseph Sparkes, an East India Company director, that, after failing to get his cloth legally freighted on the Company ship *Earl of Oxford*, he had made other arrangements. His Calcutta agent would freight the cloth "on the Tranquebar D.E.I. [Danish East Indiaman] consigned to Messrs De Conig and Prieson of Copenhagen." From Copenhagen, his agents in Lon-don, the Messieurs Goslings, would illegally transship the cloth and get it into Sparkes's hands in Britain. Williams wrote apologetically to Sparkes, "My reason for employing the Goslings was that I was apprehensive you wou'd not choose to have your *name* appear on any transaction of this nature." As a Company director, Sparkes likely would not want to be obvi-ously engaged in such a trade. Selling cloth in Britain that he bought in India allowed Williams to transfer his Indian capital for his retirement. The profits, in this case around 40 percent, made such scheming especially worthwhile.[36]

Additionally, British merchants continued to adopt various European identities in the India trade. The directors knew that private British mer-chants trading to Asia still used the Austrian-Netherlands port of Ost-end as well as other European ports. They knew also of specific ventures such as that of William Bolts. Bolts, originally Dutch, was a disaffected employee of the Company deported to England from Bengal. He sailed back to India under "Imperial Colours" with the seven-hundred-ton ship *Joseph and Theresa*, which was part of "a Company in Germany to carry on a Commerce between Trieste and the Coast of Choromandel where the House of Austria means to establish a new Factory." The ship carried a

fol. 221v, BL; Commercial Letter to Bengal, Apr. 12, 1786, IOR/E/4/630, 169, 249–250, BL; "London, Oct. 31," *New-Haven Gazette*, Feb. 10, 1785, 1 ("only").

36. Bill of Lading and Facture, *J Reali Arciduchi di Toscana*, Captain Francois Monte-merli, Calcutta, Jan. 17, 1788, box 19, D2025, Gloucestershire Archives, United Kingdom, Joshua Williams to Joseph Sparkes, Feb. 22, 1787, Letter Book, 1786–1790, Williams, "Par-ticulars of J. Williams's Remittances to England," Williams to W. M. Carnac, Sept. 19, 1786. For an example of one of Williams's legal shipments to London through the Company's li-cense, see "Register of Piece Goods Shipped on the Princess Amelia Which Were Received into the Honble Company's Export Warehouse for Exportation to Europe, on the Private Account and Risque of Individuals," Feb. 29, 1788, box 19, D2025, Gloucestershire Archives.

party of Austrian Lutheran soldiers and was accompanied by an English brig loaded with provisions. Similar to Bolts, John Mullins, born in Portsmouth, England, spent several years in India. After obtaining citizenship papers from Trieste in the early 1780s, he sailed as a supercargo with a largely British crew on a Triestine-registered vessel to Canton and Malabar. On the return voyage, his ship stopped in the United States to obtain new papers for Ostend. In the 1790s, he switched to sailing to India under the Genoese flag, before settling briefly back in Britain. He then traveled to Calcutta under the Danish flag, ultimately obtaining Danish citizenship papers in Copenhagen. For many Britons, however, a U.S. flag and U.S. citizenship papers would be the most convenient, given similarities in language and culture.[37]

The first ship to arrive in British India with a U.S. flag, the *Hydra,* illustrates the mutually beneficial opportunities that American independence brought to both British and American merchants who worked together by adapting older patterns of interloping. In the middle of 1784, Christopher Champlin of Rhode Island claimed ownership of the *Hydra* to the U.S. Congress. He successfully petitioned Congress for "sea-letters" that vouched for the ship as American and for captain John Clark and supercargo William Green as American citizens. Congress hoped they would "prosper in their lawful affairs." Champlin, however, had lied about nearly every aspect of the voyage and its legality. Green and Clark were both "of the City of London," not American. Green had been employed in several roles with the Royal Navy during the Revolutionary War. Champlin, moreover, did not own the ship, nor was it at anchor in Rhode Island. Green owned the ship, which was in London, but Congress knew this last point, which itself was not illegal. Green and Champlin drew up a contract explaining that the voyage was to be performed "under cover of an American house [Champlin], whose name must be used for the Proforma, through the whole Transaction, and the Ship of course to be navigated under American Colors." A bill of sale from Green to Champlin created a legal

---

37. "Account of Exports from Europe to India, Including Foreign Companies," IOR/H/399/1, 2–5, 31, BL; Directors to Ft St George, Dec. 1776, IOR/E/4/867, 91 (quotations), BL. Bolts was one of the early voices condemning the Company's conduct in Bengal in the 1760s, though the Company, for its part, also criticized his conduct. He had become wealthy himself in Bengal before he was deported. For more on Bolts's battle with the Company, see Miles Ogborn, *Indian Ink: Script and Print in the Making of the English East India Company* (Chicago, 2007), 203–205. On John Mullins, see James H. Thomas, *The East India Company and the Provinces in the Eighteenth Century,* I, *Portsmouth and the East India Company, 1700–1815* (Lewiston, N.Y., 1999), 354.

veneer for the voyage. As he awaited the news of the pass from Congress, Green stressed, "This pass is so indispensable an Instrument to cover the real nature of the Voyage, that I cannot proceed without it." Green agreed to pay for the cost of any legal defenses and damages if the ship was found out. For the use of his name, the U.S. flag, and his services in obtaining false citizenship papers, Champlin earned a 2.5 percent commission on the outward bound cargo from London and Madeira.[38]

Before the ship departed, Green needed to find a replacement captain experienced in the Indian Ocean who would willingly participate in the venture and keep up the charade. Clark had fallen ill. Green's agent identified and hired the Briton John Haggey in London. Haggey had been a mate in the East India Company's service, giving him the intimate and necessary knowledge of the route to India. He had also been fired by the Company, giving him additional motive to interlope. With Haggey on board, Champlin requested a new sea letter from Congress. Champlin bolstered his request by reminding Congress, "The object of this undertaking is to endeavor to open an advantageous Trade between the United States and the different Parts of India, as well as of China." This was not a lie, but the primary advantage was to go to a Briton.[39]

Once everything was set, Green cleared the ship in London to sail to Madeira and Rhode Island, leaving out the journey to Bengal, which would occur between the two named destinations. Green warned Champlin never to refer to him as anything but an American supercargo and to trust letters "covertly" only to a Suetonius Heatly in Calcutta and a Mr. Wilkinson in London. When the *Hydra* arrived in Calcutta, Green intended to trade using the U.S. flag at the Dutch factory of Chinsurah. Instead, the British Company's governor general, John Macpherson, al-

38. Ford et al., eds., *Journals of the Continental Congress,* July 8, 1784, XXVII, 577–578; "The Ship 'Hydra': Articles of Agreement between Christopher Champlin Esq. of Newport in the State of Rhode Island in America, and William Green Esqr. of the City of London," *Commerce of Rhode Island, 1726–1800,* 2 vols., Massachusetts Historical Society, *Collections,* 7th Ser., X (Boston, 1915), II, 202–204; Green to Champlin, June 14, 1784, ibid., 211. On Green in the Royal Navy, see Henry S. Fraser, "The Memoranda of William Green, Secretary to Vice-Admiral Marriot Arbuthnot in the American Revolution," Rhode Island Historical Society, *Collections,* XVII (1924), 54–55. In his memoirs, Green claimed to have been naturalized as an American at this time. His letters show that this was not the case, although he wrote of moving to Rhode Island after the voyage. Champlin was the uncle of Green's wife. See Fraser, "Memoranda of William Green," ibid., XVIII (1925), 118–119.

39. Fraser, "Memoranda of William Green," R. I. Hist. Soc., *Colls.,* XVIII (1925), 124–127; S. Hardy, "Memorial to the Continental Congress," *Commerce of Rhode Island,* MHS, *Colls.,* 7th Ser., X (1915), II, 217. The memorial mentioned the location of the *Hydra* as London.

lowed Green to sell his cargo and purchase a broad assortment of fabrics, saltpeter, tea, and spices using French papers that Green had obtained as a backup plan. Some in India "supposed" that Green was "a principal Owner." The *Hydra* then sailed back to the Atlantic and stopped at Saint Eustatius in the Dutch West Indies. There, the governor forbade Green from trading, but Green smuggled ashore goods anyway. Eventually, the *Hydra* returned back to Newport as per the terms of the contract. From its nominal home port, the *Hydra* next sailed to Ostend, probably to sell some of its Indian cargo and to begin another journey to Asia for Green and Champlin. The ship, operating under the U.S. flag, went on to China and back to Ostend before returning once again to Newport.[40]

After the *Hydra* had returned, John Adams reported to Congress that the "Hyder or Hydrea" had stranded sixteen Chinese sailors in Ostend. The sailors made their way to London, presumably because they knew that the venture they had participated in was largely British and that London was the home of the East India Company, which frequently used Asian seamen. When they arrived in London, they were disappointed in their hope for Company passage back to India. They turned next to the U.S. government for relief, which caused Adams to bring their case before Congress. Adams claimed, however, that Congress had no jurisdiction and that the sailors did not appear to have been illegally discharged. Thus, the sailors found themselves stranded in the legally dubious wake left by the *Hydra*'s owners and operators.[41]

Adams and Congress continued to see the *Hydra* as a U.S. vessel despite conflicting reports. Certainly Green and Champlin had worked vigorously to conceal the true nature of their voyage, but reports had leaked

40. Green to Christopher Champlin, Oct. 6, 1784, *Commerce of Rhode Island*, MHS, *Colls.*, 7th Ser., X (1915), II, 230–231; Fraser, "Memoranda of William Green," R. I. Hist. Soc., *Colls.*, XVIII (1925), 124–127. For Green's reception in Calcutta, see Fort William to the Court of Directors, Oct. 25, 1785, *Fort William–India House Correspondence*, XV, 511; Notes on Americans, Madras, July 25, 1785, IOR/H/605, 77 ("supposed" and "principal"), 78, BL. Green claimed, when he tried to persuade Champlin to reduce his commission, that the U.S. flag had been useless, but Green used it in future voyages. See Green to Christopher Champlin, Dec. 26, 1784, Mar. 14, 1788, *Commerce of Rhode Island*, MHS, *Colls.*, 7th Ser., X (1915), II, 236–237, 241, 358. For the next voyage via Ostend, see "Agreement with Captain Jeremiah Clarke," *Commerce of Rhode Island*, MHS, *Colls.*, 7th Ser., X (1915), II, 290–291.

41. John Jay, "Report of Secretary for Foreign Affairs on Mr. Adams' Letter of January 27, 1787," July 31, 1787, in Ford et al., eds., *Journals of the Continental Congress*, XXXIII, 444–445; John Hales to John Adams, Feb. 2, 1787, PCC, *Letters from John Adams*, VI, 423. See also Petition of John Hales to the Lords Commissioners of His Majesty's Treasury, ibid., VI, 415.

into the press in both Britain and America. A widely circulated report explained: "Two East India ships have been lately fitted out in the River Thames for the Americans. It is not believed that they were altogether owned in America; on the contrary, it is said, that some in London have chosen to open a trade to the East Indies, under the American flag, as other ports have done under the Imperial [Austrian Netherlands] flag." Adams told Congress of "a Practice then beginning to be talked of, if not practiced, for british Merchants to metamorphose a british into an american Bottom, to trade to the East Indies." He concluded, "It seems doubtful whether it does really exist, or whether it is only talked of." Adams was on record as a major proponent of an expanded direct U.S.-India trade instead of importing India goods from Europe. He also encouraged the use of American vessels to help European company servants, "particularly the English," remit their private wealth back to Europe.[42]

Rhode Island naturalized Green as a citizen of the United States in May 1786, but Green regretted his choice and felt corrupted by interloping as an American in the British empire. Later in life, he wrote of Britain as a "dear and glorious country . . . to which I was then, as I still am and ever shall be, devotedly attached" and explained that he had only become an American for "that love of lucre which had irresistibly seized on and overpowered a mind naturally thoughtful and sober." The *Hydra* would be followed by many more joint Anglo-American voyages that departed from India, Britain, and the United States, and in which British merchants took on the cloak of American citizenship to profit from their own empire for "that love of lucre."[43]

John O'Donnell (or Donnel), for example, similarly exploited his experience in British India and the confusion over citizenship caused by American independence. Born in Ireland, O'Donnell had been "a Military Officer" in Bombay as well as "a Resident and Merchant" in Calcutta. He took his Indian Ocean trader *Pallas* to Canton, where he met Shaw and Thomas Randall, who had recently arrived on the *Empress of China*

---

42. "London, March 18," *South Carolina State Gazette and Daily Advertiser* (Charleston), May 27, 1785, [3]; "London, March 24," *Pennsylvania Packet, and Daily Advertiser* (Philadelphia), June 17, 1785, [2]; "Foreign Intelligence; London, March 24," *Columbian Herald, or The Patriotic Courier of North-America* (Charleston, S.C.), June 10, 1785, [3]; Jay, "Report of Secretary for Foreign Affairs on Mr. Adams' Letter," July 31, 1787, in Ford et al., eds., *Journals of the Continental Congress*, XXXIII, 444–445; Adams to John Jay, Nov. 11, 1785, PCC, *Letters from John Adams*, V, 729–731.

43. Fraser, "Memoranda of William Green," R.I. Hist. Soc., *Colls.* XVIII (1925), 118, 120, 212.

from New York. Randall managed an investment of bonds drawn on European associates and was looking for cargo space back to America. O'Donnell and Randall agreed to operate the *Pallas* as a joint investment to the United States. O'Donnell was plainly a British subject, not an American. In his journal, Shaw recorded the *Pallas* as an English country trader. In August 1785, when O'Donnell and the *Pallas* arrived in Baltimore, he was reported as "a perfect Stranger in this Country." The voyage was therefore in clear contravention of British law forbidding private British traders from trading outside the Company's monopoly directly from the Indian Ocean into the Atlantic.[44]

With one of the first cargoes to arrive directly from Asia on the East Coast of North America in more than eighty years, however, O'Donnell made a handsome profit from his ability to join British India with independent America. He purchased two thousand acres of Maryland waterfront to make his new home. The *Maryland Journal* celebrated his rich cargo and proclaimed, "We are extremely happy to find the commercial Reputation of this Town so far increased, as to attract the Attention of Gentlemen, who are engaged in carrying on this distant but beneficial Trade." Newspapers up and down the Eastern Seaboard celebrated his arrival. This "very ingenious and enterprising artist"—and very British subject—was eagerly welcomed.[45]

In 1786, O'Donnell sent a lengthy letter to John Jay regarding the opportunities for an independent American "Empire" in the India trade. He rehearsed the standard arguments that had been used in defense of the India

44. Fort William to the Secret Committee of the Court of Directors, Dec. 14, 1787, *Fort William–India House Correspondence*, XVI, 169 (see also IOR/H/605/1, 59, BL); Phineas Bond to the Duke of Leads, June 2, 1789, Foreign Office (FO) 4/7, 205, NA; Tench Tilghman to Washington, Aug. 25, 1785, in Crackel, ed., *Papers of Washington Digital Edition*. O'Donnell and Randall's joint investment, although it was not a sale of a ship, encouraged the East India Company to forbid the sale of British vessels in its monopoly territory to Americans. The Company feared that Britons would either sell their ships for the capital or, more worryingly, pretend to sell their ships so that they could use American cover to run around the Company's monopoly. Indeed, the regulation soon thwarted another scheme cooked up between Shaw and Britons in India in 1786. For Shaw's comments, see *Journals of Major Samuel Shaw*, 182, 218, 253, 284.

45. "Baltimore, August 12," *Maryland Journal and Baltimore Advertiser*, Aug. 12, 1785, [2]; *Massachusetts Spy: Or, the Worcester Gazette*, Aug. 25, 1785, 3 ("very"). Several papers reprinted the story from the *Maryland Journal*. See, for example, "New-York, August 22," *Salem Gazette*, Aug. 30, 1785, [3]; *Vermont Gazette*, Sept. 5, 1785, [2]; *American Herald* (Boston), Aug. 29, 1785, [2]. The goods appeared for sale from Philadelphia to Charleston. See *Pennsylvania Packet and Daily Advertiser*, Sept. 26, 1785, [1]; *Charleston Evening Gazette*, Sept. 29, 1785, [4].

trade in Britain for centuries: the employment of carpenters and seamen, a fleet of great ships, and the making of copious wealth. He encouraged the United States to pursue the policy of European powers by banning the importation of goods from Asia on foreign vessels and by allowing drawbacks on reexports. In a plan similar to that proposed by William Grayson, O'Donnell also encouraged the United States to try to displace the British as the main supplier of India goods to the West Indies and Spanish America by turning Charleston, South Carolina, into a distribution hub for India goods similar to London.[46]

Additionally, O'Donnell offered to use his sixteen years of experience as a British merchant in India and his skill in Asian languages to negotiate trading treaties on America's behalf. He expected that Indian princes at war with Britain would be eager to trade with American merchants. To this end, he offered to help establish factories for the United States in Asia on the European model, a model he argued was necessary for successful trade. Nevertheless, he did not envision a joint-stock monopoly but a federally regulated trade open to all American merchants. In return, he asked for a position of title and authority that he had not achieved in the British Company as well as the right to accept presents from Asian rulers. He offered so much for supposedly so little because, he wrote, he had adopted the United States as his country "from principle." O'Donnell did not specify the principle that brought him to choose the United States in 1785, but, given his offer to negotiate treaties for gifts and his profitable exploits bringing the *Pallas* to Baltimore, his principle appears to have been personal profit. Nevertheless, like American merchants attempting to launch other ventures to Asia, he did not eschew government. He looked to government as a tool for personal advancement.[47]

O'Donnell was sure that there were many more Britons in India who would be eager, like him, to bring their capital and themselves to America. Britons trading in India found it difficult to remit their fortunes to Britain, and O'Donnell offered to take blank passports to India to encourage them to come to America instead. The young Republic would gain both vital capital and experience in the lucrative India trade. John Jay tended to agree that Britons in India might make use of American passports to the benefit of the United States, but he worried that a sovereign country should not give "false evidence" of citizenship or the ownership of prop-

46. John O'Donnell to John Jay, June 20, 1786, *PCC, Miscellaneous Letters to Congress,* XVII, 385–392.
47. Ibid., 392–397.

erty. Jay encouraged the adoption of regulations requiring shipowners and ship captains to provide real proof of citizenship for themselves and their crews. He also argued that allowing O'Donnell to negotiate treaties "would not be consistent with the Dignity of the United States." Yet, despite Jay's misgivings over both O'Donnell's ambiguous status and his proposals, Jay did not object specifically to O'Donnell's own claims of citizenship.[48]

Within a few months of O'Donnell's arrival from China in 1785, John Wingrove had come from England to similarly persuade Congress to regulate and manage the trade with a factory in India. His reception illustrates much about the motivations behind Congress's decisions and the extent to which by 1785 its members had agreed not to create a monopoly for the India trade. Wingrove wanted to become a U.S. citizen, and he was recommended to Congress by John Adams. Adams believed that Wingrove's experience in India would make him an ideal consul. Arriving shortly after O'Donnell, Wingrove put his plan to Congress shortly before O'Donnell presented his. Congress rejected both plans. But, whereas Congress adopted O'Donnell the man, it did not adopt Wingrove. Instead, it used Wingrove's British subjecthood as the reason to turn down his application to develop an American factory in India with him at the helm. Wingrove had not arrived with a celebrated and valuable cargo from India as O'Donnell had—a considerable difference in what the two men had to offer.[49]

O'Donnell's crew faced the coldest reception of all, attesting to the core interests of both Jay and Congress in adopting O'Donnell for his experience and capital from Asia. Initially, the seamen's welcome seemed promising enough. The *Maryland Journal* gushed at seeing "the Crew of this Ship, Chinese, Malays, Japanese, and Moors, with a few Europeans," all dressed in their native clothes. "It is thus," the paper went on, "Commerce binds and unites all the Nations of the Globe with a golden Chain." O'Donnell's crew was perhaps not quite so diverse, although it included more than a dozen Indian and Chinese sailors. These men, though, did not see the chains that had brought them to America as golden. They claimed that O'Donnell had forced them to sail, treated them poorly, and barely paid them. Making matters worse, John Hamilton "who plies in a skallop," kidnapped and enslaved one of the sailor's sons. Far from gaining American citizenship, the sailors could not even gain legal exceptions to allow them to work on outgoing vessels. Eventually, the men traveled to Philadelphia,

48. John Jay to Congress, Aug. 5, 1786, *PCC, Reports of John Jay*, II, 137–138.
49. John Adams to Jay, Sept. 3, 1785, *PCC, Letters from John Adams*, V, 649; Committee Report on Mr. Wingrove, Jan. 31, 1786, *PCC, Applications of Individuals*, VI, 578.

where they beseeched the Pennsylvania Assembly for financial support, the return of the boy, and permission to work on a U.S. vessel that was sailing back to their homes. Pennsylvania provided some food and clothing, but its representatives to Congress argued that Maryland should be responsible. A congressional committee decided that any assistance would be "inexpedient." The sailors' expertise was not needed, and they had no capital to offer.[50]

O'Donnell, however, continued to enjoy the prosperity enabled by his experience as a Briton in India, the Asian sailors' service to him, the position of the United States outside the British empire's regulatory framework, and the good favor of Congress. In 1787, O'Donnell built the *Chesapeake* in Baltimore and prepared it to sail to Calcutta under the U.S. flag. Congress issued him sea letters vouching that his new vessel was the property of a U.S. citizen and that its crew members were U.S. citizens. The ship's crew were, according to the East India Company, mostly British subjects, despite their commission and pass from Congress, and, of course, the Company knew who O'Donnell was. Nevertheless, the *Chesapeake* arrived back in New Jersey in May 1789 with a cargo from Bombay, Madras, and Calcutta. Local East India Company officials had much to gain from American traders. American vessels made possible the export of British-Indian capital, such as O'Donnell's, outside the severe constraints of the Company, while British-Indian capital helped solve the American difficulty of otherwise needing to export rare bullion to Asia.[51]

John Brown, of the Brown family of merchants of Rhode Island, pursued a similar opportunity to profit from the empire Americans had fought to leave by working with Britons desirous of profiting off their own Asian empire. Brown explained to his brother Moses that a Mr. Hayley, a Briton who had lived in India for seven years, "gives Good Encouragement to send the" *General Washington* to the East Indies. Hayley had just arrived and married an American woman, but he was eager to depart again to manage the ship. He recommended an outbound cargo of cannons, an-

<hr />

50. *Maryland Journal and Baltimore Advertiser*, Aug. 12, 1785, [2]. On the actual experiences of the crew, see Thomas Malden? Dec. 17, 1785, and Memorial of Keesar et al. to Pennsylvania Council and Congress, Dec. 15, 1785, *PCC, State Papers: Pennsylvania*, II, 533–534, 537; *Daily Advertiser: Political, Historical, and Commercial* (New York), Nov. 15, 1785, [2]. For another report of the sailors' origins, see Tilghman to Washington, Aug. 25, 1785, in Crackel, ed., *Papers of Washington Digital Edition*.

51. Ford et al., eds., *Journals of the Continental Congress*, Aug. 30, 1786, XXXI, 596; Fort William to the Secret Committee of the Court of Directors, Dec. 14, 1787, *Fort William–India House Correspondence*, XVI, 169 (see also IOR/H/605/1, 59, BL).

chors, iron, tar, ginseng, Madeira, and spirits. The *General Washington* left in December 1787 under Captain Jonathan Donnison and made its way to Madras, an ideal port at which to find Britons looking to cycle their savings from their Indian careers back to Britain through cargo carried on an American ship. Donnison then took the *General Washington* loaded with cotton to Canton and returned after a voyage of nineteen months.[52]

Congress's majority plan was to support such an open and peaceful trade to India, but it was not pursuing a totally laissez-faire approach. The American antimonopoly position was shared with the Commonwealthman Whigs in Britain, who had long argued against monopoly as an infringement of the Magna Carta's promise of the freedom of the seas. In the United States, the opposition to monopoly also followed the patriots' vigorous opposition to the Company during the tea crisis as well as the experiences of some American merchants smuggling tea. Independence had brought the legal freedom to trade, encroached in Britain, to America. But in neither Britain nor the United States did resistance to monopoly mean exclusion of government involvement. Congressional sea letters, for instance, legally incorporated the capital and experience of Britons such as William Green, John Haggey, and John O'Donnell into American efforts. The letters also sought to provide introductions for those American merchants who were unknown in Asia. Additionally, Congress appointed Samuel Shaw, who had been the supercargo on the *Empress of China* and was a friend of George Washington, as the first U.S. consul in Canton. As Jay explained, "Such Officers would have a Degree of Weight and Respect which private Adventurers cannot readily acquire, and which would enable them to render essential Services to their Countrymen." Consuls would have "more ready Access to and greater influence with Princes, Governors, and Magistrates" to assist merchants. In short, Congress picked out an expedient path on the India trade, rewarding Shaw with a patronage position where it was most needed to help deal with the Hong merchants in Canton, bending citizenship requirements to welcome British men to finance and guide the trade to India, and offering sea letters to ease the way for British and American merchants.[53]

52. John Brown to Moses Brown, Aug. 18, 1787, in Gertrude Selwyn Kimball, *Papers from the Historical Seminary of Brown University*, VI, *The East-India Trade of Providence, from 1787 to 1807* (Providence, R.I., 1896), 45–56. Donnison brought back Samuel Shaw, American consul to Canton, and the American-born merchants Edward Dowse and Nathaniel Shaw. See *United States Chronicle: Political, Commercial, and Historical* (Providence, R.I.), July 9, 1789, [3].

53. Jay to the President of Congress, Jan. 20, 1786, *PCC, Letters of Secretary of Foreign*

Congressmen largely agreed on the need for even more regulation, although they disagreed on the best policies. Richard Henry Lee, who would become the leader of the Antifederalists, reported to James Madison in 1785 that he feared "a Rage for East India Voyages. So that the variety of means may defeat the Attainment of the concurrent end—A regulated and useful commerce with that part of the World." John Adams and Rufus King, soon to be leading Federalists, hoped to gather support from all the states for "Duties, upon the Importation of all East India Goods from Europe. . . . judiciously calculated and made high enough to give a clear Advantage to the direct Importer from India." Because the United States was without cotton and silk manufacturers, Adams wrote, it had no reason to try to reduce direct imports from India like Britain did. The stakes were high. Adams explained, "We should attend to this Intercourse with the East, with the more Ardour, because. . . . The East Indies will probably be the Object and The Theatre of the next War." With significant experience in the India trade, the United States would gain leverage to either align with the best side or, preferably, keep neutral and profit the most. On this point, Adams would be proven correct, but not for a few decades.[54]

In the meantime, the nonviolent approach of merchants flying the U.S. flag (regardless of their actual connection to America), the treasure that they brought to India, and the opportunities they presented to remit fortunes and engage in trade encouraged acceptance by interlopers and Company servants alike. Instead of a heavy complement of guns to take treasure from India ships, like the pirate voyages of a century earlier, American ships took treasure to India. The Company's servants in Calcutta wrote to the directors, "The prosperity of Bengal depends not upon an exclusive Monopoly of its Commerce in favour of the Company's Trade, but that Foreign Nations should have every Inducement left to them to import Specie . . . in Exchange for its Manufactures." They also predicted that "No Law" could stop Britons from remitting capital through foreigners when the Company failed to offer sufficient channels. Similarly, in 1787 Company solicitor and urban improver Stephen Popham explained

Affairs John Jay, II, 125; Caroline Robbins, _The Eighteenth-Century Commonwealthman: Studies in the Transmission, Development, and Circumstance of English Liberal Thought from the Restoration of Charles II until the War with the Thirteen Colonies_ (Cambridge, Mass., 1959), 3–22.

54. Richard Henry Lee to Madison, May 30, 1785, in Smith et al., eds., _Letters of Delegates to Congress_, XXII, 418, John Adams to Jay, Nov. 11, 1785, _PCC, Letters from John Adams_, V, 729–731.

that Americans preferred to trade with British Madras rather than with French Pondicherry. He recommended to the governor of Madras that future American merchant vessels be welcomed "for the sake of the Customs and other Commercial Advantages to be deemed to Government and the Community therefrom." The governor assured Popham that he agreed. Such opportunities help explain why vessels flying the stars and stripes were generally welcomed, especially when combined with the participation of Britons from India and friends in India. By 1787, Britons and Americans had developed a new interloping empire clinging to—and in some ways reinforcing—the structures of the current and former formal empire.[55]

The Hastings Trial and America

Despite American willingness to profit from often illicit engagement with the British in India, concerns about long-standing British patterns of corruption continued to inform American thinking throughout the mid-1780s. John Adams, for instance, wrote in 1785 that, if Americans behaved in Asia with "an irreproachable Integrity, Humanity, and Civility, to conciliate the Esteem of the Natives, they may easily become the most favoured nation for the Conduct of European Nations in general, heretofore has given Us a great Advantage." By 1787, the growing furor over Hastings in Britain led Parliament to prepare impeachment proceedings, while in the United States concerns about the need for regulation in the India trade deepened. Adams argued "that the Trade of the United States to Asia, as well as to other parts of the World, should be subject to certain general Regulations; but at present, Congress cannot *ordain* such Regulations and cause them to be observed." The lack of a federal prerogative to develop regulations ensuring the value and virtue of the India trade to America was one of the justifications for the Constitutional Convention, which met in Philadelphia in the summer of 1787 to revise the Articles of Confederation. There were, of course, many other reasons for a new constitution, including the need to secure revenue for the federal government,

55. Fort William to the Court of Directors, Mar. 25, 1785, *Fort William–India House Correspondence*, XV, 405, Fort William to the Court of Directors, Oct. 25, 1785, XV, 511; Stephen Popham to Archibald Campbell, Mar. 10, 1787, *PCC, Miscellaneous Letters to Congress*, XIX, 603–604, Charles White to Popham, Mar. 12, 1787, XIX, 607. On the Pophams, see K. Narasimhachari, "Annals of Old Madras: Popham's Broadway," *Journal of Indian History*, XIX (1941), 92–95.

pay the debts incurred during the Revolution, and find a means for settling disputes among the states. Nevertheless, the Hastings trial, occurring at the same time, would inform and shape the politics of America's constitutional debates as well as the first policies that the new federal government would pursue.[56]

Immediately before and during the convention, newspapers throughout the United States ran countless columns on the Hastings trial, often explaining the impeachment as necessary for the defense of British virtue. Richard Sheridan, famous playwright and Whig member of Parliament, and Edmund Burke, both of whom had been strong opponents of British military action against the American patriots, led the case against Hastings. Sheridan's speech to the House of Commons arguing for impeachment in February 1787 was widely reprinted in Britain and America. He attacked Hastings for "plundering the Begums," "despoil[ing] the princesses of Oude," invading "the substance of justice," and demanding huge bribes. Sir Elijah Impey, chief justice of the Bengal Supreme Court, traveled, the newspapers reported, "in anxious search of calamities most kindred to his invalide imagination." Even those in Britain defending Hastings often agreed that injustices and crimes had been committed, though by whom was unclear. A letter from Calcutta published in defense of Hastings, for instance, pointed at the East India Company, not Hastings, as the culprit. Yet there was little doubt that this was to be a trial in the name of "British justice and humanity!" One British report published in America boasted that the impeachment was "a demonstration of that protection which the laws and constitution of this country are calculated to afford the subjects of the British empire in the most distant extremities of the globe, against a wanton excess of power." Some Americans certainly agreed; Arthur Lee wrote, "The national justice of that kingdom is much interested in arresting the progress of that excessive cruelty and injustice,

<hr>

56. John Adams to Jay, Nov. 11, 1785, *PCC, Letters from John Adams*, V, 729–731; Jay, "Report of Secretary for Foreign Affairs on Mr. Adams' Letter," July 31, 1787, in Smith et al., eds., *Journals of the Continental Congress*, XXXIII, 445. For more on the reasons for the Constitution, see E. James Ferguson, *The Power of the Purse: A History of American Public Finance, 1776–1790* (Chapel Hill, N.C., 1961), 239–325. For the positions of those against the new Constitution, see Jackson Turner Main, *The Antifederalists: Critics of the Constitution, 1781–1788* (Chapel Hill, N.C., 2004). For more on the impeachment, see Marshall, *The Impeachment of Warren Hastings*. For an example of the limits of state-by-state regulation under the Articles of Confederation, see Lucy Cranch to Abigail Adams, Dec. 7, 1786, in Taylor, ed., *Adams Papers Digital Edition*.

which have been practisd in India, in order to extort immense wealth from its wretched Natives."[57]

Hastings's defenders also compared his success in India to North's failure in America. The satirical print *A Convention of the Not-ables* depicted a short, portly North carrying an ax engraved "To Conquer America" and an emaciated Burke carrying impeachment papers as they joined Fox and others attempting to break into the Treasury. Their exploits had cost Britain dearly, while Hastings, one is to infer, had helped to fill the Treasury that they sought to raid. A newspaper report exclaimed, "Let not that policy, which, though it lost America, was deemed manly and honourable be pronounced systematic tyranny, when it saved and extended our territories in India." The *State Gazette of South-Carolina* reprinted another report from London that "Lord North, to excuse himself from the *odium* of the American war and its consequences, called it the war of Parliament; and now Mr. Burke for similar reasons, makes the House of Commons the accusers of Mr. Hastings." Echoing the debate over Fox's India bill, the report wondered why North, who lost America and accumulated a massive debt in the process, was revered by some while Hastings, who "saved our Indian possessions," should be persecuted.[58]

Many private and public reports immediately preceding and during

57. "Mr. Sheridan's Celebrated Speech on the Impeachment of Mr. Hastings," *Pennsylvania Herald, and General Advertiser* (Philadelphia), May 12, 16, 1787, [2]; "Extract from Mr. Sheridan's Celebrated Speech on the Impeachment of Mr. Hastings, on the 7th of February," *Charleston Morning Post and Daily Advertiser,* May 25, 1787, [2]; "London, March 17," *Independent Journal: or, the General Advertiser (New York),* May 23, 1787, [2] (on the Company's being at fault, not Hastings); "London, April 2," *Massachusetts Gazette* (Boston), May 18, 1787, [3] ("British"); "Late Foreign Intelligence . . . London, March 30," *Massachusetts Centinel* (Boston), May 19, 1787, 70; "Mr. Hastings," *New-York Journal, and Weekly Register,* Aug. 2, 1787, [2] ("demonstration"); "London, May 23," *Providence Gazette and Country Journal,* Aug. 18, 1787, [2]; Arthur Lee to Washington, May 13, 1787, in Crackel, ed., *Papers of Washington Digital Edition.* On Burke's primary motivation and goal for the trial, see Jennifer Pitts, "Empire and Legal Universalisms in the Eighteenth Century," *American Historical Review,* CXVII (2012), 107, 110.

58. *A Convention of the Not-ables,* published by S. W. Fores, [London], 1787, Prints and Photographs Division, Library of Congress, Washington, D.C., www.loc.gov/pictures /item/2004676789; "Publius's Letters of Reply; to R. B. Sheridan, Esq. And other Popular Accusers of Warren Hastings, Esq.," *World and Fashionable Advertiser,* Apr. 26, 1787, [4]; "The Charges against Mr. Hastings, and the Great Interest in India Involved in That Charge, Induce Us to Give the Speech of Major Scott on That Subject at Length," *World and Fashionable Advertiser* (London), Feb. 26, 1787, [4]; *State Gazette of South-Carolina* (Charleston), June 22, 1786, [1].

the Constitutional Convention and public ratification debate in America suggested that Britain was so corrupt that Hastings would not be convicted. From the American perspective, it probably did not matter a great deal whether Hastings or the Company was most to blame—they were branches of the same tree of corrupted British imperial governance and politics. Both William Smith and John Adams, leading Americans in London, predicted that Hastings would be let off. Smith explained that, even though some Britons despised "severity and oppression," it would not be enough. "The King and the present administration . . . ," he wrote, "will exert every nerve to shelter him from injury." Adams likewise predicted that "Hastings must be acquitted. . . . Such is the State of this Nation." American newspaper readers learned how Hastings, after committing such "shameful extortions, etc. etc.," was "courted and caressed by many of the first characters in the kingdom." One report joked that Hastings "arrived at that consummate height of wickedness, that he used to send home private intimations of his intention, to some of the Directors, written on pieces of muslin." "When this kind of evidence can be got at," the report continued, "it is always the best, because should it prove of no use to the cause, unlike other testimony, it may always be turned into something—a judicial cap—a lawn sleeve—or a habit of justice." The joke suggested that Hastings might, in effect, buy off those trying him with his Indian luxury goods. Others similarly claimed that Hastings was buying himself out of an impeachment conviction with expensive lawyers and bribes. "O money, money" would let Hastings escape his guilt. This was a replay of the corruption that had inspired the patriots to revolt.[59]

59. William Smith to Jay, June 15, 1786, *PCC, Letters from William S. Smith and Others*, 90; John Adams to Jay, Feb. 3, 1787, *PCC, Letters from John Adams*, VI, 420; "London, April 28–May 30," *Independent Journal: or, The General Advertiser* (New York), Aug. 8, 1787, [2] ("arrived"); "London, May 30," *Connecticut Gazette*, Aug. 24, 1787, [2]. For more on Hastings buying himself out of impeachment, see *Independent Gazetteer; or, The Chronicle of Freedom* (Philadelphia), Aug. 5, 1788, [2]; *American Mercury* (Hartford, Conn.), Aug. 11, 1788, [3]; "London," *Norwich Packet and the Country Journal* (Conn.), Aug. 14, 1788, [3]; "European Intelligence, Received by Captain Tate, Who Arrived at Portland (Falmouth) on Saturday . . . ," *United States Chronicle: Political, Commercial and Historical* (Providence), May 24, 1787, [2–3]; "Europe; England; London, February 18," *American Recorder, and the Charlestown Advertiser* (Mass.), May 25, 1787, [2]; "Elizabeth-Town, June 6," *New-Jersey Journal and Political Intelligencer* (Elizabethtown), June 6, 1787, [3]; "Elizabeth-Town, June 6," *Continental Journal, and the Weekly Advertiser*, June 14, 1787, [2]. Meanwhile, a series of articles defending Hastings, including testimony from Indians, also appeared across the United States, largely copied from London newspapers. See, for examples, "Mr. Hasting's Defence," *City Gazette, or The Daily Advertiser* (Charleston), Mar. 11, 1788, [2]; *Connecticut Courant*,

Likewise, the long-standing notion of the corrupting influence of Indian wealth and consumption habits was a common theme during the trial in both British and American newspapers. Critical appraisals of Hastings's apparently ill-gotten wealth and its manifestation in diamonds and lavish gifts appeared particularly in the papers of northern U.S. ports, where merchants were beginning to trade directly with India. One report claimed that Hastings's wife had diamonds worth sixty thousand pounds and that he gave a gift of "a cradle and a bulse" worth seventy thousand pounds. Another report claimed that Mrs. Middleton, the wife of Hastings's second in command, had a pair of shoe buckles made from Indian jewels that cost thirty thousand pounds. "Search all the Heaven of Beauty in Europe, America, or elsewhere, on what feet sparkle their fellows?" asked the report. But "the rub" was how the buckles had been purchased and how the money had been gained. Several newspapers reported from the *Columbian Magazine* that Hastings had even purchased his wife from her previous husband in Germany.[60]

Reports on Hastings also frequently recalled the charges that had circulated on both sides of the Atlantic against Robert Clive before the American Revolution. A report from Charlestown, Massachusetts, explained that Burke described Hastings "as a criminal who had depopulated nations, who had deposed princes; in the van of whose armies went death and desolation; and famine, meagre famine, lingered in the rear." These words directly paralleled Thomas Paine's piece on Clive from 1775. A Charleston, South Carolina, paper reported, based on letters that it had received from

and Weekly Intelligencer, Apr. 7, 1788, [1]; *Massachusetts Spy: or, The Worcester Magazine,* Apr. 24, 1788, [2]; "Charleston," *City Gazette, or The Daily Advertiser,* Mar. 13, 1788, [2]; *City Gazette, or The Daily Advertiser,* Apr. 4, 1788, [2]; "From the Hull Packet," *Massachusetts Gazette,* June 27, 1788, [1]; "Foreign Intelligence; London," *Carlisle Gazette, and the Western Repository of Knowledge* (Pa.), July 9, 1788, [2]; "Mr. Hastings," *Independent Journal: or the General Advertiser,* Aug. 30, 1788, [2]. On the importance of the public ratification debate, see Max M. Edling, *A Revolution in Favor of Government: Origins of the U.S. Constitution and the Making of the American State* (New York, 2003), 15–30.

60. "London, Dec. 13," *Salem Mercury: Political, Commercial, and Moral,* May 5, 1787, [2] ("cradle"); *Fairfield Gazette; or, The Independent Intelligencer* (Conn.), May 10, 1787, [2]; "Eastern Magnificence," *New-Hampshire Gazette, and the General Advertiser* (Portsmouth), Sept. 25, 1788, [3] ("Search"); *American Herald and the Worcester Recorder* (Mass.), Oct. 2, 1788, [2]; "From the Columbian Magazine," *Pennsylvania Packet, and Daily Advertiser,* May 26, 1788, [2]; *Connecticut Courant and Weekly Intelligencer,* June 30, 1788, [4]; *Columbian Herald, or The Independent Courier of North-America* (Charleston, S.C.), July 7, 1788, [4]; *New-Haven Gazette, and the Connecticut Magazine, for 1788,* July 10, 1788, [2]; *Fairfield Gazette; or, The Independent Intelligencer,* July 16, 1788, [4]; "Anecdote," *Essex Journal and New-Hampshire Packet* (Newburyport, Mass.), July 30, 1788, [4].

England, that Hastings was facing the charge—among others—of entering into illegal contracts and explained, "This is the ground on which Lord Clive had such difficulty to extricate himself." The East India Company had "sanctioned" everything that Hastings had done, reflecting American understanding of the corruption of the Company. Much as colonists had mocked the lameness of Parliament's Regulating Act in failing to punish the offenders before the Revolution, the author reported that the House of Lords could not impose a death penalty on Hastings, only a fine, for which he had prepared by securing his wealth in foreign funds. Few Americans who had lived through the Revolution could have failed to notice that Hastings's rise to power had occurred during the precise period in which the colonies embarked on revolution for fear of British tyranny and that the behavior of Hastings, the Company, and Parliament all followed the pattern of corruption evident in the late 1760s and early 1770s.[61]

In the summer of 1787, the Constitutional Convention offered an opportunity to move the United States farther away from the potential corruption represented by Hastings and the British government alike. A few items down from a prediction that Hastings would use his wealth to escape conviction, one New Jersey paper ran a story on the convention that wondered, "What would not the subjects of Great Britain, who complain of the defects or corruption of their government, give for this privilege" of crafting a brand-new Constitution for their country? "Let this comparison kindle in our bosoms a due sense of the value of liberty," the author explained, "and let no pains be spared in framing such a form of government, as will preserve it forever." The author feared, however, that the convention would turn out badly and warned against "a newly established court of American DESPOTS" and the loss of all that had been fought for in the Revolution. Another author ran through the problems facing Europe and wondered which country could be happier than America. The author

61. "Intelligence Omitted on Saturday Last for Want of Room; Charlestown, (Mass.) May 2," *Pennsylvania Evening Herald: and the American Monitor* (Philadelphia), May 17, 1786, 132; *Charleston Evening Gazette*, May 22, 1786, [2] (for another example, see *New-York Daily Gazette*, Aug. 8, 1789, 766); "For the Pennsylvania Magazine; Reflections on the Life and Death of Lord Clive," *Pennsylvania Magazine: or, American Monthly Museum* (March 1775), 108; *Charleston Morning Post and Daily Advertiser*, May 21, 1787, [2]. See also, *Daily Advertiser* (New York), May 12, 1788, [2]; *New-Jersey Journal, and Political Intelligencer*, May 21, 1788, [1, 4]; "Extract from Mr. Burke's Speech before the British House of Peers, on the Trial of Mr. Hastings . . . ," *Middlesex Gazette, or Federal Adviser*, June 2, 1788, [1]; "Trial of Mr. Hastings, London," *Thomas's Massachusetts Spy: or, The Worcester Magazine*, July 10, 1788, [1–2].

America's Early India Trade

exclaimed, "Let the citizens of America recollect *the past,* and they will rather wonder that they are so well, than lament that they are not better." He encouraged them to embrace a future of "prosperity and honour" dependent upon themselves.[62]

Importantly, and not surprisingly given the overlapping timelines and the tremendous amount of reporting on the trial, Americans directly connected the Hastings trial with Shays's Rebellion, the ratification debate, and the new Constitution's promise of freedom from corruption. On hearing reports of Shays's Rebellion, in which primarily rural people in Massachusetts raised an armed insurrection over a variety of mostly economic grievances, Abigail Adams argued that Americans needed to consider heavier taxation in the new Republic to be "the price of their freedom." She figured, "If Britain had succeeded against us, the same scenes would probably, have taken place, as have been acted in India, for we have no reason to doubt but that England could have produced more than one Hastings." A correspondent in New Hampshire wondered, "Who . . . can read the trial of Warren Hastings, and not be chilled with horror, or fired with pious indignation at the before unheard of and unparalleled cruelties exercised on the unfortunate people of India?" He went on: "I desire every day, and every hour of my life, to bless God, that I am no longer a subject of that nation. . . . May the Federal Constitution soon be fully and compleatly adopted." This new Constitution would help the United States to claim "wisdom, righteousness, justice and mercy" as its "distinguishing characteristics."[63]

The *New-Haven Gazette* explained that impeachment was a "necessary preservative in a free Constitution." It had often protected the liberties of people in Great Britain. "This necessary check to the rapacity of the great officers of government," the author explained, "was not overlooked in framing our own excellent constitution." The U.S. Senate would be able to justly try offenders against the Constitution. If a proper impeachment system had been in place over the last few years, the author continued, it would have protected Americans from the "rapacious" tax collection that had encouraged Shays's Rebellion. Although the author did not make the

62. "Elizabeth-Town, June 6," *New-Jersey Journal and Political Intelligencer,* June 6, 1787, [3]; "Philadelphia," *Worcester Magazine* (Mass.), III (Aug. 16, 1787), 261.

63. Abigail Adams to Isaac Smith, Sr., Mar. 12, 1787, in, Taylor, ed., *Adams Papers Digital Edition;* "Portsmouth, June 7," *New-Hampshire Spy* (Portsmouth), June 7, 1788, IV, 51. For more on Shays's Rebellion, see David P. Szatmary, *Shays' Rebellion: The Making of an Agrarian Insurrection* (Amherst, Mass., 1980).

comparison explicitly, the words and charges he claimed against the tax collectors mirrored the widespread reports of the revenue farmer Devi Singh, who had exploited Indians to satisfy Hastings. The saturation of American newspapers with reporting on the Hastings trial ensured that many Americans would have seen the connection.[64]

Some Americans also believed that the Hastings trial proved that engaging with India encouraged corruption and that Americans therefore needed to think carefully about expanding the U.S.-India trade. The *Independent Journal* ran a tongue-in-cheek report supposedly from a correspondent in Philadelphia that a pair of American merchants were sending two representatives to India where they would combine their financial and moral corruption with the supposed corruption of Catholicism. One representative, presumably like Hastings, was sarcastically seen to be qualified by "his long experience in business, his subtil and insinuating address, and above all his known contempt of private interest." His "Asiatic acquisitions" would become extraordinarily valuable and highly improved. Those who objected "'that all is sale and hollow, though his tonge drops manna,'" simply did not understand his genius. The second representative would succeed through "his talents for intrigue and irresistible attractions of his person among the fair," a possible reference to Philip Francis's notorious womanizing. In any case, the jabs at British behavior in India were clear, and in this report the corruption came, not from India, but from Britain. If readers had any doubt, this correspondence from Philadelphia was followed by a report on the Hastings trial.[65]

Some in favor of the new Constitution pressed for its adoption specifically to secure the American trade to India from the corrupting influence of the East India Company and British interlopers alike. As James Winthrop wrote under the pseudonym "Agrippa" to the Massachusetts Convention: "Exclusive companies are, in trade, pretty much like an aristocracy in government, and produces *[sic]* nearly as bad effects. An instance of it we have ourselves experienced." Before the Revolution, India goods needed to pass through the Company. In contrast, wrote Agrippa, "our trade in that quarter is now respectable" and more efficient. Most impor-

---

64. *New-Haven Gazette, and the Connecticut Magazine, for 1788,* June 26, 1788, [5–6]. For an example of a published letter discussing the Constitutional Convention and then turning immediately to the Hastings trial and the horror of British behavior in India, see "Extract of a Letter from Dr. Price, to a Gentleman *[sic]* This City, Dated Hackney, Near London, June 16," *New-Hampshire Spy,* Sept. 16, 1788, IV, 267.

65. *Independent Journal: or the General Advertiser,* Apr. 30, 1788, [2].

tant, "the evil of such companies does not terminate there." "They always, by the greatness of their capital, have an undue influence on the government," he explained. Such interests would undo a republic. "A Spectator" gushed over the lucrative possibilities of an American trade with the East Indies. "But Alas!" he blurted, "this prospect is greatly checked by British vessels and bottoms fitting out of this port under American colours." He was referring directly to the many Britons described above who took advantage of U.S. independence to evade the Company monopoly. Harkening back to accusations against the Company in the 1770s, he asked, "Will you, Americans, suffer the British to become your carriers, to the exclusion of your American merchants and American built ships?" The problem, he concluded, could only be solved by "an efficient consolidated government." The answer was not necessarily a monopoly Company but new national trading regulations to encourage and protect American traders and shipowners.[66]

Americans, with the help of considerable reporting from London, had developed discomfort, on the one hand, with a trade of monopoly and conquest like that pursued by the East India Company, its corrupt factors, Clive, and Hastings, and, on the other, with a weakly regulated trade to India that could spin out of control. Immediately after ratification of the Constitution, and as U.S. trade with India began to accelerate in earnest, U.S. newspapers emphasized the corrupting role of too much commerce, especially with India, using both Clive and Hastings as examples. A letter writer to the *Federal Gazette* claimed that, because the English were used to buying and selling "everything," the behavior of Clive and Hastings was typical. "Nations of miserable East Indians have been sacrificed to the damon of gold, by Clive, Hastings, and their countrymen," while ten thousand Africans deserved revenge for "English avarice." Of course, American merchants traded and American planters used enslaved Africans, but that did not come up.[67]

The picture that Americans had developed of British interactions with India informed the approach of Congress from its first session in 1789.

66. Agrippa XIV, *Massachusetts Gazette*, Jan. 25, 1788, [3]; A Spectator, "Mr. Humphreys," *Pennsylvania Mercury, and Universal Advertiser*, Apr. 10, 1788, [3]. For more on concerns over federal monopolies in the ratification debate, see Fichter, *So Great a Proffit*, 40–43.

67. The writer urged the editor to report more news from the perspective of continental Europe. The editor replied that he agreed with the letter writer and was attempting to find a supply of European papers. See "For the Federal Gazette," *Federal Gazette, and Philadelphia Evening Post*, Jan. 20, 1789, [3].

Using its new duty power, Congress immediately began crafting legislation to control the flow of goods from east of the Cape of Good Hope, to funnel these goods onto American vessels, and to attempt to make inroads in reexport markets, much as the British had done with the Company. In the spring of 1789, Elias Hasket Derby, now one of America's most experienced India traders, lobbied for a reexport drawback on India goods brought to the United States. Derby's son had earlier encouraged him to bring the *Peggy* to America and send it to Europe without unloading any of the cargo, thereby avoiding a duty of 5 percent but also making it possible for the goods to appear as American in origin instead of Asian. Derby believed that a drawback would further encourage him and other American merchants to become the primary suppliers of India goods to Nova Scotia and the West Indies. In June, the Senate appointed a committee to consider the "expediency of adding a clause" to the proposed duty bill "prohibiting the importation of goods from China or India, in ships or vessels, other than those belonging to the citizens of the United States." The committee included the lawyers Oliver Ellsworth and Tristram Dalton, powerful merchant and China-trade adventurer Robert Morris, Antifederalist Richard Henry Lee, and plantation owner and supporter of British trade Pierce Butler.[68]

The resulting law, notably Congress's second, shared common goals with Britain's Navigation Acts and in part the Company monopoly: to get goods into the United States on American-owned ships and to encourage direct imports from China, though not India. Additionally, much like in Britain, American merchants received drawbacks of most of the duties when they reexported Asian goods to encourage other peoples to purchase their goods from the United States. Congress crafted three separate duty scales to encourage tea to be imported on American ships as well as directly from China. On the low end, tea imported directly from Asia on American-owned vessels paid from six to twenty cents per pound. American vessels bringing such goods from Europe paid eight to twenty-six cents per pound. All other vessels from any place paid from fifteen to forty-five cents per pound. The law also imposed a duty of 12.5 percent on the importation of goods from "China or India" on foreign vessels, but there was no extra incentive to bring such goods directly from India. In-

68. Derby Junior to Derby, Jan. 23, 1788, Derby Family Papers, MSS 37, Series I, box 3, folder 4, PEM; Derby to B. Goodhue, May 9, 1789, Letter Book, October 1788–1796, Derby Family Papers, MSS 37, Series I, XIII, 50–51, PEM; *Journal of the First Session of the Senate of the United States of America* . . . (Washington, D.C., 1820), 32.

deed, Alexander Hamilton wondered whether the duty structure would be sufficient to check the significant importation of Indian goods reexported from Europe. He thought this line of competition more serious than that on foreign vessels from India.[69]

Instead of adjusting the duty structure significantly, in 1790 Congress followed the British principle of funneling Asian goods through specific ports to ease regulatory enforcement. In Britain, London enjoyed a national monopoly; no port would enjoy a similar national monopoly in America. Still, Congress enumerated specific ports for all states, and New York and Pennsylvania were allowed to clear goods from east of the Cape of Good Hope only at New York City and Philadelphia, respectively. Such regulations eased the monitoring of duty collection, although they also served to consolidate the India trade in specific ports, and in the hands of specific powerful merchants in those ports.[70]

In this context, references to an overly powerful Hastings with corrupt and illicit investments continued surfacing in American politics, particularly among those who encouraged restraints instead of incentives for wealthy "tory" merchants and bankers. The Jeffersonian Republican representative for Georgia, James Jackson, was quoted as saying that, owing to Hamilton's First Report on the Public Credit, "speculation in publick securities had increased and extended to such a degree as would make even a *Hastings* blush!" The report, laying out a plan to develop the nation's credit, had provided an opportunity for speculators to purchase government securities at heavily discounted rates to sell back to the government for large profits for themselves. In case any readers could not quickly place the reference to Hastings, the paper's publisher explained that they had reported on the "infamous wretch" who ruled British India in their very first paper. The *Pennsylvania Gazette* and *Boston Gazette* added to Jackson's comment: "A Dutch, British or New York tory speculator" would gain from the plunder of each American farmer by causing a crash in prop-

69. That the duty act was the second act Congress passed underscores the importance congressmen placed on exercising the federal government's new power to regulate commerce. See "An Act for Laying a Duty on Goods, Wares, and Merchandises Imported into the United States," July 4, 1789, in Richard Peters, ed., *The Public Statutes at Large of the United States of America* . . . (Boston, 1845), I, 25–27; Alexander Hamilton, "Report on Defects in the Existing Laws of Revenue," Apr. 22, 1790, in Syrett, ed., *Papers of Hamilton Digital Edition.*

70. "An Act to Provide More Effectually for the Collection of the Duties Imposed by Law on Goods, Wares and Merchandise Imported into the United States, and on the Tonnage of Ships or Vessels," Aug. 4, 1790, in Peters, ed., *Public Statutes at Large,* I, 152–153.

erty values based on the secretary's report. The author continued to allude to British behavior in India, claiming, "It is wished to sacrifice the *many* to a *few*—to make noblemen and nabobs of a few New-York gentlemen." The southern states, the critic explained, would continue to suffer the most. These people of "pure whig blood" would lose their wealth in government certificates to the same New Yorkers and Britons who had destroyed their states during the Revolution.[71]

Continuing concerns about the relationship among India, Britain, and America and about elite Americans shaped the approach of Congress in refusing to grant additional privileges to Americans trading directly with Asia. Over the next few years, the House of Representatives received memorials from Philadelphia, Rhode Island, and New York merchants both for and against proposed duties designed to privilege direct imports of Asian goods over imports of reexports from Europe. Those seeking additional stimulus for the trade to Asia took as correct the British belief that reexporting or transshipping goods siphoned off wealth into the reexporting country. A group of New York merchants sent a memorial, "praying the patronage and encouragement of the General Government" in the India trade through prohibitions or duties on foreign participation. As reexported tea from Europe flooded the market, Hamilton suggested that higher duties on such goods should certainly be considered. Assistant secretary of the treasury Tench Coxe was even more enthusiastic: "The proposed regulation for confining importations to our own ships and those of the nation making or producing the commodities, must prove a very efficient measure" to strike at the British East India Company and British shipping from the West Indies. The *Providence Gazette* exclaimed that the success of the ship *Calcutta*, sold for a profit of fifty thousand to sixty thousand pounds in specie, "will operate on the Minds of thinking People to do away with a Prejudice against the Trade, and convince them, that it is our Duty to encourage it, as being much more advantageous than for us to continue the Retailers of Indian Goods for European Merchants."[72]

71. *Western Star* (Stockbridge, Mass.), Feb. 16, 1790, [3]; "From the Pennsylvania Gazette," *Boston Gazette, and the Country Journal*, Mar. 15, 1790, [4]; *Norwich-Packet and Country Journal*, Mar. 26, 1790, [4].

72. *Journal of the First Session of the Senate of the United States of America*, 195–198; *Journal of the House of Representatives of the United States, Being the First Session of the Second Congress* . . . (Washington, D.C., 1826), 358, 380, 519, 523, 545; Alexander Hamilton, "Report on the Petition of the Merchants of Philadelphia Trading to India and China," Feb. 10, 1791, in Syrett, ed., *Papers of Hamilton Digital Edition;* Tench Coxe, "Enclosure: Thoughts on the Navigation of the United States, and concerning Further Means of Encour-

In 1794, Congress levied a duty of 10 percent on any goods not already taxed that were imported in foreign-owned vessels; this was not the result hoped for by the petitioners or the *Providence Gazette*. The duty made it more expensive for European-owned ships to bring Asian goods from Europe, but there was no additional incentive for Americans to bring goods directly from Asia instead of from Europe. Congress focused more broadly on the development of the U.S. carrying trade. Whether the goods came from Europe or India, the goal was to encourage them to arrive in American vessels. Congress's decisions reflected a continuing ambiguity in Britain and America over the corrupting danger of direct trade with India, a source primarily of luxury manufactured goods and the seat of Britain's greatest villains. Some Americans turned back to Clive and Hastings again as evidence that "justice is departed, or rather expelled" from Britain and used them as a warning against trading with India too much.[73]

Both the Hastings trial and the Constitutional Convention had, at their core, the problems of understanding, defining, and regulating the British empire with India and without (at least officially) the former thirteen colonies, and the former thirteen colonies without the British empire and with new opportunities in India. India and America had figured together for centuries in both imaginary and real incarnations of the British empire, and they did so still—even as much of North America was formally rendered out of the empire and more and more of India was formally rendered in. Negotiators over the new American Constitution read in their newspapers of Hastings much as they had read of Clive before the American Revolution. Despite independence, the United States still had to reckon with both the threat of Indian corruption and the potential benefits of Indian wealth. Being independent, strong, and united without becoming corrupted was at the heart of American politics and American interest in the Hastings trial. The Hastings trial helped Americans further refine their relationships with Britain and India, and, in the process, refine their definitions of their own country and the regulation of its trade.

AFTER INDEPENDENCE, U.S. merchants followed multiple trade patterns to India encouraged by the French but primarily established by private British merchants and dependent on a mixture of British financing,

aging it," Mar. 5, 1791, in Oberg and Looney, eds., *Papers of Jefferson Digital Edition; Providence Gazette and Country Journal*, Sept. 14, 1793.

73. "Savannah, June 12; Extract of a Letter to a Gentleman in This City," *City Gazette and Daily Advertiser*, June 6–19, 1794, [2]; *Daily Advertiser*, July 22, 1794, [2].

experience, and rule in India. Despite considerable efforts, the French simply could not promise the same quality of access to India as the British; nor did the French boast the same levels of capital and experience; nor, despite being allies in the American Revolution, did the French and Americans share the same language and density of personal connections as the British and Americans. American merchants, such as Derby, could launch trades into the Indian Ocean without the expertise of Britons, but success would thus come more slowly and with more difficulty and still often required British capital. The American trade to Asia looked similar to that of the weaker European powers—using ports in Europe and America outside the jurisdictions of the European monopoly companies to trade with Company servants and private merchants based in Asia and the Spice Islands, often with capital and expertise provided, in particular, by Britons.

The formal independence of the thirteen colonies was not simply a question of relations between Britain and America, or among Britain, America, and the remaining Atlantic colonies. It was fundamentally about the East Indies as well. The independent United States offered Britons familiar merchant partners and the ideal cover not only for capital but also for men and ships. American independence thereby helped to provide a level of access for private British merchants to India that they had not enjoyed since the 1690s. Many of the British participants in the nominally American trade had gained their experience in India working for the Company, and they traded with Company representatives in Company colonies. This trade was extralegal, but it was a part and product of the British empire.

But such a codependent independence was not necessarily what Americans desired, and illicit trade was certainly not loved by many Company directors or the British government. As the Hastings trial progressed and the new American Constitution was ratified, Congress shifted the framework of the American India trade toward increased regulation. Now with the power to create a unified approach to trade, including structures of tariffs and marine ownership and seamanship, Congress generated a policy environment that encouraged American merchants to trade for Asian goods on American vessels. American merchants and politicians embraced as their own the regulatory framework of the Navigation Acts and protective tariffs that Britons had developed over centuries. Still, there was ambiguity over the India trade in America, much as there was in Britain. The Company seemed to be seriously corrupted, and the failed Fox India bill, the Pitt India Act (1784), which placed the Company under a Board of Control, and the sensational unfolding of the Hastings scandal suggested that such corruption would not be easily overcome. Notably, Congress did not create a monopoly company and did not agree to significant incentives for American merchants to obtain India goods from India itself as opposed to from Europe. The British relationship with India and the scandals surrounding Clive and Hastings suggested that India carried a special risk. In any case, in the India trade and through the emerging production of India goods in Britain, codependent independence would increasingly characterize the relationship of Britain and America over the next several decades.

6   Remapping Production, Rethinking Monopolies

The old system of using America as an outlet for Indian manufactured goods was breaking down, regardless of the American Revolution. A convergence of economic, industrial, and fashion shifts in the late 1780s and early 1790s created a need for a major new imperial compromise. The parallels between this period and the period of the compromise negotiated from the 1690s to 1721 are striking. The problem now as then, during the pirate and calico crisis, was repositioning both India's production and fashions and America's markets in the imperial framework. The East India Company was again fueling new fashions for India goods, particularly fine white muslin that was difficult to emulate with industrial production. As with calico, critics denounced this influx of newly fashionable India goods for creating moral declension, while British manufacturers, now producing cottons, demanded protection. Also reflecting the 1690s, Britons and Americans continued to develop their associations in the India trade, enabled by American independence. Though not pirates, cooperating British and American merchants nevertheless challenged British law and authority and encouraged potential new imperial strategies. The convergence of these developments and more stimulated, not a rebuilding of the British empire or a shift to Asia, but a return to much older plans for remapping cultivation and production, exporting British manufactures, and importing raw materials.[1]

The omission of the colonies from the calico prohibitions in 1700 and 1721 had deviated from the longer-term goal of getting colonists in America and peoples in India to consume as many English and, later, British manufactured goods as possible, but the goal remained even after American independence. In the very years that colonists were contesting Parliament's interpretation of the constitution, fearing Asiatic influence in

1. The directors themselves noted the parallel between the protests of the cotton manufacturers and the silk weavers, arguing that they were equally misguided; see *Report of the Select Committee, of the Court of Directors of the East India Company, upon the Subject of the Cotton Manufacture of This Country* ([London], 1793), 6.

government, and eventually declaring independence, inventors in Britain were designing new machines, not so much of government, but of production. In 1764, the same year that Parliament passed the Sugar Act, James Hargreaves mechanized the production of cotton thread with his spinning jenny, thereby driving up the thread's availability and down its costs. During the height of protests over the Townshend duties, Richard Arkwright further mechanized cotton spinning by inventing the water frame, which produced strong warp thread. British producers could now make affordable fully cotton fabric. In 1774, as patriots protested the East India Company and the Intolerable Acts, successful British cotton cloth manufacturers pushed Parliament to repeal the ban on cottons dyed, printed, and stained in Britain, although the ban remained on imports from India. In this still-protected market, further advances in production occurred. These innovations in cotton cloth production would gradually displace Indian fabrics from international markets and would make U.S. citizens more dependent on fabric made in Britain than they had been as colonists.

British power on the subcontinent was certainly more significant than in the past, and it was continuing to expand through the Anglo-Mysore wars against Hyder Ali and his son Tipu Sultan, allies of the French. Expanding conquest in India seemed to some to still pose moral and political risks, but to others it promised new markets for British goods. British craftspeople renewed their attention to using product and process innovation to actively reinvent exports for India, such as hookah pipes and palanquins, a strategy that could be called export substitution. These activities mirrored attempts by British cotton producers and porcelain producers engaged in import substitution. India's fashion influence was hardly over. And America's markets were again rapidly growing. The problem, in London, was how to rebalance India and America in light of new geographies of rule and production. It was not simply a governmental problem. It was also the old problem of balancing the products of India, even those now made in Britain, with their potential threat. But as the economic element of the threat faded with increasing British success in import and export substitution, the political threats and changes remained unclear.[2]

---

2. This new story builds on Maxine Berg's work on import substitution and her claims that "good-quality fine ware" became "branded as British to the rest of the world." See Berg, *The Age of Manufactures, 1700–1820: Industry, Innovation, and Work in Britain*, 2d ed. (London, 1994), 1–4, 282; Berg, *Luxury and Pleasure in Eighteenth-Century Britain* (Oxford, 2005), 19–20, 46–86, 105–110, 113, 132–135. Britons, in effect, reinvented not only Chinese porcelain but also Indian cottons, hookahs, and palanquins. For porcelain and cottons, in particular, they tended to forget about the reinvention and instead often saw such

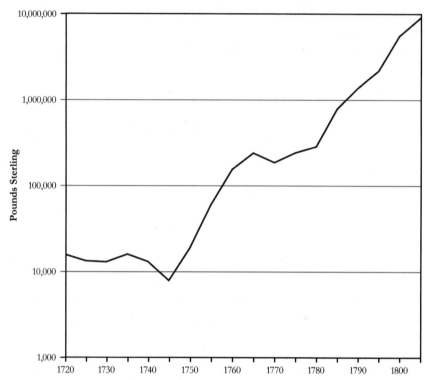

Figure 1. British-Made Cotton Cloth Exports, 1720–1810. Elizabeth Boody
Schumpeter, *English Overseas Trade Statistics, 1697–1808* (Oxford, 1960), 29–34.
Drawn by Rebecca Wrenn.

Until the 1750s, fustian exports, which are included in the totals here, generally
accounted for more than half of the cotton cloth exported. The growth after 1750 was
mostly driven by fully cotton fabric.

A New Industry, a New Fashion

By the mid-1780s, British success in imitating Indian cottons was changing the equation of the India trade and its dangers, with potentially significant implications in Britain and America alike. Historians typically rely on
graphs using a linear *y* axis to track economic data; in the case of British
cotton cloth exports, such an axis results in a sharply upturned curve. In
contrast, plotting the export data on a logarithmic axis, as in Figure 1, reveals that the growth rate of cotton cloth exports remained surprisingly

goods as their own ideas. For more on such genealogical truncation through the example of
reinvented porcelain, see Lydia H. Liu, "Robinson Crusoe's Earthenware Pot," *Critical Inquiry,* XXV (1999), 728–757.

consistent after 1745, except during the American Revolution, when export growth stalled because of war with the United States, France, Spain, and Holland. After the Revolutionary War, growth returned. In addition to the cotton production innovations of the 1760s and early 1770s, Samuel Crompton's new spinning mule reportedly allowed British spinners to produce in three hundred hours what took Indian spinners fifty thousand hours. Further British price advantages came in the mid-1780s from power looms, the mechanization of calico printing through the use of copper cylinders, and the introduction of steam power. The operation of many new powered mules, printers, and looms combined with easier peacetime access to foreign markets fueled the continuous increases in export growth.[3]

From 1780 to 1790, however, the East India Company's London sales of Indian cotton cloth and exports of British-made cotton cloth grew in parallel, as shown in Figure 2. British cloth was not so much pushing Indian cloth out of markets as expanding those markets together with Indian cloth. The popularity of Indian imports went hand in hand with the continuation of the process that had begun in the middle of the seventeenth century of associating only some India goods with corruption, thus creating a space for the fashionability and economic importance of other India goods.

As calicoes became ever more widely available and less Indian, fashionable women of the middling and upper ranks increasingly embraced pure white muslin from India, which was more difficult to industrially produce than calico, and they also adapted the style of dress for which Indians used the muslin. Britons and colonists had used muslin to make handkerchiefs, neckcloths, aprons, and decorative embroideries since the seventeenth century. Those in India went to considerable trouble to send fine muslin home to be distributed among friends and relatives. During

---

3. S. D. Chapman, *The Cotton Industry in the Industrial Revolution* (London, 1972), 20–25. Mechanized cotton thread production began in the United States on Richard Arkwright's model in 1790 when Moses Brown, whose influential family was involved in the India trade, joined with experienced English immigrant Samuel Slater to build a mill in Rhode Island. Americans were split over the benefits of increased manufacturing, with Jefferson famously arguing against it. In any case, U.S. production would be dwarfed by British production for decades. See Barbara M. Tucker, *Samuel Slater and the Origins of the American Textile Industry, 1790–1860* (Ithaca, N.Y., 1984), 45–64. For more on technology transfer, see "British Technology Transmission to the United States: The Philadelphia Experience," *Business History Review*, XLVII (1973), 24–52. For a brief overview of the divide in the United States, see Angela Lakwete, *Inventing the Cotton Gin: Machine and Myth in Antebellum America* (Baltimore, 2003), 35–36.

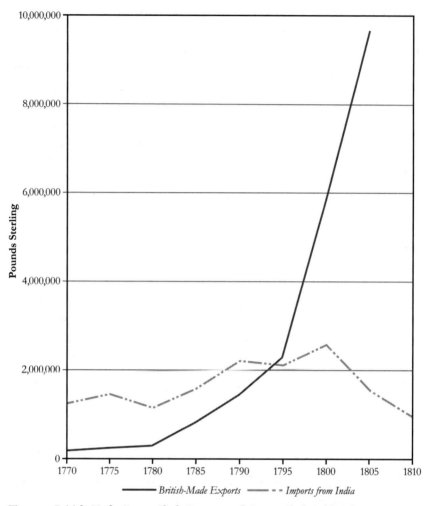

Figure 2. British-Made Cotton Cloth Exports and Cotton Cloth Sold at the Company Sales, 1770–1810. Elizabeth Boody Schumpeter, *English Overseas Trade Statistics* (Oxford, 1960), 30–34; "An Account of the Quantities of Cotton Piece Goods and Muslins Sold at the Sales of the East India Company . . . ," L/AG/10/2/5, BL. Drawn by Rebecca Wrenn

the 1770s, however, demand for muslin entered a new phase. The non-industrial, clean, white, and delicate nature of muslin helped to give it new value as a marker of higher status, but its popularity was also influenced by the growing number of Britons with experience in India. Indian women had long worn unstructured muslin dresses (Plate 16) with loose trousers underneath, and elite men also wore like attire. The evolution of muslin dresses in Europe combined this influence with other classical, theatrical, and East and West Indian influences. British women in the 1770s had begun to prefer a moderately structured but tightly laced dress, known across Europe as the *robe à l'anglaise*. This dress continued to evolve with the muslin market. By 1784, a report on "Ayder Ali Khan," republished in South Carolina, explained of the Indian ruler that his white muslin "robe is fashioned nearly the same as those of the European ladies which are called *a l'Angloise*." The report described that "the body and sleeves fit neatly, and are drawn close by strings; the rest of the robe being ample, and in folds."[4]

Meanwhile, the French further developed the robe à l'anglaise with elements of a chemise style adapted from West Indian plantation dresses, which itself was likely influenced by Asian-Indian dress. The outbreak of criticism surrounding the sensational portrait *Marie Antoinette en Chemise,* by Vigée Le Brun (1783), suggests the extent to which the style had not yet been accepted as proper public attire in Europe, but it also marks the early rise of the popular new chemise trend more broadly around the Atlantic. In 1789, the pseudonymous Christopher Curious wrote to the *Lady's Magazine* that "all the sex now—from fifteen to fifty and upwards (I should rather say downwards) appear in white muslin frocks, with broad

4. For the report, see "Particular Circumstances Relating to the Person, Habits, and Manners of Ayder Ali Khan," *South-Carolina Gazette and General Advertiser* (Charleston), Nov. 16–18, 1784, [3]. For a similar statement, see Bar[tholomew] Burges, *A Series of Indostan Letters . . .* (New York, 1790), 6–19. On influences, see Aileen Ribeiro, *The Art of Dress: Fashion in England and France, 1750 to 1820* (New Haven, Conn., 1995), 64–71, 109–113; Ribeiro, *Dress in Eighteenth-Century Europe, 1715-1789* (London, 2002), 222–228. On muslin uses, see Rosemary Crill, "Asia in Europe: Textiles for the West," in Anna Jackson and Amin Jaffer, eds., *Encounters: The Meeting of Asia and Europe, 1500-1800* (London, 2004), 271. For examples of muslin gifts, see Neil Edmonstone to Charles Edmonstone, Dec. 10, 1802, Neil Edmonstone Papers, MS Add. 7616, Cambridge University Library; T. S. Hancock to his wife, Dec. 18, 1773, MS 29236, BL; John Grose to Nash [brother], Jan. 31, 1766, MSS Eur. E284, BL; Henry Vansittart to Laurence Sulivan, Feb. 27, 1763, fol. 141, MS Eng. Hist. b. 191, Bodleian Library, Oxford University.

Plate 16. Dip Chand, Woman Smoking a Hookah with a European Side Table.
Circa 1764. Opaque watercolor, 20.9 cm. x 13.1 cm. Fullerton Collection,
Add.Or.735. © The British Library Board

sashes." By the late 1790s, several cuts of muslin dresses, particularly with increasingly high waistlines, had come in and out of fashion.[5]

London's "Committee of Buyers of East-India Piece Goods for Home Consumption" explained that the wearing of muslin dresses had spread to people of different classes within London and then geographically outward from the city. The committee sought to defend the Company's muslin imports against further restrictions that would also harm its members' businesses. It truncated the genealogy of the loosely structured muslin dress designs instead of extending them clearly to India or including the French influence. Nevertheless, the committee was correct that London was, in effect, the clearinghouse from which both the initial move toward the new muslin dresses in Europe and America and the bulk of the muslin itself were distributed. Between 1776 and 1787, the Sun Fire Office in London insured eight men and women who listed themselves, not as mere general drapers, but specifically as muslin dealers. Fashionable women, such as Barbara Johnson, who circulated between London, country houses, and Bath, brought the changing styles with them, and her album of swatches and fashion plates shows the shifts toward various muslin dresses. American women followed fashion leaders in London and Paris. As Lucy Cranch wrote to Abigail Adams, a fashionable magazine sent by the latter was in great demand. "The news was soon spread" that Cranch had received it, and *"Gentlemen* and Ladies, all borrowed it." In the fifteen years after the American Revolution, more than twelve thousand muslin advertisements appeared in American newspapers.[6]

The majority of the considerable quantities of muslin purchased by consumers in Britain, Europe, and America to supply these new fashions came through the Company's warehouses and auctions in London. Company statistics show a rapid increase of muslin imports after 1780, peaking around 1790 (Figure 3). As the quantity of pieces imported doubled, the

5. Mary Sheriff, "The Portrait of the Queen," in Dena Goodman, ed., *Marie Antoinette: Writings on the Body of a Queen* [London, 2003], 45–64; *Lady's Magazine; or, Entertaining Companion for the Fair Sex* . . . (London, 1789), 597.

6. Committee of Merchants and Drapers, Buyers of India Piece Goods to Dundas, Apr. 6, 1793, London, IOR/A/2/11, fol. 126, BL; *Indexes of the Fire Insurance Policies of the Sun Fire Office and the Royal Exchange Assurance, 1775–1787* (London, 1986), microform. For Johnson, see Natalie Rothstein, ed., *A Lady of Fashion: Barbara Johnson's Album of Styles and Fabrics* (New York, 1987), interior pages 9–39. For Cranch's magazine, see Lucy Cranch to Abigail Adams, Dec. 7, 1786, in C. James Taylor, ed., *The Adams Papers Digital Edition* (Charlottesville, Va., 2008). The total number of advertisements was calculated from searches using the database America's Historical Newspapers (Readex).

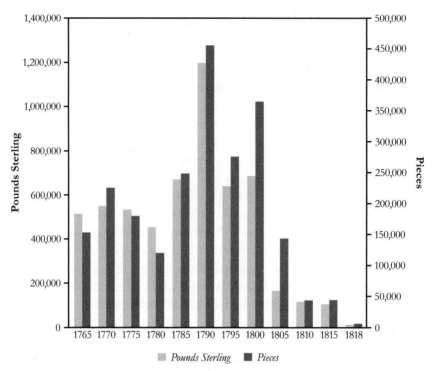

Figure 3. Muslin Sold at the Company Sales, 1765–1818. "An Account of the Quantities of Cotton Piece Goods and Muslins Sold at the Sales of the East India Company . . . ," IOR/L/AG/10/2/5, BL; "An Account of White Piece Goods Imported from the East Indies, Sold at the Sales of the East India Company . . . ," IOR/L/AG/10/2/2, BL. Drawn by Rebecca Wrenn

sales value per piece did not fall sharply. Quantities sold fell back somewhat in 1795, but prices per piece did not erode significantly, showing that demand had not yet been oversaturated.[7]

British manufacturers pressed hard to try to emulate finer and finer Indian muslin samples to secure domestic and international strength over Indian and, to a much lesser extent, French and Swiss cotton cloth producers. In the late 1780s, factory owner Samuel Oldknow, for example,

7. Governor General in Council, Commercial Department, July 23, 1806, General Letters from the Court of Directors Commercial Department, Dec. 18, 1765–Sept. 15, 1785, State Archives of West Bengal, Kolkata. Cotton calicoes for printing also came to France from India via London throughout the period; see S. D. Chapman and S. Chassagne, *European Textile Printers in the Eighteenth Century: A Study of Peel and Oberkampf* (London, 1981), 161–162.

Remapping Production, Rethinking Monopolies

requested that his associate Robert Parker in London buy sample goods from the East India Company's sales and try to ascertain the accounts of the sales to gauge pricing. Oldknow tasked his spinners and weavers to reproduce the samples as closely as possible, and wholesalers and retailers inspected the results. They reported on deficiencies and indicated whether they could successfully substitute Oldknow's goods for their Indian patterns. One customer, for instance, returned his order of handkerchiefs and muslin gowns because they fell to pieces when washed and would not sell. Parker and his partners also wrote about domestic competitors. They had obtained a British fabric "of a most currious texture and the first piece of British manufactory I ever felt like a muslin." They prevailed on Oldknow, "You must strain every nerve to excel this man, or at least keep pace with him or how shall we make drapers rever the name of *Oldknow*." Already in 1786 the directors sent samples of British-made muslin the other way to their servants in Bengal as a warning to drive down prices, or suffer the loss of the trade. As shown in Figure 3, not until about 1800 did the price per piece at the Company's sales begin to fall sharply in the face of British industrial success. Cheaper British imitations were broadly displacing Indian muslin, and the Company imported fewer and fewer pieces. By 1810, the Company imported small quantities of high-quality pieces that were still difficult to simulate.[8]

Cashmere shawls used by Indians as markers of status for centuries were even more difficult to emulate, making them also ideal new goods for fashionable Britons to display their taste and wealth. They did not become popular in Britain and America until the rise of British cotton cloth and the fashion for Indian muslin. Warren Hastings described cashmere shawls sent home for his wife as "beautiful beyond imagination" and asked, "Why should I provide paltry things for you, when I carry with me inimitables?" Neither the material nor art of producing cashmere shawls existed in Britain. Shawls were already common in Calcutta probate inventories for Britons in the 1760s. As with muslins, many Britons in India sent shawls home. Importantly, they also passed along the Indian knowl-

8. Robert Parker to Samuel Oldknow, Feb. 1788, SO/1/214, Samuel Oldknow Papers, John Rylands Library, Manchester, William Smith to Oldknow, Mar. 7, 1787, SO/1/286, Greaves, Hodgson, and Co. to Oldknow, Aug. 23, 1787, SO/1/125, John Harwood to Oldknow, Nov. 23, 1789, SO/1/138, Parker, Topham, and Sowden to Oldknow, n.d., SO/1/233; Directors' Commercial Letter to "Our Governor General and Council at Fort William in Bengal," Apr. 12, 1786, IOR/E/4/630, 254–255, BL. On European competition, see Chapman, *Cotton Industry*, 70.

edge of how to wear and use shawls and to identify their qualities and beauty. Initially, this knowledge was only readily available to middle- and upper-rank women with connections to the fashionable set in India, but prints, etiquette guides, and fashion magazines spread the knowledge more broadly. The importance of such knowledge should not be underestimated. How to wear a shawl would not have been evident to people who had never seen them before. The British and American fashion for shawls replicated standards of status common in India, including rarity, cost, and modes of use.[9]

Among critics, these newly fashionable goods and styles stimulated moral fears similar to those that had previously surrounded calicoes. A fictional letter from John Homespun in a 1785 edition of the Edinburgh-based periodical the *Lounger*, for example, attacked the behavior and fashions of the family of Mr. Mushroom, a nabob returned from India. Homespun complained that Mr. Mushroom brought home a staggering fortune

9. For Indian elites teaching Britons to give fine muslin and shawls as displays of status and respect, see Sydney C. Grier, ed., *The Letters of Warren Hastings to His Wife* (London, 1905), 336; "The Contents of Three Chests etc. for Their Most Sacred Majesties the King and Queen of Great Britain by Their Faithful and Steady Friend and Ally the Nabob of the Carnatic," H/114, 329–330, BL; [Fanny Parkes Parlby], *Wanderings of a Pilgrim, in Search of the Picturesque* . . . (1850; rpt. London, 1975), 74. For more on gifts, see Margot C. Finn, "Colonial Gifts: Family Politics and the Exchange of Goods in British India, c. 1780–1820," *Modern Asian Studies*, XL (2006), 203–231. On other shawl gifts to friends and family in Britain, see, for example, Thomas Short to Gerard Gustavus Ducarel, Feb. 27, 1788, D2091 Ducarel Family, F/14, Gloucestershire Archives, United Kingdom; Thomas Best to George Abercrombie Robinson, Jan. 21, 1787, MSS Eur F142, folder 2, BL.

Inventory analysis is based on a computerized database of more than five hundred Bengal inventories for odd years in the 1760s, 1790s, and 1820s. Typically, only people of the middle ranks and above had inventories taken at their deaths. Inventories cover Company servants, army officers, private merchants, ship's officers, partners and employees of agency houses, shopkeepers, and some unemployed women. Since English-speaking society in Calcutta had a higher proportion of middle- and upper-wealth individuals than cities in Britain or America, coverage is unusually complete. Still, virtually no inventories exist for the thousands of British army privates and other British individuals with few possessions who died in Bengal. Lois Green Carr and Lorena S. Walsh describe a range of potential difficulties with probate inventories in colonial America, particularly issues of coverage, consistency, and detail (Carr and Walsh, "Inventories and the Analysis of Wealth and Consumption Patterns in St. Mary's County, Maryland, 1658–1777," *Historical Methods*, XII [1980], 81–90). Calcutta inventories, however, tend to be more consistent and much more detailed than the inventories used in Carr and Walsh's discussion. See inventories for 1760–1769 from "Inventories of Deceased, Bengal," IOR/P/154/62–69, BL; inventories for 1790–1799 and 1820–1829 from "Accountant General's Records, Inventories and Accounts of Deceased Estates, Bengal (1780–1840)," L/AG/34/27/13–22, 69–93, BL. The database is hereafter cited as Bengal Inventories.

of one hundred thousand pounds along with a taste for excessive Indian luxury. Mrs. Mushroom wore flowered muslin, shawls, feathers, and perfumes. Additionally, the family "carpeted and cushioned" their pew in church like an Indian room, displaying a sacrilegious lack of Protestant Christian forbearance and thrift. The real trouble began for Homespun, however, when his wife and daughters began to imitate the Mushrooms. Suddenly, they had to have shawls and "muslins from Bengal," and they made "awkward attempts, by garlic and pepper to turn" their chickens "into the form of Curries and Peelaws." All these frivolities, he wrote, "not only . . . rob me of my money, but them of their happiness." Associating expensive India goods with foreignness, decadence, and a lack of spiritual fulfillment appealed to critics trying to uphold customary definitions of dangerous luxury and point out the danger of Indian corruption.[10]

As Homespun suggested, curries and other Indian foods were joining muslin and shawls in popularity among the middling and upper sorts in Britain and also, to some extent, in America. "India pickle" recipes using ginger, mustard, and turmeric had been common in cookbooks since the seventeenth century. Curry recipes also appeared in several British cookbooks, beginning with Hannah Glasse's famous cookbook in 1747. As early as 1776, in London, Mr. Jackson offered "the Nobility, Gentry, and Others . . . JACKSON'S TRUE CURRY POWDER, prepared after the original East India manner, it being allowed the wholesomest preparation made use of in the art of cookery." In 1788, Burgess's Italian Warehouse offered: "Genuine BENGAL CURRIE POWDER. A receipt given how to use it." Such curry powder commodified and simplified the preparation of a British version of Indian curry. The inclusion of the recipe suggests that, although Britons might have been interested in curry, most did not yet know how to make it, even with the premixed powder. In America, several advertisements for curry powder appeared in the 1790s in Boston, New York, and Charleston. The powder came from London suppliers, though it is not clear how popu-

10. [Henry Mackenzie], *The Lounger, a Periodical Paper* (Edinburgh), May 28, 1785, 65–68; reprinted as Mackenzie, *The Works of Henry Mackenzie, Esq.*, 8 vols. (Edinburgh, 1808), V, 169–174. Despite the fuss over nabobs, most who returned from India merged back into British life either as lower-rank soldiers or as respectable middle- and upper-rank subjects with moderate wealth; see James M. Holzman, *The Nabobs in England: A Study of the Returned Anglo-Indian, 1760–1785* (New York, 1926), 28–31, 78–82; [Joseph Price], *The Saddle Put on the Right Horse; or, An Enquiry into the Reason Why Certain Persons Have Been Denominated Nabobs* . . . (London, 1783), 22–32. Many did not return to Britain. For more on the perception of danger in nabob wealth and goods, see Tillman Nechtman, *Nabobs: Empire and Identity in Eighteenth-Century Britain* (New York, 2010), esp. 140–187.

lar it was with American consumers. After the American Revolution, imports of Indian calicoes, muslins, shawls, and, increasingly, British cottons rose to levels higher again than they had been in the colonial period. U.S. newspapers reprinted several sections of the *Lounger,* but they did not frequently, if ever, include the article on the Mushrooms.[11]

John Homespun was not a popular hero in Britain or America. Homespun was a curmudgeon fighting the perennial loss of the good old days when life was simpler and fashions were supposedly domestic and commonsensical—not to mention cheaper. The increasing production of British cotton cloth through mechanized spinning, weaving, and printing did not reduce interest in Indian fashions, but it did reduce the power of some moral arguments against cottons. The extent of the association of cottons with corruption was mostly an argument in support of domestic woolen producers. Now that domestic cotton manufacturing was becoming an impressive part of the British economy, associating it with corruption simply would not do. Even poor facsimiles of shawls were quickly reproduced in Britain, and Indian curry cooking was reproduced as curry powder. Warnings of an impending deluge of exorbitant spending on frivolous and even dangerous India muslins, shawls, and curry raised few fingers to the dikes in part because such goods had British imitations but also because the imitations were inferior. These India goods offered distinction. The Mushrooms, like other nabobs, were ahead of the flood, but they

11. For curry powder in Britain, see, for example, *Gazetteer and New Daily Advertiser* (London), Dec. 18, 1776, [4]; *Morning Herald, and Daily Advertiser* (London), June 14, 1784, [3]; *Diary; or, Woodfall's Register* (London), Mar. 27, 1790, 1; *World* (London), Dec. 17, 1788, 1; Peck's Italian Warehouse, Trade Cards 9 (95) subsect. Fruiterers and Greengrocers, John Johnson Collection, Bodleian Library, Oxford University. For curry powder in America, see for examples, *Argus* (Boston), Oct. 14, 1791, [4], May 15, 1792 [3]; *Daily Advertiser* (New York), Oct. 11, 1794, supplement; *City Gazette And Daily Advertiser* (Charleston), Oct. 11, 1797, [1]. For curry in cookbooks, see, for example, the many editions of the *Art of Cookery,* beginning with Hannah Glasse, *The Art of Cookery, Made Plain and Easy* . . . (London, 1747), 52. See also William Verral, *The Cook's Paradise Being William Verral's "Complete System of Cookery"* . . . , ed. R. L. Mégroz (London, 1948), 13; Frances Rous, Collection of Cookery, Medical and Household Receipts, 1767, MS 4288, 110, Wellcome Library, London; Stephanie R. Maroney, "'To Make a Curry the India Way': Tracking the Meaning of Curry Across Eighteenth-Century Communities," *Food and Foodways: Explorations in the History and Culture of Human Nourishment,* XIX (2011), 122–134. For an India pickle, see *The Receipt Book of Mrs. Ann Blencowe, A.D. 1694,* ed. Leander W. Smith (Cottonport, La., 1972), 34–35. An extract of a letter from Limerick, Ireland, appeared in U.S. newspapers in the summer of 1785 arguing that trading to Asia drained Britain's wealth in exchange for luxuries that poisoned the body and mind, but such examples were rare; see *New-Jersey Gazette* (Trenton), June 27, 1785, 2.

were not far outside the mainstream of respectable fashion. Consumption habits prove that most middle- and upper-sort Britons and Americans welcomed the flood; their desires for inimitable India goods, after all, caused it.

Notably, Homespun did not tell readers that Mrs. Mushroom brought back to Britain the "elephants, palanquins, and processions . . . with episodes of dancing girls" that she also prattled on about. These commodities and habits were not used in Britain by returned nabobs or fashion leaders, although those with the means continued to collect many Indian items and animals. Collecting foreign products was different from actively using them because it marked out cultural and other differences. Curiosities from India could be found in countless collections in Britain and across the Atlantic all the way to Thomas Jefferson's Monticello in Virginia. John O'Donnell even sent a hookah to George Washington, explaining that "the Bearer will shew the President's Servant It's use." It remains unclear if Washington tried the pipe. Only the regular users, especially Britons in India, of such specifically unacceptable goods as elephants, palanquins, and hookahs were corrupt. As British industrial imitation reduced the distinctive qualities of calicoes, keeping one set of India goods that were embraced by nabobs out of British and American consumer culture or confined to cabinets of curiosities continued to help make space for the adoption of other distinctive India goods.[12]

A New Market and Old Fears

British production and imitation did not necessarily result in domestic acceptance. Although Britons at home and Americans regarded palanquins and hookahs as symbols of corruption and tyranny, British producers saw in them profit. The old hope of increasing the consumption of woolens in India remained unfulfilled since cottons and silks were so much "better suited to the climate" and customs of the people. As for the new British cottons, the Board of Trade reported, "It appears to be the opinion that none of them will answer for the general consumption of the native; but that some manchester goods to a trifling amount might be sold." Conquered Indians might not be readily tempted by British manufactures, but conquest also brought more Britons to India. These people desired

12. [Mackenzie], *Lounger*, May 28, 1785, 67–68; John O'Donnell to George Washington, Sept. 9, 1790, in Theodore J. Crackel, ed., *The Papers of George Washington Digital Edition* (Charlottesville, Va., 2008).

a broad range of British goods, and they also elevated a new fusion of British and Indian fashion among Europeans and Indian elites on the subcontinent developed by craftspeople through the application of British styles, materials, and manufacturing techniques to Indian goods. Britons in India did not strive to replicate English country-estate ideals; rather, they sought to project power and status on both British and what they thought to be local terms by adapting geopolitically appropriate "rituals of rulership."[13]

After the 1760s, private merchants poured a broad range of British and European goods into British India. Each autumn, as the Company's ships sailed into port, ship's officers and auction and warehouse owners advertised goods brought as privilege cargo. The chief officer of the *Lord Camden,* for example, advertised "ELEGANT CUT GLASS HOOKA BOT-TOMS, Hanging Lamps, Wall and Reading Shades" as well as mahogany tables, stockings, chronometers, books, cider, and perry. He offered the goods for sale at the auction room of Burrell, Dring, and Company in Calcutta. Davidson and Maxwell similarly advertised a long list of goods available at their Calcutta warehouse, including British made "MANCHESTER STUFFS—of the most fashionable patterns," "QUEENS-WARE," rich-cut glass, organs, guns, and fishing tackle. One of Calcutta's leading firms, Tulloh and Company, boasted that captain John Bartlet brought an excellent cargo on the *Rose,* "laid in agreeable to an indent made out with the utmost attention in this country." This last point was essential for Britons in India—straight imports of British fashions were not enough.[14]

In particular, glassware exports to India increased substantially in the second half of the eighteenth century, with many products specifically designed for the Indian market. Building on the Company's earlier trade, London-based "Maker and Glass Engraver, Jerom Johnson," for instance,

13. Reports from the Select Committee Appointed to Take into Consideration the Export Trade from Great Britain to the East Indies for the Lords of the Committee of Privy Council for All Matters relating to Trade and Foreign Plantations, 1791? IOR/A/2/10, BL. According to Natalie Zacek, the "rituals of rulership" in the West Indies denied "the twin realities of slavery and the protoindustrial nature of plantation production" by focusing strongly on the image of an English country gentleman. See Zacek, "Rituals of Rulership: The Material Culture of West Indian Politics," in David Shields, ed., *Material Culture in Anglo-America: Regional Identity and Urbanity in the Tidewater, Lowcountry, and Carribean* (Columbia, S.C., 2009), 119. Nevertheless, Britons in the West Indies also used, and were mocked for using, simple palanquins and umbrellas; see Thomas Day, *The History of Sandford and Merton; a Work Intended for the Use of Children* (London, 1783), 13; for a somewhat later example, see William Elmes, *Adventures of Johnny Newcome* ([London], [1812]).

14. *World* (Calcutta), Feb. 11, 1792, 1, Apr. 28, 1792, 1, Sept. 15, 1792, 1, Dec. 15, 1792, 1.

sold hookahs to a private, likely privilege, exporter for India in the 1740s. In a 1752 issue of London's *Daily Advertiser,* Johnson offered "Turkish or Indian Fashion, Hubble-Bubbles, [and] Springel Glasses," available "for Exportation . . . wholesale or retail, at the lowest Rates." Glassmakers in India had neither the recipes nor skills required to make lead glass, nor the facilities and experience to cut it. After 1777, heavy new taxes on opaque glass in Britain stimulated further growth in cut glass crystal throughout the British empire and in America. Whitefriars glasshouse in East London, for example, began making glass for export to India in the 1770s. East India ship brokers, such as Hacket and Company, were regular customers of Whitefriars. They purchased a broad range of cut glass items fashionable in Britain, but they also purchased such items as hookah bottoms specifically made for the India trade. By the later eighteenth century, glassware consistently ranked near the top of exports from London to India by value, typically exceeding SR 200,000, or about £25,000 per year. This move toward cut glass crystal coincided with the increasing numbers of British merchants, administrators, military officers, and others in India with the means to purchase it. High rates of breakage owing to the long ocean voyage, the low quality of Indian roads, and frequent, large, and often energetic dinner parties combined to keep the British-Indian demand for glassware consistently high, and increasingly so for hookah pipes.[15]

Mughal works often associated the hookah with power and sexuality, associations that both attracted and alarmed Britons. Hookah pipes already had a huge, caste-crossing domestic market among Indians. Indian hookahs ranged from simple coconut shells with holes bored in them to impressive machines made from bidree, a black South Asian metal alloy inlaid with gold and silver. In the mid-eighteenth–century Rajasthani painting *Lady Yearning for Her Lover,* for example, a woman holds one of her breasts in one hand and a phallic hookah mouthpiece in the other. In

15. For glass exports, see General Account of Imports, Commercial Reports, P174/13, 17, 22, 27, 32, 37, 42, BL; John Bell, *Review of the External Commerce of Bengal, from 1824–25 to 1829–30; with Appendix of Tables, etc.* (Calcutta, 1830), 13, 31. On Jerom Johnson, see Francis Buckley, "Glass for the Eastern Market," *Glass* (April 1932), 156–157; Advertisement, *Daily Advertiser* (London), Jan. 17, 1752. On Indian glass production, see Moreshwar Dikshit, *History of Indian Glass* (Bombay, 1969), 79, 86, 90–116, 126. On taxes and cut glass popularity, see E. M. Elville, *English and Irish Cut Glass, 1750–1950* (London, 1953), 18–21. On Hacket and Company, see Customers of Whitefriars, IV, 267, MS 3096, Museum of London. The Exchange rate is from Holden Furber, *John Company at Work* (Cambridge, Mass., 1951), 349–350.

Plate 17. Francesco Renaldi, *Muslim Lady Reclining.* 1789. Oil on canvas, 57.2 × 69.9 cm. B1981.25.519. Courtesy the Yale Center for British Art, Paul Mellon Collection

Plate 16, the hookah snake sliding between the legs of the Indian woman retained a less graphic sense of the hookah's eroticism. In this case, the woman wore the style of dress from which the European muslin fashion was borrowed, sat in a European chair, and rested her hookah on a British-style tea table. The combination of Indian sexuality and Indian and British material culture disturbed those who saw India as an immoral place where objects and women both seduced British gentlemen. Late-eighteenth-century British painters in India replicated and further entrenched the Indian use of the hookah as an erotic device. Francesco Renaldi's *Portrait of a Mogul Lady* and *Muslim Lady Reclining* (Plate 17) depicted young Indian women in thin muslin suggestively directing hookah mouthpieces. To British viewers, their open pose, soft, downturned gaze, and bare feet suggested a heightened sense of eroticism and sexual availability. British women in India, upholding the image that they were more chaste and decorous than Indian women, were not depicted with hookahs, though men often were. Indeed, hookah smoking, like other forms of smoking, was seen to be more acceptable for men, as was sexual desire. Robert Home's portrait of Anthony Lambert, dated 1797, depicts Lambert at a table, gazing off in a similar plane to his hookah mouthpiece, which suggests his virility as it points out from between his legs (Plate 18).[16]

Men were certainly not immune to criticism for embracing hookahs and the sexuality that they represented. Britons outside India saw long-standing tropes of wanton heathen peoples, the corrupting effect of tropical climates, tyranny, laziness, and disorder in such depictions of hookahs. In his opening speech against British India's governor-general Warren Hastings in 1788, Edmund Burke described the extortionate revenue farmer Devi Singh's brothel, intended to seduce and bribe Britons "with the best wines of France, with an exquisite entertainment, with the perfumed India smoke." In her novel *Andrew Stuart; or, The Northern Wanderer*, Mary Ann Hanway described an Indian prince as a "freebooter, who reclined in ferocious majesty, smoking his hooka, on something like a couch." Critics asserted that when a man smoked a hookah he tended to do little else. The large apparatus impeded mobility, and the clouds of scented smoke impeded rational thought and action.[17]

16. For a discussion of the diffusion of Mughal art in Britain, see Natasha Eaton, "Nostalgia for the Exotic: Creating an Imperial Art in London, 1750–1793," *Eighteenth-Century Studies*, XXXIX (2006), 233–239. On hookah types, see Thomas Williamson, *The East India Vade-Mecum; or, Complete Guide to Gentlemen Intended for the Civil, Military, or Naval Service of the Hon. East India Company* (London, 1810), I, 226–228. Renaldi was likely born in Britain and studied at the Royal Academy; see Mildred Archer, *India and British Portraiture, 1770–1825* (London, 1979), 281, 313. For *Lady Yearning for Her Lover*, see J. C. Harle, *The Art and Architecture of the Indian Subcontinent* (London, 1986), 391, 570, fig. 310. Strong female sexuality was seen largely negatively in respectable British and American society. See Marlene LeGates, "The Cult of Womanhood in Eighteenth-Century Thought," *Eighteenth-Century Studies*, X (1976), 21–39; Patricia Meyer Spacks, "'Ev'ry Woman Is at Heart a Rake,'" ibid., VIII (1974), 27–46. On America, see Nancy F. Cott, "Passionlessness: An Interpretation of Victorian Sexual Ideology, 1790–1850," *Signs: Journal of Women in Culture and Society*, IV (1978), 219–236; Jan Lewis, "The Republican Wife: Virtue and Seduction in the Early Republic," *WMQ*, 3d Ser., XLIV (1987), 703–721.

17. Edmund Burke's speech to Parliament, Feb. 8, 1788, *The Writings and Speeches of Edmund Burke*, VI, *India: The Launching of the Hastings Impeachment, 1786–1788*, ed. P. J. Marshall (Oxford, 1991), 412; Mary Ann Hanway, *Andrew Stuart; or, The Northern Wanderer* (London, 1800), III, 188. See also [James Mackintosh], *Travels in Europe, Asia, and Africa . . .* (London, 1783), republished as "A Curious Journal, Descriptive of Anglo-Asiatic Manners," in *Asylum or Weekly Miscellany*, I (Glasgow, 1794), 75–78. On British tropes, see Durba Ghosh, *Sex and the Family in Colonial India: The Making of Empire* (Cambridge, 2006), 56; Kate Teltscher, *India Inscribed: European and British Writing on India, 1600–1800* (Delhi, 1995), 38–68. On these tropes in America, see Mark L. Kamrath, "An 'Inconceivable Plea-

Plate 18. Anthony Cardon after Robert Home, *Anthony Lambert*. London, 1806.
Stipple engraving. Harvard Art Museums / Fogg Museum, Gift of Belinda L. Randall
from the collection of John Witt Randall, R7647. Photo: Imaging Department
© President and Fellows of Harvard College

Nevertheless, the proportion of inventories for Britons in Calcutta containing hookahs nearly doubled between the 1760s and the 1820s, with most of this growth happening after cut glass hookahs entered the market in force in the 1780s. In the 1760s, the hookahs in British inventories were made from colored glass, pewter, silver, and bidree. By the 1790s, cut glass accounted for 12 percent of hookahs, rising to 19 percent in the 1820s, making it the most common material. Another portion, particularly of the latter decades, listed glass bottoms that might have been cut. Shifts in the types of hookahs ordered by experienced India captain Charles Chisholme for his outbound glass investments further document the trend toward cut glass. In 1778, he selected thirty-eight enameled and blue hookahs similar to the Indian style and only nine of the more expensive cut bottoms. By the turn to the nineteenth century, he ordered only cut class hookahs. The famous firm of Nuenburg and Nash provided several East India captains with a range of high-end glassware. It sold fifteen "Elegant Cut Glass Hooka Bottoms" to a single East India Company captain in 1801. The bottoms ranged in value, at prime cost, from £1.10 to nearly £4 each. The captain bought thirty-eight cut glass and silver muffineers for only slightly more than one hookah. In Calcutta, Nellmony Shaw ordered "Glassware from Messrs Lee and Burk" of London, including "24 Hooka Bottoms from £1.12 to £2 each," eighty shades, sixty-four lamps, and a range of table glassware. Shaw paid an advance of 50 percent and expected to receive the goods in about twenty-two months. In addition to significant growth in the market among Britons in India, some such orders were undoubtedly intended for Indians adopting the British style.[18]

---

sure' and the *Philadelphia Minerva: Erotic Liberalism, Oriental Tales, and the Female Subject in Periodicals of the Early Republic,*" *American Periodicals: A Journal of History, Criticism, and Bibliography,* XIV (2004), 3–34. Not everyone agreed that tropical climates made people sexual. James Johnson argued that this popular notion was simply an excuse to allow Britons to be profligate in India; see Johnson, *The Influence of Tropical Climates on European Constitutions; to Which Is Added Tropical Hygiene; or, The Preservation of Health in All Hot Climates* (Philadelphia, 1821), II, 287.

18. Charles Chisholme, bought from Cox Farquharson and Co., Jan. 26, 1778, MS 5462, fols. 63–64, NLS; Anthony Farrington, *A Biographical Index of East India Company Maritime Service Officers, 1600–1834* (London, 1999), 147. For examples of surviving orders, see Invoice Book, 1801, and Nellmony Shaw's Commission of Europe Goods, Dec. 26, 1801, Thomas Britten Chancery Papers, C114/82/45, NA; Rasterry Dot, List of Europe Goods, Thomas Britten Chancery Papers, C114/82/45, NA. On bidree, see Benjamin Heyne, "An Account of the Biddery (Vidri) Ware in India," *Asiatic Journal and Monthly Register for British India and Its Dependencies* (London), III (January–June 1817), 220–222. On prices, see also "The Price of Glass Goods, at the White Friars Glass House," July 6, 1812, MS 3115, Museum

Plate 19.
Hookah Bottom,
England. 1820s.
Cut glass.
22.5 cm. × 17 cm.
C.117–1998.
© Victoria and
Albert Museum,
London

A surviving early-nineteenth-century cut glass hookah bottom at London's Victoria and Albert Museum shows the extent to which cutters transferred patterns invented for British glasses, bowls, and decanters to hookahs (Plate 19). The hookah bottom incorporated four of the British cutting patterns fashionable at the time: sharp raised diamonds near the mouth and around the top of the bowl, three layers of different hollow flutes around the bowl's flare, three sections of horizontal prism cuts around the bowl, and multiple star patterns on its large flat end. The raised diamonds and hollow flutes became popular in Britain in the second half of the eighteenth century. In the last quarter of the century, the star cut became popular on cruet bottle bases, and the application on the hookah clearly follows that fashion. Finally, prism cuts did not appear

---

of London. About one-fifth of the inventories in each decade did not detail construction material (Bengal Inventories).

until the early nineteenth century and enjoyed only a few decades of popularity. The prism cuts on this example show the speed at which British cutters applied newly fashionable domestic designs to hookahs for export. Such bottoms were also finished by London silversmiths with silver accents and chillums.[19]

British influence on hookah fashion extended beyond the pipe itself. Jean Duff (Lady Grant) and Jane Grant, for instance, carefully ordered a British hookah and accompanying carpet for Company servant James Grant (respectively, their son and brother), who was in Farrukhabad. Jane's knowledge of hookahs appears to have come from family members, including her brother. She discussed in detail precisely how British style could best be adapted to this Indian pleasure. The pipe should be London cut glass and bear James's seal. As for the carpet to place under it, Jane suggested that it should measure three feet by seventeen inches. "Some like a medallion at one end for the Hookah to stand on, and others prefer it plain, just the same as a rug for a Hearth only of a neater and more elegant Pattern than is deemed requisite for that purpose," she explained. Jane included a drawing of a suitable pattern. Such carpets, which appeared often with cut glass hookahs in inventories and in Calcutta newspaper advertisements, further fused British production with British-Indian style.[20]

Josiah Wedgwood, always attuned to opportunities to profit from British conceptions of style, hoped to develop markets for Wedgwood hookahs. Wedgwood and other British pottery, inspired by Chinese porcelain, had become extremely popular in Britain and America as well as among Britons in India in the last quarter of the eighteenth century. Wedgwood worked up a few Turkish hookah designs from drawings in 1773, hoping that his partner Thomas Bentley "may either find an opportunity of introducing them into that Empire, or prevail upon our own Good People to fall in love with them." In 1790, Wedgwood began producing basalt hookah bottoms on his own with silver borders. A variety of colored, cane,

19. Elville, *English and Irish Cut Glass*, 26–31. For an example of a complete hookah pipe made in London, see J. Gendall, Mr. Blades' Upper Show Room, c. 1820, John Johnson Collection: Trades and Professions 6 (45), Bodleian Libraries, University of Oxford.

20. Jane was almost certainly Lady Grant's daughter. Correspondence suggests that Jane had not been to India. Unfortunately, the drawing is now lost. See Jane Grant to Lady Grant, Dec. 12, 1803, GD248/194/2/56, NAS, William Grant to Lady Grant, Jan. 20, 1804, GD248/197/2/25. The British in India also purchased hookah carpets from the famous Belgian carpet industry. For examples of advertisements for hookah carpets from Britain and Belgium, see *Calcutta Morning Post*, Jan. 17, Feb. 7, 28, Oct. 1, 1812. Robert Stuart owned a specifically English hookah carpet, as did A. Thellusson (Bengal Inventories).

and jasperware bottoms with decorations matching standard Wedgwood lines soon followed. It is unclear if the hookahs gained much popularity as ornaments in British houses. Probate inventories, however, show that these bottoms never gained anything near the popularity of cut glass in India. The Wedgwood versions made from more ornamental materials used for decorative objects and vases, as opposed to glazed creamware or glass used for everyday dinner services, likely did not attract British consumers in India looking to use hookah bottoms alongside their cut glass wine decanters and drinking glasses. Additionally, an opaque bottom could not show off the bubbling water inside the pipe. Wedgwood's lack of success in the Indian hookah market points to the importance of hookahs as objects of use rather than ornament for Indians in Britain.[21]

Just as Britons in India bought cut glass hookah bottoms that matched their cut glass drinking services, they desired curry dishes to match their dinner tableware services. Here, Wedgwood had another opportunity. Curry dishes were essentially slyly relabeled tureens. India trade agents wrote to Wedgwood that "the India Captains" took "Macaroni Dishes for Curries—and for Curries also narrow oval Dishes with water pans" to add to plate sets for resale. The popularity of such dishes expanded dramatically over time. Less than 1 percent of Calcutta inventories contained at least one curry dish in the 1760s, rising to 25 percent in the 1790s and more than 40 percent in the 1820s. Queensware curry dishes made up approximately one-half of all such dishes, more than double the number of silver dishes, the second-most popular type. In a single 1801 order, Shaw requested fifty curry dishes to accompany fifty tureens, fifty beef-steak dishes, and two thousand queensware plates. To enable him to hawk packaged lots, he ordered an equal number of curry dishes to match the other serving ware. As with hookahs, British styles and brands mattered a great deal to the popularity of these dishes. Tulloh and Company in Calcutta, for example, boasted of "QUEEN'S WARE. / FROM WEDGWOOD AND BYREY" in the "latest and most fashionable patterns."[22]

21. Josiah Wedgwood to Thomas Bentley, Mar. 6, 1773, E35-18444, Keele University Special Collections and Archives, Staffordshire, Eng. See also Diana Edwards and Rodney Hampson, *English Dry-Bodied Stoneware: Wedgwood and Contemporary Manufacturers, 1774 to 1830* (Suffolk, Eng., 1998), 70, 95; William Milburn, *Oriental Commerce; Containing a Geographical Description of the Principal Places in the East Indies, China, and Japan, with Their Produce, Manufactures, and Trade* . . . (London, 1813), 115; Bengal Inventories. For the use of hookahs at mealtimes, see, for example, Williamson, *East India Vade-Mecum*, I, 229.

22. Begbie and Hunter to Wedgwood, Dec. 18, 1802, L117-22435, Keele University Special Collections and Archives; Nellmony Shaw's Commission of Europe Goods, Dec. 26, 1801,

British producers also applied British design and materials to palanquins in London, but they did so even more frequently in India. In the eighteenth century, London-built carriages had risen to the pinnacle of transportation fashion in Europe. In 1778, the soon-to-be member of Parliament Frederick Robinson described a state palanquin being built in London by Samuel Vaughan for the nabob of Arcot valued at £500. Vaughan employed "upwards of twenty workmen" at his sedan chair workshop. Robinson described the palanquin as being rather different from a European sedan chair. He explained it as a sort of "vis a vis with a long kind of proboscis before and behind," fitted with red morocco leather and "very fine bronze ornaments." The nabob had a well-known and insatiable desire for the most lavish British-made style. A British-built palanquin suggested great wealth and a direct connection to the newly powerful British regime. It is unclear whether London builders such as Vaughan were responsible for first adapting British design to palanquins, but in the 1780s palanquin design in India changed sharply.[23]

Britten Chancery Papers, NA; *Tulloh and Company Respectfully Beg Leave to Acquaint Their Friends and the Public, That They Have Received Their Extensive and Choice Investments of Europe Goods* (Calcutta, [1810]), 7. Nothing officially designated as a curry dish appeared in searches through many pattern books used by Wedgwood and his competitors or through Wedgwood's correspondence; see Greens, Clarks, and Co., *Designs of Sundry Articles, of Queen's or Cream-Coloured Earthenware* . . . (Leeds, 1794 and 1814); Christies, *A Catalogue of All the Valuable Stock in Trade and Select Private Collections of the Most Rare Scarce Specimens of Mr. Charles Bond, Chinaman* ([London], 1794); Wedgwood orders and pattern books examined in Keele University Special Collections and Archives, and at Wedgwood Museum and Visitor Centre, Stoke-on-Trent, England. Unfortunately, the material used to make about half of the curry dishes was not recorded. Of those dishes for which material was recorded, 57 percent was made from queensware (Bengal Inventories). Williamson explained that British creamware was more popular than chinaware in India; see Williamson, *East India Vade-Mecum*, I, 171–172.

23. William Bridges Adams, *English Pleasure Carriages* . . . (1837; rpt. London, 1971), viii. For an example of shipments to India, see Invoice from William and Tees Campbell to Charles Chisholme, Feb. 6, 1778, MS 5462, NLS. The invoice included one chariot and two phaetons valued at £484 to be shipped on Chisholme's captain's privilege on the Company ship *Gatton*. The safety of such large and valuable objects depended on careful packing. For imports, see General Account of Imports, Commercial Reports, IOR/P/174/13, 17, 22, 27, 32, 37, 42, BL. On the palanquin for the nabob of Arcot, see Testimony of Samuel Vaughan in the Trial of Jonathan Simpson, Theft: Simple Grand Larceny, Feb. 25, 1761 (t17610225-3), *Old Bailey Proceedings Online*, Feb. 11, 2006, www.oldbaileyonline.org; Frederick Robinson to Thomas Robinson, earl of Grantham and ambassador to Madrid, Dec. 8, 1778, 30/14/333/150, Wrest Park (Lucas) Manuscripts, Bedfordshire and Luton Archives and Record Service, Bedford. The nabob appears to have contracted Alexander Tod to order and ship the palanquin for him. Tod likely took it with him as part of his privilege trade as captain of the *General Barker* on his voyage from London in 1778. See *Papers Presented to the House*

BENAREES PALKEE .

Plate 20. Robert Temple, Benares Palkee [Fly Palanquin], Bombay Views and Costume. 1810–1811. WD 315, no. 83, BL. © The British Library Board

Back in the 1760s, most palanquins were fly palanquins, which looked like "a well contrived couch with pillows, and an arched canopy over it; in these they sit, or lie at their full length," like the one shown in Plate 20. The remainder were chair palanquins, armchairs carried on men's shoulders over short distances, similar to an open version of a sedan chair in

of Commons from the East India Company concerning the Late Nabob of the Carnatic (1802; rpt. [London], 1807), 130; Anthony Farrington, Catalogue of East India Company Ships' Journals and Logs, 1600–1834 (London, 1999), 262. On the nabob's character, see J. D. Gurney, "Fresh Light on the Character of the Nawab of Arcot," in Anne Whiteman, J. S. Bromley, and P. G. M. Dickson, eds., Statesmen, Scholars, and Merchants: Essays in Eighteenth-Century History Presented to Dame Lucy Sutherland (Oxford, 1973), 220–241. Although the official statistics do not itemize palanquins, between 1800 and 1830 makers of British sedan chairs and carriages annually exported to Bengal palanquins, coaches, chariots, and phaetons worth an average of at least SR 80,000, or approximately £10,000. The widely varying values of different types of conveyances make it difficult to estimate the number of carriages this figure represented. Regardless of the exact breakdown, it likely amounted to between one and two hundred carriages and palanquins. See General Account of Imports, Commercial Reports, IOR/P/174/13, 17, 22, 27, 32, 37, 42, BL. The average exchange rate is based on Asiya Siddiqi, ed., Trade and Finance in Colonial India, 1750–1860 (Delhi, 1995), 57.

Europe or America. According to East India Company director David Scott, in the 1760s palanquins had still been the preserve of heads of state and British elites, but by 1786 "chair Palanquins . . . were not [sic] longer confined to the English Gentlemen, but likewise were common with all the Native writers under them, and in the public Offices, and others of every profession who were of any note, whether Portuguese, Armenian, Hindoo, Musleman, Persee, Arabian, or what else." Scott discussed palanquins while considering the extent to which Indians could be expected to become a valuable market for items of, as he said, "the English fashion." He positioned palanquins alongside carriages, mirrors, and English furniture as particularly English goods, dependent for their popularity on the production skills of Englishmen and the tastes of Britons in India. Palanquins had become so popular among Britons in India that Scott came to see the once-elite Indian conveyance as English. Indeed, after the fly and chair palanquin, the newest form of palanquin was shaped significantly by British taste.[24]

In the last quarter of the eighteenth century, British immigrants to Calcutta trained in European carriage building applied the materials, structures, and decorations that they and their British customers knew to palanquin construction. As India expert James Forbes explained, "Late improvements by the Europeans settled in Bengal" had transformed the palanquin. Shops such as William Lang's offered "Carriages and Palanquins of all sorts, made and repaired," to the large population of traveling Company servants. British carriage builders replaced open sides with wooden paneling and added doors fitted with windows and venetian blinds. They replaced bent bamboo poles and fabric, conventionally used to make a sun canopy, with a ceiling made from rectangular wooden framing and panels. Similarly, as in carriage construction, builders added paint and varnish finishes. These new palanquins, such as the one in Plate 21, came to be known most frequently as "mehanah" palanquins. James East, a magistrate in Calcutta, described his mehanah palanquin as "a machine not much unlike a coffin." East's "coffin" came equipped with "sliding doors on each side." His reclined posture and the palanquin's position, "supported by a pole fore and aft on the shoulders of four bearers," maintained

---

24. Mr. Scott's Paper to the Court of Directors, Papers on Private Trade, 1800, IOR/L/MAR/1/26, fol. 315, 316v, BL. On traveling by palanquin, see, for example, Burges, *Indostan Letters*, 11; John Fransham, *The Entertaining Traveller; or, The Whole World in Miniature; Giving a Description of Every Thing Necessary and Curious* (London, 1767), II, 55. For a description of the chair palanquin, see Williamson, *East India Vade-Mecum*, I, 316–318.

A MEYAUNA PALKEE.

Plate 21. Robert Temple, Mayauna Palkee [Mehanah Palanquin], Bombay Views and Costume. 1810–1811. WD 315, no. 84, BL. © The British Library Board

links with the older Indian fly palanquin. Additionally, builders made "a compound of our sedan chair with the body of a chariot" especially for British women in India. The deeper seat provided a more respectably upright and modest position in public. British-Indian palanquins also became personally distinctive. The builder and diarist Richard Blechynden fretted that he could not travel on a covert visit to his Indian lover because her family would recognize his conveyance.[25]

25. James Forbes, *Oriental Memoirs: Selected and Abridged from a Series of Familiar Letters Written during Seventeen Years Residence in India* . . . (London, 1813), plate XVI (caption), IV, 356; William Lang advertisement, *World*, Nov. 12, 1791, 1; James Buller East to Frederick Sylvester North Douglas, Aug. 5, 1816, MSS Eur. A145, BL; Richard Blechynden, Diary, Nov. 21, 1794, 183, MS 45591, BL. On English carriage construction, see Adams, *English Pleasure Carriages*, 75–76, 141–151. On mehanah style and palanquins for women, see An Officer for Fire-Side Travellers at Home [Moyle Sherer], *Sketches of India* . . . (London, 1821), 10; Williamson, *East India Vade-Mecum*, I, 319–320, 322. At the turn of the century, Calcutta boasted eight coach-making firms, all of which appear to have been owned and operated by British immigrants and many of which also produced palanquins; see John Mathison and Alexander Way Mason, *An East-India Register and Directory, for 1803*, 2d ed. (London, 1803), 100–136. A detailed census of Indian businesses in the city, in contrast, in-

Many fashionable palanquin decorations and parts were imported from British manufacturers, replacing previous Indian accessories. Decorative and expensive silver and crimson tassels in the Indian taste had given way to the similarly expensive British taste for morocco leather, silver mountings, lamps, lace, painted details, and spring suspensions. One East India Company ship from London brought "Five pair of the most fashionable full plated lamps for Chariots and Palanquins . . . 6 setts of White pull down Locks comp. for Palanquins . . . 6 setts of Gentlemans Palanquin Lace and trimmings of fashionable patterns No 7612 . . . two setts of Ladies Palanquin lace and trimmings complete of fashionable patterns No 13614." The pattern numbers suggest that the "Palanquin Lace" based on London carriage fashion was regularly made in Britain specifically for the palanquin trade. These items amounted to nearly £100. Builders also imported mass-produced British metal and glass parts. Calcutta coach builder Alexander Sunderson, for example, had seven sections of "palankeen glass," many "palankeen hinges," and a lot of plated "palankeen rollers." Altogether, a typical mehanah palanquin was worth approximately as much as a horse-drawn phaeton. Sunderson's estate auction included a completed "Handsome Mahana Palanquin lined with Satin Hair Cloth and Hair Mattross," which sold for SR 235, or the sizable sum of approximately £30.[26]

---

cluded no Indian-owned coach or palanquin businesses, though Indians certainly worked for the British firms. Some of the 150 Indian carpenters that appeared in the census might also have made palanquins. See "Account of the Different Trades Carried on in Calcutta, by Native Merchants, and Shopkeepers, with an Estimate of the Amount of the Annual Sales of Each Avocation," IOR/P/174/13, n.p., BL. Calcutta carriage makers applied similar tactics to the reinvention of Indian elephant howdahs. Charles D'Oyly explained: "The native howdas are square wooden frames, about eighteen inches deep, with bedding, and pillows behind and on each side. They sit in them cross-legged. Those used by the European sportsmen are like the body of a buggy, some with hoods and a high splashboard in front, against which they rest when standing." Several plates show the buggy-like characteristics; see [D'Oyly], *Tom Raw, the Griffin: A Burlesque Poem, in Twelve Cantos: Illustrated by Twenty-five Engravings, Descriptive of the Adventures of a Cadet in the East India Company's Service* (London, 1828), 247.

26. Harry Verelst to John Cartier, Apr. 27, 1761, MSS Eur. F218/79, fols. 20–20v, BL. Such tassels appear repeatedly in Bengal probate inventories during the early 1760s valued at up to SR 270. These tassels often cost considerably more than the palanquins that they were attached to; see Bengal Inventories. For the new British materials, see Invoice Book, 1801, Thomas Britten Chancery Papers, C114/82/45, NA; Alexander Sunderson Estate Auction, Dec. 22, 1798, IOR/L/AG/34/27/21, no. 41, BL. Palanquin lace also appeared in Calcutta price currents, further highlighting the size of the Calcutta palanquin-building trade and the importance of London part suppliers. See, for example, Price Current for Europe Goods,

At the turn to the nineteenth century, mehanah ownership was a requirement of respectable British society in India. The recently arrived Company servant James McNabb, for example, wrote home from Patna, "I must have a palanquin, so away to the coach Maker's and an amazing handsome one is now building for me." McNabb's order attested to the importance of a distinctive and elegant palanquin made with personal cues in the British coach style. He continued, "My arms are to be painted on it (which I have found out) and various other elegancies about it, which are really requisite for a *man* of such *importance* as *I* am in this country." The records for the dead show the popularity of these "coffins" among the living. Bengal probate inventories included few mehanah palanquins in the 1760s, amounting to less than 2 percent of all palanquins listed. By the 1790s, however, mehanah palanquins accounted for 40 percent of palanquins described. Additionally, "Hindoostani," a term that does not appear in records from the 1760s, was used in the 1790s as a descriptor for a few palanquins. These examples were likely fly palanquins built by Indians and not in the British style.[27]

The application of British design and techniques to palanquins helped increase their popularity among Britons in India, but it did not make them immune from associations with corruption and tyranny in Britain and America. The reclined position of the palanquin rider combined with the requirement for human bearers made the palanquin an ideal metaphor for Indian oppression. In his 1783 geography, William Fordyce Mavor singled out palanquin riding. Under his palanquin canopy, wrote Mavor, "the chief of Indostan indulges his native indolence; and whilst the wretched slaves, who support this unworthy burden, totter under it's weight, he . . . sinks into slumbers, unmindful of those who groan under the intolerable and disgraceful load." Similarly, in the 1785 morality play *The Maternal Sister,* the spoiled Miss Fowler explained, "I hate to walk on foot, and to ride in a *hackney* coach is intolerable." She desired to go to India, where, "instead of being obliged to make my own things, as I do now, shall have all my

---

Calcutta, Oct. 10, 1810, MS 10922, NLS. On phaeton pricing, see Invoice from William and Tees Campbell, Feb. 6, 1778, Charles Chisholme Papers, MS 5462, NLS; see also, Thomas Blossom, 1808–1826, MS 31621, Guildhall Library, London. The exchange rate is based on Siddiqi, ed., *Trade and Finance,* 57; Furber, *John Company at Work,* 349–350.

27. McNabb to his parents, Sept. 1, 1806, MSS Eur. F206/1, BL; Adams, *English Pleasure Carriages,* 212. The importance of coats of arms in English carriage decoration recurs frequently in Adams and Co., Estimates Letter Book, Acc 324, Westminster Archives, London. Ownership patterns derived from Bengal Inventories.

work done for me, and shall have slaves to wait on me, and carry me in a palanquin." The *Maternal Sister* was republished in New Haven in 1791, as America's India trade expanded.[28]

A report on "Asiatic Fortunes" reprinted on both sides of the Atlantic told of young Company servants "on their fine horses and carried about in sumptuous palanquins" influencing one another and going on to accumulate their fortunes "by every method of rapacity." They then return to Britain, purchase seats in Parliament, and vote for corruption and oppression. The palanquin prominently carried them literally and metaphorically into greed and tyranny. The balloonist in the fictional *Aerostatic Spy* likewise observed a corrupted and exploitative British nabob in India who "strutted with an air of consequence, and threw himself into his palanquin, attended by guards and a numerous train." His enjoyment of his princely palanquin and seraglio tied into the common associations of India with luxurious despotism and lasciviousness.[29]

Similar usages in works without significant content on India suggest the extent to which associations between palanquins and despotism were widely understood in the English-speaking Atlantic. Henry St. John, Viscount Bolingbroke, for instance, wrote that God could be seen as either a noninterventionist king watching the world from heaven or "like an Eastern monarch, carried about in his palanquin, neither seeing his subjects, nor seen by them, familiar with a few of his favorites, terrible to all the rest of his people, and known only by the pomp with which he is served, and by the severity of his government." Bolingbroke's writings influenced John Adams, Thomas Jefferson, and James Madison and had been widely read in North America for decades. In another example, an anonymous author attacking the election proceedings in the County of Down, Ireland, imagined the gentry carrying their local "despot" on their noses, "sweating under the enormous load, like the miserable Indians beneath the palan-

28. [William Fordyce Mavor], *The Geographical Magazine; or, A New, Copious, Compleat, and Universal System of Geography . . . by William Frederick Martyn*, 2 vols. (London, 1782), I, 263; P. I., *Dramatic Pieces Calculated to Exemplify the Mode of Conduct Which Will Render Young Ladies Both Amiable and Happy* . . . (London, [1785?]), II, 25, and (New Haven, Conn., 1791), II, 14.

29. "From the Morning Chronicle: Asiatic Fortunes," *General Advertiser and Political, Commercial, and Literary Journal* (Philadelphia), Jan. 26, 1791, [2]; *The Aerostatic Spy; or, Excursions with an Air Balloon; Exhibiting a View of Various Countries in Different Parts of the World; and a Variety of Characters in Real Life . . . by an Aerial Traveller* (London, 1785), I, 108–109.

quin of the proud, pampered Nabob, who oppresses them—Hail! Hail!" Palanquins as a trope of tyranny were well known.[30]

British manufacturers did not try to sell palanquin parts, tureens labeled as curry dishes, or cut glass hookah bottoms to either domestic or U.S. consumers. For consumers in Britain and America, palanquins built in London appeared just as unsuited for their consumption as those built anywhere else. David Scott's palanquins were "English" only in India. Different products, then, were succeeding in different marketplaces, though the overall pattern was one of increasing the exports of British manufactures. Birmingham-made palanquin parts and accessories, London-built palanquins, Wedgwood curry dishes, and London-made hookahs offered their owners claims on high metropolitan style—even when these objects had no metropolitan market. Increasing ownership of palanquins, hookahs, and curry dishes among Britons in India suggests that this British veneer made such goods seem more attractive and respectable, at least to Britons in India and to British producers. By applying British taste to Indian objects, British producers turned the cultural difference between Britain and colonial India to their advantage. In Britain and America, palanquins and hookahs were often pilloried as evidence of lasciviousness, corruption, and tyranny and remained rarities suitable only for collectors' cabinets crammed with alien and wonderful curiosities. Ironically, these reinvented products served, not to domesticate India's novelty, but to ossify a particular sense of difference between India and the British Atlantic.

Production and Monopoly

Only in the last third of the eighteenth century had the common belief among Protestant Britons in their political, religious, and moral superi-

---

30. Henry St. John, Viscount Bolingbroke, "LXXVI," in *The Philosophical Works of the Late Right Honorable Henry St. John, Lord Viscount Bolingbroke* (London, 1754), V, 185; Isaac Kramnick, "Corruption in Eighteenth-Century English and American Political Discourse," in Richard K. Matthews, ed., *Virtue, Corruption, and Self-Interest: Political Values in the Eighteenth Century* (Bethlehem, Pa., 1994), 56–57. Unfortunately, it is not clear whether Adams, Jefferson, or Madison had read this particular Bolingbroke essay. Jefferson certainly owned it. See William D. Liddle, "'A Patriot King, or None': Lord Bolingbroke and the American Renunciation of George III," *Journal of American History*, LXV (1979), 956, 969; Ralph Ketcham, *Presidents above Party: The First American Presidency, 1789* (Chapel Hill, N.C., 1984), 3, 56–57, 73, 94–95, 97, 99, 100–101, 106, 115, 202. For the example from Ireland, see *An Historical Account of the Late Election of Knights of the Shire for the County of Down; Together with the Petition to Parliament, Complaining of an Undue Election and Return for the Said County* . . . ([Dublin?], 1784), 82.

ority over Catholics, Muslims, and Hindus begun to align with growing, though hardly mature, British manufacturing strength in goods other than woolens. The British production of cottons and, to a lesser extent, other goods such as glassware, creamware, and palanquins combined with conquest in India and the arrival of newly independent American traders stimulated a reappraisal of the imperial compromise that had been negotiated from a similar conjuncture in the early eighteenth century. A range of Britons, including manufacturers, India goods dealers, Company leaders, private merchants, and imperial administrators, debated both old and new solutions to three major, long-standing, and interconnected problems: protecting British manufacturers, transitioning the Company to a trade in raw materials from India, and stopping interlopers and smugglers. Between 1787 and 1792, the Board of Trade and Henry Dundas, a leading voice in the Board of Control for India and in 1791 appointed by Prime Minister William Pitt as home secretary, accumulated information from many of these individuals and interest groups and contemplated solutions. Indeed, during these years Dundas would form many of his ideas on the India trade and the Company that he would invoke in the charter renewal negotiations in 1793.[31]

In 1788, Robert Parker warned muslin manufacturer Samuel Oldknow from London, "People seem here quite of Opinion Mr Pitt is circumstanced with the Company in Leaden Hall St. and receiving so much Interest and influence from that Trade you will have much to combat." The Company was still influential and valuable, and such reports encouraged the manufacturers to aggressively expound their difficulties and proposed solutions widely across the government and public. The cotton manufacturing interest in Britain had become sizable, but it still complained to the Board of Trade of the insufficiency of the already substantial duties and continuing prohibitions on Indian fabrics. Part of the difficulty came from technical barriers, especially in muslin production, and another part came from the East India Company's improved negotiating position with

31. In addition to the question of the monopoly, Dundas was considering a plan to have the British government take over much of the administration of India from the Company. Cornwallis replied that such a plan would bankrupt the Company, destroy the quality of Indian manufactures, redirect the trade away from London, and eliminate the means of moving tribute to Britain and collecting duty revenue from fine cottons. He conceded the export trade to India alone might suit being opened. See Henry Dundas to Lord Cornwallis, Aug. 8, 1789, and Nov. 13, 1790, Letters of Dundas to Cornwallis and his successors as Governor General of India, 1786–1799, MS 3387, 98, 163–164, NLS; Cornwallis to Dundas, Apr. 2, 1790, Lord Cornwallis: Letters to Mr. Dundas, 1786–1794, MS 3385, 329–339, NLS.

local weavers and merchants post conquest. The Company increased its ability to monopolize orders, standardize quality, enforce contract terms, and drive down prices. Sounding similar to English woolen and silk producers nearly a century earlier, more than one hundred cotton manufacturers from Lancaster, York, Chester, Stafford, and Nottingham told the Board in 1788 that their "valuable branches of Trade are rapidly on the decline, which has reduced many Families from circumstances of affluence to a state of insolvency, and thousands of poor people dependent on these Manufactures are in a condition little better than starving." Their situation caused both "individual distress and national loss." They had no doubt "the immense importations of similar manufactured Goods by the East India Company, which are sold at their sales much below the cost price of British made Goods" were the cause. According to the manufacturers, large quantities of India goods avoided duties by being passed off fraudulently as British.[32]

The manufacturers proposed to the Board of Trade that the Company be prohibited from importing piece goods and handkerchiefs beyond the levels reached in 1787 and that the Company should import raw materials instead. They pressed the Board of Trade for help in creating new cotton wool supplies from both the West and East Indies. To encourage the transfer of production from India to Britain, they requested that the Company import a minimum of five hundred thousand pounds of the "finest Bengal cotton, in the cleanest and most perfect state for manufacture" each year. A tract produced by the manufacturing interest made a similar case for raw cotton and silk as well as indigo and madder for making dyes. As had a long line of imperial promoters and domestic producers since the late sixteenth century, the manufacturers explained that the nation benefited most from importing Indian raw materials and exporting British-made goods.[33]

---

32. Robert Parker to Samuel Oldknow, Feb. 23, 1788, SO/1/215, Samuel Oldknow Papers, John Rylands Library, Manchester; Petition to the Board of Trade, Apr. 3, 1788, Liverpool Papers, CCII, Add. MS 38391, 72–73, BL; "The Memorial of the Undersigned Muslin and Callico Manufacturers and Cotton Spinners in the Counties of Lancaster, York, Chester, Stafford, and Nottingham" to the Right Honourable Commissioners for the Affairs of India, IOR/A/1/85A, n.p., BL. To help avoid customs fraud, British law already required British producers to stitch blue threads on one fabric edge, while tasking Indian customs officials to mark East Indian cloth with a Company stamp; see "Hearings on Commerce with France and the Negotiation of a New Treaty," Feb. 24, 1786, Liverpool Papers, CC, Add. MS 38389, 197–198/fol. 99, BL. For the Company's position with weavers, see Prasannan Parthasarathi, *The Transition to a Colonial Economy: Weavers, Merchants, and Kings in South Asia, 1720–1800* (New York, 2001), 78–100, 135–148.

33. "Propositions from Delegates of the Manufacturers of Callicoes and Muslins Pre-

Some manufacturers suggested that greater success would come not only by copying the East India Company's fabric or increasing import barriers and encouraging colonial production of raw materials but also by establishing a central wholesale distribution point for British fabric on the model of the Company's London sales. The Board of Trade conducted a series of meetings with manufacturers from throughout Britain to assess the plan. Merchants from Glasgow, for example, resolved that a consolidated sale of British cotton cloth would "support a fair Competition in the Home Market, which it is not possible to do at present while the East India Company enjoy the superior Advantage of a Public Sale, by which the whole European Buyers are collected together." Perhaps they also expected that it would reduce the advantages of Manchester and Liverpool, where British cotton manufacturing and export were centered. Manufacturers would not be required to participate in the sale and could make other deals on their own. Yet the town of Paisley's manufacturers complained that, despite legal opportunities for side deals, the market prices would be set at the consolidated sale and they would still need to travel to London frequently "to see Fashions and get new patterns." More stridently, Manchester's manufacturers wrote, "Words are inadequate to impress upon Their Lordships' Minds the general Disapprobation which this visionary Scheme has received from every Order and Description of people." They had much less to gain from consolidating their sales with those of Glasgow and other distant producers. Indeed, Manchester's manufacturers did not want support for either Scots or Indian producers, much as England's woolen weavers had argued against Scottish linen and Indian calico a century before.[34]

---

sented to the Court of Directors and the Board of Trade: Letter #1," June 2, 1788, Liverpool Papers, CCII, Add. MS 38391, 106–107, BL (Glasgow manufacturers made a similar request for cotton in 1793; see Committee of Manufacturers of Glasgow to the Court of Directors, May 1, 1793, IOR/A/2/11, fols. 145–146, BL); *Observations Relative to the Resources of the East India Company for Productive Remittance; and the National Loss Occasioned by the Importation of the Same Species of Cotton Goods Which Can Be Manufactured in Great Britain* (London, 1788), 1–11, NA. The East India Company directors responded that the manufacturers had no right to tell them how much they could trade and in what articles. They were furious that the manufacturers had considered these points "settled." See "Copy of the Court's Memorial on the Cotton Manufacture, in the Year 1788," *Report of the Select Committee . . . upon the Subject of the Cotton Manufacture*, 10–11. For more on cotton wool supplies, see Michael M. Edwards, *The Growth of the British Cotton Trade, 1780–1815* (Manchester, 1967), 75–89.

34. "Report against Granting the Prayer of Two Petitions or a Charter of Incorporation to Certain Persons Proposing to Form an Association for Promoting a More Extensive Vend

Pitt's appointed leader on the India question, Dundas, and Francis Baring, elected as Company deputy chairman in 1791 and chairman in 1792, received considerable information on the competition between the domestic manufacturers and the Company from the ideally positioned Thomas Brown. Brown was a major dealer in the "India line," with twenty to eighty thousand pounds in India goods on hand at all times; he knew several Manchester cotton manufacturers, and his son Joseph worked for the Company in Calcutta as the superintendent of piece goods. Brown's position against the manufacturers was no doubt influenced by his own and his son's businesses, but he solidly backed his arguments that further protections for domestic manufacturers were unnecessary. In 1791, Brown wrote, "I am convinced from information that I rely on" that the prices the Company could obtain for its muslin at its London sales would soon be far less than the muslin cost. He thought "it probable the consumption of India Muslins will annually grow less and soon die a Natural Death." The problem was not declining consumption of muslin; it was the rapidly declining prices and improving qualities of British imitations. Brown wrote, "I have had customers from several parts of the Kingdom within the last three months who would not buy a Piece of India who two years since would buy no British." Cotton fabrics, he explained, had driven woolens largely out of the markets to the benefit of a few wealthy cotton industrialists. The "intelligent manufacturers" had told him that they had a multitude of advantages over Indian producers.[35]

Brown could not understand why the government would consider further protecting British manufacturers, who benefited from the triple advantages of cheaper thread, lower distribution costs, and proximity to market demands. He collected information showing that mechanized spinning in Britain made thread twelve and a half times cheaper than in India. Brown's son provided details on fine muslin production that Brown forwarded to Baring. In contrast to the mechanized system used to spin thread in Britain, Indian combers used fish jaws in a lengthy combing and spinning process that could be performed only during the rainy season lest the thread break. The workers made a paltry one rupee per month. Depending on several factors, the thread would come out in different thick-

of British Cotton Manufactures," July 23, 1788, Liverpool Papers, CCV, Add. MS 38394, 55, 65, 78/fols. 28r, 33r, 39v, BL.

35. Thomas Brown to Francis Baring, September 1791, Henry Dundas, 1st Viscount Melville Collection, MS 1064, fols. 58r–59v, NLS.

nesses that the weavers needed to sort before they could begin weaving. An average weaver spent four months to produce a twenty-yard piece of superfine tanjeb. The cloth then needed washing, bleaching, stitching with gold thread, and beating with shells to create an even gloss. Although British industry had not yet matched the finest and most expensive India muslin, "the lower sorts are preferred to India, from the goodness of the make and are less troublesome to the retail Draper who consequently now recommends them in preference to India." Additionally, interest, duties, and freight added 42.5 percent to the cost of India goods imported into Britain. The proximity of British manufacturers to their consumers also gave them "power to comply with the Fashion of the moment . . . a wonderful advantage over those of India." Brown explained that many Indians were now British subjects, but they could not afford to buy British goods unless they continued to have employment making fine muslin. He wondered whether the government would fully abandon successful "old systems of import and export."[36]

While the Company faced the emerging problem of reduced demand for its Indian fabric, it also faced the opposite but related problem of paying for its popular Chinese tea. In the 1760s, tea had challenged textiles as the Company's highest value export, and in generating net profits tea had steamed ahead. The Chinese, like the Indians, had never wanted many British goods, but by exporting raw materials, including cotton, from British India and using silver brought by private traders the Company had exported only a small amount of silver from London to China since 1772. By 1785, however, the Company had run up a growing credit account in Canton, and the private exports of silver were draining Bengal. The Bengal government also correctly expected that the 1784 Commutation Act's reduction of tea duties from 119 to 12.5 percent would increase demand for Company tea in Britain, which would need to be paid for by increasing silver exports from London and India to China. The Company, therefore, explored multiple trading solutions to reduce its need for credit in Canton without transferring silver from India or Britain. These solutions depended on finding Indian goods that the Chinese wanted, much as the

36. "A Comparison between the Cotton Spinning in India, and in Great Britain 1791," Henry Dundas, 1st Viscount Melville Collection, MS 1064, fols. 61r–62v, NLS, Brown to his father, "Description of the Cotton Plant, the Mode of Culture, etc. and a Statement of the Labour and Cost Necessary to Its Manufacture," Calcutta, Aug. 19, 1791, fols. 73r–78v, Brown, "Further Information of the Advantages This Country Possesses over India in the Spinning of Cotton Thread," Apr. 9, 1792, fols. 64r–66r.

Company might soon need to find new Indian goods that Britons, Europeans, and Americans would want instead of cotton fabric.[37]

Opening a trade to China from the west coast of North America offered one new means to avoid exporting silver from London or India. The Spanish had for centuries operated a regional trade using silver galleons between the Pacific coast of South America and Manila. The Pacific coast of North America had little silver. In his journal published in 1783 about James Cook's third voyage, however, American born John Ledyard explained that they had traded with the local people for inexpensive furs, including sea otter and beaver, which, they were surprised to learn, the Chinese would pay handsomely for. James Hanna, a private trader, entered into the British Pacific pelt trade in 1785, before the Company, by using the Portuguese flag and with the support of Britons in India. Hanna proved the value of the trade by sailing from Canton to Nootka Sound, trading with the Nootka Indians for 560 sea otter pelts and selling the pelts back in Canton for a profit of $20,600. The East India Company itself, however, had also licensed expeditions from London and Bombay. When Hanna returned to Nootka Sound in 1786, he found that James Strange had come from India and purchased nearly all of the available pelts. In 1787, British newspapers celebrated the great advantage that Canada would give the empire in this new trade. American newspapers reprinted the story in the spring of that year.[38]

37. For import values, see K. N. Chaudhuri, *The Trading World of Asia and the English East India Company, 1660–1760* (Cambridge, 1978), 538–539, 540–548. Company-calculated profit data begins in 1771 and is for all goods from India and China, respectively. It is useful here nonetheless because fabric and tea accounted for the major respective exports, and tea was already producing much larger profits by this time. See IOR/L/AG/18/2/1, 17–18, BL. On China and silver, see H. V. Bowen, "Bullion for Trade, War, and Debt-Relief: British Movements of Silver to, around, and from Asia, 1760–1833," *Modern Asian Studies*, XLIV (2010), 453–454, 457–459, 471; Indrajit Ray, *Bengal Industries and the British Industrial Revolution (1757–1857)* (New York, 2011), 31–34.

38. John Ledyard, *A Journal Of Captain Cook's Last Voyage to the Pacific Ocean, and in Quest of a North-West Passage, between Asia and America; Performed in the Years 1776, 1777, 1778, and 1779* (Hartford, Conn., 1783), 70; Clarence L. Ver Steeg, "First United States Ship to China," *Pacific Historical Review*, XXII (1953), 5–6; "London, April 6," *Charleston Morning Post and Daily Advertiser*, June 5, 1787, [2]. The Russians had already taken such furs to China, but few if any Britons or Americans were aware. See James R. Gibson, *Otter Skins, Boston Ships, and China Goods: The Maritime Fur Trade of the Northwest Coast, 1785–1841* (Montreal, 1992), 12–13, 22–23. For more on Ledyard, see Edward G. Gray, *The Making of John Ledyard: Empire and Ambition in the Life of an Early American Traveler* (New Haven, Conn., 2007). On Hanna, see W. Kaye Lamb and Tomás Bartroli, "James Hanna and John Henry Cox: The First Maritime Fur Trader and His Sponsor," *BC Studies*, no. 84 (Winter

Remapping Production, Rethinking Monopolies

Indeed, American merchants then used Spanish support to move through the door to the China trade from the Pacific northwest of North America that British adventurers had opened. Richard Henry Lee wrote, "It seems to me that N. America is going, if we are prudent, to be the Entrepôt between the East Indies and Spanish America." Six American investors, led by Boston's Joseph Barrell, sent out two vessels to Nootka Sound under the command of John Kendrick, arriving in September 1788. They wintered in the sound, and, in March 1789, a Spanish naval ship appeared under the command of Esteban José Martínez. Martínez seized three British vessels for trading at Nootka Sound, which sat on land claimed by Spain. Kendrick, however, convinced him not to seize the American vessels. The Spanish looked kindly on the independent Americans and allowed Barrell's vessels and those that followed it to trade throughout the Pacific northwest. Kendrick's own son converted to Catholicism, changed his name from John to Juan, and served on Spanish vessels. The British pushed Spain to allow full British activity in the region in the Nootka Convention of 1790, but the Company was already expanding a different trade to solve its Chinese specie problem.[39]

The Bengal government had launched an aggressive and successful program to enlarge and dominate the opium trade to China from India, avoiding a Pacific crossing and making use of Company territory. Asking for the support of the directors, they wrote, "We are determined . . . to apply the Proceeds of the Opium Manufacture in future to the exclusive Business of your China Trade." By strengthening the Company opium trade, they hoped to reduce both its risk and the export of specie to China. In the 1790s, exports of opium and cotton reversed the silver flow back to India.[40]

Even better, some Company officials explained, the Company might begin cultivating Chinese commodities in India so that they did not need to be purchased in China. China would then need to pay for its opium with even more silver into the Company's coffers. The Bengal Board of Trade proposed the cultivation of "China Turmerick," using imported seeds or

1989–1990), 6–9, 17–19, 27. On Strange, see "A Narative of a Voyage to the Northwest Coast of America Most Respectfully Inscribed [to] the Honble Major General Sir Archibald Campbell Governor in Council Fort St. George by James Strange of Madras," IOR/H/800, BL.

39. Richard Henry Lee to Washington, July 15, 1787, in Crackel, ed., *The Papers of George Washington Digital Edition;* F. W. Howay, "John Kendrick and His Sons," *Quarterly of the Oregon Historical Society,* XXIII (1922), 296.

40. Fort William to the Court of Directors, Apr. 29, 1785, *Fort William–India House Correspondence,* XV, 416–420; see also X, 22–23, 28.

roots. The Board explained, "It is certainly better that any article which is carried from China should, if procurrable in Bengal, on terms as advantageous, or nearly so, be sent from hence." Returned longtime Company servant and soon-to-be director Charles Grant encouraged substantial experiments in cultivating tea plantations. Not until the middle of the nineteenth century, however, would such tea plans become a reality, and then on an almost unbelievable scale.[41]

Forward-looking Company servants, meanwhile, including Grant, also began to push for the aggressive export to Britain of a range of raw materials already produced in India. Grant optimistically hoped that British cotton manufacturers would have a difficult time selling their goods in foreign markets, where they enjoyed less protection than in Britain. Nevertheless, he feared continued British manufacturing progress at the lower end of the market, writing, "It certainly becomes highly expedient for the Company to be as little dependent on this article as possible, and to be early provided with every practicable substitute for it." Grant "supposed" a reduction of approximately half of the cloth imports from Bengal would be suitable. The money from this reduction in fabric purchases should be redirected, in order of descending value, to raw silk and indigo, used by domestic manufacturers, and sugar, saltpeter, and drugs. The Company was already encouraging increased exports of raw silk, the development of mulberry plantations, and the transferal of tobacco seeds from Virginia. Another author similarly encouraged the export of raw cotton from Bengal to supply British manufacturers. According to this author, the type of cotton, not the techniques of spinning it by hand, made fine India muslin extraordinary. He believed that the Indian climate was important for spinning but that steam could be easily and cheaply injected into the air of an "enclosed manufactory." "With this requisition," he wrote, "I have no doubt but that the British Manufactures would rival those of Bengal in their finest manufactures." Spinners in Bengal could simply transition to other employment since Bengal possessed "so many articles on which to employ its labour." There were, then, those in the Company and outside it who certainly agreed with the British manufacturers on the point of making India a source of more raw materials.[42]

---

41. "Mr. Charles Grant on the Bengal Investment," 1791? IOR/A/2/11, fol. 214, BL. For another call for tea cultivation, see Memorandum, Sept. 29, 1788, Liverpool Papers, XXXIV, Add. MS 38223, fols. 203–206v, BL; Bengal Board of Trade to Council, Feb. 24, 1792, IOR/P/155/93, 37–38, BL.

42. "Mr. Charles Grant on the Bengal Investment," 1791? IOR/A/2/11, fol. 213v–214,

John Prinsep argued "that a richer Tribute" would come by exporting such raw materials from Bengal "than is furnished by the present almost worn out System of investing it in Manufactures which are every Day falling in Estimation at Home, since European Industry has adopted such Variety of Imitation and Improvement upon the Fabrick of the East." Prinsep had spent decades in India, was a friend of Hastings, and had become, for a time, a wealthy merchant. He explained that people in both the East and West Indies under Company or crown rule were equally British subjects and therefore should be encouraged to produce raw materials for British industry. Moreover, he noted, those in India were not subject to morally offensive enslavement and were cheap to employ. Indeed, he was perhaps most important for creating an Indian supply of indigo during the American Revolution, when North Carolina indigo was difficult to procure. The directors agreed with Prinsep that "the Natives are equally British Subjects; and every Mind must revolt at an Attempt to prevent those Natives from improving the Produce of their Soil, by their Ingenuity and Labour." They also agreed that indigo could become "a beneficial article of our commerce," but they were deeply unhappy with the high prices their servants had to pay to Prinsep. They encouraged attention to the cleaning, shape, and appearance of indigo to serve the higher end of the market since Carolina indigo was again serving the lower end after the peace with the United States. The government in Bengal soon wrote in agreement of "the great importance the article in question is of to the Commercial Interest of the Company and indeed to that of the Nation at large." By 1795, Bengal provided the bulk of all indigo imported into Britain.[43]

BL; Directors to Fort William, Oct. 23, 1783, Apr. 11, 1785, *Fort William–India House Correspondence*, IX, 192–195, 419. On Virginia tobacco, see Fort William to Directors, Jan. 12, 1794, ibid., XII, 324. On cotton, see "On the Expediency of Renewing the Company's Exclusive Privilege," 1792 or 1793? IOR/A/2/11, fols. 420v, 450, BL. On allspice from Jamaica, see Fort William to Directors, Feb. 5, 1795, *Fort William–India House Correspondence*, XII, 416.

43. John Prinsep to Lord North, Jan. 25, 1780, Trade Papers, MSS Eur. D624, I, fols. 1–2v, BL; [John Prinsep], *The Right in the West-India Merchants to a Double Monopoly of the Sugar Market of Great Britain, and the Expedience of All Monopolies Examined* (London, [1792?]), 28–51; *Report of the Select Committee . . . upon the Subject of the Cotton Manufacture*, 5; Directors to Fort William, Apr. 11, 1785, *Fort William–India House Correspondence*, IX, 196–197, 201; Fort William to Directors, Mar. 7, 1786, X, 410. On Prinsep's indigo cultivation, see Joyce E. Chaplin, *An Anxious Pursuit: Agricultural Innovation and Modernity in the Lower South* (Chapel Hill, N.C., 1993), 206–207. On indigo quantities by 1795, see Comml from Court, July 27, 1796, cited in *Fort William–India House Correspondence*, XII, 6;

The directors considered the extent to which such success in India's raw material cultivation and export might threaten the trade of Britain's West Indian colonies. At a meeting of the directors in the early spring of 1792, experienced and returned Company servant George Dallas explained that everyone agreed that the best colonies were those that gave the most raw materials and took the most manufactures, but colonies must be careful not to compete with one another. He reminded the directors that "Great Britain had long pursued one settled line of conduct with regard to her distant territories." The benefits of this arrangement should not be given up for "speculation." Britain should continue to take from the East and West Indies different commodities and increase the imports of only those raw materials from the East that could not come from the West. Randle Jackson, Company proprietor, conversely argued that the West Indian planters and the East India Company should not claim monopolies for specific raw materials, such as sugar; they should both supply as much of these materials as they could to drive down prices for the benefit of consumers in Britain. He explained, "Let the East and West India Proprietors think of themselves as they were, the right and left hands of the Country." Indeed, since 1776 the Company had actively encouraged the expansion of sugar cultivation in Bengal for export. The Company supported a new "sugar works on the best plan of those in the West Indies" as well as a rum distillery. The directors allowed the transport to Bengal of "every apparatus for making Sugar, together with a small complete Model of [a] Sugar Mill." The potential of large sugar exports from India could not be ignored.[44]

Despite differences on the pursuit of sugar, all agreed that British vessels should carry such goods regardless of their origins. Jackson explained that the real threat came, not from competition between the East and West Indies, but from giving over to the Americans the sugar-carrying trade from both Indies. U.S. merchants had already set up with commercial agents in India, he noted, "where they might mock the short arm of the British Legislature." The governor of British Dominica warned that he

---

Thomas Brown to Peter Speke, "Copy of Mr Brown's Report of the Import and Export Trade of Calcutta by Sea from 1796/7," IOR/P/174/13, BL.

44. East India Company, *Debate on the Expediency of Cultivating Sugar in the Territories of the East India Company* . . . (London, 1793), 5–6, 12, 17, 22. For more on Jackson, see "Memoir of Randle Jackson," *European Magazine, and London Review*, LXXVII (May 1820), 388. On the sugar works, see Directors to Fort William, Apr. 5, 1776, *Fort William–India House Correspondence*, VII, 149. For the sugar equipment, see Directors to Fort William, Apr. 16, 1777, ibid., VIII, 87–88. For more on sugar and the Company, see IOR/Z/P/46, esp. July, August, and September 1792, BL.

was watching Americans take over the supply of East India goods in the West Indies: "The quantity of East India goods lately imported to America and to the West Indies in American vessels has totally put a stop to our supplying the foreign markets in our neighborhood with these commodities . . . from Britain." "Five American ships from India have put into the West Indies," he went on, one of which brought, not piece goods, but sugar, coffee, and pepper. The sugar, from Calcutta, threatened local production with its high quality and low price.[45]

Britons smuggling through Ostend using European and American ship registrations also posed a major problem. A letter forwarded to Henry Dundas from Ostend explained, "It is well known that five out of six, of the ships that go from this Port, to the East Indies, are British property, both Ship and Cargo, and it is likewise a well known fact, that all the fine Goods that they bring home, find their way to London." Some of these traders further undercut the Company's position in India by selling their cargoes to Tipu Sultan, the Company's primary enemy. The Board of Trade was likewise "assured" that seven-eighths of the trade from Ostend to India was British merchants evading British law. However, unlike earlier in the century, the Board thought it unwise to demand that the Austrian government stop the trade because the merchants would simply shift to another port. Additionally, Ostend was the largest port for legal exports from the Company's own sales. The solution, the Board expected, was for the Company to use their power in India to undercut the illicit adventurers.[46]

Indeed, the Company was investigating in Europe and India, seeking both to outsell and catch interlopers acting under European and American flags. A lengthy Company report noted that 5,505 tons of shipping, "entirely English," had left Ostend for India. The author wrote, "That Port is now considered as much an English Port as the Port of London, both for Exports to India and Imports from it." He reckoned that twenty-two ships per year engaged in the Ostend trade with India and that 80 to 90 percent of the property involved was English. A list of foreign ships sailing from Bengal to Ostend in 1792 included nine registered to America and three to

45. East India Company, *Debate on the Expediency of Cultivating Sugar*, 11; John Orde [governor of British Dominica] to Lord Grenville, July 31, 1791, IOR/A/2/11, fol. 210, BL. For an example of an American merchant bringing sugar from India to the Atlantic, see Elias Hasket Derby, Orders to Capt Benjamin Hodges and Joseph Moseley, Mar. 17, 1792, Derby Family Papers, box 3, folder 5, PEM.

46. R. Rontree to James Chapman, Mar. 28, 1792, IOR/A/2/11, fol. 257, BL; W. Fawkener, "Austrian Netherlands: Letter to the Duke of Leeds on the Subject of the Trade," Jan. 6, 1791, Liverpool Papers, CCV, Add. MS 38394, 275–277/fols. 138–139, BL.

Genoa. The author of the list noted, "There is not one of the above that is not British or Indian Property or supported by *their* funds of credit." The ships carried mostly sugar, followed by piece goods, cotton, and pepper, reflecting the changing nature of British and, more broadly, European demand toward raw materials.[47]

In India, Cuthbert Fenwick responded to the publication of a call from the directors for the investigation and punishment of illicit traders by reporting to the Bengal government information on several foreign vessels operating as cover for private British merchants. Fenwick had ably commanded the *Success Galley* for the Company. He presented evidence, in particular, against Captain Home Popham, the brother of Stephen Popham, the Company's solicitor at Madras who had strongly encouraged the acceptance of nominally American traders on the grounds that they provided commercial benefits to the Company. The complaints were at least in part personal, but the Bengal government proceeded to investigate the matter, despite believing that Fenwick's reports "did not in any degree arise from a zeal for the public interests." Fenwick explained that Home Popham commanded the ship *L'Etrusco* from Ostend, nominally commanded by Fransisco Coppe. Coppe died in India, and at that point Popham "openly" took formal command. Popham also retailed and auctioned the cargo in Calcutta. He then sold the ship and bought an American ship that he similarly named *Etrusco*.[48]

The Bengal government decided to fine Popham but claimed it was too risky to bother seizing his ship and cargo because the Company might lose in court. With Popham's connections to the Company's own attorneys, so it might. Even those less connected apparently risked little. The government seized none of the several other vessels or cargoes that Fenwick identified. The government's claim that failed prosecution would embolden illicit traitors seems a stretch since a lack of prosecution would surely have emboldened them more. Fenwick was vocally disappointed in the gov-

47. An additional five vessels were bound for Copenhagen and registered to Denmark. The Danish ships carried saltpeter instead of sugar. See Secret Letter from Fort William to the Secret Committee of the Court of Directors, Apr. 27, 1792, *Fort William–India House Correspondence*, XVII, 453; "Account of Exports from Europe to India, including Foreign Companies," 1792? IOR/H399/1, 2–5, 31, BL; "List of Foreign Ships That Have Sailed This Season and Are about to Sail for Europe from Bengal," 1792, IOR/A/2/11, fol. 161, BL.

48. Cuthbert Fenwick, *The Case of Mr. C. Fenwick, Late Commander of the Success Galley, an Armed Ship Employed by the Madras Government, during the Late War* . . . (London, 1789), 22–23; Secret Letter from Fort William to the Secret Committee of the Court of Directors, Apr. 27, 1792, *Fort William–India House Correspondence*, XVII, 453, 459–460.

ernment's anemic response. However weak the Bengal government might have claimed the evidence to be, when the *Etrusco* arrived in Ostend outside the protection of the Bengal government, an English frigate successfully made it a prize for being substantially British property. The unwillingness of the Bengal government to pursue illicit traders continued to be influenced by the opportunities that the traders brought.[49]

Several authors offered various solutions to the problem of illicit trading that would not rely so much on easily influenced Company servants and British customs officials. An anonymous paper, circulated in London under the title "Thoughts on Laying Open the Trade to India," pointed to the "evil" of "the illicit Trade with India which has been for some time past carried on by Britons under foreign flags, aided by the Company's servants abroad." The author proposed a trade to India based on private merchants' obtaining licenses in exchange for a tax and bond guaranteeing that they would follow necessary regulations. The British government would take over the Company's warehousing in London, where goods would be sorted by private merchants. Another report explained that the captain and crew of Company ships still regularly smuggled their own private trade onto cutters for Ostend and Dunkirk, where the goods were repackaged and shipped to London. The shippers then simply bribed the customhouse officers. Captains also continued to pretend damage to their ships so that they could drop into outports to sell their private goods. The obvious solutions, the author indicated, were to decrease duties, require duplicate cargo manifests sent separately, and use government vessels to patrol the channel.[50]

Prinsep most clearly voiced the single solution on the minds of many merchants for solving the three problems of increasing British exports, obtaining cheap raw materials, and stopping British interlopers from working with foreign associates: end the Company's monopoly. He asserted, "It will scarce be denied, but that this nation is now ripe for an abolition

---

49. Secret Letter from Fort William to the Secret Committee of the Court of Directors, Apr. 27, 1792, *Fort William–India House Correspondence*, XVII, 460–462. A biography of Popham noted that he "was a considerable loser upon this occasion" but claimed that this "event" prepared Popham to become a celebrated commodore in the Royal Navy. See "Biographical Memoir of Sir Home Riggs Popham, K.M. and F.R.S.," *The Naval Chronicle for 1806: Containing a General and Biographical History of the Royal Navy of the United Kingdom . . .* , XVI (London, 1806), 270.

50. "Thoughts on Laying Open the Trade to India," Nov. 23, 1791, IOR/A/2/11, fol. 215v, BL; "Remarks on the Private Trade of the Sea Officers in the Service of the East India Company," circa 1791, MSS Eur. D624, II, fols. 311–314v, BL.

of monopolies," and he went on to quote Adam Smith extensively. With an open trade there would be less need to interlope, and prices and freight rates would decline under competition, making both Indian raw materials and British manufactures less expensive. Indeed, Prinsep identified the East India shipowners with their lucrative Company contracts as the biggest difficulty. He called them a "monopoly within a monopoly . . . one of the most shameful, barefaced combinations ever successfully maintained." Prinsep later beseeched his associates in the Company "to effect that liberal encouragement to the trade of individuals, unfettered by restrictions, and left to pursue their own objects in their own way, which has been so clearly demonstrated to be perfectly consistent with the true interests of the corporation . . . and of the Kingdom at large." This was certainly not the first time that British merchants had pushed for the end of the Company monopoly, but the different circumstances of the late 1780s and early 1790s gave such pressure added weight.[51]

A New Imperial Compromise

The shifting geography of production had revitalized seventeenth-century hopes for both an open India trade and a trade in cheap Indian raw materials in exchange for British manufactured goods, hopes that had been largely shelved in the early-eighteenth-century compromise. The renewal of the Company's monopoly in 1793 provided the opportunity for new policies. The man with the most influence, Henry Dundas, explained to Francis Baring that he would support the monopoly only if the Company could make its freight rates cheaper than the freight rates of private merchants, thereby driving down the cost of Indian raw materials in Britain and British manufactures in India. He was particularly keen, too, to redirect British-Indian capital from clandestine channels into legal ones, furthering the use of British shipping and capital alike. Dundas told the directors that "the grant of an exclusive commerce to India, is not very material to the interests either of the East-India Company or of the Public." He proposed an "experiment" wherein the Company would set aside three thousand tons of its shipping per year to sell at fixed rates to private British merchants. He expected that this would remove some of the incentive for Britons to trade through Ostend and help British manufacturers export to India. Dundas threatened that, if the directors did not agree

---

51. [Prinsep], *Right in the West-India Merchants to a Double Monopoly*, 53, 81; Prinsep, *Proposal of a Substitute for Funding in Time of War* (London, 1797), 80.

to the plan in general, he would oversee the transition to an open trade, which he fully expected to be successful.[52]

Determining the appropriate freight rates was in many ways the crux of the plan. Dundas preferred rates of £5 per ton eastward and £15 westward, coupled with reduced duties to dissuade Britons from trading through Ostend. Dundas was not alone on these figures. William Fairlie, a powerful British agent in Calcutta, for example, had written to Company director David Scott that £15 was a reasonable rate for the voyage from India to Europe and that import duties on Indian fabric must be lowered. Lowering the duties to 15 percent would divert goods that were currently going to Ostend and Lisbon to London and do little to harm the burgeoning British cotton manufacturers. Another report indicated that private merchants typically paid substantial insurance premiums, which were unnecessary when using the Company's robustly built ships. On cargoes worth hundreds of thousands of pounds, the Company had reportedly lost goods worth only an average of £133.5.11 over the previous sixteen years, including the years of the American Revolutionary War. Supposing that insurance cost shippers on non-Company ships 8 percent, the author calculated that Company freight at £20 return was cheaper than the sum of private freight at £16 and insurance. The Manchester manufacturers

52. *Report of the Select Committee . . . upon the Subject of the Cotton Manufacture*, 6–7; Henry Dundas to Francis Baring, Feb. 16, 1793, in *Papers respecting the Negociation for a Renewal of the East-India Company's Exclusive Trade* ([London], [1793]), I, 8–9, Mar. 24, 1793, III, 57. This passage was widely quoted during the debate. See, for example, Dundas quoted by Mr. Francis in William Cobbett, *The Parliamentary History of England . . .* (London, 1817), XXX, 699. For a longer passage from Dundas including this quotation, see Friend to the Freedom of the Press, *A Letter to Richard Brinsley Sheridan, Esq. on the Proposed Renewal of the Charter of the East India Company* (London, 1793), 41–42. Dundas made the same point at other times, so it is clear that he did not believe a legal monopoly was essential. He wrote, for example, "The East-India Company greatly overvalue the advantages of an exclusive trade to India; for the same reasons that induce me to be satisfied that the merchants and manufacturers of Great Britain and Ireland are in a delusion in their expectations from a freedom in trade"; China required a different calculus. See Dundas to Baring, Mar. 27, 1793, in *Papers respecting the Negociation*, III, 15. Dundas had also expressed doubt about the efficacy of the monopoly in the mid-1780s and was already thinking about moving away from older hopes of monopolizing the entire world's India trade through London. The question of directing private British-Indian capital to Britain also had been on Dundas's mind since the mid-1780s, but it would become especially important after 1800. See Michael Fry, *The Dundas Despotism* (Edinburgh, 1992), 124–127. On Dundas's proposal, see Dundas to Baring, Apr. 18, 1793, VII, 3–9, 17, in *Papers respecting the Negociation*, VII, 3–9, 17. Dundas specifically called the new charter plan an "experiment" to determine what actions might be best in the future; see Cobbett, *Parliamentary History*, 660–685 (quotation on 683).

disagreed, however, arguing that the combined maximum needed to be £16. They estimated that £12 westward would be necessary to encourage imports of raw material, and £4 eastward to encourage exports of their products to India.[53]

The Company directors were often painted as trying to obtain freight rates too high to encourage private merchants to use Company ships, but the directors, like the manufacturers and private merchants, predicted that Dundas's high westward rates would continue to provide incentive for interloping, particularly with the American flag. True, the manufacturers' combined rate of £16 was under the Company's minimum of £20. Nevertheless, they did agree on the westward rate. The directors determined that £8 eastward and £12 westward would reduce the temptation of trading on foreign vessels through Ostend and fill their homeward-bound ships. In their opinion, Dundas's rates would not only encourage private British merchants to continue using European and American shipping but also that "with America, the supply of the West-India Islands will naturally follow." Similarly, commission agent John Cochrane wrote to Dundas, "It affords me much satisfaction to see . . . that you perceive the necessity of permitting those persons who intend trading to India to procure freight at as cheap a rate as they can." He calculated that, based on the experience of Captain Truxton of the American ship *Delaw* that sailed between Madras and Hamburg, a rate of "£10 per Ton out and home" would be competitive. A rate of £15 homeward would "totally cut out" the rice trade in particular, "a very serious consideration." Cochrane had overseen the purchase of thirty-seven hundred tons of sugar and two hundred tons of cotton at Calcutta, which, if shipped by the Company at £15, would have cost his associates an additional £15,000 over shipping with the Americans. He concluded, "If not attended to, the Americans will undermine us." The firm of Naysmith and Campbell compared the proposed rates to those common in the Jamaica trade. It reckoned that a private ship running twelve return voyages to India in twelve years would be much cheaper than the Company's ships at £15, and interloping would therefore continue. The firm acknowledged that insurance would need to be added to the cost of using

---

53. William Fairlie to David Scott, Aug. 31, 1792, IOR/A/2/10, n.p., BL; "Observations on the Company Ships," n.d., IOR/A/2/11, fols. 187v–189, BL; Dundas to Baring, Apr. 18, 1793, in *Papers respecting the Negociation*, VII, 8–9. For the manufacturers' rates, see "Minutes of a Conversation between Mr. Pitt, Mr. Dundas, and Messrs. Gregg and Frodsham, Delegates from Manchester," ibid., III, 19.

regular merchant ships but doubted that it would come anywhere near the freight premium proposed.[54]

As another author wrote to Dundas: "An American may load in Bengal and go either to Affrica, America, or Europe. The whole world is open to him, what possible injury could arrive from a British subject doing the same. The profits would ultimately centre in Britain instead of America." Nominally American merchants, offering freight at half the price of the Company, "will run away entirely with the Company Trade of India, but also with the whole of the carrying trade to Europe of sugars etc." The author correctly explained, "To be a British subject in India is now a disadvantage, and numbers to my certain knowledge deny themselves being such" so that they can trade with the advantages of foreigners in British ports. Instead of furthering cultivation, moreover, the Company had "thrown away" vast sums on conquests. The solution was to allow the Company to have a monopoly on a few selected goods, such as saltpeter, some types of fabric, raw silk, and pepper, and that otherwise "nothing short of a free trade in particular articles will ever do." Additionally, the principles of the Navigation Acts needed to be applied, requiring that the ships be British. By this dual mechanism of an open trade and British bottoms, the trade would be secured from American-registered ships. The author championed the proposal, "not only to satisfy the merchants, and people of Great Britain, who have undoubtedly a claim to have goods brought home at reasonable rates, but also to secure a proper influence in India, and to prevent foreigners from running away with the trade."[55]

Predictions that Americans and Britons masquerading as Americans would soon take over the India trade because of the Company's monopoly were also combined with criticisms of the monopoly over cotton cloth pursued by Manchester manufacturers. One author wondered that anyone could find it reasonable to charge more duty on cloth from British

54. For the Company's desired rates, see Baring to Dundas, Mar. 21, 1793, in *Papers respecting the Negociation*, III, 9–10, "Minute of the Committee of Correspondence, Dated 25th March 1793," III, 32, "At a Committee of Correspondence, the 17th of April 1793," VII, 19. On America, see "Report of the Committee of Correspondence, dated 1st April 1793," ibid., IV [misprint; should be V], 21; John Cochrane to Henry Dundas, Apr. 21, 1793, IOR/A/2/11, fols. 165–170, BL. Naysmith and Campbell estimated a far higher frequency of voyages than undertaken by the Company's ships; see Naysmith and Campbell to Henry Dundas, Apr. 2, 1793, IOR/A/2/11, fols. 163–164v, BL.

55. "Comments respecting the E I trade, Shipping, etc.," Mar. 4, 1793, IOR/A/2/11, fols. 181v–185, BL.

India than from France. He also asserted, "The plan of preventing the exportation of cotton machinery is folly in the extreme, and operates as a bounty for the emigration of the best manufacturers." But, by the same token, he claimed that the East India Company had done nothing to cultivate commodities or to build roads and canals to improve British India. The Company, moreover, had abused its dual position as government and merchant. Production in Dacca, for example, had plummeted as the Company exploited the people by demanding impossibly low prices for goods. He wrote, "The system adopted by the Company and their servants was a disgrace to any civilised country." "To compleat the ruin of the manufacturers," the Company's servants traded on their own accounts to supply foreigners with the same goods as the Company. These men created an outcry against the "free merchants and other traders." The Company's servants simply used the power and name of the Company to protect their personal trades from competition. The author claimed that, in contrast, private British merchants, now often pretending to be Americans, gave "a just and fair price" to Indians for their goods and that, in his time in India, "I never heard of any malconduct."[56]

Tension escalated over the question of the monopoly within the Company itself. Some, such as Stephen Lushington, between stints as the Company chairman and a member of Parliament, argued that the Company benefited from foreign merchants visiting India and that it had no need to monopolize exports to Europe, only Britain. Others joined Prinsep in arguing against the monopoly altogether. An anonymous owner of

56. "General Observations on Monopolists, the E I Co. in Particular," Apr. 15, 1793, IOR/A/2/11, fols. 352, 360v, 365, BL. There was significant tension among the weavers, zamindars, and the Company. See, for example, Resident at Malda to Bengal Board of Trade, June 29, 1789 (enclosed in July 7, 1789, from Board of Trade to Council), IOR/P/155/75, 496–498, BL; Mr. Scott, "No. 5 Board of Trade," Aug. 11, 1789, IOR/P/155/76, 111–113, BL; "No. 12. Regulations for Weavers Revised," Oct. 27, 1789, IOR/P/155/76, 716–735, BL. Henry Thomas Colebrooke noted that India's weavers could not be considered entirely free; see [Colebrooke], *Remarks on the Present State of the Husbandry and Commerce of Bengal* (Calcutta, 1795), 134. Company records show that Company purchases of Dacca goods plummeted but that the problem was "the very great diminution in the demand for the fabrics of this province." The Company in fact paid more to the weavers, and it claimed that it gave them freedom to work for whomever they chose, but increased prices for fabric had not kept up with inflation, and many weavers were impoverished by 1800. See James Taylor to the Bengal Board of Trade, Dec. 1, 1801, IOR/P/156/42, n.p., BL. The Bengal Board of Trade alerted the Court of Directors to problems with private merchants in Benares who would not accept advances and offered goods that deviated considerably from the musters; see Bengal Board of Trade to the Directors, Mar. 1789, IOR/P/155/74, 23, BL.

Company stock published a proposed speech arguing that the monopoly would steadily transfer the India trade from the British ports in India to those run by other European powers. This proprietor saw an open trade for Britons with low duties on imports from British India as an ideal way to offset the loss of the carrying trade to America and the duties placed by the United States on British imports. He argued that the plan to offer cargo space on Company ships would not be effective. David Scott, a former private trader with leading Indian agency houses and now supported as a Company director by Dundas, also spoke out against the need for an exclusive monopoly, particularly on the exports to India. He warned the directors that he intended to say the same to Parliament. Most of the directors disagreed, as did Company chairman Francis Baring. The East India Company's Select Committee on the monopoly question defended the monopoly by comparing the exports to India in the 1650s with those from the 1780s. The trade overall had grown dramatically, while the export share of bullion had shrunk dramatically.[57]

Some woolen producers also petitioned heavily for the continuance of the Company monopoly. Primarily to be a national service, the Company exported British woolens. Eleven different woolen manufacturing towns sent letters to Dundas explaining that any change to the Company's monopoly would destroy their business. As the woolen producers from Newton Abbot wrote, the Company was their primary buyer and thereby employed "almost the whole of the numerous poor in this and adjoining counties." The Company's regular purchasing allowed them to offer better prices and "to carry on our manufacturies to a much greater extent under their security than we could possibly venture to do, should this valuable Trade be hazard in the hands of private individuals." The Company pointed out that British cotton manufacturers were displacing woolens

---

57. East India House, *A Continuation of the Series of the Several Debates That Have Taken Place at the India-House, on the Following Important Subjects: The General Principles of the Company's New Charter and the Various Clauses Which It Contains, respecting the Political and Commercial Interests of the India Company and Its Funded Property* . . . ([London], 1793), 45, 47, 104–105; *Heads of a Proposed Speech, by a Proprietor, upon the Policy of Renewing the Company's Monopoly, etc.* (London, 1793), 7–9, 18; "Second Report of the Select Committee . . . ," in *Three Reports of the Select Committee, Appointed by the Court of Directors to Take into Consideration the Export Trade from Great Britain to the East Indies, China, Japan, and Persia; Laid before the Lords of the Committee of Privy Council* . . . (London, [1793]) 87–91, 96. For more on Scott, see Yukihisa Kumagai, *Breaking into the Monopoly: Provincial Merchants and Manufacturers' Campaigns for Access to the Asian Market, 1790–1833* (Leiden, 2012), 15–16.

and linens made from British raw materials, whereas the Company's cotton imports were largely reexported.[58]

British cotton manufacturers, nevertheless, continued to push for higher duties or total prohibitions. John Dunlop wrote on behalf of the Committee of Manufacturers of Glasgow that the Company must not be allowed to keep importing piece goods. Dunlop claimed that piece goods now made up little of the Company's trade, so neither its profits nor the duty revenue of the government would suffer much. He expected that ending the imports would employ an additional 2,088 weavers in Britain. Though if the Company's fabrics had such little effect, one might wonder why they needed to be more fully prohibited. Later that year, while Parliament was considering the Company's accounts, R. S. Moncrief complained from Glasgow that, just as British producers were recovering from a recession, they "were all put back again by the India sales of muslin—never was any thing so cruel and in my opinion so impolitic as bringing forward these sales at this time." Moncrief echoed the century-old argument that Britons were being thrown out of work in favor of Bengalis.[59]

Fearing that Dundas and the government would side with British manufacturers, Thomas Brown organized increased lobbying in defense of India piece goods. In January 1793, he had informed Baring of his willingness to gather "very readily all together the Merchants and Traders in India piece goods to urge their Interest and advantage in the Trade which has been carried on with great profit to this Country long before British Manufactures of Muslin existed." By April, Brown was helping to lead the protests of the "British Committee of Buyers of East-India Piece Goods." The Committee of Buyers repeated Brown's arguments of the previous two years that British manufacturers were "already amply protected by the high freight, insurance, interest of capital for two years, 18 P Cent. Duty, and other incidental charges, to which the India Muslins are sub-

58. For examples, see Manufacturers of Newton Abbott to Henry Dundas, Apr. 4, 1793, IOR/A/2/11, fols. 28–29v, 67–68v, BL; Manufacturers of Long Ells Residing at Wellington in Somerset to the East India Company Board of Control for the Affairs of the East India Company, Apr. 6, 1793, IOR/A/2/11, fols. 32–33v, 73–74v, BL; Manufacturers of Woollens in the Town of Ashburton, Devon, to Henry Dundas, Apr. 6, 1793, IOR/A/2/11, fols. 34–35v, 71–72v; *Report of the Select Committee . . . upon the Subject of the Cotton Manufacture*, 4–5.

59. Committee of Manufacturers of Glasgow, signed John Dunlop, to Henry Dundas? May 1, 1793, IOR/A/2/11, fols. 145–146v, BL. Moncrief had interests in John Monterth and Company, which had unsalable muslins worth fifty thousand to sixty thousand pounds. See "Extract of a Letter from R. S. Moncrief, Glasgow," Sept. 14, 1793, MSS Eur. D624, I, fols. 52–53, BL.

ject." They were astonished that prohibition might be expanded "upon the mere notion of a handful of private manufacturers, who owe to our anxious and indefitigable exertions their recent acquaintance with the nature of India Piece Goods, and consequently the very existence of their manufactories, who have not poverty for their plea, but whose chief argument arises from their incredible success." The Committee and Brown argued that the agitation coming from Manchester for a prohibition was a misguided attempt to create a monopoly for Manchester manufacturers, making that city the "depot for all goods wanted by the Draper" and shifting the economic power away from London and its merchants.[60]

In addition, the Committee of Buyers claimed that British cotton manufacturers would suffer from such a monopoly since their success depended on the allure of India's goods. British manufacturers still could not reproduce the finest India muslin, and their growing domestic and international success was aided because "a very great proportion . . . are passed for India." The manufacturers would not be able to pretend that their goods came from India if all India goods were prohibited, nor could they profit from the allure of India fashion. The Committee of Buyers explained, "A due mixture of the India manufacture is absolutely essential to preserve the reputation of the whole." A London draper similarly wrote, "British Goods fascinate Buyers by their general Eveness of Make," but "higher Wearers" found in them "an harshness." Any attempts to further restrict fine India muslin would thus lead these consumers, not to British muslin, but to "another article of Dress more congenial to their soft sensations." "There is no arguing against taste," the Committee of Buyers exclaimed, referencing the great difficulties the government had faced in other such fabric prohibitions. Brown suggested that the Company might agree to import large quantities of raw cotton from Dacca for British manufacturers in exchange for allowing India muslin to be sold in Britain at competitive prices. Brown noted that British cloth had been made from cotton from Brazil and Bourbon instead of from British colonies. Manufacturers were therefore supporting rival foreign powers. Indian cotton had a much shorter staple than these cottons, and it was difficult to spin mechanically,

60. Brown to Baring, Jan. 9, 1793, Henry Dundas, 1st Viscount Melville Collection, MS 1064, fol. 81r, NLS, Brown to Baring, 1793? fol. 205r; The Committee of Merchants and Drapers, Buyers of India Piece Goods, to Henry Dundas, Apr. 6, 1793, IOR/A/2/11, fols. 121–122, 131, BL, published as *Letter to the Right Honorable Henry Dundas, One of His Majesty's Principal Secretaries of State, from the Committee of Buyers of East-India Piece Goods for Home Consumption, respecting the Prohibition of India Muslins* (London, 1793).

a problem that had proven intractable. Brown, however, had procured different samples of raw cotton from India that some Manchester manufacturers thought they could spin.[61]

In Dundas's words, the new Company charter of 1793 would "reconcile and conciliate what were supposed to be jarring interests"—the Company, private traders, the nation's war effort against the French, British manufacturers, and the state. It would "engraft an open trade upon the exclusive privilege of the company." As expected, the charter required the Company to offer three thousand tons of cargo space to private merchants, to be increased to six thousand tons as demand required. Dundas also set the freight rates at five pounds outbound to India and fifteen pounds back, which the Company, private merchants, and British manufacturers disparaged. Such rates, if paid, would support the Company's shippers and, in the process, maintain their warlike vessels for national emergencies. Private British merchants were not allowed to trade in military stores, moreover, again reflecting the government's greater confidence in the Company, its shippers, and their robust ships. To aid the Company's transfer of tribute to Britain as well as the production of British manufacturers, private merchants were also prohibited from importing cotton or silk piece goods from India, pushing them instead to compete with the Company on the trade in raw materials to increase supply and drive down prices. The much cheaper rate of eastward freight would also operate as a "bounty" to encourage private merchants shipping British manufactures to India. Following the arguments of Brown and others, manufacturers would get no further prohibition against Indian cloth. Additionally, to draw foreign merchants to British ports instead of French or Dutch ports in the Indian Ocean and to encourage the use of the maximum amount of capital from British India, the Company's servants and others would now be allowed to act as agents for foreign merchants engaged in the India trade.[62]

61. Brown to Baring, 1793 Henry Dundas, 1st Viscount Melville Collection, MS 1064, fols. 82r–84r, 205r, NLS, Finney Sirdefield to Mr. Peel, May 8, 1793, fols. 102–103; *Letter to the Right Honorable Henry Dundas*, 10.

62. Dundas to Baring, Apr. 15, 1793, in *Papers respecting the Negociation*, VII, 4; Cobbett, *Parliamentary History*, 683. For the charter terms as proposed, see *Papers respecting the Negociation*, IX, 1–17. Lushington had defended the shipowners for their military importance and described the low outbound freight as a "bounty" (East India House, *A Continuation of the Series of the Several Debates*, 73). The benefit of preserving the Company's warlike ships during war with France was also identified in C. H. Phillips, *The East India Company, 1784–*

The new 1793 charter was followed by the Jay Treaty, negotiated in 1794 by the American John Jay and Lord Grenville, reinforcing, with America, the charter point that allowed Britons in India to act as agents for foreigners. The treaty was designed to deal with several outstanding disputes between Britain and the United States resulting from the American Revolution. Its relationship with the Company charter has attracted little attention from historians. In particular, article 13 of the treaty codified the trade of Americans with the British East Indies at the same duty levels enjoyed by Britons, but without the stipulation to purchase expensive Company cargo space that constrained British merchants. American ships, however, were required to return to the United States and unload—they could not ship British Indian goods directly to Europe, although the treaty contained no clear prohibitions against the reexport of goods from America. In a time of national emergency owing to the wars of the French Revolution, when ships and seamen were needed for the navy, British agents could work with American merchants and make use of readily available American shipping. The charter and the Jay Treaty thus together responded to Britain's wartime needs.[63]

GRENVILLE'S CONCESSIONS TO American merchants and shippers alarmed the West Indian planter and dogmatic slavery supporter Gilbert Francklyn. He pointed to "undoubted" reports of a Philadelphia proposal "to form a society, and establish a house of commerce near to Calcutta, for the purpose of carrying on a very extensive trade—not in Sugars only,

---

1834 (Manchester, 1940), 79. Holden Furber argued that the treaty terms allowing Americans to reexport India goods and to export goods from Europe to British India was an oversight, but Furber also provides evidence that Dundas was clear in supporting the wording of the terms. Furber assumed that American shippers in the Indian Ocean were a problem for Britain, but Dundas and others as shown in the next chapter saw Americans instead as a solution. See Furber, "The Beginnings of American Trade with India, 1784–1812," *New England Quarterly*, XI (1938), 244–245, 249–250.

63. On trade, the treaty included British restitution to American shipowners, improved British access to American markets and American access to British imperial markets, and provided tacit American acceptance of Britain's naval war with France. One of the seminal works on the treaty in America barely mentions the India trade: Jerald A. Combs, *The Jay Treaty: Political Battleground of the Founding Fathers* (Berkeley, Calif., 1970), 104–117, 137–152 (on France; 151 mentions the India trade). James Fichter has explored the treaty's India clause, though not its connection to the charter renewal (Fichter, *So Great a Proffit*, 176–178, 344n–345n). It remains unclear who proposed article 13, though it clearly fit with Dundas's thinking.

but on every other article" for export "to Europe or America." If the British government clamped down on foreign trade to the West Indies but allowed foreign trade to India, including what he argued was the illegal export of sugar against the Navigation Acts, British contraband would flourish and foreign states would benefit. U.S. merchants with their cheap freight, and with or without a company of their own, would soon fill all the markets in North and South America that the Company used to supply. He demanded that the Company restrict the production of sugar in India for export. "Sure I am," he wrote, that foreign trade with British India "is at present prohibited by the laws of the kingdom." "All the acts of navigation" and Company control had helped Britain prosper throughout the world, and he argued that they must be vigorously enforced, or British India sugar would lead to nothing less than the collapse of the empire.[64]

Similarly, India expert and supporter of an open trade Henry Colebrooke explained that requiring British colonies to trade only with Britain was "the principle, which has constantly been applied to the government of possessions similar to British India." Colebrooke argued that an open trade with India confined only to Britons was therefore the ideal policy. The tonnage allotted for private merchants by Dundas was insufficient, but it would not matter because the freight rates were too high. The large clandestine and foreign trade had already made the Company's trade only "nominally exclusive," and Colebrooke explained that fully opening the trade legally to Britons would not harm the Company any further. British manufacturers, meanwhile, would not be able to obtain inexpensive raw materials from India because of the costs of freight. Colebrooke was still stuck in the late-seventeenth- through mid-eighteenth-century view of the India trade in which the goal was to make London the "emporium" or "organ" for Indian commodities, beating out European, and now American, rivals. He believed that the new India trading "arrangement" was intended "to suppress clandestine trade, to make London the depot, and the British shipping the carriers from India." He could not understand how the government's compromise could possibly meet these goals. The

64. Gilb[ert] Francklyn, *Remarks on a Pamphlet, Entitled Bengal Sugar; and on the Manner in Which the Trade of the East-India Company Is Carried on in the East-Indies . . .* (London, 1795), quotations on 39, 54, 109; see also 28, 38–40, 55–59, 66–87. A printed subscription form for a Philadelphia-based "East India Company of North-America" survives from the late 1790s. This attempt might easily have been based on an earlier one, or it simply might have taken a few years to go from conception to subscription. See [William Barker], *Constitutional Articles of the Association of the East India Company of North-America* (Philadelphia, 1799).

Remapping Production, Rethinking Monopolies

answer was simple. These were not the primary goals that Dundas and Grenville ultimately had in mind.[65]

The more important goals in the mid-1790s—which Colebrooke had alluded to but had not grasped as fully as Dundas—were to bring India's raw materials to Britain, make Britain the world's manufacturer of previously Indian fabrics, and protect Britain's trade and the value of British India from war with France. These goals did not require Britain to be the hub of the global India trade, and, indeed, war with France increasingly meant that Britain could not, at least temporarily, be that hub. The war encouraged the preservation of the Company's warlike ships, the confinement of vital military materials to those ships during transport to and from India, and the employment of neutral traders. Article 13 of the Jay Treaty was similarly influenced by the war, but it was also part of the early stages in the breaking down of the East India Company monopoly and its replacement with a British manufacturing monopoly. On the American side, article 13, enabled by the Constitution of 1787 and the political success of the Federalists, reflected John Adams's argument to Jay in 1785 that the United States would benefit immensely from having a neutral India trade in a European war. The treaty was a success for American merchants trading with India, but it also made considerable sense to those in Britain who saw British manufacturing of cottons as changing the balance in the ancient debate over the East India Company's purpose. British manufacturers might soon dominate America's and India's markets, and the West and East Indies would increasingly supply the raw materials to fuel this dominance.[66]

65. [Colebrooke], *Remarks on the Present State*, 253–265 (quotations on 253 and 257), 270, 274–275, 278. Anthony Lambert, a partner in Lambert and Ross, a major Calcutta agency house trading to Europe and seeking to break the Company's shipping monopoly, claimed to have penned the first and third sections of the chapter on foreign trade. In any case, Colebrooke and Lambert shared the same views. See Anthony Lambert to Lord Cornwallis, Nov. 2, 1795, Letter Book, Donald Heald Rare Books, New York. Richard Wesley, 1st Marquess Wellesely, the governor general of India, also thought a key goal should still be to "render London the universal mart for the manufacture and produce of Asia," and he believed that much more private British shipping would help meet that goal. The extra shipping would also serve the goal of supporting British exports to India; quoted in Thomas Henchman, *Observations on the Report of the Directors of the East India Company respecting the Trade between India and Europe* (London, 1801), 167. For more on freight rates, see "Address of the Merchants of Calcutta to the Bengal Government, respecting Europe Tonnage; to the Honorable Sir John Shore . . . ," in [Colebrooke], *Remarks on the Present State*, Appendix 2, 285–290.

66. John Adams to John Jay, Nov. 11, 1785, *PCC, Letters from John Adams*, V, 729–731.

The important monopoly would not be over the India trade but over the global production of goods that had once been manufactured in India. War, conquest, and the gradual transition to British rule in India had stimulated growing markets for British manufactures, some of which Britons in India saw as symbolically necessary for their power, and which also seemed to Britons at home to prove the need for further reformation of the Company's servants and of India. The resurgence of the old goal of monopolizing export markets with British manufactures made from cheap imported raw materials combined with the Company's growing role as a government generating tax revenue from cultivation was displacing rationales for an India trading monopoly. The charter of 1793 and the Jay Treaty looked forward to the fulfillment of hopes from long in the past— British hopes for overwhelming exportations of domestic manufactures and American hopes for extensive participation in the India trade. As had been the case in other realignments of the India trading regulations, however, making the regulations did not guarantee that they could be enforced or that they would create the intended benefits.

7 The French Wars and the Refashioning of Empire

In 1794, as the Jay Treaty negotiations between Britain and America progressed, Eliza Fay, a successful British merchant in Calcutta, decided to associate with American merchants, shipowners, and captains to repatriate her Indian fortune. Fay's experiences illustrate the developing interdependence of Britons and Americans in the India trade. They show the ongoing willingness of Company officials in India to ignore the Company directors, the British use of Ostend and more recently American merchants to interlope, the American need for capital and experience, and the many opportunities and risks in the private trade. Fay had gone to India in 1779, notably without the Company directors' permission and via Britain's enemy, France. Like many other Britons, she and her husband sought to use the British empire for their own benefit, despite the regulations of the government and Company; they were, after all, British, and it was the British empire. Many Company servants shared these beliefs. Company Supreme Court judge Elijah Impey, for example, welcomed the Fays enthusiastically, commenting, "It is nothing to us whether you *had* or *had not* permission from the Court of Directors to proceed to this settlement." Fay increasingly took up trading on her own account, exemplifying, too, the role of women as India merchants.[1]

After fifteen years of accumulating a small fortune in India, Fay was ready, she later wrote, to secure "a home in my native country." She left her affairs in Calcutta in the hands of a young friend and negotiated with the Salem merchant, Jacob Crowninshield, to take her and much of her capital in the form of goods to Ostend, the long-popular hub of extra-monopoly British trade with India. During the voyage, they came across a French fleet that boasted of the success of the French Revolutionary

---

1. Fay was also dear friends with Robert and Frances Chambers; the former worked alongside Impey as a judge. Impey was a close friend of Warren Hastings and was impeached with him, connecting Fay also to the Company's greatest scandals. See Eliza Fay, *The Original Letters from India of Mrs. Eliza Fay*, new ed., ed. Walter Kelly Firminger (Calcutta, 1908), iv–vi, viii–ix, 1–11, 90, 136, 156–157.

army in seizing Ostend and much more. Instead of risking the venture in war-torn Europe, Crowninshield offered to take Fay and her investment to the United States. Fay preferred to get to Britain and asked Crowninshield to leave her at the Isle of Wight and to oversee the sale of her goods in America. Crowninshield agreed and sent Fay "a fine new vessel," the *Minerva*, as the proceeds from her investment.[2]

Crowninshield's decision—or perhaps, given the difficulties of capital in America, his need—to send Fay the *Minerva* must have been disappointing, but the best could be made of it compared to the experiences to come. Fay admitted to the fine new quality of the vessel, and Crowninshield had sent his own brother to serve as the captain. Fay outfitted and coppered the *Minerva* in London for a voyage to Boston and then Bengal. Before the ship set sail, however, it caught fire, costing Fay the small fortune of six thousand pounds. The vessel survived, and, with American cover, Fay took it to Calcutta. Fay was not overjoyed with the market for her goods, but she managed to dispatch the *Minerva* with a cargo. She stayed behind and, with Crowninshield's associates, took another interest in the *Rosalia*, bound for the United States. The actions of Crowninshield and his associates suggest that they respected Fay and her knowledge as a merchant, regardless of her gender. Unfortunately, the *Rosalia*'s American captain would not listen to her experienced advice about "deadlights" as they left Calcutta, and the ship was struck hard by an unseen wave, which made the ship unseaworthy. Fay and her cargo next went on board the *Hero*, again sailing for the United States. Fay had a low opinion of the U.S. citizens involved in the *Hero* and of the "Yankee" captain's lack of honor. Upon nearing New York, she explained, "My spirits were very low, and sunk with what I may now term a presentiment, as I approached another people and another world." Unfortunately for Fay, her trade to America would not help transport her fortune to Britain; instead, America would be her fortune's "grave." Whether they admitted it or not, the Americans needed Fay's capital and experience to learn and take advantage of the India trade. And whether it worked out or not, Fay needed American assistance to try to redeem her capital.[3]

The nominal and actual American trades to India of which Fay was a part expanded along with the spread of the French Revolutionary and Napoleonic Wars. The increase in the importance of American merchants and shipping can be seen in the Calcutta census. In 1794, the cen-

2. Ibid., 195, 198–199.
3. Ibid., 199, 217–218, 224–225.

sus showed seven "American" men living in and around Calcutta. All but one of them, a ship commander described as from "Quebec America," had lived there for at least six years and were listed as "British." The group included a writer, punch-house worker, servant, printer, and keeper of a provisions warehouse. The latter two men were apparently part of the large diaspora of loyalists caused by the American Revolution. Not one of the men was a merchant. By 1806, they had all left Calcutta. The new census listed seven different American men. Five of the seven American arrivals were merchants, and none of them appear to have been loyalists.[4]

The timing of this increase in American trade with British India was primarily a product of the addition of wartime American neutral advantages to earlier British-American cooperation and to the increasing success of American merchants in Asian trades following the patterns of Ostend traders and other Europeans. It was not evidence of overwhelming American demand, capital provision, or merchant ingenuity. American merchants in the India trade enabled better access to global markets for British Indian producers and merchants and built capital in the United States. These developments caused considerable debate about article 13 of the Jay Treaty and contributed to debates about the Company monopoly and the future of British and American economic growth. Importantly, the wars that sprung from the French Revolution, including the War of 1812 between the United States and Britain, also caused considerable concern for British manufacturers needing access to U.S. markets and, especially, raw materials. The dramatic and sustained growth of competitive British cotton manufacturing and America's place in that growth would lead to the expansion of major changes to the regulations and systems of the em-

4. "List of Europeans Residing in Calcutta [and environs]," June 10, 1794, and "General Registerr of the Europeans, not in the Service of His Majesty or of the Honble Company Residing in Calcutta and the Several Cities and Zillahs Subject to the Immediate Authority of Presidency of Fort William," 1806, O/5/26, n.p., BL. The printer was William Duane. He left America for Ireland with his mother as a young man immediately before the American Revolution, but he and his mother might have supported the patriot cause. In any case, from Ireland Duane went to London, where he was identified as a Radical Whig, and then to British India, where he largely supported the empire until 1794. After his newspaper became a threat to the Company, he was deported to London, and he returned to America in 1796. As with many people in the eighteenth century, it is difficult to assign Duane any particular national identity for much of his life, and, indeed, he seems to have switched his own identity frequently; see Nigel Little, *Transoceanic Radical, William Duane: National Identity and Empire, 1760–1835* (London, 2008), 20–32, 86, 105, 129–133. For more on the loyalist diaspora, see Maya Jasanoff, *Liberty's Exiles: American Loyalists in the Revolutionary World* (New York, 2011).

pire begun in 1793. Indian, British, and American interests, though often divergent, remained deeply enmeshed.

The Jay Treaty and the French Wars

Most immediately, global war between Britain and France caused serious difficulties for the British India trade, especially when combined with the growth of British wealth in India. As early as 1794, the Company received an alarming report of eighteen frigates and privateers from the Isle de France alone. These French vessels were seizing valuable British and Dutch ships and posing a serious threat to Company and private cargoes in the Indian Ocean. Britons in the Company's colonies, such as Fay, had accumulated considerable capital, and they needed protection. They also needed more and cheaper outlets for trade than the Company and its shippers were willing to provide. The 1793 plan of home secretary and president of the Board of Control Henry Dundas to allot space on Company ships for private British merchants had provided neither competitive freight rates nor the advantages of neutral shippers offering increased protection from privateers and access to more foreign markets. The charter clause allowing British agents to work more fully with foreigners in India and article 13 of the Jay Treaty, therefore, took on additional importance. Yet the legal limits of British and American involvement and of the American trade with British India itself, as well as just who would benefit most from the U.S. India trade, remained to be determined.[5]

In the United States, article 13 stimulated some of the old fears of the corrupting and draining influence of Britain and of the India trade, particularly among Republicans. A circular printed in Philadelphia bemoaned that the treaty was with Britain, "the universal Foe of *Liberty*," in-

5. A neutral American merchant schooner was the source for some of the information, and it counted twenty-five privateers in the East Indies. American merchants stood to benefit from British fears of privateers, and the provider of the report hoped the accounts were "much exaggerated," despite the detailed quality of the information. See John Pringle to the Secret Committee of the Court of Directors, Feb. 24, 1794, *Fort William–India House Correspondence*, XVII, 134–136. The directors dispatched the report to Bengal with instructions to defeat the privateers and seize their bases, if possible (Secret Letter from the Secret Committee of the Court of Directors to the Governor General and Council of Bengal, June 14, 1794, ibid., 134). For substantial losses, including in the India to China trade, see Political Letters from Fort William to the Court of Directors, Nov. 5, 1793, and Mar. 10, 1794, ibid., 304–305, 326–327. Other European powers also enjoyed a similarly beneficial relationship with America; see James R. Fichter, *So Great a Proffit: How the East India Trade Transformed Anglo-American Capitalism* (Cambridge, Mass., 2010), 149–172.

stead of with "avowed Friend" France, and Jay was burned in effigy for his elevation of *"English gold"* over *"Virtue, Equality, and Independence."* In a speech before the people of Charleston, South Carolina, influential Republican state legislator Charles Pinckney argued that American traders to India would exchange valuable specie for "items of mere luxury." His words against the Jay Treaty used the very terms that Britons who were worried about the India trade had used for hundreds of years.[6]

Yet his and similar utterances of fears were largely drowned out by arguments over how the treaty would work and who it would benefit. "A Federalist" explained that Americans should be thrilled with the treaty since it gave legal access to British India, allowing India goods to be purchased 25 percent cheaper in the United States than in Europe. An author named Decius, referencing the Roman Republican who rescued a Roman army from a trap, responded that U.S. merchants could obtain from other Asian ports the same goods as from the British settlements in India "upon as easy or better terms." Only to try to gain some of the American trade for themselves did the British agree to allow U.S. merchants to trade with their Indian settlements. Additionally, Decius explained, the treaty restricted U.S. merchants from trading except back to the United States. A rejoinder from A Federalist stated that nothing in the treaty prohibited reexports of India goods from America. Another Federalist, Camillus, pointed out that U.S. merchants would have far more freedom to trade with British India than private Britons and that the Company itself could trade only to London. Moreover, Americans would pay the same duties as British vessels, and U.S. merchants had real advantages in the export of certain goods to India. Americans could also bring goods directly to America and thus more cheaply, as evidenced by the growing domestic consumption of India goods. Americans could hardly expect to get, in addition, the rights to trade among British Indian ports or from these ports directly to Europe, Camillus explained, nor could they expect the unfettered right that some demanded to settle in British India. These arguments, as the pseudonyms of the authors suggested, largely followed party lines that had been developing since the debate over the new Constitution in the late 1780s.[7]

6. Circular and effigy report from Stephen Girard, quoted in John Bach McMaster, *The Life and Times of Stephen Girard: Mariner and Merchant* (Philadelphia, 1918), I, 295–296; Charles Pinckney, "Speech of Charles Pinckney," *The American Remembrancer; or, An Impartial Collection of Essays, Resolves, Speeches, etc. Relative, or Having Affinity, to the Treaty with Great Britain* (Philadelphia, 1795), I, 13.

7. "Federalist No. III," *American Remembrancer*, II, 96–98, "Decius No. V," II, 137, 140, "Federalist No. V," II, 244, "Camillus No. XXVI," III, 154–161. For an example of the desire

The same party split occurred in Congress, where both sides of the debate on article 13 invoked concerns voiced during the tea crisis and by anti-Company Britons a century before. Pennsylvania Republican John Swanwick, for instance, clearly recalled the rhetoric against the East India Company in 1773, exclaiming, "Of all the despotisms in the world, that of a mercantile monopolizing company is the worst; yet, into such hands we are to fall, and from them to solicit leave to reside or travel in the country." The British East India Company "will have here her India warehouses, and will, by her capital and resources, before long, have this trade entirely in her own hands." He explained that, since many India goods remained illegal in Britain, the Company profited by reexporting them to Europe and America. Federalist Benjamin Goodhue of Salem, Massachusetts, however, responded that the treaty gave Americans better terms to trade with India than British people outside the Company enjoyed. He wondered what British merchants must think of being treated worse than Americans by the British government. As in Britain a century earlier, the congressmen also could not agree on whether the India trade strengthened or weakened national wealth. Republican William Findley of Pennsylvania explained that it took away money for "articles of convenience" and was allowed by Britain in the treaty because it was not "advantageous to the United States." Pennsylvania Federalist John Kittera responded, sounding like Josiah Child or Charles Davenant, "I consider the East India trade a source of great wealth as we shall probably supply many of the markets with Asiatic goods." In mid-1795, the Senate assented to the treaty twenty votes to ten along party lines. In the House of Representatives, responsible for the appropriations to support the treaty, Federalist petitions and pressure convinced several middle-state Republicans to swing the vote narrowly in favor of funding, thereby supporting the version of the India trade the treaty represented.[8]

---

for the right to settle in India, see A Citizen of the United States, "Remarks on the Treaty of Amity, Navigation, and Commerce, Concluded between Lord Grenville and Mr. Jay, on the Part of Great Britain and the United States, Respectively," ibid., III, 296. Claims that the treaty reduced American commercial liberty continued. John Wood wrote, for example, "Our towns and villages were immediately stocked with British agents, Nova-Scotian tories, and French royalists"; see Wood, *The History of the Administration of John Adams* ... (New York, 1802), 2.

8. United States, Congress (4th, 1st session, 1795–1796), *Debates in the House of Representatives of the United States during the First Session of the Fourth Congress, upon the Constitutional Powers of the House, with Respect to Treaties, and upon the Subject of the British Treaty* (Philadelphia, 1796), II, 55–63, 121–122, 179–181, 195. For the many other issues in the treaty debate, the vote breakdown, and those voting against party, see Jerald A. Combs,

Many Americans and Britons, such as the operators of the *Persever-ance*, quickly tested article 13. Thomas and John Ketland of Philadelphia consigned the *Perseverance* under Captain James Williamson to Adaseer Dada in Bombay, where it attracted the Company's interest in the spring of 1796. The Bombay government still did not have the final treaty, did not know whether it was in effect, and did not have instructions for how to handle American vessels if it was. Thus unprepared, the government questioned Williamson, a Scotsman who claimed he was American. The government asked Williamson for the date that he became an American citizen; he refused to answer. Williamson stated that he had brought the vessel to Bombay via Hamburg, London, and Madeira. He intended to sail again for Hamburg with a cargo of cotton. The Bombay government asked Adaseer Dada if he knew that the vessel was British, and he responded that he was sure it was American. The Company's solicitor in Bombay advised the Bombay government that there was no doubt that the *Perse-verance* carried a British cargo on joint British and American credit. He argued that the voyage was illegal "whether they can or cannot assume the Characters of American Citizens or Agents for American Citizens." But if they were American, sailing to Europe was only illegal if the treaty was now in force. The government ordered Williamson to remoor and threat-ened to send an armed party aboard to force his compliance. Williamson explained that he would not go to Hamburg, but he would like to go wher-ever the government told him was legal. Finally, without clear instructions and with ample suspicion but little proof, the Bombay government fol-lowed years of Company servant practice accommodating interlopers and let the *Perseverance* go to Hamburg.[9]

A legal letter from the Company to Bombay explained that the *Perse-verance* should not have been cleared. The cargo and the papers furnished "abundant reason for suspicion of her being an illicit Trader in the employ of British Subjects." The letter went on, "Such illicit trade has been carried on in fictitious Names and under covered Pretences to a great extent to

The Jay Treaty: Political Battleground of the Founding Fathers (Berkeley, Calif., 1970), 161, 171, 184–187; Todd Estes, *The Jay Treaty Debate, Public Opinion, and the Evolution of Early American Political Culture* (Boston, 2006), esp. 182–187.

9. Copy of the President's Minutes and the Bombay Board's Resolution, Apr. 22, 1796, IOR/H/337, 111–114, BL; Bombay Minutes, IOR/H/337, 373, BL; William White to ?, Apr. 30, 1796, IOR/H/337, 343–344, BL; Forester Constable, Company Solicitor, Bombay to ?, Apr. 23, 1796, IOR/H/337, 171–175, BL; J. G. Richardson to Philip Dundas, Apr. 23, 1796, IOR/H/337, 167, BL; Williamson to the Bombay Board of Trade, Apr. 28, 1796, IOR/H/337, 333, BL.

the Injury of the Company and of their Commanders and Officers who are licenced to trade." The voyage was doubly illegal—for being a British interloper disguised as American and, under the terms of the Jay Treaty, for sailing directly from British India to Europe. The directors also sent the governments of their presidencies guidelines for implementing the treaty. They explained that Britons could not simply claim U.S. citizenship to trade with India. American vessels were also not allowed to take British-India goods from port to port within the Indian Ocean and China Seas. They could carry goods from British India only to the United States. Alexander Hamilton and others in America agreed with and publicized the Company's assessment of this important term.[10]

Nevertheless, even though its servants refused clearances for ports outside America, the Company had little control over where American vessels went after they left British Indian ports. The American vessel *Elizabeth,* for instance, unloaded its cargo in Calcutta and then proceeded slightly inland to the Danish port of Fredericksnagore, or Serampore, and onward to Batavia. The advocate general explained that Britons had no power to stop such movements (according to the treaty, the ship could carry its "original cargoes, or part thereof," from port to port; the latter clause provided considerable leeway), and, once the vessels went to a foreign port, that port might readily allow the ship to sail wherever it wanted, even to ports illegal under the treaty. Nor could the British refuse harbor pilots to American vessels since the treaty guaranteed they would "admit and hospitably receive American Ships." Some in the Company strongly disagreed with the advocate general's position, noting that all the piece goods loaded on the *Elizabeth* at Serampore had to be the produce of British India since Serampore was a port surrounded entirely by British Bengal. According to the treaty, the Americans could take British Indian goods only directly to the United States.[11]

10. "Extract of Law Letter to Bombay," Mar. 22, 1797, IOR/H/439/2, 491, BL; "Extract Public Letter to Bengal," Aug. 31, 1796, IOR/H/337, 615–616, BL. Hamilton saw the restriction on American vessels going to Europe from India as reasonable to protect the East India Company's trade, though he argued for more rights for Americans to trade among British settlements in Asia; see Alexander Hamilton to George Washington, Sept. 4, 1795, in Harold C. Syrett, ed., *The Papers of Alexander Hamilton Digital Edition* (Charlottesville, Va., 2011). For the agreement of American newspapers, see "New York, May 1," *City Gazette and Daily Advertiser* (Charleston, S.C.), May 18, 1797, [2].

11. "Extract Bengal Foreign Consultations," Jan. 23, 1797, IOR/H/337, 635–639 ("admit"), BL; "Extract Foreign Letter from Bengal," Aug. 28, 1797, IOR/H/337, 659–661, BL. For the text of article 13, see *Treaties and Conventions Concluded between the United States of America and Other Powers, since July 4, 1776,* rev. ed. (Washington, D.C., 1873),

The French Wars and the Refashioning of Empire

American ships voyaging directly from British India to Europe or carrying British Indian goods to other ports in the Indian Ocean openly violated the Jay Treaty, but the status of American ships going to India from Europe was less clear. In 1797, the *Five Brothers* arrived in London from the Isle de France, Bourbon, and Surat, and the London merchant William Vaughan sought permission to clear it out for Batavia and China carrying eighty thousand dollars. The Company directors attempted to stop the vessel from departing. The directors appealed to the Privy Council that the voyage was "a direct infringement of the East India Companys exclusive right of trading and for which she cannot be entitled to a clearance without their licence." The customhouse responded, however, that the Company charter regulated only British, not foreign, ships leaving Britain. The directors then argued that the ship might be allowed to go east but that the goods on board could not. As a legal opinion submitted to the Privy Council explained, "Goods, Merchandize, Treasure, and effects shipped or put on board any Ship or Ships, Vessel or Vessels, bound from Great Britain to the East Indies or parts aforesaid . . . are forfeited together with double the value and may be seized." It is unclear whether the *Five Brothers* left London with a cargo or its treasure, but it soon joined a convoy of Company East Indiamen under the protection of the British frigate *Niger* for the East Indies. Presumably, it had at least treasure on board to trade.[12]

Cases regarding participation by American and British associates in the India trade landed in courts in the West Indies and the United States as well. The contest over the Philadelphia ship *Mount Vernon* showcased the continuation of duplicitous Anglo-American partnerships and the legal risks involved. In 1796, the recently arrived Britons William Duncanson and James Ray, with wealth and experience from Bengal, purchased a new Philadelphia-built 431-ton coppered ship, the *Mount Vernon*, from

---

326. For an example of a refusal of a clearance, see Fort William to Directors, Jan. 9, 1797, *Fort William–India House Correspondence*, XIII, 523.

12. "Opinion of Mr. Rous," Oct. 2, 1797, IOR/L/MAR/C/325, n.p., BL; *Gazette of the United States, and Philadelphia Advertiser,* Jan. 10, 1797, [3]; *City Gazette and Daily Advertiser,* Mar. 15, 1797, [2]; *Salem Gazette* (Mass.), Jan. 12, 1798, [3]. The Bombay government had been unsure about what to do with the *Five Brothers* since, as with the *Perseverance,* it did not know whether the treaty was in effect when the ship arrived. The government hoped the Americans would report that the treaty had been ratified so that it could prohibit them from "Shipping any piece goods, excepting expressly for some port in America." But, without word of ratification, the government told the local "Nabob" in Surat to trade with the Americans as if the treaty did not exist. See *Gazette of the United States, and Philadelphia Advertiser,* Dec. 21, 1796, [3]; Fort William to Court of Directors, May 12, 1796, *Fort William–India House Correspondence,* XVIII, 218–219.

Thomas Murgatroyd. Unsubstantiated rumors circulated that Duncanson and Ray had come to America to avoid giving testimony in the trial of Warren Hastings. Duncanson intended to send the *Mount Vernon* to London, onward to India, and back to Philadelphia with the backing of his Philadelphia partners, Willings and Francis, a firm well connected to East India Company director Francis Baring. Thomas Willings, the senior partner, knew the India trade better than most U.S. merchants; he had overseen the sale of the cargo brought back on the *United States* in 1784. Willings and Francis believed that Duncanson had already obtained American citizenship papers to safely bypass the Company monopoly in India, but he had not. Murgatroyd, therefore, agreed to keep his name on the ship while Duncanson tried to become a U.S. citizen. Willings and Francis supplied the cargo on Duncanson's account. The partners hired George Dominick to captain the ship to London, where it was to be transferred to Duncanson under the assumption that he would by then have his U.S. citizenship. Apparently, this arrangement was an open secret; Murgatroyd and Willings and Francis warned Dominick that a French privateer intended to capture the ship for aiding the British. Dominick sailed anyway and was soon caught. The ship's captors took it to Puerto Rico to be condemned. Murgatroyd ordered Dominick to chase the *Mount Vernon* as an American citizen by using the schooner *Paragon*.[13]

Murgatroyd, Duncanson, and Dominick hoped to continue to play their nationality multiple ways, and where they failed—with their ship—others would succeed. In the French Admiralty court, Murgatroyd claimed the ship as his neutral American property and its captain as an American citizen. The court disagreed, noting that the vessel was aiding the British enemy and that the captain was not in fact George Dominick but Dominico, a Portuguese man without proper American papers. Another American named McLure bought the ship as a French prize and fought off

13. Willings and Francis to George Dominick, Apr. 26, 1796, Mordecai and Samuel Lewis Papers, Leonard Beale Collection, 1746–1892, Collection 1735, HSP. On the acrimonious partnership with Ray, the rumors of the Hastings trial, and Duncanson's real estate investment failure, see Allen C. Clark, "William Mayne Duncanson," *Records of the Columbia Historical Society, Washington, D.C.*, XIV (1911), 13–18, 22–24. On the agreement with Duncanson, see Francis to ?, June 27, 1796, Lewis Papers, Collection 1735, HSP. For the warning, see Willings and Francis to Dominick, June 5, 1796, Willings and Francis Papers, Collection 1874, box 1, folder 9, HSP. Duncanson was a fascinating character. In the late 1790s, he came to Philadelphia, headed a canal lottery scheme, became a litigant in several civil suits, and enjoyed a bloodless duel with Mr. Greenleaf; see Presly Thornton, "Alexandria, October 15," *Alexandria Advertiser*, Oct. 15, 1798, 3.

claims from both Murgatroyd and Duncanson in the U.S. Supreme Court. The plaintiffs argued that, since the seizure had been an illegal infringement of neutral rights, the ship should still be theirs. McLure responded that the ship had in fact been Duncanson's clandestine British property and thus legally seized. The machinations among Duncanson, Murgatroyd, Dominick, and Willings and Francis slowly came to light, and the court decided that the voyage broke American law forbidding foreigners, such as Duncanson, from owning a vessel with American flags. The partners lost their ship, not for breaking British law regarding the India trade, but for breaking French and American laws regarding false contracts and aiding the enemy with their backup plan. According to Duncanson, it is not clear that Willings and Francis actually lost anything. Duncanson described Willings and Francis as "damned Rascals, Villains, and Swindlers" for supposedly orchestrating the entire *Mount Venture* adventure to "defraud and Rob him" of more than forty-nine thousand dollars. In any case, the *Mount Vernon* sailed to British India in 1798 under its new ownership, where the East India Company's officials at Fort Saint George entered a rare question mark in their records under nationality. Still, Company officials let the *Mount Vernon*'s captain load piece goods and sail back to Baltimore. Apparently, where the ship had come from and whether it was owned by U.S. citizens, and thus whether it was trading legally, mattered less than that it had come to buy a few hundred tons of British Indian manufactures.[14]

14. Duncanson to Willings and Francis, December 1799, and Affidavit of James Ray, Feb. 21, 1800, Willings and Francis Papers, Collection 1874, box 1, folder 10, HSP; *Duncanson v. McLure* and *Murgatoyd v. McLure*, 4 U.S. 308 (1804), in A. J. Dallas, *Reports of Cases Ruled and Adjudged in the Several Courts of the United States and of Pennsylvania, Held at the Seat of the Federal Government*, 3d ed. (New York, 1895), IV, 308–309, 341. The defendant in this case may be the famous Baltimore merchant John McLure or one of his relatives. It could also be a British captain with this surname who was experienced in the West India–America trade posing as a U.S. citizen; see *Philadelphia Gazette and Daily Advertiser*, Aug. 26, 1800, [3]. Duncanson was swindled by Ray, and Thomas Jefferson strongly defended Duncanson's character; see Clark, "William Mayne Duncanson," *Records of the Columbia Historical Society, Washington, D.C.*, XIV (1911), 14–16, 22. The *Mount Vernon* arrived back in Philadelphia on June 7, 1797, with Captain Merrihew; see *Boston Price-Current*, June 15, 1797, 3. One month later, it appears to have cleared for Baltimore under Captain Stokes; see *Philadelphia Gazette and Universal Daily Advertiser*, July 25, 1797, [3]. For the *Mount Vernon* in India, see, "Fort St George List of Arrivals and Departures of ships from the 31st May 1798 to the 1st June 1799," IOR/L/MAR/C/547, n.p., BL. The *Mount Vernon* appears to have sailed to England or Rotterdam and onward to Batavia and Madras, arriving back in Baltimore in 1799 after a profitable voyage of fifteen months; see *Aurora General Advertiser* (Philadelphia), Mar. 26, 1799, [3]. After the voyage, the *Mount Vernon* was sold again at auction in

Indeed, the landmark 1798 British case *Wilson v. Marryat* gave legal protection to Britons with American citizenship as well as American traders departing from Britain through a broad interpretation of the Jay Treaty. The case centered on the voyage of the ship *Argonaut,* owned by Anthony Butler and John Collet and under Collet's command. Butler had been born in Britain but had lived in America since before the American Revolution. Collet had also been born in Britain, where he lived until July 1784, when he moved his family to the United States and was granted U.S. citizenship. Collet took the *Argonaut* from Philadelphia to Brest, Bordeaux, and Madeira and then toward British India. His cargo included British goods bought on credit from Wilson, the plaintiff in the case. The *Argonaut* was seized as an illicit trader near the Cape of Good Hope by the Royal Navy. The insurer, Marryat, refused to pay Wilson's claim, arguing that the voyage was illegal. Lord Chief Justice Lloyd Kenyon noted that the court was "threatened on both sides, by the one party not to touch the concerns of the *East India* Company, by the other not to irritate our allies in *America.*"[15]

Kenyon determined that, following existing precedent, the ship's captain and part owner, Collet, could not give up his British subjecthood but that the United States could, and had, granted him U.S. citizenship and the protection and opportunities of that citizenship "for the purposes of commerce." Kenyon noted that the Jay Treaty was not intended to restrict U.S. traders to the direct trade from America to India but also determined that Americans could trade from Europe to India, though not directly back to Europe. Reportedly, Grenville, the Company, and the British government believed "it was not a fair and natural interpretation of words, which authorized a commerce between two defined limits." Nevertheless, Kenyon's upholding of the citizenship precedent and his interpretation of article 13 of the Jay Treaty legalized a tremendous range of British and American merchant activity.[16]

As the legal questions were settled, less and less obstructed Britons and Americans from combining their interests and advantages. Continuing patterns from the 1780s, the United States still had undeveloped banking and private investment services and a limited capital pool. American

---

Baltimore, along with its cargo of coffee, pepper, and two hundred bales of piece goods; see *Philadelphia Gazette and Universal Daily Advertiser,* Mar. 29, 1799, [3].

15. Charles Durnford and Edward Hyde East, *Reports of Cases Argued and Determined in the Court of King's Bench* (Dublin, 1800), VIII, 31–34, 44.

16. Ibid., 44–46.

merchants trading with India had such trouble securing capital that they ran subscriptions among American farmers, attempted to sell American land to people in Calcutta, and tendered "fictitious" bills of exchange. In the early 1790s, Henry Colebrooke estimated that British capital financed two-thirds of all foreign trade from Bengal to Europe and America and that British ships under foreign colors carried much of this cargo. In 1796–1797, Americans in Calcutta drew bills on Britons amounting to approximately twice as much as on their own countrymen. More conservatively, Company directors Edward Parry and Charles Grant calculated that between 1795 and 1800 clandestine British capital accounted for one-quarter of all American expenditures in India. Another estimate suggested that British agency houses provided American merchants with two hundred thousand pounds of capital in 1799 alone. When the Company's reporter of external commerce, Thomas Brown, broke down the value of exports from Calcutta by merchant nationality instead of by the ships' recorded destinations, he found that Britons exported, not twice (as shown by the country of initial destination), but more than three times as much as Americans in 1799–1800. The difference came from the large number of Britons masquerading as American citizens or employing their capital on U.S. ships.[17]

Britons could buy cargo space on U.S. vessels, as Fay had done, temporarily adopt or pretend to hold U.S. citizenship, as Duncanson had done, or loan capital to U.S. merchants with the debts payable in Britain, as Baring had done. Britons in India further profited as agents to American merchants by earning commissions and interest that could be remitted back to Britain. Calcutta had fifteen agency houses in 1790; it had twenty-nine in 1803. Most of these houses maintained close connections with London affiliates that provided credit and facilitated sales. All of these mechanisms

17. On the capital situation in the early Republic, see R. C. Nash, "The Organization of Trade and Finance in the British Atlantic Economy, 1600–1830," in Peter A. Coclanis, ed., *The Atlantic Economy during the Seventeenth and Eighteenth Centuries: Organization, Operation, Practice, and Personnel* (Columbia, S.C., 2005), 131–133; Thomas M. Doerflinger, *A Vigorous Spirit of Enterprise: Merchants and Economic Development in Revolutionary Philadelphia* (Chapel Hill, N.C., 1986), 78. For U.S. attempts to raise capital, see "Copy of Mr Brown's Report of the Import and Export Trade of Calcutta by Sea from 1796/7" to Peter Speke, IOR/P/174/13, n.p., BL. Colebrooke was responding to an even higher estimate made in a 1791 memorial to the Court of Directors; see Henry Thomas Colebrooke, *Remarks on the Present State of the Husbandry and Commerce of Bengal* (Calcutta, 1795), 177–181, 217. For the other estimates, see Edward Parry and Charles Grant, Response to Francis Barings's Paper, October 1808, FO 353/58, fol. 162v, NA; C. H. Philips, *Correspondence of David Scott*, cited in S. B. Singh, *European Agency Houses in Bengal, 1783–1833* (Calcutta, 1966), 141; Brown to Speke, Sept. 1801, IOR/P/174/13, n.p., BL.

allowed Britons to employ their capital in the India trade via the American flag. American merchants worked alongside Portuguese, Danish, and other European merchants, offering freight and insurance rates that undercut the Company, and all often working with British associates seeking to avoid the Company monopoly.[18]

Americans and Britons using the American flag gained further opportunities from the U.S. neutral status as the French Revolutionary War with Britain intensified. Including all foreign goods, not just those from Asia, U.S. reexports increased from several hundred thousand dollars per year in the early 1790s to approximately $6,500,000 in 1794, $26,300,000 in 1796, and $49,131,000 in 1800. Reexports then plummeted to $13,594,000 during the temporary Franco-British peace from March 1802 to May 1803. An analogous pattern occurred in estimated U.S. shipping profits, which increased from $6,000,000 to 7,000,000 per year in the early 1790s to $15,500,000 in 1794 and $26,200,000 in 1800. Shipping became the single largest source of U.S. foreign exchange, and no commodity would reach comparable levels until cotton in the 1820s. In the Calcutta trade, by 1800–1801, American shipping hit a new peak, accounting for approximately one-quarter of exports beyond the Cape of Good Hope (Figure 4). The neutral advantages of protection from seizure by enemy privateers and men-of-war as well as better access to foreign markets combined to create unprecedented opportunities for U.S. merchants trading with Europe in non-American commodities.[19]

Neutral Americans also worked actively with the French to import India goods from the British empire and to offer neutral protection to goods moving among French possessions and France. In the years immediately before 1793, U.S. ships most frequently brought American tobacco, rice, and flour to Bordeaux. After 1793, they most frequently brought re-

18. On agency houses, see Singh, *European Agency Houses in Bengal*, 8–10. For freight and insurance rates, see Rates of Freight and Insurance from Calcutta in 1795/6, IOR/P/174/13, n.p., BL.

19. Douglass C. North, "The United States Balance of Payments, 1790–1860," in *Trends in the American Economy in the Nineteenth Century: A Report of the National Bureau of Economic Research, New York,* Studies in Income and Wealth, XXIV (Princeton, N.J., 1960), 576–577, 595–596; Douglass North and Alan Heston, "The Estimation of Shipping Earnings in Historical Studies of the Balance of Payments," *Canadian Journal of Economics and Political Science,* XXVI (1960), 276; Silvia Marzagalli, "The Failure of a Transatlantic Alliance? Franco-American Trade, 1783–1815," *History of European Ideas,* XXXIV (2008), 459; Marzagalli, "Establishing Transatlantic Trade Networks in Time of War: Bordeaux and the United States, 1793–1815," *Business History Review,* LXXIX (2005), 826–829.

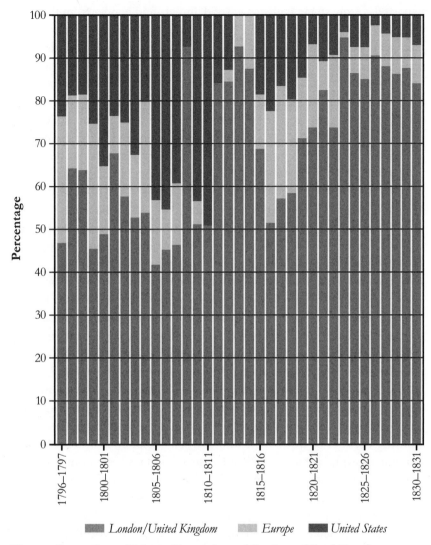

Figure 4. Proportions of Calcutta Exports beyond the Cape of Good Hope by
First Destination, 1796–1797 through 1830–1831. "Comparative Abstract Annual
Statement of Exports . . . ," IOR/P/174/17, 22, 27, 32, 42, 46, BL. Proportions are not
representative of Calcutta's export trade overall. Drawn by Rebecca Wrenn

exported cotton, sugar, coffee, dyewood, indigo, and pepper from the West and East Indies. John Crowninshield, for example, found the French merchants entirely supportive of his efforts and those of other neutrals. They were so supportive, in fact, that he was unsure whether to go back for more British Indian and other Asian goods, writing, "I hear India is full and full, of Americans in particular I mean Madras and Calcutta and Batavie etc." He was correct to be concerned. American arrivals in Madras peaked at sixteen vessels from June 1796 to June 1797, outstripping the market and falling back to an average of just more than five per year until June 1800. Although Britons in India, including many Company servants, were keen to work with Americans, there was substantial disagreement in Britain over who gained and lost more from the U.S. India trade.[20]

In 1800, Henry Dundas wrote to the Company directors explaining that, to maximize British India's value to Britain, foreign ships should bring foreign capital to British India to purchase India goods, and British Indian capital, augmented by such transactions, should be transferred back out only on the British empire's ships and only to Britain. British rule in large parts of India had allowed Britain to benefit from India's exports to the Atlantic even if the goods did not pass through London. Dundas argued that Parliament had made clear that the British India trade "should not be regulated on the principles of colonial exclusion." Under such an unwanted policy, British agents in India would not be allowed to work with foreigners, and foreigners would instead trade in non-British ports on the Indian Ocean. Those ports and their mother countries would gain the benefits of trade instead of British India, and ultimately Britain. But allowing agency did not solve the second problem of maximizing the export of British capital on British ships. He argued that the number of British and India-built ships needed to be dramatically increased, or Britons would turn to foreigners who would gain part of this capital. The issue was an imbalance between too much freight space heading east and not enough affordable British freight space heading west. Dundas recognized that the freight rates in his 1793 plan had proven too high to encourage Britons to use British instead of foreign shipping. Pointing to wartime demands, he had already pushed Parliament to legalize India-built ships

20. John Crowninshield to Crowninshield and Sons, May 21, 1797, MH 15, box 4, folder 8, Letter Book of Ship *Bellisarius*, PEM. U.S. arrivals in Madras are calculated from statistics in IOR/L/MAR/C/547, n.p., BL. On the shift in American imports to Bordeaux, see Marzagalli, "Failure of a Transatlantic Alliance," *History of European Ideas*, XXXIV (2008), 463.

The French Wars and the Refashioning of Empire

to trade as British-built. Now he pushed hard for the Company to employ them.[21]

Company director Charles Grant penned a lengthy report similarly arguing that colonial trading principles, such as the Navigation Acts designed to confine much of colonial American trade to Britain, were not suitable for India, where the goal was to maximize the export of British India goods regardless of destination. Grant saw in thoughts of settler colonization and an open trade the "Colonial principle" that had led to revolution in the thirteen colonies. He, and the directors as a group, also agreed with Dundas that a colonial monopoly in which all India goods for foreign markets must come first to Britain made no sense. India's value depended on high demand for its exports, but pushing goods for Europe or America through London would increase prices and lower demand. Britain could not control Manila, Java, or the French Islands in the Indian Ocean or the trade of those places, but it could provide incentives for foreign merchants to come to British India instead. Britons in India under the present system had become "the general Agents for the European Exports," gaining commissions while the Company in India collected duties, all in exchange for imports of foreign bullion, and all further enriching the British empire.[22]

Grant at this time saw little new or particularly worrisome in the trade of Americans, unless they became the means for transferring much more British capital. Grant found that Harry Verelst, as governor of Bengal in

21. Henry Dundas, "Letter from the Right Honorable Henry Dundas to the Chairman; dated the 2d April, 1800," in *Papers respecting the Trade between India and Europe* ([London], 1802), 1–14 (quotation on 11). On Dundas's earlier attempt, see "An Act for Allowing, for a Limited Time, the Importation of Goods from India and China, and Other Parts within the Limits of the Exclusive Trade of the East India Company, in Ships Not of British-Built . . . ," 35 Geo. III, c.115, in [Owen Ruffhead, ed.], *The Statutes at Large . . .* , 14 vols. (London, 1786–1800), XL, 399–400.

22. Charles Grant, "Observations on the Question of Enlarging the Trade of British Subjects between India and Europe," July 1800, Add MS 37277, fols. 191–227v (quotations on 214v, 274r), BL (also in IOR/H/405, 691–859, BL). The directors' resolutions on these points agree with Grant's positions; see "Minutes of the Court of Directors, Held on Wednesday, the 4th February 1801, Containing the Resolutions of the Special Committee, Adopted by the Court . . . ," in *Letters From the Right Hon. Henry Dundas to the Chairman of the Court of Directors of the East-India Company, upon an Open Trade to India* (London, 1813), 36–37, 41–45. Dundas replied that he agreed with Grant that foreign silver imports were terrific and that colonial principles, as expressed in the Navigation Acts, did not make sense for the current India trade; see Henry Dundas to Charles Grant, July 31, 1800, IOR/H/405, 863–876, BL.

1768, estimated that foreigners, including the Dutch, French, and Danes, exported 73⅔ lakh of current rupees. Grant noted that this estimate compared closely to the exports of foreigners now totaling 65 lakhs. Neutral American merchants were not expanding the foreign trade; they were helpfully taking over the trades run previously by the French and Dutch, and they were mostly trading with Calcutta instead of foreign ports in India. Nevertheless, Americans could cause problems by trading directly to Europe, providing the means for Britons in India to develop "interest and relations in America," and by engaging in clandestine trade with Britons. With Britain increasingly in control of India's ports, there were opportunities to increase the duties on foreigners, including Americans, and to lower the duties on legal imports into Britain. These duty revisions would sharply reduce the incentives for clandestine trade. Unfortunately, Grant explained, the Jay Treaty still guaranteed Americans the same duty rates as private Britons for several more years.[23]

Grant believed with Dundas that Britain needed to take full advantage of the "extraordinary" transition over the past three decades from India as a sink of British bullion to India as a generator of capital for Britain, but he came to a different conclusion about the difficulty of transferring that capital. He explained that "the Tribute paid by the British possessions has furnished the Capital of the British Trade, Public and Private." Essentially, then, "India gives her choice productions for nothing." Moreover, he explained, the Company was shifting to the export of raw materials from India, including sugar and indigo. Even when cloth exports fell, the Company would still be able to employ all available capital. Opening the trade or expanding the use of India-built ships, Grant argued, would therefore only suck capital away from Britain's other trades.[24]

The London shipbuilders and shipowners, with 350 votes in the Court of Directors, drove the Company's position against Dundas on adding shipping. The Company did not own its ships; it contracted them from private owners who formed a London lobby to orchestrate higher construction costs and freight charges than in any other trade. India-built ships were cheaper, lasted longer, and required fewer repairs with their rot-resistant teak construction. American-built ships lacked the benefits of teak, but they were still cheaper than Company ships. India- and U.S.-

23. Grant, "Observations on the Question of Enlarging the Trade of British Subjects," July 1800, Add MS 37277, fols. 230–247v, BL.

24. Ibid., fols. 251v–260, 302v.

built ships thus threatened substantial competition to London-built East Indiamen, with their elevated monopoly shipping rates.[25]

The shipping lobby defended its position in part by describing India's constitutional position in the British empire as being unlike the thirteen colonies before the American Revolution and like the United States after. Joseph Cotton, for instance, explained that the carrying trade was "the Birthright of our Countrymen." Cotton was appalled "that the Black Subjects of the Indian Domain are to have Employment, to the Exclusion of British Ship-Builders, Artificers, Tradesmen and Seamen." "Black" Indians, for Cotton, were subjects, but they were clearly neither British nor entitled to the legal trade advantages of being part of the British empire. Cotton and others who argued on behalf of London's India shipowners positioned Indians as rather different from colonists in the Atlantic. The Navigation Acts had, after all, defined Atlantic colonial ships and crews as equivalent to those from Britain itself. Cotton proclaimed the value of the Navigation Acts, but, unlike for British colonists in America, he excluded Indians from the benefits of those acts.[26]

These lobbying efforts had real consequences. In 1798, for example, the firm Lambert and Ross in Calcutta was "under considerable anxiety" as they finished seven ships for the trade to Britain, ranging from 470 to more than 900 tons. By 1800, the Company had refused to charter the ships, and Charles Lambert complained, "Shipping concerns as far as we have engaged in them to Europe, have been[?] a source of anxiety, trouble, inconvenience, and loss, and I would recommend all of them to be closed as soon as possible, and on no account continued, unless a manifest advantage appears in favour of these speculations." The shipyards, he expected, might be best employed building 400- to 600-ton vessels for the West Indian trade.[27]

25. For more on the London lobby as well as India-built ship quality and advantages, see Indrajit Ray, *Bengal Industries and the British Industrial Revolution (1757–1857)* (New York, 2011), 186–191. On the shipping lobby's votes, see Northcote Parkinson, *The Trade in the Eastern Seas, 1793–1813* (Cambridge, 1937), 170–190.

26. Joseph Cotton, *A Review of the Shipping System of the East-India Company; with Suggestions for Its Improvement, to Secure the Continuance of the Carrying Trade to This Country, and the Advantages of Indian Commerce to the Company* (London, 1799), 12, 25. Cotton's simultaneous positioning of Indians within and without the British empire followed long-standing ambiguity; see Ian Baucom, *Out of Place: Englishness, Empire, and the Locations of Identity* (Princeton, N.J., 1999), 7–15.

27. Charles Lambert to W. Thomas Gilchrist, May 1, 1798, Letter Book, MSS Eur C515, 32, BL, Charles Lambert to Anthony Lambert, July 25, 1798, 65, 32, Charles Lambert to L. Ross,

In Dundas's view, the Company's recalcitrance to offer more shipping only served to enrich foreign, notably American, merchants and their illicit British associates. He was furious that the Company would not enable private British Indian capital to be fully mobilized either by private British or India-built ships. Americans' effective immunity from the London shipping lobby allowed the employment of private capital at lower cost, without the need to officially defeat the monopolies of the Company or the London shipowners. "British Traders in India," Dundas wrote, would prefer "the liberal and advantageous allurements held out to them with avidity and kindness by our foreign Rivals" over "the niggardly and narrow minded Propositions held out to them by the Court of Directors." Dundas warned that thereby "the Surplus Wealth of India passes into the hands of Foreigners" at the permanent expense of Britain and the Company's future trade. He asserted, "The object appears to me to be, that Sir Francis Baring may enjoy the great Emoluments he receives from the Trade of the Americans to India which is daily encreasing." It is not clear, however, that Indian-built shipping would have absorbed all of the trade from U.S. ships during wartime. America's neutrality provided particular advantages in safety and market access. Indeed, during the peace from March 1802 to May 1803, much of the proportion of Calcutta's trade that had gone in American and other European ships during the previous few years went back into British ships (Figure 4). Then, when war resumed between Britain and France, causing dramatic turmoil in Europe, the neutral U.S. flag became more valuable than ever.[28]

J. Scott, and W. Hollings, Jan. 14, 1800, 250–251. The Company chartered at least one of the ships, the *Vareena*, but refused to use it again. To keep up the pressure against India-built ships, the Company's London shipowners formed a society in 1802 that "most strongly deprecated any attempt to relax those wholesome and beneficial maritime regulations, which had so conspicuously and effectually contributed to the greatness and power of the country." See Society of Ship-owners of Great Britain, "A General Meeting of Shipowners, Held the First Day of December, 1802 at the London Tavern," in *Collection of Interesting and Important Reports and Papers on the Navigation and Trade of Great Britain, Ireland, and the British Colonies in the West Indies and America* . . . [London, 1807], lxv. Parliament did not fully succumb to the lobby and reaffirmed the 1795 law that permitted India-built shipping. Nevertheless, the Company retained discretion over employing the ships. See "An Act for Making Perpetual So Much of an Act . . . to the Allowing the Importation and Exportation of Goods from India and China, in Ships Not of British Built . . . ," 42 Geo. III, c. 20, in *The Statutes of the United Kingdom of Great Britain and Ireland*, XIX, ed. Thomas Edlyne Tomlins (London, 1804), 292–293.

28. Dundas to the Earl of Dartmouth, Aug. 5, 1801, MSS Eur D624, II, fol. 193, BL, Dec. 26, 1801, fol. 247, Jan. 8, 1802, fol. 260v. For more on Baring's working with Americans in the India trade, see Fichter, *So Great a Proffit*, 142–143. Baring developed an association in

Practices and Profits

Tench Coxe advised secretary of state James Madison in October 1803:

> It appears to me probable that the English East India Company will find it difficult to dispense with our trade there at this Moment; because our silver is of great us[e] to them in India, because they want a sale for their India Manufactures, wch. are not consumable in England; because they want a vent for their Sugars and Indigo, and because our ships will be useful to that distant possession, in the present war.

Coxe was right. With the resumption of war, the total share of exports from Calcutta on neutral Portuguese and American ships resurged (Figure 4). U.S. merchants and ships were invaluable wartime tools for transferring goods out of India to foreign markets in exchange for foreign silver. According to the Company's carefully collected data, treasure accounted for 84 percent of the value of U.S. imports into Calcutta at the turn of the century. The possibilities that war expanded for American merchants in the trade of British India were not lost on merchants such as John Crowninshield, of the influential U.S. India trading Crowninshield family. Crowninshield wrote from Bordeaux, "Remember you cannot make too much money this war—drive the India trade hard." But all was not necessarily easy or cheap for U.S. merchants. And, as U.S. merchants overcame difficulties to take advantage of wartime opportunities, the Company directors became increasingly unsure whether the Americans were friends, enemies, or necessities for Britain's India trade.[29]

. Private merchants, including Americans, had different difficulties and advantages in the India trade from the Company. Instead of ordering goods in advance, as the Company did, private merchants purchased goods at bazaars and from Indian middlemen. On the one hand, they had less control over production, less opportunity to strong-arm producers for low prices, and limited abilities to contract for cloth to meet specific patterns and dimensions. On the other hand, private merchants could purchase goods much more quickly than the Company, a timeframe measured

---

1803, for example, with the wealthy and successful Philadelphia merchant Stephen Girard. See McMaster, *Life and Times of Stephen Girard*, 431–433.

29. Tench Coxe to James Madison, Oct. 16, 1803, in J. C. A. Stagg, ed., *The Papers of James Madison Digital Edition* (Charlottesville, Va., 2010); John Crowninshield to Crowninshield and Sons, July 13, 1803, Bordeaux Letter Book, 96, MH 15, PEM. On treasure, see Thomas Brown to Peter Speke, Sept. 10, 1801 (copy), IOR/P/174/13, n.p., BL.

in weeks instead of months. They could respond more quickly to changing market information, and they could bargain with a broad range of competing suppliers. Most of all, neutral private merchants had significant advantages in reduced risk at sea and increased access to foreign markets. Calcutta's reporter of external commerce estimated that more than half of the ships with papers for America simply collected replacement papers in a U.S. port without unloading before sailing to French ports. Many others ran the risk of going straight to French ports with British Indian goods.[30]

Like countless American merchants in the late 1790s and early 1800s, the wealthy Philadelphian Stephen Girard decided to enter the India trade. Girard had developed his business by trading with his native France and the West Indies. In 1803, as war between Britain and France resumed, high numbers of American and Portuguese ships poured into Calcutta. The supercargo of Girard's *Voltaire*, Leopold Nottnagel, reported that nineteen American and seven Portuguese vessels were in Calcutta as well as two Danish and two Spanish ships. "Under these circumstances," he explained, "I am very much at a Loss what to do." He wished he had the power to alter the destination of the ship, but he promised to try to buy whatever seemed reasonable. Over the next several weeks, Nottnagel managed to buy some piece goods and sugar at an "enormous" price. More ships then arrived from Salem, threatening to drive up prices further.[31]

American traders such as Girard and Nottnagel without access to the Company's procurement system needed substantial help from Indian banyan merchants, British agents, or experienced supercargoes to find and assess goods, drive bargains, and predict price movements. J. Stark, an agent in Calcutta, told Girard that he had heard U.S. merchants "invariably, and with great Justice, complain of the knavery of the Banyans . . . but whom, under the present system, they are nevertheless obliged to employ, as the medium of obtaining cargoes." U.S. merchants often needed to purchase goods "3rd, 4th, or 5th hand," with each person in the

30. J. P. Larkins, "Report on the External Commerce of Bengal for the Year 1803/4 from the 1st of June to the 31st of May 1804," IOR/P/174/15, fol. 104, BL; Larkins, "Report on the External Commerce of British India as Carried on by Individuals in the Year 1804/5," IOR/P/174/15, fol. 174v–175v, BL.

31. McMaster, *Life and Times of Stephen Girard*, I, 4, 10–11, 253–254, 275–276, 353, 383, 386, 427, 428–435; Leopold Nottnagel to Girard, Oct. 14, 1803, no. 473, reel 29, Stephen Girard Papers, 1793–1857, APS, Nottnagel to Girard, Nov. 29, 1803, no. 566, reel 29. Girard began trading to the Isle de France, India, and Batvia in the years immediately before the 1802 peace, often sending his ships east from Hamburg. Girard was also a friend of Thomas Randall of the early American trade to China.

supply chain taking profits and raising the price. Stark, however, had his own reasons to talk down the banyans. He offered to be Girard's purchasing agent for "goods fit for North or South America, the West Indies, or Europe," and he promised the lowest prices and best quality from his own "Manufactures." E. Vialar, also in Calcutta, warned Girard against both the banyans and such agents as Stark. He claimed that the influx of inexperienced U.S. and Portuguese merchants in the late 1790s and 1800s "rely blindly on the natives of this country, whom they commission to procure their merchandise . . . without paying any attention whatever to the quality." Men like Stark, meanwhile, "have a good deal of merchandise belonging to themselves or to their friends in the interior of the country to sell, and you readily understand what the result in such a case might be." Vialar also warned Girard not to rely on credit from London merchant houses in Calcutta, which demanded "onerous" terms. He advised Girard to hire only supercargoes and captains "who are themselves capable of selecting and purchasing your returns." Such supercargoes landed in Calcutta armed with Spanish dollars, British bills of exchange, and perhaps a shopping list or guide such as *A System of Exchange with Almost All Parts of the World: To Which Is Added, the India Directory, for Purchasing the Drugs and Spices of the East-Indies* by Joseph James and Daniel Moore.[32]

32. J? Stark to Girard, Nov. 29, 1803, no. 565, reel 29, Girard Papers, APS (this may be the Briton James Stark), E. Vialars to Girard, Nov. 26, 1803, no. 558, reel 29 (this is probably the merchant Eustache Vialars); Joseph James and Daniel Moore, *A System of Exchange with Almost All Parts of the World: To Which Is Added, the India Directory, for Purchasing the Drugs and Spices of the East-Indies . . .* (New York, 1800). Complaints of the deceptions of Indians had a long history. For other examples, see Gerard Gustavus Ducarel to his mother, Oct. 6, 1765, D2091/F11, Gloucestershire Archives, United Kingdom; Abraham Caldecott to Miss Pettet, Sept. 14, 1783, MSS Eur D778, n.p., BL; Henry Lee to Edward A. Newton, Oct. 19, 1810, in Kenneth Wiggins Porter, ed., *The Jacksons and the Lees: Two Generations of Massachusetts Merchants, 1765–1844* (Cambridge, Mass., 1937), II, 920.

Some merchants became extremely close with their Indian banyans. A group of thirty-five merchants from ports including Boston, Salem, and Philadelphia, for example, commissioned a portrait of George Washington to express their gratitude to the wealthy and connected banyan Ramdoolal Day; see M. V. Kamath, *The United States and India, 1776–1996: The Bridge over the River Time* (New Delhi, 1998), 62–63. Ramdoolal stayed in touch with Philadelphia merchants, such as Robert Waln. He relayed market conditions and prices of piece goods to assist Philadelphians in planning their voyages. See Ramdoolal Day to R. and W. Waln, May 6, 1808, Robert Waln Papers (1794–1825), Collection 687, HSP; William Waln and Willings and Zanus to John Powel Hare [Hare Powel] and Aaron Kelly, May 22, 1806, Series 5a, box 8, Powel Family Papers, Collection 1582, HSP. For another example, see Henry Lee to Andrew Cabot, July 7–10, 1812, and Oct. 21, 1812, in Porter, ed., *The Jacksons and the Lees*, II, 1027, 1061–1062.

American supercargoes bought up whatever they could find, even as supplies, quality, and prices fluctuated wildly. Supercargo Robert Branu wrote to Girard from Calcutta that Americans "do not care about the quality" of any kind of merchandise and that indigo and many types of piece goods "are extremely scarce." He had "repeatedly rejected whole lots of merchandise because they were absolutely different from the samples." Brokers variously applied different names to the goods, compounding the problem. At Madras, Nottnagel bemoaned the low quality and high prices of piece goods. The handkerchiefs that Girard wanted most were "of slight quality[,] false Colors[,] and unsaleable patterns." Nottnagel took it upon himself to have new patterns drawn up and to wait while handkerchiefs were produced to his specifications. Other Americans, meanwhile, purchased "great quantities" of the inferior goods. Additionally, Nottnagel reported to Girard and Thomas Osgood reported to Benjamin Pickman of Salem that U.S. vessels arrived empty from Dutch Batavia, which had become overrun with Americans looking for cargoes. With Batavia and Calcutta in frenzies, Osgood chose to buy sugar in Manila instead. Looking for more opportunities with less competition, Girard began shipping opium from Turkey to China.[33]

U.S. merchants dispersed their India goods to Africa, the West Indies, and throughout North America as well as to Europe. In late 1805, for example, John Barton brought the ship *Arab* to Salem from Tranquebar, a small Danish settlement in southern India. Tranquebar was surrounded in British territory, and it had long been used primarily by Britons, with goods and capital from British India, avoiding the Company monopoly. By trading with Tranquebar instead of Madras or Nagapattinam, American merchants could likewise legally claim that the goods were not from British India. The *Arab* brought saltpeter, pepper, and 385 bales of piece goods, the bulk of the cargo. Pepper, 489 bags, was reexported to France. More than 50,000 pounds of saltpeter and several bales of cloth went to Boston, and more bales went to Barton as his commission. The Salem

33. Nottnagel to Girard, Aug. 16, 1805, no. 490, reel 35, Girard Papers, APS, Robert Branu to Girard, July 13, 1807, no. 391, reel 41, Branu to Girard, Aug. 27, 1807, no. 487, reel 41; Thomas Osgood to Benjamin Pickman, Nov. 11, 1805, box 2, folder 3, Benjamin Pickman Papers, MSS 5, PEM. For Pickman's instructions, see Pickman to Osgood, Apr. 20, 1805, box 2, folder 2, Pickman Papers, MSS 5, PEM. During the French Revolutionary and Napoleonic Wars, U.S. merchants took control of more than half of Batavia's trade, which was enabled fully by American neutrality, as shown in Fichter, *So Great a Proffit*, 150–152. On Girard and Turkish opium, see Jonathan Goldstein, *Philadelphia and the China Trade, 1682–1846: Commercial, Cultural, and Attitudinal Effects* (University Park, Pa., 1978), 54.

merchants John Derby, Samuel Derby, and John Prince, Jr., reexported 167 bales of the piece goods to Africa, presumably to purchase enslaved people. Six months later, a further 148 of the bales went to Africa as well. Finally, 15 bales went to the West Indies, which could be a strong market with its own specific demands. Philadelphia merchant Zaccheus Collins, for example, asked his supercargoes on the *Pennsylvania Packet* to buy handkerchiefs "if they can be well purchased and of such particular patterns as W.B. knows will suit the W India market."[34]

The 1806 voyage of the *Bramin* from Philadelphia to Calcutta provides a well-documented example of the maturation of U.S. merchant activity in the India trade. The main object of the voyage was to buy piece goods from Calcutta for the Philadelphia market. Joseph S. Lewis and Company hired Samuel Parrish and Job Bacon as supercargoes. Lewis provided thirty thousand Spanish dollars for the investment as well as detailed instructions for spending it. He requested a brief stop in Madeira to pick up wine before heading around Africa. He detailed dozens of specific fabrics, noting the appropriate colors, sizes, and prices as well as the level of local demand. Gunny bags, twine, hides, rice, sugar, or, if it was legal, saltpeter made up the remainder of his shopping list. Several lesser partners, including John Evans, Zaccheus Collins, and Isaac Cathrall, all of Philadelphia, also contracted with Parrish and Bacon to manage their investments. Collins, for example, sent five thousand dollars and explained, "Madras Hkfs I don't like, Ventapoolams of good patterns and above all of *fast* colours, If you approve I would not object to." Lewis recommended that Parrish and Bacon look up two reputable banyans in Calcutta named "Callesunker" and "Doorgapers." More than anything, however, Lewis stressed time: "It is a very great object to have the ship home early next spring, as we wish to send her out again, and also to be early at market with our goods, you will therefore use every exertion to get away from Calcutta by the 10 or 20 December." American merchants and supercargoes had developed experience, networks of knowledge, and vital associations with Indian banyans.[35]

34. Account of Cargo Rec'd by Ship *Arab*, from Tranquebar, Arrived December 1805, box 1, folder 7, Barton Family Papers, MSS 110, PEM (For more examples in 1809, see Porter, ed., *The Jacksons and the Lees*, I, 635); Zaccheus Collins to Richard Bayly and James Logan, May 2, 1804, Letter Book, 1801–1804, Zaccheus Collins Papers, Daniel Parker Collection, Collection 1587, HSP; Ole Feldbaek, *India Trade under the Danish Flag, 1772–1808: European Enterprise and Anglo-Indian Remittance and Trade* (Denmark, 1969), esp. 220–229.

35. Lewis and Co. to Parrish and Bacon, May 13, 14, 1806, Parrish and Bacon, Account Book, Consignment from Calcutta, 1806–1807, Cox-Parrish-Wharton Family Papers, 1600–

These developments enabled Parrish and Bacon to quickly and success-fully react to changing circumstances on the ground in Calcutta. Parrish and Bacon wrote from Calcutta that many of the goods "mentioned in your memorandum are not to be had at any price." Even the Madeira wine "has not come to a good market" since three cargoes had already arrived. Dollars sold low, making matters worse. They found their Indian factor and spent their days touring markets buying ready-made "checks, curtas, blue gillies, and chintz the only articles at present to be had at a reason-able rate, we have been purchasing them in small parcels as we could pick them up—we have about 50 bales packed." Vessels dropped into Calcutta "daily" and were "keeping up the high price of goods." Within a month the situation had gone from bad to worse, and the supercargoes admitted that they had to ignore all the carefully written instructions. Following their own instincts, they managed to pack "about 450 bales of baftas, mam-moodies, blue goods, some gurrahs and emerities" as well as sugar, rice, pepper, ginger, and indigo. Earning a good profit came down to trusting their selections and their ship's ability to arrive before their competitors. When the *Bramin* arrived back home, Lewis listed his share of the cargo in *Poulson's American Daily Advertiser* and in the *United States' Gazette*. He offered goods privately and at auction, for reexport and retail. In this voyage, unlike many earlier voyages, Americans themselves financed, pur-chased, manned, and freighted the investments from India to America. Still, even this apparently independent venture depended upon the British government of Calcutta and its cloth-producing hinterlands.[36]

The Company, for its part, also retained advantages in the India trade, particularly in regulation, terms of sale, and the procurement of certain classes of fine India cottons. It continued to use duplicate pattern books in London and India, and it continually increased the success of its quality-

1900, Collection 154, HSP, Zaccheus Collins to Parrish and Bacon, May 14, 1806. Stopping in Madeira for wine was a common practice; for more on this trade, see Newton, Gordon, Murdoch, and Scott to Lewis and Co., May 22, 1806, Lewis Papers, Collection 1735, HSP. For similar examples of detailed orders, see William Waln, Willings, and Zanus to John Powel Hare [Hare Powel] and Aaron Kelly, May 22, 1806, Series 5a, box 8, Powel Family Papers; Patrick Tracy Jackson et al. to George Lee and Joseph Hall, Oct. 15, 1810, in Porter, ed., *The Jacksons and the Lees*, II, 870–897.

36. Parrish and Bacon to Messrs Lewis and Co., Nov. 5, Dec. 13, 1806, Account Book, Collection 154, HSP; *Poulson's American Daily Advertiser*, May 1, 1807, [2]; "Shipping News," *United States' Gazette* (Philadelphia), Apr. 27, 1807, [3]. The pepper from this voyage was not ordered by any of the investors and was sold at auction; see "Sales of Pepper Received per Ship Bramin from Calcutta," June 22, 1807, Daniel Parker Papers, 1761–1838, Collection 1587, HSP.

control measures to better satisfy consumers. Some merchants continued to supply small amounts of India goods to the United States from London. Newspaper advertisements, such as that for Guest and Bancker in 1804, offered Indian fabrics specifically imported via Britain to American consumers. Nevertheless, the streams heading from London to American markets were small. Far larger quantities were going from London to France despite the war. Only two-fifths of the Company's 1806 muslin order was intended for the home market. To the dismay of Napoleon Bonaparte, "very large quantities of Indian muslins . . . found a way to France" from the London sales. This ongoing trade was not only embarrassing for Napoleon; it was economically beneficial for the British.[37]

With such trade continuing, in 1806 Napoleon closed much of the Continent to British merchants and products with his Berlin Decree, further raising the value of neutral shipping. American shipping from Calcutta surged, taking over much of the share of continental European shippers (Figure 4). Italian merchants, for instance, encouraged neutral U.S. associates to bring more goods from India to keep markets stocked. Girard's correspondent in Livorno informed him that French troops had unexpectedly taken control of the port and tried, so far ineffectually, to seize all British property and goods. He hoped desperately that Britain and America would remain at peace and that the neutral American flag would still be able to get into the port. In 1809, Salem merchant Benjamin Pickman directed Francis Coffin not to break any U.S. laws but to take his ship *Java* with its cargo from Calcutta directly to Palermo, another Italian port. Coffin was to invest the proceeds "in unquestionable bills on London and . . . remit them to the house of P and H Le Mesurier and Co on our account." Such activities were replicated across Europe.[38]

37. On muslin exports to France, see Court of Directors to Governor General in Council, July 23, 1806, State Archives of West Bengal, Kolkata, India (quotation); Kimberly Chrisman-Campbell, "The Empress of Fashion: What Joséphine Wore," in Eleanor P. DeLorme, ed., *Joséphine and the Arts of the Empire* (Los Angeles, 2005), 160–166. For examples of merchants shipping India goods to America from the London sales, see *Poulson's American Daily Advertiser*, Apr. 30, 1804, [1], Sept. 20, 1810, [1]; James Begbie to Thomas Graham Stirling, Oct. 3, 1809, Letters of James Begbie and David and John Colvin, MS 10872, NLS; Henry Lee to Thomas Lee, Nov. 12, 1811, in Porter, ed., *The Jacksons and the Lees*, II, 987–988, 990, 991. On the Company's advantages and tactics, see Kumkum Chatterjee, *Merchants, Politics, and Society in Early Modern India: Bihar, 1733–1820* (New York, 1996), 160–171; Commercial Department to Governor General in Council, Bengal, Aug. 19, 1807, General Letters, State Archives of West Bengal, Kolkata.

38. M. Hutchinson to Girard, Sept. 10, 1807, no. 515, reel 41, Girard Papers, APS, ? to Girard, Sept. 7, 1807, no. 513, reel 41, J. C. Ulrick to Girard, Sept. 11, 1807, no. 523, reel 41;

In 1807, Denmark entered the war against Britain, removing one of the only other remaining neutral competitors to U.S. shipping. The American Joseph Pitcairn wrote to John Barton, "Denmark will gladly receive and fully protect American Cargoes—indeed, the whole Baltic is open to the American flag, Mecklenburg only excepted." Danish and British associates had long worked together to evade the Company monopoly, but now that trade came to an end. By early 1808, the British occupied Denmark's Indian settlements. The Danish and the private British merchants who used the Danish flag now had little access to India. Pitcairn said he could find good markets for West and East Indian goods, the latter including sugar, cotton piece goods, dyestuffs, and nankeens. Given the instability in Europe, he warned Barton to give his men considerable freedom to act as they saw fit. Armed with the only remaining major neutral flag, U.S. merchants alone could readily serve Continental markets with British India and other goods. By 1810–1811, the U.S. neutral flag's share accounted for the joint share of all previous non-British European exports from Calcutta; notably, the British share had not declined below its pre-American embargo level (see Figure 4).[39]

American merchants did not waste the opportunity and generated significant profits and accumulated capital for themselves and others through the India trade. In 1803, merchants estimated that they could sell goods in Philadelphia for double the prime cost in Calcutta. As the East India Company's reporter of external commerce Thomas Brown explained, "The nett profit of a voyage to Bengal if the ship brings dollars is estimated at 20 percent after the payment of every charge incidental thereto, and debiting the adventure with an interest, at the rate of 7 percent per annum." Zaccheus Collins, for example, sold a Calcutta investment to a Samuel Archer for a net profit of $1,081 on a $5,500 outlay. He netted 20 percent, just as

P. and A. Filicche to Benjamin Pickman, Dec. 29, 1804, box 1, folder 7, Benjamin Pickman Papers, MSS 5, PEM. As for the *Java*, the instructions arrived too late, and it went back to Boston. See Benjamin Pickman to Francis Coffin, Apr. 16, 1809, box 3, folder 3, Benjamin Pickman Papers, MSS 5, PEM. American merchant Patrick Tracy Jackson started bringing India goods into Europe in 1808; see Porter, ed., *The Jacksons and the Lees,* I, 627. On the extent of American ships trading India goods into Europe, see Larkins, "Report of the External Commerce of Bengal as Carried on by Individuals in the Year 1806/7—or from the 1st of June 1806 to the 32st of May 1807," IOR/P/174/18, fol. 5d, BL. On the blockade, see Frank Edgar Melvin, *Napoleon's Navigation System: A Study of Trade Control during the Continental Blockade* (1919; rpt. New York, 1970), 173–186, 240–242.

39. Joseph Pitcairn to John Barton, May 22, Aug. 3, 1810, box 1, folder 2, Barton Family Papers, MSS 110, PEM. On the effective end of Danish trade with India, see Feldbaek, *India Trade under the Danish Flag,* 229–230.

Brown predicted, but his profit would have been nearly double if he had not paid the steep wartime price of $751 for insurance. John Barton, in another example, paid $271 to insure $3,000 of property in 1804. Interest charges on long voyages, particularly those due in India, could eat up all of a merchant's profit and more. Respondentia bonds, which absolved the borrower from risk if the cargo was lost, essentially combined insurance and lending but charged even higher interest rates. Even when merchants paid such costs, their payments became revenue and potential profits for British and American insurers.[40]

Similarly, commissions, crew wages, and ship costs broadly disbursed the financial benefits of the India trade. Captain Thomas Osgood earned 4 percent of the inbound cargo of his ship and was offered a bonus of 5 percent on sales over $70,000. Parrish and Bacon earned a 4 percent commission, or SR 10,636 (about $5,700) on their purchases of SR 2,76,484. The shipowners, Lewis and Company, who were also the main investors, earned 10 percent on the value of all the goods shipped, or about SR 27,648 (nearly $15,000). Captains had to pay their officers and crew too. John Barton paid Peter Lander $22 per month and gave him a privilege of two tons to act as assistant on the ship *Arab*. Barton followed the East India Company model in offering free privilege cargo, and he was not alone. Other profits from the trade flowed to local shipbuilders; one Philadelphia builder during this period constructed three four-hundred-ton ships and two three-hundred-ton ships for the Asian trade. These ships, although not as large or expensive as those in the Company's service, were large by Atlantic standards. Merchants in the India trade thereby generated gains for others and economic growth in India, Britain, and America.[41]

40. Thomas Brown to Peter Speke, "Copy of Mr Brown's Report of the Import and Export Trade of Calcutta by Sea from 1796/7," IOR/P/174/13, BL; "Adventure per Amelia," 1804–1805, Zaccheus Collins Papers, Daniel Parker Collection, Collection 1587, HSP. For Barton's insurance, see Union Maritime Insurance Company, no. 146, Dec. 1, 1804, box 1, folder 3, Barton Family Papers, MSS 110, PEM. The high cost of insurance for getting goods to America backs up Francis Baring's argument that freight rates were a misleading indicator of the true costs of American trade. For more on insurance and freight costs, see Porter, ed., *The Jacksons and the Lees*, I, 65–67. For high interest charges, see Patrick Tracy Jackson to Ramduloll Day, Oct. 6, 1806, ibid., I, 619, and for respondentia, II, 858–860.

41. For commissions, see Pickman to Capt. Thomas B. Osgood, Apr. 20, 1805, box 2, folder 2, MSS 5, PEM; Parrish and Bacon, Consignment Notes, Account Book, Collection 154, HSP. On ship captains and crews, see Agreement with Captain Barton, Nov. 17, 1804, box 1, folder 3, Barton Family Papers, MSS 110, PEM. On ships, see Goldstein, *Philadelphia and the China Trade*, 27, 41; and for comparative ship tonnage, see Maritime Records, Ship Arrivals and Clearances, section III, vol. I, 1800–1802, 1816–1817, Inward, HSP. This data

Those investors with large amounts of capital to risk also had the biggest potential profits, but, even for experienced merchants, the India trade did not guarantee a high rate of return. In 1804, Salem merchants Benjamin Pickman, Jr., Timothy Williams, and Dudley Pickman invested $70,000 in a voyage to Calcutta for cotton cloth and bandannas. They made $111,148 after expenses on the sales of the cargo in Boston, less the initial investment, leaving $41,148. Even if they paid to fully insure the cargo at wartime rates, the profit was spectacular. Benjamin Pickman, who had fronted half the risk, came out particularly well. In 1810, in contrast, Pickman teamed up with John Derby and John Prince in a more modest venture to Calcutta, with a much more modest profit. They shipped out copper worth $17,927 and $3,000 in cash. Captain James Gilchrist sold the copper for a net loss and used the proceeds and the cash in Calcutta to buy 12,895 piece goods. These goods sold for $29,103 back in America. However, the venture incurred several costs. Duties amounted to $3,320, plus another $800 in commissions, charges, and advertisements. Once freight was subtracted, the profit had been reduced to a few thousand dollars before any insurance charges.[42]

The U.S. Treasury also generated revenue from the India trade. In the years 1802 through 1804, on imports averaging $3,530,000 from the "British East Indies," the United States collected $576,261 in gross duty revenue per year. Cotton piece goods were estimated to be the bulk of the British India imports. Altogether, goods from British India accounted for 4 percent of average gross duty revenue of $16,195,000. These goods also represented 5 percent of the total U.S. imports of $75,316,000 per year. The non-British East Indies accounted for an additional $4,856,000 in imports, primarily tea from China, which paid a further 4 percent of duty revenue. The British India and China imports were also comparable in scale to those from the British West Indies, which amounted to $4,570,000.[43]

---

suggests that the typical 400-ton arrival from the East Indies ran about double the size of those from Europe. Ralph Davis gives data for 1766 showing that ships in the British Atlantic averaged 133 to 176 tons; see Davis, *Rise of English Shipping Industry: In the Seventeenth and Eighteenth Centuries* (New York, 1962), 299.

42. Invoice of Merchandise Shipped by Dudley L. Pickman in the Ship *Derby*, May 7, 1804, Calcutta, Account of Ship *Derby*, and Sales of the Cargo of the Ship *Derby*, from Calcutta, October 1804, box 1, folder 7, Pickman Papers, PEM; John Prince to James Gilchrist, June 16, 1810, Invoice of Calcutta Piece Goods for Brig *Caravan*, Account Sales for Brig *Caravan*, box 1, folder 3, Pickman Papers, PEM.

43. Albert Gallatin, "Commerce with Great Britain and Her Dependencies, and All Parts

The extensive economic activity generated by American merchants trading directly between the East Indies, Atlantic ports, and Europe made waves that sloshed into the East India Company's offices, increasing pressure to reconsider the system routing the British India trade through London. An 1805 plan vetted in Britain and among British governors in Asia, though not implemented, suggested that India goods should no longer be routed through Britain as directed in the trading regulations developed in particular in 1721 and the East India Company charter. Instead, people and goods should flow from the East Indies directly to the West Indies. Given the revolution in Haiti, which had broken out in 1791 as the enslaved rose up and resulted in the 1804 founding of the Republic of Haiti, stabilizing British possessions and reducing dependency on enslaved African labor was a weighty issue. Robert Townsend Farquhar, the East India Company's governor of Prince of Wales Island (today Penang Island on the coast of Malaysia), explained that offering free land to Chinese settlers in Trinidad would create a stable and able new middling class of landowners who worked their own farms. He noted that it may be difficult to get sufficient numbers of Chinese women to accompany the men but suggested that women could be encouraged to go from India, other places in the West Indies, or America. Importantly, these free settlers would create "an extensive and intimate link of connection between the British Empire in the East and West Indies." The East India Company would then direct trade from Asia to the Caribbean and Americas without the costs of passing goods through London. Farquhar suggested that any reduction in British state revenues caused by rerouting goods directly to the West Indies might be offset by supplanting the "Spanish and American Trade" in India goods.[44]

---

of the World," in Walter Lowrie and Matthew St. Clair Clark, eds., *American State Papers: Documents, Legislative and Executive, of the Congress of the United States . . .* , 38 vols. (Washington, D.C., 1831–1861), 9th Cong., 1st sess., 1806, Commerce and Navigation, I, 640–644. Although Gallatin pointed out that the government simply did not collect data by item, data was collected by duty rate and origin. Cotton and silk fabrics from India paid a duty rate of 12.5 percent during these years. These fabrics made up nearly all the items from the "British Dominions in East Indies" dutied at this rate. See One of the People, *An Examination of the New Tariff Proposed by the Hon. Henry Baldwin, a Representative in Congress* (New York, 1821). It is not clear that Asian trade saved the United States from financial ruin. Such claims have been made: Sydney Greenbie and Marjorie Barstow Greenbie, *Gold of Ophir: The China Trade in the Making of America*, rev. ed with introduction by Rufus Rockwell Wilson (New York, 1937), xiii–xiv.

44. Charles Grant and George Smith to Chairman and Deputy Chairman, copy to Lord

The success of American merchants and the expiration of article 13 of the Jay Treaty also set off an intense debate within the East India Company on the benefits and drawbacks of the U.S. trade for the Company. Company director Francis Baring argued from his experience and interests that U.S. merchants succeeded largely owing to their neutrality, and he attacked the assumption underlying the Navigation Acts that the shippers who carried the goods generated the most value for the national economy. Despite the lower freight charges from India to America, he explained, Americans did not necessarily trade cheaper than the Company. American merchants had to get back across the Atlantic, they had to insure their ships at high wartime rates, and they could not obtain their goods as cheaply as the Company. The American trade expanded because neutral American merchants alone enjoyed access to both British India and continental Europe. Why pick a fight with America, Baring asked, when American neutrality saved the India trade from ruin? Americans brought their own money as well as that of the French and British to India, which they spent on Indian manufactures and Company duties. They infused large amounts of silver bullion into the Company's dominions. Baring allowed that having the trade in British ships would generate even more value for Britain, but pushing Americans out of the trade would not get the trade in British ships under wartime conditions. Without American participation, silver would not come into British India, British India goods would not be able to get into major European markets, and the East India Company would not collect export duty and internal fees on those goods. Americans were not competitors in the India trade; they were essential collaborators.[45]

Indeed, the influx of American shipping helped to maintain the overall strength of Bengal's economy and provided part of the backing for the Company's wartime assistance to Britain. American shipping brought 40 percent of all silver imports between 1802 and 1811, providing liquidity for British India's economy and helping to back the Company's new policy of transferring bullion from India to Britain. Duties on exported Bengali cloth, meanwhile, totaled between 16 and 18 percent before 1810. In 1803–

Castlereagh, Nov. 28, 1805, IOR/H/439/2, 189–190, BL; Robert Townsend Farquhar, "Observations on the Proposed Plan of Introducing Chinese Settlers at Trinidad and Our Other West India Islands, and of Opening a Direct Intercourse of Trade between the East and West Indies," Add MS 13879, 45r–52v, 58r–59v, 63r–66r, BL; Farquhar to Marquis Wellesley, Apr. 16, 1805, Add MS 13879, fols. 63–71r, BL.

45. Baring to the Directors, Sept. 15, 1807, FO 353/58, NA.

1804 alone, revenues to the East India Company on cloth exported from Calcutta by Americans amounted to approximately £132,000. The financial and shipping resources of the Company, augmented by the American trade, made it possible to ship twenty-seven cargoes of rice on British, country-trade, and U.S. ships to help alleviate famine in the home islands caused by poor harvests and reduced grain imports during the 1790s and poor harvests again at the turn of the century. The directors specifically mentioned using American shipping in their request to Calcutta for as much rice as possible in 1795. Additionally, the freight tonnage brought by the nominally American carrying trade allowed the Company to convert ten of its regular trading vessels into sixty-four-gun Royal Navy frigates and a further sixteen into troop ships. Without the East India Company's support, moreover, Britain's need for foreign borrowing would have grown after 1772, and its financial position would have become untenable after 1809.[46]

Such was the importance of American trade in Calcutta that, when it plummeted in 1808 as a result of the U.S. embargo that began in December 1807 (see Figure 4), the value of export piece goods plummeted as well. The Republicans imposed the embargo as a means to apply economic pressure on France and, particularly, Britain, and for Thomas Jefferson at least to develop American economic independence. Both the French and British had targeted U.S. neutral shipping for aiding the enemy, and the British also impressed U.S. sailors. The embargo forbade U.S. ships from

46. For silver imports, see "Papers etc. (East India Company)," Parliamentary Papers, 1812–1813, VIII, no. 136, part 5, cited in H. V. Bowen, "Bullion for Trade, War, and Debt-Relief: British Movements of Silver to, around, and from Asia, 1760–1833," Modern Asian Studies, XLIV (2010), 468–469. For export duties, see "Report on the Private Trade between England, America, and Bengal, from 1st June 1796 to 31st May 1802" (copy), IOR/P/174/13, BL. Multiplying the median duty of 17 percent by the value of American exports for 1803–1804, or SR 6,670,800, equals SR 1,134,036, or £132,304. Export data is calculated from "Comparative Abstract Annual Statement of the Exports of Merchandize from Calcutta by Sea from the 1st of June 1803 to the 31st of May 1811 (no. 8)," IOR/P/174/22, BL. In 1810, the duty structure was reorganized; see Narendra Krishna Sinha, The Economic History of Bengal, III, 1793–1848 (Calcutta, 1970), 42–43, 47. On rice shipments and frigates, see H. V. Bowen, The Business of Empire: The East India Company and Imperial Britain, 1756–1833 (Cambridge, 2006), 48–51; Singh, Agency Houses, 108. On food shortages in Britain, see John Bohstedt, The Politics of Provisions: Food Riots, Moral Economy, and Market Transition in England, c. 1550–1850 (Farnham, 2010), 188–191, 206. For the directors' request, see Secret Letter (Draft) from the Secret Committee of the Court of Directors to the Bengal Government, July 7, 1795, Fort William–India House Correspondence, XVII, 138. On national borrowing, see Javier Cuenca Esteban, "The Balance of Payments, 1772–1820: India Transfers and War Finance," EHR, LIV (2001), 65.

trading with foreign ports, effectively stopping the U.S. India trade. It was soon expanded to also prohibit exports from the United States. The embargo harmed the American economy more than the British, but its effect in Calcutta prompted the reporter of external commerce, J. P. Larkin, to agree with Baring about the importance of the American trade to British India's prosperity. He explained, "By the more enlightened politicians" in Britain, the U.S. embargo "will be considered as an attempt to aid . . . the blockade of the European Continent as proclaimed by the French Ruler in the Berlin decrees. . . in the joint expectation of destroying the commercial prosperity of Great Britain, and of thereby annihilating her existence as a Nation." Under the U.S. embargo, he argued, the British would lose their primary means of getting India goods into America and Napoleon's Europe.[47]

To Baring's exasperation, however, the Company shipping lobby as well as Company chairman Edward Parry and deputy chairman Charles Grant grew increasingly alarmed at the scale of U.S. trade and the accumulation of U.S. profits. The shipowners were "convinced [that trade with the United States] will prove highly injurious to the general interests of the Empire." They resolved "that, unless the navigation and colonial system of Great Britain be strictly adhered to in the future, the most ruinous consequences will result to the country." The London shipowners benefited from the elimination of American competition under the U.S. embargo, but they wanted more permanent protection. During the failed negotiations to replace the Jay Treaty with the United States in 1807, Parry and Grant pushed hard to have the American trade to India constrained to direct voyages in both directions. They responded to Baring that the Jay Treaty had been intended to forbid Americans from reexporting India goods, and they reiterated Grant's position from 1800 that the treaty concession limiting American duties should be ended. Baring replied that the Jay Treaty had not restricted American reexports and that the British courts had declared that it also allowed Americans to go to India from Europe. He explained, again, that the neutral trade was critical to the Company during

<hr />

47. J. P. Larkins, "Report on the External Commerce of Bengal as Carried on by Individuals in the Year 1807/8, or from the 1st of June 1807 to the 31st May 1808," IOR/P/174/19, fol. 5b, BL. Smuggling around the embargo had increased substantially by late 1808. On American politics and the embargo, see Burton Spivak, *Jefferson's English Crisis: Commerce, Embargo, and the Republican Revolution* (Charlottesville, Va., 1979), 102–111, 198–203; Reginald C. Stuart, *The Half-Way Pacifist: Thomas Jefferson's View of War* (Toronto, 1978), 44–49.

the current war, that high duties would drive neutral merchants to other ports, and that Americans brought silver and few manufactured goods. He gushed, "Trade with America is the brightest commercial jewel that we possess."[48]

Parry and Grant eventually responded, noting that Dundas had introduced the policy of allowing Britons in India to trade with foreigners in 1793, against the strong objections of the directors. They now disagreed with Baring's claim that the Americans had not taken over much of the trade to Europe before Napoleon. They also now disagreed that the Americans brought a significant supply of silver. Most upsetting, American merchants, captains, and investors had accumulated considerable profits that they reinvested in their own trade, as Dundas had predicted. Parry and Grant calculated that British capital, which had accounted for one-quarter of American capital in the period from 1795–1796 to 1799–1800, had dropped to one-tenth in the period from 1800–1801 to 1804–1805. They concluded that America "is not the *best*, but the *worst* Customer." The question of neutral Americans' trading goods from British India into Europe during the war was, to Parry and Grant, beside the point. They explained that British manufacturers would now supply the cotton piece goods that India used to supply to Europe. The India trade would change ever more to raw materials for Britain, and reexports would no longer be as important. Although they were incorrect on many points, Parry and Grant were correct on both the India trade's current profitability to Americans and the U.S. India trade's future decline as British manufacturing increased. Global war between Britain and France had created opportunities for American merchants, particularly as the countries of other formal neutral traders all ended up on one side or the other—and Americans had capitalized. Neither those opportunities nor the older opportunities for helping Britons to evade the Company monopoly would last much longer.[49]

48. Society of Ship-owners, "At a Meeting of the Committee of Ship-owners for the Port of London, Held This Day 23d Day of October, 1806," in *Interesting and Important Reports*, clxiii; Parry and Grant to the Directors, Oct. 14, 1807, IOR/H/494, 13–51, BL; Baring to Parry and Grant, Dec. 16, 1807, IOR/H/494, 132–190 (quotation on 140–141), BL.

49. Parry and Grant to Baring, October 1808, IOR H/494, 209–326 (quotation on 323), BL. On the language they wanted in the treaty and the difficulties it would pose for U.S. traders, see Jacob Crowninshield to James Madison, Apr. 7, 1807, RG 59.2.3, Miscellaneous Correspondence, U.S. National Archives and Records Administration.

Unmaking and Making Monopolies

The participation of Americans in the India trade was increasingly over-shadowed by major changes in the global geographies of cultivation and production. These changes portended new roles for both India and America in British economic growth. After many false and slow starts, in the first decade of the nineteenth century India and America alike were supplying the raw materials sought by British manufacturers, includ-ing indigo and raw cotton wool. British cotton cloth manufacturers had, meanwhile, taken control of much of the U.S. market. Nevertheless, the American embargoes and the increasing tension before the War of 1812 between Britain and the United States suggested the tenuousness of this interdependence. The Company's charter was due for renewal in 1813, and the success of America in providing raw cotton, and Britain's increas-ing dependence on that success, fundamentally changed America's im-portance to the British economy and to the debate over India policy. The old seventeenth-century language and arguments against the East India Company monopoly were revitalized by the changing economic reality. The arguments were generally not for a free trade for all in the neoliberal sense; they were for an open trade for British merchants still regulated and managed by duties, and still very much in the interests of Britain, par-ticularly its increasingly attainable goal of exporting British-made fabric to the rest of the world.

Port and customs records reveal the increasing dominance of British cotton manufacturers in American markets. From the middle of the 1790s, the number of vessels arriving in Philadelphia from Liverpool, the primary port for Manchester exports, surged dramatically (Figure 5). When Liver-pool arrivals dropped briefly in 1798, the following year additional ships arrived from Calcutta to offset the shortage of British fabric in the market-place. This was a temporary situation, however. An average of thirty-two vessels, with a low of twenty-four and a high of forty-one, arrived each year from Liverpool between 1800 and 1810, while an average of six vessels ar-rived from Calcutta, with a low of zero and a high of ten. By 1805, approxi-mately 53,000 pieces of Indian-manufactured cotton fabric, worth about $170,000, were reexported from Britain to the United States. American merchants imported additional piece goods, worth approximately $2 mil-lion, from British India directly. In contrast, however, the United States imported more than $10 million, or 13,835,989 yards, and an additional 255,143 pieces (measuring approximately 3,000,000 to 4,000,000 yards)

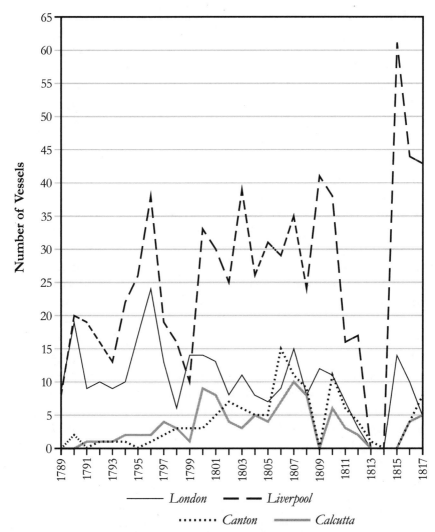

Figure 5. Ship Arrivals to Philadelphia by Point of Origin, 1789–1817. Inward Index, 1789–1817, Port of Philadelphia Custom House Records, Collection 157, HSP. Drawn by Rebecca Wrenn

of British-made "cottons," including handkerchiefs, calico, and muslin. Small additional quantities were imported from continental Europe. U.S. household production added 16,581,299 yards of cotton cloth, but American industrial production turned out only an additional 146,974 yards. Household producers could not create quality muslin and lacked the ability to dye or print fabrics to look like the calicoes arriving from India and Britain. Most homespun cotton was utility fabric or suitable only for clothing at the lower end of the market. British-made products dominated the large American fashionable cotton cloth market.[50]

At the same time, British manufacturers began to fulfill the elusive and centuries-old dream of manufacturing cotton cultivated in North America for export to the world. As the British merchant and author Henry Merttins Bird wrote in 1794, "Prudence appears to unite with a liberal policy in recommending, to increase our commercial intercourse with a nation of agriculturers [sic] whose market for manufactures must long be an object of the first importance." Historians have focused primarily on the importance of southern U.S. cotton plantations to Britain in the antebellum and Civil War eras. Information, seeds, and technologies, however, had long circulated in the Atlantic colonies. In the thirteen colonies, the boycotts of the late 1760s and the American Revolution encouraged further innovations in cotton cultivation and increased cotton cloth production to offset the loss of fabrics imported from Britain. Farmers transferred tobacco cultivation techniques and infrastructure to increase cotton yields. In the 1790s, planters in the southern U.S. followed those in the British West Indies in actively pursuing raw cotton exports to Britain. Though

50. Philadelphia Inward Index, 1789–1817, HSP; "An Account of the Goods Wares and Merchandise Being Foreign Produce and Manufacture Exported from Gt Britain to the United States of America . . . ," and "An Account of the Goods Wares and Merchandise Being British Produce and Manufacture Exported from Great Britain to the United States of America . . . ," CUST 17/27, 61Ar, 62r, NA. A "piece" would typically measure from one to two yards in width and from ten to twenty yards in length. Unfortunately, U.S. customs officials did not record quantities for India fabric since it was taxed only on its value. See "A General Statement of Goods, Wares, and Merchandise, Imported into the United States, in American Vessels, from the 1st of October, 1804, to the 30th September, 1805," and "A General Statement of Goods, Wares, and Merchandise, Imported into the United States, in Foreign Vessels, from the 1st of October, 1804, to the 30th September, 1805," in Lowrie and St. Clair Clarke, eds., *American State Papers*, House of Representatives, 9th Congress, 1st Session, 1806, Commerce and Navigation, I, 675, 681. For U.S. household production, see Tench Coxe, *A Statement of the Arts and Manufactures of the United States of America, for the Year 1810* (Philadelphia, 1814), 2–5.

the process of inventing and refining cotton gins was ongoing, particularly in the French Atlantic, Elli Whitney's cotton gin improved the prospects for American cotton. Growers focused on both quantity and quality. At the beginning of the 1790s, the United States produced 8,889 bales of cotton and exported 889 bales. Year after year the quantity increased, and in 1799–1800 the United States produced 155,556 bales, with a domestic consumption of only 35,556 bales. By 1809–1810, production had increased to approximately 340,000 bales, with a domestic consumption of 64,000 bales, leaving more than 80 percent of American raw cotton to be exported, mainly to Britain.[51]

But the American states were not British colonies anymore, even if the economic and cultural relationships between the two countries were often colonial. The 1807 American embargo cut off the cotton flow to Britain. British industrialists faced shortage, and southern cotton planters had to make due with much weaker, but patriotically supportive, domestic markets. The United States removed the embargo in 1809, but tension with Britain remained high. British manufacturers and merchant groups pushed the British government to revoke both the East India Company monopoly and the Orders in Council, which particularly targeted neutral American ships. Whereas the Company monopoly had long reduced access to Asian raw materials and markets, the Orders in Council contributed to tension with the United States, which had manifested in the 1807 embargo. American cotton was already crucial to British producers, and not easily replaced.[52]

51. [Henry Merttins] Bird, *A View of the Relative Situation of Great Britain and the United States of North America* (London, 1794), 25. Bird's London firm was indemnified by the U.S. government to provide surety for cases of captured U.S. ships; Lowrie and St. Clair Clarke, eds., *American State Papers*, Senate, 3d Congress, 2d Session, 1795, Foreign Relations, I, 512–514. For an excellent treatment of the rise of cotton cultivation in the West Indies and North America during this period, see Sven Beckert, *Empire of Cotton: A Global History* (New York, 2014), 88–119. On early efforts in cotton cultivation for export, see Daniel H. Thomas, "Pre-Whitney Cotton Gins in French Louisiana," *Journal of Southern History*, XXXI (1965), 135–148; Angela Lakwete, *Inventing the Cotton Gin: Machine and Myth in Antebellum America* (Baltimore, 2003), 26–33. On South Carolina, cotton quality, and the pursuit of British markets, see Joyce E. Chaplin, "Creating a Cotton South in Georgia and South Carolina, 1760–1815," *Journal of Southern History*, LVII (1991), 175–184, 188, 193–194. For data, see James L. Watkins, *King Cotton: A Historical and Statistical Review, 1790–1908* (1908; rpt. New York, 1969), 29.

52. Chaplin, "Creating a Cotton South," *Journal of Southern History*, LVII (1991), 194–197; Anthony Webster, "The Political Economy of Trade Liberalization: The East India Com-

Leading British administrator John Anstruther noted with dismay in 1811 that the East India Company failed to supply Britain's manufacturers with nearly enough cotton. He made use of the Calcutta statistics from the reporters of external commerce and added material from the other presidencies. The Company, he found, imported so little raw cotton that British manufacturers spent £2 million per year on American cotton. When private merchants had tried to fill the gap by exporting raw cotton from India themselves, the directors took "considerable delay," and the officials at Bombay decided to offer a bad deal to a Parsee merchant instead. Anstruther recounted that Parliament had approved Dundas's allowance for private merchants on Company ships in 1793 for the express purpose of maximizing the supply of raw materials from India and the export of British manufactured goods. Additionally, Anstruther did not accept the Company's claims that it would be impossible to significantly increase the consumption of British manufactures in India, and he believed that the Company was thwarting growth in this area. Finally, he warned that if the Company raised export duties on goods shipped by neutral traders too much it would "prevent the Exports to America," reduce consumption, and, combined with the impediments to private British traders, destroy British India.[53]

In 1812, as tension increased with the United States again, leaders in London, armed with such scathing reports of the Company, including from a parliamentary select committee, quickly moved to end the Company's monopoly upon the renewal of its twenty-year-old charter. In March, Robert Dundas, Lord Melville, who served as the president of the government's Board of Control for the East India Company, offered to compromise between private merchants and the Company by ending the monopoly while continuing to confine the India trade to London. His plan followed the earlier thinking of his father's 1793 experiment. On April 3, a group from Birmingham arrived in London to convince the public and the government of the necessity of opening the India trade to all the ports of Britain. That same day, George Rose, vice president of the Board of Trade, brought the Board into the decision on the monopoly's future. The

pany Charter Act of 1813," *EHR*, 2d Ser., XLIII (1990), 405–407; D. J. Moss, "Birmingham and the Campaigns against the Orders-in-Council and East India Company Charter, 1812–13," *Canadian Journal of History*, XI (1976), 175–186.

53. John Anstruther, "A Report upon the Commerce of the East India Company," 1811, Add MS 13821, fols. 12v, 29v–45v, BL. Anstruther had been active in the prosecution of Warren Hastings, served as the chief justice of Bengal, and was a member of the Privy Council.

The French Wars and the Refashioning of Empire

Board had severe misgivings about the Company's management of the India trade and its confinement to London. On April 4, the U.S. Congress resumed its embargo of all trade with Britain.[54]

With trade difficult in both Europe and North America, South America and the British West and East Indies took on additional importance as wartime markets for British goods, and especially as suppliers of sugar, raw cotton, indigo, rice, and a range of other materials essential to British people and manufacturers. The Board of Trade and Robert Hobart, the earl of Buckinghamshire, who had taken over from Melville at the Board of Control, expected that only private British merchants and shippers could sustain the flow of raw materials from India and find alternatives to U.S. markets. On April 19, Buckinghamshire told the Company directors that he would open the India trade to all of Britain's merchants and ports. In June, the British government repealed the Orders in Council, while the United States moved toward an official declaration of war. The Board of Control, meanwhile, canvassed the Commissioners of Customs and of Excise for thoughts on the difficulties of collecting duties in an open trade, including the outports. This interest in input from the revenue agencies paralleled that pursued by the Board of Trade in the early-eighteenth-century calico compromise. Government revenue was, as it had been, a serious factor in India trade regulation. The customs feared major problems, but the excise figured its problems to be manageable. As a partial solution, the Board proposed maintaining the Company monopoly on trade with China, which consisted mostly of duties and excised tea and consumer goods, a strategy that the customs found to "be less pregnant with the apprehended danger to Revenue." Warnings of an open trade causing violence in China also suggested the monopoly there should be retained. By the autumn of 1812, the Board of Control had ready its plan to open the monopoly, excepting China. Meanwhile, British merchants, particularly those from the outports close to the manufacturers, and the manufacturers themselves lobbied intensely to encourage the Board of Control, the Board of Trade, and Parliament to follow through.[55]

54. Webster, "The Political Economy of Trade Liberalization," *EHR*, 2d Ser. XLIII (1990), 406–410; Moss, "Birmingham and the Campaigns," *Canadian Journal of History*, XI (1976), 180–182.

55. "Report, to the Right Honourable the Lords Commissioners of His Majesty's Treasury, of the Commissioners of Customs; Relative to the Trade with the *East Indies* and *China*" and "Report from the Commissioners of Excise, *London;* on the Trade to *India* and *China*," in *Accounts and Papers, viz. Returns from the Board of Customs and Excise, Relative to the Trade with the East Indies and China* (London, 1813), 5–13 (quotation on 8), 109–110. Fich-

Merchant and manufacturer lobbying built on a long history of arguments against the Company's corruption and ill government, and the Company, too, responded much as it had for centuries. Seventeenth-century opponents of the Company had claimed it "tended to the Scandal of our Religion, to the Dishonour of the Crown and Nation, the Reproach of the Laws, the Oppression of the People, and the Loss of the Trade it self." Likewise, in 1811, Samuel Waddington, a hop merchant bucked from the Surrey light horse because of his radical views, claimed that he was "exposing a *pernicious monopoly,* and thus ULTIMATELY CONVEY *[sic]* LIBERTY AND CHRISTIAN CONSOLATION, TO FORTY MILLIONS OF UNFORTUNATE FELLOW-SUBJECTS!" The Company directors countered that their domains showed a "gratifying picture of a people raised from the lowest disorder and degradation, to a state of industry, security, and freedom." And they turned back to their own ancient defenses, that their seamen "augment the national glory"; their shipyards, "the national defence"; the fortunes of their servants, the national "capital"; and their trade, "the national fund of strength and glory." One merchant group gestured, in contrast, to the scandals over Robert Clive and Warren Hastings in which Indians were exploited and killed through the power of government for Company and private profit, writing, "The experience of thirty years has proved to demonstration, that your characters as sovereigns and merchants are totally irreconcileable *[sic].*"[56]

---

ter indicates that the Company's own reports on American trade convinced Parliament of the need to end the Company monopoly (Fichter, *So Great a Profitt,* 241–249). Certainly, the American trade was part of the argument. The Board of Control under Tory leadership had, nevertheless, long since prepared the plan that the Tory Parliament was almost certainly going to approve under the prevailing system of Tory members supporting their ministers and following public pressure. The vote's passage was seen as such a sure thing that those from the outports calling for an open trade were told not even to bother presenting evidence. For more on the key decisions being made at the Board and ministerial levels, see Webster, "The Political Economy of Trade Liberalization," *EHR,* 2d Ser., XLIII (1990), 406–413, 417; C. H. Phillips, *The East India Company, 1784–1834* (Manchester, 1961), 189–190. On party voting, see Frank O'Gorman and Peter Fraser, "Party Politics in the Early Nineteenth Century (1812–32)," *English Historical Review,* CII (1987), esp. 73–75, 87.

56. "The Humble Reply of Several Merchants and Others (Who Petitioned Your Majesty in Council on the 17 and 31 of August Last) to the Answer of Certain Persons Stiling Themselves the Governour and Company of Merchants of London Trading into the East-Indies," in *A Journal of Several Remarkable Passages, before the Honourable House of Commons, and the Right Honourable the Lords of Their Majesties Most Honoarable Privy Council: Relating to the East-India Trade* ([n.p.], [1693]), 23; *Reasons Humbly Offered against Establishing, by Act of Parliament, the East-India-Trade, in a Company, with a Joint-Stock, Exclusive of Others, the Subjects of England* ([n.p.], [1693]), 4; S[amuel] F[errand] Waddington, *The*

Those arguing against the Company monopoly at the turn to the eighteenth and turn to the nineteenth century alike also pointed to the notion that Britons had a long-standing constitutional right to trade and that such a right was a central part of British freedom. In 1691, an anonymous author had explained that all trade needs to be free, "this being every Subjects Natural Right." Several 1693 merchant petitions explained that the monopoly was in breach of "Magna Charta, and several other Statutes" that guaranteed British liberty on the seas. In 1811, Waddington similarly concluded, *"Exclusive* privileges are incompatible with the principles of a free people, and with the spirit of the GREAT CHARTER." A Mr. Spence in 1812 asked, to the cheering of a gathering of merchants from Kingston upon Hull, "If we the natives of this free kingdom have not the privilege of trading to every quarter of the globe at peace with us, wherein in this respect do we differ from the degraded vassals of a Bonaparte or any other despot?" The long-standing belief in superior British liberty in contrast with French despotism had particular resonance during the Napoleonic Wars. In 1813, the Glasgow "merchants house" claimed trade to India as the "birth-right" of all British people.[57]

Oriental Exposition; Presenting to the United Kingdom an Open Trade to India and China (London, 1811), 183–184; *Resolutions of the General Court of Proprietors of East-India Stock, Relative to an Application to Parliament for a Renewal of Their Exclusive Privileges* (London, 1813), 12, 16; "The Address and Remonstrance of the Merchants and Traders of These Kingdoms, on Behalf of Themselves and the Public, to 'The United Company of Merchants Trading to the East Indies,'" in A Member of Parliament, ed., *Free Trade to India: Letters Addressed to the Merchants and Inhabitants of the Town of Liverpool, concerning a Free Trade to the East Indies* (Liverpool, 1812), 31. Despite his support of free and open trade, Waddington was convicted of forestalling hops to raise their price; see E. I. Carlyle, "Waddington, Samuel Ferrand," rev. Stephen M. Lee, *DNB.* For more on the Company as trader and government, see William J. Barber, *British Economic Thought and India, 1600–1858: A Study in the History of Development Economics* (Oxford, 1975), 97–98.

57. "To the Queens Most Excellent Majesty: The Humble Petition of Several Merchants, in Behalf of Themselves and Others," in *A Journal of Several Remarkable Passages,* 12 (see also 32, 61); Waddington, *Oriental Exposition,* 183–184; Mr. Spence quoted in *East India Trade: Report of the Proceedings of the Meeting at Kingston-upon-Hull, 6th April 1812, on the Subject of Laying Open the Trade to the East-Indies* (Hull, Eng., 1812), 9, 20; see also F. A. Winzer, *Prosperity of England midst the Clamors of Ruin* (London, 1799), 32. For the Glasgow "merchants house," see T. C. Hansard, *The Parliamentary Debates from the Year 1803 to the Present Time . . . ,* XXIV (London, 1813), Feb. 5, 1813, 387–388. The anonymous quotation is from *Companies in Joynt-Stock Unnecessary and Inconvenient: Free Trade to India in a Regulated Company, the Interest of England; Discours'd in a Letter to a Friend* ([n.p.], 1691), 1. For more examples of the use of the language of rights as a patriotic idiom among British merchants during the French wars, see Jonathan Eacott, "Trading Language: British Merchants and Political Economy between 1793–1815" (master's thesis, Queen's University,

Using the concepts of individual rights and, especially, natural rights to argue against the Company's monopoly tied an open India trade to the increasingly popular millenarian and Newtonian understanding of the world as a natural system. In 1693, an author against the Company monopoly had explained, "MEN being reasonable Creatures, Framed for Society, and the whole Earth being given unto them; I do take it to be the Dictate of Nature, that mutual Traffick or Commerce is free, and of Right doth belong to every Man." Individual freedoms and an open trade would allow God's will to be done by natural forces. Continuing the argument in 1812, a Scottish pamphlet author detailed a common connection between individual rights, free traders, and prosperity, writing, "There is no feature, perhaps, of the policy of an unenlightened age which is more strikingly incompatible with the fair enjoyment of individual rights, or the rapid progress of general prosperity than this same system of monopolies." Adam Smith's *Inquiry into the Nature and Causes of the Wealth of Nations* (1776) was the most effective and comprehensive statement of the long-standing political economy of natural law and liberty. As one anonymous author in 1812 wrote, "To those who are not already satisfied of the evil tendency of Monopoly, on general principles, I would recommend the fourth book of Smith's Wealth of Nations *[sic]*, and almost every political writer of modern times . . . as a general question of *theory*, no one seems to doubt that the Monopoly, should cease."[58]

Opponents to the Company's charter during previous renewal debates had argued that private merchants promised cheaper prices, access to more ports, and a bigger supply of more diverse Asian products. They

2001); Fichter, *So Great a Proffit*, 235–236. On British liberty and Napoleon, see Linda Colley, *Britons: Forging the Nation, 1707–1837* (New Haven, Conn., 1992), 30–42, 111–113, 354. Merchant emphasis on legal rights might have been connected to Jeremy Bentham's utilitarian philosophy that all rights were man-made and that the notion of natural rights was chimerical. In any case, utilitarian philosophy also emphasized limited government intervention, a stand poorly adapted to the claims of monopolists. See Peter N. Miller, *Defining the Common Good: Empire, Religion, and Philosophy in Eighteenth-Century Britain* (New York, 1994), 393–395.

58. *Reasons Humbly Offered against Establishing, by Act of Parliament, the East-India-Trade, in a Company, with a Joint-Stock, Exclusive of Others* . . . ([n.p.], [1693]), 1; *The Question as to the Renewal of the East India Company's Monopoly Examined* (Edinburgh, 1812), 3–4, 11; Waddington, *Oriental Exposition*, 168; *Letters on the East India Monopoly, Originally Published in the Glasgow Chronicle, with Additions and Corrections*, 2d ed. (Glasgow, 1812), 4. For one of countless examples of thinking from the *Wealth of Nations*, see A London Merchant, *Observations upon the Supplies of Provisions to the Metropolis, and upon the Means of Their Continuance in Case of Invasion* (London, 1812), 20.

pointed to the success of British merchants in the West Indies, English merchants during the open trade to India in the reign of Oliver Cromwell, and British interlopers to India operating out of Europe and, briefly, the Atlantic colonies. It was in this established line that those against the Company monopoly in the early nineteenth century pointed to the success of American merchants as evidence for the superiority of an open trade. In their resolutions for Parliament demanding free trade, merchants in Kingston upon Hull noted that "the Americans have gradually established, and actually enjoy an extensive and flourishing Commerce in every quarter of India." Alderman Wray claimed that American trade "rivalled, perhaps exceeded in amount and in tonnage, that of the East India company." An anonymous author posited that "the mercantile adventurers of America have been allowed to participate so largely, that they have had the supply, not only of their own market, as well as that of South America, but have actually competed to good purpose, with the company itself, in the general market of Europe." The effectiveness of the invocation of American merchants is difficult to judge, but only twenty-seven of ninety petitions sent to the House of Commons in 1812 and 1813 on the monopoly specifically mentioned American merchants' entering the India trade, and several more mentioned neutral and foreign traders in general.[59]

The records of the Glasgow East India Association Committee against the monopoly, made up of merchants and manufacturers, further help to illustrate the package of arguments used against the monopoly and the place of America in that package. In its first petition to Parliament, the committee argued that the monopoly acted "contrary to the Rights of British Subjects, and to those Principles of liberal Policy by which this nation is governed." The committee did not refer to U.S. merchants in its initial discussions, but, after corresponding with other groups against the trade, it added to a later petition that "every objection which can be

59. For examples from the 1690s, see *A Regulated Company More National Than a Joint Stock in the East-India-Trade* ([London], [169–?]), 1–2; "The Humble Petition of Several Merchants and Others, on Behalf of Themselves and Other Your Majesties Subjects," in *A Journal of Several Remarkable Passages*, 51; *Reasons Humbly Proposed for Asserting and Securing the Right of the Subjects to the Freedom of Trade, until They Are Excluded from It by Act of Parliament* ([London], [1695]), n.p.; R[oger] C[oke], *A Treatise concerning the Regulation of the Coyn of England, and How the East-India Trade May Be Preserved and Encreased* (London, 1696), 36. For the later period, see *East India Trade*, 3, 7; *Question as to the Renewal of the East India Company's Monopoly*, 23, 57, 63, 72. See also *A Demonstration of the Necessity and Advantages of a Free Trade to the East Indies; and of a Termination to the Present Monopoly of the East-India Company* (London, 1807), 135–139.

preposed to this measure, is at once experimentally and satisfactorily removed by the success which *[sic]* the American traffic." It also argued: "This intercourse has been allowed to Foreign States at amity with his Majesty, while it has been denied to his own subjects; and, as it now appears in the case of the united states of America, has contributed at once to relax the resources of this Country and to strengthen the sinews of the enemy." The other America was perhaps as important. In April 1813, the committee explained, "It is of the utmost importance that some relaxation of the Navigation Laws should be obtained and some provision made in an enactment for the regulation of the Trade with India, for permitting an intermediate traffic, particularly with the South American Colonies." This concern with South America reflected the arguments of Charles Davenant and others a century before. Finally, the committee's report documenting the successful effort to end the Company monopoly discussed the more general success of "foreigners" and did not single out Americans, nor did the committee mention the American trade in their summary of the debate in Parliament.[60]

Similar arguments against the monopoly had not worked for more than a few years back in the seventeenth century; something was new in 1813. True, antimonopoly theories had increased in sophistication, particularly at the hand of Adam Smith. The stack of charges against the Company's behavior in India had also continued to mount, as had its territory. American merchants had joined the India trade, and the U.S. flag had taken over from many other neutral and interloping flags. But these were largely incremental changes, and the issue raised over the American trade was not so much about its success in serving the U.S. market as about its success in serving European markets, which largely followed the earlier trades through Ostend and paralleled trades through Portugal and Denmark. The activities of U.S. merchants in the India trade did not cause the end of the Company's monopoly. America mattered more to the ending of the

60. See the following sources in Glasgow East India Association Committee Minute Book, 1812–1813, MS 891001/1, Glasgow Mitchell Library, Glasgow, Scotland [microfilm]: Resolutions of the Committee, Mar. 25, 1812, fol. 3; "The Petition of the Subscribed Merchants and Manufacturers in the City of Glasgow," Minutes of the Committee of Correspondence, Mar. 27, 1812, fol. 5v; "To the Honourable the Common of the United Kingdom of Great Britain and Ireland, in Parliament Assembled; the Petition of the Subscribers Merchants and Manufacturers in the City of Glasgow," fols. 28v–29; Minutes of the General Committee, June 16, 1812, fol. 18v; Minutes of the General Committee, Apr. 15, 1813, fol. 41v (they also conceded the China trade to the Company, 42); "Report of the Glasgow Committee to the Subscribers," Oct. 29, 1813, fols. 64v, 70.

monopoly because of what it grew. The U.S. embargoes and the War of 1812 underscored the dangers of relying on the politically independent United States for raw materials to feed British industry, in particular cotton. Anstruther, the Board of Trade, and the Board of Control all had explicitly referenced the overreliance on U.S. raw cotton as a strong reason to end the monopoly.

As much as some Company directors wanted to retain their monopoly system, advances in British simulations of India goods combined with Company conquest in India had increasingly shifted the means through which the Company was useful to the British state. In 1813, the Company's great projected value—and it could still be a significant financial, military, and economic prop for Britain—stemmed from the Indian revenue it acquired through conquest, its ability to further the cultivation of raw materials suitable for British industry, and even its promise to provide growing markets for British goods. None of that depended on the monopoly. The merchants and manufacturers who lobbied hard for the government to end the monopoly were pushing for a decision that had been made already in the Board of Control, but their lobbying reflects the shared interest in an India trade that would be in raw materials. The merchants' target customers for India goods were not the fashionable people of London and beyond; they were the industrialists of Manchester and Glasgow who were demanding raw materials. In turn, they intended to ship out British, not Indian, fashionable goods made with those raw materials. Confining the trade through London, far from the industrial outports, thus needed to end. The new charter, moreover, ended the Company monopoly with India, but not with China, from which manufacturers had not expected to gain the quantities and types of raw materials they hoped to gain from India. Indeed, as shown earlier, China was importing raw cotton from India itself. The monopoly was long intended as a means to constrain British trade with India while still deriving revenue benefits. The British government ended the Company monopoly in large part because that monopoly now seemed to constrain the development of another more promising monopoly of British manufacturers over domestic and foreign markets.[61]

THE PROBLEMS WITH INDIA for Britain had always been its manufacturing success, the strength of its domestic regimes, and its seductive and

61. On the British industrial monopoly, see Bernard Semmel, *The Rise of Free Trade Imperialism: Classical Political Economy, the Empire of Free Trade, and Imperialism, 1750–1850* (London, 1970), 6–8, 157.

corrupting luxury. The East India Company's monopoly and the Calico Acts had been designed to allow Britain to profit from India's productive superiority by funneling India's goods through London, while preventing Britain itself from being swamped by India goods. The value of the fabric trade from India had long been under suspicion as a sink of wealth and a displacer of domestic manufactures. Although conquest had initially reduced the outflow of bullion from Britain, it had also seemed to draw in more corruption, and, from the mid-1790s to 1805, India again took in an influx of silver from London and, particularly, America. Between 1802 and 1807, American merchants brought an average of nearly $3 million in silver per year into British India, compared with only $432,000 of merchandise. Manufacturers in Britain, meanwhile, made major technological advances in cotton production to remove the threat of India's manufactures. The French Revolutionary and Napoleonic Wars as well as the War of 1812, which eliminated the support of American merchants, markets, and materials, put added pressure on India as a source of raw materials, including cotton, but also indigo and a growing range of other commodities. Taking advantage of India now demanded the greatest volume of trade possible, making obsolete the Company's monopoly, the Calico Acts, and many of the complex and cumbersome imperial regulations designed to constrain and direct Britain's global India trade.[62]

During the lengthy series of wars with France, American merchants filled multiple roles for Britain: they provided the cover of neutrality, brought huge quantities of silver into India, and were a useful means of extracting capital out of India to Britain. Of course, that capital went to America, too, and enriched countless American merchants and their associates. Americans were not, however, competing with British manufacturers exporting to India. In American markets, even as American merchants became major players in the India trade, British cotton cloth had largely displaced Indian fabric. This displacement would continue to draw the United States toward Britain as the entrepôt, not for Indian manufactures, but for British-made simulations of those manufactures. It would

---

62. Adam Seybert, *Statistical Annals: Embracing Views of the Population, Commerce, Navigation, Fisheries, Public Lands, Post-Office Establishment, Revenues, Mint, Military and Naval Establishments, Expenditures, Public Debt, and Sinking Fund of the United States of America: Founded on Official Documents* . . . (Philadelphia, 1818), 289. For more on the influx of bullion into India, see Bowen, "Bullion for Trade, War, and Debt-Relief," *Modern Asian Studies*, XLIV (2010), 459–460.

also increasingly draw the United States toward supplying Britain's demand for raw cotton.

Parliament could now follow the seventeenth-century logic of Richard Hakluyt, John Smith, Samuel Purchas, and John Cary. Britain would have an open India trade not just to ease supply fears in war but also to facilitate a new (or, rather, old) vision of an even more lucrative imperial system, making Asian goods in Britain using raw materials from America and Asia. Britain could now pursue a monopoly, not of trade or reexports, but of production in Britain for the world. As Cary had written in 1695, "If a Manufacture of *Wool* will not please, why may not one of *Cotton*, the *Primum* of which *Calicoes* are made, whereof we have great quantities imported every Year from our own Plantations in *America*, and no doubt we might in a short time attain to an excellency therein, not only to supply ourselves, but also Foreign Markets." It would be an imperial monopoly that London's seventeenth-century woolen lobby, with its fabric inferior to cotton, could only have dreamed of. Cary's vision had come a hundred years too soon.[63]

63. John Cary, *A Discourse concerning the East-India Trade Shewing It to Be Unprofitable to the Kingdom of England, Being Taken Out of an Essay on Trade* (London, 1696), 7.

8   Conversions

At approximately thirty years old, Sarah Farquhar became seriously ill in New York and was advised to take a "long voyage to a hot climate" to recuperate. The events that followed in Farquhar's life illustrate many of the British and American commercial and religious interconnections with India, particularly the connections among individual merchants and missionaries. Andrew Smith, the son-in-law of Farquhar's teacher and mentor Isabella Graham, happened to be a merchant engaged in the India trade. In May 1804, Smith planned a new voyage with his ship *Allegany* to London and Madras, and he took Farquhar on board as a passenger. In August, they arrived in Britain, where the nondenominational London Missionary Society (LMS) was keen to dispatch doctor John Taylor and W. C. Loveless to begin a new mission in Surat. The East India Company, however, had become concerned that missionaries might destabilize the political situation in India and refused to grant them passage. Smith, with his American flag, agreed to take Taylor and Loveless on the *Allegany* to evade the Company's restrictions on missionaries, much as he and many other British merchants used the American flag to evade the Company's monopoly. Smith himself had been born in Scotland, where he retired, suggesting that his U.S. citizenship was just such a matter of convenience.[1]

1. Richard Knill, *The Missionary's Wife; or, A Brief Account of Mrs. Loveless, of Madras, the First American Missionary to Foreign Lands* (Philadelphia, 1839), 3–4. On Andrew Smith's life, see William M. MacBean, *Biographical Register of Saint Andrew's Society of the State of New York* (New York, 1922), I, 342. Sources alternately spell the ship's name *Allegany* and *Alleghany*. In his advertisements, Smith used the former; see, *Mercantile Advertiser* (New York), May 12, 1804, [1]. Smith's partner was Divie (also Devie) Bethune, a prominent Presbyterian evangelical who reportedly paid for the printing of ten thousand religious tracts. Bethune was the brother-in-law of Farquhar's mentor. On Bethune's life and trade, see "Deaths," *New England Historical and Genealogical Register,* XVI (July 1862), 292; "Shipping News," *Commercial Advertiser* (New York), May 10, 1802, [3]. On Smith's arrival in the spring, see "New-York, April 21," *United States Gazette* (Philadelphia), Apr. 23, 1804, [3]. On the summer voyage of 1804, see *Mercantile Advertiser* (New York), May 12, 1804, [1]. On Farquhar as a passenger on the *Allegany*, see Knill, *Missionary's Wife*, 4. On the *Allegany's* arrival in Britain, see *Daily Advertiser* (New York), Oct. 19, 1804, [3]. Taylor

In December 1804, the *Allegany* set sail for British India: an American vessel, departing from a British port, operated by a merchant alternately British, American, and British again, with an American woman and two British missionaries aboard. After becoming close during the long voyage, Farquhar and Loveless married in Madras, where they remained for two decades. Their union personified the growing union of British and American missionaries in India, interdependent entities with a common cause. Indeed, similar to Smith, Farquhar's citizenship, subjecthood, and identity had become uncertain. One British commentator wrote that she was "scarcely American, as she was adopted and educated by a Scotch lady; she spent the vigor of her life in British India," was married to an English missionary, and retired to England. Smith and Farquhar represented the blending and crossing of British and American identities encouraged by interests in India. Taylor and Loveless were clearly British, but their missionary activities nevertheless depended on nominally American assistance, and the American flag was used to further their British goals. The emerging missionary movement brought Americans and Britons together, blurred and merged their similarities, and took advantage of their differences, much as did the India trade.[2]

---

and Loveless were following a pattern begun in the 1790s; see, for example, Samuel Stennett, *Memoirs of the Life of the Rev. William Ward, Late Baptist Missionary in India* . . . (London, 1825), 76–77.

2. To allow the couple to remain in the Company's territory, Loveless became "superintendent of the Military Orphan Male Asylum," where he also proselytized. The couple built, and she managed, a missionary chapel that bore their name. See Knill, *Missionary's Wife*, 4–8; "Sarah Loveless," in W. H. Carey, ed., *Oriental Christian Biography, Containing Biographical Sketches of Distinguished Christians Who Have Lived and Died in the East* (Calcutta, 1850), I, 183–185. For definitions of Farquhar, see Thomas Timpson, *Memoirs of British Female Missionaries* . . . (London, 1841), 200. Knill opened, "Mrs. Loveless was an American," but concluded, "She was born in America, spent the vigour of her days in India, and died in the city of Canterbury, in England . . . her spirit is, we believe, with her 'Precious Jesus'" (Knill, *Missionary's Wife*, 3, 20). Knill's work was reprinted in *A Series of Tracts on the Doctrines, Order, and Polity of the Presbyterian Church in the United States of America* (Philadelphia, n.d.), II, 325–344.

The cooperation of British and American missionaries in this period has not figured significantly in histories of missionary work in India. See, for example, Anna Johnston, *Missionary Writing and Empire, 1800–1860* (Cambridge, 2003), 65; and Penelope Carson, *The East India Company and Religion, 1698–1858* (Woodbridge, U.K., 2012), 103, 159, 167–168. Historians have documented tensions among missionaries, merchants, planters, and political figures in empire. See, for example, Andrew Porter, "An Overview, 1700–1914," in Norman Etherington, ed., *Missions and Empire*, 40–62; John L. Comaroff, "Images of Empire, Contests of Conscience: Models of Colonial Domination in South Africa," *American Ethnologist*, XVI (1989), 661–685.

For various Britons, both religious and economic conversion in India appeared to be finally within reach in the early nineteenth century through the combined forces of conquering armies, Anglo-American merchants and missionaries, British manufacturing, and American and Indian raw materials. Long after American independence, the United States' relationship with Britain remained in many ways a codependent one, furthered substantially by relations with India. Many Britons and some Americans also expected that economic and religious changes in India would go hand in hand. How to achieve those changes, however, remained a problem of considerable debate. Not all evangelicals agreed that it was appropriate when, in the words of the British evangelical Melville Horne, "thus were Missions connected with manufactures and commerce, and gain became a pedestal for godliness to stand upon." Whether, moreover, officially independent America or officially conquered India would prove most useful and most under British influence, too, remained in doubt.[3]

Missions in the Making of Loyal American Subjects

Active missionary work, although often proclaimed and at times practiced, had not been a central part of English and, later, British conquests or plantation settlement in America or in either of the Indies. A transatlantic awakening of evangelical interest in Britain and America in the late eighteenth and early nineteenth century, however, stimulated a new emphasis on missionary work in the new and expanding British territories in North America, the West Indies, India, and beyond. On the subcontinent, the Company had defeated Tipu Sultan in 1799, and by 1804 it ruled the east coast and large parts of the west coast as well as much of the inland south and a large swath of territory in the north (Plate 22). The Company had become India's dominant power, holding considerable sway over a range of subsidiary and protected states, and it continued to exert its strength against the Maratha empire, which had earlier taken over much of India from the Mughal empire. Shared British and American concerns with the corruption of expanding Company rule fit readily with evangelical ideals, particularly as the Company had recently resisted evangelical efforts in its domains and refused missionaries passage to India on its

3. Melville Horne, *Letters on Missions; Addressed to the Protestant Ministers of the British Churches* (Bristol, 1794), 28. Horne's influential work was printed on both sides of the Atlantic; see Horne, *Letters on Missions, Addressed to the Protestant Ministers of the British Churches* (Andover, Mass., 1815), 50–51.

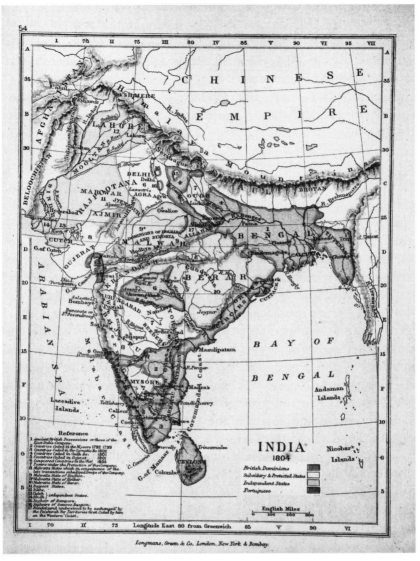

Plate 22. [F. S. Weller], "India, 1804." From Samuel Rawson Gardiner, *A School Atlas of English History,* new imprint (London, 1902), 106. Image provided by the University of Connecticut Libraries Map and Geographic Information Center (MAGIC)

ships. The latter restrictions made American merchants and ships, such as Smith and his *Allegany,* particularly useful to British evangelicals. But power, including in Atlantic evangelical circles, was asymmetrical. Missionary projects in India potentially enhanced British influence over like-minded American citizens more than over conquered Indian subjects.[4]

The LMS, for instance, used the inclusive language of "union" when courting the assistance of the Connecticut Missionary Society to proselytize at the turn of the century, but the LMS also took a stance of superiority, hoping to direct the Connecticut Society's efforts. The LMS suggested in 1798 that the Connecticut Society, given its nearness to "multitudes of the Heathen" and America's gospel history, might fix its efforts close to home. Under the LMS's guidance, "large bodies of Ministers and Christians, remote from each other in earthly situations," would "harmonize in zealous concern for the extension and prosperity of his kingdom." Two years later, the LMS explained that they were working to "send . . . ample assistance" to their one missionary in India and stated that British North America and the West Indies "strongly excite our prayers, that the Lord of the harvest would send forth more labourers." These laborers, the LMS hoped, would come from the Connecticut Society. In response to such requests, the Connecticut Society remarked that they did not see it as appropriate to send missionaries into the colonies of a foreign power. In truth, the Connecticut Society was not keen to engage with indigenous peoples in Canada, the United States, or India and worked instead with white settlers, in contrast and resistance to the designs of the LMS. The LMS nevertheless made clear that they valued their correspondence "with our dear Brethren in America with whom we have the double union of blood and of grace." Britons and Americans, they claimed, shared bonds even in political independence that set them fundamentally apart from others. Such bonds might not have obtained assistance for the LMS from the Connecticut Missionary Society, but they would prove valuable in other instances, particularly among the Baptists.[5]

4. On English missionaries in America, see Francis Jennings, *The Invasion of America: Indians, Colonialism, and the Cant of Conquest* (Chapel Hill, N.C., 1975), 53–54, 228–253.

5. John Love for the LMS to Messrs Timothy Dwight, Dana, and Trumbull, Feb. 23, 1798, Papers of the Missionary Society of Connecticut, reel 13, Joseph Hardcastle, John Eyre, Robert Cowrie et al. [London Missionary Society (LMS)] to the Directors of the Connecticut Missionary Society, October 1801; "Letter from the Directors of the London Missionary Society, to the Trustees of the Missionary Society of Connecticut," *Connecticut Evangelical Magazine,* II, no. 8 (February 1802), 309–312. On Canada and resistance to doing missions to nonwhites, see LMS to Connecticut Society, Aug. 9, 1804, Papers of the Missionary Society of

Accordingly, a stream of British missionaries obtained passage to India on American vessels from the last years of the 1790s through the early 1800s. In 1799, the British Baptist Missionary Society (BMS) sent William Ward, Joshua Marshman, William Grant, and Daniel Brunsdon to India via Philadelphia with Captain Benjamin Wickes on the American ship *Criterion*. The Company turned the missionaries away from Calcutta. Instead, they joined the British Baptist missionary William Carey, who had covered his missionary efforts by running an indigo plantation but had since moved to Serampore. In 1804, four more British Baptist missionaries and their wives traveled through New York to India. In 1805, Farquhar, Taylor, and Loveless arrived with Smith for the LMS. In 1806, Wickes brought two more British Baptists from London for free.[6]

BMS missionaries further gained emotional, material, and financial strength from Americans. Such support was vital because missionaries reported that "almost the universal opinion amongst Europeans" in India was "that our design is utterly chimerical." In 1800, evangelicals in Philadelphia sent supplies and positive messages to the missionaries in Serampore. Carey thanked them for the "very luxurious feast" and wrote, "It gives us great pleasure to find that we are thought of, and prayed for in so distant a quarter of the globe." He hoped for letters "by every opportunity," particularly in the face of the limited success the missionaries were experiencing amid the "deplorable state" of the "heathens" and Europeans in India alike. The Brahmins, he reported, were "literally . . . pickled in vice." Carey went on to laud Captain Wickes for his support and explained that "the glorious work going on in America, the establishment of Mis-

Connecticut, reel 13, Connecticut Society to LMS, Mar. 20, 1805, reel 14, LMS to Connecticut Society, Aug. 22, 1803, reel 13. Similarly, Carey had earlier also proposed that British Baptists would focus on India while U.S. Baptists would concentrate on North America; Carey to Andrew Fuller, Mar. 23, 1797, in Baptist Missionary Society (BMS), *Periodical Accounts Relative to the Baptist Missionary Society* (London, 1800–1819), I, 373. On the tension between the LMS and the Connecticut Missionary Society over missions to indigenous peoples, see Kariann Akemi Yokota, *Unbecoming British: How Revolutionary America Became a Postcolonial Nation* (New York, 2011), 159–164. Yokota argues that this tension was part of a larger one between the LMS as a sort of parent and the Connecticut Society as a child seeking respect and equality. Her reading is not necessarily in opposition to the language of union. Union need not suggest equality or constant agreement.

6. Stennett, *Memoirs of the Life of the Rev. William Ward*, 76–80; "Memoir of Rev. William Ward, One of the Serampore Missionaries," *American Baptist Magazine*, n.s., V, no. 1 (January 1825), 6–7; William Staughton, *The Baptist Mission in India: Containing a Narrative of Its Rise, Progress, and Present Condition; a Statement of the Physical and Moral Character of the Hindoos . . .* (Philadelphia, 1811), 61, 69, 298–301.

sion Societies, and the like, call for our most lively thanks, and have given us very great encouragement." Similarly, Ward was "amazed and encouraged" by Wickes's accounts of current revivals in America, and Marshman took comfort and inspiration from the British Atlantic evangelical hero Jonathan Edwards's "Dissertation *God's last end in creation.*" The BMS also used Wickes to transfer money and supplies to their missionaries free of charge. In 1805, Wickes and wealthy American merchant Robert Ralston spearheaded a funding drive in the United States that supposedly doubled the financial assets of the BMS.[7]

Even during the tense years before the War of 1812, Americans continued to funnel British and American missionaries and financial support to India while they vigorously publicized that East Indian missions were enabled by the legacy of British conquest in America. In 1809, the LMS sent William Lee to America to gain passage to India as a missionary, and from there he departed for Bengal. In 1811, the British Baptists William Johns and John Lawson, with their families, traveled to America, from where they embarked for India. They sold a $1 American edition of the *Brief Narrative of the Baptist Mission in India,* revised by D. S. of Philadelphia, to publicize their work. Overall, they raised $4,624 in Boston and Salem for their mission. They commented that it was rare to hear anything disparaging against missions to India in America. That same year, the editor of the *Connecticut Evangelical Magazine* encouraged Americans to donate to the British Baptists to support their translations, exclaiming, "What American Christian, who is acquainted with the oppression and poverty, under which his forefathers fled to these wilds, would have supposed, that one purpose, in the counsels of infinite wisdom was, here to prepare a part of the means, through which the rich Indies of the East, should read the gospel, in their own language!" This story echoed that of English imperial adventurers in the seventeenth century and since: the ex-

---

7. Stennett, *Memoirs of the Life of the Rev. William Ward,* 90; Carey to Dr. Rogers, Dec. 30, 1800–Jan. 9, 1801, *Gospel News; or, A Brief Account of the Revival of Religion in Kentucky, and Several Other Parts of the United States; Likewise, Some Pleasing Late Accounts of the Success and Prospect of the Everlasting Gospel in the East-Indies* (Baltimore, 1801), 15–17, "Extract of a Letter on Christian Friendship," 24; "From Mr. Ward's Journal," July 22, 1803, BMS, *Periodical Accounts,* II, 482. Jonathan Edwards helped to lead the First Great Awakening in the British Atlantic during the 1730s and 1740s; see "Mr. Marshman's Journal," Dec. 29, 1803, BMS, *Periodical Accounts,* II, 511. On Wickes's transferring money and supplies, see "Proceedings of the Committee," BMS, *Periodical Accounts,* III, 123–125. On the 1805 funding drive, see Staughton, *Baptist Mission in India,* 69; "Proceedings of the Committee," BMS, *Periodical Accounts,* III, 125–127.

pansion of the English and, later, British empire was God's plan. Britons were now leading the charge of the gospel, and their American offspring were called on to support evangelical designs in Asia.[8]

Americans, meanwhile, produced their own celebrations of the British missionary cause, supported by sharp attacks on Hinduism. In his 1811 *Baptist Mission in India*, the British-born American and leading Baptist William Staughton portrayed Indians as depraved, horridly immoral, ill clothed, and either frightfully poor or "immensely rich," both extremes evidence of corruption and other failings to readers in the early Republic. Nevertheless, Staughton believed India's peoples and animals to be capable of great moral improvement. He included a passage from Carey explaining that wild Indian buffalo were "one of the most dangerous and mischievous animals . . . remarkably stupid and savage, and their disposition precarious." Yet tamed buffalo were productive and could be made even more so with British intervention: "Their milk is very good: their flesh coarse, but well tasted; and might be improved by feeding. The animal might be harnessed to the plough or the cart." With the help of good Christians, "what is now a curse might be made a blessing, if properly attended to; an event which the spread of the gospel, by promoting civilization, will no doubt produce." Indians had domesticated buffalo since antiquity, a point that simply did not fit into Carey's schema. American readers received an even more negative impression of Hindu people from Noah Webster's *History of Animals*. Webster claimed, "They are an effeminate, cowardly people, and have always been conquered when invaded, by the more hardy natives of the north. They make poor soldiers, but good slaves." For Webster, such people could never be equal to Britons or Americans, but for evangelical readers such claims did not invalidate efforts at spreading the gospel.[9]

8. "William Lee," in Carey, ed., *Oriental Christian Biography*, 51–52; "Address," *Connecticut Evangelical Magazine*, IV, no. 3 (March 1811), 116–117; William Johns and John Lawson, Dec. 21, 1811, BMS, *Periodical Accounts*, V, 34, 45–46 (they finally arrived in India in August 1812); Timothy D. Whelan, ed., *Baptist Autographs in the John Rylands University Library of Manchester, 1741–1845* (Macon, Ga., 2009), 415. For another $6,000 raised, see "Translations of the Bible," *Connecticut Evangelical Magazine*, IV, no. 12 (December 1811), 479–480.

9. Staughton, *Baptist Mission in India*, 119–121 (Carey on buffalo), 125–164, 181–198, 204–205, 215–217. Noah Webster wrote that American Indians descended from more northern "Asiatics" and had many more good qualities. See Webster, *History of Animals* . . . (New Haven, Conn., 1812), 18–20. Among many important positions, Staughton would go on to become chaplain of the United States Senate in 1823. On perceptions of wealth, see Drew McCoy, *The Elusive Republic: Political Economy in Jeffersonian America* (New York, 1982),

The British Reverend Claudius Buchanan's *Memoir of the Expediency of an Ecclesiastical Establishment for British India* also appeared in an 1811 American edition with a special preface by its "American Editor" emphasizing the importance of cooperation among British and American evangelicals. The editor noted that, although the subject might have to do with British India, "America is cooperating with Europe in this benevolent and pious design." "Contributions have been forwarded from this country to India, towards procuring translations of the Scriptures . . . and some of our young men had already devoted themselves to the Indian Mission." The editor did not mention American women who had traveled to India and the essential role of American captains in getting the missionaries into India. Still, the claim on cooperation was a strong one.[10]

Also in 1811, the new American Board of Commissioners for Foreign Missions actively embraced the LMS's plans, whereas the Connecticut Missionary Society had earlier refused them. The Board set plans in motion to send Protestant missionaries east to India and west to the "Caghanawaga" people in Lower Canada specifically to help the British. The Board positioned themselves as postcolonial agents of British power over other peoples colonized by Britain, helping, in their minds, to support the overburdened but just British evangelical, and also imperial, apparatus. The Board explained, "The Christians of Great Britain are, indeed, ardently engaged in the glorious work of evangelizing the nations; but in imparting the word of life to hundreds of millions ready to perish in Asia and Africa, they need and they desire our help." Such a union made sense because "we derive our origin, our language, our laws, and our religion" from Britain. Britain and the United States were the only countries with the "inclination, or the ability," to convert the world's peoples, but Britain was already burdened by the expenses of a great war with France—"a power which threatens to subjugate the civilized world"—as well as by its own domestic and global charity. The Board clearly positioned the British empire as the champion and ultimate model of civilization, not just against the heathen but also against the Catholic French.[11]

1–75; Joyce Appleby, *Capitalism and a New Social Order: The Republican Vision of the 1790s* (New York, 1984), 11–14, 50, 74–75, 80–81, 90–91.

10. Claudius Buchanan, *Memoir of the Expediency of an Ecclesiastical Establishment for British India . . .*, 1st American ed. (Cambridge, Mass., 1811), vi.

11. The language of the Board's plan also paralleled earlier letters in other places, notably in a reference to "Elliot and Brainard" as examples to be followed; see "An Address to the Christian Public," *Connecticut Evangelical Magazine*, V, no. 2 (February 1812), 50–56 (quotations on 51, 53, and 55).

To begin to fulfill its plan, the Board sent two couples, Adoniram and Nancy Judson and Samuel and Harriet Newell, to India. The Board instructed its missionaries to consider all other Protestant missionaries "as your brethren" and to "cheerfully co-operate, as far as consistently you can." After arriving in Serampore, Nancy Judson wrote, "Our blessings have been given in answer to the prayers of our christian friends in America." The East India Company, however, directed them to leave. The editor of the *Connecticut Evangelical Magazine* expressed a commonly shared disappointment among evangelicals but reckoned that, since the two countries were now embroiled in the War of 1812, little else could have been expected. Harriet Newell soon passed away, and the remaining missionaries bumped around the Indian Ocean. Eventually, the Judsons succeeded in revitalizing the British mission in Burma. Several British missionaries had struggled to establish a lasting mission there outside the Company's territory, including Carey's son Felix. In Burma, the Americans could bolster a faltering British project to spread Protestantism while avoiding the Company's restrictions.[12]

After peace returned among Britain, the United States, and France, many Americans spoke out in favor of supporting British missions and British rule in India. Assessing the extent of such opinions in the United States is tricky, but certainly they were not uncommon. William Staughton reassured the missionaries at Serampore: "Missionary ardour in the United States is growingly vigorous, and opposition is like a ball of snow in a furnace of fire. The work is the Lord's, and the people feel it such from Georgia to Maine, from the Atlantic to the Mississippi." He explained that "Brother Rise [Luther Rice]" had been traveling throughout America "exciting our brethren" to support the missions in Asia. The directors of the Fairfield County Bible Society in Connecticut bubbled that foremost among all the missionary organizations was "the British and Foreign Bible Society—the brightest star that ever rose upon her 'sea girt isles;' the center of the most resplendant constellation, that mortal eyes ever beheld." American-born University of Pennsylvania medical student Richard Harlan, who traveled to Calcutta as a ship's surgeon, believed that the British

12. "Instructions, Given by the Prudential Committee of the American Board of Commissioners for Foreign Missions, to the Missionaries to the East, Feb. 7, 1812," *Connecticut Evangelical Magazine*, V, no. 12 (December 1812), 465; "American Missionaries to the East Indies," ibid., VI, no. 2 (February 1813), 67; Nancy Judson to Keziah Punchard, June 30, 1812, Fam. MSS 515, Nancy Judson Papers, PEM. Nancy's given name was Ann. For a brief history of the two couples, see "Samuel Newell" and "Ann Hasseltine Judson," in Carey, ed., *Oriental Christian Biography*, I, 23–25, 239–250.

were saving India from despots, such as Tipu Sultan. He saw Tipu Sultan as a clear example of the debilitating effects of the "luxury of an Eastern monarch." India would have been fully "desolated" by its Muslim rulers "had not the British, by their conquests, exterminated its ambitious oppressors, and restored peace." He noted, "Time and long intercourse with the Europeans may eventually do away these barbarous customs." Even though Harlan supported British rule, he still doubted how readily Indian cultures might be changed.[13]

Indeed, between India and Britain, whose influence would be stronger on the other remained unclear, but, between Britain and the United States, the direction of cultural exchange was more certain. British evangelicals had gained few Indian converts, but they did gain the support of many Americans by using the promise of conversions in India. The new British evangelical vision of India as a space of active Protestant conversion persuaded many American evangelicals to support British rule in India, if not the Company, with its corruption and resistance to the spread of the gospel. In assisting Britons in importing various forms of religious supplies and passengers into India, many American evangelicals were active in supporting British evangelical goals. Many American evangelicals were, in some measure, thereby complicit in subordinating American goals to British goals. Early on, the Connecticut Missionary Society pushed back, seeing local work among white settlers as most in their interests, but the American Board and many other American evangelicals increasingly saw

13. W[illiam] Staughton to the Brethren at Serampore, Oct. 24, 1816, *Circular Letters Relative to the Baptist Missions in India, Including Miscellaneous Intelligence respecting the Progress of the Gospel*, X (April 1817), 67–68; Lucius Bolles to William Ward, Dec. 24, 1816, ibid., X (June 1817), 109; H. Humphrey, "Second Annual Report of the Directors of the Fairfield Bible Society," *Religious Intelligencer*, I, no. 21 (Oct. 19, 1816), 331; Richard Harlan, Apr. 10, 11, June 17, 1817, Richard Harlan Journal, Mss.B.H228, 28, 32 (quotations), 37, 46, APS. Harland's brother, Josiah, eventually rose to substantial fame for his own exploits working with the East India Company and various rulers in India and Afghanistan. Josiah Harlan's life has been explored in Ben Macintyre, *Josiah the Great: The True Story of the Man Who Would Be King* (London, 2004). The Company had evicted Rice with the Judsons. He returned to America to raise support for missions in India. See "Ann Hasseltine Judson," in Carey, ed., *Oriental Christian Biography*, 241. The American Respectable Society was also busy raising additional funds (Mrs. Rowe copied to Ward by J. Rowe, Dec. 16, 1816, *Circular Letters*, X [July 1817], 125). Interactions during the war were sharply limited but not ended entirely. For example, the governor-general, Lord Minto, ordered a large group of American missionaries and their families out of Bengal; they found refuge in Bombay under a more sympathetic British governor. See Carson, *East India Company and Religion*, 102–104, 158–159, 167.

British goals in British possessions as preeminent. The United States, they argued, had already benefited from British religion, culture, and ideals, and now it was the Americans' turn to help Britons spread the gospel in other parts of the globe.

Cargoes of Civilization

Questions about the potential dangers and benefits of British and American efforts to convert India's peoples to Protestantism, meanwhile, were connected to questions about the appropriate standards and objectives for British rule and the means to increase the export of British manufactured goods to India. Evangelicals often tied the need for religious conversion to old associations between India's moral corruption and its consumption practices and fashions. As William Ward put it, "Almost all of the first impressions of mankind are derived from the objects around them; and in this way the characteristic features of every order of human societies are formed." Indian fashions and possessions reflected the hold of tyranny. Carey wrote that their brass bangles, for instance, made "a noise in walking like prisoners in their irons." Evangelicals both within and without the Company largely believed that Britons needed to resist converting to such supposedly despotic Indian norms that had long been seen as corrupting on both sides of the Atlantic. Many with Company experience in India, in contrast, believed in the need to accept Indian cultures and faiths and to continue to convert British modes of rule into terms that they thought Indians understood and respected. As the longtime Company servant and military officer Thomas Munro quipped to the House of Commons, "If civilization was to become an article of trade between the two countries, I am convinced that this country [Britain] will gain by the import cargo." These evangelical and general Company positions, despite their stark differences, were both often shaped by prejudice. They were also both attempts to incorporate Indians into larger global English-speaking communities and into forms of British subjecthood for political and economic benefits. The cargoes of civilization were metaphorical and material.[14]

14. William Ward, *View of the History, Literature, and Mythology of the Hindoos: Including a Minute Description of Their Manners and Customs, and Translations from Their Principal Works,* new ed. (London, 1822), I, xxviii (preface); Carey to Mr. [John Webster?] Morris, Dec. 5, 1797, in BMS, *Periodical Accounts,* I, 385; Thomas Munro, Apr. 12, 1813, in T. C. Hansard, *The Parliamentary Debates from the Year 1803 to the Present Time* (London, 1813), XXV, column 786.

Some British evangelicals, encouraged by the East India Company's territorial expansion, proposed replicating earlier British patterns of militant agricultural settlement in America to convert India's peoples, their habits, and their fashions. In a revealing example, Granville Sharp, an Anglican evangelical who gained most of his fame in the abolition movement, wrote to the Reverend John Mitchell regarding Mitchell's prize-winning essay on the best means to civilize Britain's Asian subjects. Sharp and Mitchell agreed that, following the model of early settlement in New England, Britons should be encouraged to settle in India in orderly towns and townships. Each settler would be granted one acre in a town and an additional two and a half acres in the corresponding township. Each township would be defended by fences, earthworks, ditches, and a local militia. They also agreed on the need to eliminate India's legal code, which they saw as "both *cruel* and *unjust*." Caste would need to be abolished, as would polygamy and suttee, which were as odious as enslavement and the trade in enslaved people. Men must be forbidden from wearing women's clothing, or at least clothing that appeared to be women's clothing to British men. All these practices were unnatural and crimes against God. Much like many English commentators in the seventeenth century, Sharp noted that Hindus and papists were in fact analogous: Satan ruled them both. With dramatic Protestant reforms, India's plenty could become ordered, positive, godly, and properly British, instead of corrupting.[15]

Though certainly not keen for such settlement plans, the Company, too, considered the means to order and rule Indian society on terms that it hoped would avoid corruption, but questions about what counted as corruption persisted. From 1805 to 1809, the British resident at Hyderabad,

15. Granville Sharp to John Pattison for John Mitchell, June 20, 1806, D3549/13/1/P7, Gloucestershire Archives, United Kingdom. Carey also expressed deep concern in his correspondence with Dr. Rogers about the continuance of enslavement in the U.S. South. Many British evangelicals imagined the U.S. North to have developed without enslaved labor. See Carey to Dr. Rogers, Dec. 30, 1800–Jan. 9, 1801, *Gospel News,* 17. Granville Sharp had become an expert on enslavement and was important in the 1772 Somerset case, which had found no legal basis for enslavement in Britain. He then worked with Dissenting Quaker evangelicals as chairman of the Society for Effecting the Abolition of the Slave Trade; see E. C. P. Lascelles, *Granville Sharp and the Freedom of Slaves in England* (London, 1928), 16–34, 50–55, 69–80. For more on Sharp, the abolition of the slave trade, and America, see Christopher Leslie Brown, *Moral Capital: Foundations of British Abolitionism* (Chapel Hill, N.C., 2006), 161–206. Mitchell's plan used British settlers, unlike that of Alexander Dow in 1772; see Chapter 4, above. For a similar American statement on the Catholics being like the heathen, see "American Missionaries to the East Indies," *Connecticut Evangelical Magazine and Religious Intelligencer,* VI, no. 2 (February 1813), 67.

Thomas Sydenham, and the secretary to Bengal's governor-general, Neil Edmonstone, engaged in a lengthy debate over the appropriate concessions to India's cultures in order to maintain control. Sydenham argued for the necessity of display on Indian terms, whereas Edmonstone argued for frugality and British-derived marks of power. Their debate reflected a larger one taking place throughout the Company and outside it. "It is my Duty to state," wrote Sydenham, "that the reductions which have lately taken place in the retinue, and expences of the Residency, have produced a strong impression on all ranks of People, very unfavourable to the former notions of our Power and resources." Worse for Sydenham, "they have led even the Soubardar to imagine that my diplomatic Powers and Rank were not equal to those of my Predecessors." Of course, he acknowledged, it was "ridiculous" to think that British right and might had declined, and Sydenham could still fall back on Britain's increasingly successful military power. However, he explained, the ability to exercise power peacefully and in any sort of medium- or long-term capacity depended on Indian perceptions of the wealth, habits, and state equipage of their British rulers.[16]

After finding his more general explanations for the need to look like Indian rulers unsuccessful, Sydenham began sending Edmonstone lists of what he bought and why. He wrote that he had to buy new umbrellas and pay for repairs to his prestigious silver umbrella, which he claimed possessed a vital lineage of local authority. The umbrella had been used by the previous British resident, who had obtained it from the famous army officer and highly experienced British negotiator to Indian and Persian courts Colonel John Malcolm, who had bought it from Hyder Ali Khan, who had used it in his "celebrated invasion of the Carnatic." Additionally, Sydenham needed new spears and camel decorations as well as a new elephant howdah (a sort of carriage placed on an elephant's back). The old bits had worn out, and his retinue depended upon a regal Indian show.[17]

"It is the Opinion of the Government," Edmonstone replied, "that the dignity and respectability of the British Representatives should be made to rest, as in fact it does, on more solid foundations than the maintenance of state and splendour, borrowed from the manners and habits of the Natives of India, and in great degree inconsistent with our character." Here was the nub of the issue. Some splendor was required for the highest Company officials in inland establishments, but the governor had directed that such splendor must befit a Briton and appear British. The government would

16. Thomas Sydenham to Neil Edmonstone, July 16, 1806, IOR/F/4/311/7096, 14–15, BL.
17. Sydenham to Edmonstone, July 21, 1808, IOR/F/4/311/7096, 19–20, BL.

provide only the annual allotment set out in 1805, leaving Sydenham to cover all of the additional costs.[18]

Edmonstone's instructions made sense to many in London and certainly to evangelicals in India, including Governor-General John Shore, whom Edmonstone had served with for several years in the mid-1790s. Nevertheless, the instructions contradicted the common practices of many British officials in India, particularly those living outside major British settlements. Edmonstone himself had bought an elephant and a range of Indian status items, including a prized hookah, soon after arriving in the Indian countryside in the late 1780s. He had an Indian partner who bore him children. And even Shore specifically rode an elephant to install Saadat Ali Khan as the new nawab in Lucknow during a coup in 1798. Edmonstone boasted, "I never saw so grand a sight." Why Edmonstone encouraged a different approach from the one he followed is unclear, but Edmonstone's letters to Sydenham did not reflect changing attitudes at the top. Despite the elephant, Shore was already disappointed in the behavior of Company servants who embraced Indian culture in the 1790s. In 1803, however, Edmonstone had married a British woman, which might have reflected or instigated his own harsher line against Indian culture. In any case, these contradictions within Edmonstone's own attitudes underscore the dilemma many Britons perceived in securing rule in India.[19]

In 1806, as Sydenham and Edmonstone debated the need to abide by elite Indian consumption and display habits, a dramatic mutiny emphasized the stakes in ignoring the consumption practices of India's peoples. The Indian sepoy troops, upon whom the British relied to maintain power, killed nearly two hundred Britons in Vellore, part of the Madras Presidency. John Craddock, the local commander in chief, argued that imprisonment of the recently defeated Mysore princes had stimulated the mutiny. But Craddock had also recently passed new regulations that forbade the Company's sepoys from wearing caste marks and earrings, required the trimming of beards, and reworked the turban to be more like a British shako hat with a leather cockade, which, according to many Indian faiths and cultures, risked polluting those who touched it. The governor of the Madras Presidency, William Bentinck, argued that these new, more

18. Edmonstone to Sydenham, May 27, 1809, IOR/F/4/311/7096, 27, BL.

19. Neil Edmonstone to William Edmonstone, Apr. 29, 1797, Neil Edmonstone to Archibald Edmonstone, Apr. 21, 1798, "Narrative of the Revolution at Lucknow," all in Correspondence and Papers of Neil Benjamin Edmonstone, MS Add. 7616, Department of Manuscripts and University Archives, Cambridge University Library.

European-style dress regulations had provoked the violence and would appear to Indians as evidence that the government intended to convert them to Christianity. The Vellore mutiny redoubled concerns held by many within the Company about missionary activity and particularly about changes to local practices of consumption and reduced cultural accommodation as threats to British power.[20]

Certainly aware of such concerns, Baptist missionary Joshua Marshman wrote from Serampore: "No one in Leadenhall street, nor even in Britain, more ardently wishes for the permanence and prosperity of the British empire in India than myself. . . . I am fully convinced that one of the most effectual means of perpetuating the British dominions in India will be the calm and silent, but steady and constant, diffusion of Christian light among the natives." He predicted that Hindus would always be ruled by people practicing other religions and that, even once Indians became Christian, they would remain incapable of governing themselves. Therefore, the Company need not fear missionary work in India, and Britons should ensure that, for the sake of India's people, Britain and not some other foreign power ruled the subcontinent. For Hindus, "Mahometanism, ambitious and blood-thirsty in its very nature," he argued, using a centuries-old stereotype, was a much worse faith under which to be ruled. In reality, India's Muslim rulers tended to be tolerant, a pragmatic position for a small minority ruling a much larger majority of a different faith. Edmonstone took the same position when he warned Marshman against aggressive attempts to convert Hindus and forbade the Baptists from proselytizing in areas of significant tension between Hindus and Muslims. He was thus seen by some missionaries as a powerful enemy, although he was not absolutely against the dissemination of the gospel. Edmonstone's thinking again defied easy categories.[21]

20. The sepoys likely rebelled over reductions in their right to negotiate the terms of their service more than over the issue of dress. But many Britons argued that the dress regulations were the central issue. See Carson, *East India Company and Religion*, 70–73, 90–94; James W. Frey, "The Sepoy Speaks: Discerning the Significance of the Vellore Mutiny," in Gavin Rand and Crispin Bates, eds., *Mutiny at the Margins: New Perspectives on the Indian Uprising of 1857*, IV, *Military Aspects of the Indian Uprising* (Thousand Oaks, Calif., 2013), 1–23.

21. "Occurrences at Serampore," Oct. 11, 1807, and Nov. 28, 1807, in BMS, *Periodical Accounts*, III, 397, 412–413 (quotations). The material cited here was also reprinted in America; see "Interesting Extracts from the Last Report of the Baptist Mission Society," *Connecticut Evangelical Magazine; and Religious Intelligencer*, III, no. 3 (March 1810), 115–117. For more on Edmonstone's warning, see Carson, *East India Company and Religion*, 101.

Despite the mutiny in Vellore, between 1807 and 1810 Company directors Edward Parry and Charles Grant increasingly tried to shift the Company and the British government toward support for missionary work. In India, Grant had lost two children to smallpox and gambled away much of his family fortune, facilitating his evangelical awakening. Grant began working with the famous member of Parliament William Wilberforce in the 1790s on both the abolition of the trade in enslaved people and the expansion of the missionary movement in India. In 1807, they wrote a vigorous defense of missionaries to Robert Dundas, Lord Melville, the president of the Board of Control. They claimed that converting Indians to Christianity needed to be a primary Company goal, for "in every thing which usually unites the Rulers and the Subjects of a State, as identity of descent, of Country, Language, Education, Religion, Laws, Manners and Character, we and the Indian People whom we govern, are totally dissimilar." By sharing with Indians the Protestant religion, "infinitely superior . . . in light and purity to their own," common bonds would be created that would attach Indians more firmly and positively to British rule. They later explained, "It is indispensible to recognise as a principle that it is the duty of this Christian Country as well in obedience to the dictates of its Religion as from regard to the welfare of its heathen Subjects, to endeavour by prudent and proper methods to communicate the light of the Gospel." The Company did not need to pursue this work directly, but the country and Company alike needed to "promote the prudent and safe exertions" of individual missionaries. The letter apparently appealed to Dundas, who expressed concern that prohibitions against missionaries would further sink the Company in the opinion of the British public.[22]

The opposition from within the Company was vigorous. In one sense, the resistance was analogous to West Indian planters who feared that missionaries proselytizing among the enslaved and arguing for abolition would stimulate violent uprisings. In the Company, however, the primary fear was not that radical Dissenters would stimulate uprisings among newly Christian Indians; it was that missionaries would stimulate uprisings among confirmed Hindus and Muslims angry at being mocked and fearful that the Company intended to force conversions. John Scott

22. Edward Parry and Charles Grant to Robert Dundas, June 8, 1807, MS Eng. Hist. c. 210, 4, Bodleian Library, Oxford University, Minute from Edward Parry and Charles Grant, Aug. 16, 1808. Some of Grant's gambling was on bad investments. Many evangelicals supported the end of the monopoly, but Grant feared that an open trade would destabilize the Company and its rule. See Carson, *East India Company and Religion*, 25, 34, 76–80, 110.

Waring, a Company stockholder and military officer, requested that the Company call back all missionaries and prohibit support for any further missionary activity. He described Dissenting evangelical missionaries as obsessive radicals. Another leading Company stockholder published a letter to Parry arguing that missionaries would cost the Company its power in India. Similarly, a member of the Company's medical establishment published a tract with the Company's booksellers arguing that pushing Indians to convert to Christianity would lead them to join Napoleon. The author posited: "Under the able but unprincipled despotism of Buonaparte, France would conquer England on the banks of the Ganges." To avoid this dire outcome, "our principal efforts must be directed to assure the whole of our Indian subjects and neighbours, that. . . . we shall continue to respect those usages which they hold sacred: that they shall always remain unmolested in the exercise of their customs, laws and religion." Rule, as it had for the Mughals, depended on such tolerance.[23]

Fear of revolts was not, however, the only argument mobilized against missionary activity and other cultural conversions in India. Charles "Hindoo" Stuart strongly defended Hindu beliefs and practices in his *Vindication of the Hindoos from the Aspersions of the Reverend Claudius Buchanan.* Buchanan had argued in favor of forced conversions in India in his *Memoir of the Expediency of an Ecclesiastical Establishment for British India.* Stuart, who rose up the ranks of the army to major general, embraced many aspects of Indian culture in his personal life and his writings. His views built on a series of generally sympathetic late-eighteenth-century accounts of India's cultures by a group of British writers known as "orientalists." The leading orientalist, philologist Sir William Jones, publicized the idea that Sanskrit originated in the same language family as Latin and Greek. India's current peoples were the heirs of a great classical civilization responsible for significant advances in learning.[24]

23. David Hopkins, *The Dangers of British India, from French Invasion and Missionary Establishments* . . . (London, 1808), 7, 48–52 (quotation on 49), 151 (quotation), 152. Some radical Dissenting evangelicals expressed considerable sympathy for the French Revolution, and many evangelicals were against enslaved labor. In Jamaica, Dissenting evangelical ministers were imprisoned, and in Demerara blacks were forbidden to assemble for worship or missionary instruction during daylight hours. See Carson, *East India Company and Religion,* 45, 81–86, 114–115.

24. Claudius Buchanan, *Memoir of the Expediency of an Ecclesiastical Establishment for British India; Both as the Means of Perpetuating the Christian Religion among Our Own Countrymen; and as a Foundation for the Ultimate Civilization of the Natives* (London, 1805), 27–28. For more on Stuart's life and the debate over the authorship of his works, see Liz Woods, "Stuart, Charles (1757/8–1828)," *DNB.* William Jones had supported the Ameri-

Stuart extended Jones's thinking to counter Buchanan's claim that the great civilization of ancient India was dead like those of Rome and Greece. Stuart explained that Hindus believed in one supreme God, saw the divine spirit in everything around them, disavowed material wealth and luxury, lived soberly, guarded their sexual virtue, respected the elderly, and feared the hellish bodies that sinful people would be destined to after transmigration. What, he asked, could missionaries teach to such people? Neither Christians in Britain who believed in fairies and ghosts nor Hindus who believed in reprehensible customs followed the truth of their faiths. "Whenever, therefore, the Christian Religion does as much for the lower orders of society, in Europe, as that of Brahma thus appears to have done for the Hindoos," he proposed, "I shall cheerfully vote for its establishment in Hindostan." For Stuart, the goodness of Hindus was reason enough not to force them to convert to Protestantism, which might even take them a step backward.[25]

Like many others on both sides of the debate, Stuart associated Indian commodities and fashions with his perceptions of its people. Shortly after publishing *A Vindication of the Hindoos,* Stuart advocated for British women to further adopt Indian fashion in a series of articles that had first appeared in the Calcutta *Telegraph.* Stuart explained, "Nothing can be more becoming than the Indian stays; of pliant gauze, Benares silk, or fine reticulated muslin." Stuart simply could not understand why some British women still insisted on the discomforts and distortions of hoops: "Does it proceed from indifference about pleasing; from affectation of refined decorum; from mistaken prejudice against all customs *Hindostanee?* or do they think they shall be less attractive in our eyes?" Stuart thought it delightful that "the Hindoo robe . . . leaves little room for deception; and does nature more justice than any dress I have ever seen." "Maria," in a letter to the editor of the *Telegraph,* responded that Stuart was "depraved" and ridiculously championed "our sooty sisterhood!" "Rhapsodist," in another letter to the *Telegraph,* claimed to agree with Maria, but only because "the superior refulgence of European charms, blazing through the thin medium of a Brahmin dress, might endanger our magazines, or set

can Revolution and considered moving to America. For more on Jones, see Garland Cannon, *The Life and Mind of Oriental Jones: Sir William Jones, the Father of Modern Linguistics* (Cambridge, 1990), 82, 92, 114, 135–137, 183.

25. [Charles Stuart], *Vindication of the Hindoos from the Aspersions of the Reverend Claudius Buchanan . . .* (London, 1808), 24–44, 62–63, 69, 79, 102 (quotation), 126–127.

our bungalows on fire. Ladies do mischief enough, already." Stuart fought a winning battle against his critics on this issue.[26]

Since relatively unstructured muslin dresses had already been adopted by large numbers of British, European, and American women, it was difficult to make negative associations stick. Thomas Williamson, the author of the Company's semiofficial guide to India, *The East India Vade-Mecum*, explained that Indian attire was "the robe from which our ladies have taken their present dress, but which they have modestly closed before" (Plate 23). In her *The Mirror of the Graces*, popular on both sides of the Atlantic, "A Lady of Distinction" recommended such relatively unstructured dresses, British and Indian muslin, Chinese and Indian silks, and cashmere shawls as well as rose water, popular in India, preferably mixed with brandy, for the skin. She wrote that a woman of status must carefully assemble "the empire of all her personal charms," positively and directly connecting personal fashion to the empire at large.[27]

As with India's calicoes in the mid-seventeenth century, some writers actively separated Hindu dress from criticisms of Hindu people. Army officer and Calcutta botanical garden founder Robert Kyd, who was generally more critical of Indians than Stuart, remarked of Indian clothing that "the contour and configuration of the whole person, if gracefully formed is shown to greater advantage, as well as the reverse if defective," compared to "European complicated clothing." The missionary William Ward did not recommend Indian dress for Britons, but he did find it "happily suited to the climate" and productive of "a very graceful effect." India expert James Forbes noted that the dress of Indian women had both form and function in its favor. But, like Ward, he still attacked Hinduism, writing, "Those who best know the Hindoos, know them to be immersed in ignorance, superstition, and idolatry!" For Forbes, as for the many British and

26. [Charles Stuart], *The Ladies' Monitor, Being a Series of Letters, First Published in Bengal, on the Subject of Female Apparel, Tending to Favour a Regulated Adoption of Indian Costume* (London, 1809), 5, 20, 31.

27. Thomas Williamson, *The East India Vade-Mecum; or, Complete Guide to Gentlemen Intended for the Civil, Military, or Naval Service of the Hon. East India Company* (London, 1810), I, 375, II, 2. A Lady of Distinction feared signs of a return to the corset and stays. See A Lady of Distinction, *The Mirror of the Graces; or, The English Lady's Costume; Combining and Harmonizing Taste and Judgment, Elegance and Grace, Modesty, Simplicity and Economy, with Fashion in Dress* (London, 1811; New York, 1813), plates X–XII, 34, 40, 64–65, 81. It was published in Boston with a different subtitle in 1831 and on both sides of the Atlantic into the 1840s. See, for example, *The Mirror of the Graces* (Boston, 1831).

Plate 23. Rudolf Ackermann, "Promenade Dresses." From *Repository of Arts, Literature, Commerce, Manufactures, Fashions, and Politics*, II (Aug. 1, 1809). Los Angeles County Museum of Art, Los Angeles, California, U.S.A. Digital Image © 2015 Museum Associates / LACMA. Licensed by Art Resource, NY

American women who had modified and naturalized the muslin dress, it was not a manifestation of such corruption.[28]

Similar to such fashions, curries and other Anglo-Indian foods continued to become increasingly naturalized in Britain. Of thirty distinct cookbooks first published in Britain between 1780 and 1830, two-thirds contained curry recipes. Many cookbooks in the early nineteenth century also explained how to make curry powder at home to save for later and how to use it in Anglo-Indian recipes. In her highly influential 1807 work, *A New System of Domestic Cookery,* Maria Rundell included recipes based on curry powder for the very British cod, lobster, and prawns as well as both difficult and easy chicken curry recipes. She explained that "a dish of rice boiled dry must be served" and pointed readers to her rice recipe. She further recommended that "slices of under-done veal, or rabbit, turkey, etc. make excellent currie." John Armstrong, who tailored his recipes to the "middle" and "poor" sorts, included Rundell's curry recipes. Additionally, Rundell and Armstrong both highlighted rabbit curries in their menu suggestions. In 1809, apparently hoping to capitalize on this growing trend, the Patna-born Indian Dean Mohamed opened the first Indian restaurant in the English-speaking world outside India. He advertised a new sort of place where "the Nobility and Gentry . . . might enjoy the Hookha with real Chilm tobacco and Indian dishes of the highest perfection." Yet Mohamed's curry house failed to attract a significant British clientele, and he went bankrupt after two years. Britons did not necessarily want curries served among Indian decorations and bubbling hookah pipes, but they did want them naturalized at home and in conventional British taverns.[29]

---

28. Robert Kyd, "Some Remarks on the Soil and Cultivation on the Western Side of the River Hooghly," [1791], MSS Eur. F95, fol. 75, BL; William Ward, *Account of the Writings, Religion, and Manners of the Hindoos* . . . (Serampore, 1811), I, 101; James Forbes, *Oriental Memoirs: Selected and Abridged from a Series of Familiar Letters Written during Seventeen Years Residence in India* . . . (London, 1813), I, 74, 230 (quotation).

29. Maria Rundell, *A New System of Domestic Cookery: Formed upon Principles of Economy and Adapted to the Use of Private Families* (London, 1807), 10, 20, 85–86, 315; John Armstrong, *The Young Woman's Guide to Virtue, Economy, and Happiness,* 6th ed. (Newcastle upon Tyne, [1817]), viii, 174, 184, 703. For curry powder recipes, see Ignotus, *Culina Famulatrix Medicinae; or, Receipts in Modern Cookery; with a Medical Commentary,* 3d ed. (York, U.K., 1806), 164–165; R. House, *The Family Cookery, Combining Elegance and Economy: Instructions for Preparting Soups, Gravies, Sauces, and Made Dishes* . . . (London, [1810]), 101. By the late 1820s, Dalgairns also included a curry chapter; see Dalgairns, *The Practice of Cookery, Adapted to the Business of Everyday Life* (Edinburgh, 1829), 162–165. "This common and favourite dish is at once economical, convenient at table, and of

Americans, without territory in India and with many fewer returned migrants from India in their midst, downplayed a taste for curries in their published cookbooks. Amelia Simmons, the earliest American cookbook author, first published her widely reprinted and pirated recipes, "adapted to this country," in 1796. She targeted her work at women who adhered "to those rules and maxims which have stood the test of ages, and will forever establish the *female character*, a virtuous character—altho' they conform to the ruling taste of the age in cookery, dress, language, manners etc." Her recipes did not include curries or curry powder, though they did include both American and Asian spices. Such spices, including curry powder, at least in large port cities, remained readily available. The producer of the 1803 American version of Susannah Carter's much older cookbook selected British recipes and added several American recipes. Curry recipes were not included. An American Lady's 1805 cookbook included recipes from Simmons, plus some additional recipes, but not for curries. The absence of curry recipes suggests that all three women considered such dishes unacceptable and un-American, unlike British authors, who naturalized them as British, and unlike those unknown number of Americans who were buying curry powder from local shops.[30]

---

easy preparation," explained Margaret Dods in the late 1820s; see Margaret Dods [Christian Isobel Johnstone], *The Cook and Housewife's Manual: A Practical System of Modern Domestic Cookery and Family Management,* 4th ed. (1829; rpt. London, 1988), 314; Michael H. Fisher, *The First Indian Author in English: Dean Mohamed (1759-1851) in India, Ireland, and England* (Delhi, 1996), 239–240, 256–257, 275. E[lizabeth] M. Collingham places the popularity of curry somewhat later; see Collingham, *Curry: A Tale of Cooks and Conquerors* (New York, 2006).

    30. Amelia Simmons, *American Cookery; or, The Art of Dressing Viands, Fish, Poultry, and Vegetables, and the Best Modes of Making Pastes, Puffs, Pies, Tarts, Puddings, Custards and Preserves, and All Kinds of Cakes, from the Imperial Plumb to Plain Cake* . . . (1796; rpt. New York, 1958), [3]; Susannah Carter, *The Frugal Housewife; or, Complete Woman Cook* (New York, 1803); An American Lady, *New American Cookery; or, Female Companion* . . . (New York, 1805). For a pirated copy of Simmons's work, see Lucy Emerson, *The New-England Cookery; or, The Art of Dressing All Kinds of Flesh, Fish, and Vegetables and the Best Modes of Making Pastes, Puffs, Pies, Tarts, Puddings, Custards, and Preserves and All Kinds of Cakes from the Imperial Plumb to Plain Cake; Particularly Adapted to This Part of Our Country* (Montpelier, Vt., 1808). See also Winterthur Recipe Book Database, Winterthur Museum and Library, Delaware. The only purportedly American cookbook containing curry recipes during this period, [Maria Rundell], *American Domestic Cookery, Formed on Principles of Economy* . . . (Baltimore, 1819), was not really American. Rundell simply rebadged her British cookbook and bolstered it with a few American recipes. Curry appeared in a few other British cookbooks republished in Philadelphia, such as Colin MacKenzie, *Five Thousand Receipts in All the Useful and Domestic Arts, Constituting a Complete and Universal Practical Library, and Operative Cyclopaedia* (Philadelphia, 1827), 244. A well-used hand-

Britons wanted curries adapted to British tastes, much like calicoes in the seventeenth century, or muslin dresses more recently. "Ignotus," a pseudonymous cookery author, included "observations" by the character Archaeus after many of his recipes. The name Ignotus translates as a sort of everyman, and the Anglo-Indian forms of curry that the book suggested closely matched the balance between old standards and new flavors that many middling Britons had begun to embrace. "Archaeus," according to the Paracelsians, represented a person's vital force. This force was not in the heart or brain; it was in the stomach. Archaeus conceded curry's nutritious qualities. He noted, however, that "the taste is certainly an acquired one, as at first tasting a curry, it does not convey to the palate an extraordinary sensation of pleasure." In reference to a particular recipe, Archaeus protested, "This is a good curry, and is sure to be well received by those who have lived under a burning sun; but it cannot be made familiar to the inhabitants of a cold country." For Indian "Burdwan" stew, his observations cut deeper still: "Plain eaters suffering themselves to be led astray by dishes, that never were intended for them" risked health, happiness, and virtue. Ignotus recommended tempering the Burdwan by substituting chili for cayenne pepper and mild onions for hot. Spicey hot foods, he explained, suited hot climates. The author included several curry recipes, though his implementation of the Archaeus character suggested that readers must carefully balance the positive and negative material outcomes of adapting Indian cooking to Britain.[31]

Even as Britons naturalized such Indian goods and foods, however, British support for missionary work in India continued to strengthen, as evidenced by the debate over the Company's 1813 charter. The charter would include a compromise on religion encouraged in part by American activities, the successful movement to end the Atlantic trade in enslaved people, and the desire to support British manufacturers. As the editors of the *Christian Observer* wrote, "Now that the African slave trade has re-

written recipe book from 1820s Ohio contains a mango pickle recipe. The recipe was marked with a star, presumably indicating that it was used often or turned out particularly well; see Bertha E. Josephson, "An Ohio Recipe Book of the 1820's," *Mississippi Valley Historical Review*, XXXVI (1949), 99–100. For an example of backcountry spice distribution, see David Chambers, Daybook, 1827–1830, fol. 136, Winterthur Museum and Library. For a few of many examples of curry powder advertisements, see *Eastern Argus* (Portland), Feb. 6, 1812, [4]; *Baltimore Patriot and Evening Advertiser*, May 29, 1815, [1]; *New-York Courier*, Feb. 27, 1816, [1]; *Columbian Centinel* (Boston), Apr. 2, 1817, [3]; *City Gazette And Daily Advertiser* (Charleston), Nov. 20, 1818, [3].

31. Ignotus, *Culina Famulatrix Medicinae*, 164–186, 222–223.

ceived its sentence, the question respecting the diffusion of Christianity, throughout Asia, strikes us as the most important." Wilberforce, in particular, exercised his skills, contacts, and experience from the fight over the trade in enslaved people. He spoke powerfully in Parliament, lobbied behind the scenes, and organized a campaign that produced 908 petitions in favor of missionaries, more than seven times the number of petitions presented both for and against the ending of the Company monopoly. The petitioners, from the Church of England and Dissenting churches, used patriotic language focusing on their right as Britons to work as missionaries in India, much as private merchants focused on their right as Britons to trade with India. The LMS explained that they were still "obliged to send" their missionaries to India on the "circuitous route" via America, though some continued to be rejected by the Company on arrival. Some argued that Christianity would expand British trade. Reflecting a broader political shift toward support for the evangelical missions, the House of Commons in 1813 published Company director Charles Grant's *Observations on the State of Society among the Asiatic Subjects of Great Britain*, which he had written for private distribution in 1792.[32]

Grant defended the Company's record as ruler of Bengal and explained that converting Indians to Christianity would lead Indians to convert themselves to British culture and fashions more broadly. Peace, order, godliness, and consumption of British goods went together. He claimed that the famine in Bengal before the American Revolution had not been the Company's fault and blamed the nawabs and native revenue collectors. The Company, he argued, had substantially improved conditions compared to the 1760s. The problem, as Grant saw it, was that Indian men inclined readily to dishonesty, tyranny, barbarism, and licentiousness, dragging the women down with them. The difference between British and Indian morals was "analogous to the difference of the natural colour of the two races." Yet he also argued that the deficiencies of India's peoples were moral, not physical. India's peoples were, therefore, redeemable and correctable. The Company must encourage the reform of India's peoples by teaching them English and European literature and culture and leading them to Christianity. Without Christianity, legal and political

---

32. *Review of a Letter of Thomas Twining, Esq. . . . and of Pamhplets by Major Scott Waring . . . Extracted from the Christian Observer* (London, 1808), Part II, 1; "London Missionary Society," *Connecticut Evangelical Magazine*, VI, no. 10 (October 1813), 381, 383. For much more on evangelical lobbying regarding India, see Carson, *East India Company and Religion*, 122–127, 133–143.

reforms would be ineffective. The successful conversion of the character, morals, and faith of India's peoples, moreover, would make them affluent and align their tastes with British tastes. A Protestant India, such arguments suggested, would be a profitable India for British manufacturers.[33]

In the summer of 1813, as part of the charter debate, Parliament peppered several Company servants with questions about ending the Company monopoly, increasing the sale of British goods, expanding missionary activity, and developing settlement colonization in India, underscoring the extent to which these issues were interconnected. Many Company men, such as Warren Hastings and William Cowper, saw the threat of an open trade and unregulated missionary activity as similarly dangerous to the British government of India. Hastings also pointed to private Americans and Britons alike as threatening to stability. In their questions, the members of Parliament were particularly interested in the best means to increase Indian consumption of British manufactures. Hastings, Cowper, and many others in the Company agreed that neither private merchants nor missionaries would successfully increase such consumption. Thomas Munro explained that Indians primarily ignored British goods because of the "excellence of their own manufactures." Christianity, therefore, would not increase consumption of British goods among Indians. Alexander Fraser Tytler, a Company judge, explained that British goods were culturally and climatically unsuitable to India, they needed to be shipped great distances, and they sold at high prices in a country where vast numbers of people lived in poverty. Even rich Bengalis, he wrote, would not furnish, dress, eat, or drink as Europeans, and those few who did had little understanding of taste and arranged their European objects in a "ludicrous" manner. With active missions, an open trade, and peace among Britain, France, and the United States, it remained to be seen which expectation would be most accurate: Grant's belief that Hindus would convert to Christianity and adopt British consumption practices or the belief of Hastings, Cowper, Munro, and Tytler that Indians would convert to neither Christianity nor British fashion.[34]

33. Charles Grant, *Observations on the State of Society among the Asiatic Subjects of Great Britain, Particularly with respect to Morals; and on the Means of Improving It* ... (London, 1813), 12, 14, 26–40 (quotation on 31), 76–78, 109–112.

34. Responses of Warren Hastings, Mar. 30, 1813, Responses of William Cowper, Mar. 31, 1813, in Hansard, *Parliamentary Debates*, XXV, columns 418–428, 448–452, 777; Alexander Fraser Tytler, *Considerations on the Present Political State of India* ..., 2d ed. (London, 1816), I, 397–398, II, 329–342, 353–356. Tytler is not to be confused with his father of the same

The end of the Company's monopoly over the trade between India and Britain soon culminated in the Company's complete conversion into a government in India, but as a government it was still interested in the consumption habits of India's peoples for revenue and rule. Now, however, government revenue was distinct from commercial revenue and depended more than ever on political stability for tax collection. India's goods continued to play a prominent role in debates over how to maintain and, perhaps, enhance that stability. The Company was not alone in still worrying about the relationship between consumption practices and influence. As British and American missionaries expanded their operations and sought to develop the stability of their missions and their influence among Indians, evangelicals faced many of the same dilemmas about Indian goods that Company administrators faced. British and American evangelicals went too far in claiming that the Company had always resisted missionaries or that the charter "unbars India to the missionaries of the cross." The Company retained the discretion to control missionary admittance, movement, and designs. Indeed, both inside and outside the Company and in India, Britain, and America, disagreement continued over the relationships among consumption, missionary activity, and Company rule.[35]

In the late 1810s and early 1820s, an intense debate broke out among evangelicals in India, Britain, and America over the spending habits of longtime Baptist missionary Joshua Marshman, particularly his food and palanquin expenses. The debate echoed the one in the Company between Sydenham and Edmonstone. Fellow missionary William Carey pointed out that people in London could not judge what was necessary for Marshman's missionary life in India. Marshman ran a college for upper-rank Indian students who might spread the gospel. To keep such students, Carey

---

name. For more on Tytler's life, see John W. Burgon, *The Portrait of a Christian Gentleman: A Memoir of Patrick Fraser Tytler* . . . , 2d ed. (London, 1859), 118–119.

35. *Connecticut Evangelical Magazine; and Religious Intelligencer*, VII, no. 2 (February 1814), 75; "An Address to the Christian Public on the Subject of Missions to the Heathen, and Translations of the Scriptures," ibid., VI, no. 12 (December 1813), 473. The Company had pursued conversion sporadically for a century, and some officials had recently accepted missionary activity in their areas. For more on overblown claims about the charter; see Carson, *East India Company and Religion*, 151–167; Frykenberg, "Christian Missions and the Raj," in Etherington, ed., *Missions and Empire*, 109–112. On the Company's rapidly declining trade with India after 1813, see H. V. Bowen, *The Business of Empire: The East India Company and Imperial Britain, 1756–1833* (Cambridge, 2006), 253–255.

explained, Marshman needed to look respectable to Indian families and offer first-rate Indian-style accommodations. He stated, "As a missionary, I could go in a straw hat and dine with the judge of the district, and often did so; but as a Professor in the College, I cannot do so." One simply had to look the part to get access to leading Indians. Pointedly, Carey wrote, "I have no doubt but my collection of plants, aviary, and museum would be equally impeached as articles of luxury and lawless expenses," if the BMS leadership in London had known about them. Carey expected that the complaints against Marshman had been started by recently arrived missionaries in Calcutta who were asked by someone in England to "spy out our conduct." The division between missionaries with more and less experience in India was so sharp that Marshman and Carey separated from the BMS, writing that they had been tasked with supporting themselves instead of relying on donations from abroad. They could not abide being attacked for profligacy.[36]

Americans also debated the merits of Carey's and Marshman's mission and their consumption habits. An author calling herself "Sophronia" wrote to Philadelphia's *Reformer* condemning British and American missionaries for corrupting the true purpose of the gospel. She wrote that U.S. missionaries should devote their attention to the poor in their midst before traveling "13000 miles," sounding on this point like the Connecticut Missionary Society two decades earlier. But much more critically, she asked, "What are the benefits and blessings which the inhabitants of India have derived from the christians?" before answering, "*carnage and bloodshed.*" When Hindus compared missionaries who were living upon a few thousand dollars per year with the Brahmins who were satisfied with twenty-five dollars, they would be "confirmed" in the superior virtue of their own religion. "Surely," Sophronia wrote, "he must think the virtue of his Bramin far superior to the effeminate christian missionary, whose delicate frame compels him to be carried about in a *palanquin.*" Sophronia's arguments fused concerns over Christian violence and the embrace of luxury,

36. Carey wrote back to the society in England in 1793 warning, "The grandeur, the customs, the prejudices of the settlers are exceedingly dangerous. . . . Their profuse way of living being so opposite to his [the missionary's] character, and so much above his ability." And he conveyed similar concerns in 1809, yet he vigorously defended Marshman. See William Carey to the BMS? Nov. 26, 1793, BMS, *Periodical Accounts*, I, 69, Carey to Andrew Fuller, Oct. 25, 1809, IV, 86; Carey to John Dyer, July 15, 1819, in *Letters Official and Private from the Rev. Dr. Carey, Relative to Certain Statements Given in These Pamphlets Lately Published by the Rev. J. Dyer, Secretary of the Baptist Missionary Society* . . . , 2d ed. (London, 1828), 3–13, Carey and Marshman to the BMS, Nov. 15, 1827, 38.

and her example of the palanquin connected to long-standing associations of the conveyance with despotism.[37]

In an oft-reprinted piece originally published in the *Reformer*, a pseudonymous author turned to reports from Harriet Newell to criticize how Carey, Marshman, and Ward spent the money raised in America on their behalf. He quoted Newell, "Dr. Carey's house appeared like a palace to us," and "The missionaries enjoy *all* the comforts of life." The author wondered, "If the sole object of these missionaries had been honour and self-agrandizement, could they have pursued any other course, that . . . enabled them to wallow in such luxury and pride?" Moreover, Newell did not mention a single "Heathen" in the mission's schools, which formed such an important part of the fundraising appeals. Americans were donating, not to save Hindus, as they had been told, but to educate Europeans and support "missionaries living in such princely style." The author further explained that the missionaries wanted more than one thousand dollars per year to live, whereas a Hindu family needed only sixty-five dollars to live "comfortably." The editor of the *Reformer* reported that the missionaries had now declared themselves independent of their society and claimed the mission as their own property, which "fully exhibited their true character." These were despotic and corrupted people living in Asiatic luxury.[38]

The evangelical British immigrants Divie Bethune, merchant, and William Colgate, founder of the company that would be famous for toothpaste, responded in New York's *Commercial Advertiser*, ultimately persuading the editors of the *Christian Herald and Seaman's Magazine*, who reprinted the exchange. Bethune and Colgate pointed out that Newell's words were being twisted to a rather different meaning from what she intended. They claimed that Ward drew all the money for his expenses from England and that he invested every dollar he raised in the United States in a local canal company with an interest of 6 percent directed to India. Bethune, Colgate, the influential William Staughton, and Robert Ralston, who had spearheaded earlier funding campaigns, acted as trustees of the investment. Bethune and Colgate agreed that Carey, Marshman, and Ward

37. Sophronia, "The Impartial Observer, No. I," *Reformer: A Religious Work* (Philadelphia), I, no. 1 (Jan. 1, 1820), 16–17.

38. "From the Reformer," reprinted in "Rev. W. Ward and the Serampore Mission," *Christian Herald and Seaman's Magazine*, VIII, no. 20 (Mar. 2, 1822), 614–616; originally printed as Marcus, "Communicated from a Correspondent in Connecticut," *Reformer*, II, no. 22 (Oct. 1, 1821), 226–232; see also "From the Philadelphia Reformer," *Gospel Herald*, II, no. 28 (Oct. 27, 1821), 220–223; "Extracted from the Journal of the American Missionaries at Ceylon," *Reformer*, IV, no. 37 (Jan. 1, 1823), 7–8.

were financially successful in India, but this success was used to support the mission. They concluded, "Lord Teignmouth, the Bishop of Gloucester, Sir James McIntosh, Sir William Borroughs, Wilberforce, and many distinguished associates, patronize this society." If such leading lights in Britain, including no less than Wilberforce himself, supported the mission, it was worthy of the support of Americans. Marcus fired back, reiterating that the large dinners and beautiful homes that Newell described were signs of pride and luxury and objecting to the notion that Americans should follow eminent British evangelicals. He turned to the comments made by the BMS in 1810 that Christianization was the only means to secure British power in India, concluding that, "with such powerful motives presented," it was easy to see that the British mission was corrupted.[39]

To head off concerns about India's corrupting influence, missionary societies carefully instructed their missionaries in proper behavior and fashions. The American Board of Commissioners for Foreign Missions wrote of "the very urgent importance of observing strict economy, in regard both to your time and expenditures." The Scottish Missionary Society wrote that missionaries should have "a spirit of deadness to the world; a holy indifference to earthly comforts." They warned that the secretary for one missionary society in India had proclaimed, "We uniformly find, that a few years residence in India, causes our brethren to imbibe insensibly to themselves, liberal ideas on the subject of expense, which may occasion much perplexity to their friends at home, and against which it is therefore necessary to put them on their guard at the outset." "Missionaries," the society wrote, "are apt to attach far too much importance to worldly respectability." They also quoted the Anglican Church Missionary Society, which instructed its departing missionaries to avoid acting like European gentlemen in India. The missionaries must live "above the world and at a visible

39. Divie Bethune and William Colgate, Dec. 19. 1821, and Nov. 22, 1822, reprinted as "From the Commercial Advertiser," in "Rev. W. Ward and the Serampore Mission," *Christian Herald and Seaman's Magazine*, VIII, no. 20 (Mar. 2, 1822), 616–622; Marcus, "Serampore Missionaries," *Reformer*, III, no. 26 (Feb. 1, 1822), 45. Newell did not intend her words to be used in criticism of Carey, Marshman, and Ward, which is apparent by the original context and her expressions of fondness toward them. The quotation on the palace was in reference to their previous "little room," and the "comforts of life" quotation had no italics and continued, "and are actively engaged in the Redeemer's service." Newell's letters to her family also suggested no disdain for the missionaries and their habits. See Harriet Newell's Diary for 1812 and Newell to Elizabeth Atwood, July 14, 1812, in Newell, *Memoirs of Mrs. Harriet Newell: American Missionary to India . . .*, new ed. (Glasgow, 1823), 144 (quotations), 166 (letter).

distance from it, in your habits of life, purposes, and desires, — having few things in common with the gentry of India." "Endeavour to bring your-selves down to their [Hindus] habits and customs, and to become famil-iar with their language," it wrote; "you can scarcely identify yourselves too much with them." By incorporating themselves into the life of India's poorer peoples, those peoples would be more easily incorporated into the Protestant community.[40]

Evangelicals by and large continued to see the Devil's work in the con-sumption practices and habits of Britons in India. A petition sent to the Company directors and backed by nine pages of signatures in 1824 re-quested that more chaplains be sent to India. Britons in India needed res-cuing "from that moral and mental deterioration to which the seducing effect of heathen example, the propensities of ungoverned youth, and the long disuse of religious observances have reduced them." Evangelicals in Britain and the United States continued to attack William Carey for living in a palace and riding "in a palanquin on the shoulders of men." Far from converting Hindus, Carey's own son Felix, they believed, had converted to the "pagan faith." This claim was based on Felix's brandishing ceremonial betel boxes and state umbrellas as an ambassador for the king of Burma in Calcutta. It reflected the old theory that the material luxury of an Indian way of life inevitably reflected moral corruption. Felix's own father wrote, "The honours he [Felix] has received from the Burmese Government have not been beneficial to his soul." Such decline, for those sending money, threatened the failure of the missionary project and the hopes for a godly global empire.[41]

The debate over the implications of India dress continued to rage as

40. "Instructions, Given by the Prudential Committee of the American Board of Com-missioners for Foreign Missions, to the Missionaries to the East, Feb. 7, 1812," *Connecticut Evangelical Magazine; and Religious Intelligencer*, V, no. 12 (December 1812), 466; *Letter of Instructions from the Directors of the Scottish Missionary Society to Their Missionaries among the Heathen* (Edinburgh, n.d.), 59–61; *Proceedings of the Church Missionary Society* (London, 1822), 227, cited in *Letter of Instructions from the Directors of the Scottish Mission-ary Society*, 63; *Instructions of the Committee of the Church Missionary Society, to Mission-aries Proceeding to North and South India, Ceylon, New Zealand, and West Africa* (London, 1819), 1–3.

41. Copy of a Petition to the Directors, Aug. 25, 1824, IOR/L/PJ/3/140, fols. 434 (quota-tion), 434a–k, BL. For the attack on Carey and his son, see "The Exploder," *Correspondent* (New York), III, no. 24 (July 5, 1828), 381–382; Sunil Kumar Chatterjee, *Felix Carey: A Tiger Tamed* (Calcutta, 1991), 52; Carey quoted in George Smith, *The Life of William Carey, Shoe-maker and Missionary* (Teddington, U.K., 2006), 98. See also D. G. E. Hall, "Felix Carey," *Journal of Religion*, XII (1932), 479–492.

well. The leading evangelical writer Mary Sherwood, for instance, wrote, "The dress of the women [in India], though not unpleasant in a picture, is so disgustingly indelicate in real life . . . consisting of a single web of cloth so put on as to form a scanty petticoat, with a veil leaving one arm and breast totally bare." Britain and America should convert Indians to their faith and fashions, not vice versa. In contrast, another British author explained in 1828 that Hindu women had a "classic simplicity of dress . . . admirably suited for the study of the sculptor." Additionally, she stressed that it revealed an "elegant action in walking." A British woman experienced in India wrote: "English dresses are very unbecoming, both to Europeans and Asiatics. A Musulmanī lady is a horror in an English dress; but an English woman is greatly improved by wearing a native one, the attire itself is so elegant, so feminine, and so graceful." The Company servant and artist, Charles D'Oyly, agreed: "Indian dress too's so demure and pretty, / Contrasted with the *bareness* of our belles, / That if 'tis not adopted 'tis a pity." Despite wearing "transparent" muslin, he wrote, their "silken trowsers . . . scarce a little naked foot expose." Consciously or not, D'Oyly thus responded to critics who believed that Indian dress was too revealing.[42]

The American Nathaniel Ames, who had spent time in India as a merchant, wrote sarcastically, "It is sincerely to be hoped that the time is not far distant when these 'poor ignorant heathen' will be compelled to eat pork and lace tight, when intemperance, fraud, adultery, murder and all other 'evidence of christianity' will be introduced among them." Ames explained that many fakirs might appear disgusting on the outside, but they were saints on the inside, compared to European and American "saints," who looked respectable to Americans but were disgusting on the inside. Bringing to mind the debate in the early 1820s, he commented that American missionaries in Serampore reportedly had a great house, plenty of money, and nothing to do. Nobody seemed to know anything about the missionaries, and he had not heard any convincing stories of their success.

42. [Mary Martha Sherwood], *The History of George Desmond; Founded on Facts Which Occurred in the East Indies, and Now Published as a Useful Caution to Young Men Going out to That Country* (Wellington, Salop (Shropshire), U.K., 1821), 91; [Mrs. Monkland], *Life in India; or, The English at Calcutta*, 3 vols. (London, 1828), II, 35; Fanny Parks, *Wanderings of a Pilgrim in Search of the Picturesque* (London, 1850), I, 386; [Charles D'Oyly], *Tom Raw, the Griffin: A Burlesque Poem, in Twelve Cantos; Illustrated by Twenty-five Engravings, Descriptive of the Adventures of a Cadet in the East India Company's Service . . .* (London, [1828]), 181. In the 1810s, English fashion began switching back to hoops; see C. Willet Cunnington and Phillis Cunnington, *Handbook of English Costume in the Eighteenth Century* (London, 1957), 382.

He argued that all of the celebratory reports in America of the missions in India were fantasies. Ames also did not think the splendor of British life in India contributed to British rule; it was just more frivolous expense.[43]

Within the Company, however, many continued to express considerable concern over the impression of government support for missionary activities and disagreement with the belief that Indian goods and fashions were corrupting or a sign of corruption or frivolousness. Thomas Munro, at this point governor of Madras, charged that subcollector John Allen Dalzell "was manifestly converting his official character into that of a missionary." In a passage striking for its understanding of, and also its rejection of, the exercise of imperial power to change religions and cultures, Munro explained that Dalzell did not force Indians to convert to Christianity, "but he [Dalzell] did, and will continue to use, unknown to himself, something very like compulsion; open interference, official agency, the hope of favours, the fear of displeasure . . . there can be no real freedom of choice, where official authority is interested deeply and exerted openly." Munro echoed countless Company officials before him, noting, "Where the Rulers are so few, and of a different race from the people, it is the most dangerous of all things to tamper with religious feelings." Munro's friend and colleague in the Madras government, William Thackery, wrote to the Board of Control that, "since the late Mahratta Conquests, there is every appearance of our assuming the insolence of Conquerors." In contrast, he claimed that, when the Company "observed and maintained with all respect the Customs and even all the prejudices of the Country; we became popular; were confided in." British power in India was "founded not on national strength, but on opinion; we have established ourselves and maintained our power by the sufferance, consent, and good will of the natives, and the good opinion our wisdom, faith, and valor have established." In these opinions, the Company had to vigorously resist the temptation to try to control the daily lives of Indians and convert them to Christianity or suffer the fate of the Portuguese.[44]

43. [Nathaniel Ames], *A Mariner's Sketches, Originally Published in the Manufacturers and Farmers Journal* (Providence, R.I., 1830), 40 (quotation), 44, 48, 56–57.

44. Thomas Munro, Minute of the President #10, Extract from Fort St. George Secret Consultations, Nov. 29, 1822, IOR/F/4/960/27324, BL; William Thackery, Minute #11 to the Board of Control, IOR/F/4/960/27324, BL. Thackery was the uncle of the famous author by the same name. The Company shifted Dalzell around to a new post, though concerns continued that the Company could do more to educate the local people to ease the operation of British rule, without the religious component. See Extract from a Revenue Letter to Ft. St George, May 18, 1825, IOR/F/4/960/27324, BL.

The Company's own semi-official guide to life in India encouraged acceptance of local customs and the adoption of a broad range of Indian consumption habits for Company servants. The *East India Vade-Mecum* was published in 1810 and was revised and republished with modest revisions in 1825 as *The General East India Guide and Vade Mecum,* both by the Company's booksellers. Thomas Williamson, the original author, and John Borthwick Gilchrist, the 1825 editor, argued that Britons must view their Indian territories "not as colonies, but as conquests, of a peculiar description, to which our laws and privileges are every way either unsuitable, or unwelcome." Both editions included Williamson's argument against missionaries as dangerous and his advice that Britons should simply explain to Indians that they believed "that morality in Europe, and morality in Asia, are the same thing; that 'whether we do our duties in a black skin, or in a white one,' matters not; that men were born to aid each other, and not to be made the slaves of party, sect, color; and, that he who knows most regarding the works of the Creator, is most likely to have a proper sense of his bounty." Many would then become Christian. Both versions also provided copious details on the continued need for and role of a range of servants and Indian equipage to conduct business, protect health, and project status. The message was widely shared and believed. A former indigo planter in Tirhoot, for instance, explained that Company servants needed to exhibit pomp and ceremony to gain the respect of Indians, lest the empire collapse.[45]

Indeed, many Company servants in India in the 1820s continued to embrace particularly significant aspects of Indian culture as marks of both their British and Indian authority. Hookah ownership, for instance, rose to a new peak among Britons in Calcutta. By the 1820s, two-thirds of elite Britons in the city owned at least one hookah, compared to approximately 40 percent of middling Britons and 15 percent of Britons in the lowest wealth categories. Several elite men owned lavish silver hookah bottoms, and most owned a range of complementary items, including hookah carpets and precious mouthpieces. The lead character of Charles Dibdin's

45. Williamson, *East India Vade-Mecum,* I, 7 (quotation), 220, 228, 299–325, 468, II, 2, 318–319 (quotation); J[ohn] B[orthwick] Gilchrist, *The General East India Guide and Vade Mecum: For the Public Functionary, Government Officer, Private Agent, Trader, or Foreign Sojourner, in British India . . .* (London, 1825), 10, 102–105, 114, 121, 165–179, 212, 416. Planter William Huggins also hoped that the mixed-race children of Europeans and Indians might be used to help generate respect and understanding between the government and people, but on this point Williamson and Gilchrist disagreed; see Huggins, *Sketches in India . . .* (London, 1824), 68–84 (quotations on 78, 79).

novel, *Henry Hooka,* played upon these gentlemanly associations with the pipe. Henry Hooka returned to England a genial, rich nabob. With his Indian wisdom and wealth, he brought proper order to the disordered lives of his son, his son's mistress, his son's manservant, and even his son's childhood teacher. *Henry Hooka* was available on both sides of the Atlantic. Increasing hookah popularity and acceptance among Britons in India, if not at home, was reflected in Gilchrist's revisions to Williamson's India guide. Gilchrist generally changed little of the text, but on hookahs he deleted several critical lines that suggested that the hookah caused men to be irrational and despotic and that it gave the Indian *hookah-burdar* control over his English master, possibly even the ability to kill him undetected. Gilchrist left in place lengthy descriptions of how to use the pipe and added information on suitable tobacco.[46]

A painting of Charles D'Oyly overseeing the weighing of opium in an Indian warehouse highlights the use of the hookah and umbrella to project the image of a British gentleman of distinction firmly in control of his Indian workers (Plate 24). D'Oyly is the largest figure in the painting, and he is the only figure with a hookah and umbrella. The viewer's eyes are drawn to D'Oyly at the center of the image, to the tube leading from his mouth, and then behind the chair to the prominent hookah bottom. Smoking a complicated hookah required money, dedicated servants, and skill, attributes that together showcased gentlemanly rank and power. Smoking the hookah properly acted as a ritual, transferring the hookah's

---

46. [Charles] Dibdin, *Henry Hooka: A Novel,* 3 vols. (London, 1807). For Hooka's wisdom and skill in solving problems, see most of volume III. For an example of the novel in America, see *New-York Evening Post,* Dec. 9, 1807, [3]. Additionally, Gilchrist deleted Williamson's use of the term "blacky." See Williamson, *East India Vade-Mecum,* I, 220–226, 307; Gilchrist, *General East India Guide and Vade Mecum,* 117–119, 169–170.

Parsing ownership data by wealth is not a straightforward task since defining groups based on the net wealth of decedents, particularly in India, would not accurately reflect an individual's rank. Individuals spent what they felt necessary for a person of their rank, even if that was much more than they could afford. Many Britons in India accumulated staggering debts to pay for items of status, and these items, in turn, helped to show that they were worthy of credit. Grouping individuals by the value of their possessions offers a sense of the level of consumption that each individual believed was necessary to maintain his or her status. Individuals were grouped into three levels of total ownership reflecting three general ranks of Britons in Calcutta in the 1820s: SR 1–500 (37 individuals), SR 501–4,000 (105 individuals), and SR 4001–20,000 (18 individuals). A fourth group of Britons, including regular soldiers, sailors, and general laborers, owned too little to have inventories recorded at their death. These wealth ranges were selected based on an assessment factoring in employment status and diversity and quality of objects owned. Only inventories thought to be complete that included valuations were included. See Bengal Inventories.

Plate 24. Charles D'Oyly, Charles D'Oyly Smoking a Hookah. 1820s. Watercolor. Scrapbook, Hastings Albums, WD 4403, fol. 40, BL. © The British Library Board

associations with wealth, skill, and power to the smoker. In the painting, the hookah bottom sits in the middle of the frame at the base of a central pillar. The artist thus associated the hookah with the pillar, a common European symbol of power and strength. Additionally, the artist framed and accentuated the hookah by the bright blue umbrella propped up behind it. This umbrella is the largest and most brightly colored object in the work. D'Oyly's fine hookah marked his status while he was indoors; his fine umbrella would, the viewer is to understand, project his status while D'Oyly was on the move under the sun. These two Indian items functioned as the dominant symbols of D'Oyly's importance and power.[47]

47. On the pillar, see Jack Tresidder, ed., *The Complete Dictionary of Symbols* (San Francisco, Calif., 2004), 390. On ritual, see Grant McCracken, *Culture and Consumption: New Approaches to the Symbolic Character of Consumer Goods and Activities* (Bloomington, Ind., 1988), 60, 84.

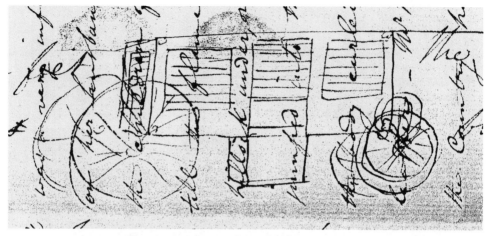

Plate 25. William Peacock, Palanquin. 1828–1829. Pen sketch.
MSS Eur C180, BL. © The British Library Board

During the early decades of the nineteenth century, Britons also continued to adapt the palanquin to elite British tastes and concerns by replacing the bearers with wheels and horses. A recently arrived indigo planter drew such a carriage and commented: "There are very few close *[sic]* carriages here except the Palankin carriages . . . the little box underneath is where we place our feet. The windows are all made with venetian blinds and sometimes with glass as well" (Plate 25). As with earlier palanquins, these, too, were made in India as well as imported from London. A story on Lord Combermere preparing for his appointment in India made note of "a new carriage, the body of which is in the palanquin style, gorgeously finished, now building for his Lordship, which will go out with him to the east." The wheeled palanquin of one British colonel accommodated four people and was "on eliptic springs . . . finished in the best possible manner, the lining of superfine drab cloth and yellow Morocco seats and rich corresponding trimmings, the body painted a fashionable green, having Princes metal mountings, lamps, double roof and light dickey, complete with venetians and glasses." The addition of wheels removed the single most distressing aspect of palanquin travel to British critics: its associations with despotism and the oppression of the men carrying it. Suggesting that a sort of tipping point in discomfort with human bearers had been reached, the related sedan chair simultaneously fell out of favor in Britain and America. Wheels, however, also made the palanquin less suitable for navigating narrow lanes and trails. Palanquins carried by men, therefore, did not disappear and remained useful in India for Company officials, so-

Conversions

ciety ladies, and missionaries alike. Still, frequent India resident Eliza Fay quipped in 1817, palanquins "are often beautifully ornamented and appear in character with the country and with the languid air of those who use them." Palanquins could not entirely shake their negative associations.[48]

In contrast to Britons continuing to use a range of Indian goods and fashions, even if adapted to British tastes and often made in Britain, Indians had not become a great new market for British goods. Indians were not buying large quantities of British woolens, ale, ham, cutlery, or footwear, nor were they buying many of the British-made hookahs and palanquins purchased by Company servants and, as evangelicals were learning, missionaries, too. Unlike culturally foreign and inappropriate hams and cutlery, or expensive British hookahs made of cut crystal, or palanquins made as British carriages, the cotton cloth made in British factories was essentially a direct simulation of much of the cotton cloth made by Indian artisans. It was also, compared to those other goods, inexpensive. In America, British cotton cloth had already made substantial inroads into consumer markets in the last decades of the eighteenth century. Still, American consumption of cottons, if not of hookahs or palanquins, might be further increased. And, although other British goods found little support among Indians, Indians might yet become important consumers of British cotton cloth.

An Industrial Empire

In the late 1810s and 1820s, British cotton cloth manufacturers vigorously pursued both American and Indian markets, stimulating considerable concern among new producers in the former and old producers in the latter. Though American factories produced a small fraction of the cot-

48. [D'Oyly], *Tom Raw*, 79; William Peacock to Anna, n.d. [1828–1829], MSS Eur. C180, BL; *Times* (London), Mar. 30, 1825, [3]. For Colonel Mackenzie's palanquin carriage and another example, see *Calcutta Gazette*, Dec. 8, 1814, [3], Dec. 15, 1814, [3]. By 1821, only one regular stand remained for picking up sedan-chair fares in London; see Harold W. Hart, "The Sedan Chair as a Means of Public Conveyance," *Journal of Transport History*, V (1962), 213. On the continuing use of palanquins and bearers, see Eliza Fay, *The Original Letters from India of Mrs. Eliza Fay; a New Edition with Introduction and Notes by the Rev. Walter Kelly Firminger* . . . (Calcutta, 1908), 124; "Brother Thompson's Journal," Feb. 13, 1817, in *Circular Letters*, X (April 1817), 65. Probate inventories show that only a small proportion of Britons in Bengal owned palanquins specifically denoted as "palanquin carriages." These inventories cannot, however, be accepted as proof for limited ownership of the style because 80 percent of all palanquins listed in the 1820s received no descriptive adjectives (Bengal Inventories).

ton produced in Britain or India, the conversion of America to a minor producer of factory cottons (as opposed to its longer history of homespun cottons) positioned American and Indian producers alike on the defensive against British industrialists. The rise of American and, particularly, British factory production also created fundamentally new conditions in the U.S.-India trade that in turn created new—or, perhaps in some ways, old—challenges. How the U.S. government might compromise among competing interests shaped by India and its goods was unclear, much as in Britain a century earlier. It was also unclear whether and how British industry could expand its markets in India, as it continued to do in America. These issues proved tightly intertwined.

The War of 1812 had dramatically limited U.S. access to cotton cloth from both India and Britain, pushing American merchants, including those in the India trade, toward domestic manufacturing. In the context of America's capital shortage, the relative capital strength of several families of American India merchants made their reallocations of experience and capital from the India trade to domestic cloth production more important than India-trade capital for industrialization in Britain. In Philadelphia, for example, Robert Waln, Jr., and Lewis Waln brought in fabrics from India from 1796 through the late 1810s, and the elder Robert Waln opened a cotton factory in New Jersey in 1812. In Massachusetts, William Phillips traded with Britain and India for a variety of goods including cotton fabric, whereas his son and grandson shifted the family attention to their new cotton mill, Lewis, Phillips, and Company. Also in Massachusetts, Patrick Tracy Jackson moved from the India trade to cotton cloth production. Such American manufacturers imitated fabrics from Britain and India and emulated British technologies and processes by attracting British artisans and weavers with the promise of higher wages and better standards of living. Americans used British expertise as they had in the India trade and now felt their own version of older British fears of competition.[49]

49. Robert Waln Papers, Collection 687, HSP; Smith-Waln Papers, Series III–IV, Collection 1628, HSP; Phillips Family Business Records, Part I, Account Book, 1793–1807, Part II, Day Book, 1825–1830, Collection 1924, Hagley Museum and Library, Wilmington, Del.; Kenneth Wiggins Porter, ed., *The Jacksons and the Lees: Two Generations of Massachusetts Merchants, 1765–1854* (Cambridge, Mass, 1937), I, 746–747, 757. The Company did not invest in British cotton manufacturers, and Britons who returned from India invested more in land; see P. J. Marshall, *East Indian Fortunes: The British in Bengal in the Eighteenth Century* (Oxford, 1976), 256. Marshall makes use of François Crouzet, ed., *Capital Formation in the Industrial Revolution* (London, 1972), 24, 215. For examples of returned Scots

The new American cotton manufacturers mobilized many of the same arguments against Indian manufacturers and the India trade that Britons had used in the early eighteenth century. The cotton manufacturers of Providence, R.I., for instance, petitioned Congress in 1815, disparaging Indian cotton fabric "as of little intrinsic value compared with the substantial and durable manufactures of our own country." They then demanded protection from these supposedly inferior products following the contorted logic used in the 1790s by British producers. Additionally, echoing centuries of British critics of imported India cottons, they argued that only a few wealthy capitalists and an insignificant number of ships and seaman benefited from the U.S.-India trade, at the expense of many domestic manufacturers and the poor that they employed. Manufacturers called for a prohibition on cottons from India and heavy duties on cottons from other places, particularly Britain.[50]

Several American authors and political leaders noted that with its growing industrial strength Britain angled to "keep America in a state of dependence, without factories and without current coin." *Niles' Weekly Register*, edited by the Republican Hezekiah Niles, was particularly active in pushing this position. Niles reprinted an article from a London paper as evidence of the British scheme. The author of the British article explained that British cottons were better and cheaper than American ones, notwithstanding American improvements during the war. "Manufactures," the Briton wrote, "belong to an old and rich country." Superior British capital and technology allowed it to dominate markets in Europe and America alike. Surveyor and cotton manufacturer Isaac Briggs argued in Niles's paper that, if the United States focused on exporting raw materials and importing manufactures, the country would be driven slowly into "poverty and weakness," though the southern states would hold on longer than the northern and western ones. But the South would fail eventually, too, as Britain perfected the cultivation of Bourbon cotton in India

---

investing their India money in local industry, including cotton manufacturing, see George McGilvary, *East India Patronage and the British State: The Scottish Elite and Politics in the Eighteenth Century* (London, 2008), 194. For more on American merchants' generating capital in the India trade and investing it domestically in corporations, banking, and manufacturing, see James R. Fichter, *So Great a Proffit: How the East Indies Trade Transformed Anglo-American Capitalism* (Cambridge, Mass., 2010), 254–277. On the movement of artisans, see Mary B. Rose, *Firms, Networks, and Business Values: The British and American Cotton Industries since 1750* (Cambridge, 2000), 41–43, 89.

50. "Cotton Manufactures," *Niles' Weekly Register* (Baltimore), IX (Nov. 18, 1815), 189–190.

suitable for machine production. Even Thomas Jefferson had adjusted his view on American manufacturing. Niles reprinted Jefferson's statement: "He, therefore, who is now against domestic manufactures, must be for reducing us to a *dependence upon foreign nations.—*I AM NOT ONE OF THESE." Manufacturing, despite the many social and urban changes it presented, must be pursued to keep the United States from becoming ever more an economic tributary of Britain.[51]

Niles also reprinted the report of the congressional committee of commerce and manufactures, which claimed that one hundred thousand men, women, and children worked in American cotton factories as a result of the War of 1812. The committee echoed the Providence petitioners that cottons from British India were inferior to American cottons but that American manufacturers needed to be protected from such competition. Whether from India or Britain itself, the British dominated global production. The committee noted, "In the hands of Great-Britain, are gathered together and held many powers, which they have not accustomed hitherto to feel and exercise." The committee did not impute any "improper motives" to the British, but it worried about the balance of trade and feared U.S. dependence on Britain "for defence, for comfort, and for accommodation." Notably, the committee drew a direct connection between military strength and consumption. Congress took these issues seriously.[52]

In June 1816, Congress passed new tariffs targeting, in particular, British India and Britain. Congress levied a duty of 25 percent on woolens and cottons as well as a minimum rate of 6.25¢ per yard on cotton cloth that cost less than 25¢. Congressmen largely supported the duties as a means to generate revenue to rescue the federal budget from the expenses of the War of 1812, much like English and British governments had used duties on cotton cloth for centuries. Higher prohibitive rates would not be profitable for the state. Despite the new tariff rates, therefore, in the year 1816–1817, merchants exported goods worth nearly £750,000 directly from Bengal to the United States, with more than half the value in piece goods. The value of cotton piece goods remained significant until 1820–1821. American customs statistics also show millions of dollars of goods paying the 25 percent duty entering from British India over these years. This large trade did not escape the notice of many American manufactur-

51. "British Manufactures," *Niles' Weekly Register,* IX (Feb. 17, 1816), 423; Isaac Briggs, "Manufactures—Very Interesting," ibid., X (Mar. 23, 1816), 49–50. Jefferson's statement was widely published. See ibid., IX (Feb. 24, 1816), 451.

52. "Report on Manufactures," *Niles' Weekly Register,* IX (Feb. 24, 1816), 447–450.

ers, writers, and politicians. As such, the tariffs did not quell the pressure for further protection, much as woolen and later cotton manufacturers in Britain had not been quieted easily in the face of continuing Indian competition despite duties and prohibitions.[53]

After the 1816 tariffs passed, Niles continued to condemn the British plan to rule the world, including America, with the combined forces of British manufactures and the detestable East India Company. Niles wrote that steeper tariffs or prohibitions were necessary, not owing to "'hostility to England,'" as some claimed, but "for the benefit of the people of the nations so doing, in encouraging a home-supply." "We, in the United States," Niles wrote, "calmly look on, talk about independence, and quietly bend our necks to the yoke—being tributaries to England, and relieving her wants at the cost of our own distress." To prove the British strategy, he quoted Henry Brougham, an opposition member of the British Parliament, who had said, "It is well worth while to incur a loss on the first exportation, in order, by the glut, to stifle in the cradle those rising manufactures in the United States." Niles also turned to the familiar old argument that the British East India Company acted with "inordinate ambition" and was responsible for "the greatest ravages ever committed on an unoffending people." Those who could remember the American Revolution or the Hastings trial would have known immediately what he was referring to, but so, too, would many who had heard only the more recent stories from missionaries of the Company's unwillingness to support evangelism.[54]

Politicians, petitioners, and officials spoke out against this form of British rule. Congressmen Thomas Gold exclaimed in a published letter, "Britain's creed is short: *to manufacture for the whole world and suffer no nation to manufacture for her.*" Gold went on, "Would our own government do for manufactures one half Great Britain has done for hers . . . we might soon bid defiance to all the efforts to crush our establishments." A memorial from Baltimore to the Congress noted, with less hyperbole, that

53. For trade data, see "Exports to North America," in Horace Hayman Wilson, *A Review of the External Commerce of Bengal from 1813–1814 to 1827–1828* (Calcutta, 1830), "Tables": 36–37; Wm. H. Crawford, "Imports for the Year Ending September 30, 1819," in Walter Lowrie and Matthew St. Clair Clarke, eds., *American State Papers: Documents, Legislative and Executive, of the Congress of the United States . . .* , 38 vols. (Washington, D.C., 1831–1861), 16th Cong., 2d sess., 1820, Commerce and Navigation, II, 480. For the duties, see F. W. Taussig, *The Tariff History of the United States: A Series of Essays* (New York, 1888), 18–19, 30.

54. "Foreign Articles," *Niles' Weekly Register,* XI (Sept. 21, 1816), 59; "American Manufactures," ibid., XI (Jan. 4, 1817), 297–298.

Britain would not allow manufactures from foreign countries to compete in the domestic market but that it cheaply dumped its own manufactures into foreign markets. The memorialists asked for an increase of the duty by 10 percent on foreign manufactures and encouraged all members of the government to wear and use only American-made goods. Tench Coxe also promoted the establishment of many more textile factories in the United States to avoid dependence on the productive capacity of the British empire, for which he had the support of outgoing president James Madison. Republican congressman Adam Seybert similarly supported duties against British manufacturers and shippers. He explained in his *Statistical Annals* that the India trade was also "disadvantageous" because it drained bullion out of America. Nevertheless, he went on, since the goods were mostly reexported to Europe, the resulting increase in American shipping and European payments for such goods offset the loss of bullion to India.[55]

Although Seybert used part of Company director Thomas Mun's 1621 argument that the balance of trade must be calculated across all trades, and not simply for each bilateral trade, his arguments did not satisfy the Federalist authors in the *North American Review*. The reviewer of *Statistical Annals* more fully used Mun's arguments, explaining that U.S. goods, such as cotton, rice, nails, and shoes, brought greater profits in the West Indies and Europe than in India, and those profits were turned into bullion to send to India to purchase goods cheaper than they could be purchased anywhere else. Buying goods for domestic consumption cheaper than they could be made at home was not impoverishing, as Seybert and those in Britain supporting the calico prohibitions had earlier argued, it was enriching. The reviewer argued that the bullion shipped to India for such goods was not to blame for shortages of specie in America since it had never entered the money supply. The reviewer and another author

55. Thomas Gold, "Manufactures," ibid., XII (Mar. 22, 1817), 50–51; Tench Coxe, *A Memoir, of February, 1817, upon the Subject of the Cotton Wool Cultivation, the Cotton Trade, and the Cotton Manufactories of the United States of America* (Philadelphia, 1817), 1–16; Adam Seybert, *Statistical Annals: Embracing Views of the Population, Commerce, Navigation, Fisheries, Public Lands, Post-Office Establishment, Revenues, Mint, Military and Naval Establishments, Expenditures, Public Debt, and Sinking Fund of the United States of America: Founded on Official Documents* . . . (Philadelphia, 1818), 280–281. See also George Logan, *A Letter to the Citizens of Pennsylvania, on the Necessity of Promoting Agriculture, Manufactures, and the Useful Arts*, 2d ed. (Philadelphia, 1800), 4, 16–23. For James Madison's support, see Madison to Tench Coxe, circa Mar. 11, 1817, in J. C. A. Stagg, ed., *The Papers of James Madison Digital Edition* (Charlottesville, Va., 2010).

in the *Review* who made many of the same arguments, echoed Thomas Papillon: "It is perfectly immaterial whether our payments to foreigners be made in specie or in merchandise. Every thing we purchase must be paid for at last by our own productions." It was preposterous, the author exclaimed, that a trade that had enriched American merchants had impoverished the nation.[56]

Some India merchants and their supporters argued that the protection of American manufacturers was destroying their livelihoods, again sounding like the Company a century before, despite all of the changes in the India trade. One author in the *North American Review* explained that the existing tariff had already ruined the importation of cheap India cottons. He claimed that from Salem alone the number of ships traveling to India had fallen from fifteen in 1817 to two in 1819, owing entirely to the tariffs. The tariffs supposedly raised little revenue because the products they were applied to had thus become too expensive to be imported. Another Salem merchant, Nathaniel Kinsman, wrote in 1819 of "some failures already, and a great many more expected." However, he privately pointed to a rather different cause. He pinned the failures on a general economic recession in Europe and America. Kinsman was closer to the mark in the short term, but an even bigger threat loomed to the U.S. trade with British India.[57]

Protectionist tariffs and cyclical economic stagnancy were not the main problems for U.S.-India traders. Given the structural economic issues at play, there was little that politicians could have done to hold off the impending decline, let alone create it. Rather, the main problem stemmed from British cotton cloth production shifting India away from supplying finished goods and toward raw materials, a shift accompanied by a corre-

56. Review of Adam Seybert, *Statistical Annals* . . . , *North American Review and the Miscellaneous Journal*, IX (1819), 224–228; T[homas] M[un], *A Discourse of Trade, from England unto the East-Indies: Answering to Diverse Objections Which Are Usually Made against the Same* (London, 1621), 8, 25–26, 30, 34–35, 40, 48; "Addresses of the Philadelphia Society for the Promotion of National Industry," *North American Review*, X (1820), 332–333; Thomas Papillon, *The East-India-Trade a Most Profitable Trade to the Kingdom; and Best Secured and Improved in a Company, and a Joint-Stock* . . . (London, 1677), 2–12. On the *North American Review* and Federalists, see Marshall Foletta, *Coming to Terms with Democracy: Federalist Intellectuals and the Shaping of an American Culture* (Charlottesville, Va., 2001), 9–15, 73–75.

57. "Report of the Committee of Merchants and Others of Boston, on the Tariff," *North American Review*, XII (1821), 71–72; Nathaniel Kinsman to Mrs. Kinsman, June 4, 1819, Private Collection, quoted in Mary Kinsman Munroe, "Nathaniel Kinsman, Merchant of Salem, in the China Trade," *Essex Institute Historical Collections*, LXXXV (1949), 13.

sponding series of structural and competitive disadvantages for American traders. U.S. manufacturers, U.S.-India traders, and Indian weavers working for export markets all suffered from this same cause.[58]

Competition from British manufacturers forced some weavers in India to petition the Company for relief, much as English woolen producers had sought protection from India cottons in their woolen markets and American cotton manufacturers now sought protection from both British and Indian producers. The weavers at Kurpoy, for instance, explained: "For some years the Company's Orders of Investment have been much smaller than they formerly were. Besides the purchases of the Danish, American and Dutch have entirely Ceased at these Aurungs which makes our Situation most severely distressing." The weavers had, following their custom, borrowed money locally to produce fabric in anticipation of orders; when the orders failed to come in, they could not repay their debts without selling their homes. The Company, quickly losing significance as a merchant body, instead acted as a government, buying at least some of the unprofitable fabric to help the weavers avoid destitution. Yet the Company impressed upon the weavers that these emergency purchases would not set a precedent for future years.[59]

In 1819, the directors told their men in Fort Saint George that the export of piece goods for Europe was over. The situation had changed completely since the 1790s. British manufacturers could now supply all of Europe, and France and Holland were also developing their own cotton industries. Duties continued to protect British manufacturers and increased the prices of India cottons to create an effective prohibition on their import. There was simply no prospect of selling even the goods on hand except at big losses. Given this new reality, the directors instructed their servants to disband many of the piece-good trading factories and consoli-

58. Historians have generally seen the decline of the U.S. trade as a result of American and, to a lesser extent, British political decisions. Holden Furber claimed that Thomas Jefferson's 1807 embargo, subsequent nonintercourse acts, and the War of 1812 combined to reverse the U.S. India trade, but these were only temporary issues; see Holden Furber, "The Beginnings of American Trade with India, 1784–1812," *New England Quarterly*, XI [1938], 263–264. More recently, Ranjan Chakrabarti has pointed to private British merchants freed from the Company's monopoly and U.S. tariff policies; see Chakrabarti, "American Merchants, Bengali *Banias* and Trade in the Bay of Bengal, 1787–1819," in S. Jeyaseela Stephen, ed., *Trade and Globalisation: Europeans, Americans, and Indians in the Bay of Bengal, 1511–1819* (Jaipur, 2003), 320.

59. Translation of Weavers' Petition, July 21, 1815, IOR/P/158/22, #32, BL; Governor in Council to George Uduy (Calcutta Board of Trade), July 26, 1815, IOR/P/158/22, #33, BL; Calcutta Board of Trade to Governor in Council, Nov. 3, 1815, IOR/P/158/25, #2–3, BL.

date the officers overseeing the remainder. The warehouse department, too, needed to be sharply curtailed. This was a much different response from the one after the passage of the Calico Acts, when the directors had continued placing large cloth orders, and the difference underscored the scale of changes caused by the remapping of the geography of cotton production.[60]

Instead of Indians being producers of cotton cloth for Britons and Americans, they were becoming consumers of British cottons. In 1813–1814, private British merchants sent £91,835 of cotton cloth to India. The total slipped back the following year, but then it began to rise quickly. In 1817–1818, the total was more than £1 million. Calcutta agent James Fraser expected an even greater change in the consumption habits of Indians, writing, "The present glut of European produce is favourable to this extention of commerce and relations . . . those who scarce knew the smallest article of European produce or manufacture will soon be unhappy if he has not the means of enjoying them." Fraser also breathlessly noted that "the former most valuable branch of piece goods is now totally gone all manufactures are let alone for the rich and extensive stores of raw materials of every kind while the manufactures of our country originally imitations of this—as muslins and calicoes are—poured into India from them, at a profit." Fraser soon marveled that enquiries in Benares, Mirzapur, Lucknow, Agra, Gwalior, Delhi, Punjab, Kabul, and locations throughout India indicated that "of the finer fabricks of cotton few are now worn but those imported from Britain." He went on: "The Dacca fabrics once so famous are now scarcely called for and are comparatively very little wrought. British goods may be had so much cheaper in price, that tho' they do not last so long, they are far cheaper and better on the whole." As for printed chintzes and calicoes, "those from England are so much more bright and tasteful and the whole work so much better that the preference is now given to them even over the finest stuffs of this country, the demand accordingly is great and increasing." By 1821, the total exports of cotton cloth by British merchants to India reached a new high of nearly £4.7 million. In less than a decade, private British exports of cotton cloth to India had increased more than fifty times.[61]

60. Director's Commercial Letter to Ft. St George, Sept. 15, 1819, IOR/E/4/923, 363–369, BL.

61. James Fraser to John Gladstone, Dec. 30, 1817, MSS Eur. Photo 150, 13, BL, to Messrs Read and Fraser, Jan. 8, 1818, 14–15, to Mr. Mackintosh, Apr. 4, 1821, 219. Exports hovered between £2.5 and £5 million throughout the 1820s, until beginning a new ascent in the

The houses of Stewart and Ritchie in Bombay and MacKintyre and Company in Calcutta reportedly dominated the trade. Sounding rather like the East India Company's scheming against interlopers and European competitors' importing cottons to Britain in the eighteenth century, Fraser explained that MacKintyre and Company could be beaten with "a most particulare and minute attention to *quality*, pattern and price. . . . Oeconomy in the management: great activity and some local knowledge in this country by which a market might be obtained for the goods when they should have reached India." Still, he explained, British policy made India wealthier and protected property, but the wealth was concentrated in the elite, so the British were missing out on creating a large consumer class from the poor. Some manufacturers found a partial answer to this problem by shipping cheap industrially produced thread to India for use by Indian weavers.[62]

Overall, India, and particularly Bengal, was transitioning to supplying Britain with low-volume luxuries and high-volume raw materials, the latter driving up the overall value of exports. As Fraser noted, "It is a most curious speculation" that India now exports "the Raw material for these fabricks which she now receives from those she once supplied of a quantity [and] texture superior to her own." During the 1810s and 1820s, the Company and private merchants in Calcutta exported to Britain small quantities of select highly profitable piece goods as well as saltpeter, grains, shellac, hemp, cotton, hides, and, especially, indigo and raw silk (Figure 6). Indigo was the most consistent export, prompting a correspondent from Calcutta to tell the leading British merchant John Palmer, "I consider no trade safe now, but Indigo." In the 1820s, raw silk quickly became a major commodity. India raw cotton, however, failed to successfully compete with growing supplies from the southern United States. Despite high expectations, it only accounted for a significant share of exports for a few years between 1814 and 1820. As for the decline of Indian cotton cloth exports, by 1830–1831 British merchants exported less than four thousand pounds' worth of it from Calcutta to Britain. Nevertheless, India's exports of raw

---

early 1830s. For data, see House of Commons, Parliamentary Papers, 1831–1832, X, pt. 2, Appendix 4, cited in Indrajit Ray, *Bengal Industries and the British Industrial Revolution (1757–1857)* (New York, 2011), 65.

62. Fraser to Mackintosh, Apr. 4, 1821, MSS Eur. Photo 150, 220, 234, BL, to Gladstone, Jan. 28, 1819, 90. For more on exports of cloth and thread to India, see Benjamin Buchanan and Co. to McConnel and Kennedy, Jan. 20, Mar. 31, June 14, 1825, McConnel and Kennedy and McConnel and Co. Papers, MCK/2/1/31, John Rylands Library, Manchester, U.K.

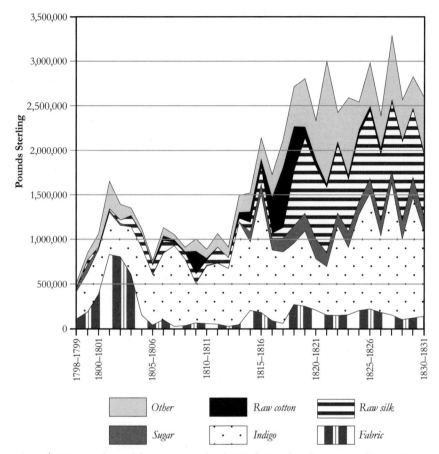

Figure 6. Exports from Calcutta to London/United Kingdom by Commodity, 1798–1799 through 1830–1831. Fabrics were mostly cotton until the 1820s, when cotton nearly disappeared and silk fabric increased. The increase in "Other" after 1817–1818 is mostly saltpeter, with spikes of treasure. "Comparative Abstract Annual Statements of Exports . . . ," IOR/P/174/17, 22, 27, 32, 42, 46, BL. Converted from SR using annual exchange rates in Asiya Siddiqi, ed., *Trade and Finance in Colonial India, 1750–1860* (Delhi, 1995), 57. Drawn by Rebecca Wrenn

materials dramatically expanded the size of the trade to Britain and its value to British merchants and industrialists.[63]

63. In the 1810s, the sale value of Indian fabric in London did not fall as sharply as the exports of it from Calcutta. There are several possible explanations, including high demand for the specific goods selected and the sale of goods stockpiled from earlier years in London. Piece goods from Surat and the coast also sold for more in London than those from Calcutta. "An Account of the Amount of All Goods, Sold at the East India Company Sales from 1st May

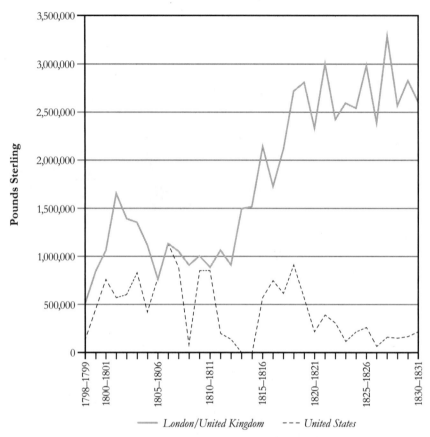

Figure 7. Exports from Calcutta to London/United Kingdom and the United
States, 1798–1799 through 1830–1831. "Comparative Abstract Annual Statements of
Exports . . . ," IOR/P/174/17, 22, 27, 32, 42, 46, BL. Converted from SR using annual
exchange rates in Asiya Siddiqi, ed., *Trade and Finance in Colonial India, 1750–1860*
(Delhi, 1995), 57. Drawn by Rebecca Wrenn

Private British merchants in British India, better tied into the imperial
system and British manufacturing than Americans, quickly took firm control of the trade after the end of the Company monopoly (Figure 7). British
agency houses in Calcutta in the late 1810s and early 1820s did business

———
1810/11 to 30th April 1819/20," L/AG/10/2/5, BL; Bowen, *The Business of Empire*, 235; Wilson, *Review of the External Commerce of Bengal*, 84; J. S. Browning to John Palmer, Aug. 12,
1821, MSS Eng. Lett. d.105, Bodleian Library, Oxford University. For examples of American
purchases, see William Gray to Nathaniel Kinsman, Dec. 15, 1821, Private Collection, quoted
in Munroe, "Nathaniel Kinsman," *Essex Institute Historical Collections*, LXXXV (1949), 17.

with associates from all over the world. John Palmer's large firm, for instance, worked with American and French supercargoes. Once the Company monopoly with India had ended, Palmer had sixteen ships of his own trading with Mauritius, China, America, Sydney, the Cape of Good Hope, and Java in addition to "regular traders to England and back." The country trade had been legal before the 1813 changes to the East India Company charter, but not the ships to America and England. British freight rates, meanwhile, plummeted with the end of war and the opening of the India trade. Competition for U.S.-India traders and shippers had increased dramatically.[64]

Furthermore, American merchants faced a range of competitive disadvantages. British merchants did not depend on bullion shipments to finance their exports from India to the extent that American merchants did. The United States followed only China in imports of bullion into Bengal after the War of 1812 until the late 1820s. As the clerk of an American merchantman wrote from Batavia Road, their cargo had not sold well, but they brought it "merely to cover the ship from Pirates." The real cargo was eighty thousand Spanish dollars to purchase goods in Calcutta. Profit would, therefore, accrue only from the return leg of the voyage. This was not an ideal business. British merchants profited on the sale of goods from both their outward and inward cargoes. It made little economic sense, moreover, to ship more expensive American products or to transship British products back through the United States. In some ways, American trade with India paralleled that of England with India in the 1680s and 1690s, but Britain, as far as the production and export of manufactures was concerned, was now more like India had been then. It was Britain, not India, that primarily supplied Americans with cottons. In 1820–1821, American cotton cloth exports from Calcutta sunk. Silk piece goods briefly surged but fell back by the late 1820s. American consumers still demanded shawls, handkerchiefs, and drugs from India, but the former were accessories, not the material of entire wardrobes, and the latter could often be purchased easily elsewhere and were not bulk commodities in any case.[65]

U.S. producers, meanwhile, had little need for most of India's raw materials. As cotton piece goods collapsed, the value of raw materials, par-

64. William Prinsep, Memoir, circa 1870, MS Eur. D1160, I, 318–321, BL. On freight rates, see James Baillie Fraser to Messrs Read and Fraser, Jan. 8, 1818, MSS Eur. Photo 150, BL.
65. Charles W. Lovett to his parents, Feb. 14, 1822, Ship.Mss.40, Acc. 14.482, PEM; Wilson, *Review of the External Commerce of Bengal*, 83, "Tables": 34–35; Ray, *Bengal Industries*, 36.

ticularly sugar, indigo, and saltpeter, dropped as well. Unlike in Britain, such goods, suitable accompaniments to the previously valuable cloth trade, lacked enough demand in America to drive the trade on their own. Sugar was readily available in the Atlantic, and the southern states produced large quantities of indigo. The United States was still not producing much raw silk, but it did not have much demand for it either—the country did not have an established silk-weaving industry. There was insufficient demand in the United States to push the value of these exports of raw materials higher to replace, let alone supersede, the value of the old cotton cloth trade, as happened in India's trade with Britain.[66]

The experiences of Philadelphia merchants Joseph Archer and John Rulon, who founded a trading house in Calcutta in the late 1820s, illustrate the variety and creativity now necessary for the few American traders in British India. Archer's father advised, "Send at least a part of your first shipment of Madras and bentapolum hkfs of the latest patterns made to *order* from *this city* if practicable." He continued, following the muster system developed by the Company 150 years earlier, "I will forward you patterns from time to time as received and give you advice if possible how to assort them for different markets." Still, handkerchiefs were not suitable to be staples in a large trade. When the elder Rulon told his son to charter "a *British* vessel," he requested that it be laded with "as much saltpetre as she *would carry,* filling up with goat skins, cow hides, hemp, shellac, gunney bags, sienna leaves and some twine; and to finish with an *elephant*— and possibly some other *strange* animals." Archer had found a buyer willing to pay five thousand dollars for the live elephant. The elephant order caused considerable enthusiasm, and, in early 1830, Rulon and Archer wrote back with satisfaction that they had shipped a selection of goods much like the one the elder Archer had requested, including not only an elephant but also a last-minute rhinoceros. The elephant was not the first in America, but the excitement over it as a means to find profit in an India trade that used to value the mass exportation of cottons is a marker of the changes in the geography of production, the decline of the U.S. trade with British India, and the continuing resonance of India's wonder.[67]

As a more profitable alternative, American merchants in the East Indies increasingly focused on tea, coffee, and spices from ports outside

66. Wilson, *Review of the External Commerce of Bengal,* "Tables": 36–37.

67. Samuel Archer to Rulon and Archer, June 12, Oct. 7, 1829, Rulon and Archer to Archer, Feb. 9, 1830, May 13, 1830, all in Rulon Papers, Collection 1691, HSP; John Rulon to Marmaduke Burrough, Jan. 18, 1830, Marmaduke Burrough Papers, Collection 1701, HSP.

British India. Such was the success of Americans in the Chinese tea trade that it caused alarm in the government of Lower Canada. In 1822, John Richardson, a member of Lower Canada's legislative assembly, alerted Company director John Inglis that smugglers from the United States had taken over the supply of the local market in Asian goods. Reflecting major shifts in both the geography of production and taste, Richardson worried in particular about smuggled tea, and not so much the calicoes or arrack that had exercised the Company, Board of Trade, and colonial governors in the 1720s. Some people estimated that the Canadians were drinking two or three cups of tea per day. Another memorial pointed out that it was the U.S. Treasury, not the British, that was gaining ninety thousand pounds in duties from tea reexported to Canada as New York and Boston became the hubs for Chinese tea legally imported into the United States and then illegally reexported. In Boston, "Every store is a tea warehouse and every store keeper a smuggler." The site of the 1773 Tea Party against the Company's excess tea now overflowed with its own tea and pushed it into Canada.[68]

But the United States had a much more important new role in supplying raw cotton to the British empire that dwarfed any British losses to such smuggling. The 1818–1834 letter book of Boston merchant William Rufus Gray documents the major price advantages that American cotton increasingly had over Indian cotton. Gray continued the business of his father, also William, who had traded to Calcutta and Manila. In December 1818, the younger Gray received 290 bales of Surat and an additional 100 bales of extra-fine cotton. He offered it for sale in New York at 18¢ and 22¢ per pound, respectively. In January 1819, he shipped 74 bales of Bombay and Bengal cotton to Liverpool for British cotton manufacturers. He had the proceeds remitted to Thomas Dickason and Company of London, who were still backing American merchants. That summer, he was hoping to receive "prime Cotton" from New Orleans at 16¢ per pound. Gray was, however, still dealing in India piece goods; he sent 6 bales to New Orleans. In the autumn, he wrote to George Prescott in Charleston, South Carolina, asking to barter Calcutta piece goods for first- or, at worst, second-quality

---

68. John Richardson to John Inglis, Sept. 2, 1822, IOR/H/706, 1–2, BL; "Report of the Joint Committee of the Legislative Council and the House of Assembly, on the Subject of Tea," IOR/H/706, 49–51, 68–69, BL; Memorial of the Committee of Trade at Quebec to Earl Bathurst, Apr. 24, 1823, IOR/H/706, 6–10, BL; Capt. Weltden to Chairman and Deputy Chairman, Dec. 23, 1823, IOR/H/706, 14–31 (quotation on 17), BL. For more examples of smuggled goods from Asia, see J. Stewart to James Daniell, Apr. 26, 1823, IOR/H/706, 5, BL.

Carolina cotton. He ordered more Carolina cotton valued at $54,000 at a maximum price of 18¢ per pound. By 1827, in contrast, Gray was paying only 8.5¢ a pound for thirty thousand pounds of Carolina cotton, half of what he had paid in 1819. As Carolina cotton became more readily available and inexpensive, it made little sense to buy more distant and expensive cotton in India.[69]

The bulk of American cotton was exported to Britain, followed distantly by France. Only one-eighth to one-fifth of U.S. cotton was used for domestic production per year through the 1830s. Cotton was the single largest U.S. export and the biggest driver of significant export growth. Cotton plantations began to dominate much of the American South, and the number of enslaved people producing cotton continued to climb. Their lives were emotionally and physically brutal, and a horrific domestic human traffic developed to keep the plantations operating. The bulk of cotton in the 1820s came from coastal southern states, particularly Georgia and South Carolina. Because of high demand, plantations cultivating cotton had, however, already spread westward into Mississippi, Alabama, and Louisiana, and, by the late 1820s, they extended out of the United States into Texas. Cotton had been grown by the Spanish in Texas, but U.S. planters brought new systems and linked directly into the ruthless labor regime from the southern states. Cotton would soon transform Texas. As Britain increasingly conquered India, officially independent America became Britain's dominant supplier of cotton, fulfilling the colonial role imagined in the late sixteenth and early seventeenth centuries.[70]

The entire system of trade had changed. The new Company charter and British peace with France eliminated the primary American advantages in

69. William Rufus Gray to Messrs C Goodhue and Co., Dec. 10, 1818, Gray to Messr Thomas Dickason and Co., Jan. 8, 1819, to Thomas Hewes, Aug. 27, 1819, Sept. 1, 1819, to George Prescott Co., Sept. 20, 1819, Nov. 27, 1819, Mar. 28, 1820, to Ms. Goodhue, Jan. 1, 1826, to Robert C. Mackay, Supercargo Ship *Emerald,* Aug. 15, 1826, to D. Crockersil?, May 7, 1827, all in William Rufus Gray Letter Book, 1818–1834, I, MSS 115, Gray Family Papers, PEM. See also Douglass C. North, *The Economic Growth of the United States, 1790–1860* (New York, 1966), 87.

70. North, *Economic Growth of the United States,* 67–77; Roger L. Ransom, *Conflict and Compromise: The Political Economy of Slavery, Emancipation, and the American Civil War* (New York, 1989), 53–60, 75, 78–79; John Hebron Moore, *The Emergence of the Cotton Kingdom in the Old Southwest: Mississippi, 1770–1860* (Baton Rouge, La., 1988), 7–18, 77–114; Randolph B. Campbell, *An Empire for Slavery: The Peculiar Institution in Texas, 1821–1865* (Baton Rouge, La., 1989), 14, 32–34; Sven Beckert, *Empire of Cotton: A Global History* (New York, 2014), 102–123; Walter Johnson, *Soul by Soul: Life Inside the Antebellum Slave Market* (Cambridge, Mass., 1999).

Conversions

providing private British merchants and missionaries access to India, protecting cargoes from privateers, and penetrating foreign markets. British merchants simply did not need American support as they had before. Most of all, however, the change was driven by new global patterns of production and cultivation shaped by Britain's long-term imperial development and industrialization. Britain had developed massive markets for Indian cottons in the Atlantic; it now almost completely displaced Indian fabric with its own simulations in these same markets. British producers flooded markets in Britain, Europe, America, and western Africa with goods made with the resources of its current and former colonies. British cotton cloth production and the limited American need for India's raw materials gave American merchants little reason to trade with British India. Indians purchasing British cotton cloth, meanwhile, provided for Britain an ideal solution to the recurring difficulty of finding sufficient exports for India and supported British manufacturers, though Indian producers continued to make large quantities for domestic and regional consumption beyond the 1820s. In many ways, after the War of 1812, which some historians have called the Second War for American Independence, both India and the United States functioned more as economic colonies of Britain than ever before.[71]

BY THE MID-1820S, Britons had attempted a series of related political, economic, religious, and cultural conversions in the India trade and in India. By ending the Company's monopoly and the restriction of the India trade to London, Parliament effectively finalized the Company's conversion into a government. The Company could still trade, and still held its monopoly to China until 1833, but in India there was no question that its merchant business fell away. Economically, the conversion to private traders was more or less complete, but the conversion of India into a mass British market was still under way. The hopes of many evangelicals, heightened by the 1813 charter, for widespread religious conversions in India were not fulfilled, nor (by 1830, at least) were hopes of eliminating the trappings and fashions adopted and adapted by British Company servants. Evangelicals even found their own missionaries adopting and adapting Indian commodities, and Britons and, to a lesser extent, Americans at home continued to adopt and adapt some, too. The biggest con-

71. On British cotton cloth displacing Indian cloth in western African markets in the first three decades of the nineteenth century, see Joseph E. Inikori, *Africans and the Industrial Revolution: A Study in International Economic Development* (New York, 2002), 443–447.

version, alongside the conversion of Britain into a cotton cloth–producing power, was the conversion of America into a cotton cultivating power, an India, not in name, but in the raw material that it provided. This conversion, hoped for by some in Britain since the turn to the seventeenth century, had been a very long time coming.

America's extensive participation in the direct trade to India was an anomaly; lengthy periods when people in America were not trading substantially with India were far more usual. It was far more usual, too, for people in America to buy their cottons from Britain, despite the shift in where those cottons were produced. Disagreement over the potential threats and opportunities of India's goods also continued, much as they had for centuries, although now with a more strident evangelical perspective in the mix. That perspective, moreover, was largely shared among Britons and Americans, and it reflected centuries-old connections tying India, Britain, and America together, generally with Britain as the center, as it had become again after the end of the French Revolutionary and Napoleonic Wars. In some ways, then, after wartime disruption and despite many major economic and political changes, including the independence of the thirteen colonies, America reverted to a pre-1783 commercial and cultural relationship with both Britain and the trade with India. Britain, however, had now asserted itself, not simply as a trading pivot between the Indian and Atlantic Oceans but also as a powerful military, manufacturing, and cultural force. After two hundred years, the empire of Protestant fellowship and British trading and manufacturing dominance that used America to rival India—the erstwhile generative idea of the early English empire—was in many ways a reality. Instead of colonial rule in America and trade with an independent India, however, the formula had become trade with an independent America and colonial rule in India.

Conclusion

Britain had made itself into an India. It had adapted many fashions from India, and it had become the world's most efficient producer of India's fabrics. It had accumulated great wealth to rival India. New England, Virginia, Jamaica, Bengal, and many places more had all been Indias in the sense explained by Edward Wynne and many other early-seventeenth-century Britons. Over time, Britons used these Indias together, exploiting each in different ways to eventually make Britain the most powerful India of all.

Britain had also, in many ways real and imagined, become corrupted by this pursuit. Great wealth had not so much stimulated laziness; nevertheless, Wynne had been correct in 1623 that riches were "the readie waie to povertie" for many of Britain's factory workers, for many Indians reduced by the combined power of the East India Company and British industry, and for many enslaved people in the cotton fields of America. Political corruption was not learned from India's rulers, but it was fomented by imperial ideas and by imperial adventurers determined to find and tap Indias to draw riches to themselves. Many in Britain and America argued that the corruption stimulated by such pursuits could be seen in multiple restrictions on their self-proclaimed British liberty, from the chartering of monopoly companies to launch the empire, to the mimicking of supposed Mughal and Catholic tyranny in India and potentially America in the 1760s and 1770s, and to the adoption of supposedly Indian customs of rule. After and despite the American Revolution, this concern over particularly Asiatic and heathen luxury and corruption encouraged American evangelicals to support their British counterparts in the project of converting both India's economy and its faiths.[1]

In several ways, the so-called first British empire finally came to fruition in the early nineteenth century as British cotton industrialists imported raw materials from India and America and distributed back British

---

1. Edward Wynne, "The British India, or a Compendious Discourse Tending to Advancement," 1623? Royal 17 A LVII, fol. 6v, BL.

manufactures. This transition, however, built on a preexisting, transatlantic mass consumer society significantly shaped by London's import and reexport of India's manufactured goods, from cottons and silks to arrack. The Company had supplied information to producers in India from merchants and consumers throughout the Atlantic world to stimulate and meet demand and standardize production long before the Manchester cotton producers pursued similar ends in the second half of the eighteenth century. Indeed, Indian weavers had long produced standardized cotton and silk fabrics in quantities that must be considered mass. British factories imitating India goods accelerated production, lowered costs, and tightened standardization, thereby further broadening consumption patterns. British industrialists and traders also made progress on the age-old problem of increasing the flow of goods from London into the markets of Asia, markets that Adam Smith had described as "greater and more extensive than both Europe and America put together." Britons failed in creating huge markets for British woolens in India, but they instead took advantage of India's already huge markets for cottons. Industrialization, therefore, followed and did not lead the shift to consumer societies with standardized and essentially mass-produced goods, but it nevertheless fundamentally shifted labor modes and geographies of production.[2]

The problem posed to Britain by the independence of the thirteen colonies, if indeed it even was a problem, was in many ways addressed by Britain's increasing ability to emulate Indian products through industrialization and with American cotton. The transition from Indian to British cotton cloth at the same moment that American merchants began to engage directly with India helped to keep the United States within the British imperial orbit. Soon-to-be Pennsylvania representative to the U.S. Senate George Logan noted in 1800, "We are dependent on Great Britain for almost every Article of Clothing we wear." Americans could not compete with the exploited "Subjects of England, either in Europe, or in India." English woolen and silk weavers and their supporters in the late seventeenth century had accused calicoes of being the means through which the Muslim Mughal empire would conquer Britain. Calicoes were now, in a sense, a means of British reconquest in America. Patriot fears in America during the 1770s of being enslaved like Bengalis to Britain and the East India

2. Adam Smith, *An Inquiry into the Nature and Causes of the Wealth of Nations*, ed. R. H. Campbell and A. S. Skinner (Oxford, 1976), II, 632; Giorgio Riello, "The Globalization of Cotton Textiles," in Riello and Prasannan Parthasarathi, eds., *The Spinning World: A Global History of Cotton Textiles, 1200–1850* (Oxford, 2009), 282.

Company had in a less hyperbolic sense become a reality. In this reality, however, white Americans were the ones enslaving African Americans, increasingly to produce cotton for British industry. The resulting cotton cloth, like the Indian cloth before, was shipped to western Africa to purchase the ancestors of many of the enslaved, and, indeed, perhaps themselves. The U.S. southern states were, more than ever before, a cultivator for Britain. And, even as American manufacturing capacity grew based on British precedents in the middle of the nineteenth century, America was, until after the Civil War, a predominantly agricultural economy.[3]

India and America had become more alike as cultivators of raw materials for Britain, and America remained an important subject and enabler of British strength. Britons did not manage to draw sufficient quantities of raw cotton from India to satisfy their demand. They did, however, draw from India vast quantities of indigo, raw silk, and other essential raw materials as well as, in a later story, increasingly displace China's supply of tea to Britain. British laws, moreover, continued to apply over growing swaths of India and British North America alike, and Britain applied British laws to some of those claiming U.S. citizenship, including in the India trade. In trade and then in missions in India, Britain and the United States had a dramatically unequal and sometimes politically broken, yet still intensely close, interdependence. Indeed, in 1830, an Indian woman in Calcutta asked American merchant Nathaniel Ames whether "America was not in England."[4]

From the perspective of conventional political narratives, it seems ironic that the vision of a British empire that made use of America as the way to gain Asia's riches ultimately succeeded after American independence and as British conquest in Asia accelerated. By tracing patterns of production, trade, and consumption in the exercise of imperial power, however, the British use of the post-Revolutionary United States to cultivate Asian raw materials and consume British cottons appears as the logical culmination of two centuries of imperial political economy. Historians have debated the extent to which the War of 1812 solidified American independence. Keeping India in the frame provides another perspective. Both white and

3. George Logan, *A Letter to the Citizens of Pennsylvania, on the Necessity of Promoting Agriculture, Manufactures, and the Useful Arts* ([Philadelphia], 1800), 4, 16–23. See also Tench Coxe, *A Memoir, of February, 1817, upon the Subject of the Cotton Wool Cultivation, the Cotton Trade, and the Cotton Manufactories of the United States of America* ([Philadelphia], 1817), 1–16.

4. Nathaniel Ames, *A Mariner's Sketches, Originally Published in the Manufacturers and Farmers Journal* . . . (Providence, R.I., 1830), 78.

probably many black people in the United States were more amenable to British influence than the majority of India's peoples. Cultural forms in the United States often imitated those in Britain, and British manufacturers happily supplied American consumers. Even though the United States went to war with Britain in 1812, soon after the peace U.S. cotton and markets helped to enable the British empire, much as, previously, Indian cloth and riches had seemed to enable the empire. That the grand imperial vision of using America to cultivate Asian raw materials—the leading justification for empire before the refiguring of the colonists and enslaved Africans as cultivators of tobacco and, especially, sugar, and as consumers of both British and Asian products—succeeded after the American Revolution suggests that scholars might have to rethink when, which parts, and in what ways America effectively became independent.[5]

Which territories were formally part of the empire and when often matters less than the products, laborers, lands, and trades that imperial thinkers, adventurers, and rulers saw as the founts of imperial strength. The geography of imperial thinking, and imagined and real imperial systems, did not correlate directly to the geography of imperial rule. Like the United States remained even after independence, India was already central to English and, to some extent, Scotland's imperial thinking, strategies, and systems in the seventeenth century, before England exercised any substantial territorial empire in India. Likewise, the relationships among British and American missionaries as well as their activities within and beyond the empire do not easily correspond with the boundaries on maps of rulers and ruled.

Whether India was more important for British economic and international power in the seventeenth, eighteenth, nineteenth, or twentieth centuries is an open question. Yet it seems possible that India was most productive economically and most significant to English and British thinkers, merchants, consumers, and government leaders before it was a massive British colony covering much of the subcontinent. In any case, by the 1830s India was no longer a leading manufacturer for the empire and the world, although it retained significant production for its domestic economy. It also provided valuable raw materials to Britain. In one sense, neither consumer markets nor access to raw materials were nec-

5. For more on continuing British cultural influence in the United States, see Kariann Akemi Yokota, *Unbecoming British: How Revolutionary America Became a Postcolonial Nation* (New York, 2011), 62, 65, 80, 89, 92; Elisa Tamarkin, *Anglophilia: Deference, Devotion, and Antebellum America* (Chicago, 2008), esp. 178–246.

essarily dependent on a place having been subject to British conquest, as evidenced by extensive British trade with South America in the nineteenth century. In another sense, the South American trade clearly built on Britain's earlier trading, colonial, and industrial exploits in both the Atlantic and Indian Oceans, and the same could be said of imports of Indian raw materials and Indian consumption of British goods.[6]

British thinking about, trade with, and conquest in India changed Britain and America in many ways, and people continually shifted the connections among economics, politics, and the aesthetics of India goods. Individuals themselves also shifted how they made and saw such connections. Young East India Company servant Frederick Shore, for instance, arrived in India in 1818 with the culturally superior attitude often attributed to colonial rulers. Like many Britons since the early seventeenth century, he came to India with a clear schema in mind: decadent Indian life on the one hand, and respectable British life on the other. To his sister in London, Shore wrote, "I do not wish to give way to these Indian customs, which are in fact nothing but the customs of laziness." "Calcutta," he complained, "is a miserable place." "I keep up as much as possible all English customs," Shore went on, "so that when I come to see you all again I hope you will find me just as much of an Englishman, as I was before I left it." To his aunt, Shore explained that the best houses in Calcutta were the most English in design. He did his early traveling by buggy. Even tropical Indian commodities, he claimed, such as coconuts and pineapples, were inferior to those grown in British hothouses. Many Britons in Calcutta smoking British-made hookahs and in London wearing British-made cottons would have agreed that Britons produced Indian products better than Indians. Whereas in the seventeenth century many Britons had been awed by Indian products and by the capabilities of Indians to emulate any European goods, by the turn to the nineteenth century Britons celebrated British emulation of India's goods.[7]

Shore's experiences, however, complicate notions of hardening British attitudes toward India's cultures in the early nineteenth century. Gradually, Shore became familiar with the use of a growing range of Indian ob-

6. Britain's cotton textile exports to South America, for instance, rivaled and even exceeded those to the United States in much of the nineteenth century; see Manuel Llorca-Jaña, *The British Textile Trade in South America in the Nineteenth Century* (New York, 2012), 45 (on cotton fabric exports), 141–184 (on remittances in bullion, bills, and raw materials).

7. Frederick Shore to his sister Anna, Nov. 23, 1818, MSS Eur. E307/6, fol. 1v, BL; Shore to his aunt, Nov. 13, 1818, MSS Eur. E307/4, n.p., BL.

jects and customs. His diary, spanning his early years in India, showed an increasingly sophisticated understanding of India's peoples and their cultures. In 1821, he began to record trips in his palanquin instead of his buggy. In 1824, he smoked a hookah with a group of Indians, though it was still an unusual activity for him. Around the same time, Shore became heavily involved in tiger hunting, which fused his belief in his role as a protector of Indians with his participation in an activity of India's elite. Shore's own daughter learned Hindi before English. In 1827, he sent a small collection of curiosities home to his father, including Hindu daggers and tiger skulls, to be dispersed among his favorite authors.[8]

After a decade in India, Shore's opinions aligned much more with those Britons and Americans, such as Nathaniel Ames, on both sides of the Atlantic who had argued, particularly since Robert Clive's conquest of Bengal in 1757, that Britons who ruled India were corrupted by wealth and power, and the pursuit of both, not by corruption inherent to India and its goods. In 1828, Shore wrote to his father denouncing the same prejudice against Indian culture that he had championed on his arrival. "The English," he wrote, "are nationally the most bigoted and illiberal people I have ever seen or heard of." To illustrate this new realization, he described a scenario whereby a man threw a January dinner party in England without a fire, with open windows, and a requirement that guests smoke and wear light linen clothing. "Would not fool or madman be the epithet applied to him?" he asked. "Yet would that be more absurd . . . Than for a man in India to invite a party, and intimate that they must be dressed in broad cloth, and must not bring their hookas, and would be expected to dance; and this in June or July?" He came to detest a parochial Britishness. He concluded that the Indian practice of growing beards and shaving heads was as rational as the British custom of growing hair and shaving beards. He now defended the hookah pipe against British "prejudice." Objects and practices that he had associated with laziness and degeneracy he now associated with the specificities of the local environment or, notably, with an acceptable range of cultural difference. With his changing habits, his overall perspective on British rule had inverted: "Summarily my opinion is this; that the English govt is oppressive to the natives in the extreme;

8. Shore, Diary, May 7, 1821, May 20, June 15, 1822, MSS Eur. E307/1, [39], [41], [66], BL. For smoking, see ibid., Apr. 6, 1824, MSS Eur. E307/1, 144, BL. For his daughter, see Shore to his father, Dec. 23, 1833, MSS Eur. E307/5, fol. 45v, BL. For the collection, see Shore to his father, Jan. 3, 1827, MSS Eur. E307/5, fols. 23–34, BL.

and that the natives detest us." He averred, "The majority of English soldiers and sailors" agree.[9]

In a single person, Shore provides evidence of the two extreme poles
Britons developed in thinking about the matter of India, while belying
easy narratives of Britons' becoming much less introspective, more rigid,
and increasingly disgusted by Indian life. Domestic perceptions were typically less laudatory than Shore's yet still nuanced on the matter of India.
Britons at home who wanted to be comfortable with imperial rule in
India, as well as Britons and Americans who sought to convert Indians to
Christianity, had, consciously or not, naturalized the Indian products that
Anglo-American consumers had adopted, such as calicoes, silks, shawls,
and umbrellas, while making other aspects of Indian material life, especially hookahs and palanquins, appear as markers of supposedly sharp differences and Asiatic corruption. There was, however, nothing at all natural about this split; it was an invention as much as was the Calico Act, the
spinning jenny, or the wheeled palanquin carriage.

The world's different places, products, and peoples are often wondrous,
appalling, and frightening because of how we think about them, not because of what we claim they are. And yet the systems we create with our
ideas and with the buying, selling, and consuming of our possessions are
real, and they have real implications. From the ideas of countless thinkers, adventurers, and leaders—including Edward Wynne, John Smith,
John Cary, William Keith, Dean Mohamed, James Hargreaves, Eliza Fay,
Henry Dundas, Francis Baring, and Sarah Farquhar—and from the labor
of countless more, the global British empire gradually developed. The empire's development did not always follow the path its schemers expected,
and yet it ultimately fulfilled most of their biggest expectations. Britain
superseded Catholic and Muslim powers, creating an empire of cultivation and consumption to support a nation of industrial might. To these
ends, it replaced native regimes in eastern North America and the West
Indies with societies of enslaved cultivators and eager consumers, and it
conquered India. The vaunted consumer economy of the United States is

9. Shore to his father, July 10, 1828, MSS Eur. E307/5, fol. 41, BL. In the early 1830s,
after spending a year and a half in Britain, Shore returned to India and published several
articles in the *India Gazette* attacking British rule. In 1837, these articles were collected
together and published as Frederick John Shore, *Notes on Indian Affairs*, 2 vols. (London,
1837). For a condensed modern reprint, see Shore, *The Rebel Bureaucrat: Frederick John
Shore (1799-1837) as Critic of William Bentinck's India*, ed. Peter Penner and Richard Dale
MacLean (Delhi, 1983).

in many ways a product of English and, later, British imperial and trading policy concerning India as well as of British industrialization in imitation of India's goods. The phenomenon of dominant British and, particularly, American manufacturing was a historically recent and relatively brief one. As industrial production and consumer culture expand on the subcontinent, and Indian corporations buy up hallowed old British marks such as Tetley tea, South Asia is becoming globally powerful again. The terms on which it does so have been set in part by India's role in the making of Britain and America.

Index

Dunbar, David, 129–130

Dunbar, Jeremiah, 128–130

Duncanson v. McLure, 342, 343

Dundas, Henry, 307, 310, 311n, 317, 320–323, 325–331, 336, 348–350, 352, 367, 372, 443

Dundas, Robert, 372, 398

Dutch East India Company, 227, 229; competition of, with British, 28–29, 33–34, 41, 45–46, 52, 56, 59, 61, 68, 77, 111, 149, 185, 205, 227, 328, 350; as model for conquest, 28, 42, 55, 153; cooperation of, with British, 96, 135; and reexports to America, 100, 108, 136, 159, 185, 205, 217, 227–231

Dutch empire: competition of, with Britain, 47–49, 52, 61. *See also* Dutch East India Company

Duties: British, 30, 55, 69, 87, 91, 92, 97, 100, 111, 131, 134, 151, 155–157, 163, 164, 170n, 184, 185, 188–190, 198, 224, 238, 240, 307, 308, 311, 319, 321, 325, 326, 337, 349, 350, 367, 368, 372, 373, 423, 426, 433; on the colonies, 156–159, 163, 164, 180, 182, 183, 185–187, 189, 190, 192, 194, 209n, 210, 211; and the American Revolution, 163, 164, 170n, 183, 188–190, 194, 205, 206, 210, 211, 218, 224, 238, 277; U.S., 245, 260, 270, 272, 274, 362, 364, 366, 421, 422, 424, 425; British-Indian, 329, 349, 350, 364, 365, 372. *See also* Taxation

East India Company: and colonial settlement plans, 2, 29, 40, 46, 71n, 154, 155, 184, 221, 349, 363, 394; and tensions with servants, 3, 4, 142, 143, 148, 155, 211, 213, 217, 252, 253, 333; contribution of, to state revenue, 3, 18, 33, 55, 69, 75, 84, 91, 92, 100, 101, 107, 108, 121, 159, 160, 165, 181–183, 190, 194, 196, 197, 206, 216, 217, 232, 235, 238, 263, 363, 373, 379; de-

fenses of, 22n, 29, 30–34, 45, 52, 67, 68, 77, 82, 101, 107, 108, 111, 112, 114, 120, 126, 152, 159–161, 181, 185, 204, 210, 211, 283, 349, 365, 374, 406, 407; diplomacy of, 28, 47, 76, 81, 84, 85, 91, 92, 134, 135, 166, 168, 229, 353, 364, 384; and Protestantism, 36, 52, 81, 155; and cloth procurement and sorting, 42, 52, 85, 141–146, 148, 149, 151, 165, 193, 308, 353, 358, 359; militancy of, 55, 153, 154, 163, 164, 167, 168, 286n, 331, 365, 379, 384, 393, 399; constitutional position of, 73, 84, 95, 108, 166, 170, 195, 196, 202–204, 206, 207, 211, 213, 216, 220, 221, 223, 231, 262, 350; conflict of, with the new Company, 84, 85, 89, 92, 134; and Indian revenue, 120, 121, 153–157, 167–169, 181, 189, 197, 204, 206, 307n, 326, 349, 364, 365, 379, 407; and its shipowners, 138, 159, 164, 320, 328n, 336, 350–352, 366; relations of, with Indian weavers, 143, 165, 166, 307, 324, 426; and missionaries and proselytizing, 155, 382, 384, 387, 391, 393, 397–399, 414, 415

East India Company charter, 2, 42, 73, 75, 84, 113, 134, 159, 204, 211, 218, 341, 363, 376; of 1600, 21, 22; of 1609, 22; of 1657, 52; of 1661, 55, 56n, 70; of 1793, 307, 320, 328, 329, 332, 336, 341; of 1813, 368, 372–379, 405–408, 431, 434, 435

Edmonstone, Neil, 395–397

Elephants, 33n, 38, 51, 65, 165, 171, 172, 199, 201, 235, 289, 303n, 395, 396, 432

Elizabeth (ship), 340

Elizabeth I, 19, 21, 29, 35, 39

Embargo of 1807, 365, 366, 371

Empress of China (ship), 242–244, 254

Enslaved people, 13, 15, 170, 178, 187, 198, 201–203, 209, 210, 213, 214, 216, 219, 221, 222, 224, 233n, 257, 329,

394n, 398, 438; trade in, 3, 4, 17, 53,
54, 108, 113, 114, 118, 135, 160, 165,
185, 208, 269, 357, 394, 398, 405, 406,
434, 439; labor of, 3, 14, 46, 52, 53,
56, 80, 99, 166, 269, 304, 305, 363,
389, 399, 434, 437, 440, 443; and
clothing, 70, 80, 173; patriot fear of,
209, 210, 214–216, 219, 221, 438

Etrusco (ship), 318, 319

Eugene (ship), 114

Exports to India, 18, 28, 29, 33, 55,
91–93, 153, 159, 163, 164, 277, 289–
291, 295–299, 303, 306, 317, 325, 332,
406, 407, 419, 427, 428, 435, 441

Fairfield County Bible Society, 391

Fame (ship), 121–124, 129

Farquhar, Sarah, 382, 383, 387, 443

Fay, Eliza, 333, 419, 443

Fenwick, Cuthbert, 318

Fitzwilliam, Richard, 123, 124

Five Brothers (ship), 341

Fox, Charles James, 233, 263; and India
bill, 233–235, 263, 274

Fox (ship), 128

France, 13n, 31, 33n, 59, 61, 67, 69, 72,
135, 179, 216, 224, 232, 240, 277,
279, 293, 324, 328n, 331, 333, 336,
354, 359, 367, 390, 391, 399, 426,
434; and the supply of India goods to
America, 227–230, 237–239; in U.S.-
India trade, 241–244, 246–249, 274,
329n, 356, 365, 380, 407, 434. *See also*
French East India Company; Lorient

Francis, Philip, 231, 232, 233n, 268

Franklin, Benjamin, 178n, 188, 205, 214

Fraser, James, 427, 428

Freight rates, 159, 311, 320–323, 326,
328, 330, 331n, 336, 346, 348, 350,
361n, 362, 364, 431

French East India Company, 148, 152,
230

French Revolutionary and Napoleonic
Wars, 331, 333–336, 346, 352–354,

356n, 359, 360, 365–367, 380, 399,
436

Furniture, 50, 56, 64–66, 68, 71, 95, 102,
115, 120, 157, 159, 172, 180, 193

Fustian, 58, 98, 113, 133, 140, 153, 179,
237

Ganj-i-Sawai (ship), 73, 82

General Washington (ship), 258, 259

Gilchrist, John Borthwick, 415, 416

Girard, Stephen, 337n, 353n, 354–356,
359

Glasgow, 309, 326, 375, 377, 378n, 379

Glassware, 65, 91–93, 153, 290, 291, 306,
307, 418

Glorious Revolution, 72, 75, 76n, 104

Gold, 14, 16, 20, 27, 31, 33, 38, 46, 52–54,
57, 61, 67, 70, 77, 82, 85, 88, 94, 107,
161, 269, 291, 311, 337

Gordon, Patrick, 122–124, 130

Grand Turk (ship), 247–248

Grant, Charles, 314, 345, 349, 350, 366,
367, 398, 406

Grant, William, 387

Green, William, 251–254

Grose, John Henry, 180, 202

Guinea Company, 46, 52

Guns, 18, 119, 132, 260, 290, 365

Haitian Revolution, 363

Hakluyt, Richard, 18–20, 38n, 154, 381

Hamilton, Alexander, 235, 271, 272, 340

Hanna, James, 312

Harlan, Richard, 391, 392

Hastings, Warren, 204, 228, 231–233,
271, 285, 315, 374, 407; impeachment
trial of, 261–269, 271, 273–275, 293,
342, 423

Hemp, 36, 156, 428, 432

Hinduism: negative views of, 41, 42, 62,
201, 389, 394, 397, 401; positive views
of, 49, 50, 399, 400, 409, 413

Hobart, Henry, 82, 83, 89n

Hobart, Robert, 373

140, 156, 159, 161; Scottish, 62, 104–
106, 110, 115, 309; British, 98, 133,
140, 157, 163, 179, 237, 326; Irish, 179
Liverpool, 10, 309, 368, 433
London Missionary Society (LMS), 382,
386–388, 390, 406
Longcloth, 46, 52, 142
Lord, Henry, 40, 41, 43
Lord mayors, 30–32, 36, 39. *See also*
Mayoral pageants
Lorient, 229, 239
Loveless, W. C., 382, 383, 387
Lower Canada, 433
Luxury and corruption, 1, 28, 29, 37–39,
42–44, 56, 63–65, 67, 68, 70, 81, 159,
161, 162, 165, 178, 190, 194, 198, 201,
202, 207, 225, 232–235, 264, 265,
273, 276, 277, 286–288, 291–293,
305, 306, 337, 380, 389, 392–395,
400, 408–412, 418, 419, 437, 441–443

Mackintosh, William, 232, 233
Madagascar, 46, 70, 75, 88, 89, 113, 114,
118, 136, 246
Madison, James, 245, 260, 305, 305n,
353
Madras, 84, 91, 142–144, 149, 155, 166,
168, 233, 258, 259, 261, 318, 322, 348,
356, 357, 382, 383, 396, 414, 432
Magna Carta, 75, 259, 375
Manchester, 113, 209, 289, 306, 309, 310,
321–323, 327, 328, 368, 379, 438
Maratha empire, 7, 384
Marshman, Joshua, 387, 388, 397, 408–
411
Martin, David, 101, 102
Martin, Henry, 108
Mayoral pageants, 30–32, 171
Merchant lobbying: British, 76, 187, 188,
239, 319, 323, 326, 327, 351, 352, 366,
371, 374–379, 390; U.S., 270, 272, 425
Middleton, Thomas, 31, 33
Minerva (ship), 334
Missionaries, 5, 22n, 198, 382–384, 386,

389, 397–401, 405–412, 414, 419, 423,
435, 440; U.S. support of British,
382, 383, 387–392, 406, 410. *See also*
East India Company: and missionaries and proselytizing; *individual
missionaries; individual missionary
societies*
Monopoly, 245, 259; and East India
Company, 2, 54–56, 68, 72, 75, 77,
84, 107–109, 111–121, 125, 159–161,
163, 164, 184, 188, 189, 194, 228, 231,
238, 268–271, 274, 319–321, 323–325,
338, 371–380, 408; and the colonial
system, 47–48, 53, 54, 56, 74, 114,
116–118, 125, 130, 207, 208, 348, 349;
and Royal African Company, 52–54,
72, 109n; industrial, 53, 79, 115, 323,
331, 332, 381, 421–424, 438; and
the American Revolution, 208, 209,
213–218, 224, 230, 231; and U.S.-
India trade, 231, 249, 256, 257, 259,
269–271, 275; and East India Company shipowners, 320, 350, 351. *See
also* East India Company charter
Moore, John, 121–124, 129–130
Morris, Robert, 242, 270
Mount Vernon (ship), 341–343
Mughal empire, 5–7, 16, 23, 27–29, 34,
36, 38, 49, 57, 68, 73, 76, 81, 82, 84,
91, 202, 216, 224, 384, 399, 437, 438
Mullins, John, 251
Mun, Thomas, 33, 34, 37, 39, 45, 59, 424
Munro, Thomas, 393, 407, 414
Murgatroyd v. McLure, 342, 343
Museums, 51, 171, 409. *See also*
Collecting
Muslin: Indian, 28, 62, 65, 66, 91, 100,
123, 140, 147, 152, 156, 159, 165, 172,
179, 183, 191, 240, 276, 279, 283–285,
287, 288, 292, 307, 310, 311, 314, 326,
327, 359, 400, 401; British, 98, 99,
284, 285, 307, 310, 326, 327, 370, 401,
427; and dress fashion, 281, 283, 287,
292, 400–403, 405, 413

Nabobs: negative views of, 201, 202, 232, 234, 235, 272, 286, 287n, 299, 305, 306; defenses of, 232, 416

Native Americans, 7, 13, 14, 15n, 20, 25, 26, 29, 36, 49, 147, 153, 169, 170, 187, 202, 214, 222, 224, 389n, 443

Navigation Acts: of 1651, 46–48; of 1660, 54; English, 69, 73, 74, 116, 120, 121, 125, 126, 270, 274, 323, 330, 351, 364, 378; U.S., 270, 272, 273

Newell, Harriet, 391, 410, 411

Newell, Samuel, 391

New Jersey, 75, 87, 258, 266, 420

New York, 75, 88, 116, 185, 239, 240, 287, 334

Nightingale, Samuel, junior, 193, 239

Nine Years' War, 72, 82

Nonimportation movements, 188, 191–194, 370

Nootka Sound, 310, 313

North, Frederick (Lord North), 206, 213n, 214, 218, 225, 231, 233–235, 263

Northwest Passage, 20, 23, 24n

Northwest Passage Company, 23, 31

Nova Scotia, 129, 207, 270

O'Donnell, John, 254–259, 289

Oldknow, Samuel, 284, 285, 307

Opium, 204, 313, 356, 416

Orders in Council, 118, 371, 373

Ostend, 93–96, 113, 118, 119, 130, 131, 133–135, 137, 251, 269, 317–322, 333, 334, 378; Company, 134, 135

Ottoman empire, 5, 15–17, 18n, 19, 23, 24, 28, 66n, 156n

Paine, Thomas, 217, 222, 224, 265

Palanquins, 12, 51n, 171, 199, 307, 442; debate over, 50, 64, 232, 289, 290n, 305, 306, 408–410, 412, 419, 443; innovations in, 277n, 299–304, 418, 419, 443

Pallas (ship), 254–256

Papillon, Thomas, 59, 61, 75, 76n, 84, 425

Parry, Edward, 345, 366, 367, 398, 399

Party politics, 337, 338, 374n. *See also* Republicans; Tories; Whigs

Perseverance (ship), 339

Philadelphia, 83, 87, 121, 137, 140, 141, 147, 149, 172, 173, 176, 186, 191, 193, 211, 217, 222, 223, 239, 240, 244, 245, 257, 261, 268, 271, 272, 329, 330n, 336, 357, 360, 361, 368, 387, 409, 432

Pigou and Booth, 193

Piracy, 15, 32, 33n, 73, 75, 77, 114, 118, 248; in the Indian Ocean and Red Sea, 6n, 21, 72, 76, 77, 81, 83, 89, 118, 241, 249; in the Atlantic Ocean, 74–77, 81–83, 88, 242, 249. *See also* Protestantism: and piracy

Pitt, William, the Elder, 188, 198

Pitt, William, the Younger, 274, 307, 310

Pitt India Act (1784), 274

Plymouth Company, 23

Political economy, 29, 30, 33, 34, 45, 59, 61, 67, 68, 77–79, 104, 106–108, 159–163, 180, 184–186, 191, 238, 241, 259, 260, 269–273, 308, 316, 319, 320, 338, 374, 376, 424, 425, 439

Popham, Home, 318, 319n

Popham, Stephen, 260, 261

Portuguese empire and trade, 14, 18, 20, 21, 27, 28, 34, 47n, 48, 55, 61, 176, 177n, 233n, 243, 245, 301, 312, 342, 346, 353–355, 378, 414

Postillion (ship), 114

Powel, Samuel, 135, 137–141, 146, 147, 151, 152

Pownall, Thomas, 183, 184

Price, Joseph, 232, 233, 238, 287n

Princess Amelia (ship), 126–129

Prinsep, John, 315, 319, 320

Privilege trade, 92, 113, 127, 138, 243n, 290, 291, 295, 298, 299n, 361

Profit, 23, 28, 29, 56, 77, 79, 82, 157, 164, 171, 172, 212, 271, 289, 323, 346, 367, 380, 407, 422, 424; as motivation, 17, 21, 22n, 24, 28, 40, 55, 153, 254, 256, 258; hoped for, from India trade, 28,

Smuggling, 87, 97, 119, 120, 126, 127, 129, 137, 151, 159, 184, 187, 240, 253, 307, 366n, 433; criticism of, 5, 96, 101, 119, 124, 125, 128, 130, 132, 135, 163, 164, 317, 319, 433; into colonies, 87, 96, 118–129, 135, 149, 159, 183, 184, 189, 190, 194, 204–206, 211, 224, 227, 240, 253, 259, 316, 433; into Britain, 90, 93–95, 100, 112, 119, 120, 130–133, 138, 317, 319, 433; defense of, 122–125, 130, 131, 158, 205, 208, 211, 245. *See also* Interloping

Smythe, Thomas, 23

Society for Promoting Christian Knowledge, 155

Somers Isles Company, 23

South Carolina, 67, 76, 79, 80, 99, 161, 177n, 240, 256, 265, 281, 337, 371n, 433, 434

South Sea Bubble, 105

Spanish America, 15, 48, 69, 70, 108, 256, 313, 377, 434; as model, 14, 15, 20, 35; British trade with, 82, 87, 105, 160, 185, 225, 313, 330, 363, 373, 378

Spanish empire, 4n, 6, 15, 18n, 19, 20, 34, 35, 37, 38n, 40, 47, 48, 53, 57, 69, 70, 82, 87, 107, 108, 158, 160, 177n, 185, 225, 256, 312, 313, 354, 363, 434

Spice Islands, 18, 34, 35n, 48, 249, 274

Spices, 18, 28, 30–32, 35, 40, 46, 49, 50, 56, 57, 65, 68–70, 85, 95, 137, 139, 140, 171, 179, 182, 191, 193, 208, 232, 253, 355, 404, 405n, 432; pepper, 5n, 15n, 18, 28, 30, 47, 51, 56, 59, 65, 68, 86, 123, 152, 155, 156, 171, 179, 225, 287, 317, 318, 323, 348, 356, 358, 405; ginger, 15, 50, 179, 287, 358; cloves, 30, 48, 139, 179; mace, 30, 139, 179; nutmeg, 48, 138, 139, 179; cinnamon, 139, 179; curry powder, 287, 288, 403, 404, 405n

Stamp Act (1765), 188, 194, 196

Staughton, William, 389, 391, 410

Sugar, 9, 11, 14, 47, 53, 54, 56, 70, 77, 119n, 138, 153, 156, 160, 172, 183, 232, 440; from India, 44, 155, 314, 316–318, 322, 323, 329, 330, 348, 350, 353–358, 360, 373, 432

Sugar Act (1764), 183, 184, 188, 190, 277

Sugarcane, 38, 80, 138

Surat, 27, 28, 39, 41, 44, 73, 84, 85, 91, 97, 143, 341, 382, 433

Sydenham, Thomas, 395, 396

Tariffs. *See* Duties

Taxation, 169, 187, 188, 195, 198, 210, 213–218, 241, 267, 268, 319, 408. *See also* Duties

Taylor, John, 382, 383, 403

Tea, 113, 156, 159, 164, 178, 179, 189, 225, 237, 238, 253, 270, 272, 311, 362, 373, 432, 433; Indian, 12, 314, 439, 444; hopes for American cultivation of, 99; smuggling of, 120n, 121, 130–132, 205, 206, 208, 211, 227; in colonial politics, 169, 170, 178, 179, 189, 190, 192, 193n, 194, 204–214, 217, 222, 223, 231, 259, 338. *See also* Tea Act; Commutation Act

Tea Act (1773), 115, 169, 205–208, 210, 211, 224, 338

Terry, Edward, 49, 50, 57, 62–64

Tigers, 51, 172, 173, 442

Tin, 18n, 155

Tipu Sultan, 277, 317, 384, 392

Tobacco, 15, 40, 63, 53, 54, 56, 70, 160, 178, 204, 237, 314, 346, 370, 403, 416, 440

Tomkyns, John, 182, 185

Tories, 61, 76n, 77n, 83, 92, 93, 220, 222, 271, 374n

Townshend, Charles, 158n, 189, 190, 194, 204

Townshend, Charles, Second Viscount, 157

Townshend Acts (1767), 189, 191, 192, 205, 206, 211, 277

Travel narratives, 15, 26, 37, 50, 63, 64, 201, 232, 312

Treaty of Paris (1783), 230, 233

Treaty of Vienna (1731), 135
Tryon, Thomas, 79, 80
Tucker, Josiah, 163, 164, 195
Turbans, 41, 43, 44, 173, 187, 219, 234, 235, 396. *See also* Banyan caps
Tyranny, 15, 18, 35, 38, 39, 41, 42, 65, 70, 104, 195, 201–203, 207, 208, 211, 212, 216, 217, 219, 221–224, 228, 231, 235, 263, 266, 289, 293, 304–306, 338, 375, 392, 393, 399, 406, 410, 416, 418, 437

Umbrellas, 12, 24, 43, 51, 74, 176, 180, 193, 199, 395, 412, 416, 417, 443
United States (ship), 244, 342
U.S. citizenship, 243, 251, 254, 257, 382, 383, 439; false claims of, 252, 324, 339, 341–343, 382; extension of, 256, 257, 344. *See also* Interloping: under U.S. flag

Vellore mutiny (1806), 396–398
Virginia, 14, 20, 23–25, 27, 32, 35, 36, 40, 46–50, 67, 70, 114, 191, 245, 314
Virginia Company, 22n, 25, 31, 32; and charter of 1606, 21, 22; and charter of 1609, 23

Walsingham, Francis, 19
Ward, William, 387, 388, 393, 401, 410, 411
Waring, John Scott, 399

War of 1812, 315, 368, 379, 380, 388, 391, 420, 422, 426n, 431, 435, 439, 440
War of the Austrian Succession, 152, 165, 166
War of the Spanish Succession, 92
Washington, George, 221, 237, 242, 259, 289
Waterhouse, Edward, 14, 15
Webster, John, 32, 33, 173
Wedgwood, Josiah, 297, 298, 299n, 306
Western Design, 48
Whately, Thomas, 184, 185, 195
Whigs, 59, 61, 75, 77n, 83, 84, 93, 108, 112, 259, 262, 272, 335n
Wickes, Benjamin, 387, 388
Wilberforce, William, 398, 406, 411
Williamson, Thomas, 401, 415, 416
Willings and Francis, 342, 343, 358n
Wilson v. Marryat (1798), 344
Woddrop, John, 237
Woolens, 18, 57, 58, 66, 77, 79n, 82, 86, 90, 92, 93, 95, 99, 111, 114, 133, 157, 159, 163, 191, 208, 289, 307, 310, 381, 419, 422, 423, 426, 438; colonial production of, 66, 78, 81, 112, 115, 162n; arguments in favor of English, 72, 78, 80, 81, 89, 91, 100–107, 109, 110, 112, 115, 132, 133, 153, 161, 162, 288, 309, 325
Worsley, Henry, 118, 119, 127–130
Wynne, Edward, 1, 14, 169, 437, 443

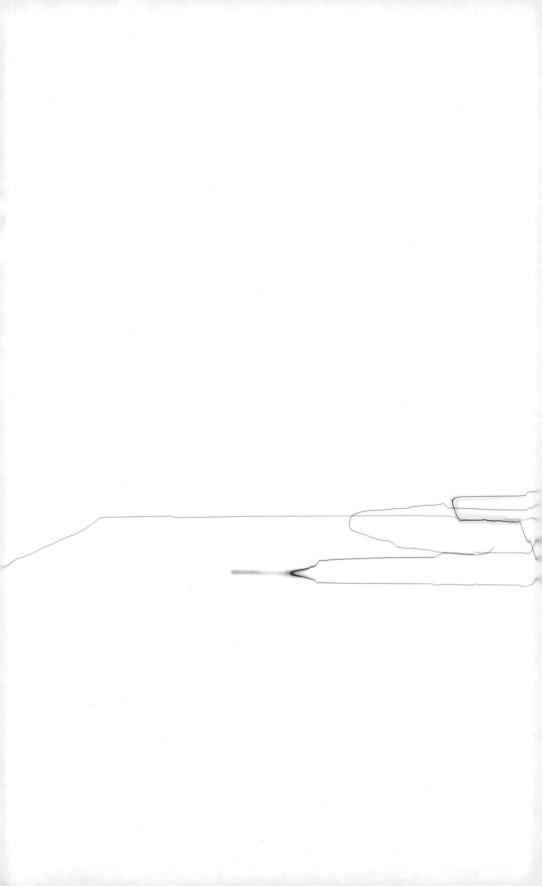